WORK, INDUSTRY, AND CANADIAN SOCIETY

Third Edition

HARVEY J. KRAHN & GRAHAM S. LOWE

University of Alberta

an International Thomson Publishing company

Toronto • Albany • Bonn • Boston • Cincinnati • Detroit • London
Madrid • Melbourne • Mexico City • New York • Pacific Grove • Paris
San Francisco • Singapore • Tokyo • Washington

I(T)P® International Thomson Publishing
The ITP logo is a trademark under licence
www.thomson.com

Published in 1998 by
I(T)P® Nelson
A division of Thomson Canada Limited
1120 Birchmount Road
Scarborough, Ontario M1K 5G4
www.nelson.com

Visit our Web site at **http://www.nelson.com/nelson.html**

Canadian Cataloguing in Publication Data

Krahn, Harvey
Work, industry, and Canadian society

3rd ed.
Includes index.
ISBN 0-17-605609-2

1. Work — Social aspects — Canada. 2. Industrial sociology — Canada. I. Lowe, Graham S. II. Title.

HD6957.C3K72 1998 306.3'6'0971 C97-932055-0

Team Leader and Publisher Michael Young
Acquisitions Editor Charlotte Forbes
Project Editor Evan Turner
Production Editor Jim Gifford
Art Director Angela Cluer
Interior Design Ken Phipps
Cover Design Julie Greener
Production Coordinator Brad Horning
Composition Analyst Nelson Gonzalez

Send your comments by e-mail to the production team for this book:
college_arts_hum@nelson.com

Printed and bound in Canada

1 2 3 4 (WC) 01 00 99 98

CONTENTS

List of Tables and Figures xii
Preface xiv
Introduction xv

CHAPTER 1 Capitalism, Industrialization, and Postindustrial Society 1

Introduction 1
The Origins of Industrial Capitalism 3
  Early Capitalism 4
  The Great Transformation 5
Canada's Industrialization 6
  Work in Pre-Industrial Canada 7
  The Industrial Era 7
  The Decline of Craft Work 8
Rethinking Industrialization 10
  The East Asian Tigers 11
  Signs of Capitalism in China and the Former Soviet Union 14
Theoretical Perspectives 16
  Karl Marx on Worker Exploitation and Class Conflict 16
  Adam Smith: Competition, Not Conflict 18
  Diverse Perspectives on the Division of Labour 19
  Max Weber on Bureaucratic Organizations 21
  The Managerial Revolution 23
Postindustrialism and Globalization 24
  Postindustrial Society 24
  Industrial Restructuring 26
Globalization 27
Canada and Free Trade 29
The Role of the State in Today's Economy 31
Conclusion 33
Notes 34

CHAPTER 2 Canadian Employment Patterns and Trends 37

Introduction 37
Data Sources 38
The Demographic Context of Labour Market Change 39
Workforce Aging 39
Greater Workforce Diversity 42
A Better Educated Workforce 43
Labour Force Participation Trends 46
Gender Differences in Labour Force Participation 47
Labour Force Participation among Youth 49
Labour Force Participation among Older Canadians 50
Unpaid Work 52
Industrial Changes: The Emergence of the Service Economy 54
Service Sector Growth 54
Employment Diversity within the Service Sector 55
Gender and Age Differences in Service Sector Employment 56
Occupational Changes 58
Blue-Collar and White-Collar Occupations 59
Gender and Occupational Location 59
Self-Employment Trends 64
The Canadian Labour Market: Regional Variations 65
Industry Differences across Regions 65
Unemployment Trends 68
Counting the Unemployed 68
Canadian Unemployment Rates over Time 69
Regional Variations in Unemployment 71
Gender and Unemployment 72
Youth Unemployment 73
Causes of Unemployment 74
International Comparisons 76
Hours of Work and Alternative Work Arrangements 78
Nonstandard Work Arrangements 80
Varieties of Nonstandard Work 80
Part-Time Work 84
Temporary Employment and Part-Year Work 86

Future Trends 87
Notes 89

CHAPTER 3 Labour Markets and Jobs: Opportunities and Inequality 93

Introduction 93
Good Jobs and Bad Jobs 95
Income Differences 96
Other Employment Benefits 99
Risks to Personal Health and Safety 101
Computer Use in the Workplace 104
Occupational Status 106
Canada's Class Structure 108
Marx on Social Class 108
Postindustrial Class Structure of Canadian Society 109
The Human Capital Model of Labour Market Processes 111
Social Structure and Occupational Choice 113
Equality of Educational Opportunity 114
Economic Advantage and Cultural Capital 115
Differences by Gender and Region 117
Occupational Mobility Research 117
Status Attainment Research 119
Labour Market Segmentation 122
Dual Economies 122
Internal Labour Markets 125
Labour Market Shelters: Unions and Professions 126
Barriers to Primary Labour Market Entry 127
Historical Patterns of Racial and Ethnic Discrimination 129
Disadvantaged Groups in Today's Labour Market 131
New Patterns of Labour Market Segmentation 135
Labour Market Polarization 136
Rising Income Inequality 137
Policy Responses to Labour Market Barriers and Growing Inequality . . 139
Conclusion 142
Notes 142

CHAPTER 4 Women's Employment 149

Introduction 149
Women's Economic Role in Historical Context 150
    Industrialization and Women's Work 151
    The Family Wage Ideology 152
Female Labour Force Participation Patterns 154
    Influences on Women's Employment 154
Work and Family 158
    Changing Family Forms 159
    The Domestic Division of Labour 159
    Balancing Work and Family 162
Gender Segregation in the Labour Market 165
    Female Job Ghettos 165
    Trends in Labour Market Gender Segregation 167
    Gender Stratification within Occupations 173
The Wage Gap 178
    Gender-Based Inequality of Earnings 178
    Accounting for Women's Lower Earnings 181
Theoretical Perspectives on Work-Related Gender Inequities 183
    Human Capital and Labour Market Segmentation Models 183
    Gender Role Socialization 185
    Gender Inequality and the Organization of Work 186
Achieving Workplace Equality 189
    Employment Equity 190
    Pay Equity 193
Conclusion 195
Notes 195

CHAPTER 5 The Organization and Management of Work 199

Introduction 199
What's Wrong with Bureaucracy? 200
    Weber, Bureaucracy, and Capitalism 201
    The Ills of Bureaucracy 201
    Bureaucracy and Fordism 203
Theoretical Perspectives on Organizations 204

- Structures, Systems, Strategies 205
- Change Strategies 207
- Understanding Organizational Change 208

The Role of Managers 210
- Management Ideology and Practice 210
- Managers as Decision Makers 211

Scientific Management 213
- Taylorism 213
- The Legacy of Scientific Management 215

The Human Relations Movement 216
- Toward Normative Control: Workers as Human Beings 217
- The Hawthorne Studies 218
- Re-Evaluating Human Relations Theory 219
- Cooperation and Conflict in Human Relations Theory 220

Organizational Culture 221
- The Informal Side of Organizations 222
- Organizational Culture 224
- Managing Consensus through Culture 225
- Do Organizations Have Different Cultures? 226
- A Learning Culture 227

In Search of a New Managerial Paradigm 228
- The Critique from Within 229
- The Quality Mission 232
- The Downside of Downsizing 234
- Revolution or Evolution? 236

Work Humanization, Job Redesign, and the High-Performance Workplace 237
- Swedish Work Reforms 238
- North American Quality of Working Life Programs 239
- Shell's Sarnia Chemical Plant 241
- The High-Performance Workplace 243

Japanese Influences on Management and Organizations 244
- The Japanese Employment System 245
- The Japanese Approach in North America 246
- Flexible Specialization 248
- The Flexible Firm 250

Lean Production 251
Conclusion 253
Notes 255

CHAPTER 6 Conflict and Control in the Workplace 259
Introduction 259
Marx on Employment Relationships within Capitalism 262
The Labour Process Perspective 263
Harry Braverman on the "Degradation of Work" 263
Braverman's Contribution to the Sociology of Work 264
Models of Managerial Control 266
The Skill Debate 270
Technology and the Labour Process 274
Technology and Social Inequality 274
The Information Technology Revolution 276
Skill Requirements of New Technologies 277
New Technologies and Control of Workers 280
Job Creation or Job Loss? 281
Technological, Economic, or Social Determinism? 283
New Management Approaches: A Critical Perspective 285
Quality of Working Life (QWL) 285
Total Quality Management (TQM) 286
Flexible Specialization 287
Lean Production 288
High-Performance Workplaces 289
New Management Approaches: A New Labour Process? 290
A Critical Perspective on Workplace Health and Safety 291
The Politics of Workplace Health and Safety 292
The Labour Process and Workplace Health and Safety 294
Industrial Democracy: Rethinking Workers' Rights 297
Industrial Democracy in North America 298
Institutionalized Industrial Democracy in Germany 300
Sweden: Industrial Democracy as a National Goal 302
Globalization and Industrial Democracy 304
Workers Taking Over Ownership 304

Employee Share Ownership Plans 305
Employee Buyouts 306
Producer Cooperatives 307
Conclusion 310
Notes 312

CHAPTER 7 Unions, Industrial Relations, and Strikes 315
Introduction 315
Theoretical Perspectives on the Labour Movement 317
Why Do Workers Unionize? 317
Conflict and Cooperation in Union–Management Relations 318
Unions as "Managers of Discontent" 320
What Do Unions Do? 321
Public Opinion about Unions 322
The Economic Impact of Unions 323
The Development of the Canadian Labour Movement 324
Craft Unionism 325
Industrial Unionism 326
Quebec Labour 328
The Role of the Canadian State in Industrial Relations 329
Union Membership Trends 332
Canadian Union Membership Growth and Stabilization 332
A Comparative Perspective on Canadian Unions 334
The Decline of U.S. Unions 337
The Current State of Unions in Canada 338
Membership Patterns 338
The Rise of Public Sector Unions 343
"Canadianizing" Unions 344
Women and Unions 346
Management Opposition to Unions 350
Positive Labour Relations 350
Unions in an Era of Continuous Restructuring 353
The Nature of Collective Action 354
The Dilemmas of Collective Action 355
The Mobilization Process 356

Strikes 358
What Are Strikes? 358
Canadian Strike Trends 361
A Comparative Perspective on Strikes 364
Explaining Strikes 366
Worker Militancy and Class Politics 367
Comparative Perspectives on Working-Class Radicalism 368
Class and Politics in Canada 370
The Future of Worker Militancy 371
Conclusion 374
Notes 375

CHAPTER 8 The Meaning and Experience of Work 381
Introduction 381
Defining Work Values, Work Orientations, and Job Satisfaction 382
Work Values across Time and Space 383
Historical Changes in the Meaning of Work 383
The Protestant Work Ethic 385
Work as Self-Fulfillment: The Humanist Tradition 386
Experiencing Unemployment: Identifying the Meaning of Work in Its Absence 387
Cultural Variations in Work Values 389
A Need for New (Nonpaid) Work Values? 392
Work Orientations 394
Instrumental Work Orientations 395
Gender and Work Orientations 397
Changing Orientations to Work 398
Work or Leisure as a Central Life Interest? 399
The Work Orientations of Youth 400
Welfare Dependency and an Emerging Underclass? 403
Anxious Workers: Growing Anxiety over Job and Income Security 406
Job Satisfaction and Dissatisfaction 407
The Prevalence of Job Satisfaction 407
Age and Job Satisfaction 408

Gender and Job Satisfaction 410
Educational Attainment and Job Satisfaction 411
Job Conditions, Work Orientations, and Job Satisfaction 412
Canadian Research on Intrinsic Job Rewards 413
Consequences of Job Satisfaction and Dissatisfaction 416
Work and Alienation 417
Karl Marx and Alienating Work within Capitalism 418
The Social–Psychological Perspective on Alienation 419
Robert Blauner on "Alienation and Freedom" 420
Work and Stress 421
Defining Work-Related Stress 421
Causes and Consequences of Work-Related Stress 422
The "Demand–Control" Model of Work-Related Stress 423
The "Person–Environment Fit" Model 425
Conclusion: The "Long Arm of the Job" 426
Notes 429

Conclusion 435
Notes 441
References 442
Index 493

LIST OF TABLES AND FIGURES

Table 1.1 Social and Economic Indicators for Selected Countries, 1994
Table 2.1 Industry by Gender, Employed Population, Canada, 1996
Table 2.2 Classifying Occupations by Skill Type and Level–The National Occupational Classification
Table 2.3 Occupation by Gender, Employed Population, Canada, 1981 and 1996
Table 2.4 Industry by Region, Employed Population, Canada, 1996
Figure 2.1 Age Distribution of the Labour Force by Gender, Canada, 1975 and 1996
Figure 2.2 Educational Attainment of the Labour Force by Gender, Canada, 1975 and 1996
Figure 2.3 Labour Force Participation Rates by Gender, Canada, 1946–1996
Figure 2.4 Unemployment Rate, Canada, 1946–1996
Figure 2.5 Employees' Work Arrangements and Preferences, Canada, 1995
Figure 2.6 Non-Standard Work, Canada, 1989 and 1994
Figure 2.7 Non-Standard Work by Industry, Canada, 1989 and 1994
Figure 2.8 Non-Standard Work by Age and Gender, Canada, 1994
Figure 2.9 Reasons for Part-Time Work, Canada, 1975 and 1995
Table 3.1 Real Annual Earnings and 1981–1993 Percentage Change in Real Annual Earnings by Sex and Age
Figure 3.1 Employer-Sponsored Benefits by Full-Time/Part-Time and Permanent/Nonpermanent Work, Paid Employees Aged 15 to 69, Canada, 1995
Figure 3.2 Work-Related Fatality Rates by Industry Canada, 1976–1981 and 1988–1993
Figure 3.3 Computer Use in the Workplace by Occupation, Canada, 1994
Table 4.1 The Five Leading Female Occupations in Canada, 1901, 1951, and 1991

Table 4.2 Average Employment Income of Full-time, Full-year Workers in the Ten Highest-Paying Occupations, Canada, 1990

Figure 4.1 Labour Force Participation Rates in Seven Industrialized Countries, Women Aged 25 to 54, 1975 and 1994

Figure 4.2 Female Labour Force Participation Rates by Selected Characteristics, Canada, 1996

Figure 4.3 Average Time Spent Daily by Employed Women and Men on Unpaid Household Work by Family Status, Canada, 1992

Figure 4.4 Time-Crunch Stress Reported by Full-time Dual Earners by Age of Youngest Child, Canada, 1992

Figure 4.5 Employment Concentration and Occupational Distribution of Women, Canada, 1996

Figure 4.6 The Ten Most Highly Nontraditional Occupations with Greatest Increases in Female Representation, Canada, 1986–1991

Figure 4.7 Women as a Proportion of Total Full-time University Enrolment, Canada, 1972–1973 and 1992–1993

Figure 4.8 Average Earnings in Constant (1995) Dollars for Full-Time/Full-Year Workers, by Gender, Canada, 1969–1995

Figure 4.9 Job Benefits Received by Employees Aged 25 to 54, by Gender, 1995

Table 7.1 Ten Largest Unions, Canada, 1996

Table 7.2 Work Stoppages Involving One or More Workers, Canada, 1976–1996

Figure 7.1 Union Membership in Canada, 1911–1996

Figure 7.2 Union Density and Collective Bargaining Coverage in Selected Industrialized Countries, 1990

Figure 7.3 Unionization Rates by Province, Canada, 1994

Figure 7.4 Unionization Rates by Industrial Sector and Gender, Canada, 1994

Figure 7.5 Unionization Rates by Occupation, Canada, 1994

Figure 7.6 Strike Volume in Selected Industrialized Countries, Annual Averages, 1970–1992

PREFACE

As in the previous editions of this text, we acknowledge the collective nature of textbook writing. Research assistance was provided by Trish McOrmond, Sandra Rastin, and Karen Robson. Their willing help in locating research articles, organizing references, and proofreading is gratefully acknowledged. Karen Hughes and Deborah Hurst suggested a large number of useful new references. We have also received helpful advice about additions and changes to this text from various colleagues across the country who use the book in their teaching. Equally important, feedback from undergraduate students at the University of Alberta has led to other modifications. At ITP Nelson, Charlotte Forbes encouraged us to take on another revision and Evan Turner graciously put up with several missed deadlines. Jim Gifford and the rest of the production staff made the work of revising our text as trouble-free as possible.

As for ourselves, we continue to work as equal partners on this and other academic projects. Even if we might want to take individual credit for specific ideas, by now it is difficult to remember where an idea originated. Similarly, there is no point in identifying who wrote which sections since, after substantially editing each other's contributions, the results have become a collective effort.

This third edition began with plans to update as much of the statistical trend data as possible, to incorporate new research findings throughout the text, and to build in more international comparisons. We believe we have met these goals although, as with previous editions, completely up-to-date data on some subjects were not available. We had not planned to reorganize the structure of the text. However, by the time we had finished, ten chapters had become eight, and quite a number of subsections had moved from one chapter to another. We think these are improvements, and hope that users of the text will agree.

Harvey J. Krahn and Graham S. Lowe
University of Alberta
Edmonton, July 1997

INTRODUCTION

Work is undeniably one of the most essential of all human activities. It is the basis for the economic survival of individuals and society. Beyond this, an individual's work activity structures much of her or his time and, one hopes, provides a source of personal fulfillment. An occupation also shapes one's identity and, in the eyes of others, largely determines an individual's status or position in society. Stepping back to gain a wider perspective, one also sees that Canadian society and the quality of life we have come to enjoy are the historical products of the collective work efforts of millions of women and men. Thus, while the *sociology of work and industry* may at first glance seem as potentially boring as the part-time job you just quit at your local shopping mall, it is not difficult to justify the subject's social relevance.

When we wrote the second edition of this book we began by noting that the pace and scope of change in Canadian workplaces, the national labour market, and the global economy had increased in the 1990s. Five years later we find ourselves drawing the same conclusion. Global economic restructuring continues, but there are some new powerful national economies involved, particularly in East Asia. In North America, a continental free trade agreement has begun to leave its mark. While unemployment rates remain high, public sector downsizing can now be added to the list of causes, along with continued layoffs in the private sector. The trend towards more non-standard employment has not slowed down, and computer-based technologies are further reshaping the world of work. The composition of the Canadian labour force continues to change. Labour legislation and some aspects of the social safety net (unemployment insurance, for example) are being adjusted in response to demands from employers. Unions continue to struggle to maintain their role in the labour market while employers continue to experiment with new models of management. Overall, labour market polarization continues and social inequality has increased. We have tried to examine and assess all of these, as well as other important trends, in this third edition.

In the following eight chapters, we examine these trends while addressing a broad spectrum of questions about the changing nature of work in Canada. In particular, we are concerned with the consequences of different types of work arrangements for both the individual and society. As the book's title suggests, a sociological analysis of work must be grounded in its industrial context—hence, our emphasis on the underlying economic forces that have shaped and continue to shape work opportunities. But a comprehensive understanding of the world of work also requires us to consider other features of society. For example, there are basic connections between a person's paid work and her or his family responsibilities. Society-wide value systems influence the work expectations of employees, as well as the behaviour of employers. The state plays a pivotal role in determining the nature and rewards of work through its employment standards and labour legislation, various labour market programs, and the educational system. Consequently, our discussion of work, industry, and Canadian society frequently ranges well beyond the work site.

The sociology of work and industry is not a neatly defined area of scholarship. This is an advantage, in our view, because more than is the case for most sociological specialties, we are forced to incorporate the insights of related disciplines. Classic sociological theory, political economy, organization studies, industrial relations, labour history, labour economics, macroeconomics, women's studies and feminist theory, stratification, race and ethnic relations, and social policy are some of the diverse literatures upon which we draw. Because of this scope, our coverage of the literature is far from exhaustive. Instead, we selectively examine theoretical discussions and research findings in an attempt to highlight key themes and debates in the sociology of work and industry. Our goal is to introduce students to the many important and interesting questions in this field, to show ways in which they have been approached theoretically, and to consider how such theoretical explanations stack up against available empirical evidence.

A few brief definitions may be useful. First, *work* refers to activity that provides a socially valued product or service. In other words, through our work we transform raw materials as diverse as information, iron ore, and wheat into something that is socially desirable or necessary. The emphasis in this definition is on activity; action verbs such as cook, hammer, clean, drive, type, teach, sculpt, or serve are what we typically use to describe work. Obviously, such a definition is very broad, including both paid and unpaid work, activities ranging from the legal to the illegal, and from the highly esteemed to the undesirable and despised.

But, with a few exceptions, we have restricted our focus to *paid work*. This approach recognizes the centrality of the employment relationship in modern capitalist societies, both in terms of the production of wealth and the quality of life. Hence, we discuss housework and child care—the major forms of unpaid work in our society—only briefly. Similarly, volunteer work receives only a few comments, as does work in the expanding "informal economy," where goods and services may be exchanged without cash transactions, and work in the traditional hunting and gathering economies that still exist among some of Canada's Aboriginal peoples. By omitting these nonpaid forms of work we are not suggesting they are unimportant, but that they warrant careful study in their own right.

While a job is an economic necessity for the vast majority of working-age Canadians, throughout the life course, paid work is variously combined with school work, child rearing, care of dependent relatives, household work, and community volunteering. Therefore, we do examine the interaction of paid employment with some of these other types of work. But this is only one vantage point; it would be equally interesting to look at the labour market and at work organizations through the eyes of parents of young children, women with substantial domestic responsibilities, people actively involved in community organizations as volunteers, and participants in the informal economy. We have tried, therefore, to reference a number of other books and articles that take such a perspective.

The relationship between employer and employee forms the cornerstone of the sociological study of work. By centring our analysis on workplace relations and the organizational structures in which these are embedded, we are able to address many of the core themes of classical sociological theory, including *inequality* and the distribution of scarce resources, *power* and how it takes shape in authority relations, and the shaky balance between the ever-present potential for *conflict* and the need for *cooperation* and *consensus*. A basic problem in all societies involves the distribution of wealth, power, and prestige. Paid work is central to this dilemma of distribution. Put more concretely, who gets the well-paying, interesting, and high-status jobs? Who is most vulnerable to unemployment? How does cooperation among employees and between management and employees occur? To what extent are employees integrated into their work organizations? Are there inherent conflicts of interest between employers and employees?

Another key theoretical concern in research on the sociology of work and industry is the interplay between the actions of individuals and the constraints exerted on them by social structures. For us, the *agency–structure debate* translates into some very basic and practical questions: How limiting and restrictive are work organizations of the actions of individuals (individually or collectively)? How much can employee actions reshape these structures? It is easy to detect the themes of *stability* and *change* just beneath the surface of these questions. In addressing these obvious tensions between individual action and social structures, it is helpful to distinguish between *macro* (social structure) and *micro* (individual) *levels of analysis.* At the macro level, we focus on the changing global economy, labour markets, industries and occupations, bureaucracies, unions and professional associations, and a variety of institutions that "structure" or establish regular and predictable patterns of work activity in society. We must be careful, however, not to place too much emphasis on social structures, because in doing so we risk losing sight of individuals who are engaged in performing the work.

As a counterbalance to this macro view, a more individual-level micro perspective on work in Canadian society is needed. This we provide by asking questions such as: How do individuals experience their work situation? What are the ingredients of job satisfaction? Or, looking at the negative side, what causes job dissatisfaction, alienation, and work-related stress? What types of work values are held by Canadians? Do different types of people seek different kinds of work? Do most individuals accept their work situation, or do they attempt to change it? If so, how? In short, a micro-level analysis investigates how people experience their jobs, how they adapt to working conditions that are often far from ideal, and how, in some instances, they attempt to improve these conditions within the confines of what is possible given existing work institutions.

To elaborate this point, while an individual's work options may be constrained by social structures, there is nothing inevitable about the daily work routines, employment relationships, and legislative frameworks found in capitalist societies. Thus, we will argue that work can be demeaning or rewarding, depending in large part on how it is organized and who has authority. Further, we will highlight some of the possibilities offered by more egalitarian and humanized forms of work. However, we stop well short of advocating a utopian vision of work. Instead, we approach the subject of work from a *reformist perspective*, arguing that even within the confines of post-industrial capitalism the quality of working life can be improved for many. We believe that through careful theoretical reasoning and rigorous empirical research, sociologists can further the development of enlightened public policy and help individuals create better workplaces for themselves.

It will quickly become clear that we are not presenting a strictly Marxist analysis of work. Similarly, we go beyond a simplistic Weberian approach that gives undue emphasis to employees' understandings of their work situations. And we certainly do not advocate a functionalist or Durkheimian model of the work world that allows the need for social integration and stability to take on a larger-than-life presence. To varying degrees we have been influenced by all of these theoretical orientations, although our starting point is, more than anything, that of a *conflict perspective* of the social world. Thus, a Marxist perspective has strongly influenced the book's emphases on inequality, power, conflict, and control. The Weberian approach sensitizes us to the centrality of individual actors, and their beliefs and behaviours, in sociological analysis. The Durkheimian tradition reminds us that social integration, consensus, and stability within work organizations is the motivation for much management theory and practice.

In short, our objective in this textbook is to provide a comprehensive overview—both theoretically and regarding specific subject matter—of the sociology of work and industry from a Canadian perspective. At the same time, we have incorporated more comparative material than in previous editions, recognizing that our understanding of work in Canada can be enhanced by comparisons with other capitalist societies.

Thus, this third edition of *Work, Industry, and Canadian Society* retains the basic themes and guiding questions addressed in the first two editions. However, a considerable amount of new material has been added since we last revised the book in 1993, while a few sections have been eliminated. We also reorganized a number of sections under eight chapter headings rather than the ten employed in the second edition. As much as possible, statistical trend data have been updated to 1996.

As with the previous editions, the book is written with university undergraduates in mind. But it could also be used profitably by graduate students seeking a general assessment of the literature from a Canadian perspective, and by non-students seeking a better understanding of contemporary work trends. We have provided an extensive guide to sources, allowing readers to find their way into the literature in pursuit of answers to their own research questions. Readers might also wish to examine articles on the same topics contained in *Work in Canada: Readings in the Sociology of Work and Industry* (Lowe and Krahn 1993), a collection of readings that could serve as a supplement to this textbook.

Chapter 1 of this book begins with an overview of the industrialization process and the rise of capitalism in Europe. This short history lesson provides a backdrop against which we can compare the somewhat later Canadian industrialization experience and the even more recent process of industrialization in a number of Asian countries. This first chapter also introduces some aspects of the theoretical writings of Karl Marx, Adam Smith, Max Weber, and Emile Durkheim. These social philosophers developed their assessments of the problems and prospects of work in industrial capitalist societies from their observations of how Europe was transformed during the Industrial Revolution. But the global economy, the industrial structures of advanced capitalist societies, and the employment opportunities found within them have all changed dramatically over the course of the twentieth century. Thus, we also examine a number of more recent theoretical perspectives on work in postindustrial society. Both the classical and contemporary theories resurface throughout the text as we focus on more specific topics within the sociology of work and industry.

Chapter 2 offers a detailed sketch of the major industrial, labour market, and labour force trends in Canada. We begin by examining changes in the composition of the labour force over the past few decades, and then focus on how the industrial and occupational distribution of employment has also changed. Labour force participation patterns and unemployment rates are then examined, along with the rise in nonstandard forms of work (temporary and part-time, for example).

Labour markets are central institutions in the contemporary work world, basically determining who gets the good jobs and who ends up in the less desirable ones. Chapter 3 examines how the Canadian labour market operates by comparing recent findings with the predictions of two competing theories, the human capital model and the labour market segmentation approach. This chapter also focuses directly on the problem of growing labour market polarization and increasing social inequality.

The growing labour force participation of women is clearly one of the most remarkable social changes of the twentieth century. The question of how gender affects labour market outcomes is woven into the discussions in Chapters 2 and 3. But, given the importance of gender issues in the workplace, Chapter 4 provides an in-depth analysis of women's employment. This chapter outlines the transformation of women's economic roles, emphasizing the ways in which gender has become a source of entrenched divisions both within the labour market and within work organizations. The current push for gender equality is also highlighted, with specific reference to employment equity and pay equity programs.

Chapter 5 shifts the focus to how work activities are typically organized and managed in large bureaucracies. Here we discuss organizational theories that attempt to explain the structure of large organizations, as well as how change occurs within them. Equally important, we introduce the range of management theories that have been developed over the past decades. We examine these models of management with particular attention to whether they counter some of the problems of bureaucracy and attempt to humanize working conditions, and whether they offer workers more autonomy or managers more control.

Chapter 6 is, in some ways, a debate with the mainstream management approaches. Our starting point is the *labour process perspective,* a much more critical assessment of employer–employee relationships in capitalist society. We examine different methods managers have used to control and gain compliance from workers, and ask whether new computer-based technologies, as well as the new management approaches, really provide workers with more autonomy and a chance to enhance their skills. Then, looking for alternatives, we discuss current approaches to addressing health and safety concerns in the workplace since, to some extent, they require co-management by workers and management. Going further afield, we conclude by discussing different forms of industrial democracy as well as examples of worker ownership, arguing that these approaches to organizing and managing work do have something to offer.

Unions receive some comment in earlier chapters, but Chapter 7 is devoted to this subject. We discuss various theories about the origins and functions of unions, and document the development of the organized labour movement in Canada. We also describe the legal framework for regulating union–management relations that has emerged. This chapter concludes by examining worker militancy, particularly strike patterns, and by asking whether unions represent a revolutionary or reformist collective response by workers to the greater power of employers.

We conclude, in Chapter 8, by examining the individual experience of work. After commenting on society-wide work values and how they vary across time and culture, we then discuss work orientations, asking what individual employees seek to obtain from their work. Are their work orientations (or preferences) perhaps shaped by the work opportunities available to them? Equally important, are we seeing the emergence of new work orientations in response to growing employment insecurity and income inequality? From here we go on to discuss a wide array of research findings on job satisfaction, alienation, and workplace stress. A major theme developed in this chapter is that negative work experiences can have serious and lasting effects on individuals.

Finally, in a short conclusion, we review the trends described and the main conclusions drawn in the previous chapters. We also raise some important questions about the future of work in Canada. Work humanization through job redesign, industrial democracy, occupational health and safety initiatives, the information technology revolution, and the forces of industrial restructuring all hold out possibilities for creating better workplaces. But these trends could as easily have negative effects on the quantity and quality of work. We do, however, have some control and room to manoeuvre. What Canada needs is a wide-ranging debate, involving workers, employers, organized labour, and government, which would address work democratization, new technologies, industrial restructuring, and economic renewal strategies.

1 CAPITALISM, INDUSTRIALIZATION, AND POSTINDUSTRIAL SOCIETY

INTRODUCTION

Nellie McClung, a Western Canadian political activist who championed the right of women to vote, was also, like many other women in the early decades of the twentieth century, involved in the Women's Christian Temperance Union. The story is told of her visits to schools where she would try to convince children about the evils of alcohol. Her method involved bringing two glasses into the classroom, one filled with water and the other with whiskey. She would then take a worm from a box and, after dropping it in the water, pull it out to show the children that it was still alive and healthy. She would then drop the same worm into the whiskey where it would quickly die. When asked what they had learned, children would usually comment that whiskey was not healthy, and could even kill you. However, after one such demonstration, Johnny, waving his hand excitedly from the back of the classroom, was asked what he had learned. "It looks to me," he said, "that if you drink whiskey, you won't get worms."[1]

This anecdote highlights an important principle of sociological analysis. The conclusions we draw about our immediate world, about the significance of particular social patterns, and about what we might like to see changed, are greatly influenced by our vantage point, by the comparisons we make, and by our assessment of what is desirable and good. This book examines the types of paid work done by Canadians today. Most work for wages or a salary in bureaucratic organizations. In two out of three two-adult households, both partners are employed outside the home. Seven out of ten Canadians work in the service sector. Almost one in four are working either in temporary or part-time jobs. For every nine employed Canadians, at least one is unemployed.

These present labour market realities become more interesting when we realize that only a generation ago some of these trends had just begun to emerge. And going back a century, the differences in work patterns are huge. What social and economic forces led to the shifts from agriculture to manufacturing, then to services? Why are women still under-represented in better jobs? Why are many jobs in today's "high-tech" information economy so mindless? Why have two-earner households become the norm, and what are the social consequences?

To answer these and many other related questions, we examine the complex process of industrialization by looking back in history and at other societies. This historical and comparative approach will help us to understand present patterns and trends, assess their significance for individuals and society, and respond to the future challenges they pose.

Industrialization refers to the technical aspects of the accumulation and processing of a society's resources. *Capitalism* is a term used to describe key aspects of the economic and social organization of the productive enterprise. An industrial society is one in which inanimate sources of energy such as coal or electricity fuel a production system that uses technology to process raw materials. But labelling a society "industrial" tells us little about the relationships among the individuals involved in the productive process. A capitalist system of production is one in which a relatively small number of individuals own and control the means for creating goods and services, while the majority have no direct ownership stake in the economy and are paid a wage to work for those who do.

Studying the rise of capitalism requires us to make sense of large, complex processes spanning generations and leaving no aspect of daily life unaffected. The theoretical writings of Adam Smith, Karl Marx, Emile Durkheim, and Max Weber help us to explain, not just describe, the causes and consequences of capitalist development. But as we will see, the sociological concepts of *power, control, inequality,* and *conflict* that these early social scientists used to analyze changes in their times continue to be central to today's debates about the nature of twenty-first century postindustrial society. Therefore, in this chapter and later in the book we address questions such as: Is the rise of a knowledge-based, "high-tech" economy creating more flexible ways of organizing economic activity that benefits both workers and employers? How are new information technologies transforming the content and organization of work? Are there more losers than winners as a result of the "economic restructuring" of the past two decades? Are well-educated knowledge workers becoming a new elite in society? Is economic globalization increasing the power of transnational corporations at the expense of national governments? And with the astonishing economic growth in East Asia and the collapse of the Soviet Union, do we need to rethink our explanations of capitalist development?

THE ORIGINS OF INDUSTRIAL CAPITALISM

Capitalism and industrialization dramatically reshaped the structure of European society, economically, socially, and spatially. These changes occurred over centuries, with a different pace and pattern in each country. While the details of these changes differed internationally and regionally within countries, the result was profound change in how, where, for whom, and under what conditions individuals worked.

The emergence of capitalism in Europe consisted of two basic periods: *mercantile* or *commercial capitalism,* which began in the 1500s, and *industrial capitalism,* which evolved somewhat later.[2] In the mercantile period, merchants and royalty in Spain, Holland, England, and France accumulated huge fortunes by trading internationally in a variety of goods, including spices, precious stones and metals, sugar, cotton, and slaves. An elaborate trading network evolved, linking Africa, Asia, and the American colonies with Europe. This global trade and the pillage of cultures (slaves from Africa, for example, and vast amounts of gold and silver from Central and South America) provided wealth that would subsequently fuel the growth of industrial capitalism in Europe (Beaud 1983: Chapter 1; Amin 1976; Worsley 1984: 1–16).

Yet Europe was still a *feudal society* and the *Industrial Revolution* had not yet begun. Most people still lived in the countryside. The class structure of these agrarian societies consisted of a relatively small aristocracy and merchant class, most of whom lived in the cities, a rural landowning class, and a large rural peasantry. Work typically involved peasants farming small plots of land they did not own. Landowners received rent, usually in the form of agricultural produce, little of which was sold for cash. Generations of peasant families lived and died on the same feudal estates.

Thus, feudal Europe was predominantly a *pre-market economy* in which the producer was also the consumer. It also was a *pre-capitalist economy* because wage labour was rare and a business class had not yet become dominant. Feudal lords accepted rent and expected services in the form of manual labour required for the upkeep of the estate. In return, they allowed historical tenancy relationships to continue and provided some protection, if necessary, for their tenants. Thus, feudalism was built upon a system of mutual rights and obligations, reinforced by tradition. One's social position was inherited. But this relatively stable society also stifled economic progress.[3]

Did the decay of feudalism lead to the rise of capitalism, or was it the other way around? Scholars are divided on this question. Some argue that factors internal to feudal society, such as growing rural populations, deterioration of land, and landlords demanding more rent, forced people off the land and into the cities where they could form an urban working class. Others counter that as mercantile capitalism developed in urban areas, and as the market economy slowly began to make an impact on rural life, cities began to attract landless serfs. This debate is difficult to resolve, since the two processes influenced each other (Hilton 1976; Aston and Philpin 1985). What is undisputed is that capitalism brought with it an entirely new social order.

Early Capitalism

Industrial capitalism began to emerge in the early 1700s. The production of goods by artisans, or by the home-based *putting out system* in which merchants distributed work to peasant households, led to larger workshops ("manufactories") that made metal, cloth, glass, and other finished goods (Beaud 1983).

By the late 1700s, various inventions were revolutionizing production techniques. James Hargreaves's spinning jenny transformed work in textile industries. Growth in trade and transportation, the construction of railways, and military demand for improved weapons encouraged new techniques for processing iron and other metals. Inventors also were devising ways of harnessing water and steam, as exemplified in James Watts's steam engine.

These early inventions facilitated a new form of work organization: the *industrial mill*. A technical breakthrough that involved harnessing many machines to a single inanimate energy source, the mill also had immense social implications, consolidating many workers under one roof and the control of managers (Beaud 1983: 66–67; Burawoy 1984). A growing class of impoverished urban wage-labourers endured horrific working conditions in early industrial mills. Some workers resisted this trend, particularly artisans who previously had controlled their own labour. Episodes of destroying textile machinery occurred between 1811 and 1816 in a number of British communities. The unemployed craftsmen involved (called *Luddites*) were not unthinking opponents of technological innovations, but skilled workers frustrated by changes that were making their skills obsolete. These uprisings were quashed by the state; some participants were jailed or deported, others were hanged (Beaud 1983: 65; Grint 1991: 55).

The emergence of industrial capitalism also changed the *gender-based division of labour*. While women, men, and children had done different types of work in feudal times, much of it at home, they were often engaged in parallel work activities (Middleton 1988). The putting out system, particularly in the textile industries, brought many women into the paid labour force along with men, since they could work out of their home and still carry out domestic work and child care. Early textile factories also employed men, women, and children (Berg 1988). But as manufacturing developed and expanded, it became the preserve of men. While a gendered division of labour had long existed, it became more pronounced with the rise of industrial capitalism.[4]

The Great Transformation

In only a matter of decades, factory production dominated capitalist societies. The urban landscape also changed as manufacturing cities grew to accommodate the new wage-labour force. Mechanization and the movement to factory-based production proceeded even faster in the 1800s than it had in the previous century. Manufacturing surpassed agriculture in its annual output. Industrial production in Britain, for example, increased by 300 percent between 1820 and 1860. The portion of the labour force employed in agriculture in Britain, France, Germany, the United States, and other industrializing countries declined, while employment in manufacturing and services rose rapidly. By the end of the nineteenth century, industrial capitalism was clearly the dominant system of production in Western nations.

For Karl Polanyi, the *great transformation* that swept Europe with the growth and integration of capital, commodity, and labour markets—the foundation of capitalism—left no aspect of social life untouched.[5] The struggle for democratic forms of government, the emergence of the modern nation-state, and the rapid growth of cities are all directly linked to these economic changes.

Along with new technologies, the replacement of human and animal sources of energy with inanimate sources and the emergence of an integrated market system for finance, commodities, and labour, this era also saw dramatic changes in how work was organized. In time, the relatively stable landlord–serf relationships of feudalism were replaced by wage-labour relationships between capitalists and labourers. Employers paid for a set amount of work, but also determined exactly how, and under what conditions, work would be done. Previously independent artisans lost out to the factory system. In the end, the result was a higher standard of living for most residents of the industrialized countries. But the interrelated processes of change that created a market economy also led to new problems of *controlling, coordinating,* and *managing* work—central themes in this book.

CANADA'S INDUSTRIALIZATION

The process of industrialization in Canada lagged behind Britain and the United States, and can be traced back to the mid-1800s.[7] As a British colony, Canada's role had been to provide raw materials, rather than produce finished goods that would compete on world markets with those of the mother country. Canadian economic elites focused on traditional activities such as exporting *staple products* like timber and fur to sell on world markets, and developing transportation networks (particularly railways) that could link the resource-producing regions of the country with the port cities involved in export trade.

Work in Pre-Industrial Canada

The first half of the nineteenth century, then, was a pre-industrial economic era in Canada. Canada still had a pre-market economy, since most production and consumption took place in households. In fact, given the peculiarities of a colonial economy dependent on Britain, even land was not really a marketable commodity. By the mid-1830s, less than one-tenth of the vast tracts of land that had been given by the French, and later British, monarchy to favoured individuals and companies had been developed for agriculture.

At the same time, immigration from Europe was increasing. Shortages of land for small farmers, potato famines in Ireland, and dreadful working conditions in many British factories fuelled immigration to the New World. Large numbers of immigrants landed in Canada, only to find shortages of urban factory jobs and little available agricultural land. Thus, the majority of these immigrants sought employment in the United States, where factory jobs and land were more plentiful (Teeple 1972).

Some of the immigrants who stayed in Canada were employed building the Welland and Rideau Canals—the first of many transportation megaprojects—in the first half of the nineteenth century. The influx of unskilled workers created a great demand for such seasonal jobs, which often involved fourteen to sixteen hours a day of very hard and poorly paid work. Consequently, poverty was widespread. In the winter of 1844, the *St. Catharine's Journal* reported that:

> the greatest distress imaginable has been, and still is, existing throughout the entire line of the Welland Canal, in consequence of the vast accumulation of unemployed labourers. There are, at this moment, many hundreds of men, women, and children, apparently in the last stages of starvation, and instead … of any relief for them … in the spring … more than one half of those who are now employed must be discharged.[7]

The Industrial Era

By the 1840s, Canada's economy was still largely agrarian, even though the two key ingredients for industrialization—an available labour force and a transportation infrastructure—were in place. Prior to Confederation in 1867, some of Canada's first factories were set up not in Ontario or Quebec, as we might expect, but in Nova Scotia. Shipbuilding, glass, and clothing enterprises were operating profitably in this region before the Maritime Provinces entered Confederation (Veltmeyer 1983: 103). After 1867, manufacturing became centralized in Ontario and Quebec, resulting in the *deindustrialization* of the Maritimes. A larger population base, easy access to U.S. markets, and railway links to both Eastern and Western Canada ensured that the regions around Montreal and Toronto would remain the industrial heartland of the country.

At the time of Confederation, half of the Canadian labour force was in agriculture. This changed rapidly with the advance of industrialization. By 1900, Canada ranked seventh in production output among the manufacturing countries of the world (Rinehart 1996; Laxer 1989). The large factories that had begun to appear decades earlier in the United States were now springing up in Toronto, Hamilton, Montreal, and other central Canadian cities. American firms built many of these factories to avoid Canadian tariffs on goods imported from the United States. This began a pattern of direct U.S. foreign investment in Canada that continues today.

These economic changes brought rapid urban growth and accompanying social problems. Worker exploitation was widespread as labour laws and unions were still largely absent. Low pay, long hours, and unsafe and unhealthy conditions were typical. Workers lived in crowded and unsanitary housing. Health care and social services were largely nonexistent. In short, despite economic development in the decades following Confederation, poverty remained the norm for much of the working class in major manufacturing centres (Copp 1974; Piva 1979).

The Decline of Craft Work

Traditionally, *skilled craft workers* had the advantages of being able to determine their own working conditions, hire their own apprentices, and frequently set their pay. Some worked individually, while others arranged themselves into small groups in the manner of European craft guilds. But this craft control declined as Canada moved into the industrial era. Factory owners were conscious of the increased productivity in American factories obtained through new technology and "modern" systems of management. By dividing craft jobs into many simple tasks, work could now be performed by less skilled and lower-paid employees. Mechanization further cut costs while increasing productivity.

As these systems entered Canada, the job autonomy of craft workers was reduced, resulting in considerable labour unrest. Between 1901 and 1914, for example, over 400 strikes and lockouts occurred in the ten most industrialized cities of southern Ontario (Heron 1980; Heron and Palmer 1977). While these conflicts may look like working-class revolt, they are more accurately seen as a somewhat privileged group of workers resisting attempts to reduce their occupational power. While there were large numbers of skilled workers who experienced the "crisis of the craftsmen" (Heron 1980; also see Rinehart 1996), there were larger numbers of unskilled manual labourers whose only alternative to arduous factory work was seasonal labour in the resource or transportation industries, or unemployment.

There were, in fact, thousands of workers employed in the resource extraction industries throughout Canada, and many others worked on constructing the railways. In *The Bunkhouse Man*, Edmund Bradwin estimates that up to 200,000 men living in some 3,000 work camps were employed in railway construction, mining, and the lumber industry during the early twentieth century. These workers were from English Canada, and Quebec, as well as from Europe and China. Employers considered immigrants to be good candidates for such manual work, as they were unlikely to oppose their bosses. This hiring strategy often did ward off collective action, although immigrants sometimes were the most radical members of the working class.[8]

The creation of a transcontinental railway led to a high demand for coal. Mines were opened on Vancouver Island and in the Alberta Rockies, with immigrants quickly taking the new jobs. Mine owners attempted to extract a lot of work for little pay, knowing they could rely on the military to control unruly workers. It has been estimated that in the early 1900s, every 1 million tons of coal produced in Alberta took the lives of 10 miners, while in British Columbia the rate was 23 dead for the same amount of coal.[9] These dangerous conditions led to strikes, union organization, and even political action. In 1909, Donald McNab, a miner and socialist, was elected to represent Lethbridge in the Alberta legislature. The same year, the Revolutionary Socialist Party of Canada elected several members to the British Columbia legislature (Marchak 1981: 106; Seager 1985). But, although the labour movement did take root in resource industries, it never had the revolutionary spark that some of its radical leaders envisioned.

RETHINKING INDUSTRIALIZATION

Our overview of European and Canadian industrialization had several goals. One was to highlight issues of power, conflict, and inequality in what is sometimes viewed as simply a period of rapid technological change and economic growth. An equally important goal was to draw attention to differences in patterns of industrialization.

But while countries differ in the timing, pace, and form of industrialization, there still appears to be some similar underlying dynamics and processes. Industrialized countries tend to be highly urbanized; production typically takes place on a big scale using complex technologies; workplaces tend to be organized bureaucratically; and white-collar workers comprise most of the workforce. Citizens are reasonably well educated, and generally an individual's level of education and training is related to her or his occupation. Such similarities led American social scientists in the 1950s to claim

> The world is entering a new age—the age of total industrialism. Some countries are far along the road, many more are just beginning the journey. But everywhere, at a faster pace or a slower pace, the peoples of the world are on the march towards industrialism. (Kerr et al. 1973: 29)

This is the *logic of industrialism* thesis, a deterministic and linear argument about the immensity and inevitability of industrial technology. It contends that industrialism is such a powerful force that any country, whatever its characteristics at the outset, will eventually come to resemble other industrialized countries. Hence, this argument is also known as the *convergence thesis.* Yet, as we will see in later chapters, comparisons of work patterns in various industrialized countries do not support this prediction. For example, there are pronounced national variations in unemployment rates, innovative forms of work organization, unionization and industrial relations systems, and education and training.

Returning to our historical overview, we also see that Canada's industrialization occurred later and was shaped by its colonial status, immigration was a major factor in creating a workforce, and resource industries played a central role. Other countries such as Sweden and Japan also industrialized later, but their experiences differed from Canada's. In recent decades, Central and

South American nations such as Mexico and Brazil have undergone much more rapid industrialization. Again, the process differed. In particular, inequality has become even more pronounced in these countries (Chirot 1986: 251–55). By reflecting on the experiences of the most recently industrialized nations of East Asia, and on the stirrings of capitalism in China and the former Soviet Union, we will come to appreciate even greater diversity in this process. Other than at the broadest level of analysis, basically there does not appear to be an inherent "logic of industrialism."

This becomes clear when we compare the twenty countries in North and South America, Asia, and Europe presented in Table 1.1. Keep in mind that comparing nations at different phases and levels of development presents methodological challenges, mainly because perfectly compatible data are lacking. However, the World Bank has constructed basic comparative measures that perhaps are as precise as we can get, so we use these in Table 1.1. Canada provides a useful "benchmark" for interpreting the relative socioeconomic conditions in other countries. After noting which countries are included in Table 1.1, scan each column to get a sense of the huge differences in population, urbanization, per capita income, average annual economic growth rate, proportion of the labour force in agriculture, women as a proportion of the total labour force, and inequality (share of all income or consumption accounted for by the top and bottom *quintiles*, or equal groupings of 20 percent). Of course, these basic social and economic development indicators raise a host of questions about the underlying historical, cultural, and political contexts in which countries industrialize. Also interesting are the consequences for work and workers of the current level and form of industrialization in a country. These are big topics, so we will explore them from several angles at various places in this chapter and elsewhere in the book.

The East Asian Tigers

The *Four Tigers* of East Asia—Singapore, Hong Kong, Taiwan, and South Korea—are attracting much attention from scholars, businesses, and politicians around the world. In a few decades, these economies have become highly industrialized and have either surpassed (the first two) or are fast approaching (the last two) per capita incomes in the major western industrial nations. For example, it took Britain 58 years (1780 to 1838) and the U.S. 47

TABLE 1.1 *Social and Economic Indicators for Selected Countries, 1994*

	Population 1994 (millions)	Urban Population as % of Total (1994)	GNP per capita (PPP) 1994 Current International Dollars (A)	Average Annual Growth per capita 1985–94 (B)	% Labour Force in Agriculture (1990)	Labour Force % Female (1994)	% Share of Income or Consumption in Lowest 20% of Income Earners	% Share of Income or Consumption in Highest 20% of Income Earners
Canada	29.2	77	19,960 +	0.3	3	44	5.7	40.2
United States	260.6	76	25,880 +	1.3	3	45	4.7	41.9
Brazil	159.1	77	5,400 a	−0.4	23	34	2.1	67.5
Mexico	88.5	75	7,040 b	0.9	28	32	4.1	55.3
Chile	14.0	86	8,890 a	6.5	19	31	3.5	61.0
India	913.6	27	1,280 c	2.9	64	32	8.5	42.6
China	1,190.9	29	2,510 d	7.8	72	46	6.2	43.9
Indonesia	190.4	34	3,600 a	6.0	55	40	8.7	40.7
Thailand	58.0	20	6,970 c	8.6	64	47	5.6	52.7
South Korea	44.5	80	10,330 c	7.8	18	40	—	—
Hong Kong	6.1	95	—	5.3*	1	36	5.4	47.0
Singapore	2.9	100	21,900 e	6.1	0	37	5.1	48.9
Japan	125.0	78	21,140 +	3.2	7	40	8.7	37.5
Russian Federation	148.3	73	4,610 +	−4.1	14	48	3.7	53.8
Ukraine	51.9	70	2,620 +	−8.0	20	48	9.5	35.4
United Kingdom	58.4	89	17,970 +	1.3	2	43	4.6	44.3
Germany	81.5	86	19,480 +	—	4	41	7.0	40.3
Sweden	8.8	83	17,130 +	−0.1	—	47	8.0	36.9
France	57.9	73	19,670 +	1.6	5	44	5.6	41.9
Switzerland	7.0	61	25,150 +	0.5	6	40	5.2	44.6

(continued)

TABLE 1.1 *(cont.)*

Source: World Bank, *World Development Report 1996: From Plan to Market* (Oxford: Oxford University Press, 1996), Selected World Development Indicators. Reprinted with permission.

A) Parity Purchasing Power. The PPP conversion factor is defined as the number of units of a country's currency required to buy the same amount of goods and services in the domestic market as one dollar would buy in the United States.

B) GNP is calculated using the *World Bank Atlas* method. GNP measures the total domestic and foreign value-added claimed by residents. It comprises Gross Domestic Product plus the net factor from abroad, which is the income residents receive for factor services (labour and capital) less similar payments made to nonresidents who contribute to the domestic economy. GNP per capita is calculated using the resident population in the corresponding year.

a. Extrapolated from 1980 U.N. International Comparision Programme estimates.

b. Extrapolated from 1975 U.N. International Comparision Programme estimates.

c. Extrapolated from 1985 U.N. International Comparision Programme estimates.

d. World Bank Estimate.

e. Based on regression estimates.

* Data refer to GDP (gross domestic product).

** World Bank Estimate.

+ Extrapolated from 1993 U.N. International Comparision Programme estimates.

years (1839 to 1886) for per capita gross domestic product (the total output of the economy) to double; it took South Korea only 11 years (1966 to 1977) (*The Economist,* 16 October 1993: 80). In the same region, another set of *newly industrializing countries* (NICs)—Thailand, Indonesia, and Malaysia—is following just behind the Four Tigers.

The World Bank (1993: 277) considers rapid economic growth and greater reductions in income inequality than in other developing nations to be the signal features of the "East Asian miracle." But other factors are also important, such as rising output and productivity in agriculture at the same time that a manufacturing export sector was developing, steep declines in birth rates so that population growth was constrained, and heavy investment in human resources through the expansion and improvement of educational systems.

But this overstates the similarities among these nations; in fact, there are striking differences. For example, capitalism has taken distinctive forms in the Four Tigers.[10] A few giant diversified corporations (called *chaebol)* that have close ties to the state dominate the South Korean economy. Taiwan's dynamic export sector is sustained by a network of highly flexible small and medium-sized manufacturing firms with extensive *subcontracting systems* that often extend into the "informal" sector of the economy. In Hong Kong (and also Taiwan) the main organizing unit of business is the Chinese *family enterprise.* These firms give utmost priority to the long-term prosperity and reputation of the family—a very different concept than the "rugged individualism" of North American capitalism. Singapore is set apart by the prominent role of the state in setting the direction of industrialization, which has involved much greater reliance on direct investment by foreign multinational corporations. These variations in business systems account for diverse industrialization paths and approaches to work organization within firms. In Richard Whitley's (1992) view, these business systems are rooted in each nation's unique history, cultural values, political system, and traditional authority relations.

Signs of Capitalism in China and the Former Soviet Union

We've all seen media reports of rich "peasants" in China buying German luxury cars, and of the garishly lavish lifestyles of Russia's new "entrepreneurs." Does this mean that capitalism has taken hold in the two pillars of the communist world? Social scientists have asked this question, attempting to understand the complex transitions these societies are undergoing. Recent research has looked beyond "markets" in a narrow economic sense, attempting to present a more comprehensive explanation of what influences the economic behaviour of individuals in these societies. The emergence of market structures, and how individuals pursue opportunities within these structures, is influenced by factors such as the society's customs, culture, and norms, as well as by existing social networks, how work has been organized, and state policies (Nee and Matthews 1996: 403).

China was the leading recipient of foreign direct investment by the capitalist world's multinational corporations in the 1980s, a trend that continues.[11] As the world's most populous nation, with some 1.2 billion inhabitants, China is seen by these corporations as a huge market to conquer. Its workers also are being integrated into the global economy; "Made in China" now appears on a growing number of consumer items that Canadians buy. Between 1980 and 1995, China experienced an unprecedented annual economic growth rate of just under 10 percent (compared with slightly more than an average of 2 percent in all the major Western industrial economies) (*The Economist,* 9 March 1996: 5).

Is communist China being overtaken by capitalist free enterprise? The short answer is no, but there is a remarkable transformation occurring, mostly localized in a few coastal industrial regions. Market reforms in China began in the mid-1970s. But the Chinese version of an entrepreneurial spirit is deeply rooted, and can be seen in the rich and powerful dynasties established by mainland Chinese families who migrated throughout Asia around a century ago (*The Economist,* 9 March 1996: 10). Chinese-style capitalism, influenced of course by the Western version, built Hong Kong, Singapore, and Taiwan. Now that Hong Kong has been reunited with China, it will be interesting to observe how China responds both politically and economically to the free market ways of this former British colony.

Unlike the former Soviet Union, where privatization is now widespread, state ownership of property remains dominant in mainland China. But the rules have changed: farming has shifted from collective farms to households, giving farmers full return on anything they produced over a set quota. And while state-owned enterprises are still very prominent, at the local level hybrid corporations straddling the state sector and the private sector are permitted. Even in Guangzhou, a booming industrial centre, less than one-third of the jobs are in the market or private sector. As Nee and Matthews (1996: 417) conclude, "the Chinese approach did not conform to textbook economics ... Chinese reformers emphasized piecemeal incremental change, not by design, but by trial and error ... " The looming question now is if and when these economic reforms will precipitate political reforms and increased human rights.

The fall of the Berlin Wall in 1989 marked the collapse of the once powerful Soviet Union. Robert Brym observes that a "strange hybrid of organized crime, communism and capitalism grew with enormous speed in the post-Soviet era" (Brym 1996: 396). Private enterprise, or market liberalization, was introduced in the mid-1980s, but competitive capitalism as we know it failed to emerge. The reason, in Brym's view, is that the old Communist Party elite, along with organized criminal gangs that had prospered in the corruption of the Soviet economy, were well placed to take advantage of any new opportunities. The result is a predatory and primitive kind of capitalism that enriches a small elite while breeding corruption and making life worse for ordinary Russians.

A broadly similar pattern is typical of other Eastern block nations. Former Communist Party elites, who still control state resources and have good business networks, benefit from the transition to a market economy, while living standards for the majority have declined (Rónas-Tas 1994; Szelényi and Kostello 1996). Unlike earlier transitions to capitalism in western Europe and North America, what is occurring in the former Soviet block does not involve the rise of a new economic elite or the creation of a working class—both of which existed in different forms under communism. Thus, Polanyi's "great transformation" from feudalism to a market economy in nineteenth-century Europe represented a unique experience of social and economic change. Subsequent transformations to industrial capitalism have taken some unexpected twists and turns.

THEORETICAL PERSPECTIVES

Now that we have some historical and comparative background on industrialization and capitalism, we can examine major explanations of the causes and consequences of these changes. The following sections present a range of classical and contemporary theories of social and economic change. After acquainting ourselves with these theories and their analytic concepts, we can apply their insights throughout the book when considering specific work issues.

Karl Marx on Worker Exploitation and Class Conflict

Karl Marx spent a lifetime critically examining the phenomenon of industrial capitalism. His assessment of this new type of society was presented within a very broad theoretical framework. He called the overall system of economic activity within a society a *mode of production*, and he identified its major components as the *means of production* (the technology, capital investments, and raw materials) and the *social relations of production* (the relationships between the major social groups or classes involved in production).

Marx focused on the manner in which the ruling class controlled and exploited the working class. His close colleague, Friedrich Engels, documented this exploitation in his 1845 book, *The Condition of the Working Class in England*. Engels (1971: 63) described one of London's many slum districts, noting that other industrial cities were much the same:

> St. Giles is in the midst of the most populous part of the town, surrounded by broad, splendid avenues in which the gay world of London idles about.... The houses are occupied from cellar to garret,

> filthy within and without, and their appearance is such that no human being could possibly wish to live in them. But this is nothing in comparison with the dwellings in the narrow courts and alleys between the streets, entered by covered passages between the houses, in which the filth and tottering ruin surpass all description .... Heaps of garbage and ashes lie in all directions, and the foul liquids emptied before the doors gather in stinking pools. Here live the poorest of the poor, the worst paid workers with thieves and the victims of prostitution indiscriminately huddled together.

It was from such first-hand observations of industrializing Europe that Marx developed his critique of capitalism.

Class conflict was central to Marx's theory of social change. He argued that previous modes of production had collapsed and been replaced because of conflicts among class groups within them. Feudalism was supplanted by capitalism as a result of the growing power of the merchant class, the decline of the traditional alliance of landowners and aristocracy, and the deteriorating relationship between landowners and peasants. Marx identified two major classes in capitalism: the capitalist class, or *bourgeoisie*, which owned the means of production, and the working class, or *proletariat*, which exchanged its labour for wages. A third class—the *petite bourgeoisie*—comprising independent producers and small business owners, would eventually disappear, according to Marx, as it was incorporated into one of the two major classes. Marx argued that capitalism would eventually be replaced by a socialist mode of production. The catalyst would be revolutionary class conflict, in which the oppressed working class would destroy the institutions of capitalism and replace them with a *socialist society* based on collective ownership of the means of production.

Marx sparked ongoing debate regarding the nature of work and of class conflict in capitalist societies (Zeitlin 1968; Coser 1971). Ever since, social, political, and economic analysts have attempted to reinterpret his predictions of a future worker-run socialist society. No capitalist society has experienced the revolutionary upheavals Marx foresaw. And the collapse of the Soviet communist system in Eastern Europe ended speculation that communism would evolve into true socialism. In fact, Marx probably would have been an outspoken critic of the Soviet communist system, given its extreme inequalities in power distribution and harsh treatment of workers. He would also have condemned the inequalities in today's capitalist Russia.

Marx's critique of capitalism also has shaped research in the sociology of work and industry, as analysts attempt to refine or refute his ideas. First, Marx emphasized how the capitalist profit motive is usually in conflict with workers' desires for better wages, working conditions, and standards of living. Second, Marx argued that the worker–owner relationship led to workers losing control over how they did their work and, hence, to the dehumanization of work. Third, Marx predicted that the working class eventually would organize to more actively oppose the ruling capitalist class. In short, Marx wrote about inequality, power, control, and conflict. His enduring legacy for sociology was this more general *conflict perspective.* He recognized that the relations of production in industrial capitalist society typically are exploitative, with owners (and their representatives) having more power, status, and wealth than those who are hired to do the work. Almost all of the debates about better ways of organizing workplaces and managing employees, the need for unions and labour legislation, and the future of work in our society stem from this basic inequality.

Adam Smith: Competition, Not Conflict

Adam Smith wrote *The Wealth of Nations* in 1776, during the early Industrial Revolution in England, extolling the wealth-producing benefits of capitalism. Thus, he is often portrayed as the economic theorist whose ideas outlasted those of Marx who, when writing some time later, predicted the eventual downfall of capitalism. Even today, Adam Smith's ideas are frequently used to call for less government intervention in the economy, the argument being that "the unseen hand of the market" is best left alone.

It is important to note, however, that Adam Smith did not condone the exploitation of workers. He recognized that working conditions in the industrializing British economy were far from satisfactory, and actually argued that higher wages would increase the productivity of workers and the economy as a whole (Weiss 1976; Saul 1995: 150). But Smith was very clear about what he saw as a key underlying principle of capitalism. *Competition among individuals and enterprises*, each trying to improve their own position, led to growth and the creation of wealth. As he put it: "It is not from the benevolence of the butcher, the brewer, or the baker, that we expect our dinner, but from their regard to their own self-interest" (Smith 1976 [1776]: Book 2, Chapter 2: 14).

Thus, for Adam Smith, the "profit motive" was the driving force of capitalism. Individuals and firms in aggressive competition with each other produced the "wealth of nations." Where Marx (some decades later) saw conflict, exploitation, and growing inequality, Adam Smith saw competition leading to greater wealth.

These different perspectives continue to underpin arguments for, on the one hand, restructuring employment relationships to reduce inequality and, on the other, eliminating barriers to competition that are perceived to be holding back the creation of wealth. These counter-positions highlight a central contradiction of capitalist economies. Many people like to believe that the "marketplace" is best left unchecked if greater wealth is to be produced. At the same time, it is clear that social inequality increases without labour legislation, employment insurance, and other programs that smooth the rough edges of capitalism. The question, then, is "what kind of society do we want?"

Diverse Perspectives on the Division of Labour

Human societies have always been characterized by a basic *division of labour*—essentially, how tasks are organized and distributed among workers. In primitive societies, work roles were assigned mainly according to age and gender. But with economic development these roles became more specialized, and the arrival of industrial capitalism further intensified this process. Once a certain scale of production was reached, it was much more efficient to break complex jobs into their component tasks.

Pre-industrial skilled craft workers are often idealized. C. Wright Mills, for example, emphasized the personal satisfactions derived from being involved in all aspects of the creation of some product, being free to make decisions about how the work should be done and to develop one's skills and abilities (Mills 1956: 220). Obviously not all pre-industrial workers were fortunate enough to be craft workers, but it is clear that such opportunities were reduced with the growth of industrial capitalism. Part of the change was due to the loss of control over work that accompanied the spread of wage-labour. Equally significant was the division of work processes into simpler and smaller tasks, each done by an individual worker.

In *The Wealth of Nations*, Adam Smith identified the division of labour as a key to capitalism's success. Using the example of a pin factory, he described how productivity could be greatly increased by assigning workers to specific tasks such as stretching wire, cutting it, and sharpening it. Whereas individual workers might produce 20 pins a day each by doing all of the operations themselves, with a well-defined division of labour, 10 people could make 48,000 pins a day. The greater productivity, Smith reasoned, came from the increased dexterity a worker could master in repeating a single task over and over again, the time saved in not having to change tasks and shift tools, and the added savings obtained from designing machines that workers could use to repeat the single task (Smith 1976; Braverman 1974: 76). The real advantage of this form of work organization would only be realized when factories made large quantities of a product—precisely the goal of industrial capitalism.

In 1832, Charles Babbage translated Smith's principles into practical cost-cutting advice for entrepreneurs. By subdividing tasks, he argued, less skill was required of any individual worker. Consequently, employers could pay less for this labour. Workers with fewer skills simply cannot demand as high a reward for their work (Braverman 1974: 79–83). The early history of industrialization is full of examples of this basic economic principle at work. The advent of factories with detailed divisions of labour invariably replaced skilled craft workers with unskilled factory workers who were paid less—just the sort of outcome that Marx criticized.

Returning to Mills's description of the craft ideal, we can easily see some of the problems. A central feature of *craft work* was the degree to which one individual was involved in all aspects of the creation of some product. The resulting sense of pride and self-fulfilment was an early casualty of industrialization. Furthermore, the minute subdividing of tasks in an efficient mass-production factory or administrative system inevitably led to repetitious, boring work. Little wonder, then, that many craft workers actively resisted factory-based production.

Marx's discussions of work in capitalist society focused on the negative consequences of an excessive division of labour. For him, capitalism itself was the source of the problem. The division of labour was simply a means to create greater profits from the labour of the working class. The development of huge *assembly-line factories* in the early twentieth century epitomized this trend. Henry Ford, the inventor of the assembly line, took considerable pride in recounting how his Model T factory had 7,882 specific jobs. Ford calculated that about half the jobs required only "ordinary men," 949 required "strong, able-bodied men," while the rest could be done by women, older children, or men who were physically disabled, he reasoned. These observations do not reflect a concern for disabled workers, but instead highlight the extreme fragmentation of the labour process, to the point that even the simplest repetitions became a job.[12]

Emile Durkheim, an early twentieth century French sociologist, provided the alternative conservative assessment of capitalist employment relations, particularly the division of labour. He noted that industrial societies contained diverse populations in terms of race, ethnicity, religion, occupation, and education—not to mention differences in beliefs and values. Durkheim pointed to evidence in European industrialization of group differences creating conflict over how scarce resources should be distributed, over rights and privileges, and over which beliefs and values set the standard. Durkheim saw the division of labour as a source of *social cohesion* that reduced this potential for conflict.[13] He reasoned that individuals and groups engaged in different tasks in a complex division of labour would recognize their mutual interdependence. In turn, this would generate tolerance and social harmony.

Durkheim believed that individuals in modern society are forced to rely on each other because of the different occupational positions they fill. In simple terms, lawyers need plumbers to fix their sinks while plumbers need teachers to educate their children. By the same logic, capitalists and their employees are interdependent. Without cooperation between the two groups, the economy would grind to a halt. We will see in later chapters how Durkheim's positive assessment of the division of labour influenced management theories that assume shared interests in the workplace. While Marx has influenced conflict perspectives on work in modern society, the conservative assumptions of Durkheim's general model are the backbone of the *consensus approach.*

Max Weber on Bureaucratic Organizations

Max Weber, a German sociologist also writing in the early twentieth century, addressed yet another major change accompanying capitalist industrialization—*bureaucracy.* Weber noted that Western societies were becoming more rational, a trend most visible in the bureaucratic organization of work. Small, informal relationships among workers, and between workers and employers, increasingly were being replaced by more formal, impersonal work relations in large bureaucracies. Rules and regulations were now determining workers' behaviour. While Weber was concerned about the resulting loss of personal work relationships, he believed that this was far outweighed by greater organizational efficiency. For Weber, bureaucracy and capitalism went hand in hand. Industrial capitalism was a system of rationally organized economic activities; bureaucracies provided the most appropriate organizational framework for such activities.

What defined Weber's "ideal-type" bureaucracy was a precise division of labour within a hierarchy of authority (Weber 1946: 196–98). Each job had its own duties and responsibilities, and each was part of a chain of command in which orders could be passed down, and rewards and punishments used to ensure that the orders were followed. But the power of the employer could not extend beyond the bureaucracy. The contract linking employer and employee was binding only within the work relationship. Also necessary for efficiency were extensive written records of decisions made and transactions completed.

Recruitment into and promotion within the bureaucratic work organization were based on competence, performance skills, and certifications such as educational credentials. Individual employees could make careers within the organization as they moved as far up the hierarchy as their skills and initiative would carry them. Employment contracts assured workers a position so long as they were needed and competently performed the functions of the office. In short, rationality, impersonality, and formal contractual relationships defined the bureaucratic work organization.

Yet bureaucracies were not unique to nineteenth-century capitalism. A somewhat similar form of centralized government had existed in ancient China, and European societies had been organizing their armies in this manner for centuries. What was unique, however, was the extent to which workplaces became bureaucratized under capitalism. At the beginning of the twentieth century, increased competition and the development of big, complex industrial systems demanded even more rationalized production techniques and worker control systems. Large bureaucratic work organizations would become the norm throughout the industrial capitalist world. But bureaucracy also became the norm during the twentieth century in industrialized communist countries of the former Soviet block. So, while closely intertwined, bureaucracy and capitalism are, in fact, separate phenomena.

The Managerial Revolution

Large corporations had begun to dominate the Canadian economy by the early twentieth century. Formerly, most manufacturing enterprises had been owned and controlled by individuals or families. Then came the joint-stock companies in which hundreds, sometimes thousands, of investors shared ownership and profits. Such a diverse group of owners obviously could not directly control the giant corporation in which they had invested. Consequently, a class of managers who could run the enterprise became essential (Berle and Means 1968).

As this pattern spread, observers began to question the Marxist model of industrial capitalism that portrayed the relations of production as a simple two-class system: capitalists who owned and controlled the means of production versus workers who had little choice but to exchange their labour for a wage. An alternative model became popular. The *managerial revolution* theory predicted a new era of reduced conflict and greater harmony in the workplace (Burnham 1941). The theory held that *managers*, who were salaried workers and not owners, would look beyond profits when making decisions; the good of both the company and the workers would be equally important. Since ownership of the firm was now diffused among many individuals, power and control of the enterprise had essentially shifted to a new class of professional managers.

Several decades of debate and research later, it is generally agreed that this perspective on industrial relations in capitalist society exaggerated the degree of change (Zeitlin 1974; Hill 1981: 71–76; Scott 1988). First, family ownership patterns may be less common, but they certainly have not disappeared. In Canada, the prominence of names like Molson, McCain, and Bronfman demonstrate the continuing role of powerful families in the corporate sector. Furthermore, while ownership of corporations involve more individuals, many corporations are still controlled by small groups of minority shareholders. Individuals who serve as directors of major corporations are linked in a tight network of overlapping relationships, with many sitting on the boards of several major corporations simultaneously. Another postwar trend has been the corporate ownership of shares. Concentration of ownership increased as a few large holding companies replaced individual shareholders. Thus, the belief that the relatively small and very powerful capitalist class described by Marx has virtually disappeared is not supported by current evidence.[14]

Advocates of the managerial revolution theory also must demonstrate that, compared with earlier capitalists, the new breed of managers is less influenced by the bottom line of profit. But research continues to show that senior managers and corporate executives think and act in much the same way as capitalist owners. They share similar worldviews, often come from the same social backgrounds as owners, and hold large blocks of shares in the corporation, where they frequently serve as directors as well. In brief, the optimistic predictions of an era of industrial harmony brought on by new patterns of corporate ownership and management are largely unfounded.

POSTINDUSTRIALISM AND GLOBALIZATION

Postindustrial Society

Continuing social and economic change has led some social scientists to argue that we have moved out of the industrial era into a *postindustrial society.* Daniel Bell, writing in the early 1970s, was among the first to note these transformations in the U.S. occupational structure.[15] The Industrial Revolution had seen jobs in the manufacturing and processing sectors replace agricultural jobs. After World War II, jobs in the service sector had become much more prominent. The number of factory workers was decreasing, while employment in the areas of education, health, social welfare, entertainment, government, trade, finance, and a variety of other business sectors was rising. White-collar workers were beginning to outnumber blue-collar workers.

Bell argued that postindustrial societies would engage most workers in the production and dissemination of knowledge, rather than in goods-production as in industrial capitalism. While industrialization had brought increased productivity and living standards, postindustrial society would usher in an era of reduced concentration of power (Bell 1973: 358–67). Power would no longer merely reside in the ownership of property, but also in access to knowledge and in the ability to think and to solve problems. *Knowledge workers*—technicians, professionals, and scientists—would become a large and important class. Their presence would begin to reduce the polarization of classes that had typified the arrival of the industrial age. In contrast to the managerial revolution thesis, which envisioned a new dominant class of managers, Bell proposed that knowledge workers would become the elite of the postindustrial age.

A decade after Bell published his ideas about postindustrial society, John Naisbitt popularized them in *Megatrends*. By including occupational groups as diverse as secretaries, data entry clerks, lawyers, librarians, and scientists in his category of "information workers," Naisbitt observed that a majority of the workforce in the United States was employed in the information sector. He argued that knowledge, unlike property, cannot be possessed by a small elite. Since a majority of the population is involved in creating, processing, and distributing information, society must be moving into a new, more democratic era. "The new source of power is not money in the hands of a few but information in the hands of many," he concluded (Naisbitt 1982: 7).

While continuing to focus on knowledge workers in his book, *The Work of Nations,* Robert Reich disputes the arguments of Bell and Naisbitt about declining inequality. Reich distinguishes *symbolic analysts* (engineers, scientists, consultants, and so on) from the many individuals performing *routine production work* (most manufacturing employees, along with data entry clerks and many other lower-level white-collar workers) and from those providing *in-person services* (retail sales clerks, workers in the food services, and security guards, for example) (Reich 1991: 174–76). Reich recognizes that inequality has increased in American society in the past decades. He argues that the symbolic analysts whose skills are in great demand have become wealthier, while other American workers have become poorer (Reich 1991: 174–76).

Why the optimism in the early theories of postindustrial society? These explanations of social and economic change were developed in the decades following World War II, a time of significant economic growth in North America.[16] White-collar occupational opportunities were increasing, educational institutions were expanding, and the overall standard of living was rising. This context influenced the optimistic tone of the social theories being developed. Yet, as we discuss at various points in the book, other commentators paint a negative picture of the rise of service industries and an expanding white-collar workforce. These critical perspectives point to job deskilling, reduced economic security, the dehumanizing impact of computers, and widening labour market polarization—trends that seem more pronounced since the early 1980s.

Industrial Restructuring

Technological change is accelerating at a time when the international economy is in upheaval. The deep recessions of the early 1980s and early 1990s, fierce international competition, multinational free-trade arrangements, and the spectacular growth of Asian economies have had a major impact on Canada. In fact, it is becoming more difficult to think in terms of discrete national economies. In the words of Robert Reich (1991: 6), "[m]oney, technology, information, and goods are flowing across national borders with unprecedented rapidity and ease." This *globalization* of economic activity continues to bring about fundamental readjustments in the Canadian economy and labour market, including plant shutdowns, job loss through "downsizing," corporate reorganization and mergers, and the relocation or expansion of company operations outside Canada.[17]

But are these new trends? Writing in the early twentieth century, economist Joseph Schumpeter considered *industrial restructuring* a basic feature of capitalism. According to Schumpeter, this process of "creative destruction" involved breaking down old ways of running industry and building up more competitive, efficient, and high-technology alternatives.[18] North American industry clearly is engaged in this process today. But while necessary for the economy as a whole, industrial restructuring can also have negative effects on the quality and quantity of work for individuals. Job losses may be part of the process for some, while others may find themselves with much less job security.

Industrial restructuring involves interrelated social, economic, and technological trends. Crucial is the shift from manufacturing to services. Canada's service industries have rapidly grown in recent decades, compared with declining employment in agriculture, resource, and manufacturing industries. Indeed, both Canada and the United States have experienced *deindustrialization.* This concept refers to declining employment due to factory closures or relocation, typically in once-prominent manufacturing industries: steel, automotives, textiles, clothing, chemicals, and plastics. Once mainstays of the Canadian and U.S. economies, these industries are now sometimes referred to as "sunset industries," because they have failed to adapt quickly to shifting consumer demands. Factories have been sold off, shut down, or relocated to areas such as Mexico, China, or other developing nations where labour is cheap and employment rights and environmental standards are lax. As

Bluestone and Harrison (1982: 9) observe, "left behind are shuttered factories, displaced workers, and a newly emerging group of ghost towns."

Canada has been more vulnerable than the United States to deindustrialization. As Daniel Drache and Meric Gertler note, by 1990 dozens of large multinationals, encouraged by the Canada–U.S. free trade agreement, had announced or implemented plant closures in central Canada, seeking cheaper labour and fewer regulations.[19] More recently, after purchasing the Bauer hockey equipment company, Nike announced in 1997 that it was closing the Ontario factory. But Canadian-owned firms have also been making similar moves. As Canadian corporate giants like Bombardier and Nortel (Northern Telecom) have become global competitors, they have shifted more of their operations (and many of the jobs they provide) out of the country. For example, at the beginning of the 1990s, Nortel reduced its Canadian workforce by almost half while increasing recruitment in its U.S. operations.[20]

GLOBALIZATION

The term *globalization* has become part of everyday language, but what does it really mean, and can evidence document such a trend? As we noted regarding industrial restructuring, the basic idea is not new; in Canada's colonial past, the masters of the British Empire no doubt envisioned their reach as global. Yet searching for a definition of globalization, one is struck by the great many meanings it conveys. Advocates of globalization echo earlier themes in this chapter: the logic of industrialism's belief in the inevitable spread of capitalist markets and national convergence, and the postindustrial vision of economic progress through technology and information. As Gordon Laxer (1995: 287–88) explains, globalization typically refers to four interrelated changes:

> Economic changes include the internationalization of production, the harmonization of tastes and standards and the greatly increased mobility of capital and of transnational corporations. Ideological changes emphasize investment and trade liberalization, deregulation and private enterprise. New information and communications technologies that shrink the globe signal a shift from goods to services. Finally, cultural changes involve trends toward a universal world culture and the erosion of the nation-state.

Corporations, and often governments, promote globalization as a means by which expanding "free markets" will generate economic growth and elevate living standards. Signs of an increasingly global economy are visible in trade arrangements and financial markets. The following are good examples: regional trade liberalization agreements such as NAFTA, the European Union, the Association of South East Asian Nations, and recent initiatives by the larger Asia-Pacific Economic Co-operation forum; international regulatory frameworks such as the World Trade Organization and the Multilateral Agreement on Investment (MAI); and the integration of financial markets through information technology. Critics—and there are many—detect more sinister aspects of globalization. For example, in Canada the proposed international investment treaty (MAI) has raised concerns reminiscent of the earlier debates over free trade. Such treaties are seen as threats to Canadian culture, workers' rights, environmental regulations, and, ultimately, national sovereignty (*The Globe and Mail,* 3 April 1997: A1).

In a truly global economy, corporations would operate in a completely transnational way, not rooted in a specific national economy. But research suggests that there are few such corporations (Hirst and Thompson 1995). McDonald's, IBM, and General Motors may do business in many countries, but they are still U.S.-based. The United States, Japan, and Europe still account for most of the world's trade, largely through corporations located in these countries. While multinational corporations account for 25 percent of the world's production, they only employ 3 percent of the labour force (Giles 1996: 6). Even so, global production is becoming more of a reality. Personal computers are a good example, with financing, design, manufacturing components, assembly, and marketing involving a network of suppliers from many countries. But as Anthony Giles (1996: 6) cautions, "Beyond the obvious technological, economic and logistical hurdles, there are a host of cultural, legal, political and linguistic factors which complicate the development of genuine globally integrated production systems."

It is much easier to imagine production systems spanning several continents than it is to envision a largely global labour force. Despite expanding international markets for some goods and services, labour is still a local resource. According to Hirst and Thompson (1995: 420), "Apart from a 'club-class' of internationally mobile, highly skilled professionals, and the desperate, poor migrants and refugees who will suffer almost any hardship to leave intolerable conditions, the bulk of the world's populations now cannot easily move." In fact, Canada plays an important role in this regard, being one of the few nations to accept relatively large numbers of immigrants annually.

Although labour might not be part of a global market, globalization may still have an impact on labour practices, notably through the public's growing concern about the labour practices of nationally based firms operating in developing countries (one could say the same about environmental practices). Global media coverage has helped to raise the awareness of North Americans. Recently, multinational corporations like Nike have been the targets of public campaigns because of their labour practices in Asian countries (Heinzle 1997). Reflecting these concerns, a 1997 survey of 98 of Canada's largest corporations by the Montreal-based International Centre for Human Rights and Democratic Development found that while 42 percent of the responding firms agreed that international business has a role to play in promoting human rights and sustainable development, only 14 percent had a code of labour standards that protects basic human rights—freedom of association, nondiscrimination, and elimination of child labour and forced labour.[21]

CANADA AND FREE TRADE

The 1989 Free Trade Agreement (FTA) with the United States and the 1994 North American Free Trade Agreement (NAFTA) that included Mexico committed Canada to a policy of more open, less regulated markets. As a NAFTA proponent commented: "Free trade is Darwinian. In the absence of tariff protection, the inefficient expect to be weeded out if incapable of competing" (Dana 1992: 7). He was referring to inefficient industries and firms, but individuals, families, and communities end up being the real victims. It is not clear what the effects of the FTA have been, given that a severe recession began soon after the agreement was signed.[22] While claims of massive job losses directly from the FTA and the NAFTA have not been borne out, the permanent factory closures and job losses that occurred in central Canada as this decade began have partly been linked to free trade. Significant industrial restructuring was already taking place, but the FTA probably accelerated the process, allowing the individuals and communities negatively affected less time to respond. Between the first quarter of 1990 and the second quarter of 1991, Canada lost 273,000 manufacturing jobs, a decline of 13 percent in the industry as a whole. As the Economic Council of Canada (1992a: 4) concluded, "Many of the jobs that were lost will not return." NAFTA does include an accord on labour, and a commission for labour cooperation to track labour market trends in the three NAFTA countries and to address complaints about workers' rights, collective bargaining, and labour standards, so, presumably, these issues are being monitored.[23]

To put NAFTA in perspective, the three participating countries had a combined labour force of 183 million workers in 1995: 72 percent in the U.S., 20 percent in Mexico, and 8 percent in Canada (Secretariat of the Commission for Labor Cooperation 1996: 8). Mexico's labour force has been growing at a considerably faster rate than have the labour forces of its two northern neighbours, but since 1990 manufacturing employment in that country has actually declined (Arsen 1996: 46). The migration of jobs from Canada or the U.S. to Mexico was a major concern of NAFTA opponents. There is little doubt that the *maquiladora* factories along Mexico's northern border have been booming. In January 1995, for example, there were 300 new maquilas started by Canadian and Japanese investors and 6,000 new workers hired (Kopinak 1996: 197). Were these "new" jobs, or relocated jobs from high-wage Canada or Japan? From available evidence, it seems that fewer jobs than expected have migrated south.[24] And much of the new foreign investment in Mexico is from firms based in Japan, East Asia, and Europe seeking a base from which to supply the North American consumer market.

Jobs may be migrating south, but only in some manufacturing industries, and if these employers are in search of low wages, they would likely relocate to China, not Mexico. Actually, there is as much concern that competitive pressures from NAFTA in some manufacturing industries, such as auto and auto parts manufacturing, have accelerated the trend toward *nonstandard or contingent* work (part-time, temporary, contract) in the U.S. and Canada (Roberts, Hyatt, and Dorman 1996). Thus, perhaps the group most negatively affected by NAFTA is Mexican workers. Drawing our attention to Mexico's industrial and social development, one commentator notes: "Of the many arguments against NAFTA the most cogent was the case made by many Mexican opposition activists: that it would artificially prop up a decadent political monopoly, delaying democratic reform and ultimately making it harder for Mexico to modernize" (Orme 1996: xxv).

It is not difficult to find supporting evidence for this view. Mexico's industrialization in the 1980s led to increased social and economic inequalities. The workers in the border maquiladora factories numbered about half a million prior to NAFTA. While their dollar-an-hour pay, lack of rights, and working conditions may be deplorable by Canadian standards, they were part of an emerging middle class in Mexico, able to "cross-border" shop in the U.S. But few workers were spared the ravaging effects of the devaluation of the Mexican peso in late 1994, which saw per capita income instantly plummet from $4000 to $2600 U.S. (Orme 1996: xi). Maquiladora workers, already advantaged by Mexican standards, had the most militant response to this devaluation, and, through illegal strikes, did gain better pay and benefits (Kopinak 1996: 199). Furthermore, NAFTA debates tended to overlook the circumstances of the majority of Mexicans—the rural poor. The Zapatista uprising in the rural state of Chiapas briefly drew the world's attention to those who would not benefit from NAFTA.

The Role of the State in Today's Economy

Clearly, the information technology revolution, industrial and labour market restructuring, and economic globalization are proceeding in a political context where laissez-faire beliefs that advocate free markets with little or no government interference are dominant.[25] In a sense, this political environment is also a key determinant of Canadians' future employment prospects. These three large trends have the potential to either improve employment opportunities for Canadians, or lead to further labour market disruptions. It is difficult to predict just what their ultimate impact might be, but it is important to consider how these forces could be shaped to our collective advantage. Public policy in other industrial countries in Europe and Asia has been more proactive in attempting to influence the course of technological, labour market, and economic change.

The FTA and NAFTA were negotiated by governments, and have been hotly contested political issues in all three countries affected. These trade agreements underscore the evolving role of the state (or government) in the economy and the labour market. The history of industrial capitalism is replete with instances of different forms of state intervention. For example, in the early industrial revolution, the French government forced unemployed workers into factories in an attempt to give manufacturing a boost. We noted, above, that in the early nineteenth century the British government dealt harshly with the Luddite protests against new technologies. And the Canadian government adopted its National Policy in 1879 to promote a transcontinental railway and settlement of the West.

In fact, as Canada industrialized, the government heavily subsidized the construction of railways in order to promote economic development. It also actively encouraged immigration to increase skilled labour for factory-based production and unskilled labour for railway construction. At times, it provided military assistance to employers combating trade unionists, and introduced laws discriminating against Chinese and other nonwhite workers. But the Canadian government also passed legislation that provided greater rights, unemployment insurance, pensions, and compensation for workplace injuries. While some might argue that these initiatives were designed mainly to ensure industrial harmony and to create an environment conducive to business, it is still true that these labour market interventions benefited workers.

A consensus, or compromise, was reached between employers and workers (mainly organized labour) in the prosperous post–World War II period. Acting on *Keynesian economic principles* that advocated an active economic role for the state, the Canadian government attempted to promote economic development, regulate the labour market, keep unemployment down, and assist disadvantaged groups—in short, develop a "welfare state." While the Canadian state was never as actively involved in the economy and the labour market as some European governments, it nevertheless saw itself playing an important role.[26]

But industrial restructuring in the 1980s was accompanied (some would say facilitated) by new conservative political doctrines based on free-market economics (Marchak 1981; Saul 1995; Kapstein 1996). Ronald Reagan in the U.S., Margaret Thatcher in Britain, and Brian Mulroney in Canada argued that economies would become more productive and competitive with less state regulation and intervention. Public policy was guided by the assumption that free markets can best determine who benefits and who loses from economic restructuring. The ideas of Adam Smith were used to justify the inevitable increases in inequality. High unemployment came to be viewed as normal. In some jurisdictions, labour rights were diluted, social programs of the welfare state came to be seen as a hindrance to balanced budgets and economic competitiveness, and government-run services were privatized.[27] As John Ralston Saul (1995) argues, these free-market ideologies erode democratic freedoms, threatening what he calls "the great leap backward." Similarly, with the rapidly developing economies of East Asia, governments routinely use economic imperatives to restrict individual and collective rights.

Thus, in today's economic climate of globalization and restructuring, proponents of free-market economics seem to have more influence. But as we noted when discussing the ideas of Adam Smith, an unchecked marketplace generally leads to greater inequality. So, when answering the question, "what kind of society do we want?" it will be important to determine how the functions of the state will contribute toward this end. Given that Canadians are concerned about labour market inequalities, unemployment, workers' rights, and employers' responsibilities to communities, then clearly the state will continue to play an active role in economic life (Betcherman and Lowe 1997; Tobin 1996; Lonnroth 1994).

CONCLUSION

From feudalism to NAFTA, we have covered a lot of territory in this chapter. We began with an historical overview of the origins and development of industrial capitalism, then discussed various theories that explain and evaluate the causes and consequences of this complex process. As economies and societies continually evolve and the nature of work is transformed, new social theories have been constructed accordingly.

We have highlighted important social and economic changes initially unleashed by the Industrial Revolution in Europe. As feudalism gave way to capitalism, markets grew in importance. A new class structure evolved and a predominantly rural society became urban. Factory-based wage labour became the norm, while craft work declined. Larger workplaces demanded new organizational forms and, in time, bureaucracies evolved to fill this need. And while industrial innovations led to substantial increases in productivity, it was some time before the standard of living of the working class began to reflect this increase. These far-reaching social and economic changes were the focus of early sociologists like Marx, Durkheim, and Weber, and economists like Adam Smith. Having had a brief look at the changing worlds that these social theorists were observing, we are now better equipped to understand their concerns and conclusions.

Our overview of the industrialization experience in Canada and several other countries takes us into the present. Much larger workplaces, new technologies, a more complex division of labour, growth in white-collar occupations, and a new class of managers were among the changes observed as industrial capitalism matured in twentieth-century Canada. Once again, these changes generated a variety of new social theories dealing with technology, social inequality, skill, knowledge workers, increasing convergence, and labour–management cooperation. But the optimistic predictions of reduced inequality and conflict in a postindustrial era are not well supported by the data. Instead, as we will see in the next chapter, employment trends suggest a growing gap between more and less advantaged workers.

We have also highlighted a number of global economic and technological forces now reshaping employment patterns. Like other advanced capitalist societies, Canada has become a service-dominated economy. The information technology revolution is having a major impact on both the quantity and quality of work in the Canadian labour market, as are processes of industrial and labour market restructuring. The eventual outcomes of these trends are still unclear. We also will have to confront the limits to growth, as environmental sustainability becomes a more pressing global problem (World Commission on Environment and Development 1987). We may see a general improvement in the standard of living and the quality of working life. Alternatively, the benefits might go primarily to those who already have better jobs, thus contributing to increased polarization in the labour market and in society as a whole. In subsequent chapters, we will return frequently to this basic question about increasing or declining inequalities.

NOTES

1. We thank Pat Armstrong for this story.
2. Beaud's (1983) history of capitalism is a major source for our brief discussion; also see Grint (1991: 48–83) on pre-industrial and early industrial work patterns.
3. Over the centuries, however, technological innovations did lead to important changes in work patterns. See, for example, White's (1962) detailed historical analysis of the impact of draught horses and the wheeled plough on agriculture, and of the effects of the invention of the stirrup on the practice of warfare.
4. Grint (1991: 69–73); Cohen (1988: 24) concludes that industrialization in Canada did not lead to a sharper gender-based division of labour since, as was not the case in England, such segmentation already existed prior to industrialization.
5. Polanyi (1957). See Boyer and Drache (1996: 8–12) for an application of Polanyi's ideas to the current era.
6. This discussion is drawn from a variety of sources, many cited individually below. For a useful overview of this period in Canadian history, see Ryerson (1968), Laxer (1989), Kealey (1995: Part One), Palmer (1992), and the Canadian labour studies journal, *Labour/Le Travail*.

7. Bleasdale (1981: 13); see Wylie (1983) on the building of the Rideau Canal.
8. See Bradwin (1972); see Avery (1995) and Creese (1988–89) on strikes and radical behaviour among immigrant workers.
9. Mine accidents that took the lives of many miners at one time are mainly responsible for these high averages. For example, 189 miners died in a mine explosion in Hillcrest in 1914. See McCormack (1978: 9) on British Columbia, and Caragata (1979: 16–21) on Alberta coal miners during this era.
10. See Whitley (1992), Shieh (1992), and Hsiung (1996) for detailed accounts of economic development in the region.
11. $33.8 billion U.S. was invested in China between 1981 and 1992. *The Globe and Mail* (5 September 1994: B5).
12. Toffler (1980: 50) provides the quote from Henry Ford.
13. Durkheim (1960) did allow that a "forced" division of labour, where individuals have no choice over how they participate in the productive system, would not lead to increased social solidarity. But he argued that this and other abnormal forms of the division of labour would disappear as industrial capitalism matured further.
14. See Antoniou and Rowley (1986) on family ownership patterns; Dhingra (1983) on concentration of ownership; and Carroll et al. (1982) on crosscutting directorship ties.
15. Bell (1973); current and more critical perspectives on postindustrial society are reviewed by Kumar (1995), Clement and Myles (1994), and Nelson (1995).
16. The managerial revolution perspective (Burnham, 1941; Berle and Means, 1968) was developed earlier, during an era when corporate concentration in North America was proceeding rapidly and when concerns about the excessive power of the corporate elite were being publicly debated (Reich, 1991: 38).
17. See Betcherman and Lowe (1997) for analyses of industrial restructuring in the Canadian economy. Also see Drache and Gertler (1991), Boyer and Drache (1996), and Barnet and Cavanagh (1994: Part Three) for critical perspectives on restructuring, globalization, and work.
18. Schumpeter's views are discussed in Bluestone and Harrison (1982: 9).
19. Drache and Gertler (1991: 13); also see Lush (1987), Grayson (1985), and the Canadian Labour Congress (1991). See Heinzl (1997) on Nike's closure of the Bauer factory.
20. Drache and Gertler (1991: 12). Also see Mahon's (1984) analysis of restructuring in the Canadian textile industry.
21. International Centre for Human Rights and Democratic Development, 1997. A report on this survey is available at the organization's web site: (http://www.idhrdd.ca).
22. The Canadian Labour Congress (1991) places the blame directly on the agreement. See the assessments of the FTA in Drache and Gertler (1991), as well as positions on both sides of the debate in Gold and Leyton-Brown (1988).
23. For current information, see the North American Institute's web site (http://www.santafe.edu). The Institute monitors the North American Agreement on Labor Cooperation. Two recent complaints, one in Mexico and the other in the U.S., concerned management opposition to union membership and collective bargaining.

24. Orme (1996: 13); Arsen, Wilson, and Zoninsein (1996); for different perspectives on NAFTA, see Bognanno and Ready (1993).

25. See Saul (1995) for a critique of this ideology.

26. Smucker and van den Berg (1991) provide a useful comparison of Swedish and Canadian labour market policies.

27. See Rubery et al. (1989) on British government labour market policies in the past decade; Kalleberg and Berg (1987: 208–12) and Rosenberg (1989) on the U.S. experience; Drache and Gertler (1991) on neoconservatism in Canada; and Haiven et al. (1991) for articles on Canada, Britain, and Sweden. Block (1990: 1–5) discusses how free market economics have come to dominate social and economic thought in North America.

CANADIAN EMPLOYMENT PATTERNS AND TRENDS

INTRODUCTION

Pick up a copy of any Canadian daily newspaper and flip through it, looking for features on job and career trends. You'll likely come across articles based on labour force statistics collected by Statistics Canada, or by some other public or private sector data collection agency. Most common are the unemployment rates, which are updated on a monthly basis. But the media frequently also carry stories on a wide range of other labour force topics, including income patterns, industry and occupational changes, gender differences in employment opportunities, part-time work, strikes, and workplace health and safety.

Many of these labour force statistics are examined in this chapter. Becoming more statistically literate is an important goal: in a society in which the media constantly bombard us with the latest figures on one social trend or another, it is helpful to have some understanding of the definition and source of these numbers, and even more important, to be able to interpret them critically. Hence, we will discuss these trends with reference to some of the broad theories of social and economic change discussed in Chapter 1. At the same time, this statistical overview will provide us with the background needed to evaluate, in Chapter 3, competing theories of how labour markets operate.

We begin by outlining key demographic factors shaping the workforce. We then go on to discuss labour force participation trends and Canada's occupational and industrial structures, emphasizing the rise of the service economy. Discussions of Canada's unemployment trends, and the growth in nonstandard jobs in this country are other central components of this chapter. We conclude with an analysis of where current labour market trends may be taking us, raising important issues about the future of work.

DATA SOURCES

A major data source is the Canadian census, a survey of the entire population of the country. The most recent national census was completed in 1996, although the results are not fully available in time for this edition of the book. The huge effort and cost involved in collecting information on the 29 million people in the country means that only a limited number of questions can be asked about each household and the individuals within it. Furthermore, because a census takes place every five years, results are seldom up to date. Despite this, it provides the most complete and accurate picture of the Canadian industrial and occupational structures at specific points in time, and allows us to accurately plot historical changes.

A second useful source is the monthly *Labour Force Survey* conducted by Statistics Canada. Unlike the census, which attempts to cover a range of areas, this random sample survey is designed to collect only work-related information and so provides much more detail. Because the survey is done every month, information is always updated. In order to get precise estimates of the labour market behaviour of Canadians aged 15 and older, a large sample is needed. Approximately 62,000 households (roughly 115,000 respondents) are included in the sample.[1] Households remain part of the sample for six months before being replaced.

The *Labour Force Survey* provides, for example, monthly estimates of unemployment rates, labour force participation rates, and the industries and occupations experiencing job growth or decline. The survey content has recently been revised and expanded to better reflect changes in the labour market.[2] Frequently, more detailed surveys, designed to study specific work-related topics, are piggybacked onto the *Labour Force Survey.* Examples of such topics include student summer employment, involuntary part-time work, and job search behaviour. Many of the statistics cited in this chapter are obtained from this useful source.[3]

THE DEMOGRAPHIC CONTEXT OF LABOUR MARKET CHANGE

Whether our focus is on the labour market today or 10 to 20 years in the future, there is no denying that *demographic shifts* (population changes) under way in Canadian society set some basic parameters. Of all the employment trends we will consider in this chapter, those related to the demographic composition of the labour force are perhaps the only ones we confidently can project into the future. So while economists debate whether the unemployment rate may stay high or decline next year, demographers (who specialize in studying the structure and dynamics of population) can quite accurately estimate birth rates, life expectancy, population growth, age distributions of the population, and related trends. Three of these trends deserve our attention: aging, cultural diversity, and educational attainment.

Workforce Aging

While we might dispute David Foot's claim in his best-selling book, *Boom, Bust and Echo,* that "[d]emographics explain about two-thirds of everything," we do agree that Canada's demographic trends influence many economic and social changes.[4] Foremost among these demographic factors is *population aging,* which has many implications for job opportunities, pensions, work values, and organizational structures. The *baby boom generation,* born between 1946 and 1964, is the largest generation in Canadian history. In the words of historian Doug Owram (1996: xiv), "Economics, politics, education, and family life would all have been considerably different without the vast demographic upsurge of births after the Second World War." As baby boomers went through the life course, they left few institutions unchanged—from popular music in the 1960s, to the rapid expansion of post-secondary institutions in the 1970s, to the burgeoning mutual fund industry of the 1990s. Coupled with smaller birth cohorts following in their wake, due to sharply declining birth rates, the aging of the baby boom has fundamentally altered the demographic shape and social structure of Canada. When baby boomers were entering the workforce in droves in the early 1970s, the median age of the labour force was around 27; by 1996 this had increased to 35, and it is projected to rise to just over 40 by 2016 (Dumas 1995).

This huge bulge in the workforce has affected the career opportunities of many Canadian workers. The baby boom generation entered the workforce when the economy was still expanding, and many obtained good jobs. The smaller generations that followed them into the labour force have been less fortunate, since higher unemployment and global economic uncertainties have led to lay-offs, not hiring. Yet many baby boomers are facing career blockages. This is because most work organizations are pyramids. Success has been defined in terms of climbing a ladder that has room for fewer and fewer people on each higher rung. Many baby boomers are finding that their careers have plateaued, as opportunities for upward movement disappear. For younger workers who have difficulties finding entry-level jobs, this may not seem a serious problem. But, for long-term employees who have learned to view success as upward movement, career blockages can be very unsettling (Foot and Venne 1990). Generally, work organizations have not adapted to changing demographic pressures, maintaining pyramidal structures and recruitment policies that are no longer appropriate and focusing on downsizing for the past decade (Foot and Stuffman 1996: Chapter 4).

Figure 2.1 details the workforce aging process by profiling the *age distribution* of labour force participants in 1975 and 1996. Note the decline in the relative proportion of teenagers (15 to 19 years) and young adults (20 to 24 years) between 1975 and 1996. Compare this with the increased size of the 35- to 44-year-old cohorts over this period. What is also interesting is the decline in the proportion of 55- to 64-year-olds in the workforce since 1975. This marks the trend toward "early" retirement, in part due to older workers being affected by labour market restructuring, and organizational "downsizing" in the 1980s and 1990s. Overall, improvements in health have increased life expectancies; thus, people are living longer.

In 1971, 8.2 percent of Canadians were 65 years of age or older. In 1991, 12 percent of the Canadian population were in this age group, and this is projected

FIGURE 2.1 *Age Distribution of the Labour Force by Gender, Canada, 1975 and 1996*

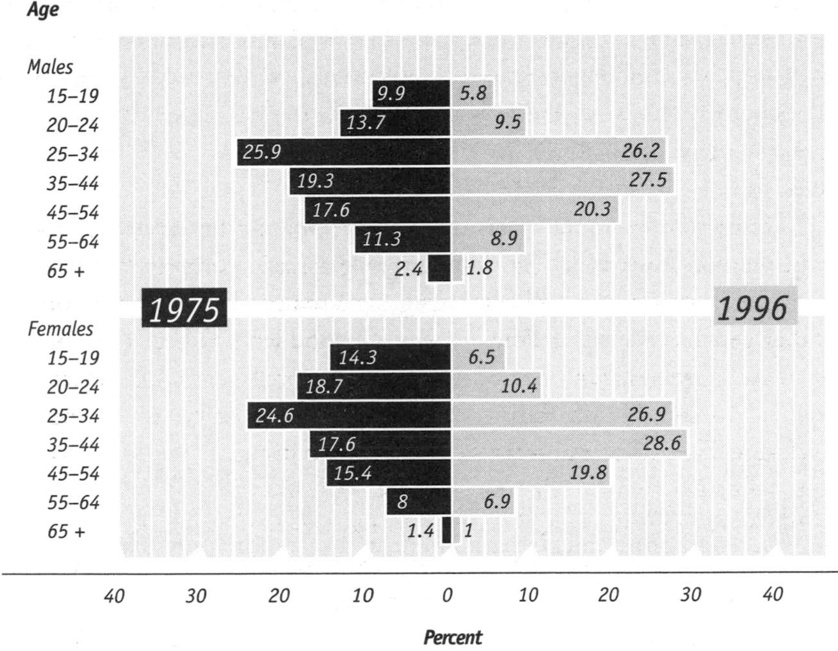

Source: Statistics Canada, "Age Distribution of the Labour Force by Gender, Canada, 1975 and 1996," adapted from "Labour Force Annual Averages, 1989–1994," Catalogue No. 71-529; and "Labour Force Annual Averages," Catalogue No. 71-220. Reprinted with permission.

to rise to about 23 percent by 2031.[5] The relative size of the working-age population that funds government old-age security programs through payroll contributions will shrink during this period. The first wave of baby boomers is now turning 50, and issues of retirement or career changes are foremost in their minds. Hence, pensions have become a public concern. Will the Canada/Quebec Pension Plan (C/QPP), one of Canada's main *social safety nets*, be able to support all the retiring baby boomers, or will today's youth have to cover the added costs? Reforms to the C/QPP in 1997 increased monthly premiums to address this concern. Will employer-sponsored pension plans be adequate, considering that less than half of employees, and fewer women than men, presently have one? Many workers do not have adequate means of support planned for their retirement. In 1993, for example, while 90 percent of the labour force participated in the C/QPP and, therefore, will receive small government pensions, only 35 percent made Registered Retirement Savings Plan (RRSP) contributions, and 35 percent participated in employer-sponsored registered pension plans (Statistics Canada 1996c).

It would seem reasonable to expect that workforce aging would open up opportunities for younger workers, who are far outnumbered by middle-aged baby boomers (Easterlin 1980). This has not been the case yet, mainly because employers have been downsizing rather than hiring. Consider the relatively small size of the 15- to 19-year-old and 20- to 24-year-old cohorts (Figure 2.1). In ten to fifteen years, when the baby boomers enter retirement, there is a distinct possibility of labour shortages—or at least a drop in the unemployment rate. Even so, we need to be concerned about the generation in-between, which currently is having difficulty finding good jobs.

Greater Workforce Diversity

Immigration is an important determinant of Canada's population mosaic. For centuries, Canada has been a country of immigrants. In the post–World War II era, Canadian governments have attempted to tailor immigration policy to labour market trends, partly in anticipation of labour shortages in key areas. Immigration levels have been kept low when unemployment was high, but have been allowed to rise when economic expansion required extra workers. In fact, there have been times (around 1910, for example, when the Western provinces were being settled) when immigration levels were considerably higher than they are today. For over two decades now, birth rates have been below replacement level, so low that our population would have declined unless supplemented by immigration.

Quotas are now set around 200,000 immigrants per year (less than one percent of the total population), with an emphasis on business immigrants who can make substantial investments in the Canadian economy. Despite concerns in some quarters that immigrants are taking jobs away from native-born Canadians, research shows that this is rarely the case. Immigrants frequently create their own jobs, or are willing to take jobs that others do not wish to have, and are carefully selected to match shortages of workers in specific occupational categories. Between 1986 and 1991, 28 percent of the increase in Canada's overall employment was accounted for by immigrants. And, given the impending shortage of labour force participants a few decades ahead, maintenance of current levels of immigration is a necessary policy decision.[6]

While the majority of immigrants are selected for their occupational, educational, and financial credentials, Canada also continues to accept a significant number of refugees from impoverished and politically unsettled countries for humanitarian reasons. Not all of these immigrants are equipped to compete successfully in our labour market, and many require training in English and other skills, as well as other social supports—all increasingly difficult for communities to provide at a time of government cuts to social programs.

The source countries for immigration to Canada have changed dramatically in the past few decades. This has created greater cultural diversity, in society and in workplaces. Until recently, the majority of immigrants to Canada were from European countries; most were white. Today most immigrants are arriving from Asia, Africa, and Central and Latin America. Half of recent immigrants are from Asia (Chui and Devereaux 1995: 19). Canadian immigration policies no longer favour European immigrants but, more importantly, the demand to immigrate to Canada has declined in Europe, while it has increased dramatically elsewhere. Consequently, more immigrants are members of visible minority groups with distinctive cultural backgrounds.

According to the 1991 Census, 31 percent of the population reported ethnic origins other than British or French (Renaud and Badets 1993: 20). In 1991, *visible minorities* accounted for 1 in 10 Canadians, and this is projected to increase to 1 in 5 by 2016, assuming medium population growth and a continuation of present immigration policies.[7] The largest visible minority group in Canada in 1991 was the Chinese (about 666,000 individuals), followed by South Asians and Blacks (*Canadian Social Trends,* Summer 1996: 3; Dai and George 1996). Moreover, 3.9 percent of the nation's population is of Aboriginal origin, and this is expected to increase to over 4 percent by 2016 (Loh 1995: 35). Given that immigrants and Aboriginals tend to be younger than the population as a whole, they will comprise a growing share of the workforce as older Canadians retire. As discussed in later chapters, these demographic trends have prompted governments and employers to develop employment equity policies to facilitate greater workplace cultural diversity and reduce the potential for labour market discrimination.

A Better Educated Workforce

On the whole, Canadians are becoming increasingly well educated, a trend which has also fundamentally changed the character of the labour force.

Figure 2.2 shows the dramatic change in *educational attainment* of the labour force between 1975 and 1996. In 1975, more than 50 percent of females and 45 percent of males in the labour force had a high school education; only 7 and 10 percent, respectively, had a university degree. In subsequent decades, large numbers of both men and especially women obtained post-secondary credentials. Specifically, 17 percent of labour force participants had a university degree in 1996.

This rising educational attainment has been the backdrop for a debate over the role of education in a rapidly changing and increasingly global and technological economic environment. Some analysts believe that a well-educated workforce is now a nation's key resource in a global marketplace (Reich 1991; Drucker 1993). Business and government have argued that additional education and training, and an overhaul of the education system that makes it more

FIGURE 2.2 *Educational Attainment of the Labour Force by Gender, Canada, 1975 and 1996*

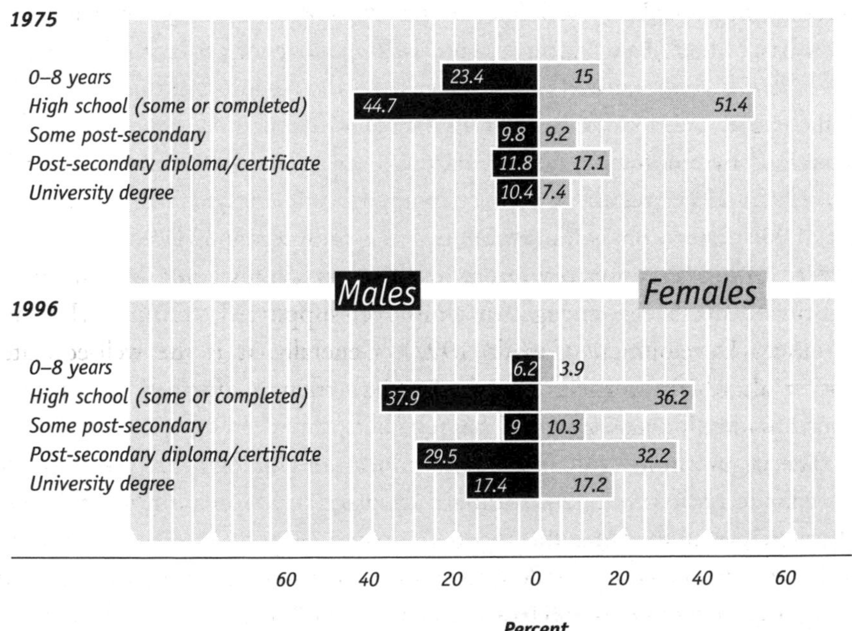

Source: Statistics Canada, "Educational Attainment of the Labour Force by Gender, Canada, 1975 and 1996," adapted from "Labour Force Annual Averages, 1989–1994," Catalogue No. 71-529; and "Labour Force Annual Averages," Catalogue No. 71-220. Reprinted with permission.

job-relevant, will help Canada improve its "competitive edge" (Economic Council of Canada 1992a). The latest variant of this perspective is found in the concepts of *lifelong learning* and *learning organizations*.[8] Essentially, these refer to continuous education, both formally and informally, in educational institutions and at work and home, throughout one's adult life. Speaking on behalf of the corporate sector, the Conference Board of Canada has been promoting "business–education partnerships" to ensure that education becomes more relevant to the new economy (Bloom 1990). Educators, parents, and students have responded by raising concerns that closer links between education and the economy might mean too much business influence over what is taught at all levels of the educational system (Barlow and Robertson 1994).

By international standards, Canadians indeed are well educated if one looks at post-secondary credentials and enrolment levels (Oderkirk 1993). But there is more to developing a nation's human resources than the acquisition of formal education. No doubt there are educational reforms (current or prospective university and college students, for instance, likely would advocate lower tuition and improved student loan programs) which could help us graduate more skilled, flexible, and enterprising labour force participants. Even basic literacy and numeracy are lacking in small pockets of the workforce.[9] But work-related training is not only the responsibility of the education system. Canada has a poor record of workplace training provided or sponsored by employers. A 1990 comparison of 23 industrialized countries ranked Canada sixteenth in terms of the proportion of gross domestic product (GDP) spent on work-related training (Economic Council of Canada 1992b). And according to a recent national survey, just over one-quarter of full-time employees engage in employer-supported training (Human Resources Development Canada 1997). Generally, it is the well-educated worker already in a good job who receives training, further accentuating labour market inequalities (see Chapter 3).[10]

The assumption underlying the education and training solution to Canada's recent economic difficulties is that our workforce is not sufficiently educated and trained, yet the above discussion suggests there is more to the problem. For one thing, while unemployment is higher among the less educated, a considerable number of Canada's unemployed are well educated. In addition, many Canadian workers are in jobs that require little education or training. In 1994 almost 1 in 4 (23 percent) of employed Canadians (aged 15 to 64) reported that they were overqualified for their job.[11] This "underemployment" highlights the need to also examine how job content and skill requirements could be upgraded—in short, how the "demand" for educated labour could be improved. Clearly, there are deeper problems in the structure of our economy as well, and concerted efforts by government, the private sector, organized labour, and professional associations are needed to address them. As two American sociologists recently concluded about the United States: "The problem is a shortage of good jobs to a greater extent than it is inadequate training and development."[12]

LABOUR FORCE PARTICIPATION TRENDS

Now that we understand the basic demographic profile of the workforce, we can examine key labour market and employment trends that define where, how, and for whom Canadians work. *Labour force participation* is the main indicator of a population's economic activity, at least from the perspective of paid employment. Whether relying on census or monthly Labour Force Survey data, calculations of labour force size or participation rates are based on the number of individuals 15 years of age or older who are working for pay (including self-employed without employees and those employing others) and those who are looking for work. Hence, the *unemployed* (those out of work but who have actively looked for work in the past four weeks) are counted as part of the labour force. However, individuals performing unpaid household and child care work in their home are not included in official labour force calculations, even though their labour makes essential economic and social contributions.

Using the official definition to look at work patterns at the beginning of the century, 53 percent of Canadians (15 years of age and older) were participating in the labour force in 1901. The rate increased to over 57 percent by 1911 but did not go much higher until the 1970s (Figure 2.3). By 1981 almost two-thirds (64.8 percent) of the eligible population was in a paid job or seeking one. Participation rates peaked in 1989, just prior to the recent economic recession, at 67.5 percent. Rates fell during the recession and the so-called "recovery" period to about 65 percent in 1996. Rates for both males and females have fallen, although more so among the former, and the sharpest declines of all are found among youth (15 to 24 years). It appears that as jobs became harder to find, some Canadians decided to leave the labour force.

FIGURE 2.3 *Labour Force Participation Rates by Gender, Canada, 1946–1996*

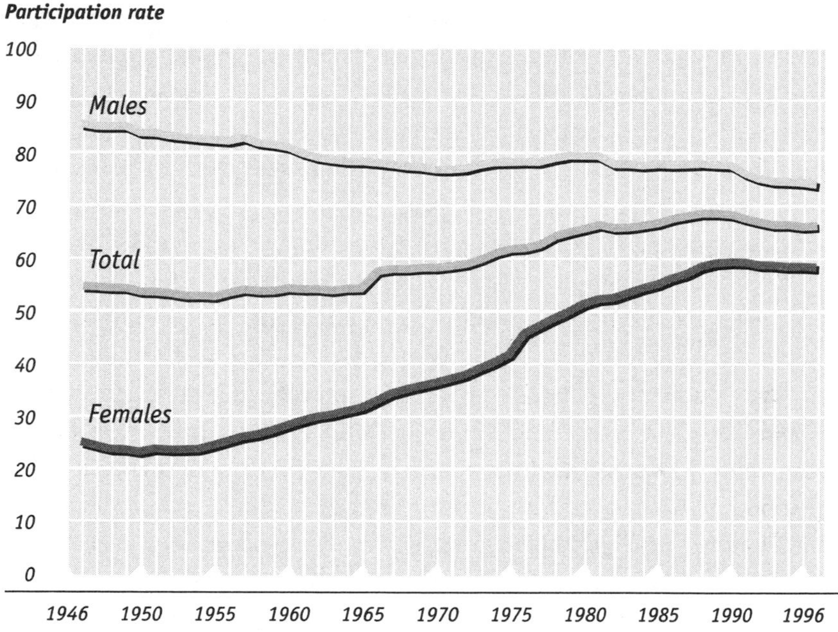

Source: Statistics Canada, "Labour Force Participation Rates by Gender, Canada, 1946–1996," adapted from "Labour Force Annual Averages, 1989–1994," Catalogue No. 71-529; "Labour Force Annual Averages," Catalogue No. 71-220; and "Historical Statistics of Canada," Catalogue No. 11-516. Reprinted with permission.

Gender Differences in Labour Force Participation

Breaking down the participation rate by gender, we find striking differences. In 1901 only 16.1 percent of women aged 15 or older were in the paid labour force. However, this rate increased with each ten-year census. By the post–World War II period, the size of these increases was substantial (Figure 2.3). Between 1960 and 1975, female labour force participation jumped from 28 percent to 41 percent, and the following decade saw it rise to 55 percent. The landmark year was 1980, the first in which a majority of Canadian women were part of the officially defined labour force.

Women's labour force participation rate peaked at about 59 percent in 1990 and 1991 (again, before the recession), then dropped slightly to just over 57 percent in subsequent years. This ended a steady four-decade climb in women's participation rates (Basset 1994; Butlin 1995). Even so, it is hard to underestimate the impact of this long-term trend on workplaces, families, and society as a whole. During the 1960s and 1970s, much of the growth was due to larger numbers of women returning to paid employment after their children were in school or had left home. Much of the female employment growth in the 1980s occurred among mothers with children at home. *Dual-earner families* now account for 3 in 5 of all families, and 15 percent of all mothers in the workforce are single parents.[13]

While female participation rates have gone up over the decades, male rates have declined, although not as steeply. Between 1901 and 1931, male participation rates remained close to 90 percent, dropping to the mid-80 percent range in the pre– and post–World War II decades. In the 1970s and 1980s, male rates fluctuated between 76 and 78 percent. However, the rate has declined from 77 percent in 1989 to just over 72 percent in 1996. In comparison with the female rate, this recent decline in the male labour force participation rate has been greater and continuous.

Thus, long-term growth in total labour force participation rates is the product of substantial increases for women and somewhat less dramatic declines for men. The latter change reflects two trends: men are living longer (with more men living past the conventional retirement age, the proportion of all men out of the labour force is increasing) and more men are retiring early (that is, before the accepted retirement age of 65). The causes of growing female labour force participation, which are more complex, are discussed in Chapter 4. A similar convergence of female and male rates has occurred in other industrialized countries (the United States, Britain, Germany, France, Italy, and Japan, for example) but, over the past few decades, Canada has experienced the largest jump in female labour force participation.

It is important to note that these labour force participation rates are annual averages. Given the seasonal nature of some types of work in Canada (jobs in agriculture, fishing and forestry, and construction and tourism, for example), higher levels of labour force participation are typically recorded in the spring, summer, and autumn months. Furthermore, taking a full twelve-month period, we observe higher proportions of Canadians reporting labour force participation at some point during the year. Thus, annual averages do not reveal the extent to which Canadians move in and out of different labour market statuses. A 1993 analysis of labour market activity showed that 27 percent of individuals who were in the labour force at some point that year experienced a change of status, either entering or exiting the labour force, becoming unemployed, or finding a job.[14]

In addition, there are a number of groups that continue to have much lower than average rates of labour force activity. Many Native Canadians are economically marginalized, facing huge barriers to paid employment. For example, the 1986 census revealed a labour force participation rate for male Aboriginal Canadians living off reserves of 66 percent, compared with 77 percent for all Canadian men. Comparable statistics for Aboriginal women living off reserves and all Canadian women were 45 percent and 55 percent, respectively.[15] Similarly, research shows that disabled Canadians are much less likely to be in the paid labour force, even if their disabilities only restrict them from certain types of employment.[16]

Labour Force Participation among Youth

The labour force participation of youth (aged 15 to 24) rose steadily from an annual average of 63.8 percent in 1977 to 70.6 percent in 1989. Like the overall participation rates, since then the youth rate also declined, but much more steeply. By 1996, the rate had fallen below its 1977 level, to 61.5 percent.[17] In 1996, the participation rate for teenagers (aged 15 to 19) was 47.3 percent, compared with 75.5 percent for young adults (aged 20 to 24). Not only have youth been finding it more difficult to obtain well-paying jobs after graduating, but in addition, throughout the 1980s there was a pervasive decline in youth wages, more so than for any other age group in the labour market (Betcherman and Leckie 1997). Young people have responded to this tightening of the labour market by staying in or returning to school. For example, 77 percent of the 15- to 20-year-old population attended school during the 1993–94 school year, up considerably from 59 percent in 1981–82 (Bernier 1995: 12). However, with rising post-secondary education costs, this option may not continue to be open to as many youth.

As we note below in our discussion of Canada's growing service economy, many of the part-time jobs created in the lower-level service industries have been filled by students (and women). Thus, part-time employment appears to have become part of youth culture (in Canada and the United States), typically providing spending money for teenagers and helping to pay education and living expenses for young adults. While the advantages to college and university students are obvious, some observers have questioned whether teenage employment, particularly if it requires many hours each week, might have negative effects on educational performance and individual adjustment.[18]

Labour Force Participation among Older Canadians

Moving to the other end of the age continuum, we also are observing a decline in labour force participation among older men (aged 55 to 64). For example, in 1996 only 59.3 percent of 55- to 64-year-old Canadian men were in the labour force, compared with 76 percent in 1975 (Lindsay and Devereaux 1991; Statistics Canada 1997c). With improved social service benefits provided to the elderly by government, compared with a generation or two earlier, and with the larger numbers of older men who have company-sponsored pensions as well as other personal savings (RRSPs, for example), income security among older men has increased. Consequently, a greater percentage before the age of 65 are opting to retire.[19] In 1994, 14 percent of males 55 to 59 years were retired, as were 45 percent of those 60 to 64 years. The average retirement age was 61 years.

However, there are also other reasons for early labour market exit by men. Among all retired men, the 1994 General Social Survey found that health was the most frequent reason given for retirement (by 25 percent), followed by choice (24 percent). One in ten had been forced into retirement by unemployment (Statistics Canada 1995b). Looking just at retired men ages 55 to 64, in 1993 only 48 percent of this group had the support of employer pension plans. For many men in this age group, retirement means subsisting on a very low income (Gower 1995). So it is not surprising that we also note a trend to re-employment after retirement. In 1994, for example, 16 percent of men who had ever retired re-entered employment after their first retirement; one-quarter cited financial reasons for doing so, while some 20 percent wanted to occupy their free time, and a similar percentage cited personal choice (Monette 1996b). These recent trends challenge the traditional three-stage model of the work life—education, employment, then retirement. Instead, researchers are now using a *life-course perspective* that views individuals' roles as more fluid, and examines the choices and constraints underlying transitions across roles.[20]

Older men who lose their jobs have more difficulty finding work, since many employers are reluctant to hire and retrain older workers. In addition, older men are more likely to be employed in industries where employment is declining (manufacturing and the resource-based industries, for example). Hence, the chances of being rehired by a former employer are lower than average (Tindale 1991: 15, 16). Consequently, many unemployed older men decide to retire. Some do so because they are offered early retirement packages by employers attempting to downsize their workforce, while others decide that "retired" would be an easier label to live with than "unemployed." Thus, while a shortage of jobs may have pushed some men over the age of 55 out of the labour force, for an equal number an adequate pension encouraged them to retire voluntarily.[21]

A similar shift toward earlier retirement has not been observed for older women (aged 55 to 64). Only 9 percent of women aged 55 to 59 are retired from a paid job, as are 22 percent of the 60 to 64 age group. However, defining retirement for older women is not straightforward, given that some who consider themselves retired were last employed prior to having children, while others define their own retirement in terms of their husband's status or the receipt of a government pension (Monnette 1996a: 10). And only 8 percent of women who ever retired reported returning to paid employment, which is half the proportion of men who did so (Monnette 1996b). Since a smaller number of women are employed in manufacturing and resource-based industries, fewer older women are being pushed into retirement by downsizing in these industries.

In fact, labour force participation among older women (aged 55 to 64) has been increasing slowly, reaching 36.9 percent in 1996, despite recent declines in the overall female labour force participation rate. Rather than seeking to leave the labour force early, more older women appear to be re-entering. There is probably an underlying financial factor. Women earn less on average than men and receive fewer benefits, including pensions. Hence, compared with men of the same age, fewer older employed women may have the financial resources needed to retire before the age of 65. Furthermore, the growing trend toward wives becoming the sole wage earner in families is most evident in families with husbands aged 55 or older (Crompton and Geran 1995: 28). In some of these families, women may have continued to work after their husbands became unemployed or retired.

Unpaid Work

As stated in the Introduction to this book, our emphasis is on paid work since this is the primary type of work for the majority of adults in an industrialized capitalist economy. Nevertheless, using the definition of work as activity that provides a product or service used or valued by others in society, it is obvious that paid work constitutes only a portion of all work done in Canada. The largest and most serious omission is *unpaid household and child care work.* In fact, time-use studies reveal that Canadians, on average, spend as much time in their unpaid work as in paid work. If given a dollar value, this unpaid work would have added $235 billion, or another one-third, to Canada's 1992 gross domestic product (GDP) (Frederick 1995: 7; Jackson 1996: 29). The biggest share (approximately two-thirds) of this type of unpaid work continues to be done by women, a topic explored in Chapter 4.

Also omitted from labour force participation rates and employment statistics are those Native Canadians (and a few non-Natives) typically resident in the northern parts of the country, who continue to live and work in traditional hunting and gathering societies. Such groups form only a small part of Canada's population; nevertheless, their *subsistence work* clearly provides useful and valued goods and services for their families and communities.

In addition, *volunteer work* is overlooked if we rely only on official labour force statistics. A national survey of Canadian adults revealed that in 1987 about 5 million unpaid workers contributed their time and energy in over 9 million volunteer jobs. Most of these jobs involved only a few hours per week, but they amounted to over 1 billion hours during that single year. Recognizing that many volunteers do not view their contributions as work, we can still treat their efforts in 1987 as equivalent to more than half a million full-time, full-year jobs. If paid at minimum-wage levels, this work would have cost more than $75 million each week (Pold and Wong 1990).

Volunteer workers are found in a wide variety of clubs and associations, as well as in religious and political organizations. However, a very large number work in the publicly funded service industries, assisting in the provision of health, social, recreational, educational, environmental, and other types of services. In recent years, as government departments at all levels have attempted to cut costs and reduce payrolls, volunteers have also been replacing paid employees. This trend will no doubt continue, so volunteer work is likely to become an even larger part of the total amount of unpaid work performed by Canadians.

Official labour force participation statistics also omit some Canadians working in the *hidden economy*, or, as it is sometimes called, the underground or irregular economy. Such work might involve illegal activities like selling drugs, prostitution, gambling, or, alternatively, legal work done for cash or in exchange for some other services. Mechanics working out of their homes and not reporting this income, and farmers assisting their neighbours in return for similar help at another time would be examples of this noncriminal group, some of whose members would be represented in labour force surveys through their real jobs. Others, if surveyed, might report themselves unemployed or out of the labour force in order to avoid detection by tax authorities. There is little research on the subject, since there is no direct way of systematically studying behaviour that people do not wish to have publicly documented.[22] But the research available suggests that participation in the hidden economy is relatively common. During the mid-1980s, an assessment of concealed employment (legal but unreported work) in Western industrialized countries concluded that up to 1 in 5 adults might be involved at some point in a given year, although, for most of these individuals, this would reflect relatively few hours of work. Canadian researchers estimate that about 15 to 20 percent of total economic activity in Canada was not being reported to tax authorities in 1994.[23] The introduction of the Goods and Services Tax (GST) several years earlier may have prompted more independent self-employed workers to begin asking for "under-the-table" payment.

In short, official statistics clearly underestimate the number of working Canadians and the value of their work. Various types of informal work (household and child care work, volunteer work, work in subsistence economies, and work in the hidden economy) are overlooked. This reflects how society values individuals' unpaid activities. Indeed, there is growing discomfort with conventional approaches to measuring economic activity. As articulated by three American economists, "the GDP [the nation's economic output] ignores the contribution of the social realm—that is, the economic role of households and communities. This is where much of the nation's most important work gets done, from caring for children and older people to volunteer work in its many forms. It is the nation's social glue" (Cobb, Halstead, and Rowe 1995: 76). Furthermore, it appears that informal work may be increasing. However, we could not even begin to provide an adequate overview of both paid employment and the various types of informal work in one volume. Consequently, with some exceptions, the rest of this book focuses on paid employment (including self-employment in the formal economy), which continues to represent the largest share of work performed by Canadians.

INDUSTRIAL CHANGES: THE EMERGENCE OF THE SERVICE ECONOMY

The work done by labour force participants can be categorized in several ways. We begin by discussing industrial shifts and then examine occupational changes in the following section. *Industry* classifications direct our attention to the major type of economic activity occurring within the workplace. In the broadest sense, we can distinguish the *primary sector*, including agriculture, mining, forestry, and other resource extraction industries, from the *secondary sector* (manufacturing and construction), where goods are produced from the raw materials supplied by the primary sector, and the *tertiary sector*, where services rather than products are provided. A service, simply defined, is the exchange of a commodity that has no tangible form (Price and Blair 1989: 2). These general industrial categories can be further subdivided into more specific industries. The service sector, for example, includes among others the finance, education, retail trade, government (public administration), and health service industries.

Service Sector Growth

In 1891, the primary industries accounted for 49 percent of the Canadian labour force, the secondary sector for 20 percent, and the service sector for the remaining 31 percent (Matthews 1985: 36). In the following half-century, the primary sector lost its dominance, while the manufacturing industries expanded. At the same time, the service industries were also increasing in size. By 1951 almost half (47 percent) of all employed Canadians were working in the service industries, while the secondary sector accounted for almost one-third (31 percent) of employment (Picot 1987: 11). The relative size of the primary and secondary sectors have been declining steadily. For example, between 1961 and 1995, agricultural employment fell from 11 to 3 percent of the total, and the decline in manufacturing was from 24 to 15 percent of the total (Betcherman and Lowe 1997: 26). The portion of workers in the service sector has more than doubled over the past century, and now accounts for close to three-quarters of the labour force. This sector has also come to represent a much larger share of the total value of goods and services produced in the Canadian economy.[24]

These few statistics clearly demonstrate that we are now living in a service-dominated economy. A similar transition from a pre-industrial to an industrial to a service economy occurred in other capitalist countries such as the United States, the United Kingdom, Japan, and Germany. Compared with these countries, manufacturing never played as great a role in Canada's development. Consequently, compared with the industrial structure of most of these countries, the service industries account for a somewhat larger share of the Canadian labour force today (Price and Blair 1989: 15).

The rise of the service sector can be attributed to a combination of factors. Productivity gains due to new technologies and organizational forms in manufacturing, but also in the resource industries, have meant that fewer people could produce much more. In primary industries, the growing size and declining number of farms in Canada is perhaps the best indicator (McSkimmings 1990). Toward the end of the nineteenth and into the early twentieth century, factory mechanization doubled workers' productivity, despite a reduction in hours worked (Pomfret 1981: 123). In the last few decades, automated production systems (robotics and information technology) have meant an acceleration of this trend. Thus, the expansion of production in the primary and secondary sectors has not been accompanied by a proportional increase in the demand for more employees.

Industrial expansion and productivity gains over the years have led to higher incomes and increased amounts of leisure time. These factors, in turn, have fueled the demand for a wide range of services, particularly in the last few decades when the recreation, accommodation, and food service industries have been growing rapidly. In addition, the expansion of the role of the state as a provider of educational and social services and a funder of health services has contributed significantly to the growth of the service sector. However, governments' vigorous pursuit of deficit reduction in the 1990s has resulted in reduced program funding, downsizing, and privatization—trends that do not bode well for public sector employment.

Employment Diversity within the Service Sector

Specific industries within the broad service sector have been categorized in a number of different ways. The standard Statistics Canada classification system lists the following five categories: transportation, communication, and other utilities; trade; finance, insurance, and real estate; public administration and defence; and community, business, and personal services. Yet this typology hides some important differences. In particular, the community, business, and personal services category, the largest of the five and the one that has been expanding most rapidly in recent years, contains a range of diverse industries within which working conditions vary significantly (Pold and Wong 1990b: 5).

A clearer picture emerges from an alternative classification system that separates the service sector into six industry groups: distributive services (transportation, communication, and wholesale trade); business services (finance, insurance, real estate, and other services to business); the education, health, and welfare sector; public administration; retail trade; and other consumer services. Distributive services differ from the others by being the final link in the process whereby raw materials are extracted, transformed, and then delivered to the ultimate consumer. Business services also provide support to the primary and secondary industries (the goods-producing sector), but in a less tangible way. Like public administration, the education, health, and welfare sector contains primarily noncommercial services provided by the state, while retail trade and other consumer services (for example, food and beverage, accommodation, and the tourism industries) are commercial services aimed directly at consumers. The same typology subdivides the goods-producing sector into agriculture, natural-resource based industries (other primary industries including utilities), manufacturing, and construction.[25]

It is useful to further divide the six service categories into an *upper tier* (distributive, business, education, health and welfare, and public administration) and a *lower tier* (retail trade and other consumer services) since, as we will demonstrate later, many more good jobs are located in the former.[26] Table 2.1 uses the ten-category classification system to profile the industrial distribution of Canada's employed. Other tables in this chapter are also based on only the employed members of the labour force. In 1996, just over one-quarter (25.9 percent) of employed Canadians were working in the goods-producing sector, while 74.1 percent were employed in the service industries. Table 2.1 shows that almost one-half (47.4 percent) of the employed are located in the upper-tier services, and approximately one-quarter (26.8 percent) have jobs in the lower-tier service industries.

Gender and Age Differences in Service Sector Employment

Table 2.1 also reveals distinct gender differences in industrial locations. In 1996, almost 4 out of 10 men were employed in the goods-producing sector, compared with only 14 percent of women. However, women were much more

TABLE 2.1 *Industry by Gender, Employed Population, Canada, 1996*

Industry	*Total*	*Female* %	*Male*
Goods-producing sector (total)	25.9	13.7	36.1
Agriculture	3.3	2.4	4.1
Natural resource-based	2.1	0.7	3.2
Manufacturing	15.2	9.5	20.1
Construction	5.3	1.1	8.7
Service sector (total)	74.1	85.2	62.5
Upper-tier services (total)	47.3	54.3	41.5
Distributive services	12.1	7.2	16.1
Business services	12.6	14.3	11.1
Education/health/welfare	16.6	26.8	8.3
Public administration	6.0	6.0	6.0
Lower-tier services (total)	26.8	32.1	22.4
Retail trade	12.6	14.0	11.5
Other consumer services	14.2	18.1	10.9
Total percent	100.0	100.0	100.0
Total (in 000s)	13,676	6,197	7,479

Source: Statistics Canada, "Industry by Gender, Employed Population, Canada, 1981 and 1996," adapted from "Labour Force Annual Averages 1996," Catalogue No. 71-220. Reprinted with permission.

likely to be employed in the lower-tier services (32 percent compared with 22 percent of men). Within the upper-tier services, women were much more heavily concentrated in the education, health, and welfare industries than were men, while the latter were somewhat more likely to be employed in the distributive services (transportation, communication, and wholesale trade).

Age plays an important part in further stratifying the employed labour force across these industrial categories. Younger workers (aged 15 to 24) are much less likely to be employed in the upper-tier services. Instead, many young workers, particularly women, hold jobs in the lower-tier retail trade and consumer service industries.[27] Many of these young workers are students in part-time jobs, as noted above in our discussion of labour force participation rates. Thus, the expansion of the lower-tier service industries (for instance, shopping malls, fast food restaurants, and tourism) since the 1970s has relied largely on the recruitment of student workers, creating a distinct segment of the labour force. However, older female workers are also much more likely than older male workers to be employed in the retail trade or other consumer service industries.

OCCUPATIONAL CHANGES

While the industrial classification system is based on what is being produced, we also can sort workers according to their *occupation.* Occupational distinctions are determined by the kind of work that an individual typically performs, the actual tasks that she or he completes. Thus, secretaries, managers, or accountants (occupational titles) work in mining companies, automobile factories, and government bureaucracies—that is, in the primary, secondary, and tertiary (or service) sectors of the economy. Other occupations are sometimes found only within specific industrial sectors. Teachers, nurses, and retail clerks are occupational groups typically found in the service sector, for example. So the two classification systems parallel each other to an extent but also overlap considerably. In fact, Canada's Standard Occupational Classification (SOC) system has a "service occupation" category, which includes occupations such as hairdressers (personal services), police officers (protective services), and waitresses (food services).

A basic limitation of the SOC system is that it does not adequately capture the skill content of jobs. From our earlier discussions of education and training, it is clear that developing human resources—the skills of the workforce—has become a public policy priority. How can we provide a detailed skills profile of the workforce that will assist individuals, employers, and policy makers to plan where to make educational and training investments? Human Resources Development Canada recently teamed up with Statistics Canada to devise a methodology for addressing this question. The result was the National Occupational Classification (NOC).[28]

Table 2.2 displays the structure of the NOC with selected examples of occupations in each category. Essentially, the NOC identifies two dimensions of *skill,* providing information on skill level and generic skill type for each of the 25,000 detailed occupations in the Canadian labour market. Four basic skill levels are used, plus a separate level for management occupations, and each is directly related to the education and training required. For example, occupations in skill level A are mainly the professions and require a university education; occupations in skill level D require no formal education and only short demonstrations or some on-the-job training. The nine skill types indicate the kinds of tasks performed. Note that the highest skill groups are concentrated mainly in what we earlier referred to as "upper-tier services," while skill level D occupations are in lower-tier services and goods production.

Blue-Collar and White-Collar Occupations

Many but not all of the people employed in the primary and secondary industries would be classified as blue-collar workers, while most of those working in the service industries would be identified as white-collar workers. The term *blue-collar* has traditionally been used to distinguish occupations (for example, farmer, miner, truck driver, construction worker, and factory worker) with potentially dirty working conditions from *white-collar* (including clerical, sales, managerial, and professional) occupations. The explanation, of course, is that for the former jobs wearing a white collar would be inappropriate, since it would not stay clean. Thus, in the past, white-collar occupations tended to be viewed as having higher status. However, with the expansion of the service industries, including the lower-tier services where poorly paid, part-time jobs are quite common, the white-collar occupational category has come to include the majority of the labour force, including many people in less desirable jobs.

As primary sector industries became less important over the course of this century, we saw a huge decline in the size of some occupational groups and a proportional increase in others. A number of specific examples can help make the point. The 1911 census revealed that 34 percent of the labour force was in agricultural occupations, compared with only 4 percent in clerical occupations, and a similarly small proportion in professional occupations. By 1951, agricultural occupations had declined to only 16 percent of the labour force, compared with 11 percent in clerical occupations and 7 percent in professions (O'Neill 1991: 10). The 1996 Labour Force Survey shows 3 percent of the labour force in agricultural occupations, along with 14 percent in clerical occupations, and the same proportion in management and administrative occupations. In short, the expansion of the service economy has greatly increased a wide range of white-collar occupations.

Gender and Occupational Location

Many of the new white-collar positions have been filled by women, while the remaining blue-collar jobs in the primary and secondary sectors are still typically held by men. In fact, given the heavy concentration of women in clerical, sales, and service occupations, the term *pink collar* has been used to describe these occupational categories.

Table 2.2 *Classifying Occupations by Skill Type and Level—The National Occupational Classification**

	Occupational Skill Type								
Skill Level	**Business, finance & administration**	**Natural & applied sciences**	**Health**	**Social sciences, education, government service, religion**	**Arts, culture, recreation, sport**	**Sales and service**	**Trades, transportation & equipment operators**	**Primary industries**	**Occupations unique to processing, manufacturing & utilities**
Management occupations	*Senior managers, legislators, managers*								
Skill level A	*auditors, accountants, human resource professionals, investment professionals*	*engineers, architects, systems analysts, computer programmers, physical and life science professionals*	*physicians, dentists, chiropractors, pharmacists, registered nurses, therapy professionals*	*judges, lawyers, professors, teachers, psychologists, social workers, clergy, probation officers, policy and program officers, researchers, and consultants*	*librarians, writers, translators, public relations professionals, creative and performing artists*				
Skill level B	*clerical supervisors, administrative occupations, secretaries*	*technical occupations in physical and life sciences, engineering, architecture, electronics*	*medical and health care technologists and technicians*	*paralegals; social service, religious, and education occupations not classified above*	*technical occupations in libraries, museums, galleries; photographers, graphic artists, technical occupations in motion pictures, broadcasting, performing arts; announcers; athletes and coaches*	*sales and service supervisors, technical sales specialists, insurance and real estate sales, chefs and butchers, police officers, and firefighters*	*supervisors, machinists, electrical trades and telecommunications occupations, plumbers, carpenters, other construction trades, mechanics, train crew, tailors, jewelers*	*supervisors, underground miners, logging machine operators, fishing vessel operators, fishermen/women; contractors, operators, and supervisors in agriculture*	*supervisors, central control and processing operators*

(continued)

Table 2.2 *(Cont.)*

Skill Level	*Occupational Skill Type* Business, finance & administration	Natural & applied sciences	Health	Social sciences, education, government service, religion	Arts, culture, recreation, sport	Sales and service	Trades, transportation & equipment operators	Primary industries	Occupations unique to processing, manufacturing & utilities
Skill level C	*clerical occupations, office equipment operators, library clerks, mail and message distribution occupations*		*assisting occupations in health services*			*retail sales clerks, travel and accommodation occupations, tour and recreational guides, food and beverage service occupations, childcare and home support workers*	*motor vehicle and transit drivers, heavy equipment operators, installers, repairers, and servicers*	*logging and forestry workers, mine service workers, oil and gas drilling operators, agriculture workers, fishing and trapping workers*	*machine operators and related workers, assemblers*
Skill level D						*cashiers, food counter attendants, security guards, cleaners*	*trades helpers, labourers*	*labourers*	*labourers*

* This table gives examples of occupational groups (based on 3-digit Standard Occupational Classification). For a complete list, see *Job Futures 1996, Volume One: Occupational Outlooks* (Ottawa: Minister of Supply and Services Canada, 1996), xv–xviii, 455–57.

Source: Employment and Immigration Canada, *National Occupational Classification* (Ottawa: Canada Communications Group, 1993). Reproduced with the permission of the Minister of Public Works and Government Services Canada, 1997.

Using the SOC to maintain comparability with earlier data, Table 2.3 provides a detailed gender breakdown of occupational distributions for 1981 and 1996. Again, we are examining a subset of the total labour force: the currently employed. Considering first the total distributions (female and male combined), it is apparent that over the past 15 years, managerial and administrative occupations have become considerably more common (an increase from 8.1 percent to 13.9 percent of all employed). At the same time, employment in manufacturing occupations has declined (going from 15.2 percent to 12.1 percent), mostly due to the massive restructuring in this sector outlined in

TABLE 2.3 *Occupation by Gender, Employed Population, Canada, 1981 and 1996*

	1981			*1996*		
Occupation	***Total*** **%**	***Female*** **%**	***Male*** **%**	***Total*** **%**	***Female*** **%**	***Male*** **%**
Managerial/administrative	*8.1*	*5.5*	*9.9*	*13.9*	*13.7*	*14.0*
Natural sciences	*3.7*	*1.5*	*5.2*	*4.0*	*1.8*	*5.8*
Social sciences	*1.4*	*1.8*	*1.2*	*2.2*	*3.0*	*1.6*
Religion	*0.2*	—*	*0.4*	*0.2*	*0.1*	*0.3*
Teaching	*4.2*	*5.8*	*3.0*	*4.6*	*6.6*	*3.0*
Medicine and health	*4.6*	*8.6*	*1.8*	*5.4*	*9.6*	*2.0*
Artistic/recreational	*1.5*	*1.5*	*1.5*	*2.3*	*2.3*	*2.4*
Clerical	*17.7*	*34.3*	*6.4*	*14.2*	*25.0*	*5.3*
Sales	*10.3*	*10.1*	*10.4*	*10.0*	*10.2*	*9.9*
Service	*13.4*	*18.3*	*10.1*	*13.9*	*17.5*	*10.8*
Agriculture	*4.6*	*2.7*	*5.9*	*3.4*	*2.0*	*4.6*
Fishing/hunting/trapping	*0.3*	—	*0.5*	*0.2*	—	*0.4*
Forestry and logging	*0.5*	—	*0.9*	*0.4*	—	*0.7*
Mining and quarrying	*0.7*	—	*1.2*	*0.4*	—	*0.7*
Manufacturing (processing, machining, fabricating)	*15.2*	*7.3*	*20.5*	*12.1*	*5.1*	*18.0*
Construction	*6.0*	*0.2*	*10.0*	*5.0*	*0.3*	*8.9*
Transportation	*3.8*	*0.6*	*5.9*	*3.8*	*0.8*	*6.3*
Materials handling/other crafts	*3.8*	*1.8*	*5.2*	*3.6*	*1.7*	*5.1*
Total percent	*100.0*	*100.0*	*100.0*	*99.6*	*99.7*	*99.8*
Total (in 000s)	*11,001*	*4,445*	*6,556*	*13,676*	*6,197*	*7,479*

* Dashes indicate estimates of less than 4,000 workers, which Statistics Canada does not publish given the small number of Labour Force Survey respondents from which such estimates would be obtained.

Source: Statistics Canada, "Occupation by Gender, Employed Population, Canada, 1981 and 1996," adapted from "Labour Force Annual Averages 1996," Catalogue No. 71-220. Reprinted with permission.

Chapter 1. What also deserves our attention is the drop in clerical employment, from 17.7 to 14.2 percent. This trend reflects a complex set of related changes, from advancing information technology to downsizing to the upgrading of some of these jobs to administrative categories. Shifts in the proportion of the employed labour force in other occupational categories, meanwhile, have not been as substantial.

Chapter 4 focuses on the unequal employment experiences and rewards of women and men, so we will comment only briefly at this point on the gender differences in Table 2.3. The 1996 data show a more even distribution of men than women across the occupational structure. Women are more heavily concentrated than men in several occupational groups (the "pink collar" occupations mentioned above), with 53 percent employed in clerical, sales, and service occupations (compared with 26 percent of employed men). Women are also relatively overrepresented in teaching and health occupations.

However, it is important to note the changes since 1981 in the gender composition of the occupational structure. In 1981, only 1 in 20 (5.5 percent) employed women were in managerial or administrative occupations. Fifteen years later, about 14 percent of women were working in these higher-status white-collar occupations—the same proportion as for employed males. Table 2.3 also shows a small increase over time in the proportion of women in social sciences, teaching, and medicine and health occupations. Conversely, the proportion of Canadian women employed in sales and service occupations has declined. But the largest relative decline has been in clerical work, shrinking from over one-third of all employed women in 1981 to one-quarter in 1996.

To conclude, there have been some shifts in the gender composition of the occupational structure, although female–male differences have not disappeared. But we must remember that these are broad occupational categories. Medical occupations, for example, include doctors, nurses, orderlies, nursing assistants, and other support workers. Women are still more likely to be in the lower-status occupations within these broad categories, and are still typically supervised by men (Boyd et al.1985; Clement and Myles 1994). Hence, it is necessary to look in more detail at the specific occupations within which women and men typically are employed, as we do in Chapter 4.

SELF-EMPLOYMENT TRENDS

As in other industrialized capitalist economies, self-employment has dropped sharply over the past century. In 1946, for example, 33 percent of employed Canadians were self-employed. By 1981 this figure had fallen to 10 percent (Riddell 1985: 9). This shift toward paid labour can be explained to a great extent by changes in the agricultural sector. Early in this century, roughly 75 percent of those employed in agriculture were owner–managers, while most of the rest were unpaid family workers. Since then, the proportion of paid workers in agriculture has been slowly increasing. By 1991, the 448,000 Canadians employed in agriculture consisted of paid workers (32 percent), unpaid family workers (9 percent), and self-employed individuals (59 percent). At the same time, the number of farms in Canada has declined from a high of 733,000 in 1941 to only 280,000 in 1991. Thus, while wage–labour has become more common in agriculture, a huge reduction in the number of family farms has also meant fewer self-employed individuals and unpaid family workers.[29]

Over the decades, self-employment in the secondary and service sectors also declined slowly. However, a reversal of this trend appeared about 15 years ago. By 1996, 17 percent of all employed Canadians (including those in agriculture) were self-employed, up from 14 percent in 1986 and 10 percent in 1981 (Akyeampong 1997a). A similar increase was observed in most other industrialized capitalist economies during the 1980s. In Canada, the number of employers (the self-employed who also hire others to work for them) and own-account self-employed (without employees) are roughly similar, but there are signs that the latter group may be growing faster (Krahn 1995). Self-employment still is largely a male status, but since the 1980s, women's share has grown rapidly. They now make up 34 percent of the independent (own-account) self-employed, and 24 percent of the self-employed whose businesses employ others (Gardner 1995: 27).

The 1981–82 and 1990–92 recessions in Canada are, no doubt, linked to the small increase in own-account self-employment. Many employers in both the private and public sectors reduced the size of their labour force, and this led to higher rates of unemployment than had been observed in the 1960s and 1970s. But it is not clear that those who lost their jobs were the same individuals who set up their own businesses. An overview of self-employment in Western industrialized countries (including Canada) suggests that the majority of the self-employed come directly from the ranks of wage-earners.

Furthermore, managerial, professional, and technical workers are more likely to become self-employed than are clerical and manual workers (the groups most affected by unemployment) (OECD 1986: Chapter 2). The self-employed are more highly educated than the rest of the labour force, suggesting that at least some of the growth in self-employment is a response by more advantaged workers to potential job insecurity.

The self-employed are dispersed across a wide range of occupations, with considerable variation in income and other rewards. For example, excluding agriculture, employers had higher employment incomes in 1990 than employees, while the own-account self-employed earned less than employees. This partly reflects the fact that many professionals—doctors, dentists, lawyers, and accountants—are counted as employers. In contrast, the most common jobs for own-account self-employed women are in child care, sales, and hairdressing, and for men in sales, carpentry, and truck driving—all relatively low paying (Gardner 1995: 29).

THE CANADIAN LABOUR MARKET: REGIONAL VARIATIONS

Industry Differences across Regions

So far we have treated Canada as a single economic entity, putting aside important regional differences. Anyone who has driven across Canada will have strong impressions of its regional diversity. The fishing boats and lumber mills of the West Coast are left behind, replaced by oil wells and grain elevators as one begins to head east across the Prairies. The flat landscape disappears a few hours after leaving Winnipeg, and one is faced by the rocks, forests, and water of the Canadian Shield. The smokestacks of Sudbury and other mining communities are reminders of the natural resource base of that region, but they eventually give way to the old gray barns of Ontario, symbols of an agricultural economy older than the one observed several days earlier. But this is unlikely to be the only memory of the trip through Ontario and into Quebec. The huge Highway 401 pushing its way past miles of warehouses and suburban factories will also leave a strong impression as it takes one through the industrial heartland of the country. Then, repeating the pattern observed in the West (but in reverse, without the mountains and on a smaller scale), the farming economies of Quebec and the Atlantic provinces begin to merge with a forest-based economy. Eventually, one returns to a region where fisheries are once again important. In short, regional diversity means economic diversity.

This description obviously overgeneralizes. There are high technology firms in the Fraser Valley, factories in Calgary, and oil wells off the East Coast. And in the northern parts of Canada, energy development and mining compete uneasily with traditional Aboriginal hunting, fishing, and trapping. Still, it is essential to take into account the regional distribution of industries when considering work opportunities available to Canadians. Some regions are much more economically advantaged than others, as we point out below in our discussion of unemployment trends. Labour force participation rates also vary significantly across provinces. For example, in 1996, Alberta's labour force participation rate of 72.1 percent was much higher than the 52 percent rate in Newfoundland.

A brief comparison of industrial patterns of employment in 1996 highlights these regional variations (Table 2.4). For example, 11.1 percent of the employed labour force in Manitoba and Saskatchewan and 6.7 percent in Alberta had jobs in agriculture, compared with around 2 percent in the other regions. Larger-than-average concentrations of workers in the resource-based industries reflect the presence of the fishing industry on the East Coast and in British Columbia, forest-based industries in the Atlantic provinces, Alberta, and British Columbia, and the oil and gas industry in Alberta (Apostle and Barnett 1992; Marchak et al. 1987). Meanwhile, 18 to 19 percent of workers in Quebec and Ontario had jobs in manufacturing, compared with only 8.6 percent in Alberta. It is also interesting to note that Alberta and Ontario, the two provinces taking the lead in scaling down government, have the lowest employment in public administration.

Canada is not unique in having some regions in which primary industries are most important, and others in which manufacturing is concentrated. But its economic history is marked by a reliance on exports of raw materials such as furs, fish, timber, wheat, coal, natural gas, and oil. This was Canada's colonial role in the British empire, but even as an independent industrialized nation it has continued to provide natural resources to the global economy. The *staple theory of economic growth* developed by Harold Innis and others documents the economic, political, and social consequences of this dependence on the export of unprocessed staple products. The theory argues that overcommitment to extraction and export of a single or few resources makes a nation or region vulnerable

TABLE 2.4 *Industry by Region, Employed Population, Canada, 1996*

Industry	*Total* %	*Atlantic Provinces* %	*Quebec* %	*Ontario* %	*Manitoba/ Saskatchewan* %	*Alberta* %	*British Columbia* %
Goods-producing sector							
Agriculture	3.3	1.8	2.4	2.2	11.1	6.7	1.9
Natural resource-based	2.0	4.6	1.2	0.8	2.5	5.5	2.8
Manufacturing	15.2	10.3	18.0	18.6	9.3	8.6	11.5
Construction	5.3	5.6	4.2	5.0	4.4	6.6	7.0
Service sector							
Upper-tier services							
Distributive services	12.1	11.8	11.8	11.7	12.7	13.0	12.7
Business services	12.5	8.1	12.1	13.8	9.2	12.2	13.7
Education/health/welfare	16.7	19.0	17.9	15.8	18.2	15.0	16.0
Public administration	6.0	8.1	6.5	5.5	6.7	5.2	5.9
Lower-tier services							
Retail trade	12.6	14.8	12.3	12.6	12.5	12.2	12.6
Other consumer services	14.2	14.7	13.5	13.8	13.2	15.1	16.0
*Total percent**	99.9	98.8	99.9	99.8	99.8	100.2	100.2
Total (in 000s)	13,678	948	3,213	5,311	987	1,413	1,806

* Columns may not add to 100 percent in these cases because of unreported data due to estimates of less than 4,000, the combining of provinces (the four Atlantic provinces have been combined, as have Manitoba and Saskatchewan), and recategorization of industries.

Source: Statistics Canada, "Industry by Region, Employed Population, Canada, 1996," adapted from "Labour Force Annual Averages 1996," Catalogue No. 71-220. Reprinted with permission.

in world markets. The relative absence of manufacturing industries means that large portions of the workforce remain employed in lower-skill primary and tertiary sector jobs. In addition, a weak manufacturing sector does not encourage significant quantities of research and development, and does not generate spinoff industrial activity. These factors create a "staples trap" in which there are few economic development alternatives (Watkins 1997, 1991).

Indicative of Canada's natural resource base is the number of single-industry communities scattered across the country. These towns and cities, often situated in relatively isolated areas, exist only because the extraction of some natural resource requires a resident labour force. While some of these communities have attempted to diversify their economies, few have been successful. Instead, their economic activity remains dominated by the primary resource extraction industry (oil in Fort McMurray, Alberta, for example, or nickel in Sudbury, Ontario). If the market for the staple declines or the resource is depleted, the economic base of the community will crumble. Mine shutdowns in Uranium City, Saskatchewan, and Schefferville, Quebec, are examples from the first half of the 1980s, while the dramatic drop in the population of Elliot Lake, Ontario, between 1986 and 1991 (a decline of 21.7 percent, which represented a loss of about 3,900 residents) identifies another single-industry community more recently hit by hard times. One critic suggested that ghost towns are an appropriate symbol of Canada's resource development policies.[30] By contrast, a stronger world market for oil has made it economically feasible to invest in oil-sands production, creating another economic boom in Fort McMurray and other northern Alberta communities.

Over the decades, the prospects of better jobs and higher incomes have led many thousands of people to "go down the road" to the industrial cities of central Canada. But many have also been attracted to the resource towns of the hinterland for the same reasons. Such communities have historically provided work for unemployed or underemployed migrants from other regions of the country. However, the life cycle of resource towns, as they move through fairly predictable stages of development, is one in which work opportunities for residents and migrants do not remain constant. Moreover, since mining, forestry, the railway, and other blue-collar industries have traditionally been male occupational preserves, women have had trouble finding satisfactory employment. Many single-industry towns are located in areas with sizable Aboriginal populations, yet these groups seldom benefit from the employment opportunities generated by the towns.

UNEMPLOYMENT TRENDS

Counting the Unemployed

Annual averages show that during 1996, there were 15,145,000 Canadians aged 15 and older in the labour force and 13,676,000 of them were employed. The unemployed, numbering almost 1.5 million, made up the difference. To put this in perspective, the number of unemployed people in 1996 is roughly equivalent to the total population (children included) of Newfoundland, New Brunswick, and Prince Edward Island combined.

The official *unemployment rate* is calculated by dividing the number of individuals out of work and actively looking for work (the unemployed) by the total number of labour force participants (including the unemployed). Such calculations reveal the percentage of labour force participants who are unemployed at a particular point in time (an annual average provides the average of twelve monthly estimates). But over the course of a year, many people find jobs while many others quit or lose them. Consequently, if we were to count the number of people who had been unemployed at some point during a year, this alternative unemployment rate would be considerably higher. For example, in 1993 the annual average unemployment rate was 11.2 percent, but over the course of the entire year, 22 percent of individuals and 35 percent of all families had experienced unemployment (Noreau 1996: 36).

The official definition of unemployment, whether we calculate rates for a single point in time or over the full year, identifies a state of being without paid work (including self-employment). It excludes students who do not wish to work while studying, individuals performing unpaid work in the home, the disabled who are not seeking work, and the retired, all of whom are considered to be outside the labour force. It also excludes potential labour force participants who, believing there is no work available in their community or region, have not actively sought employment in the previous four weeks. In the wake of the 1981–82 recession, the Labour Force Survey estimated the size of the *discouraged workers* group at 197,000 (March 1983). The number of discouraged workers declined as the economy recovered, and did not rise as high again during the recession that began in 1990, peaking at 99,000 in March 1992. This lower number of discouraged workers in the most recent recession is rooted in other basic labour market changes during the 1980s, already mentioned: declining youth labour force participation, rising educational enrolments and participation in training, and early retirement.[31] What this discussion points out, of course, is that the official unemployment rate understates the magnitude of the problem.

Canadian Unemployment Rates over Time

Canadian unemployment rates, according to the official definition, reached their highest point this century (around 20 percent) during the Depression of the 1930s (Brown 1987). But these hard times were quickly replaced by labour shortages during World War II and in the immediate postwar years. The average national unemployment rate was only 2 percent during the 1940s. Since the end of World War II, unemployment has slowly climbed higher, responding to successive business cycles of recession and expansion. Still, the long-term upward trend is clearly apparent from Figure 2.4. The average national unemployment rate was 4 percent in the 1950s, 5 percent in the 1960s, 6.7 percent in the 1970s, 9.5 percent in the 1980s, and 10.1 percent so far in the 1990s.[32]

During the 1980s, unemployment peaked at 11.9 percent (the highest point since the Depression) and then began to fall again, going to 7.5 percent in 1989. But this respite was short, as a sudden recession at the end of the decade again pushed rates up to just over 11 percent in 1992 and 1993. A disturbing long-term trend is apparent in Figure 2.4. While declines in unemployment have been observed during several post-recession periods during the

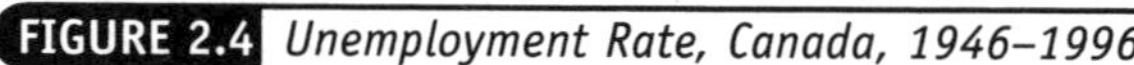

FIGURE 2.4 *Unemployment Rate, Canada, 1946–1996*

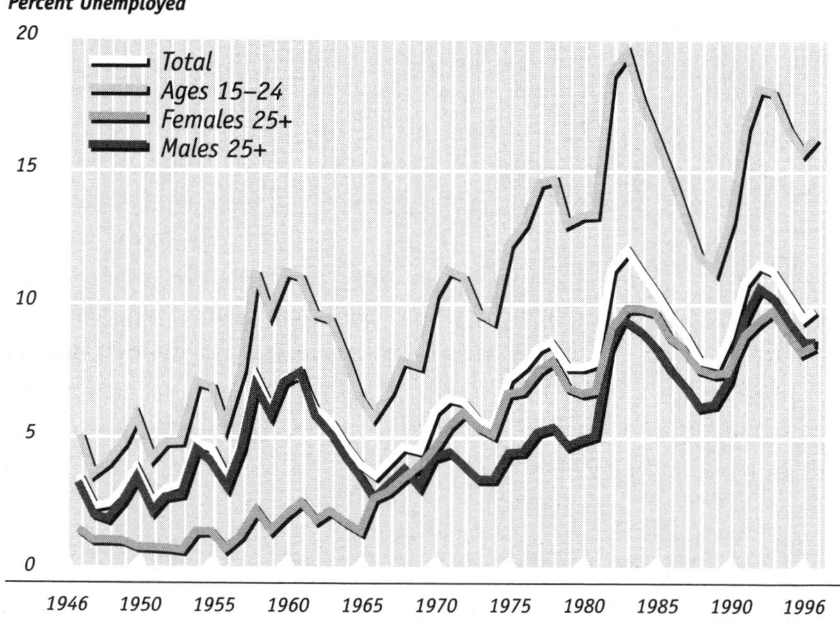

Source: Statistics Canada, "Unemployment Rates, Canada, 1994 to 1996," adapted from "Labour Force Annual Averages, 1989–1994," Catalogue No. 71-529; "Labour Force Annual Averages," Catalogue No. 71-220; and "The Labour Force," Catalogue No. 71-001, November 1995. Reprinted with permission.

last few decades, these declines have typically not brought unemployment down to the pre-recession level. Thus, some analysts argue that without a complete rethinking of government economic policy, shifting the emphasis away from deficit reduction and low inflation and toward active job creation measures, unemployment during the 1990s is unlikely to drop to the levels observed in the economically buoyant 1960s.[33]

As unemployment rates have slowly climbed, the duration of unemployment has also increased. In the late 1970s, the average spell of unemployment was about 15 weeks. This figure rose to 21 weeks in the mid-1980s, dropped to around 17 weeks in 1990, then rose to 28 weeks in 1996. In 1996, about one-quarter of unemployed Canadians had unsuccessfully tried to find work for 6 months or longer. Older workers laid off during the recessions of the early 1980s and 1990s were most likely to experience prolonged periods of unemployment.[34]

Regional Variations in Unemployment

National rates of unemployment conceal the great degree of variation across regions of the country. In 1996, Newfoundland's unemployment rate averaged 19.4 percent, compared with 12.6 percent in Nova Scotia, 11.8 percent in Quebec, 9.1 percent in Ontario, 7 percent in Alberta, and 6.6 percent in Saskatchewan. The Atlantic provinces, particularly Newfoundland, have had higher-than-average rates of unemployment for decades, while the manufacturing provinces of Ontario and Quebec have typically had lower rates. Historically, the regions most dependent on a few natural resources have experienced the most severe unemployment. The extent of regional inequality, as measured by unemployment, appears to have increased. The more economically diversified regions recovered much more quickly from the recession of the early 1980s, resulting in a larger gap between the unemployment rates of the more and less advantaged provinces (Gower 1989, 1995; Gera 1991: 6). What has added to this hardship is the 1996 tightening of unemployment insurance regulations—renamed Employment Insurance to emphasize a focus on training—that reduces eligibility.

Unemployment also tends to be concentrated within specific occupational groups and industrial sectors. Seasonal work like fishing, logging, and construction carries a high risk of unemployment, and helps account for some of the higher levels of unemployment in the natural-resource-dependent regions of the country. Manufacturing jobs are also prone to unemployment, since economic downturns often lead to layoffs and plant shutdowns. On the other hand, professional and technical occupations tend to be somewhat more protected from unemployment.

Aboriginal peoples continue to experience exceptionally high rates of unemployment. When combined with lower than average rates of labour force participation, it is clear that this group faces serious disadvantages in the labour market. For example, Aboriginal people aged 15 to 54 living off reserves in 1986 had an unemployment rate of 21.3 percent, more than double the comparable rate among non-Aboriginals. The spread is even greater when only youth are compared.[35] These levels of unemployment are probably low compared with estimates for Aboriginal Canadians living in northern Manitoba, Saskatchewan, and Alberta, as well as in the Territories. The isolated Native communities in these regions offer few employment opportunities. In addition, low levels of education, limited work experience other than in short-term, low-skill jobs, minimal access to information about jobs and those doing the hiring, and discrimination in hiring have all contributed to high rates of Aboriginal unemployment both on and off reserves.

Gender and Unemployment

A comparison of female and male unemployment rates in the post-war years reveals some interesting shifts in relative position (see Figure 2.4). Looking at adult workers (25 years and older), during the 1950s and early 1960s male unemployment rates were generally about twice as high as those for females. The two rates converged in the mid-1960s, and by the 1970s, female rates were typically about 2 percent higher than male rates. This trend continued until the recession of the early 1980s. In both 1982 and 1983, male unemployment rates were a fraction higher than female rates. For the rest of the 1980s, female rates of joblessness were again higher than male rates, but the difference was always less than 1 percent. Because of the 1990–92 recession and its aftermath, men were again more likely to be unemployed. By 1996, the rates again were similar, at around 8.5 percent for workers 25 and older.

A far more detailed analysis than is possible here would be needed to explain these shifts in female and male unemployment rates. Nevertheless, a large part of the explanation would focus on women's locations in the labour market. Female labour force participation was much lower in the 1950s and 1960s, and women were employed in a limited number of traditionally female occupations. Unemployment then, as now, was considerably higher in the blue-collar occupations, in which few women were found. Since that time, women have been making their way into a broader range of service sector jobs alongside men. But many women continue to be employed in lower-level, less secure positions. Thus, during the past few decades, women have been somewhat more vulnerable to unemployment. However, the recessions at the beginning of the 1980s and 1990s led to widespread layoffs in blue-collar industries (manufacturing, for example). Since men continue to be overrepresented in these industries, unemployment rates for them rose rapidly and passed the female rates when the economy weakened.

Youth Unemployment

Young Canadians (aged 15 to 24), particularly those with the least education (high school dropouts, for example) have experienced high rates of unemployment for several decades (Figure 2.4). We should point out three important differences between youth and adult unemployment patterns: young people have shorter spells of unemployment; relatively few of them have access to Employment Insurance; and they are disproportionately represented among discouraged workers (Betcherman and Leckie 1997: 10–14). Youth unemployment fluctuated between 9 and 14 percent in the 1970s. The 1981–82 recession pushed the rate to about 20 percent, but it had dropped to 11.2 percent by 1989. The recession that began in 1990 reversed this decline; rates in the 18 percent range were reached in 1993 and 1994. Even though youth unemployment is affected by the same economic forces that determine the risk of joblessness for the adult labour force, it is clear that young workers have fared much worse since the early 1980s.

A shifting age distribution partly explains changing youth unemployment rates. Canada experienced an exceptionally large "baby boom" during the 1950s and 1960s. The last of the children born in that era of high birth rates were making their way into the labour force during the early 1980s, just as a severe recession was reducing employment opportunities. The next cohort of school leavers was considerably smaller and entered the labour force in the mid-1980s when the economy was considerably stronger. Thus, competition for jobs typically held by young workers was somewhat reduced.[35]

However, as already noted, youth unemployment rose again in the 1990s as the economy weakened. Since the most recent cohort of school leavers was considerably smaller than the cohort ahead of it, we might expect high unemployment to have moved to a higher age group. But comparing the unemployment rates of teenagers and young adults (those aged 20 to 24) shows that teenage rates have been higher since the mid-1970s. Compared with teenagers, young adults are somewhat more likely to find employment since they are typically better educated and have more work experience. In 1996, for example, the unemployment rate for 15 to 19 year olds was 20.1 percent, compared with 13.6 percent for 20- to 24-year-olds.

While the majority of teenagers are still in school, many young adults have left the education system and are attempting to start careers and set up independent households. Teenage labour force participants usually look for work (typically part-time) in lower-tier service industries, while most young adults seek better paying, full-time jobs in upper-tier services or goods-producing industries. The 1990–92 recession saw many manufacturing firms lay off workers. Private and public sector employers in the throes of downsizing also reduced the recruitment of young graduates. The retail industries were also affected, but not as severely. Consequently, current labour market trends have forced many young adults to take part-time and temporary jobs when they would prefer full-time and more secure employment.

Causes of Unemployment

We have already hinted at some of the causes of rising unemployment. Obviously, there is a demographic factor to consider. The sizable increase in the birth rate in the years following World War II resulted in the increase in labour force numbers several decades later. In addition, the increased proportion of women entering the labour force led to a greater demand for jobs. But people working for pay are also people with money to spend, and the growth in labour force participation itself led to substantial job creation. Thus, econometric analyses conclude that these demographic shifts have had very little impact on the overall increase in unemployment in the past two decades (Gera 1991: 3).

One common explanation of unemployment focuses on the jobless themselves. Such arguments are typically supported by anecdotal evidence and little else. One version suggests that many of the unemployed could be working if only they would accept the less attractive jobs that are available, or had better work skills and attitudes. But in many communities, the number of jobless far exceeds the total number of available jobs (Marsh et al. 1990). Furthermore, many of the jobs that may be available (and perhaps are even hard to fill) are part-time positions in the lower-tier services with pay rates so low that it would be impossible to support oneself, let alone a family. For many of the unemployed, accepting such work would be economically irrational, since it would force them to try to survive on very little income and discontinue actively searching for a better job.

Another popular explanation of unemployment traces the problem to the presumed laziness of the unemployed in combination with the generosity of the government. But it is hard to believe that more than a few Canadians would prefer the low level of government social assistance (or unemployment benefits) to a higher and more secure income. In fact, relatively fewer workers are participating in the Employment Insurance program. Comparing the peaks of the 1981–82 and 1990–92 recessions, the proportion of the labour force receiving unemployment benefits declined.[36] Furthermore, research on Canadians' work values (reviewed in Chapter 8) shows that few would choose the economic hardship and the stigma of unemployment over a regular job.

Economists offer a different view, distinguishing *cyclical unemployment*, which rises during recessions and then declines as the economy recovers, from *frictional unemployment*. The latter results from the ongoing movement of workers in and out of jobs as they seek to match their skills and interests with the jobs offered by employers. Some unemployment, therefore, is normal, even in the strongest economy, since a perfect match between jobs and workers is never possible. However, research suggests that periods of cyclical unemployment over the past few decades have had the permanent effect on the Canadian labour market of increasing the "natural rate of unemployment" to such a degree that it is now unlikely to go back down. Economists recognize that Canada has developed a serious problem of *structural unemployment*. More deep-rooted and permanent than cyclical or frictional unemployment, this requires new approaches to economic policy.[37]

Some of the emerging industrial and employment trends discussed in the previous chapter have contributed to the high and persistent level of unemployment in Canada. With industrial restructuring, many corporations have shifted their activities to countries and regions where labour costs are lower, and where government legislation regarding labour relations, worker safety, and environmental protection is less developed. Automation and information technologies are replacing workers in some industries. The role of technology in creating mass global unemployment is now hotly debated, as seen in reactions to Jeremy Rifkin's book, *The End of Work*.[38] In both the private and public sectors, many employers have responded to fiscal problems by downsizing, cutting full-time jobs, and relying increasingly on temporary workers. In addition, parts of Canada's staple-based economy have been hit hard by recent global economic shifts. Some of our basic resource industries (oil, wheat, and lumber, for example) have lately encountered unstable world markets. Others, such as the East and West Coast fishing industries, are suffering because of declining resource stocks.

As noted in Chapter 1, the impact of government policies on unemployment trends is equally important and must also be scrutinized. High unemployment has been linked to the government's pursuit of a low inflation policy, with the latter receiving priority. Further, a policy of high interest rates in the 1980s also likely aggravated the unemployment problem.[39] With a market-oriented approach to economic development that included entry into a continental free trade agreement, the Canadian government may have made it easier for large corporations to close factories and lay off workers.

International Comparisons

How do Canadian unemployment rates compare with those of other industrialized countries? In 1996, the gap between the Canadian rate (9.7 percent) and the U.S. rate widened, as the latter declined to 5.4 percent. By comparison with other countries that form the group of major industrialized nations often known as the G-7, Canada's unemployment rate is high. France and Italy were both over 12 percent in 1996, but Germany and the United Kingdom were around 7 and 8 percent, respectively, and Japan's rate was 3.4 percent.[40]

Given that these countries are struggling with economic problems similar to those of Canada, why do some have high unemployment while others have nearly full employment? In terms of labour market policies, Canada lies between the laissez-faire, or free-market approach, of the U.S. and the more interventionist European approach. Research by economists has attempted to explain the large Canada–U.S. gap. Some of the interesting findings are that while both economies have generated more jobs than Europe in the last several decades, the two countries differ in both the higher level of unemployment insurance coverage in Canada and the greater likelihood of Canada's unemployed remaining in the labour market searching for work (Riddell 1996). The greater propensity of unemployed Americans to leave the labour market, partly due to a weaker unemployment insurance program, means that larger numbers are not officially counted as unemployed. In addition, the U.S. is a society that imprisons many more of its citizens. In 1993, 13 percent of young males (25 percent of young black males) were either in prison or on parole or probation. While jobless, many of these young men would not be counted as unemployed.[41]

Canada has typically relied on the marketplace to reduce unemployment, while instituting unemployment insurance and social assistance programs to help deal with the social problems created by persistently high levels of unemployment. The present public policy challenge is how to create more employment opportunities for unemployed job seekers. Countries like Japan, Sweden, and Germany have been much more interventionist in this regard. Employers, organized labour, and governments frequently have worked together toward a common goal of full employment. In Canada, this kind of collective effort is missing, as is a well-developed industrial strategy that might counter some of the global economic forces negatively affecting our economy. In the low-unemployment countries, labour market programs have typically been proactive. For example, in Sweden, 90 percent of government funds spent on labour market programs goes toward training, job creation, and assistance for workers moving to new jobs. In Canada, the government has relied on the private sector to create jobs and to train and retrain workers, even though it has not had a particularly good record in this regard.[42]

While other countries have devised more effective approaches to dealing with unemployment, we cannot simply import solutions. Canada has a unique economic history and industrial structure, a complicated political system where federal and provincial responsibilities are separate (and frequently disputed), and its own unique business and labour institutions. In short, we will have to fashion our own solutions. Nevertheless, the examples provided by other countries demonstrate that long-term high levels of unemployment need not be seen as inevitable, and that employers, the government, and organized labour will all have to be active participants in any attempts to solve our structural unemployment problem.

HOURS OF WORK AND ALTERNATIVE WORK ARRANGEMENTS

In 1870, the standard number of hours in a work week (the number beyond which overtime would typically be paid to full-time workers) in the Canadian manufacturing sector was 64 (Reid 1985: 146–50). This was subsequently reduced because of trade union pressures and the introduction of new manufacturing technologies that could produce more goods in a shorter time. By 1901, 58.6 hours per week was standard in manufacturing. Twenty years later, 50 hours per week was typical, but this average changed little until after World War II.

Between 1946 and 1949, the manufacturing standard dropped quickly from 48.7 hours per week to 43.5 hours. It then fell to 40 hours by 1957, fluctuated slightly around this point for the next two decades, and dropped to around 39 hours per week by the mid-1970s. Since then we have seen a small further decline: In 1996, the average number of hours worked per week for the total employed labour force was 37.7, compared with 39.0 in 1976. Canadians spend considerably less time at work than they did a century ago, but recent changes have been minimal.

Even shorter work weeks have recently been negotiated in several western European countries, in part to reduce unemployment by sharing work among a larger number of workers. For example, German autoworkers negotiated a new deal with Volkswagen in order to preserve jobs, achieving a reduced work week with little pay loss. Longer vacations also help spread work within a society. But compared with a number of European countries where vacations of four weeks or longer are required by law, many Canadian workers continue to have only two weeks per year of paid vacation (in addition to statutory holidays). For the majority of Canadian employees, vacation entitlements might rise to three or four weeks per year only after many years in the job (Kumar et al. 1991: 388–89).

There is also growing interest in alternative work schedules. While shift work has long been common in some industries, *teleworking* (working at home or in a remote site, often using computer technology) and *flextime* (choosing the time to start and stop work) have been receiving more attention. These work options can help parents balance child care with their jobs. But they also have drawbacks, given that such arrangements often provide fewer benefits and can deprive workers of interactions with coworkers. But how common are flexible work arrangements in Canada, and do employees want this option? According to the national Survey of Work Arrangements, in 1995, most workers had Monday to Friday and "9 to 5" schedules (Figure 2.5). Just under one-quarter had flexible start and end times, and less than one in ten worked at home all or part of the time. Historical comparisons are not available, but it seems that widespread flexibility in work arrangements is a long way off in most workplaces.

Shorter work weeks offer a potential solution to Canada's unemployment problem. Advocates claim that reducing full-time jobs a few hours a week could generate thousands of new jobs. A 1994 federal government advisory group, which included labour and industry representatives, recommended ways to redistribute work hours.[43] One Canadian organization, the Work-Well Network, is actively promoting a 30-hour work week. Speaking on behalf of the Network, Bruce O'Hara (1993: 3) concludes that "working harder is the problem, not the solution" to Canada's economic difficulties. What is interesting,

FIGURE 2.5 *Employees' Work Arrangements and Preferences, Canada, 1995**

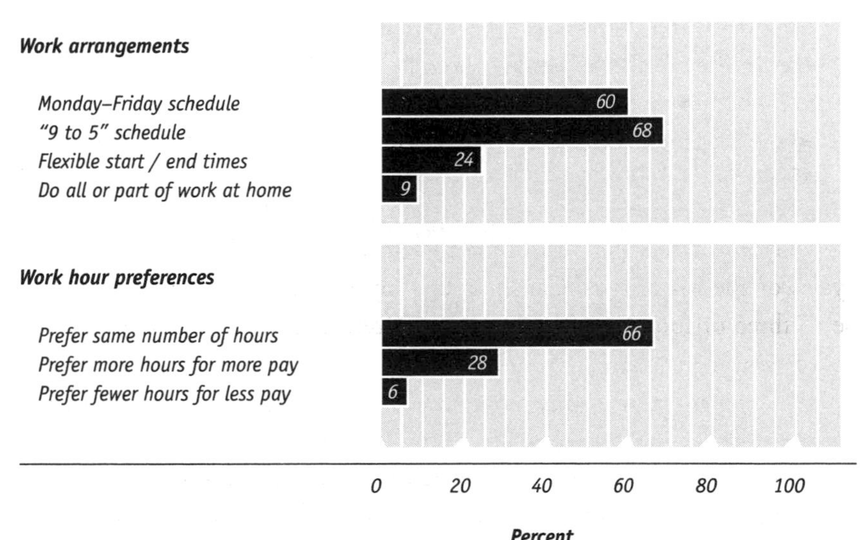

* Paid workers not enrolled full-time in school, excluding self-employed, aged 15 to 69.
Work arrangement percentages do not add up to 100 percent due to overlapping categories.

Source: Statistics Canada, "Employees Work Arrangements and Preferences, Canada, 1995," adapted from "Perspectives on Labour and Income," Catalogue No. 75-001, Spring 1997, Volume 9, Number 1, pages 48–52. Reprinted with permission.

though, is that two-thirds of workers in Canada prefer the same number of work hours, and those desiring a change want more hours, not less (Figure 2.5). These preferences need to be interpreted, however, in the context of declining earnings (discussed in the next chapter) and high levels of concern about economic security (see Chapter 8). Such factors make reduced work hours and pay difficult to imagine.

Returning to the subject of weekly hours of work, a closer look at the 1.3 hour per week decline in the past 20 years reveals a very important shift in Canadian work patterns. In 1996, full-time workers were putting in an average of 42.4 hours per week, compared with 17.7 hours for part-time workers. These averages have changed little since 1976 but the proportion of part-time workers has risen. Thus, a polarization in the distribution of working hours is under way, especially since the 1981–82 recession. In 1993, 61 percent of paid workers put in 35 to 40 hours weekly, down from 71 percent in 1976 (Sunter and Morissette 1994: 9). Youth experienced the largest drop in work hours, which is linked to their declining earnings since the early 1980s. But we have also seen longer hours for adult workers, particularly males. In fact, if we look only at full-time workers, we observe that the proportion working long hours (50 or more hours per week) has actually increased, in part because of increases in the number of workers holding more than one job (Cohen 1992). In the following discussion of nonstandard work arrangements, we examine both the part-time phenomenon and the incidence of multiple-job holding.

NONSTANDARD WORK ARRANGEMENTS

Varieties of Nonstandard Work

Most employed Canadians have a full-time, year-round, permanent, paid job. However, alternatives to this standard type of employment arrangement are increasing not just in Canada, but in all industrialized societies.[44] *Nonstandard work* takes various forms. Part-time work has become quite common, and the number of multiple-job holders appears to be increasing slowly. The own-account self-employed category has grown moderately. There are indications that temporary (contract or "contingent") work has become somewhat more common. When these four types of nonstandard work are combined (not counting overlaps), they accounted for 28 percent of all employed working-age (15 to 64 years) Canadians in 1989, rising to one-third by 1994 (Figure 2.6).

Nonstandard work also can be classified according to whether it has been instituted by employers or initiated by individual workers. Many employers, in both the private and public sectors, have responded to the economic difficulties of the past decades by replacing full-time with part-time workers (and sometimes part-year workers), and by eliminating permanent positions and replacing them with temporary (limited-term contract) positions. These employment strategies allow employers greater flexibility in responding to uneven demands for goods and services, and reduce labour costs. This "flexible firm" model is discussed in Chapter 5. At the same time, a slowly increasing number of labour market participants have chosen to set up their own

FIGURE 2.6 *Non-Standard Work, Canada, 1989 and 1994*

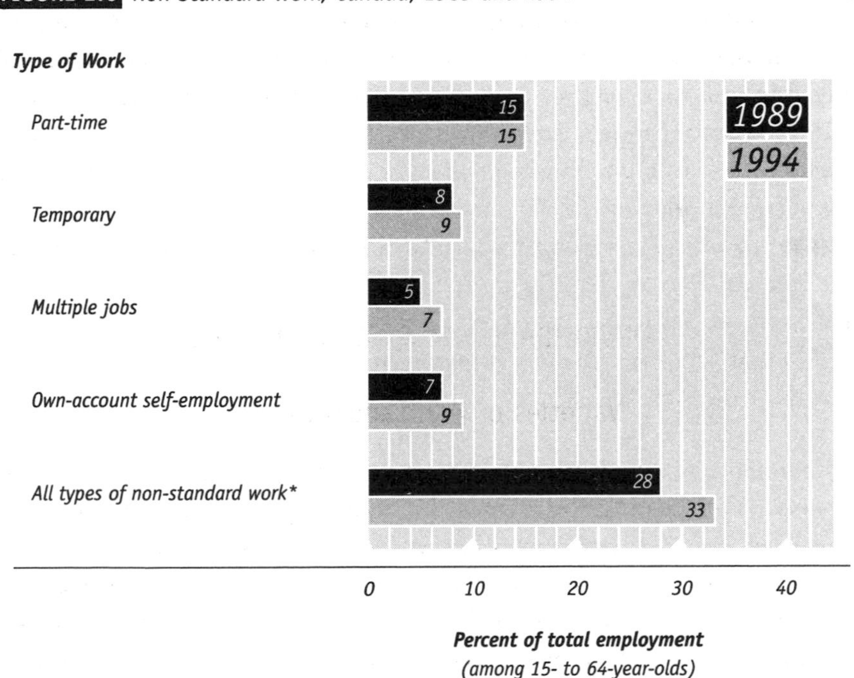

* Persons in more than one type of nonstandard work are counted only once.

Source: Statistics Canada, "Non-Standard Work by Industry, Canada, 1989 and 1994," adapted from "Perspectives on Labour and Income," Catalogue No. 75-001, Winter 1995, Volume 7, Number 4, page 37. Reprinted with permission.

business (the own-account self-employed) or to take on a second job.

Some workers choose alternative forms of employment (part-time work or self-employment, for example) because of personal preference. But for many others, such choices are a response to a difficult labour market. Workers may create their own jobs because few paid jobs are available; accept temporary or part-time work only when permanent, full-time jobs are scarce; or take on a second job because their first job pays poorly. Since nonstandard jobs typically pay less, provide fewer benefits, are less likely to be covered by labour legislation, and have less employment security, an increase in nonstandard employment also means an increase in the precariousness of employment (and income) for many Canadian workers.

We have already commented on the small increase in *own-account self-employment* in the past decades. Roughly 9 percent of employed working-age Canadians are in this category, which includes farmers, doctors, lawyers, and business consultants, as well as the small entrepreneurs we typically associate with self-employment (Figure 2.6). Multiple-job holding increased from 5 percent in 1989 to 7 percent in 1994. People take on a second job for a variety of reasons, including topping up an inadequate income, paying off debts, and saving for the future. Economic hard times undoubtedly have contributed to the growth in multiple-job holding. However, since the majority are supplementing a full-time job, and since about one-third have a professional or managerial first job, we should be cautious about assuming that all Canadians with more than one job are in a precarious financial or employment situation. The same applies to the own-account self-employed.

Nonstandard jobs are more common in some sectors of the economy, and a worker's demographic characteristics influence her or his likelihood of being in this kind of work. In terms of industry variations, Figure 2.7 shows that agriculture has the highest rate of nonstandard work, and that this is rising. A large proportion of these nonstandard workers are the own-account self-employed. But it is the lower-tier industries—retail and other consumer services—that are the main source of nonstandard employment, given their relative size in the economy. There is also considerable nonstandard work in upper-tier services, particularly in social services and business services. Pronounced age and gender differences also define the nonstandard work trend. As Figure 2.8 shows, young workers are most likely to be in nonstandard jobs. Older workers (55 to 64 years) also have somewhat higher rates of

FIGURE 2.7 *Non-Standard Work* by Industry, Canada, 1989 and 1994*

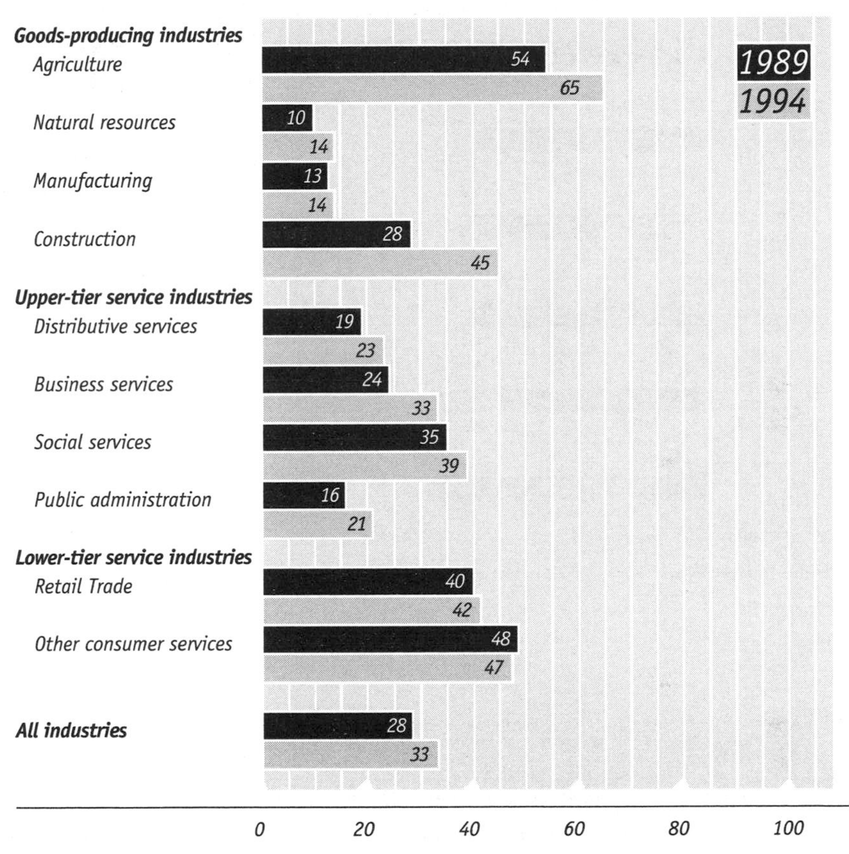

* Paid workers 15 to 64 years old. Includes one or more of part-time work, temporary work, own-account self-employment, or multiple job-holding (people in more than one type of nonstandard work are counted only once).

Source: Statistics Canada, "Non-Standard Work by Industry, Canada, 1989 and 1994," adapted from "Perspectives on Labour and Income," Catalogue No. 75-001, Winter 1995, Volume 7, Number 4, page 40. Reprinted with permission.

nonstandard employment. In all age groups, women are more likely to have nonstandard work arrangements than men, with young women having the highest rate of any age or gender group.

FIGURE 2.8 *Non-Standard Work* by Age and Gender, Canada, 1994*

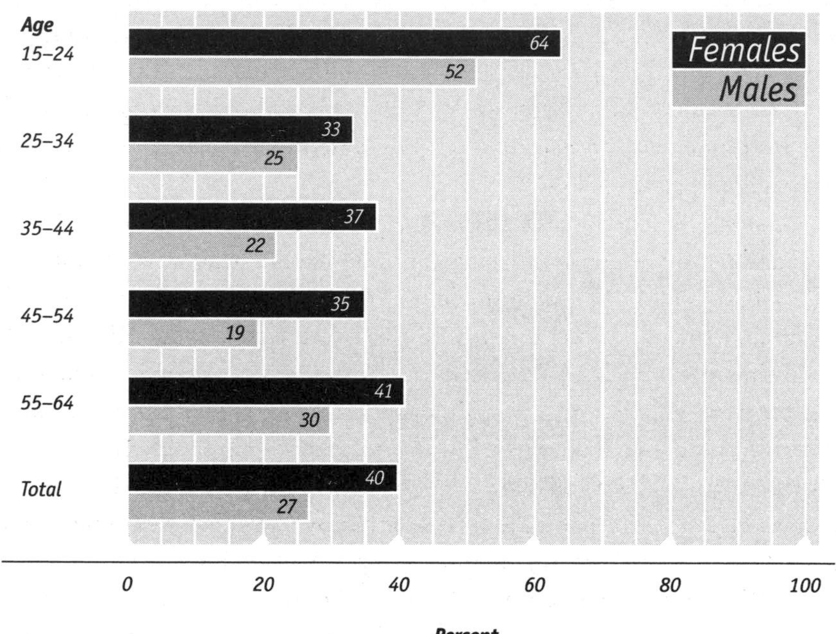

* Paid workers 15- to 64-years-old. Includes one or more of part-time work, temporary work, own-account self-employment, or multiple job-holding (people in more than one type of nonstandard work are counted only once).

Source: Statistics Canada, "Non-Standard Work by Age and Gender, Canada, 1994," adapted from "Perspectives on Labour and Income," Catalogue No. 75-001, Winter 1995, Volume 7, Number 4, page 40. Reprinted with permission.

Part-Time Work

Part-time work is the most common type of nonstandard employment. Part-time work was long defined by Statistics Canada as less than 30 hours per week in total, even if more than one job was held. But with the rise in multiple-job holding, especially among part-time workers, this definition was changed in 1996. Thus, part-time workers are now defined as those who work less than 30 hours per week in their main job.

At mid-century (1953), less than 4 percent of the employed held part-time jobs, but during the 1960s and 1970s, part-time work became more common.

By 1977, part-time work accounted for 13 percent of all employment in Canada. Since the recession of the early 1980s, part-time job creation has outstripped full-time. By 1996, 18.9 percent of workers were part-timers. This amounts to almost 2.6 million workers. Some 36 percent of part-timers are youth (15 to 24 years) and close to half (45.6 percent) of all young workers are in such jobs. Among adult workers (25 years and older) the gender difference is striking, with 76 percent of all part-timers female. Close to 1 in 4 adult women hold part-time jobs.[45]

Some people choose part-time work because it allows them to balance work and family responsibilities, to continue their education while still holding a job, or simply to have more leisure time. Others, *involuntary part-time workers*, are forced to accept part-time jobs because they cannot find one that is full-time. The monthly Labour Force Survey asks part-time workers why they are working part-time, providing the following possible answers: cannot find a full-time job (involuntary); going to school; personal/family responsibilities; do not want a full-time job (no specific reason provided); and other reasons. Figure 2.9 displays the reasons given by Canadian part-time workers in 1995 and in 1975 when part-time rates were much lower.

In 1975, more than one-third (37 percent) of part-time workers stated that they did not want a full-time job. In 1995, this reason was given by a smaller portion (22 percent) of part-time workers. However, in 1995, involuntary part-time workers made up 31 percent of the over 2.5 million part-time workers in Canada, compared with only 11 percent of the roughly 1 million part-time workers in 1975. Thus, a significant factor influencing part-time employment growth over the past decades has been employers seeking ways to cut labour costs rather than because of changing worker preferences.

Age and gender have an impact on the reasons for part-time work. For a majority of young part-time workers, this nonstandard work arrangement may fit with their educational pursuits. Adult women, especially those with children, are likely to cite personal or family reasons, or simply state that they do not want full-time work. Had these women been asked whether they would still prefer a part-time job if they had access to adequate and affordable child care, it is likely that some would have expressed interest in full-time employment. In other words, traditional assumptions about female child care roles together with a shortage of affordable, quality child care may create an underestimate of the real level of involuntary part-time employment among women.[46]

FIGURE 2.9 *Reasons for Part-Time Work, Canada, 1975 and 1995*

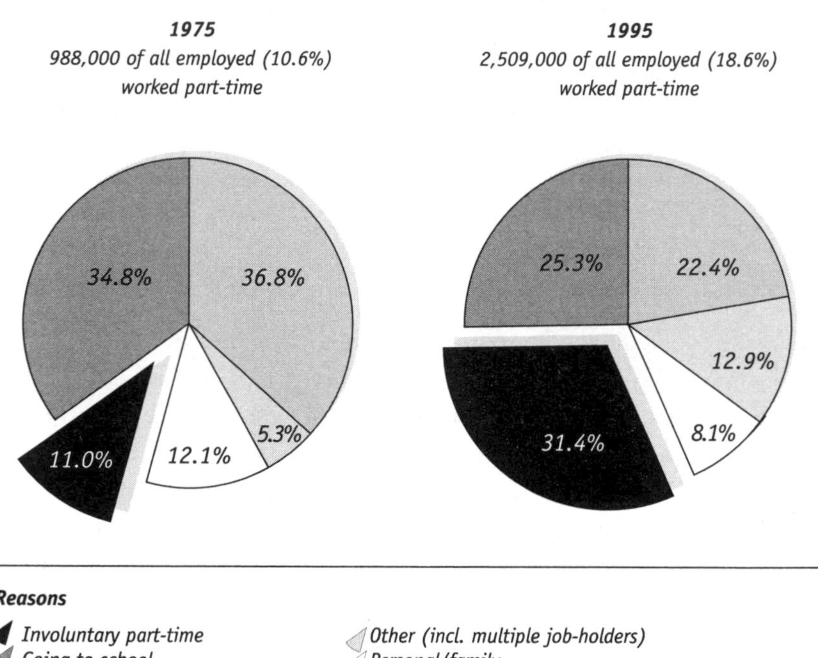

Reasons

- *Involuntary part-time*
- *Going to school*
- *Did not want full time*
- *Other (incl. multiple job-holders)*
- *Personal/family*

Source: Statistics Canada, "Reasons for Part-Time Work, Canada, 1975 and 1995," adapted from "Labour Force Annual Averages, 1989–1994," Catalogue No. 71-529; and Labour Force Annual Averages," Catalogue No. 71-220. Reprinted with permission.

Temporary Employment and Part-Year Work

We know considerably less about the growth in *temporary employment*, which could be either full- or part-time, since Canadian data collection agencies have not been monitoring this phenomenon on a regular basis. However, the 1994 General Social Survey revealed that 9 percent of working-age (15 to 64) paid employees (employers and the own-account self-employed were excluded) were in a job that had a specific end date, up only slightly from 1989 (Figure 2.6). But compared to 10 or 20 years ago, this figure clearly appears to have risen. There is evidence that temporary help agencies have been hiring greater numbers of workers to be sent out on assignment to employers seeking to fill a temporary employment need. Many more private and public employers have begun to hire more employees on a limited-term (perhaps six months or a year) contract basis, rather than offering permanent positions as was the custom a decade or two ago.[47]

Younger workers are more likely to find themselves in temporary positions. In 1994, 16 percent of 15- to 24-year-old employed Canadians held temporary jobs, up from 13 percent five years earlier. Young student workers are more likely to be employed in the lower-tier consumer services, where temporary jobs are more common. Also, in the upper-tier services (the education and health and welfare industries, for example), it is much easier to offer a new (young) employee a contract position than to move someone already in a permanent position to a contractually limited job. Quite often, contract employees work alongside permanent employees, performing similar tasks and for comparable pay, but without the guarantee of continued employment beyond six months or a year. While some people, often those with highly marketable skills, find such arrangements quite satisfactory, others are frustrated and worried by their employment and income insecurity.

Part-year work has also received little systematic research attention, although many of Canada's resource industries, including fishing, forestry, and agriculture, rely heavily on part-year workers, as do construction and tourism, two other industries that are also crucially affected by the weather. In fact, part-year work and part-year unemployment frequently form the annual labour force cycle for workers in these industries. There is no standard definition of part-year work, but since the definition of part-time work (less than 30 hours per week) is roughly 75 percent of a 40-hour week, we can define part-year workers as those who ordinarily work 9 or fewer months per year (that is, in their main job, if they have more than one). According to this definition, 7 percent of employed 15- to 64-year-old Canadians had part-year jobs in 1989. Again, at 14 percent, young workers were overrepresented in this type of nonstandard work. Older men, who are more likely to be employed in agriculture, the resource-based industries, and construction were also somewhat more likely to be part-year workers.[48]

FUTURE TRENDS

The twentieth century has recorded profound changes in how, where, and for whom Canadians work. The late nineteenth and early twentieth centuries were times of rapid industrialization and workplace rationalization. The years that followed saw further growth in white-collar occupations, expansion of the service sector, and a decline in self-employment. By the 1960s, the Canadian paid work world had been largely transformed. But, as our examination of more recent trends has shown, we are witnessing further restructuring of the Canadian labour market as we approach the next century.

The service sector has expanded enormously, producing both good and bad jobs, with many more of the latter in the lower-tier service industries. Meanwhile, manufacturing industries have continued to contribute less to employment growth in Canada. We have seen a substantial increase in part-time employment, with indications that other forms of nonstandard work (temporary or contract work, for example) have increased. Unemployment rates remain alarmingly high, and the public is understandably concerned about economic insecurity in the years to come. Not all aspects of these trends are negative, but there are clear signs of growing employment difficulties for significant numbers of Canadians.

What lies ahead? By simply posing this question, we enter the debates and controversies surrounding the future of work. There is a burgeoning literature on the future of work, offering a bewildering range of contradictory scenarios. Students of the sociology of work and industry should be encouraged to critically appraise these writings for themselves. From our perspective, the evidence presented in this chapter does not support the extreme positions taken by many futurists. The trends we have documented suggest neither a "workerless world" as technology displaces humans[49] nor do they support a "dejobbed world" in which work is repackaged into a variety of more flexible and rewarding entrepreneurial forms for a majority of Canadians (Bridges 1994).

We can be fairly certain that several of the trends we documented will continue. Demographic factors are a given, especially workforce aging. In addition, we can expect some continued expansion in the service sector's share of total employment. And nonstandard work seems to be slowly on the rise. The big unknown is unemployment: when and how will rates decline? Unemployment rates have gone both up and down in the past 30 years, but the long-term trend has been upward. Is an unemployment rate of, say, 5 percent even a remote possibility? How would public policy have to mesh with employers' strategies to create adequate numbers of jobs?

Examining Canadian work trends most likely to affect the future, Gordon Betcherman and Graham Lowe identify a cluster of interacting forces creating considerable economic anxiety for Canadians. Foremost among these are persistently high levels of unemployment and underemployment, especially among young people; the uncertainties created by spreading nonstandard work; and the creation of a more polarized labour market, resulting in the economic marginalization of poorly educated or unskilled individuals. By throwing more of the risks associated with economic change onto individuals and families, and by widening the gulf between "haves" and "have-nots," these trends are eroding our sense of social cohesion.

Some of these trends—higher levels of structural unemployment, declining employment in manufacturing, and increasing nonstandard employment—are linked to global economic restructuring. An unstable world market for some of Canada's staple products has reduced the prospects of regions most dependent on primary industries. Increased international competition has prompted some Canadian-based firms to rationalize their operations, shut down or relocate, replace workers with automation, or resort to low-cost nonstandard employment. Canada's economy, then, is not insulated from global economic forces. As we have argued earlier, the Canadian government's laissez-faire labour market policies have, in some ways, made working Canadians more vulnerable to the negative effects of these economic changes.

NOTES

1. Excluded are residents of the Yukon and the Northwest Territories, residents of Native reservations, full-time members of the armed forces, prison inmates, and others living in institutions such as hospitals or nursing homes.
2. See Statistics Canada (1995a) for an overview of these changes.
3. Unless otherwise noted, the 1996 estimates presented in this chapter are from the annual averages compiled by Statistics Canada (1997c) from these monthly surveys. Other data sources are individually identified.
4. Foot and Stuffman (1996: 2) provides a fascinating account of how demographic trends influence society. However, in our opinion, he under estimates the effects of the profound economic changes that are also occurring.
5. Maser (1996: 14). Also see Statistics Canada's quarterly publication, *Canadian Social Trends*, for various articles on demographics, pensions, and retirement; and *Perspectives on Labour and Income* (Spring 1995).
6. See Logan (1991) on immigration trends during the 1980s, and the Economic Council of Canada (1991b) on the economic and social impacts of current immigration policies. A survey of Canadian employers conducted by the Hudson Institute (1991) shows that the majority are concerned about possible labour shortages, although concrete actions to deal with this future problem are rare.

7. Dai and George (1996: 29). See Kutscher (1995) for similar trends and projections in the United States, where the Black, Hispanic, and Asian populations are growing most rapidly.

8. On learning organizations, see Senge et al. (1994); Jones and Hendry (1994). For a critical perspective on lifelong learning, see Livingstone (1993).

9. See Statistics Canada et al. (1996) on adult literacy

10. On work-related training, see Betcherman (1993); Lowe and Krahn (1995); Crompton (1992).

11. Statistics Canada (1995b). On underemployment, see Redpath (1994); Livingstone (1993); Krahn and Lowe (1997a).

12. Bellin and Miller (1990: 187); also see Green and Ashton (1992) on the debate over competitiveness and presumed skill shortages in Britain.

13. Statistics Canada, *The Daily* (9 May 1994); Logan and Belliveau (1995: 25).

14. These observations about movements in the labour market are based on findings from the Survey of Labour and Income Dynamics (SLID). See Statistics Canada, *The Daily* (26 June 1996). Also see Statistics Canada (1992a, 1992b) and Ross and Shillington (1991) for an earlier perspective on labour market transitions.

15. McDonald (1991: 5). See Hagey et al. (1989) and Drost (1996) for overviews of the labour market activity and economic conditions of Aboriginal Canadians.

16. Shain (1995). Statistics Canada estimates that there were 1.4 million Canadians aged 15 to 64 with disabilities that might affect their employment (Michaud, George, and Loh, 1996). Disability refers to any restriction or reduced ability to perform work activities due to disease or injury.

17. Statistics Canada (1996d: 8); also see Betcherman and Leckie (1997) and Lindsay et al. (1994).

18. Tanner and Krahn (1991); Lowe and Krahn (1992); also see Gilbert et al. (1993), Bernier (1995), and a special issue of *Youth and Society* (vol. 22, 2: December 1990).

19. Gower (1995); Monette (1996a, 1996b); Lowe (1991b). On older workers and retirement issues, see Centre for Studies of Aging (1996); McDonald and Wanner (1990); Tindale (1991).

20. On the life-course perspective, see Riley (1988). Myles and Street (1995) apply this perspective to pension reform.

21. Findings from a study by Lars Osberg (*Perspectives on Labour and Income*, 1990). See Meyer and Quadango (1990) for a similar study of older male workers in the U.S. automobile manufacturing industry.

22. Methods of studying work in the irregular economy include unofficial surveys (assuming one can gain the confidence of respondents), examination of law enforcement records (in an attempt to estimate amounts of illegal economic activity), and assessments of the amount of cash in circulation in an economy (compared with taxation reports of the total amount of reported income). See the OECD (1986; Chapter 3) and Harding and Jenkins (1989: Chapters 5 and 6). See Felt and Sinclair (1992) for an interesting study of unpaid work in rural Newfoundland.

23. Minus et al. (1994). Revenue Canada has intensified its investigation of individuals operating in the underground economy in an effort to recover unreported taxes. See Revenue Canada's website: http://www.revcan.ca.

24. See the Economic Council of Canada's (1991a) overview of the service economy.

25. See Krahn (1992: 17–18) for details on this industry typology, based on the classification system used by Myles et al. (1988), and similar to the typology used by Lindsay (1989). All three typologies can be traced to the classification work of Singelmann (1978). Compared with the standard industrial classification system, the ten-category typology shows a larger proportion of the labour force in the resource-based industries, since utilities, as well as wood, paper, primary metal, coal, and petroleum industries are included here rather than in manufacturing.

26. This reduced classification system is quite similar to the industry typology developed by the Economic Council of Canada (1990, 1991a) in its studies of the service sector. The Economic Council distinguished *dynamic services* (distributive and business services) from *nonmarket services* (education, health and welfare, public administration) and *traditional services* (retail trade and personal services).

27. Data from the 1989 General Social Survey show 58 percent of young female workers and 37 percent of young male workers with jobs in the lower-tier services (Krahn, 1992: 45). Also see Betcherman and Leckie (1997).

28. See Human Resources Development Canada's (1996b) *Job Futures* for a detailed discussion of current and future labour market prospects for 211 occupational groups classified according to the NOC. This is a very useful guide for career planning.

29. Statistics Canada, *The Daily* (4 June 1992); also see Winson (1996). Ilg (1995) documents the same trend in the United States.

30. Watkins (1977: 90). See Lucas (1971), Bowles (1982), Clemenson (1992), Statistics Canada, *The Daily* (28 April 1992), and Angus and Griffin (1996) on Canada's single-industry communities.

31. This discussion is based on Akyeampong (1992); also see Economic Council of Canada (1982: 53–58) and Akyeampong (1989).

32 For discussions of unemployment trends and policy responses, see Gera (1991), Cohen (1991), and MacLean and Osberg (1996).

33. Alternative policy options are presented in MacLean and Osberg (1996), a special issue of *Policy Options* (July–August 1996), Betcherman and Lowe (1997), and Freeman and Soete (1994).

34. Cohen (1991: 44) notes that when you multiply the average number of unemployed in 1980 times their average length of unemployment, you obtain a figure of 12.7 million person-weeks of unemployment, compared with 18.2 million person-weeks in 1987, even though the unemployment rate in both years was 7.5 percent. Gera (1991: 6) presents data on the duration of unemployment from 1976 to 1989; 1990 data are from Cross (1992: 7–8); and 1996 data are from Akyeampong (1997a: 16).

35. Drost (1996: 181). Also see Hagey et al. (1989), Ross (1992), and Statistics Canada (1994a) on the labour force activity of Aboriginal Canadians. See Waldram (1987), Stabler and Howe (1990), and Niezen (1993) regarding employment opportunities for Aboriginal Canadians in northern communities.

36. Foot and Li (1986). In 1982, youth (aged 15 to 24) made up 24 percent of the total Canadian population, compared with only 18 percent in 1990 (Thompson, 1991: 7).

37. Picard (1994: 29). Also see Corak (1993) on the characteristics of workers who participated in the Unemployment Insurance program.

38. See the analysis and debates in Gera (1991); MacLean and Osberg (1996); *Policy Options* (1996).

39. Rifkin (1995) predicts a future in which masses of the population will be deprived of employment because of technological change. See Betcherman and Lowe (1997) for counterarguments.

40. A number of prominent economists express this view, such as Fortin (1996); also see Donner (1991).

41. Akyeampong (1997a: 16); also see Sorrentino (1995). See Sherman and Judkins (1995: 49–57) on measurement problems in comparisons of national unemployment rates.

42. Sherman and Judkins (1995: 53) on measurement problems in comparisons of national unemployment rates.

43. Drache and Gertler (1991: 19–22). For comparative perspectives on government industrial policy, see Campbell (1991: 31–34), Muszynski and Wolfe (1989). Also see Tobin (1996) and Lonnroth (1994) on the role of government in creating jobs.

44. Human Resources Development Canada (1994); also see Yalnizyan et al. (1994).

45. See the International Labour Organization's (1997) comparative analysis; for the United States, see the entire issue of the *Monthly Labor Review* on "contingent" forms of work (October 1996); and for the United Kingdom, see Felstead, Krahn, and Powell (1997).

46. The 1996 figures are based on the new definition, that is, a worker is defined as part-time if her or his main job is less than 30 hours weekly. The source is Statistics Canada (1996d). We should note that the Labour Force Survey measure of part-time employment is higher than the General Social Survey (Figure 2.6), both because the GSS used the old definition and because its smaller sample led to less reliable estimates.

47. Duffy and Pupo (1992). Also see Warme et al. (1992) on part-time work.

48. Krahn (1995) discusses estimates of nonstandard work in Canada based on data from the 1989 and 1994 General Social Surveys. Also see Schellenberg and Clark (1996) for a detailed analysis of temporary employment trends in Canada. The Economic Council of Canada (1990: 12) reports on the growth of temporary help agency work in Canada. See Henson (1996) for a personal account of temporary employment.

49. See Krahn (1991) for estimates of part-year work in Canada in 1989, and Crompton (1995b) for 1983–93 trends in full-year employment.

50. This futurist literature is summarized in Betcherman and Lowe (1997). This is the position taken by Rifkin (1995).

LABOUR MARKETS AND JOBS: OPPORTUNITIES AND INEQUALITY

INTRODUCTION

WHY DO HIGH SCHOOL TEACHERS EARN MORE than retail sales clerks, or engineers more than construction workers? Presumably, these income differences are a result of teachers and engineers investing in extra years of education that, in turn, lead to more skilled and responsible jobs. So why do dentists make more money than child care workers? While dentists spent more years training for their profession, caring for and teaching young children is also a very complex and responsible task. Why are the children of middle-class parents much more likely to go to university, compared with the children of less affluent Canadians? Why are women, the disabled, Aboriginal Canadians, and members of visible minority groups overrepresented in less rewarding jobs?

Such questions about variations in educational outcomes, career patterns, job security, and other job rewards are central to the sociological study of labour markets. We can define a *labour market* as the arena in which employers seek to purchase labour from potential employees who themselves are seeking jobs suitable to their education, experience, and preferences. In the labour market, workers exchange their skills, knowledge, and loyalty in return for pay, status, career opportunities, and other job rewards (Kalleberg and Berg 1987: 48–49).

A number of other institutions and organizations support or interact with the operation of the labour market. Among their other functions, schools and families prepare individuals for entry (or re-entry) into the labour market. Government legislation affects how labour markets operate—minimum wage laws and legislation governing the activities of trade unions are examples. Government agencies may also assist the unemployed with financial support or job-training programs. Unions and professional associations are active in the labour market, looking after the interests of their members by bargaining for additional job rewards and, sometimes, by limiting access to better jobs. Organizations representing employers also try to influence labour market operations, lobbying governments to change laws regarding unions or encouraging schools to include more employment-related subject matter in their teaching.

Labour economists and sociologists study many of these institutions and how they influence labour market operations.[1] Of particular interest to sociologists are the distributive aspects of the labour market. Specifically, does the labour market provide opportunities for hard-working individuals to improve their social position and quality of life, or does it reinforce patterns of inequality in society? Perhaps it does both.

The previous chapter discussed Canada's changing industrial and occupational structures, rising unemployment, and growth in nonstandard jobs. It demonstrated that some jobs are much more rewarding than others and that some people are at much greater risk of unemployment. This chapter pursues these issues. It begins by reviewing some of the criteria by which individuals evaluate the desirability of jobs. We then ask several basic questions: Who has the good jobs? How did they get them? And how do they manage to keep them? Our attempt to answer these questions is built around a comparison of two alternative approaches to explaining labour market outcomes in societies like ours, the human capital model and the labour market segmentation perspective.

According to *human capital theory*, jobs requiring more effort, training, and skill typically receive greater rewards. The theory assumes that labour market participants compete openly for the best jobs, and that the most qualified people end up in the jobs requiring their particular skills. The outcome should be an efficient and productive economy and a fair allocation of job rewards. But in reviewing research on differences in job rewards, educational and occupational choice, status attainment, and labour market segmentation, we observe that the labour market does not always operate in this manner. In fact, there is evidence that the open competition assumptions of human capital theory need to be seriously challenged, and that a segmented labour market often allows the perpetuation of social inequalities.

Thus, the study of labour markets is not only about who gets better or worse jobs; it also addresses broader questions about social stratification and class structure.[2] Consequently, this chapter also discusses class inequalities within Canadian society and the growing polarization of living standards and life chances.

GOOD JOBS AND BAD JOBS

We have already begun to assess the quality of different jobs in our discussion of nonstandard employment relationships. Compared with being unemployed, a part-time or temporary job may be preferable. For most labour force participants, though, a full-time, full-year, permanent job would be much more desirable because of the income security it provides. Thus, recognizing that some Canadians do prefer nonstandard jobs for educational, personal, or family reasons, and allowing that some nonstandard jobs (business consultants working on a contractual basis, for example) might pay very well, we would still classify only a minority of nonstandard jobs as "good jobs."

Clearly, the criteria for deciding whether a particular job is a good or bad job are not universal. Individuals compare the rewards a job provides against their own needs and ambitions, and against the personal costs of working in such a job. Since most workers are concerned about maintaining or improving their standard of living and quality of life, material or *extrinsic job rewards* are very important. How much does it pay? What kinds of benefits come with the job? Is it dangerous? Is it full-time and permanent?

In the following section, we examine variations in pay and other employment benefits in the Canadian labour market. We also present data on work-related injuries and deaths, our rationale being that a job with few risks to personal health and safety is, in a crucial sense, a better job. We then comment on the types of jobs that require workers to use computers. Recognizing that not all jobs involving computer use are highly rewarding, a subject we will return to in later chapters, we reason that computer use provides workers with technology skills that could enhance their future employment prospects. Finally, we discuss occupational status (the prestige ranking of a particular job), even though it is not really an extrinsic job reward in the same sense as pay and benefits. However, occupational status is also not as subjectively (individually) determined as are the more *intrinsic job rewards* (the chance to be creative, to work independently, to develop friendships in a job, and so on) discussed in Chapter 8. While power relationships within Canadian workplaces are obviously also central to discussions of good jobs and bad jobs, we will introduce them briefly in this chapter and then provide a fuller discussion in Chapter 6.

Income Differences

Statistics Canada collects income information annually, using various surveys. We draw on several of these data sources to highlight some of the most important factors influencing income differences in the Canadian labour market.

Considering only *paid employees* (that is, excluding the self-employed), incomes in the service industries are about 20 percent less than in the goods-producing industries. In 1994, average weekly earnings (excluding overtime) were $518 in the former, compared to $664 in the latter. However, there is more variation in employees' incomes within the service sector, with workers in the upper-tier industries earning much more than those in the lower-tier industries. For example, in 1994, paid employees in engineering, architectural, and computer-related services earned an average of about $800 per week, almost four times as much as those in food and beverage services.[3]

Comparing incomes of several major occupational groups in 1995, we find that managers reported average annual earnings (wages and salaries, and net income from self-employment) of $41,352. Canadians in teaching occupations had 1995 average earnings of $35,330, while medicine and health professionals earned almost as much ($34,410). In contrast, clerical (office) workers had considerably lower average annual earnings ($21,825), but these were still higher than the average earnings ($17,160) in service occupations (for example, waitresses, hairdressers, and security guards).[4]

Some of these differences in earning patterns are a result of larger proportions of part-time and part-year workers in service occupations and in the lower-tier service industries. Higher earnings in some goods-producing and upper-tier services, and in managerial and professional occupations, can be traced, in part, to the presence of unions and professional associations that have bargained for higher incomes (and full-time work). It is also apparent that workers with specific professional skills (for example, doctors, teachers, and engineers) are generally paid much more than those with less training. Thus, some of the industrial and occupational differences in earnings are due to supply and demand factors in a labour market that rewards educational investments. Also important are differences in the bargaining power of the various groups participating in the labour market.

These occupational earning patterns hide large gender differences. Thus, female managers reported average annual earnings in 1995 of $32,306, two-thirds of the earnings of their male counterparts ($48,753). In the medicine and health category, women earned $29,557 in 1995, only 54 percent of the average annual earnings of men ($55,211) in this category. Similar gender differences are observed in all of the broad occupational groupings, although the *female-to-male earnings ratio* does vary across these categories. As Chapter 4 documents, this ratio is influenced by the specific occupations typically held by women and men within the larger categories. Men are more likely to be medical doctors, for example, while women are overrepresented in nursing.

Overall, larger proportions of women than men are employed in the lower-tier services and in clerical, sales, and service occupations where incomes are considerably lower. In addition, women are more likely to be in part-time jobs. As a result, in 1995 the average earnings of all employed women in Canada ($20,219) represented only 65 percent of the average earnings of all employed men ($31,053). When we restrict our analysis to the full-time, full-year employed, male average earnings increase to $40,610, while the female average climbs to $29,700. This translates into women receiving, on average, 73 percent of what men earned in 1995, up from about 60 percent in 1970.

The *gender wage gap* has been decreasing for several decades primarily because women's earnings have been rising slowly while the earnings of men, on average, have stalled. Perhaps the rising incomes of women simply reflect more women investing in higher education and, as a result, gaining access to better-paying jobs. This explanation might account for a small part of the income trend, but it is not a sufficient explanation. While, overall, *educational attainment* has been increasing steadily, there has been virtually no difference in the median years of schooling of Canadian women and men for the past two decades (Statistics Canada 1996a: 191–92). Similar numbers of women and men participate in post-secondary education (see Chapter 2). So we need to examine other features of the labour market (for example, hiring and promotion practices, and the presence or absence of unions) and its related institutions (for example, how do families and schools influence educational, occupational, and career choices) to obtain a more complete explanation of the remaining gender differences in income (see Chapter 4).

By restricting our discussion to broad occupational categories, we also overlook the extreme ends of the *income distribution* in the Canadian labour market. At the top of the earnings hierarchy, chief executive officers (CEOs) of Canada's largest firms typically earn huge incomes (based on salaries, performance bonuses, and options to purchase stocks in their company at below-market value). In 1996, the 100 highest-paid CEOs all earned in excess of $700,000. At the top of the list, Laurent Beaudoin of Bombardier Inc. received a total compensation package worth $19.1 million. It would take the average Canadian employee, with annual earnings of about $30,000, over 600 years to accumulate this much money.[5]

At the other end of the income scale are a great many Canadian workers with very low incomes. Legislated minimum wages in Canada have always been very low, and in the past twenty years they have not kept up with inflation. Thus, in 1995 if a worker earning a minimum wage worked 40 hours a week for 52 weeks in the year, she or he would earn $9,880 annually in Newfoundland and Prince Edward Island (provinces with the lowest minimum wage), $10,400 in Alberta and New Brunswick, $12,480 in Quebec, $14,248 in Ontario, and $14,560 in British Columbia (the highest minimum wage) (Schellenberg and Ross 1997: 42, Table 23).

Many, but not all, of these lowest-paid workers are students working in the lower-tier services (retail trade and consumer services), frequently part-time. Some older, full-time workers also have minimum wage jobs, but many more are hired at pay rates only a few dollars above the minimum wage. As a second income in a household, such salesclerk, waitress, cashier, and service station attendant jobs might help pay some bills. However, if this were the only income, the household, especially if it contained children, would likely be living well below the official *low income (or poverty) line.*[6]

Hourly wage rates in blue-collar occupations such as construction or manufacturing are typically at least twice as high as the minimum wage. Yet even with a $12-per-hour wage, and working full-time and year-round, these earnings would still make it very difficult to raise a family in most major Canadian urban centres. Furthermore, many of these blue-collar jobs are seasonal and are subject to frequent layoffs. Consequently, when we look closely at the characteristics of Canadian families living below the poverty line, we find that low wages, insufficient work (part-time or part-year), and periodic unemployment are usually the problem (Schellenberg and Ross 1997; Crompton 1995). Some of the working poor lack education or marketable skills, but many simply cannot find well-paying and secure employment.

Other Employment Benefits

Additional employment benefits (a form of indirect pay) are an important dimension of the quality of jobs. In the 1950s, benefit costs made up approximately 15 percent of Canadian employers' total labour costs. By 1989, the cost of benefits had more than doubled to 33.5 percent of gross payroll costs. Benefits required by law (employer contributions for Employment Insurance, Canada/Quebec Pension Plan, and Workers' Compensation) make up only about one-sixth of the cost of all employee benefits provided in Canada. A much larger portion of the indirect income provided through employment benefits comes from paid vacation and statutory holidays, and from employer contributions to private pension and employee health and dental plans.[7]

Thus, in 1995 almost three-quarters of paid employees in Canada received some vacation pay, while between 50 and 60 percent had an employer-sponsored pension plan, health plan, dental plan, and paid sick leave (Figure 3.1). A much smaller proportion (21 percent in 1994) received formal work-related training, paid for by their employer.[8] Such training can lead to promotions, higher income, and an improved ability to compete for other jobs.

Additional employment benefits are unequally distributed. Individuals employed in the lower-tier services, particularly in nonstandard jobs, receive relatively few benefits. In fact, full-time and permanent workers are about three times as likely as their part-time and temporary counterparts to have

FIGURE 3.1 *Employer-Sponsored Benefits by Full-Time/Part-Time and Permanent/Non-Permanent Work, Paid Employees Aged 15–69, Canada, 1995*

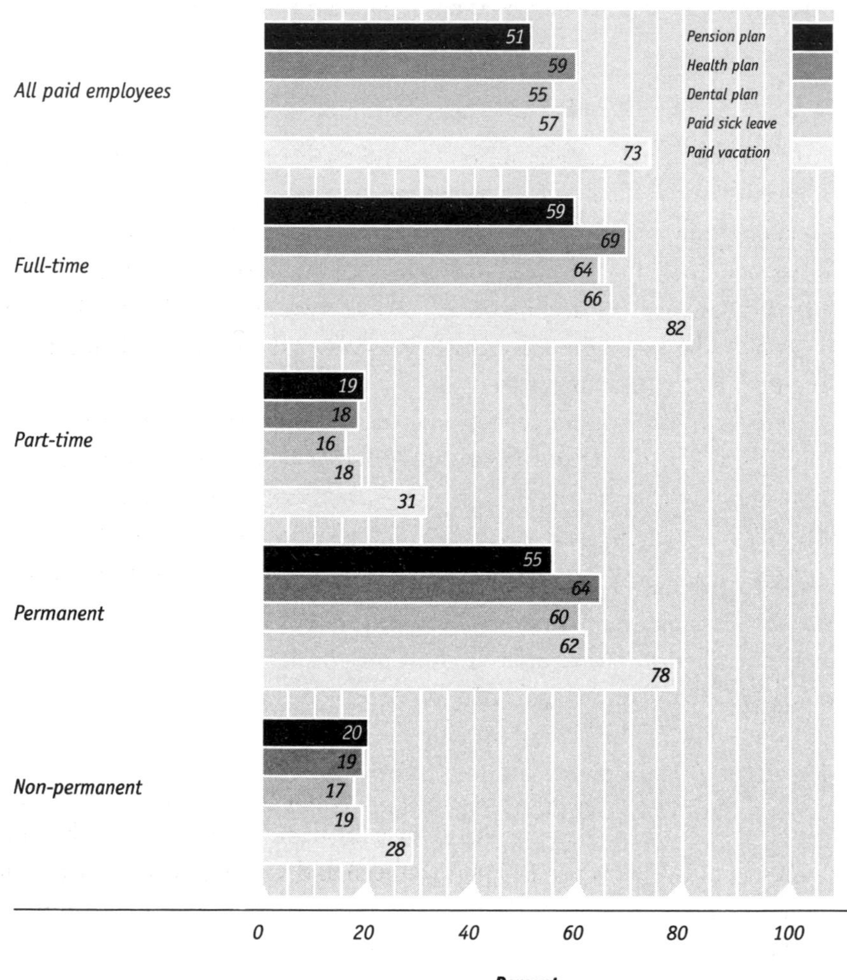

Source: Statistics Canada, "Employer-Sponsored Benefits by Full-Time/Part-Time and Permanent/Non-Permanent Work, Paid Employees Aged 15–69, Canada, 1995," adapted from "Perspectives on Labour and Income," Catalogue No. 75-001, Spring 1997, page 52. Reprinted with permission.

employer-sponsored pension, health, and dental plans, and paid sick leave and vacation pay (Figure 3.1). The same benefits are also more frequently available in larger firms (where pay is also typically higher) and in unionized workplaces.

Similarly, better-educated workers, those employed in larger firms, and those in full-time positions are more likely to receive employer-sponsored work-related training.[9] It is apparent, then, that pay differences within the Canadian labour market are accentuated by the uneven distribution of fringe benefits.

Risks to Personal Health and Safety

We can extend this discussion of job quality by examining the personal risks of different kinds of jobs. For example, every year hundreds of Canadian workers die from work-related injuries or illnesses. In 1993, 758 work-related fatalities were recorded, bringing the total since 1976 to over 17,000.[10] While industrial fatalities have declined over the past two decades (Figure 3.2), the chances of being killed on the job are still greater than those of being killed on the road by a drunk driver.

Industrial fatality rates are lowest in the service industries, with a few exceptions (Figure 3.2). Government services (a sector including workers in parks and prisons, for example, as well as offices) have somewhat higher rates (an average of 5 deaths per year per 100,000 paid workers), followed by manufacturing (an average of 8 deaths annually). However, the construction and transportation industries have much higher fatality rates, with almost two dozen work-related deaths per year per 100,000 workers. These rates are dwarfed by those found in the resource extraction industries: between 1988 and 1993, the annual fatality rates were 63 (per 100,000 workers) in mining, 82 in logging and forestry, and 113 in fishing and trapping.

Some jobs within these industries carry extremely high risks. The most dangerous are those involving cutting, handling, and loading of materials in the mining industry (281 deaths per 100,000 workers) and working with insulation in the construction industry (246 deaths). However, since relatively small numbers of people work in these and other high-risk jobs (including fishing and trapping), the three leading causes of work-related death are exposure to harmful substances (20 percent of all industrial fatalities between 1988 and 1993), accidents involving transportation vehicles (19 percent), and being struck by an object. Since the high-risk jobs are typically filled by men, 96 percent of the workers who died because of work-related reasons between 1988 and 1993 were men.[11]

The incidence of disabling injury and illness rose in Canada during the 1970s and 1980s, but then began to decline in the early 1990s. Some of this

FIGURE 3.2 *Work-Related Fatality Rates by Industry, Canada, 1976–1981 and 1988–1993*

Industry	1976–81	1988–93
Agriculture	9	10
Fishing/Trapping	182	113
Logging/Forestry	97	82
Mining/Oil	79	63
Manufacturing	9	8
Construction	32	23
Transportation	36	25
Communication	6	4
Wholesale trade	11	7
Retail trade	2	1
Finance/Insurance	1	1
Government Services	8	5
Other Services†	3	2

0 40 80 120 160 200

Annual Fatality Rates (per 100,000 workers) *

* Rates per 100,000 paid workers (averaged over five years); data from Workers' Compensation Boards.
† Includes business, education/health/welfare, and other consumer services.

Source: Statistics Canada, "Work-Related Fatality Rates by Industry, Canada, 1976–1981 and 1988–1993," adapted from "Perspectives on Labour and Income," Catalogue No. 75-001, Summer 1996, Volume 8, Number 2, page 27. Reprinted with permission.

improvement may be due to increased efforts to reduce risks, but the onset of the recession in 1990 also put more people out of work and reduced working hours for others. Both of these trends would have had an immediate impact on the number of work injuries recorded. Even so, in 1993, Workers' Compensation Boards and Commissions across the country compensated 423,184 individuals for work-related injuries and illness resulting in time loss and permanent disability. Almost half of these claims involved sprains and strains (45 percent of all compensated injuries), increasingly associated with use of computers and other automated technologies. Back injuries were most common (29 percent of all injuries), and overexertion was most often the root cause (29 percent) (Statistics Canada (1994b).

Not all work-related injuries and illnesses get reported and compensated, and the effects of some do not become apparent for many years. Hence, it is useful to also look at research on *workplace hazards* that might be harming workers' health. A 1991 national survey, for example, indicated that 38 percent of Canadian workers had experienced one or more serious stress-inducing work situations in the previous year. The same study revealed that 34 percent of employed respondents (representing 4.9 million workers) in the previous 12 months in their job had been exposed to dust or fibres in the air. One in four (26 percent) reported exposure to loud noise, 22 percent had been exposed to poor quality air, and 18 percent said they had been exposed to dangerous chemicals or fumes. Blue-collar workers were much more likely to be exposed to dust or fibres, loud noise, and dangerous chemicals, while white-collar workers were more likely to report poor quality air in their work environment.[12]

There are a number of important conclusions to be drawn from this brief discussion of workplace health and safety in Canada. First, it is clear that work-related stress, injuries, illnesses, and fatalities constitute an extremely serious social problem. Hundreds of Canadians die in work-related injuries each year, and hundreds of thousands are injured or become ill. But even though work time lost to injuries and illnesses continues to far exceed the time lost due to strikes and work stoppages in Canada (see Chapter 7), the latter is much more often perceived to be a problem.

Second, workplace health and safety problems constitute a huge cost for employers. In addition to the direct costs of compensation, there are indirect costs resulting from production losses, lower efficiency, decreased employee morale, and lost supervisory time. Although such costs are notoriously hard to calculate precisely, estimates are typically in the billions of dollars annually. Third, industrial and occupational differences in injuries and fatalities demonstrate that the risks of injury, illness, and death are an additional important dimension of overall job quality. Some of the best-paid groups within the labour market experience many fewer risks to their personal health and safety.

Computer Use in the Workplace

The impacts of new *information technologies* (IT) on employment opportunities and on the quality of work are hotly debated topics in the sociology of work. Proponents of the new technologies point to long-term increases in employment as new types of jobs appear, and to increased skill requirements in jobs employing computers and automated technologies. Critics remind us that new technologies have frequently led to job loss for many workers as employers have used the technology to cut labour costs. They also draw attention to examples of jobs that have been *deskilled* as automated systems have replaced some of the previously required manual and cognitive skills of workers. We will return to this larger debate in Chapter 6, focusing here on which workers actually use computers in their jobs. With respect to characteristics of good jobs and bad jobs, we reason that computer use on the job provides workers with technology skills that might enhance their future employment prospects (Oderkirk 1996; McMullen 1996).

The 1994 General Social Survey revealed that 48 percent of employed Canadians used a computer (personal computer, mainframe, or word processor), the most common form of information technology, in their main job. This figure had risen substantially from 35 percent five years earlier. However, computer use was far from equally distributed across industries and occupations. While 82 percent of workers in the business service and finance industries used computers in their job, along with 71 percent of those employed in public administration, only about half of Canadians working in the education, health, and welfare sector (51 percent) and in distributive services (53 percent) did so. Below-average computer use was observed in the primary industries (31 percent), manufacturing (41 percent), construction (20 percent), retail trade (39 percent), and in the personal services sector (24 percent) (Lowe 1997).

Figure 3.3 demonstrates that computer use is clearly highest among managers, professionals in the natural and social sciences (the latter would include

FIGURE 3.3 *Computer Use in the Workplace by Occupation, Canada, 1994*

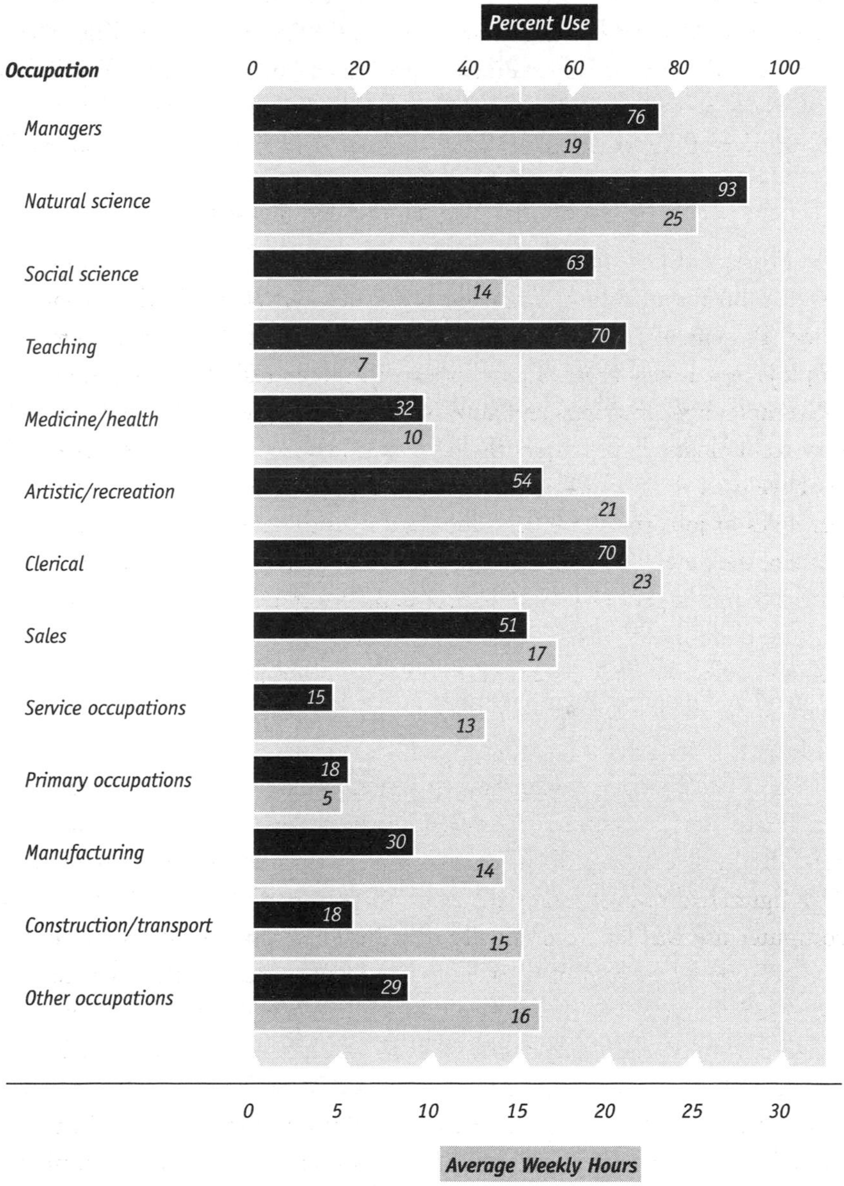

Occupation	*Percent Use*	*Average Weekly Hours*
Managers	76	19
Natural science	93	25
Social science	63	14
Teaching	70	7
Medicine/health	32	10
Artistic/recreation	54	21
Clerical	70	23
Sales	51	17
Service occupations	15	13
Primary occupations	18	5
Manufacturing	30	14
Construction/transport	18	15
Other occupations	29	16

Source: Statistics Canada, "Computer Use in the Workplace by Occupations, Canada, 1994," adapted from "Perspectives on Labour and Income," Catalogue No. 75-001, Summer 1997, Volume 9, Number 2, pages 27–28. Reprinted with permission.

lawyers), and teachers. It is also quite high among clerical (office) workers, but very low in the blue-collar and service occupations. To some extent, in the occupations where computer use is more common, average weekly hours of use are also higher. For example, 93 percent of natural science professionals used computers in their job in 1994, averaging 25 hours per week. In contrast, only 18 percent of construction workers used computers for, on average, 15 hours per week.

These patterns of computer use parallel the distribution of other work rewards in the Canadian labour market. Workers with better pay, more benefits, and more access to training are also more likely to be using computers, thus acquiring skills that might be transferable to other employment situations. These survey results correlate with other research showing that more affluent households are more likely to own personal computers (Dickinson and Sciadas 1996). However, there are two important exceptions. First, clerical workers (most of whom are women) are typically not as well paid as are managers and professionals, but they report high levels of computer use. Second, manufacturing, construction, and primary sector workers, a largely male group that has been reasonably well paid, exhibit low workplace computer use. Thus, to understand how computer use and skills fit into the good jobs–bad jobs equation, we also need to look at how this new technology is actually used and at the gendered patterns of employment in the labour market.

Occupational Status

We seldom find doctors, lawyers, scientists, or professors blushing when they are asked, "What do you do?" But for clerks, janitors, parking lot attendants, and many others, the same question might elicit an apologetic "I'm just a…." In short, there is consensus in our society about which jobs have higher status. While less important than income and benefits (which directly determine one's standard of living) and job security (which ensures continuity of that standard), *occupational status* is something we must also consider when comparing different jobs. To a great extent, our self-image and the respect of others is determined by our occupation.

Not surprisingly, there is a strong relationship between occupational status and income. It may seem that both higher pay and higher status are a direct result of the greater skill and responsibility required by certain jobs. Generally, higher status jobs do require more education, cognitive ability, and skill.[13] It is also possible that some occupations have come to be seen as more prestigious because, over time, incomes in this line of work have risen. Higher incomes, in turn, might be the result of skill increases, but they may also reflect the ability of a powerful occupational group to limit entry into its field. It is also quite clear that some occupations have traditionally had higher social status because they were viewed as men's work rather than women's work, a topic we examine in the next chapter.

The links among income, education, and occupational status have led to widespread use of *socioeconomic status* (SES) scales in sociological research. In Canada, the most frequently used SES measures are the *Blishen scores.* Bernard Blishen began with the results of a mid-1960s national study that asked respondents to rank the "social standing" of almost two hundred detailed occupational titles. He calculated the statistical relationships between these prestige rankings and the average education and income (from Census data) of men employed in these occupations, and then estimated SES scores for almost five hundred occupational titles. An updated version of this SES scale, based on 1981 Census data for both men and women, began to address one of the major criticisms of the original scale—it was biased toward traditionally "male" jobs.[14] This version of the Blishen scale ranges from low status scores, such as 17.8 for newspaper carriers and 21.5 for service station attendants, to high evaluations for professionals such as nuclear engineers (75.4), university teachers (75.9), and physicians (101.3).

A useful alternative occupational classification system consists of a sixteen-category typology developed by Peter Pineo and others from the occupational codes used in the 1971 Census and subsequently updated from 1981 Census information. This ranking focuses more on the work tasks done by different occupational groups, the skill and knowledge levels required, and the nature of the employment relationships. Self-employed professionals (doctors and lawyers, for example) are at the top of the list. Further down, we find categories such as semiprofessionals, technicians, middle management, skilled clerical, semiskilled manual workers, and so on. Compared to the Blishen scores which remain numbers with no meaning in themselves, the advantage of the Pineo scale is that the title assigned to a rank (for example, semiskilled clerical, sales, and services) actually tells us something about the occupations included.[15]

CANADA'S CLASS STRUCTURE

The question of who has better and worse jobs in the Canadian labour market is really a question about social inequality. Therefore, answering the question requires us to examine the class structure of our society. The term *social class* is used in a variety of ways by social scientists. Some treat it as equivalent to socioeconomic status, discussed above, referring to an individual's position in a fluid social hierarchy determined by occupation, education, or income. However, social class can have a much more precise meaning. It refers, at one level, to a particular position within a stratified social structure and, at the same time, to the power relationships among groups directly engaged in the production process. These "relations of ruling"[16] have an impact on individuals' life chances (their living standard and the opportunities to improve it), and, sometimes, on the way they perceive the social world around them and react to it.

Marx on Social Class

Class relationships were central to the social and economic theories of Karl Marx. In his analysis of capitalism, Marx focused primarily on the relationship between the class of *capitalists* who owned the means of production and the *proletariat*. The latter class owned no production-related property, and so had little choice but to exchange labour in return for a wage. Marx also discussed the middle class of small business owners (the *petite bourgeoisie*) and predicted that, in time, it would largely disappear; small businesses would be swallowed up by bigger competitors, and self-employment in agriculture would gradually be replaced by wage labour. The result would be an even more polarized society. Conflict between an increasingly impoverished class of workers and the capitalist class would eventually lead to the emergence of a new type of egalitarian society.

As documented in Chapter 2, historically Canada has moved in the direction of less self-employment, as have other industrialized capitalist societies. However, we have also observed an increase in self-employment in the past decade. In addition, expansion of the service industries, a growing number of skilled (and well-paid) workers in white-collar occupations, and the emergence of distinctly different patterns of employment for women and men force us to rethink Marx's model of social class relationships. What, then, are the characteristics of Canada's class structure?

Postindustrial Class Structure of Canadian Society

Marx's original classification system cannot accurately map the complexities of social class in Canadian society today. For example, while an individual whose store has three employees is classified as an employer, her or his responsibilities, power, and job rewards are hardly comparable to the president of a corporation employing thousands of workers, wielding a great deal of power, and taking home a pay package in excess of a million dollars a year. Similarly, while both a senior manager in a large corporation and a sales clerk in a retail store may be paid workers, their work experiences and rewards are very different. Consequently, a variety of attempts have been made to incorporate such important distinctions into theories of social class.

A widely used approach was developed by Eric Olin Wright (Wright et al. 1982). In his classification of labour force participants, Wright took into account ownership, the employment of others, the supervision of others, and control over one's own work. He distinguished between large employers and small employers, two groups that have legal ownership and also employ others, and the *petite bourgeoisie*, who own their businesses (or farms) but do not have others working for them (the own-account self-employed). Large employers (the group most closely resembling Marx's class of capitalists) are in a different category from small employers with only a handful of employees, since the latter would typically be directly involved in the production process (working alongside employees).

The large class of paid employees was separated by Wright into managers, who, while not owning the enterprise, would be involved in decision making, along with (or in the absence of) the legal owners; supervisors, who are not involved in planning and decision making but who nevertheless exercise authority over others; and workers, who have no ownership rights, decision-making power, or authority over others. One final class grouping, *semi-autonomous workers* (for instance, social workers, university professors, and other salaried professionals), are identified by the relatively greater control they retain over their own work.

Census and Labour Force Survey data do not contain the detail needed to classify the labour force in this manner. However, a 1982 national survey designed to examine class issues suggested the following class distribution: large employers (1 percent); small employers (3 percent); the self-employed (12 percent); managers (14 percent); supervisors (11 percent); semi-autonomous workers (16 percent); and workers (43 percent). While a small sample size (less than 1800 respondents) means that these estimates are not precise,[17] the study does demonstrate that the large class of paid workers contains several distinct types. Within this category, some workers (in unionized blue-collar settings, for example) would be much better paid and receive more benefits compared to workers in less secure jobs in the lower-tier services.

Wallace Clement and John Myles use the same data to develop a more concise typology of class relationships. They identify four main classes based on whether an individual controls the means of production and/or commands the labour power of others. In brief, the *capitalist-executive class* contains self-employed owners with three or more employees, along with senior executives and managers who make strategic decisions about how an organization operates. The *new middle class* contains individuals who control and manage other employees, while the *old middle class* are the self-employed with two or less employees. The *working class*, the largest category, contains all other employed labour force participants. Thus, the capitalist-executive class controls both production and the employment of other workers. The working class does neither. According to this classification system, in 1982 the majority of employed Canadians (58 percent) were in the working class. About 6 percent were members of the capitalist-executive class, 25 percent were in the new middle class, and 11 percent were in the old middle class (Clement and Myles 1994: 17–18).

By focusing explicitly on power relationships and using a smaller number of categories, Clement and Myles downplay some of the "ownership" distinctions made by Wright, as well as his emphasis on semi-autonomous workers. They also go beyond Wright's class analysis by integrating gender differences in employment outcomes into their model of class relations in post-industrial society.[18] The Wright model placed 43 percent of employed Canadians in the working class, in contrast to 58 percent according to the Clement and Myles model. Whichever approach we use, these are still large groupings that disguise major differences in job rewards. Consequently, there is merit in continuing our discussion of labour market outcomes by examining other approaches to the subject.

Furthermore, the class-based approach does not directly address questions about how a society allocates better or worse jobs to individuals and groups, how individual workers might improve their employment situation, or how some groups of workers might manage to exclude others from access to better jobs. Such questions about *labour market processes* are central to the human capital and labour market segmentation perspectives discussed in the remainder of this chapter.

THE HUMAN CAPITAL MODEL OF LABOUR MARKET PROCESSES

We have argued that, on a variety of dimensions, some jobs are better than others, while recognizing that some jobs also require more skills and training. Ideally, jobs with specific requirements would be filled by individuals most suited for these positions. If being suited for a particular job meant that one must first obtain an advanced education, then it would seem only reasonable that, having done so, one would be rewarded with a better job. Stripped to its essentials, these are the basic premises of *human capital theory*, a major economic explanation of how the labour market operates.

This theoretical perspective assumes that a job's rewards are determined by its economic contribution to society. It also predicts that more dangerous and unhealthy jobs should be paid more, since workers would have to be compensated for these greater risks. The model assumes that labour market participants are all competing for jobs in a single, open labour market. Information about available jobs is widely circulated. All potential employees with the necessary qualifications have equal access to job openings. When it comes to choosing whom to hire, employers make rational decisions, based on an assessment of an individual's ability.

In order to "get ahead," it makes sense for job seekers to get more education and training. But this means delayed entry into the labour market and foregoing immediate earnings. Yet this is not a permanent loss because by obtaining more education one is investing in *human capital*, which can later be "cashed in" for a better job. In short, the human capital model emphasizes the *supply side* of labour markets, and largely overlooks the behaviour and characteristics of employers and work organizations (the *demand side*). It also ignores questions about class structure and unequal power relationships within the labour market. The human capital perspective on labour markets is premised on a "consensus" view of society, in contrast to the more explicitly "conflict" assumptions underlying class-based and labour market segmentation approaches.[19]

The basic logic of human capital theory is compelling, given the evidence that better-educated individuals generally are less likely to be unemployed and more likely to hold well-paying, higher-status jobs. But it is also difficult to ignore the contrary evidence. The most dangerous and unhealthy jobs are not necessarily the best-paid jobs. There are many examples of well-trained and highly motivated people working in poorly paid, low skill jobs. For example, although most recent university graduates have managed to find reasonable jobs, compared to graduates a decade or two ago, a larger minority have had difficulty finding full-time, permanent work that matches their training.[20] The problem is clearly not one of insufficient education or effort.[21] Instead, much of this youth underemployment can be traced directly to large-scale cutbacks in the hiring of entry-level workers by employers in both the public and private sectors.

Similarly, many of the wealthiest members of our society are no more educated than the rest of us. In fact, many of them appear to have had a head start in the career race. A 1986 study of the CEOs of large U.S. companies provides a good example. It showed that almost two-thirds of these wealthy and powerful individuals came from upper-class or upper-middle-class families. Thus, the social class of one's family can strongly influence later labour market outcomes. Effort and competence do not always correlate neatly with labour market rewards. Indeed, a 1996 Canadian study by KPMG (a consulting firm) revealed that the CEOs of poorly performing large firms on the Toronto Stock Exchange actually received higher total compensation packages (an average of $682,000) than did the CEOs of the best-performing firms ($657,000).[22]

Thus, the relationships among initiative and effort, education and training, and risk, on the one hand, and occupational attainment and income on the other, are not nearly as consistent as the human capital model would suggest. In fact, research shows that some groups are systematically less likely than others to have benefited from their investments in human capital, and that reasonable returns on education and training are obtained only in certain industrial sectors or only from some types of employers. Furthermore, a great deal of evidence shows that some groups in society are more likely to have access to higher education. To understand who gets the good jobs, we must look beyond the labour market to families, schools, and other institutions that shape labour market outcomes.

Social Structure and Occupational Choice

The human capital model attempts to explain how people are sorted into different occupational positions by focusing on the characteristics of individual workers. People with skills and abilities more valued by society, and who have invested more in education and training, will be leading candidates for the better jobs, according to the model. Another assumption it makes is that individuals choose among work options, eventually settling in the occupational niche that best suits them. But to what extent do individuals actually have a choice from among the wide range of occupations? Does everyone start the "career race" from the same position, or are some groups disadvantaged at the outset? Perhaps chance plays a role in matching individuals and jobs.

We probably all know a few people who accidentally ended up in their present job, with little planning, or who landed a great position by being in the right place at the right time. We probably also know people who, as children, decided they wanted to be a teacher or a doctor, and then carefully pursued the educational route to these goals. Such behaviour and outcomes are consistent with human capital predictions, although the theory does not ask why these individuals had such high occupational goals.

In fact, we can easily imagine how socioeconomic origins might influence career patterns. It would be hard to picture a member of the wealthy Bronfman or Eaton families aspiring to be a bus driver. Similarly, many people who make their living as farmers would probably cite growing up on a farm as a major career influence, while growing up in a working-class family in a single-industry community would likely channel a youth into one of the local mills or mines. Turning from class to gender, it is also clear that many women in today's labour force were constrained in their career choices by society's attitudes about appropriate gender roles. Until quite recently, it was typically assumed that women could work as teachers and nurses, for example, but not in a wide range of traditionally "male" occupations (see Chapter 4).

For many working Canadians, family circumstances, social class background, and community of origin, along with personal attributes such as gender, race, and ethnicity, are important determinants of occupational position. The research literature on *occupational choice* concludes that, to a considerable extent, choices are limited for many labour market participants, and that factors other than skill and training influence occupational outcomes to a considerable degree.[23] Such findings clearly show the limitations of the individualistic human capital model.

Equality of Educational Opportunity

One of the core values underlying our education system is that of *equality of opportunity*. This is the belief that gender, race, ethnicity, family background, region of residence, or other individual characteristics should not be an impediment to obtaining a good education and, through this, access to good jobs and a decent standard of living. As we have already noted, gender differences in levels of education are small (although, as Chapter 4 discusses, there are substantial gender differences in types of educational choices). But research continues to show large differences in educational attainment depending on one's family background.

By way of example, analysis of data collected in a 1994 national survey reveals that, among Canadian adults aged 26 and over, a total of 16 percent had acquired a university degree. But among those from families where one or both parents had a degree, 59 percent had completed university, compared to only 12 percent of those from families where neither parent had a degree. Thus, among previous generations of potential university students, being a member of a family with a tradition of university attendance increased the chances of completing university by almost five times.[24]

How do such patterns of *intergenerational transfer of advantage* develop? An important study from several decades ago began (in 1970) by surveying 9,000 Ontario students (grades 8 through 12), as well as some of their parents. The researchers found that middle- and upper-class parents had high expectations of their children and also served as role models for successful entry into the labour market. Furthermore, more advantaged children had higher assessments of their own ability. All of this translated into higher *educational aspirations* (Porter et al. 1982: 311–19). The original sample members were re-interviewed several years later and asked about their educational attainment. As expected, given their higher aspirations and the financial advantages provided by their parents, middle-class youth were much more likely to have completed high school and gone on to obtain a university education.

Since this Ontario study was completed, the proportion of Canadian youth going on to post-secondary education has risen dramatically because of the opening of new post-secondary educational institutions, continued demand by employers for higher qualifications, and the introduction of new student finance systems.[25] Have social class differences in educational attainment been reduced? Research reveals that the efforts to improve access to higher education basically eliminated gender differences in attendance and reduced class differences somewhat. Even so, children from more affluent and better-educated families continue to be overrepresented among university students (Guppy and Pendakur 1989; Wotherspoon 1995).

A few findings from a more recent study of young Canadians in transition from school to work reinforce the conclusion that family background continues to have a powerful impact on educational attainment. In 1985, we began a longitudinal study of high school graduates in three Canadian cities (Edmonton, Sudbury, and Toronto). As in the 1970s Ontario study, we found much higher educational aspirations among young people from higher SES families. For example, 64 percent of high school graduates from families where at least one parent had a supervisory, managerial, or professional occupation planned to obtain a university degree, compared with only 38 percent of those from lower SES families. Four years later in 1989, we observed that 43 percent of our respondents from higher SES families had attended university during at least three of the four intervening years, compared with only 21 percent of those from lower SES families. By 1992, in the Edmonton sample, 64 percent of respondents from families where at least one parent had a university degree had themselves graduated from university, compared to only 33 percent of those from families without a university-attendance tradition.[26]

Economic Advantage and Cultural Capital

The process whereby advantaged backgrounds translate into educational success and better jobs begins long before students reach the end of their high school studies. Statistics Canada's National Survey of Children and Youth reveals the disturbing fact that children in Canada's poorest families are three times more likely than children of the wealthy to be in remedial education classes at school. In contrast, the most advantaged children are twice as likely to be in classes for "gifted" students (Mitchell 1997). A long list of studies has also demonstrated that, even though the high school dropout rate has been declining over the past few decades, teenagers from less affluent families are still much more likely to leave school without a diploma.[27]

Children in Canada's poorest families frequently go to school hungry. Parents with low incomes may have to work long hours to cover basic living costs, and will have less time and money to invest in their children's education. The schools in poorer neighbourhoods may also have fewer resources. These are among the more obvious explanations of the relationship between economic disadvantage and less successful educational outcomes.

In his analysis of social stratification systems, Pierre Bourdieu introduces the concept of *cultural capital* to further explain why middle-class youth perform better in the education system. Schools encourage and reward the language, beliefs, behaviour, and competencies of the more powerful groups in society. Middle-class youth bring more of this cultural capital to school with them, and so have a distinct advantage. They are more likely to speak like their teachers, to be comfortable in a verbal and symbolic environment, to know something about the subjects being taught, to have additional skills (music training, for example), and to have access to learning resources in their home.[28]

A 1994 national survey of Canadian adults provides some examples of this process. Considering only those respondents with children aged 6 to 18, 78 percent of those with a university degree reported that their children read every day for pleasure, and 70 percent stated that their children had a specified daily time for reading. Among parents without a university degree, only 41 percent said that their children read daily, while 49 percent reported a specified daily time when their children read at home.[29]

Thus, schools are not neutral institutions. Instead, they are part of the process whereby structural inequalities and power differences within society are reproduced, within and across generations, because the culture of the more powerful classes is embedded within them. Obviously, not all middle-class youth do well in school, and not all children from less affluent families do poorly. But the probability of doing well in school, graduating from high school, successfully completing post-secondary studies, and choosing an educational path that leads to a higher-status, better-paying job is much greater for middle-class youth.

Differences by Gender and Region

Several decades ago, Canadian studies showed that young women had lower educational and occupational aspirations. More recent studies of high school graduates show equivalent aspiration levels among young women and men,[30] although female and male teenagers still report quite different types of specific career goals. As female labour force participation has increased and gender role attitudes have slowly changed, the proportion of young women going on to higher education has risen to match the male rates. However, young women are still more likely to enrol in traditional "female" areas of study such as education, nursing, and the arts and humanities. As the next chapter documents, gender differences in educational choice continue to shape labour market outcomes for women and men.

The Ontario studies from the 1970s also examined the effects of students' region of residence on educational and occupational aspirations. The researchers noted that rural youth were less likely to plan on higher education, and speculated that the more "limited horizons" of rural youth might be due to their underexposure to attitudes favouring higher education. In addition, the absence of local institutions of higher learning forces rural youth to leave their communities to go to college or university, making the transition more difficult. A recent study in Nova Scotia reinforces such conclusions about problems faced by rural youth—whether planning to look for work or to continue their education, many rural youth are forced to leave their home community.[31]

Occupational Mobility Research

The term *social mobility* generally describes how individuals or groups move from one position within a social hierarchy to another. For example, we might find immigrant groups that arrived in Canada several generations ago having a much higher status today than upon arrival. Or we might document the misfortunes of previously well-off individuals (and their families) who, because of industrial restructuring, lost their jobs and became downwardly mobile.[32] Because social standing is to a great extent influenced by occupational position, most social mobility research has examined occupational mobility.

We can usefully distinguish between *intergenerational* and *intragenerational* mobility.[33] The former involves comparisons between an individual's occupational status and that of someone in a previous generation, most frequently his or her parent (or grandparent). The latter involves mobility within a generation, comparing an individual's present and previous occupations.

There is also an important difference between *structural mobility* and *circulatory (or exchange) mobility*. Chapters 1 and 2 documented massive changes in industrial capitalist societies over the past century: a huge decline in agriculture and a parallel expansion of the urban workforce, the rise of large bureaucracies, and extensive growth in the service industries. These changes precipitated enormous growth in white-collar occupations. Because of this occupational shift, we would expect to find much larger proportions of labour force participants in middle-level occupations today than a generation or two ago.

Using data from surveys asking respondents about their occupation and the occupations of their parents, researchers employ sophisticated statistical techniques to determine how much structural mobility has been occurring within a society. Such research addresses a potentially more interesting question: how much intergenerational mobility do we observe independent of the effects of changing occupational structures, or phrased differently, how open is a given society to occupational mobility?

A basic democratic value is that the "best" people end up in the more responsible and rewarding jobs. If this were the case, we would observe a great deal of circulatory mobility across generations, rather than a closed society in which occupational positions are typically inherited. Theoretically, circulatory intergenerational mobility occurs when those with more talent, skill, training, and motivation are able to move into the higher occupational positions. Merit, not social origin, determines occupational position. But no society has ever realized the goal of becoming a true *meritocracy*, raising the question: to what degree are occupational position and social status inherited in a given society?

An equally interesting question is whether different societies are more or less open to occupational mobility. Early mobility studies examined intergenerational mobility across three basic occupational categories—agricultural, manual, and nonmanual work. In 1959, Seymour Martin Lipset and Reinhard Bendix compared the United States with a number of European countries. Many might have predicted that occupational inheritance would be more pronounced in European countries with their entrenched class structures, and less significant in the United States with its stronger democratic values. However, few important cross-national differences were observed.[34] Studies using more recent data (from the 1970s and 1980s) and a larger number of occupational categories suggest few differences between mobility patterns and trends in Canada and the United States. However, they do indicate that Canada may have a somewhat more "open" stratification system than Sweden, the United Kingdom, France, and the Netherlands.[35]

To examine shifts over time in Canadian mobility patterns, researchers have compared results from two national surveys on occupational mobility, the first completed in 1973 and the second in 1986. For both women and men, the Canadian occupational structure became somewhat more open but in different ways. The steep decline in agricultural employment since the middle of the twentieth century meant that many men moved out of the agricultural occupations held by their fathers. For women, the shift was away from the housework that had been the main female occupation for their mothers' generation. For both, expansion of educational opportunities, leading to higher status occupations, played an important role.[36]

These Canadian mobility studies find only a limited amount of direct occupational inheritance across generations and conclude that the occupational stratification system became somewhat more open during the 1970s and 1980s. Yet those at or near the top of the occupational hierarchy are still more likely to pass their advantages on to their children: "Canada is still a stratified society characterized by a considerable amount of inheritance of privilege" (Wanner 1995: 175). However, the most recent study was conducted in 1986. Since then, there have been profound changes in the Canadian labour market. As we have seen, young Canadians have been particularly disadvantaged. If another Canadian occupational mobility study were to be conducted, would we still find the trend toward a more open stratification system?[37]

Status Attainment Research

Social mobility and *status attainment* studies address similar questions, but the latter focus more explicitly on intragenerational mobility and on the role of education in determining occupational outcomes. The most recent national Canadian status attainment study was conducted in 1986.[38] The researchers used Blishen scores to index the status of respondents' current and first occupations, as well as those of their fathers. The study found that the most important determinant of an individual's current job is their first job, that is, the level at which they enter the labour market. In turn, the status of that first job is heavily influenced by the amount of education obtained.

Taken alone, these findings lend support to the human capital model—greater investments in education allow one to enter the labour market at a higher level, and, consequently, to move up to even higher status positions.[39] However, the intergenerational component of the status attainment model also yields clear evidence of status inheritance by way of education. Canadians with more education (and, hence, who have entered the labour market at higher levels and have advanced further) tend to come from families with well-educated fathers in high-status occupations.

While these are not new insights, they do reinforce our earlier conclusions. First, education strongly influences occupational outcomes. Second, parents' occupational status is often transmitted to their children via differences in the amount of children's educational attainment. Status attainment studies do not explain how social origin affects labour market opportunities, but we have already mentioned some of the processes. Obviously, wealthier parents can afford more (and better) education for their children, and can provide the cultural capital needed to succeed in school. They can have a strong influence on aspirations. Being better situated in the labour market, they may also be able to provide more information about how to find good jobs or to put their children in touch with useful contacts.

The 1986 General Social Survey also revealed that, compared with men, women in the Canadian labour force had completed more years of schooling (12.9 years versus 12.3 years). This translated into a slightly higher-status first job, but the advantage ended there since men had experienced more upward mobility within their own career (intragenerational mobility). Canadian-born men had moved up 3.6 points on the Blishen occupational status scale, compared with 1.6 points for Canadian-born women. The comparable figures for foreign-born men and women were 1.9 and 0.2 points, respectively (Creese et al. 1991: Chapter 7).

Despite marginally higher levels of education, women are less able to "cash in" these credentials for jobs with career potential. This may partly be due to the different types of education completed by women and men. If women become nurses and men become engineers, for example, then perhaps the higher status (and pay) of men's jobs makes sense. But this line of reasoning simply raises other questions: Why do traditionally female jobs have lower status and less pay? Are the contributions made by individuals in these occupations really less valuable to society?

A large part of the female–male difference in career mobility is a function of the gender-segregated nature of the labour market; women are more likely to be employed in industries and occupations where promotion opportunities are limited. Some of the gender difference in mobility also can be traced to women's interrupted careers due to child-rearing responsibilities. The human capital model would predict that less career experience (as a result of interruptions) would mean less upward mobility. To fully understand the careers of women and men, we must also examine the societal values and institutions that put the biggest share of responsibility for child-rearing on women (see Chapter 4).

The 1986 study also demonstrated that foreign-born Canadians had higher-status social origins, more education, and higher-status first jobs. The explanation is quite simple: Canadian immigration policies over the last few decades have favoured well-educated and higher-status applicants. But these more advantaged beginnings did not translate into more upward career mobility. Foreign-born Canadians, particularly women, experienced little upward movement in the course of their careers. Limited knowledge of the labour market, language difficulties, licensing requirements that keep some immigrants from practising in their area of training, and discrimination in hiring and promotion might create career barriers. Furthermore, not all immigrants are well educated. A minority are refugees, often with little formal education, who were admitted to Canada for humanitarian reasons. These individuals often find work in low-skill, low-paying jobs where career opportunities are very limited.

In summary, we have found some support for the human capital model by identifying the central role education plays in determining one's occupational status and income. However, this must be weighed against evidence of considerable status inheritance, frequently passed on through the better education obtained by children in more well-to-do families. The fact that access to good education is not all that equal suggests that, to some degree, the issue of who gets the good jobs is class-based rather than an outcome of merit-based labour market processes.

By further examining the status attainment process, we observed that the Canadian labour market is not equally open to all labour force participants. Some groups of workers, men and individuals born in Canada, for example, are better able to "cash in" their education and training for higher-status and higher-income jobs. So there may be more than one labour market in operation, a possibility not considered by the human capital model. And factors other than skill, training, and effort may determine access to preferred jobs.

LABOUR MARKET SEGMENTATION

Labour market segmentation researchers begin with the proposition that there is not a single, open labour market operating in our society. Instead, better and worse jobs tend to be found in different settings and are usually obtained in distinctly different ways. Certain types of labour force participants (women and visible minorities, for example) are concentrated in the poorer jobs.

Segmentation theories also highlight the slim chances of moving out of the *secondary labour market* into jobs in the *primary labour market.* This is a key proposition, since the human capital model does not deny that some jobs are much better than others; it simply maintains that those individuals with the most ability and initiative, and who have made the largest investment in education and training, will be more able to obtain the more highly skilled and rewarding jobs. However, the segmentation perspective emphasizes the barriers that limit access for many qualified individuals into the primary labour market, along with the ability of primary labour market participants to maintain their more advantaged position.[40]

There are actually several varieties of labour market segmentation research. All share these basic propositions, but they differ in their explanations of the origins of segmentation and in their breadth of analysis. The broader dual economy approach has evolved out of the work of Marxist scholars tracing the growth of dual economic sectors in industrial capitalist societies. The narrower approach has grown out of studies of labour market dynamics within private sector firms and government bureaucracies (internal labour markets), and out of examinations of tactics used by various occupational and professional groups to restrict entry into their field of work (labour market shelters).

Dual Economies

The *dual economy* model assumes that an earlier era of *competitive capitalism* was succeeded in the twentieth century by an age of *monopoly capitalism.*[41]

Thus, a few large and powerful firms came to dominate automobile manufacturing, the oil and mining industries, the transportation sector (airlines and railways), and the computer industry, for example. Similarly, the finance sector came to be controlled by a handful of large banks, investment firms, and insurance companies. These dominant firms exert considerable control over suppliers and markets and are also able to manipulate their political environment. Examples of the power of such firms would include instances in which automobile manufacturers have been able to limit foreign imports, oil companies have influenced government pricing policies, and mining and forestry companies have lobbied legislators regarding environmental protection legislation.

Although global economic restructuring during the last decade has led to more intense competition among some of these large *core sector* firms, they still operate in an economic environment very different from the *periphery sector* where we find numerous smaller firms. Because they have less control over their environment and generally face more intense competition, such businesses have a much greater chance of failure. Many lower-tier service sector firms (for example, small retail shops and restaurants) would be found here, as would some smaller firms in the upper-tier services (for example, small office supply firms in the business services) and in the goods-producing sector (for example, small manufacturing companies).

Such enterprises are typically less profitable since they cannot control their markets and suppliers, they have low capital investments, and they are often less technologically advanced and generally more labour intensive. Compared with the core sector firms, these enterprises typically do not require the same level of skill, education, and commitment from employees. Indeed, replaceable unskilled or semiskilled employees are often ideal.

This segmentation model basically proposes that the core sector contains a primary labour market with better jobs, while the periphery sector contains secondary labour markets. Capital-intensive core enterprises, by definition, require fewer workers to equal or exceed the productivity of firms that are more labour intensive, although they frequently require workers who are more highly trained and better educated than those hired in the periphery sector. The large and bureaucratic nature of these enterprises means that there are reasonably good opportunities for upward mobility. The workers in these types of enterprises tend to be well paid, have good benefit packages, are more likely to receive training, and may have greater job security.[42] Some segmentation writers have classified government employees in the primary labour market because of the above-average job rewards that they typically receive.[43]

Why would core sector employers be willing to pay more than the going rates in the secondary labour market? Part of the answer lies in the collective strength of labour unions and professional associations which have been far more active in the primary sector. Labour market segmentation theorists have also argued that it would be too costly for core sector firms not to pay well. These enterprises have sizable capital investments and, thus, wish to avoid costly shutdowns due to labour disputes. High labour turnover would lead to the expense of training many new employees. Hence, it is simply good business practice to offer job security (negotiated with a union, if necessary), provide generous wage and benefit packages, and attempt to improve working conditions. Besides, higher profit margins mean that these employers can afford to pay more.

In the peripheral sector, employers are much less likely to provide high wages, extensive benefits, and long-term job security. We may also find more unhealthy working environments in this sector. Here, smaller profit margins, more intense competition, difficulties in imposing increased labour costs on customers, and greater vulnerability to economic cycles keep wage levels down. In addition, labour turnover is less of a problem for periphery sector employers; lower skill requirements and little on-the-job training make workers easily replaceable. Consequently, low-paying jobs are common and labour turnover is high, making union organizing more difficult.[44] The term *job ghettos* has frequently been used to describe work in such labour markets. Job insecurity, higher chances of unemployment, and irregular career earning patterns are a fact of life in secondary labour markets.

An interesting example of work in a secondary labour market is provided by Ester Reiter (1991) who writes about the time she spent working in a Burger King restaurant in Toronto. The restaurant, like most other enterprises in the fast-food industry, relied heavily on student labour, since few other workers would be available to work at a job that was part-time, had irregular hours, paid very little, and offered virtually no additional benefits. However, some middle-aged women were also employed in this industry, since such work allowed them to arrange their hours of work around family responsibilities. In addition, the industry employed recent immigrants who could not find better jobs.

Reiter describes how, in her particular restaurant, shifts were shortened to three hours so that employees could be expected to work hard for the duration of the shift without taking a break. The company actively discouraged the unionization of its employees, believing that its ability to control workers and the speed of work would be handicapped (as would its ability to pay very low wages). The work was highly standardized; the food-preparation and cash-register technology, along with specific rules for almost all tasks, left workers with virtually no opportunity to make decisions of any kind. In short, employees were interchangeable and easily replaced, as they are in many such workplaces.

Internal Labour Markets

There are typically fewer chances for career mobility within firms in the periphery sector. A carwash attendant or a mechanic in a small automobile repair shop would have few promotion prospects simply because their workplace would not have a bureaucratic hierarchy with well-defined career ladders. But many employees of IBM, Shell Canada, and other large private sector firms do have such mobility opportunities, as do university professors, government employees, and many health care workers. In contrast to the often dead-end jobs within secondary labour markets, most large corporations and public institutions have a well-developed internal training and promotion system, or what may be called an *internal labour market.* From the perspective of the work organization, such internal labour markets help retain skilled and valuable employees by providing career incentives, and also transmit important skills and knowledge among employees. From the perspective of employees, internal labour markets mean additional job security and career opportunities (Stark 1988: 327).

Researchers who study internal labour markets have usually sidestepped larger questions about the changing nature of capitalism, concentrating instead on specific features of these self-contained labour markets. Focus has been on *ports of entry*, specifically, the limited number of entry-level jobs that are typically the only way into such an internal labour market; *mobility chains*, or career ladders, through which employees make their way during their career within the organization; and training systems and seniority rules, which govern movement through the ranks.[45] Essentially, these concepts elaborate Max Weber's theory of bureaucracy while also emphasizing the career advantages held by workers in such labour markets.

There is some obvious overlap between studies of internal labour markets and the broader dual economy perspective. Early segmentation researchers tended to assume that all core sector firms contain well-developed internal labour markets open to all employees. However, there are important exceptions. For example, many major corporations have long career ladders, but these are open to only some of their employees. Clerical workers (usually women) are often restricted from moving into higher ranks (Diprete and Soule 1988; Hachen 1988). Some large corporations, like Burger King, consist of many small workplaces that have all the characteristics of a secondary labour market. In addition, corporation and government downsizing, and increased use of temporary and other nonstandard workers means that the number of advantaged workers in internal labour markets has declined.

Labour Market Shelters: Unions and Professions

Most internal labour markets have been put in place by employers. In contrast, unions and professional associations have tried to improve job and income security for their members by setting up *labour market shelters*, sometimes within specific work organizations but more often spanning a large number of similar types of workplaces.[46] Some occupational groups have restricted access to certain types of work since government legislation requires that such tasks be completed only by certified trades (for example, electricians). Public safety is the rationale for this legislation, but it also serves to protect the jobs and (relatively high) incomes of members of these often unionized trades.

Industrial unions, such as the Canadian Auto Workers, bargain collectively with employers to determine the seniority rules, promotion procedures, and pay rates within manufacturing establishments (see Chapter 7). Such contracts shelter these industrial workers from the risk of job loss or pay cuts for a specified period of time. Negotiated staffing restrictions also restrict nonmembers from access to the better jobs by giving laid-off members priority if new jobs open up.

Professional associations using tactics different from those of unions also serve as labour market shelters for their members. *Professions* have been distinguished from occupations in a variety of ways, but certain key features appear in most definitions.[47] Professionals such as doctors, lawyers, engineers, and psychologists work with specialized knowledge acquired through extensive formal education in professional schools. They enjoy a high level of work autonomy and are frequently self-regulating, policing themselves through their own professional associations. Professionals also exercise considerable power over their clients and other lower-status occupational groups, and typically emphasize the altruistic nature of their work.

For example, doctors spend many years training in medical schools where they acquire knowledge specific to their profession. They go on to determine their own working conditions in virtually all health care institutions. In fact, in the past decades, many doctors have increased their work autonomy by setting up professional corporations. Through their own professional associations, doctors can censure colleagues who have acted unprofessionally in the course of their work. Doctors have a great deal of power over their patients and those in assisting occupations, such as nurses and medical laboratory technicians. Finally, members of this profession emphasize their code of ethics, by which they are committed to preserving human life above all other objectives.

In short, professions are far more powerful than occupations. Randall Collins (1990) uses the term *market closure* to describe the ability of professionals to shape the labour market to their advantage, rather than simply responding to it, as do most occupational groups. Like the craft guilds of an earlier era, or higher castes in India's caste-stratified society, professional groups in contemporary Western society can restrict others from doing their type of work by controlling entry into their profession. Professional associations have close relationships with their (typically university-based) professional schools and can strongly influence both course content and entrance quotas. Many professional groups have actively lobbied for and obtained legislation that both requires practitioners of their profession to be officially licensed and prohibits anyone else from performing certain tasks. Over time, however, some occupational groups have gained more autonomy and power, while others may have experienced a process of de-professionalization.[48]

Barriers to Primary Labour Market Entry

Returning to our original focus on structural barriers to labour market movement (Jacobs 1983), we can now see how internal labour markets and labour market shelters not only provide more work rewards to some groups of labour market participants but also contribute to their ability to maintain labour market closure. Generally, there are only a limited number of positions within the primary labour market, and entry is often restricted to those with the proper credentials—a degree, union membership, or professional certification. Often, superior credentials (an MBA from a prestigious university, for example) will further improve one's chances of getting into the system and moving up through it. And, as we argued earlier in our discussion of social mobility and status attainment, a higher SES background typically gives one a significant head start.[49]

Specific credentials are not needed for all jobs in the primary labour market, but information about vacancies is not always widely distributed. In some cases, it may only be passed through small and informal networks. Since a large portion of all jobs are obtained through personal referrals, it is clear that access to information is extremely important. Without contacts within the primary labour market, qualified applicants might never be aware of job openings.

Barriers to mobility out of the secondary labour market may also be more subtle. For some individuals, a history of employment in marginal jobs may itself act as a barrier. In some regions of Canada, the prevalence of seasonal work means that many people are forced into an annual cycle where income is obtained from part-year jobs, employment insurance, and welfare assistance. A work record showing frequent layoffs or job changes may simply be reflecting the nature of the local labour market. But it could also be interpreted as an indication of unstable work habits, locking an individual into a "bad job syndrome."[50]

Thus, geography itself can limit one's work opportunities. A highly motivated and skilled worker living in Newfoundland where the cod fishery has been decimated, or in Uranium City after the mine was closed, is clearly at a disadvantage compared with residents of large cities in central Canada where unemployment rates have historically been much lower. Our discussion in Chapter 2 of employment opportunities in single-industry communities made the same point. There are simply fewer good jobs available outside of the metropolitan heartland of Canada.

In addition, residents of the hinterland regions are less likely to have obtained the credentials necessary for participation in primary labour markets. Dianne Looker's study of rural Nova Scotia youth leaving high school and entering the labour market highlights some of these geographic disadvantages. Compared with urban youth in Halifax and Hamilton, rural youth had less work experience, fewer course options while in school, and less knowledge about the labour market. They were also more likely to evaluate local labour market opportunities negatively, and were much more likely to conclude that they would have to leave their communities to find reasonable jobs (Looker (1993).

Some years ago, a research team in Atlantic Canada spent considerable time examining that region's employment opportunities. They argued that the high level of poverty and unemployment in the region cannot simply be explained with reference to inadequate education, training, or effort on the part of local residents. A "casualty" model of poverty, which would hold that most of the poor are incapable of working, or of working in good jobs, does not fit the facts. Rather, an explanation that focuses on the nature of the local labour market is much more useful. In short, many Atlantic Canadians have spent their working lives in a *marginal work world* where low pay, few benefits, limited career opportunities, and little job security are a way of life.[51]

Historical Patterns of Racial and Ethnic Discrimination

Employer *discrimination* in hiring and promotion can also block movement into better jobs, thus contributing to the overrepresentation of specific disadvantaged groups in secondary labour markets. Before we discuss the forms such discrimination might now take, it is instructive to look back in Canadian history at some examples of officially sanctioned racial and ethnic discrimination.

After Canada was colonized, members of various Aboriginal nations frequently participated in the pre-industrial labour market, acting as guides, fighting for the French against the English (and vice versa), and providing the furs sought by the trading companies for their European markets.[52] But as central Canada began to industrialize, and later as the West was opened for settlement, the traditional economies of the Aboriginal nations in these regions were largely destroyed. Usually the presence of Aboriginal groups was seen as an impediment to economic development. The most common solution was to place them on reservations, out of the way.

Nevertheless, some Aboriginal workers were employed in the resource industries (forestry, mining, and commercial fishing and canning, for example), and in railway construction, particularly in Western Canada. But the decline in demand for large numbers of unskilled and semiskilled workers in Canada's resource and transportation industries also meant declining wage-labour opportunities for Aboriginals. Even when jobs were available for Native workers, racist attitudes and labour market discrimination were rampant (Knight 1978). This should not be surprising in a society that clearly viewed members of First Nations as second-class citizens, not even allowing them to vote until 1960.

As Canada industrialized in the late nineteenth century, manufacturing enterprises began to take root in Quebec and Ontario. However, patterns of ethnic stratification based on English ownership of key industries meant that French-Canadian workers were typically underrepresented in the higher-status, better-paying positions. For example, in 1938 in the Quebec industrial town of "Cantonville," French Canadians provided most of the factory labour while English-speaking outsiders filled the management and technical positions (Hughes 1943: 46; Clark 1978: 98). French-Canadian men frequently also worked as labourers in the natural resource sector and in railway construction where discrimination on the part of English-Canadian employers and supervisors was common.

During the 1880s, many Chinese men were recruited to work on railway construction in Western Canada and in the resource-based industries. They were generally paid about one-half to two-thirds of what others received for the same job, and encountered a great deal of hostility from the white population (Anderson 1991: 35). Labour unions lobbied for legislation restricting Chinese workers from entering specific (better-paid) trades. Chinese workers were forced into marginal jobs in a racially split British Columbia labour market. In addition, the British Columbia government passed legislation that severely restricted the civil rights of Chinese residents of the province. For its part, the federal government required Chinese immigrants to pay a "head tax" on entering Canada, while other immigrants did not, and, later, passed the Chinese Immigration Act which, for several decades, virtually stopped all Chinese immigrants from entering the country (Li 1982; Anderson 1991).

Perhaps the discrimination faced by Chinese workers was the result of white workers' fears that they would lose their jobs to nonwhites who were willing to work for lower wages. However, studies of this era suggest that racist attitudes—fears about the impact of too many Asian immigrants on a white, Anglophone society—were frequently the underlying source of publicly expressed concerns about job loss and wage cuts. White workers seldom tried to bring Chinese workers into their unions (a tactic that would have reduced employers' ability to pay lower wages to nonwhites), even though the latter frequently showed interest in collectively opposing the actions of employers.[53]

Peter Li has described how, in the first half of the twentieth century (1910 to 1947), Chinese Canadians living in the Prairie provinces encountered similar forms of racial discrimination. Barred from entry into many trades and professions, Chinese workers were mostly restricted to employment in *ethnic business enclaves* where, by supporting one another and working extremely hard, they could make a living. Hence, Chinese restaurants and laundries provided employment for many members of the Prairie Chinese community.[54]

Similar experiences of racial discrimination were encountered by Black Canadians, many of whom were former American slaves who had settled in the area west of Toronto to the Detroit River. During the mid-nineteenth century, white residents frequently lobbied to have Blacks sent back to their former owners in the United States (Pentland 1981: 1–6). By the 1860s, officially sanctioned discrimination against Blacks had largely disappeared, but labour market discrimination continued. For example, many Blacks worked for railway companies but were restricted to a limited number of lower-paying jobs, such as sleeping-car porter. White workers were found in the better-paying, less menial jobs such as sleeping-car conductor or dining-car steward. The system was supported by societal values that took for granted that Blacks should work in menial jobs. It wasn't until 1964 that the arrangements (embedded in the contracts between railway companies and their unions) that legitimized this *racially split labour market* were completely abolished (Calliste 1987).

Disadvantaged Groups in Today's Labour Market

Today, labour laws and human rights legislation make it difficult for employers to discriminate against specific types of labour market participants. Nevertheless, there are still some groups that are severely disadvantaged in the labour market. Some of this inequality of employment opportunity results from unequal access to higher education and specialized training. Some of it is a product of regional differences in employment opportunities. But there is also evidence of continued patterns of discrimination in hiring and promotion in the Canadian labour market, although it is typically not as blatant and institutionalized as in the past.

By 1991, visible minorities made up about 9 percent of the adult (aged 15 and older) Canadian population (a total of 1.9 million people). Compared to the rest of the adult population, the nonwhite group was more likely to have a university degree and more likely to be in the labour force, in part because of their somewhat younger age profile. Despite this, they were also somewhat more likely to be unemployed (Latin American, South Asian, and Black Canadians were more likely to be unemployed, while Chinese and Japanese Canadians had lower-than-average unemployment rates). As for occupational differences, visible minority males were over-represented in both lower- and higher-status occupations, while nonwhite women were heavily over-represented in lower-paying, low-skill jobs (Moreau 1991; Côté 1991; Kelly 1995).

Since Canadian immigration policies favour better-educated immigrants, the higher education and higher-status occupations (at least for men) are not surprising. Nevertheless, it is also apparent that large proportions of visible minority women, along with many men, are employed in the secondary labour market. Language difficulties, few personal contacts within the primary labour market, and professional licensing regulations that often keep well-educated immigrants from practising their professions are part of the explanation. In addition, prejudiced attitudes on the part of employers continue to keep some members of visible minority groups from improving their employment prospects.

A 1984 study in Toronto compared the experiences of Black and white subjects, with equivalent qualifications, in applying for the same job. Blacks obtained fewer interviews and job offers, and were frequently told that the advertised position was filled, even though, in some cases, a white member of the research team was offered the same job only minutes later. In another part of the same study, subjects with names and accents identifying them as members of nonwhite or immigrant groups telephoned for job interviews. Out of a total of 237 advertised positions, South Asian subjects were told that the job was no longer available 44 percent of the time, while 36 percent of Black West Indians and 31 percent of white immigrant subjects were told this. But only 13 percent of white nonimmigrant subjects got this response (Henry and Ginzberg 1985).

A 1989 replication of this study revealed no discrimination against Blacks in the in-person portion of the study. However, the telephone survey showed that employers still favoured job applicants who had no accents (Economic Council of Canada 1991b: 30). Thus, there is some evidence that prejudiced attitudes against hiring visible minorities may be decreasing, at least in Toronto where the proportion of visible minorities is the highest in the country. Or employers may have become more cautious about discriminating in a face-to-face situation. In fact, other research findings show that racial discrimination continues to handicap visible minorities seeking to improve their employment situation.[55]

Thus, while some members of visible minority groups (usually men with higher educational credentials) find professional, technical, and managerial jobs in the primary labour market, many others are concentrated in a limited number of marginal occupations in the secondary labour market—taxi drivers, janitors, domestic workers, parking lot attendants, security guards, and workers in ethnic restaurants are obvious examples. Because of the high proportion of workers from specific ethnic groups in some of these occupations (airport taxi services in some Canadian cities, for example), we might call them ethnic business enclaves.[56]

A somewhat different picture emerges of the underlying causes of Aboriginal Canadians' severely disadvantaged labour market position. Aboriginal labour market participation rates have been low for decades. In turn, unemployment and poverty rates in their communities have been extremely high. Aboriginal Canadians living in larger urban centres also have a much more precarious labour market status. When employed, either in their own communities or elsewhere, they have been heavily overrepresented in the secondary labour market.[57] Why?

On average, Aboriginal Canadians are not as well educated as other Canadians (Bowier 1991; Ross 1992; Statistics Canada 1994a). Access to good schooling has been a serious problem for generations, as has racism and discrimination within the education system (Pauls 1996). But lack of education does not fully explain their marginal labour market position. Many live in isolated communities where employment opportunities are severely limited. Large industrial megaprojects in Northern Canada (mines, mills, dams, and so on) have typically offered only limited employment to residents of local Aboriginal communities while, at the same time, these projects have often damaged traditional hunting, trapping, and fishing economies and have had negative impacts on traditional culture (Waldram 1987; Stabler and Howe 1990; Niezen 1993).

Aboriginal Canadians who seek employment in larger urban settings consequently bring with them a patchy employment record, which can seriously restrict entry into the primary labour market. They may also often encounter prejudice among employers which, along with a lack of contacts and limited job-search resources (such as transportation), further handicap them in their search for satisfactory employment. Thus, an explanation for the disadvantaged labour market position of Aboriginal Canadians must examine the many other factors that contribute to the segmenting of the Canadian labour market.

Disabled Canadians are another group characterized by low labour force participation and high unemployment rates, fewer hours of work, and lower incomes. As with the Aboriginal population, the disabled who do manage to obtain employment are frequently found working in low-skill, poorly paid jobs in the secondary labour market.[58] A study from the early 1990s estimated the number of working-age disabled Canadians at 1.8 million, and concluded that about 80 percent were either unemployed or underemployed (McKay 1991). While some of these individuals were incapable of paid employment of any kind, many could have been making much more useful contributions in the workplace.

Huge barriers keep the disabled from obtaining satisfactory employment. Many employers, and even some of those involved in assisting the disabled, assume that all those with visual, hearing, cognitive, and movement handicaps are equally impaired, though many of these individuals could cope well in a variety of jobs, with limited assistance. Some employers are uncomfortable with or fearful of the disabled. While a significant number of employers say they would hire disabled workers, few actually do so. In addition, many of the disabled also face serious transportation problems and are held back by buildings designed without their special needs in mind.[59] While there has been some progress in improving their labour market position,[60] the disabled continue to be overrepresented in the secondary labour market; in fact, many find work only in special institutional settings where pay rates are low and career opportunities are nonexistent.

Women have faced prejudice and discrimination in the Canadian labour market for decades. Employment and human rights legislation have eliminated much of the systematic discrimination against women in recent decades, but more subtle forms of discriminatory hiring and promotion behaviour remain. For example, male employers or managers may sometimes decide that a female applicant, no matter how qualified, does not have the personality supposedly needed for a particular high-level position, or the career commitment that the corporation thinks it requires. We will address such labour force difficulties and the extent to which they relegate women to secondary labour market positions in more detail in the next chapter.

This discussion of discrimination has focused so far on the experiences of visible minorities, Aboriginal Canadians, the disabled, and women, the four groups of labour force participants designated for special attention in the federal government's efforts to promote *employment equity* (Moreau 1991). But there are other groups that can also encounter discrimination and that are not necessarily protected by legislation.

Age discrimination occurs when older workers, laid off in a plant shutdown and applying for another core sector job, are rejected in favour of younger applicants because of the belief that older workers are harder to retrain and will have difficulty adapting to new technologies. On the other hand, youth attempting to find their first permanent job also face age discrimination. Finding employment in the part-time student labour market within the lower-tier services is generally much less difficult than getting an interview for a full-time career position in a major corporation or a government department, even if one has the necessary educational qualifications. "Lack of experience" is a term heard all too frequently by unsuccessful young job applicants.

Discrimination on the basis of sexual orientation may be prohibited by human rights legislation, but this does not ensure that all employers act accordingly. In Alberta, a postsecondary educational institution (with funding from a specific religious denomination) fired a gay instructor in 1991, arguing that his sexual orientation was not acceptable among the supporters of the school. The courts rejected his claim that this discriminatory behaviour on the part of the school was unacceptable, and the case is being appealed to the Supreme Court of Canada.[61] This example, and the range of other research reviewed above, demonstrate that employer discrimination continues to be one of the factors accounting for patterns of labour market segmentation in Canada.

NEW PATTERNS OF LABOUR MARKET SEGMENTATION

In a sweeping historical analysis of labour market segmentation trends in the United States, David Gordon and his colleagues separate the last two centuries into three major epochs (Gordon et al. 1982). During the period of *initial proletarianization* from about 1820 to 1890, a large, relatively homogeneous industrial working class was emerging. While modern forms of capitalist management were still in their infancy, craft workers were beginning to lose control over the labour process. However, this trend did not develop fully until the era of *homogenization of labour*, from the end of the nineteenth century until the start of World War II. This period saw extensive mechanization and deskilling of labour, the growth of large workplaces, and the rise of a new managerial class within American capitalism. The period following World War II to the early 1980s (when these authors wrote their book) has been one of *segmentation of labour*, in which distinct primary and secondary labour markets emerged.

Canada began to industrialize later and has always remained more of a resource-based economy. Thus, the same three stages do not precisely describe our economic history, although there are some similarities (see Chapter 1).[61] However, the emphasis on change in this historical overview encourages us to ask: Are further changes in labour market segmentation occurring in the 1990s? The answer is yes. There is considerable evidence of fundamental realignments in the industrial and occupational structures, and in the nature of employment relationships, not only in Canada, but also in the United States and other Western industrialized countries.

Labour Market Polarization

We have observed a significant decline in the goods-producing industries since the 1980s. Factory closures due to increased overseas competition and the movement of manufacturing bases to low-wage countries have led to what Barry Bluestone and Bennett Harrison (1982) have called the "deindustrialization of America." The widespread introduction of computer technology has allowed many industries to maintain production levels with fewer employees (Sherman and Judkins 1995; Menzies 1996). A similar situation has developed in Canada's resource industries where unstable world markets, in combination with technological innovations that reduce the need for labour, have led employers to substantially reduce their workforces.[62] During the 1990s, *downsizing* and hiring cutbacks have been the norm in many large corporations in the business and distributive service industries. Similar trends emerged in the public sector as governments (both federal and provincial) cut deficits by laying off employees and privatizing some of the services they had previously provided directly to the public.[63]

Although a shrinking workforce has been observed in both the goods-producing and service sectors, there has still been employment growth over the past two decades. Most of it has been in the service industries. While some new high-skill, well-paying jobs have been created—leading some observers to proclaim the emergence of a "knowledge economy" (Reich 1991; Drucker 1993)

—there has also been a significant increase in the proportion of jobs in the secondary labour market. Many of the new jobs created have been part-time or temporary, paying less and offering fewer benefits and career opportunities than the full-time, permanent jobs that have disappeared. In addition, workers in some industries have experienced substantial wage rollbacks and have had their full-time positions changed into part-time jobs. In other work settings, traditional employment relationships have been altered when workers retired—temporary positions and contract work have replaced the previously permanent positions. Thus, nonstandard jobs with less security have been increasing (Krahn 1995).

The industrial realignment and the growth in nonstandard work, along with a decade or more of high levels of unemployment, have led to *labour market polarization.* Compared to the 1970s and 1980s, there are more Canadians unemployed, and fewer people employed in the reasonably well-paying, full-time, permanent jobs that used to be taken for granted. Put another way, the primary labour market has shrunk, and fewer workers now have access to its good jobs, as defined by income, benefits, and job security.

Within the broadly defined secondary labour market, two relatively distinct new segments appear to have emerged. The first is a *student labour market,* consisting mainly of part-time jobs, most of them in the lower-tier consumer services and retail trade industries. Many young Canadians participate voluntarily in this labour market, using their part-time jobs to earn discretionary income or to pay for their education. But this part-time workforce also contains nonstudents, women who cannot work full-time because of their family responsibilities, and others who simply cannot find a full-time job (see Chapter 2). The new *temporary/contract labour market* exists in both the upper- and lower-tier service industries. As employers in both the private and public sectors have come to rely more heavily on temporary workers for both low- and high-skill jobs, a larger proportion of well-educated young adults are finding themselves spending a number of years in contract work before they are able to obtain more secure employment.

Rising Income Inequality

A clear result of labour market polarization has been an increase in individual-level income inequality in Canada. While real earnings (taking inflation into account) rose systematically in Canada in the three or four decades following

World War II, this trend stopped in the 1980s. For many workers, real incomes have declined since then. A smaller proportion have seen their real incomes increasing. Compared to women's incomes, polarization of men's incomes has been more pronounced (Beach and Slotsve 1996: 43).

Even more significant has been the growing income differences across age groups. Despite their high levels of education, on average, the real earnings of young Canadians have been dropping over the past two decades. For example, between 1981 and 1993, the real annual earnings of 17- to 24- year-old males dropped by 33 percent, while the earnings of women in this age cohort declined by 23 percent. In the 25- to 34-year-old cohort, female earnings rose marginally (by only 3 percent) while male earnings dropped by 16 percent (see Table 3.1).[64] Corporate and public sector hiring freezes, the growth of the part-time student labour market, and the emergence of the temporary/contract labour market have seriously disadvantaged Canadian youth in the labour market.[65]

At the household level, however, there is less evidence of an increase in earnings inequality. While the growth in real family incomes that characterized Canadian society in the 1950s, 1960s, and 1970s has stopped, the rising proportion of employed women and dual-earner families has meant that family income inequality has increased much less than has individual income inequality.[66] But we have seen a significant change in the composition of low-income households. In the 1970s, the elderly made up a sizable portion of Canada's poor. Since then, improvements in income security for senior citizens

TABLE 3.1 *Real Annual Earnings and 1981–1993 Percentage Change in Real Annual Earnings by Sex and Age*

	Male		*Female*	
Age	*Average Earnings*	*% Change*	*Average Earnings*	*% Change*
17–24 years	*$8,589*	*–33.2*	*$7,367*	*–23.2*
25–34 years	*$22,034*	*–16.3*	*$15,671*	*3.0*
35–44 years	*$28,620*	*–11.1*	*$18,090*	*11.9*
45–54 years	*$32,122*	*0.6*	*$18,966*	*25.5*
55–64 years	*$28,502*	*1.8*	*$15,560*	*2.6*

Source: Gordon Betcherman and Norman Leckie, *Age Structure of Employment in Industries and Occupations* (Ottawa: Human Resources Development Canada, Applied Research Branch Research Paper R-96-7E, Table 2, 1995), page 5. Data from Statistics Canada's "Survey of Consumer Finances." Reproduced with the permission of Human Resources Development Canada.

have somewhat reduced poverty among the elderly. However, the combined labour market trends noted above point to an increase in problems of poverty among working-age Canadians. The *working poor* have become a larger group in the Canadian labour market, and "young" households have been particularly hard hit.[67]

Some observers have used the term *declining middle class* to describe these trends toward greater inequality. Others have commented on the emergence of an *underclass* of citizens, individuals largely marginalized from the labour market. But neither concept has been precisely defined. Some writers use the term "declining middle class" to refer to a declining proportion of well-paying blue-collar and mid-level white-collar jobs. Others emphasize growing income inequality without necessarily distinguishing between individual and family income.[68] Similarly, when proposing that an underclass has emerged, some users of the concept are referring to a growing number of long-term unemployed. Others include people unable to work and dependent on declining levels of social assistance in the category, while still others reserve the term to describe the homeless and absolutely destitute.[69]

Because of this conceptual confusion and the need for more research to test some of the assumptions underlying these concepts, we prefer to use the broader term labour market polarization to refer to the interrelated trends we have described—industrial and occupational realignment, rising levels of nonstandard work, and growing individual income inequality. Nevertheless, we strongly emphasize that social inequality has increased as a result of these polarizing trends. Greater inequality means fewer labour market opportunities and reduced life chances for more Canadians.

POLICY RESPONSES TO LABOUR MARKET BARRIERS AND GROWING INEQUALITY

What might be done to create better jobs and to counter the trend toward greater labour market polarization? Responses based on a human capital perspective would primarily emphasize access to education as the most important public policy goal. In fact, this has been a central concern of Canadian governments throughout the second half of the twentieth century, particularly during the 1960s and 1970s when a wide array of new post-secondary educational institutions were opened and student loan systems were introduced.

These policy efforts did have an effect, as we have noted earlier. The average educational attainment of the Canadian population has risen dramatically, and some of the systematic barriers to equal access to education were reduced. Even so, research continues to show that not all groups in Canadian society have equal educational opportunities. Consequently, continued policy responses targeting this goal are needed. In fact, with rising post-secondary tuition costs occurring as a result of government reductions in funding for post-secondary education, we may well see a reversal of the slow trend toward greater equality of educational opportunity that characterized the latter decades of the twentieth century.

During the 1980s and 1990s, government education policies shifted from building schools to encouraging young Canadians to stay in school and promoting skill upgrading among older labour force participants, particularly the unemployed. At the same time, more emphasis was placed on policies promoting formal training and skill upgrading in the workplace.[70] Reducing labour market inequalities gave way to concerns about Canada's competitive position in the global economy. Unemployed youth, older workers affected by industrial restructuring, and the marginal labour market position of other groups came to be seen not so much as social problems of inequality, but as economic problems. Unless we invested even more heavily in and took more advantage of current stocks of human capital, it was argued, Canada would fall behind in the global economy.[71] At the same time, greater investments in education and training should help disadvantaged groups (the unemployed, for example, and residents of economically depressed regions) to improve their labour market position.

Clearly, greater investments in education and training are important. Indeed, some groups of Canadian labour force participants continue to be educationally disadvantaged. Some could clearly benefit from improvements in their literacy skills. The Canadian record on workplace training is not very good.[72] Thus, with global competitiveness as the goal, greater investments in human capital are part of the longer-term solution.[73] We also need to look at other structural factors including inflation-fighting interest rate policies that appear to have slowed economic growth and kept unemployment high, the currently popular and misguided (in our opinion) belief that governments have no role to play in stimulating the economy when unemployment is high,[74] a limited emphasis on research and development by Canadian firms, and trade agreements that have been more beneficial to some sectors (and regions) than others.

If reducing labour market inequalities is our goal, human capital investments are only part of the solution. We know that additional education and training would assist some Canadians in improving their labour market position. But we are also aware that about 1 in 4 working Canadians consider themselves to be overqualified for their jobs, including 22 percent of those with university degrees. Research on literacy requirements in the workplace document large proportions of workers who are seldom required to use their literacy skills in their jobs.[75] Thus, *underemployment* is a serious problem in the Canadian workplace. While unemployment is lower among the better educated, many of Canada's unemployed have good educational qualifications. Simply put, there are not enough good jobs. Or, as John Myles recently concluded in a critique of "market based" solutions to social inequality in Canada, "[t]he ultimate Achilles heel of the job training strategy is the assumption that the problem is mainly on the supply side."[76]

While the human capital explanation of labour market processes focuses our attention on education as the key policy variable, the labour market segmentation perspective encourages us to identify the barriers that keep large numbers of qualified individuals out of better jobs. Obviously, a shortage of good jobs is part of the problem. Beyond that, we will also continue to need strong legislation that discourages discrimination against disadvantaged groups in the Canadian labour market.[77] Equity programs that help disadvantaged groups to catch up with mainstream labour market participants are also part of a policy package that could help reduce labour market inequality. Improved school-work transition programs that assist young people in their search for rewarding jobs and careers are needed, given that young Canadians have been particularly affected negatively by labour market polarization trends.[78] Finally, we believe that unions have a larger role to play in the Canadian labour market. If more Canadian workers were covered by union contracts, some of the inequality within the labour market could be reduced. If unions were involved on a more equal basis in decisions about national and firm-level industrial strategies, we might also move further toward the goal of global competitiveness. We will return to many of these topics in the following chapters.

CONCLUSION

After profiling good jobs and bad jobs in terms of income, benefits, risks to personal health, and other extrinsic work rewards, we began our analysis of these patterns by discussing the class structure of Canadian society and the power relationships that underlie it. In order to answer questions about who gets the better jobs, we shifted our attention to the human capital and segmentation explanations of labour market processes. While the human capital model highlights the central role of education in determining occupational outcomes, it fails to adequately account for the many examples of qualified and highly motivated individuals working in unrewarding jobs, and ignores intergenerational transfers of advantage. In contrast, the segmentation approach recognizes inequalities in labour market outcomes and provides a better account of how such power differences are created and maintained. In turn, studies of status attainment demonstrate both the importance of educational attainment and the extent to which status and power can be inherited (frequently through unequal access to higher education).

While not directly employing the concepts of class analysis, our descriptions of structured patterns of labour market inequality, intergenerational transfers of advantage, labour market polarization, and the manner in which gender and race/ethnicity intersect with these inequalities address the same issues examined in class analyses. Questions about who gets the good job and why are essentially questions about social inequality and the power relationships that underlie it. In the following chapters on gender, management strategies, conflict in the workplace, and industrial relations we will revisit this central theme.

NOTES

1. See Van den Berg and Smucker (1997) on the neoclassical economic approach and more sociological analyses of labour markets.
2. See Ashton (1986), Clement and Myles (1994), Westergaard (1995), and Breen and Rottman (1995) on labour markets, social inequality, and class analysis.
3. Grenon (1996) presents data collected from Canadian businesses through the monthly Survey of Employment, Payrolls, and Hours (SEPH). Hence, self-employed professionals, along with those employed in agriculture, fishing and trapping, private household services, and military services are not included in this survey.

4. All income data reported in the rest of this section, including gender differences, were obtained from the Survey of Consumer Finances (SCF) conducted annually by Statistics Canada as a supplement to the Labour Force Survey (Statistics Canada, 1997a).
5. Saunders (1997) lists the 1996 earnings of Canada's 100 best-paid CEOs.
6. Ibid., 42. Statistics Canada's "low income line" (LICO) is the measure most often used to measure "poverty" in Canada (see Statistics Canada, 1996b; National Council of Welfare, 1997). A family (of a given size) is considered to be in the low income category if, compared to the typical Canadian family of that size, it spends at least 20 percent more of its total income on food, clothing, and shelter. LICOs are calculated separately for communities of different sizes since the cost of living is higher in larger communities.
7. Kumar et al. (1991: 373) provide Canadian data (covering 1953–1989) on employee benefit costs, by type of benefit.
8. Human Resources Development Canada (1997) reports data from the 1994 Survey of Adult Education and Training in Canada.
9. See Krahn (1992: 94–95) on benefit differences across industries and standard/non-standard jobs; Akyeampong (1997: 52) reports differences by size of firm; Crompton (1992: 31) and Human Resources Development Canada (1997: 1–2) profile training patterns in different-size firms; for U.S. data on better benefit packages in larger firms, see Wiatrowski (1994), Mergenhagen (1994), and Kalleberg and Van Buren (1996).
10. Statistics Canada (1994b); over-time data from Marshall (1996).
11. Marshall (1996); for U.S. data showing similar industry and occupation patterns, see Toscano and Windau (1993) who report over 6,000 work-related deaths in 1992.
12. Geran (1992) reports data on work-related stress, and Grayson (1994) describes self-reported work hazards, both using data from the 1991 General Social Survey.
13. See Hunter and Manley (1986) on the relationship between occupational status and skill requirements in a job.
14. Pineo and Porter (1967) conducted the original study of occupational prestige; Blishen et al. (1987) provide the most recent version of the Blishen SES scale; see Fox and Suschnigg (1989) on gender bias in SES scales.
15. Even so, the Pineo (1984) occupational ranking system is highly correlated with the Blishen scores (Hunter and Manley, 1986: 64; Creese et al., 1991: 36). While not as up-to-date (in terms of newly emerging occupations) as the 1993 National Occupational Classification (NOC) discussed in Chapter 2, the Pineo rankings are more finely differentiated in terms of skill (the NOC contains only four skill levels), and also distinguish the self-employed from paid workers. For a recently developed international index of occupational status, see Ganzeboom et al. (1992).
16. Clement and Myles (1994); also see Hunter (1986) and Grabb (1990) on differing conceptions of social class.
17. Black and Myles (1986: 162); note that the estimate of the percentage self-employed from this small-sample survey is considerably higher than the estimates provided by the

much larger Labour Force Survey (see Chapter 2); see Clement (1990) for comparisons of these Canadian data with results from similar surveys completed in Sweden, Norway, Finland, and the United States.

18. Clement and Myles (1994) also address a range of other important issues relevant to class analysis, including the extent to which race and ethnic differences influence class relationships, the question of whether the working class has been deskilled over time, and the debate about individuals or households as the appropriate unit of analysis for studies of social class.

19. Becker (1975: first published in 1964) is generally credited for developing human capital theory, although its basic premises originate in neoclassical economics; as we describe it here, the model is closely linked to the functionalist theory of stratification (Davis and Moore, 1945); Thurow (1975) and Hunter (1986) critique the premises of the human capital model, while Van den Berg and Smucker (1997: 1–7) present a useful overview of neoclassical and sociological approaches to the study of labour markets.

20. See Krahn and Lowe (1990), Redpath (1994), Davies et al. (1994), Krahn (1995), Marquardt (1996), and Betcherman and Leckie (1997) on problems of underemployment among Canadian youth.

21. See Oderkirk (1993) on the high educational attainment of Canadian youth, compared to young people in other Western industrialized countries. Krahn and Lowe (1995) and Human Resources Development Canada (1997: 1) also demonstrate that young labour force participants are the most likely to invest in additional job-related education and training.

22. See Boone et al. (1988) on the origins of U.S. CEOs, and Church (1996) on the pay packages of Canadian CEOs.

23. Chen and Regan (1985: 39–62) present a useful overview of this literature, which they separate into the "fortuitous, rational decision-making, and socio-cultural influences" approaches.

24. Unpublished analysis (by the authors) of data from the 1994 Canadian component of the International Adult Literacy Survey. Survey respondents who did not know their parents' education were coded as if their parents had not completed university. See Statistics Canada and Human Resources Development Canada (1996) for more details about this study.

25. Osberg et al. (1995: 162); see Statistics Canada (1996a) for statistics on educational enrollments and attainment.

26. The study was not continued in Toronto and Sudbury after 1989; see Krahn and Lowe (1990, 1991, 1993) for additional results from this study. Similar research demonstrating how family background influences educational aspirations and outcomes has been conducted in Nova Scotia (Looker, 1994), Newfoundland (Sharpe and White, 1993), and British Columbia (Bellamy, 1993).

27. See Gilbert et al. (1993) and Tanner et al. (1995) for literature reviews and Canadian data on high school dropouts and their labour market experiences.

28. Bourdieu (1986); also see Teachman (1987) and Looker (1994) on how more affluent parents use their resources to create a home environment that can improve the educational success of their children.

29. Unpublished analysis (by the authors) of data from the 1994 International Adult Literacy Survey. See Statistics Canada and Human Resources Development Canada (1996) for more details on this study.

30. See Anisef et al. (1980), Porter et al. (1982), and Looker and McNutt (1989) on gender differences in aspirations several decades ago; Krahn and Lowe (1993), Looker (1993), and Mandell and Crysdale (1993) report results from the 1980s, while Lowe et al. (1997) examine 1996 Alberta results.

31. See Porter et al. (1982: 67) on the more limited horizons of rural youth, Anisef et al. (1980: xxiv) on having to leave home to continue one's education, and Looker (1993) on gender and urban–rural differences in the transition from school to work. Furlong et al. (1996) develop similar ideas in their study of how neighbourhood contexts affect occupational aspirations of Scottish youth.

32. See Swift (1995) on the downward mobility experiences of Canadian families in the 1990s; Newman (1989) and *The New York Times* (1996) tell similar U.S. stories about restructuring in the 1980s and 1990s.

33. See Wanner (1993) for a useful discussion of social mobility definitions and the important stratification questions addressed by social mobility research.

34. Lipset and Bendix (1959: 12). More recently, Kerckhoff et al. (1985) have again concluded that there are few differences between the United States and Britain in occupational mobility opportunities.

35. Wanner (1993) reports results from recent comparative studies of mobility patterns; see Wanner and Hayes (1996) on similarities and differences in the mobility patterns of men in Canada and Australia; and Breen and Rottman (1995; Chapter 5) on social mobility patterns in Britain.

36. Wanner (1993) compares results from the 1973 and 1986 mobility studies. Also see Creese et al. (1991) for additional analyses of the 1986 survey data.

37. In 1992, Krymkowski and Krauze projected occupational mobility patterns in the United States to the year 2000, and predicted less upward mobility and perhaps even downward mobility, on average, particularly for men.

38. Most status attainment studies have been modeled on Blau and Duncan's (1967) study of status attainment among American men. Boyd et al. (1985) describe research based on the first national status attainment/social mobility study conducted in Canada (in 1973). Creese et al. (1991; Chapter 7) present status attainment results from the 1986 replication of the 1973 study.

39. Knottnerus (1987) discusses the "images of society" underlying status attainment research, suggesting that its basic assumptions are congruent with human capital and structural–functionalist theories of stratification.

40. See Hirsch (1980), Clairmont et al. (1983), Blaug (1985), Ashton (1986; Chapter 3), and Rubery (1988) on segmentation theory; Kalleberg (1988) and Stark (1988) comment on crossnational differences in segmentation.

41. Edwards (1979), Hodson and Kaufman (1982), and Gordon et al. (1982) are examples of this perspective on labour market segmentation.

42. See Akyeampong (1997b: 52), Crompton (1992: 31), and Human Resources Development Canada (1997: 3) for Canadian data, and Kalleberg and Van Buren (1996) for U.S. data.

43. Such broad generalizations have led writers like Piore (1975) and Edwards (1979) to distinguish between the *independent* and *subordinate* levels of employment within the primary labour market. The latter contains primarily blue-collar unionized workers, while the former consists of managerial, professional, and technical workers whose jobs involve more general skills, require more education, and allow more individual control over the work itself.

44. Gordon et al. (1982) argue that the emergence of dual economies and segmented labour markets in the United States divided the working class and reduced class conflict. Essentially, some workers were "bought off" at the expense of others.

45. See Piore (1975) for some early theoretical observations about internal labour markets, and Althauser (1989) and Smith (1997) for overviews on research in this area. Examples of specific studies on internal labour markets include Osterman (1984), Diprete (1987), Diprete and Soule (1988), Bernard and Smith (1991), Ospina (1996), and Walsh (1997).

46. Althauser and Kalleberg (1981) distinguish between *firm* and *occupational* internal labour markets; we use the term labour market shelter to refer to the latter; see Ashton (1986; Chapter 3) on labour market shelters.

47. See Hodson and Sullivan (1990; Chapter 10) for defining characteristics of professions, and MacDonald and Ritzer (1988) for an assessment of research on the sociology of professions.

48. See Cant and Sharma (1995) on the "professionalization" of practitioners of nontraditional medicine, Randle (1996) on the "deprofessionalization" of scientists, and Wallace (1995a: 830) on whether the distinction between professional and nonprofessional occupations is still useful.

49. Useem and Karabel (1986) discuss the advantages of an upper-class background and a degree from the "right" school; Boone et al. (1988) demonstrate the link between higher-status social origins and entry into senior management positions.

50. Butler (1980), and Burchell and Rubery (1990) document the liabilities of irregular work histories in Canada and Britain, respectively.

51. See Clairmont et al. (1983) and Apostle et al. (1985) on the Marginal Work World research project. Apostle and Barrett (1992) and Osberg et al. (1995) present more recent research conducted in the same region.

52. See Jenness (1977: 250–51) and Patterson (1972); Pentland (1981: 1–3) reports that some Aboriginals were also kept as slaves in Quebec, but this practice had largely disappeared by the early 1800s.

53. See Baureiss (1987) and Creese (1988–1989); Anderson (1991: 159–63) documents an example of racist attitudes that, ironically, resulted in discrimination against white employees. In 1919, worried about contact between white women and Chinese men, members of the British Columbia legislature passed a law prohibiting the employment of white women in Chinese restaurants. Twenty years later, the law was still being enforced by some police officers in Vancouver.

54. Li (1982). Also see Avery (1979) and Sunahara (1981) on the treatment of immigrant groups and visible minorities in Canada's past.

55. Satzewich and Li (1987); Shadd (1987); Reitz (1988); James (1990); Reiter (1991: 146), das Gupta (1996).

56. See Bonacich (1972) for a theory of ethnically split labour markets; also see Kaufman (1986) and the 1987 special issue of *Sociological Perspectives* (Vol. 30, 4).

57. See Drost (1996), Statistics Canada (1994a), McDonald (1991), Moreau (1991), and Bowier (1991) on labour market problems faced by Aboriginal Canadians.

58. See Moreau (1991), Shain (1995), and Hum and Simpson (1996) on the labour market status of disabled Canadians.

59. Rioux (1985) and McKay (1991) discuss employment barriers faced by the disabled in the labour force; see Wilgosh and Skaret (1987) on employers' attitudes toward hiring the disabled.

60. The proportion of 15- to 64-year-old disabled Canadians who were employed increased from 40 percent in 1986 to 48 percent in 1991 (Shain, 1995: 13).

61. "Vriend firing set for higher court hearing" (*Edmonton Journal*, 17 August 1997: B2).

62. Heron and Storey (1986) apply a modified version of this theoretical model to Canadian history.

63. Clement's (1981) case study of technological change at INCO documented the beginning of this trend; see Osberg et al. (1995) for more recent examples.

64. Myles et al. (1988); Economic Council of Canada (1990); Krahn (1992); Gera (1993); Betcherman et al. (1994); Swift (1995); Osberg et al. (1995); Sherman and Judkins (1995); Menzies (1996); Hughes et al. (1996); *The New York Times* (1996).

65. Rashid (1993); Myles (1992; 1996); Morissette et al. (1994); Betcherman and Leckie (1995); Beach and Slotsve (1996). Also see Grubb and Wilson (1989), Schwartz (1992), Ryscavage (1995), and *The New York Times* (1996) for similar trends in the United States, and Westergaard (1995) and Sherman and Judkins (1995) for growing income inequality in Britain.

66. Betcherman and Leckie (1995: 5); also see Myles and Wannell (1988), Myles (1992), Morissette et al. (1994), Beach and Slotsve (1996), Sunter (1997), and Betcherman and Leckie (1997).

67. On changes in family income in Canda, see Evans and Chawla (1990), Pold and Wong (1990), Love and Poulin (1991), Crompton (1995a), Beach and Slotsve (1996), and Schellenberg and Ross (1997).

68. Beach and Slotsve (1996: 44). Also see Economic Council of Canada (1992c: 3–7) and Schellenberg and Ross (1997) on the working poor.

69. On the "declining middle class," see Kuttner (1983), Newman (1989), Reich (1991), Duncan et al. (1992), and Beach and Slotsve (1996).

70. In some media accounts, the term "underclass" is used to describe poor families who, *presumably* having become dependent on social assistance, have passed such values of "welfare dependency" along to their children. For discussions of the term "underclass" and/or criticisms of the notion of "welfare dependence," see Praeger (1988), Duncan et al. (1988), Edin (1991), Morris and Irwin (1992), Payne and Payne (1994), Breen and Rottman (1995: 91–93), Westergaard (1995: Chapter 8), and Wilson (1997).

71. See Economic Council of Canada (1992b), Gilbert et al. (1993), Betcherman (1993), Tanner et al. (1995), Gaskell and Kelly (1996), Statistics Canada and Human Resources Development Canada (1996), and Human Resources Development Canada (1997).

72. See Reich (1991) for one of the most widely cited discussions of the knowledge-intensive nature of work in the new global economy; see Economic Council of Canada (1992b) on Canada's competitive position.

73. Sharpe (1990); Economic Council of Canada (1992b); Betcherman (1993).

74. Osberg et al. (1995: Chapter 6); see Swift (1995: Chapter 4), Reid (1996: 293), and Osberg and Fortin (1996: Chapter 7) for critical analyses of the training "solution" to high rates of structural unemployment in Canada.

75. See Osberg and Fortin (1996) for discussions of the role of government in stimulating the economy and the impact of inflation-fighting policies on unemployment in Canada.

76. Krahn (1992: 10) reports 1989 data on self-assessed underemployment in Canada; also see Boothby (1993). Angus Reid Interactive (1996) provide a similar estimate from a 1996 public opinion poll; on literacy underutilization, see Krahn (1997) and Krahn and Lowe (1997a).

77. Myles (1996: 18); see Leadbeater and Suschnigg (1997) on the inadequacy of a "training solution" for communities where the economic base that provided employment has disappeared. Bellin and Miller (1990), and Green and Ashton (1992) take a similar "not enough jobs" position in their critiques of training policies in the United States and Britain, respectively.

78. See Dei (1996) and other papers in a special issue of the *Canadian Review of Sociology and Anthropology* (1996: Vol. 33, no. 3) on efforts to counter racism in schools and the workplace.

79. Ashton and Lowe (1991); Anisef and Axelrod (1993). Also see Pauly et al. (1995) and Stern et al. (1995) on U.S. school–work transition programs.

4

WOMEN'S EMPLOYMENT

INTRODUCTION

THE LAST THREE DECADES HAVE BROUGHT WIDE-ranging change to the economic roles of women. In 1970, 38 percent of all adult women in Canada worked outside the home for pay. By 1996, this figure had jumped to 58 percent.[1] Traditional barriers to female employment have slowly been eroding. Feminism challenged the conventional wisdom about women's capabilities. Rising education levels and job expectations made more women career-minded, and the economic necessity to be self-supporting or to contribute to the family income left some women little choice but to find a paying job.

This chapter examines these transformations in women's employment patterns. We will review the dramatic increases in female labour force participation rates during this century, showing how the labour market has become segmented into men's and women's jobs. We will also discuss two seemingly contradictory trends: on the one hand, significant gains in women's employment opportunities and rewards, and on the other, the persistence of major work-related gender inequities. A central theme is that women's work has been undervalued and poorly rewarded throughout history. Consequently, gender remains a key determinant of inequality in our society. The chapter ends optimistically, however, by reviewing two significant policy initiatives—employment equity and pay equity—that have started to redress this long-standing problem.

To better grasp the causes and consequences of gender inequity in the work world, we shall address the following questions: What forces have either pushed or pulled women out of the home and into paid employment in recent decades? Why are women concentrated in a limited range of jobs at the bottom of the occupational ladder? How did these jobs come to be labelled female, and, conversely, how have the most challenging and rewarding jobs come to be defined as male? What barriers still prevent equality of opportunity and rewards for women in the labour market? And finally, but perhaps most importantly, how can greater equality for women be achieved in the workplace?

A word of clarification before we proceed. To avoid confusion, we should define how we use the terms *sex* and *gender.* Basically, sex is the biological distinction between men and women; gender is socially constructed in the sense that it refers to how a particular society defines masculine and feminine roles. Thus, one can observe the sex segregation of occupations. But to explain this it is necessary to look at how jobs are *gendered,* that is, how they take on societal images of appropriate male or female behaviour. We tend to prefer the term gender, given that male–female differences in employment are almost solely a product of socially created gender roles and ideologies.

WOMEN'S ECONOMIC ROLE IN HISTORICAL CONTEXT

Although history has for the most part been written from the perspective of men, even a quick glance back to the past reveals that women have always performed a vital, if somewhat unacknowledged, economic role. Native women, for example, were indispensable to the fur trade, the major industry during much of Canada's colonial period. White male traders relied on Native women to act as interpreters, prepare food, clean pelts for market, and teach them wilderness survival skills.[2] Little wonder that fur traders sought out Native women as wives. When an agrarian economy began to develop in Upper Canada (Ontario) during the nineteenth century, the family was the basic production unit, in which women played a key role. Men worked the fields, while women looked after all domestic work associated with child rearing, tending the livestock and garden, making clothes, and preparing food.[3] On the Prairies during the 1920s, women were seen as contributing to agricultural development by making the farm home "a haven of safety and healthfulness."[4]

Industrialization and Women's Work

In Chapter 1, we noted that one consequence of the rise of large-scale factory production was a growing separation between men's and women's work. Men were drawn into the industrial wage-labour market; women were increasingly confined to the domestic sphere of the household. Marjorie Cohen's feminist analysis of economic development in nineteenth-century Ontario reveals that, prior to wide-scale industrialization, an integration of family and household existed within the emerging market economy (Cohen 1988). Traditional theories of industrialization, Cohen points out, tend to ignore the contribution of households to the economy. Ontario's early economy was primarily based on two staple exports, wheat and timber, which were subject to unstable international markets. Consequently, women's household labour had to fulfil two functions: generate family income by producing agricultural goods to sell in the local consumer market, and perform the domestic chores necessary for the family's survival. Cohen's research underlines the importance of examining how the public and private spheres of market and household have been intertwined in diverse ways during all phases of economic development, with women always performing pivotal roles, albeit quite different from those performed by men.

The absence of a wage-labour market and the necessity of contributing to the household economy meant that few women were employed outside the home prior to the rise of industrial capitalism. Even in late nineteenth-century Canada, only a fraction of women were engaged in paid employment. In 1891, for example, 11.4 percent of girls and women over the age of 10 were employed, accounting for 12.6 percent of the entire labour force.[5] But as factories sprang up in the late-nineteenth century, they began to redefine women's economic role. Employers in some light industries, such as textiles, recruited women as cheap unskilled or semiskilled labourers who, according to prevailing stereotypes, would be less likely to unionize and more tolerant of boring tasks.

By only focusing on paid employment, we risk ignoring the work activities of the vast majority of women during this era. The *unpaid domestic labour* of women—raising the future generation of workers and feeding, clothing, and caring for the present generation of workers—was an essential function within capitalism. Out of these competing pressures on women emerged a gendered division of labour that persists today. As we document below, in the 1990s this takes the form of the *double day* (or, in equally graphic terms, the *second shift)*, whereby most married women spend their days in paying jobs, yet still assume most of the responsibilities of child care and domestic chores when they get home.

Early twentieth-century attitudes about women's economic roles distinguished between single and married women. Expanding manufacturing and service industries had an almost insatiable demand for both blue- and white-collar workers. The employment of young, single women prior to marriage came to be tolerated in domestic, clerical, sales, and some factory jobs. Once married, women were expected to retreat into the matrimonial home. Of course, some wished to remain in the labour force and still others were forced to stay through economic necessity. In these cases, married women laboured at the margins of the economy in domestic and other menial jobs that usually had been abandoned by single women.[6]

Industrialization accentuated age and gender divisions in the economy. Examining the work patterns of working-class women in Montreal, Canada's first large industrial city, Bettina Bradbury documents how age and sex determined who was drawn into wage-labour. Women made up about 35 percent of the city's industrial workforce during the 1870s. In certain industries, such as domestic work and the sewing and dressmaking trades, 4 out of 5 workers were women, and the vast majority of them were single. Given the scarcity of wage-labour for wives because of strong sanctions against their employment, such women could make a greater contribution to the family economy by being *household managers*. In this role, wives stretched the wages of male family members and single daughters as far as possible, occasionally supplementing this by taking in boarders or turning to neighbours or charities for help (Bradbury 1988).

The Family Wage Ideology

Powerful social values justified this division of labour. Especially influential in perpetuating women's subordinate role as unpaid family workers was the ideology of the *family wage*. As working-class men began organizing unions to achieve better wages and working conditions, one of the labour movement's demands was that wages should be high enough to allow a male breadwinner to support a wife and children. The labour movement's successes in this regard had the effect of drastically reducing women's presence, and the cheap labour they provided, in the workplace (a policy that was typical of unions until a serious male labour shortage arose in World War I). Middle-class reformers also lobbied for restrictions on female industrial employment due to its presumed harmful personal and social effects. In response, employers limited their hiring mainly to single women, further reinforcing this ideology. Despite its sexist tone, the family wage ideology indirectly may have benefited those women who were dependent on a husband by raising the standard of living in working-class families. The price, of course, was the restriction of women's labour market opportunities to areas in which they would not compete directly with men—hence the endurance of the term male breadwinner.[7]

However, the family wage ideology tells only part of the story of women's lives during early industrialization. Joy Parr's case studies of two Ontario industrial towns, Paris and Hanover, between 1880 and 1950, caution us against thinking in binary oppositions—masculine/feminine, market/non-market, public/private, waged/nonwaged (Parr 1990: 8). Parr shows how the specific combinations of community context, gender roles, household forms, and industrial development patterns interacted to fashion different gender ideologies. One of the revealing points of her study is to show that, within the broad contours of the work patterns we described above, variations existed such that outcomes were not predetermined.

On the surface, both Paris and Hanover appear to be small, thriving manufacturing communities. Parr probes beneath the surface, documenting how the knit-goods industry based in Paris relied on a largely female workforce, while in Hanover's large furniture factory the workers were almost exclusively male. Consequently, different gender identities based on women's employment patterns arose to maintain each town's labour force. In turn, these were reinforced by attitudes and behaviour in households and the community. Certainly Paris was the exception at the time in Ontario. Nonetheless, its flow of daily life during the 80 years of Parr's study force us to reconsider a model of industrialization based on one dominant mode of production in which males are the breadwinners.

This brief historical sketch has identified a number of prominent themes. First, although their widespread participation in the paid labour force is a recent development, women have always made essential economic contributions. Second, women's entry into paid employment occurred in ways that reproduced their subordinate position in society relative to that of men, although the specific forms this took varied across time and place. Third, the changing interconnections among households, families, and the wage-labour market are crucial to understanding women's roles in the continuing evolution of twentieth-century capitalism.

FEMALE LABOUR FORCE PARTICIPATION PATTERNS

Few changes in Canadian society since World War II have had as far-reaching consequences as evolving female employment patterns. Virtually all industrial nations have experienced rising *female labour force participation rates* since the end of World War II. This trend has been especially rapid in Canada. Figure 4.1 provides a comparison of labour force participation rates among women aged 25 to 54 (the prime years for employment) for seven major industrial nations between 1975 and 1994.[11] Note that rising female employment levels is a general crossnational trend. But Canada's increase was greater than the others. In 1975, Canada rated in the lowest level of employment for women in the 25 to 54 age cohort. The tremendous expansion of white-collar service sector jobs, coupled with rising educational levels and a declining birth rate, drew millions of Canadian women into employment at an accelerated rate. By 1994, Canada's female labour force participation rate had surpassed all the advanced industrial nations except France and Sweden, the latter a country where women's employment outside the home has been actively encouraged by state policies.

Influences on Women's Employment

What social and economic factors account for this remarkable increase in Canada's female labour force participation? Clearly there was no single cause. The huge post-war baby boom generation was completing its education and flooding into an expanding job market by the late 1960s. Young women were becoming much better educated, which raised their occupational aspirations and made them more competitive with men in the job market. Traditional

FIGURE 4.1 *Labour Force Participation Rates in 7 Industrialized Countries, Women Aged 25–54, 1975 and 1994*

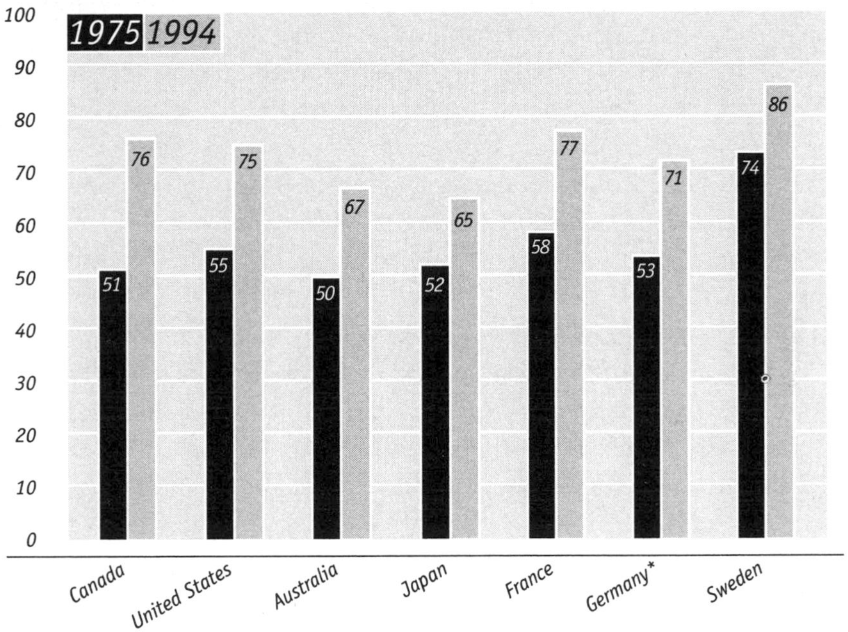

*West Germany in 1975; the unified East and West Germany in 1994.

Source: ©OECD, 1995, *Labour Force Statistics 1973–1993*. Reprinted by permission of the OECD.

stereotypes of women's work no longer fit reality. The massive expansion of white-collar service sector jobs boosted the demand for female labour, and the growth of feminism contributed to more liberal social values regarding women's work roles. As we have seen, service sector growth also fueled a trend to part-time jobs, which often are convenient for women with family responsibilities. Shrinking family size allowed married women to pursue employment more readily. Moreover, rising separation and divorce rates forced a growing number of women to find their own source of income. And in many families, the reality (or threat) of declining living standards made a second income essential.

The interaction of this multitude of supply and demand factors underlay the sharp rise in female employment.[9] Interpreting the overall impact of these changes on women's lives, Charles Jones, Lorna Marsden, and Lorne Tepperman (1990: 58–59) point out that as more women have entered paid employment, their work patterns have not come to mirror those of men. Rather, largely because women are heavily concentrated in the secondary labour market and often have to juggle family responsibilities with a job, their lives have become increasingly individualized. Compared with their mothers' generation, younger women today have adopted new ways of combining work, education, and family. Hence, since the 1950s, there is now much greater variety, fluidity, and idiosyncrasy in women's roles. For Jones, Marsden, and Tepperman, the *individualization process* is defined by these elements: (1) variety, through greater opportunities for employment and education; (2) fluidity, in terms of increased movement among these roles and domestic/household roles; and (3) idiosyncrasy, in the sense that it is now exceedingly difficult to predict if, when, and where a woman will be working for pay.

There is no question that many factors have a bearing on the likelihood of a woman participating in the labour force. Figure 4.2 identifies important variations in 1996 participation rates by region, age, educational level, marital status, and family circumstances. Provincially, women in Alberta have the highest participation rate (65 percent), followed by those in Ontario (59 percent). Newfoundland and New Brunswick have the lowest (45 and 53 percent, respectively). Certainly local and regional job opportunities have a direct bearing on female participation rates, as do regional differences in age structure and educational attainment. For example, Alberta has a relatively strong service sector and a young and well-educated workforce—hence its high rate of labour force participation for both women and men. In contrast, Newfoundland has limited employment opportunities for women (and men) due to chronic economic underdevelopment and the decline of the fisheries. Consequently, much work occurs outside the sphere of paid employment in a thriving informal economy and through self-provisioning (Sinclair and Felt 1992).

Personal characteristics also influence work patterns. Single women, for example, have higher participation rates than those who are married. Indeed, 82 percent of single women between the ages of 25 and 44 are in the labour force. Interestingly, the participation rate for married women (78 percent) in this age cohort is also well above the national average. By comparison, just

FIGURE 4.2 *Female Labour Force Participation Rates by Selected Characteristics, Canada, 1996*

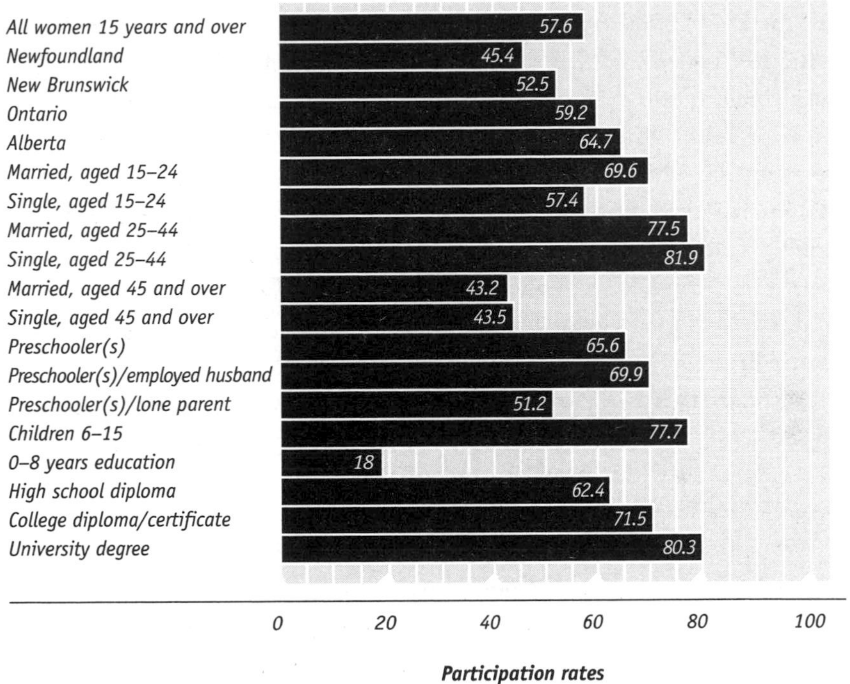

Source: Statistics Canada, "Female Labour Force Participation Rates by Selected Characteristics, Canada, 1996," adapted from "Labour Force Annual Averages," Catalogue No. 71-220. Reprinted with permission.

over four in ten women aged 45 or older are in the labour force. Women with higher levels of educational attainment are more active in the labour force—80 percent of women with university degrees compared with 62 percent who have a high school diploma. Family situation also matters. However, because a high proportion of mothers with children under the age of 15 are relatively young and well educated, their labour force participation rates are above average. For example, 66 percent of mothers with preschool children participate in the labour force.

Financial necessity is a major factor, often the most important one, in many women's decisions to seek employment. Generally, wives in low-income families, or women who are lone parents, may be compelled to work to meet, or help meet, basic expenses. In fact, the most common dual-earner family combination in Canada is a blue-collar husband and a wife in a clerical, sales, or service job (Chawla 1992: 24). The participation rate for single mothers with preschool children at home was 51 percent in 1996, while the rate for mothers of preschoolers who had an employed husband was 70 percent. For many single mothers, finding or keeping a job may be difficult, given such factors as lower educational attainment and difficulties arranging adequate and affordable child care. The number of mother-led families with preschool children has more than doubled over the past two decades, and low-paid, unstable work is a major reason for the high incidence of poverty in this group.[10] Growing concern about child poverty in Canada is clearly linked to the difficulties lone-parent females face in the labour market.[11] In contrast, better-educated, urban middle-class women, who are married and whose spouse or partner is a professional or a manager, have greater opportunities and the luxury of choice with regard to employment (Lowe and Krahn 1985: 4). Among families with the highest incomes in Canada, it is very likely that the female partner is a high-earning manager or professional.[12]

Women's organizations, such as the National Action Committee on the Status of Women, and social policy experts point to these trends to support their calls for better child-care facilities, higher minimum wages, and less punitive welfare programs. Such reforms would remove some of the barriers that economically disadvantaged mothers of young children now face in the labour market.

WORK AND FAMILY

Traditional gender roles and values have defined women's work as household tasks and child-rearing. This enduring male–female division of labour underlies much of the gender inequality we see today. For example, domestic responsibilities continue to limit women's availability for paid work, keeping many married women financially dependent on their husbands. Feminists argue that women's subordination results from the combination of two systems of domination: capitalism and patriarchy. Capitalism incorporated earlier patriarchal social arrangements. Broadly speaking, *patriarchy* refers to male domination over women, but more specifically it describes forms of family organization in which fathers and husbands hold total power.[13] Remnants of patriarchy still reinforce stereotypes of women as cheap, expendable labour.

Furthermore, women's traditional family roles of wife and mother often restrict their employment opportunities and, for those who are employed, create a *double day* of paid and unpaid work.

Changing Family Forms

Women in the 1950s saw the home as their major priority. They sometimes were employed before having children, stayed home to raise them, and then returned to the labour force at middle age after the children had grown up.[14] Because most wives in the 1950s and 1960s responded to the demands of child rearing by leaving the labour force, employers assumed that women must have a weaker attachment to paid work than men. A 1952 national study found that the major reason married women under the age of 40 left their employment was for child-raising responsibilities (Boyd 1985). Similar family constraints on employment for women still exist. For example, a study we conducted in Edmonton in the early 1980s found that the major factor preventing wives from taking a paid job was having children under the age of six in the home (Lowe and Krahn 1985). However, between 1981 and 1991, there was a pervasive national trend for mothers with children at home to seek paid jobs, with this group accounting for most of the increase in female participation.[15] As a result, many more women are facing the stresses and conflicts of juggling paid work with family roles.

Today, however, far fewer women leave the labour force, and those who do leave for a shorter time. Consequently, the dual-earner family is now the norm in Canada. Since the 1960s, the traditional family in which the husband was the sole earner has been eclipsed by dual-earner families, which now comprise over 60 percent of all husband–wife families (Oderkirk et al. 1994; Chawla 1992). At the same time, the number of lone-parent families is on the rise. According to the 1991 Canadian Census, 20 percent of families with children present are headed by lone parents, over 80 percent of whom are women.[16]

The Domestic Division of Labour

While there are some indications of greater equality in the gender division of household chores, changes in this area of domestic life have not kept pace with the rising employment rate of married women. Evidence gleaned from *time budget studies*, which ask people to record in detail how they spend their time, leads to the conclusion that many employed wives often work what Arlie Hochschild calls a "second shift" in the home.[17] After putting in seven or eight hours on the job, some wives return home to cook, clean, shop, and look after children—the domestic chores their mothers and grandmothers did as full-time housewives. This echoes the findings of a 1971 study by Martin Meissner and his colleagues, which found that taking a job outside the home meant a decrease of 13.5 hours per week in leisure time for a sample of British Columbia wives. Yet their husbands experienced no loss of leisure time because they had not shared the housework to begin with.[18] The researchers concluded that time pressures and added workloads create a "double burden" for many employed wives.

Recent investigations show some change, but women still continue to shoulder this double burden. Statistics Canada's 1992 General Social Survey documented that employed women with a partner and a child under age 5 devoted an average of 5.3 hours daily to primary child care, household work, and shopping (Figure 4.3). The comparable figure for women with partners but no children was 3.7 hours daily. Generally, women spent about 2 hours more on these daily activities than men in similar family circumstances. Moreover, the time women spend on all household work has increased since 1986 (Statistics Canada 1994c: 48–49). In dual-earner families in which both spouses had full-time jobs, over half of the wives had sole responsibility for housework (meal preparation and cleanup, cleaning, and laundry); these tasks were shared equally in just 1 in 10 such families.[19] Yet there are considerable variations in the domestic division of labour. For example, younger and university-educated women have less traditional roles.

Population aging also has implications for women in that they often provide care to elderly and dependent parents and relatives. *Elder care* is becoming a high-profile issue amid predictions of a "care-giving crunch," as fewer women are available to meet such demands because of the constraints of jobs, which would not have been the case a generation ago (McKinnon and Odynak 1991: 31). Actually, elder care has become quite common, as the 1991 Alberta Survey documented: 41 percent of full-time employed women in the province and 35 percent of full-time employed men reported they are currently providing assistance to an elderly relative.[20]

FIGURE 4.3 *Average Time Spent Daily by Employed Women and Men on Unpaid Household Work* by Family Status, Canada, 1992*

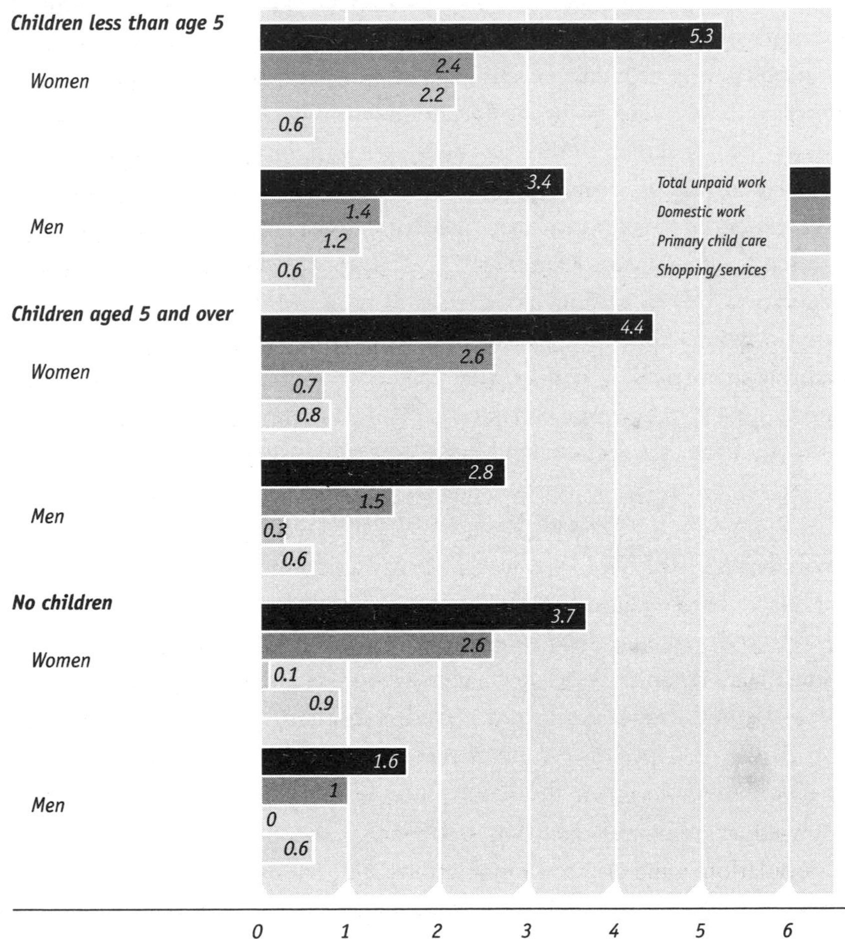

* Includes primary child care, meal preparation, meal cleanup, cleaning and laundry, and shopping and services performed by employed individuals with spouses.

Source: Statistics Canada, "Average Time Spent Daily by Employed Women and Men on Unpaid Household Work by Family Status, Canada, 1992," adapted from "Women in the Labour Force, 1994," Catalogue No. 75-507, page 54. Reprinted with permission.

Wives' household work varies, depending on their social class position and their husbands' occupation. Working-class wives have a higher probability of facing the combined stresses of poverty and menial employment. Women married to managerial and professional men may be expected to comply with the traditions of a two-person career. It has been commonly assumed in large corporations that male managers climbing the career ladder will have the unpaid services of a wife. Success in the corporate world demands unwavering dedication to one's career, often resulting in very low family involvement. Wives are expected to put on dinner parties, accompany their husbands to company social functions, make travel arrangements, and plan household moves. They are what Rosabeth Moss Kanter (1977: Chapter 5) calls "unpaid servants of the corporation." These antiquated vestiges of male corporate culture are eroding as more women pursue their own careers. However, women attempting to establish themselves in management still face disadvantages, given lingering expectations about two-person careers. Unfortunately, their husbands are seldom willing to take on extra child-care and housework responsibilities.

Balancing Work and Family

"Work has changed. Women have changed," writes Arlie Hochschild. "But most workplaces have remained inflexible in the face of the family demands of their workers and at home, most men have yet to really adapt to the changes in women. This strain between the change in women and the absence of change in much else leads me to speak of a 'stalled revolution'" (Hochschild 1989: 12). Perhaps the most pervasive consequence of this stalled revolution is the rise of *job–family conflict.* When the Conference Board of Canada surveyed 11,000 employees across Canada during 1988–89, it discovered that two-thirds had some difficulty balancing work and family (McBride-King 1990; Stone 1994). Similarly, the Alberta Government and the Alberta Union of Provincial Employees documented in a 1990 study of over 18,000 public employees that the majority of those—both female and male—with dependents reported the combined demands of work and family to be stressful.[21]

For employees, increased stress, lost career opportunities, and reduced quality of family life are major costs of job–family conflict. Balancing the demands of job and family also can affect one's quality of life. As Figure 4.4 documents, over one-third of women in dual-earner families who are employed full-time and have a child under age 10 reported feeling severely "time crunched" in the 1992 General Social Survey. This is more than twice the rate reported by men in comparable family and employment situations. It is also considerably higher than among full-time employed women who do not have children under age 10. That this difference is very small among men reflects the fact that, overall, men are much less involved in primary child care. However, men increasingly are expressing more interest in family-friendly policies, and some are contributing to the changing configuration of work, gender, and family by redefining their roles.[22] This is no doubt an area of research that will attract more attention in coming years.

For employers, the negative impacts include increased absenteeism, turnover, and recruitment problems if their policies are not perceived as family-friendly. Absenteeism is undoubtedly the greatest source of lost productivity for employers due to employees trying to balance competing job and family demands. Indeed, Statistics Canada documents that while male rates of absenteeism remained constant between 1977 and 1993, female rates rose steadily, mainly due to family or personal obligations as growing numbers of

FIGURE 4.4 *Time-Crunch Stress* Reported by Full-Time Dual Earners by Age of Youngest Child, Canada, 1992*

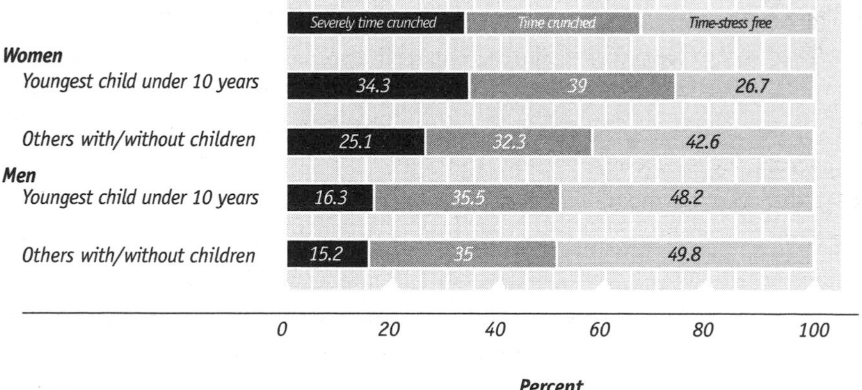

* Agreement with 7 or more of 10 statements about time pressures in your daily life (for example, consider myself a workaholic, worry I don't spend enough time with family and friends, feel trapped in a daily routine, cut back on sleep when I need more time) indicates "severe time crunch," while agreement with 4 to 6 indicates "time crunch."

Source: Statistics Canada, "Time-Crunch Stress Reported by Full-Time Dual Earners by Age of Youngest Child, Canada, 1992," adapted from "Canadian Social Trends," Catalogue No. 11-008, Winter 1995, Number 39, page 18. Reprinted with permission.

mothers with preschool children sought employment (Akyeampong 1992; 1995).

Both the Conference Board and the Alberta surveys asked employees what type of employer support would help them to better integrate their job, family, and personal life. Common responses included child-care support, flexible work hours and schedules, improved personal and family-related leave, and a more understanding approach by management to employees' nonwork needs. Slowly, in part due to studies such as these, heightened awareness of the economic and individual costs of job family conflict is challenging employers to reconsider some long-standing policies. Yet on-site child-care facilities are rare, as noted above; many managers seem rigidly locked into a nine-to-five day and five-day-week schedule; and paid maternity leave, paternity leave, or elder care support are provided by only a minority of employers.[23] Of all these needs, perhaps the issue of child care requires the most urgent attention. According to the 1988 National Child Care Survey, arranging child care that is affordable, of high quality, and convenient presents an ongoing problem for many parents (Crompton 1991). In 1992, there were about 350,000 supervised day care spaces in Canada, a number insufficient to meet the demand. Most children of working parents are looked after informally by sitters, neighbours, nannies, or relatives. In 1990, just over one-quarter of children under age six receiving care were in day care centres—only 3 percent were in workplace centres (Statistics Canada 1994c: 49–50). So far, Quebec is the only jurisdiction in Canada to make a concerted effort to address these issues, having introduced in 1997 a comprehensive program of universal subsidized day care, early childhood education, support for parental leaves, and improved family allowances (Philp 1997).

All in all, what we have just documented surely amounts to a "stalled revolution." Almost a decade ago, the Conference Board predicted that more employers would respond to these needs as the drain on productivity became more visible and employee pressure for such policies mounted (Paris 1989). Unfortunately for many working parents, there are few tangible signs of this happening. And for some employees who do have flexible work arrangements, recent research suggests that these may not meet expectations in terms of reducing the stresses of balancing job and family. After examining a variety of alternative work arrangements, Janet Fast and Judith Frederick (1996) concluded that self-employment, flex-place (working some hours at home), and shift work had no effect on workers' perceived time stress. Both women and men in part-time jobs are less time-stressed than full-timers, although far more women than men choose part-time work for family-related reasons. Flextime (employees choose when their work day starts and stops) helps to reduce time pressures, but it is less available to women than to men. Compressed work weeks (fewer days per week with longer hours each day) seem to increase women's level of time stress, likely because they interfere with family routines. Job sharing, which now is available to only 8 percent of part-time workers, was not examined in this study, but it may have the potential to contribute to reduced time pressure and better integration of work and family (Marshall 1997).

GENDER SEGREGATION IN THE LABOUR MARKET

At the heart of gender inequality in the work world is the structuring of the labour market into male and female segments. *Occupational gender segregation* refers to the concentration of men and women in different occupations. A potent combination of gender-role socialization, education, and labour market mechanisms channel women into a limited number of occupations in which mainly other females are employed.

Female Job Ghettos

Female *job ghettos* typically offer little economic security and little opportunity for advancement; furthermore, the work is often unpleasant, boring, and sometimes physically taxing. Women in job ghettos lack ready access to the more challenging and lucrative occupations dominated by men. These male segments of the labour market operate as *shelters*, conferring advantages on workers within them through entrance restrictions.[24] The concepts of ghettos and shelters emphasize the unequal rewards and opportunities built into the job market on the basis of a worker's sex. It is especially important to recognize that job opportunities determine an individual's living standard, future prospects, and overall quality of life—in Max Weber's words, her or his *life chances.*

Simply put, women in Canada are more likely to be poor than men. Poverty among employed women has grown at five times the rate of growth among men since the early 1970s. The root causes of this can be traced to a combination of gender-based labour market segmentation and domestic and child-care responsibilities. Gunderson and Muszynski explain the broader context of these realities:

> ... working poverty has not decreased and appears to be on the increase, highlighting the fact that something is fundamentally amiss in the labour market. The fruits of economic growth are not being shared evenly. The evidence of this is striking. Regional disparities in employment opportunities in Canada are glaring. The labour market is volatile with international competition, technological change, and deindustrialization leading to layoffs and plant closures, creating hardship and leaving many people out of work. The quality of the jobs now being created is in question, as part-time and low-wage service sector jobs have proliferated. These are the jobs that tend to be open to women, and they are the jobs that produce working poverty. (Gunderson, Muszynski, and Keck 1990: 220)

One of the fundamental mechanisms underlying segmentation is the *gender labelling* of jobs. Employers do not always make hiring decisions on strictly rational grounds, despite what economics textbooks would have us believe. If all hiring decisions were totally rational, women would have been recruited much earlier in the industrialization process and in far greater numbers, given their cost advantage as cheap labour. As already mentioned, men typically opposed the employment of women in their occupations for fear of having their wages undercut. Furthermore, traditional values narrowly defined female roles as child-rearing and homemaking. Women, therefore, were relegated to the less rewarding jobs that men did not want. Because these occupations came to be labelled "female," future employers would likely only seek women for them, and, regardless of the skills demanded by the job, pay and status would remain low.

Dominant social values about femininity and masculinity have long been used to define job requirements. For instance, by the late-nineteenth century, teaching, social work, nursing, and domestic work were socially acceptable for women. Society could justify this on the ideological grounds that these occupations—caring for the sick, the old, and the unfortunate, transmitting culture to children, and performing domestic chores—demanded essentially female traits. Exclusive male rights to the better jobs and higher incomes thus were unchallenged; the role of women as homemaker and wife was preserved. Once a job was labelled male or female, it was difficult for workers of the opposite sex to gain entry.[25]

Trends in Labour Market Gender Segregation

In Chapter 2, we outlined gender differences in the occupational distribution of the labour force. Figure 4.5 explores this further, summarizing for 1996 two major trends associated with occupational gender segregation. The left-hand set of bars in Figure 4.5 identify the percentage of employees in each occupation who are women. Clerical jobs and medicine and health-related occupations have the highest concentrations of women (80 percent of all employees in each occupation). Teaching, social sciences, and service occupations (for example, jobs in restaurants, bars, hotels, tourism, hairdressing, and child-care facilities, and domestics and building cleaners) are between 57 and 65 percent female. All these could be labelled job ghettos in the sense that the

FIGURE 4.5 *Employment Concentration and Occupational Distribution of Women, Canada, 1996*

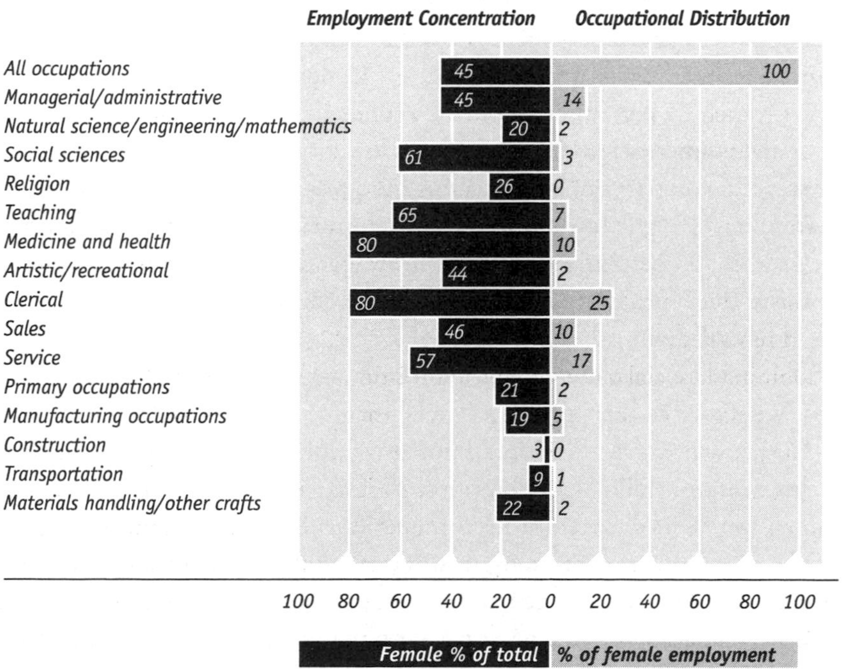

Source: Statistics Canada, "Employment Concentration and Occupational Distribution of Women, Canada, 1996," adapted from "Labour Force Annual Averages," Catalogue No. 71-220. Reprinted with permission.

majority of employees are women, although the pay and security provided in some (particularly nursing and teaching) is relatively good. By contrast, one in 5 or fewer workers in natural sciences, engineering and mathematics occupations, manufacturing, transportation, and construction are women.

The right-hand series of bars in the figure show the distribution of the female labour force across all occupations. Clerical occupations employed 1 in 4 women workers in 1996 (down from 1 in 3 in 1991). By adding women in service and sales jobs to those in clerical jobs, we can account for over half of the female labour force. This attests to women's overrepresentation in lower-status occupations.

For a more complete understanding of where men and women are located in the labour market, we need to investigate the industrial distribution of employment. You will recall from Chapter 2 that Canada's service-based economy is generating polarization between good and bad jobs. How then are men and women distributed within the upper and lower tiers of the service sector? Referring back to Table 2.1 will help to answer this question. Close to 40 percent of men work in the goods sector. Potentially this has negative implications for the male labour force, given the massive restructuring occurring in manufacturing. Women's jobs are far more likely to be found in service industries. Overall, 85 percent of employed women in 1996 were in the service sector, with about one-third employed in its lower tier (retail trade and consumer services). In comparison, 22 percent of men worked in the lower-tier services. Interestingly, a higher proportion of women than men also worked in upper-tier services (54 percent and 42 percent, respectively). The main explanation for this is the concentration of women in the education/health/welfare sector. But in overall terms, our discussion of service sector jobs in Chapter 2 suggests that relatively more women than men are in nonstandard, low-quality jobs. We return to this important issue below.

How much has gender-based job segregation diminished over the course of this century? Table 4.1 shows that in 1901, 71 percent of all employed women were concentrated in five occupations. Within this small number of socially acceptable women's jobs, that of domestic servant employed the greatest portion of working women at 36 percent. Next in importance were seamstressing and school teaching, each employing roughly 13 percent of the female labour force. These three occupations fit our description of a job ghetto, given that three-quarters or more of all workers in the job were female.

TABLE 4.1 *The Five Leading Female Occupations in Canada, 1901, 1951, and 1991*

Occupation	*Number of Employed Women*	*Percent of Total Female Employment in Occupation*	*Females as Percentage of Employment in Occupation*
1901			
1. Domestic servants	*84,984*	*35.7*	*87*
2. Seamstresses	*32,145*	*13.5*	*100*
3. School teachers	*30,870*	*13.0*	*78*
4. Office clerks	*12,569*	*5.3*	*78*
5. Farmers and stockraisers	*8,495*	*3.6*	*2*
All five occupations		*71.1%*	
1951			
1. Stenographers and typists	*133,485*	*11.5*	*96.4*
2. Office clerks	*118,025*	*10.1*	*42.7*
3. Sales clerks	*95,443*	*8.2*	*55.1*
4. Hotel, café, and private household workers n.e.s.+	*88,775*	*7.6*	*89.1*
5. School teachers	*74,319*	*6.4*	*72.5*
All five occupations		*43.8%*	
1991			
1. Secretaries and stenographers	*449,580*	*7.1*	*98.5*
2. Sales clerks and sales persons	*379,820*	*6.0*	*53.9*
3. Bookkeepers and accounting clerks	*337,185*	*5.3*	*84.3*
4. Cashiers and tellers	*296,965*	*4.7*	*88.2*
5. Nurses (registered, graduate, and in training)	*242,170*	*3.8*	*94.8*
All five occupations		*26.9%*	

+n.e.s.: Not elsewhere specified. Excludes a few persons seeking work who have never been employed.

Source: Statistics Canada, "The Five Leading Female Occupations in Canada, 1901, 1951 and 1991," adapted from "Women in Canada: A Statistical Report," Catalogue No. 89-503; "Labour Force—Occupations and Industries," from 1951 Census of Canada Data, Table 4; "The Nation, Population and Dwelling Characteristics: Occupation," Catalogue No. 93-112, Table 1; and "The Nation, Industry and Occupation," Catalogue No. 93-327, Table 1. Reprinted by permission.

This was not the case, however, for the two other main female occupations. Clerical work at the turn of the century was still a man's job, although by the 1940s the gender balance had shifted toward women. Interestingly, clerical work was one of the few traditionally male jobs to undergo this *feminization* process. Behind this change was the rapid expansion of office work accompanied by a more fragmented and routinized division of labour. As a result, a layer of new positions emerged at the bottom of office hierarchies, opening office doors to women.[26] Finally, the fact that farmers and stock raisers appear as one of the five prominent female occupations may seem peculiar. Considering that Canada was an agricultural economy in 1901, it is understandable that women would form a small part of the paid agricultural workforce.

The twentieth-century march of industrialization saw a decline of some female jobs, such as domestic work and seamstressing, and the rise of new employment opportunities in booming service industries. By 1951, the two leading female occupations were in the clerical area. Along with sales clerks, hotel, café, and domestic workers, and teachers, they comprised 44 percent of the female workforce just after World War II.

As we have seen, female job ghettos still exist. Office and sales jobs have topped the list throughout the post–World War II period. However, women are now entering a broader range of occupations. For example, according to the 1991 Census, the five main female-dominated job titles accounted for only 27 percent of the entire female labour force. This is a positive sign of occupational diversification, but how far have women moved into nontraditional (in other words, male-dominated) occupations? Karen Hughes's analysis of the 484 detailed occupations in the 1971 Census discovered that 86 percent of women worked in traditionally female occupations.[27] Over the next 15 years, the proportion of women in these traditional occupations declined to 79 percent, then changed little between 1986 and 1991.

Yet, at the same time, women were making gains in what can be called *nontraditional jobs*, where men have predominated. Figure 4.6 summarizes Hughes's analysis of women's movement into highly nontraditional jobs—in which women made up less than half of their overall share of the labour force—between 1986 and 1991. The vertical line down the right side of the figure indicates when women's share of an occupation matches their overall share of the labour force. A *coefficient of representation* measures this difference, with a value of zero telling us that there are no women in an occupation, and of one indicating that women's representation in a particular occupation is identical to the total labour force (by using this standardized scale, the coefficient of representation adjusts to changes in the latter). Figure 4.6 reports the ten most highly nontraditional occupations in 1971, showing that women's

FIGURE 4.6 *The Ten Most Highly Nontraditional Occupations with Greatest Increases in Female Representation, Canada, 1986–1991**

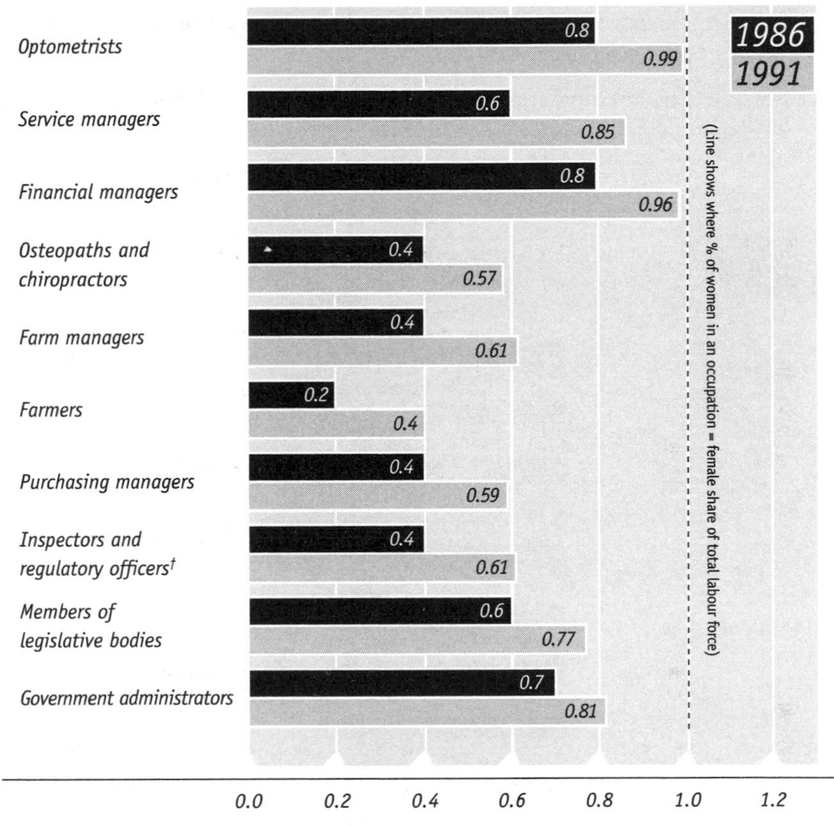

* Nontraditional is defined as a female coefficient of representation of less than 0.50 in 1971. Data are for individuals who worked mostly 30 hours or more per week for 49 to 52 weeks in the reference year and who were employed in the week prior to the census, and, if unemployed, had worked at some time in the prior 18 months (the "experienced labour force").

† Nongovernment only.

Source: Statistics Canada, "The Ten Most Highly Nontraditional Occupations with Greatest Increases in Female Representation, Canada, 1986–1991," adapted from "Perspectives on Labour and Income," Catalogue No. 75-001, Autumn 1995, Volume 7, Number 3, page 16. Reprinted with permission.

employment grew rapidly in the late 1980s. Note that women have achieved equal representation with men in optometry and financial management, and are approaching this in sales management and government administration.

Additional insights can be gleaned about the shifts taking place in female employment by focusing on professional occupations. Because professions are organized around specific bodies of knowledge and expertise, usually acquired through a university degree, women's access to these jobs should improve as their level of education rises. The proportion of all university degrees granted to women has been rising steadily. Women's share of undergraduate enrolment jumped from 43 to 53 percent between 1972–73 and 1992–93, and there were

FIGURE 4.7 *Women as a Proportion of Total Full-Time University Enrolment, Canada, 1972–1973 and 1992–1993**

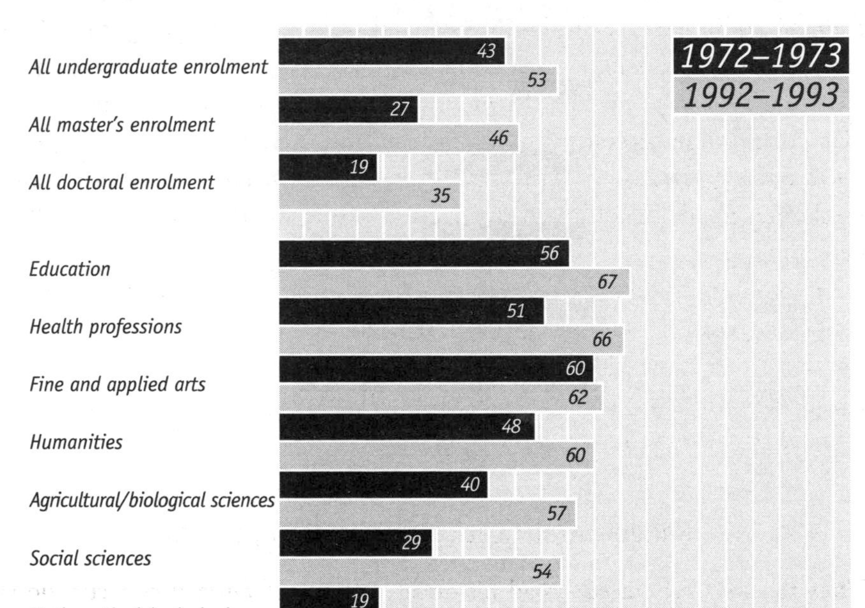

* Includes undergraduate and graduate students, except those in graduate certificate and diploma programs.

Source: Statistics Canada, "Women as a Proportion of Total Full-Time University Enrolment, Canada, 1972–73 and 1992–93," adapted from "Canadian Social Trends," Catalogue No. 11-008, Winter 1995, Number 39, page 18. Reprinted with permission.

also large increases at the master's and doctoral levels (see Figure 4.7). All major program areas saw rising female enrolments. Math, science, and engineering fields are the only disciplines in which women do not comprise over half of all students; in fact, women are significantly underrepresented in these areas.

Consistent with the direct connection between educational and occupational attainment discussed in Chapter 3, Katherine Marshall's research indicates that women accounted for two-thirds of the growth in professional occupations between 1981 and 1986.[28] Especially strong gains were made in male-dominated professions. Over half of the growth in all male-dominated professions between 1981 and 1986 was due to the entry of women. Thus, women's employment increased from 17 to 35 percent of all veterinarians, from 42 to 50 percent of pharmacists, and from 17 to 21 percent of physicians. But there are still many traditionally male occupations where such gains have not been observed. Furthermore, there was considerably less movement of men into female-dominated occupations. To give one example, between 1982 and 1993, women's share of nursing and other health-related professions (excluding medicine and dentistry) actually rose slightly, from 85.1 to 85.8 percent.[29]

Two points summarize these trends. First, to the extent that occupational gender segregation is breaking down, it is due to women moving into male-dominated areas, not vice versa. Second, despite the changes that Hughes and Marshall outline, women still have considerably fewer occupational and career avenues open to them.

Gender Stratification within Occupations

Thus far, we have traced broad historical patterns of *horizontal* occupational gender segregation. Now we will examine a related obstacle women face, *vertical* segregation. This refers to how a gendered division of tasks, statuses, and responsibilities exists within specific occupations. As a rule, men tend to be in positions of greater authority in organizations and, consequently, usually receive better job rewards than women. Consider the example of elementary and secondary school teaching. Even though women made up 70 percent of all school teachers in 1991, they occupied only 38 percent of school administrative positions. Approximately 42 percent of the women in teaching are in elementary school classrooms, while men are concentrated in the higher-status, better-paying jobs in universities, colleges, high schools, and educational administrations. Similarly, 63 percent of the women in sales jobs are sales clerks, the bottom of the ladder in this occupation, while men are overrepresented in sales supervisory positions (Statistics Canada 1993: Table 1).

The situation is much the same in other professions. Women have made significant inroads recently, particularly in law and medicine, although there is a tendency for them to opt for lower-status specialties such as family law or general medical practice.[30] This reinforces assumptions often made by the male establishment in these professions about female colleagues being best suited to tasks calling upon their "natural instincts" as wives and mothers.

In their probing investigation of the changes in legal careers in Canada, John Hagan and Fiona Kay portray a gender-stratified profession in which work environments are not family-friendly. Large numbers of women entered law in the 1970s and 1980s, when the profession was expanding and reorganizing into larger firms. According to Hagan and Kay (1995: 182):

> … women were recruited into the profession during a period when they were needed to fill entry- and intermediate-level positions and were perceived to be compliant employees.… It is possible that … many partners in law firms were encouraged by the belief that as in the teaching profession of an earlier era, women would assume entry-level positions in the profession, work diligently for a number of years, and then abandon their early years of invested work to bear children and raise families, leaving partnership positions to men assumed to be more committed to their occupational careers.

These assumptions were largely borne out in research findings. The changing professional climate of the 1980s restricted opportunities for both men and women to attain partnerships—a financial and management stake in the firm that results in much higher earnings. However, women lost out even more than men, mainly because of the conflicts and compromises created by the interplay of professional demands and expectations with family roles. Still, women who continue to practise law full-time after having children have high work commitment and high job satisfaction, despite lower earnings than men. As Hagan and Kay point out, law firms have long accepted that work and family are compatible roles for men, but this will only be achieved for women by reforms aimed at eliminating discrimination (Hagan and Kay 1995: 182).

During the 1970s, women also made major breakthroughs in the male domain of management and administration. This trend continues, for in 1996 women made up 45 percent of managers and administrators—equal to their representation in the labour force—accounting for 14 percent of the entire female labour force (Figure 4.5). How does this compare with other advanced industrial countries? The general category of managerial and administrative work in Canada, the United States, and Australia was over 40 percent female in 1993, well ahead of Japan (9 percent), Germany (19 percent), and Mexico (20 percent).[31] This selective comparison suggests that labour market and cultural barriers to women may be more resistant to change in some countries than in others.

However, a detailed analysis of the managerial and administrative category reveals that women are clustered in the least responsible and lowest-paying jobs. By reviewing detailed occupational titles contained in the 1991 Census, we learn that women accounted for 19 percent of general managers and other senior officials (see Table 4.2). Moreover, few women have entered management positions in natural sciences and engineering, or in the mining and oil sector—all economic activities dominated by men. Conversely, women managers are concentrated in predominantly female enclaves within organizations, such as office administration, personnel, and sales. A broader perspective on women in management is provided by Wallace Clement's and John Myles's crossnational study of class and gender relations in postindustrial societies. They document that, despite women having entered management in sizable numbers in North America and Europe, real power and decision-making authority is still exercised by male corporate executives and directors (Clement and Myles 1994: Chapter 6).

Women still encounter a *glass ceiling*—subtle barriers to advancement that continue to exist despite formal policies designed to eliminate such barriers. Looking at the 373 employers covered by the federal Employment Equity Act (discussed in more detail below), in 1995 women comprised 44 percent of the 587,400 employees. Yet close to two-thirds of these women worked in clerical jobs. And their representation in management ranks was inversely related to the authority and rewards of these positions. That is, women's representation in upper-level management was 14 percent, compared with 46 percent in

TABLE 4.2 *Average Employment Income of Full-Time, Full-Year Workers*[1] *in the Ten Highest-Paying Occupations, Canada, 1990*

	Men	Women	F–M earnings ratio	Total number employed	Number of women employed	Women as % of total
Judges and magistrates	$109,313	$79,204	72.5%	2,435	475	19.5%
Physicians and surgeons	111,261	73,071	65.7%	31,435	7,320	23.3%
Dentists	99,280	67,997	68.5%	6,775	760	11.2%
Lawyers and notaries	86,108	50,012	58.1%	41,180	10,430	25.3%
General managers and other senior officials	74,425	40,633	54.6%	129,225	24,580	19.0%
Other managers and administrators in mines, quarries, and oil wells	73,281	39,151	53.4%	3,870	950	24.5%
Air pilots, navigators, and flight engineers	66,087	31,026	46.9%	7,490	375	5.0%
Osteopaths and chiropractors	68,404	45,368	66.3%	2,470	440	17.8%
Management occupations, natural sciences and engineering	66,668	41,800	62.7%	14,305	1,785	12.5%
University teachers	65,671	49,000	74.6%	29,335	6,350	21.6%
Ten highest-paying occupations	79,463	48,609	61.2%	268,220	53,460	19.9%
Ten lowest-paying occupations	18,794	13,673	72.8%	235,455	170,230	72.3%
All other occupations	36,957	26,354	71.3%	7,215,105	2,795,195	38.7%

[1] A person who worked mostly 30 hours per week for 49 to 52 weeks in 1990. Athletes were in the top-ten paying occupations, but because of small numbers, their income statistics are not reliable and therefore are not reported here.

Source: Statistics Canada, "Average Employment Income of Full-Time, Full-Year workers in the Ten Highest Paying Occupations, Canada, 1990," adapted from "The Daily," Catalogue No. 11-001, April 13, 1993, page 11. Reprinted with permission.

middle management, and 63 percent among front-line supervisors. But equity policies have made a small difference, considering that in 1989 women made up only 6 percent of upper-level managers in this group of employers.[32] Still, it has been exceedingly difficult for women to gain entry into the executive suites of major corporations. Despite some recent appointments of women to the top corporate jobs of president, chief executive officer (CEO), or "chairman" (such as at Ford Motor Company of Canada and General Motors Canada), less than one percent of these posts are held by women, and only about 2 percent of corporate vice-presidents are women.[33]

In sum, although the evidence of wider employment horizons for women bodes well for the future, progress toward full gender equality in the workplace is halting and uneven. As Figure 4.6 illustrates, achieving this goal would

FIGURE 4.8 *Average Earnings in Constant (1995) Dollars for Full-Time/Full-Year* Workers, by Gender, Canada, 1969–1995*

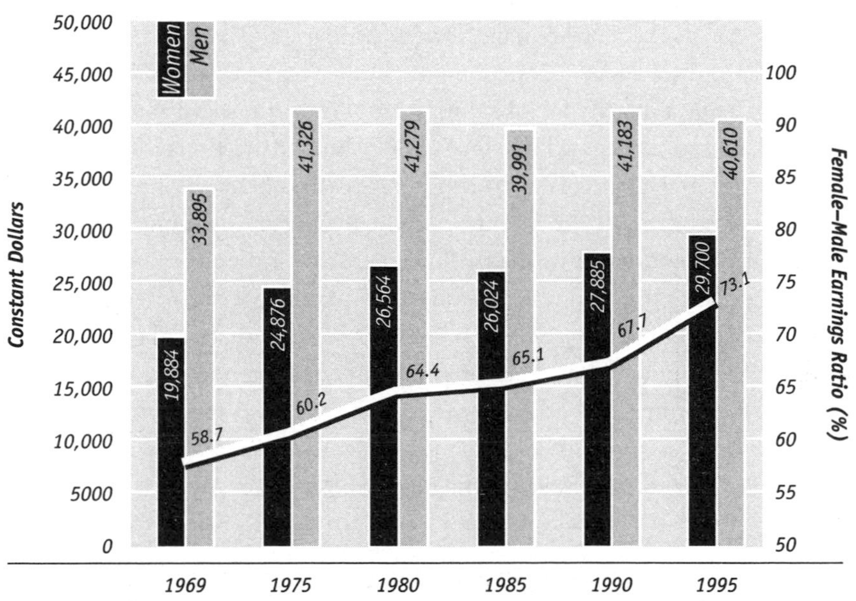

• A person who worked mostly 30 hours or more per week for 49 to 52 weeks in the reference year.

Source: Statistics Canada, "Average Earnings in Constant (1995) Dollars for Full-Time, Full-Year Workers, by Gender, Canada, 1969–1995," from "Earnings of Men and Women, 1995," Catalogue No. 13-217. Reprinted with permission.

see women represented in each occupation proportional to their overall share of the labour force, which is now at 45 percent. This immediately raises the question (which we address shortly) of how best to reach this objective. But would women want full access to all male jobs, given that a good number are dirty, dangerous, physically exhausting, insecure, low-paying, or at risk of being restructured out of existence? The implication, of course, is that unless all jobs at the bottom of the occupational hierarchy are upgraded in terms of pay and working conditions, gender equality as defined above would only be a partial advance for women.

THE WAGE GAP

One of the most obvious consequences of labour market segmentation is the *gender wage gap* (or female–male earnings ratio, as we labelled it in Chapter 3). Figure 4.8 shows that women who work full-time for the entire year earned an average of 73 percent of what similarly employed men earned in 1995. This is an accurate way to compare male–female earnings differences, because part-time or part-year workers, who have lower earnings and are disproportionately female, are not included. Despite women entering some of the higher-paying managerial and professional jobs during the 1980s, the wage gap has narrowed by less than 9 percentage points since 1980. This partly reflects the way in which employment growth trends often counteract each other. During the 1970s, the number of women in the twenty highest-paying occupations swelled more than fourfold, compared with a twofold increase for men (Boulet and Lavallee 1984: 19). But this trend was offset by an expansion of female employment at the lower end of the pay scale. While not used in our calculation of the wage gap, the big rise in the number of part-time jobs is important because it has reduced the earning potential of many women. This distinction between full- and part-time earnings reflects the growing employment disparities among women and between the sexes in the service economy.

Gender-Based Inequality of Earnings

Trends in earnings between 1975 and 1995 deserve brief comment. Figure 4.8 displays *real earnings,* which means that the effects of inflation have been eliminated by adjusting earnings for all years to 1995 dollars. This provides the startling realization that male earnings have actually declined somewhat since 1975, while women's earnings have nudged upward. Quite different labour market and organizational processes underlie these divergent earnings profiles. While women were being recruited into intermediate-level professions and junior and middle-level management, males were losing ground as traditionally well-paying (often unionized) manual occupations became less common and downsizing pushed older professionals and managers (mostly men) into early retirement. Within the labour market as a whole, some of men's loss was women's gain. A rising proportion of employed women, with incomes somewhat higher than the incomes of women a generation earlier, have kept family incomes from dropping as far as they otherwise might have. Without the wife's income, many husband–wife families now in the middle or working class would likely join the ranks of the poor.

Wages are a basic indicator of overall job quality. Recall from Chapter 3 that high wages also are part of a larger package of extrinsic and intrinsic job rewards. Stated simply, in addition to paying relatively well, "good jobs" usually offer other advantages: a range of benefits, job security, advancement opportunities, and interesting and challenging work. Turning to Figure 4.9, we find that female employees aged 25 to 54 are less likely than men in this age group to receive benefits. Paid sick leave is the only benefit not to show a major gender difference. Furthermore, 40 percent of female workers in 1994 were in nonstandard jobs, compared with 27 percent of men (Krahn 1995: 40). Men are also more likely to receive promotions. Jobs occupied by men tend to offer more decision-making authority, have higher skill requirements, and are less repetitive (Krahn 1992: 96). In short, the gender wage gap is part of a broadly based discrepancy between the quality of jobs performed by men and women.

Women's lower earnings also mean reduced living standards. In other words, women in Canada are more likely than men to be poor. Some 43 percent of families headed by employed women were living below the poverty line in 1995, compared with only 7 percent of dual-earner families with children.[34] Along with female lone-parents, women over the age of 65 are among the groups in Canadian society most vulnerable to poverty. In 1995, 51 percent of all elderly unattached women lived in poverty, mainly due to inadequate pensions. On the positive side, this is down from 72 percent in 1980 (Statistics Canada 1996b: 32–33).

FIGURE 4.9 *Job Benefits Received by Employees Aged 25 to 54, by Gender, 1995*

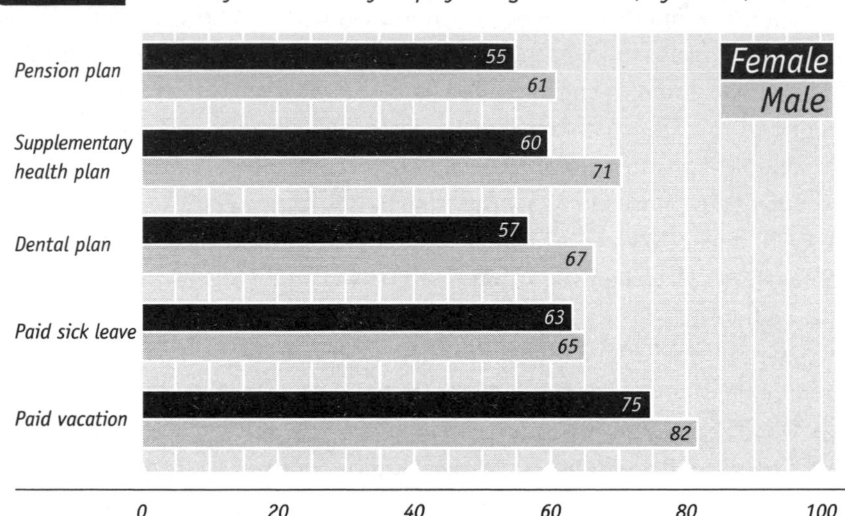

Source: Statistics Canada, "Job Benefits Received by Employees Ages 25–54, by Gender, 1995," from "1995 Survey of Work Arrangements," Catalogue No. 71M0013XDB. Reprinted with permission.

Shifting our focus from the bottom to the top of the income distribution, male and female earnings in the 10 highest-paying occupations are displayed in Table 4.2. First observe that the female–male earnings gap is somewhat greater in this top range of jobs (61 percent) than in other occupations (over 70 percent; also see Figure 4.8). The gap is narrowest for judges and magistrates (73 percent), and widest among pilots, navigators, and flight engineers (47 percent). Thus, in the most well-paying occupations, as elsewhere, women have a greater chance of receiving a lower salary. Of course, women who do succeed in entering Canada's top-paying occupations can expect to earn much higher incomes than women in other jobs. The average female income (for full-time, full-year workers) in the 10 highest-paying jobs was $48,609, compared with $13,673 in the 10 lowest-paying jobs, and $26,354 in all other occupations (Table 4.2). But we also need to note that all of the highest-paid occupations are male-dominated.[35] In fact, if we examine the list of Canada's 50 best-paid CEOs in 1995, we find that none were women.[36]

When interpreting such data, we must keep in mind that because of the quite recent entry of women into managerial and professional jobs, gender differences in age and experience will account for part of the earnings gap but by no means all of it. This is underscored when we examine earnings of recent university graduates. Studies comparing men and women who have identical university education, who are similar in age, and who have comparable work experience have found that a wage gap existed (albeit a small one) immediately after graduation.[37]

Accounting for Women's Lower Earnings

Two forms of discrimination affect female earnings. The first is *wage discrimination*, whereby an employer pays a women less than a man for performing the same job. The second stems from the gender-segregated structure of the labour market documented earlier. Occupational gender segregation results in lower female wages by channelling women into low-paying job ghettos which, in turn, provide few opportunities for mobility into more rewarding jobs.

To what extent does each form of discrimination contribute to the overall wage gap? To answer this question, one must look at an employee's education, training, and work experience, as well as at the occupation, industry, and geographic location of employment. These factors may influence a worker's productivity and, through this, his or her earnings. Research by Morley Gunderson, a labour economist, shows that when these productivity factors are taken into account (or are statistically controlled), the wage gap in Ontario is reduced from around 60 percent to between 75 and 85 percent.[38] Differences in work experience, combined with the segmented structure of the labour market, emerge as the main determinants of gender differences in earnings. Applying this analysis to men and women employed in the same jobs within a single establishment, the earnings ratio narrows even further to between 90 and 95 percent. In short, there is little direct pay discrimination by employers, at least in Ontario; rather, it is the division of the labour market into male and female jobs that creates pay inequality.

Human capital theory emphasizes that education is the great equalizer in the job market. Ideally, people with identical educational credentials should have the same amount of human capital and, therefore, be equally competitive in their earning power. But as Chapter 3 emphasized, human capital theory fails to explain why some individuals with equivalent education are much better paid. Nonetheless, education does matter. In post–World War II Canada, obtaining a good education has been a route to upward mobility for many young people, particularly males from working-class families.

Does the same hold true for women? There is little doubt that women have become better educated. Between 1975–1976 and 1988–1989, women's enrolments made up 73 percent of the increase in university enrolments in undergraduate degree programs.[39] Women also entered a wider range of programs during this period and more of them went on to graduate studies. Dramatic gains were made in male-dominated professional faculties, notably law and medicine. For instance, women received 51 percent of law degrees and 44 percent of degrees in medicine in 1993, representing huge increases from 9 percent and 13 percent, respectively, in 1971. However, women continue to be concentrated in education faculties; in 1993, education degrees accounted for 18 percent of all bachelor's degrees granted to women (compared with 8 percent of those granted to men).[40]

Professional training for science- and technology-based careers remains heavily male-dominated. For example, in 1993, only 18 percent of the students in Canadian engineering faculties were women.[41] The challenge of attracting more women into engineering was the focus of a study jointly sponsored by the federal government and the engineering profession. In its 1992 report, the Canadian Committee on Women in Engineering highlighted the complex social and cultural barriers that have obstructed women's way into engineering:

> The cultural influences that channel girls and young women away from non-traditional roles start with parents and other caregivers in pre-school years. Once in school, many girls and young women continue to be discouraged from pursuing interests in mathematics and science and from considering careers in engineering by teachers and guidance counsellors who are not sensitive to gender stereotyping. Because there are so few female science and mathematics teachers and even fewer women engineers to act as role models, young women are not likely to meet and interact with them. These influences are compounded by the perception that engineering is a male profession, that high grades are needed to succeed in engineering studies, and that engineers only build bridges and roads.[42]

Given that more women than ever before are graduating from university, a question worth considering is, have they been able to find the types of jobs for which they have been educated? Overall, a university education is a good predictor of higher occupational attainment for both women and men. However, this generalization requires careful qualification to account for the combined impact of gendered enrolment patterns, mentioned above, and occupational gender segregation. And, as also documented above, a well-educated woman cannot expect to earn as much as a comparably educated man. In short, human capital theory alone fails to explain the employment realities of Canadian female university graduates.

THEORETICAL PERSPECTIVES ON WORK-RELATED GENDER INEQUITIES

Our key question is, how has occupational gender segregation become so deeply entrenched? Once we can answer this, we will be better able to inform public policy discussions about strategies for achieving equality in the workplace. However, a comprehensive theoretical model capable of adequately explaining the origins, development, and perpetuation of work-related gender inequities has yet to be formulated. Feminist analysis has provided a necessary antidote to the long-standing male bias in much of the sociological research on work. Feldberg and Glenn characterized research in the 1970s in terms of *job* and *gender models* of the workplace. Studies of male workers focused on working conditions and organizational factors (the job model); explanations of women's employment discussed their personal characteristics and family roles (the gender model).[43] Since then, feminist debates about women's work have emphasized the necessity of integrating private and public spheres of domestic work and paid employment into a unified framework.[44]

Human Capital and Labour Market Segmentation Models

Nonetheless, most theories remain narrowly focused, dealing selectively with gender-role socialization, the family division of labour, the operations of the labour market, employee attitudes and behaviour in organizations, and so on. But the problem of occupational gender segregation is multifaceted, resulting from "the interaction of a well-entrenched and complex set of institutions that perpetuate the inferior position of women in the labour market, since all pressures within society, be they familial, legal, economic, cultural, or historical, tend to reinforce and support occupational segregation" (Reagan and Blaxall 1976: 2).

The two main competing theories of how labour markets operate are *human capital theory* and *labour market segmentation* (or *dual labour market) theory* (see Chapter 3). We have already criticized the human capital model for its inability to explain the persistence of gender segregation.[45] While the human capital model is concerned with factors influencing the characteristics of workers—the supply side of the labour market—the segmentation model examines how job requirements within organizations create a demand for particular kinds of workers. Labour market segmentation theory distinguishes between secondary and primary labour markets. Secondary labour markets are located in marginal, often uncompetitive industries that must struggle constantly to keep wages and operating costs down. In contrast, corporations and state bureaucracies in the primary sector can afford to provide employees with relatively high wages, decent benefits, job security, and pleasant working conditions. Furthermore, internal labour markets are found almost exclusively within the primary sector. Employers thus obtain a stable, committed workforce by providing employees with opportunities to develop careers within the organization.

For the segmentation model to accurately explain why men and women hold different kinds of jobs, women would have to be concentrated in the secondary segment of the labour market. This is partly true, since, it will be remembered, relatively more women than men are employed in lower-tier service industries, which form a large part of the secondary sector. However, critics point out that many women are also employed in job ghettos as typists, cleaners, or food servers within the primary sector. In short, an overly general segmentation perspective does not adequately account for gender differences in employment within the same industry or establishment, or inequalities among women. Moreover, the model cannot explain how gender segregation developed in the first place.[46]

Additional factors need to be considered in order to explain why gender is a major source of inequality in the labour market. Some researchers, for instance, link women's labour market position to their traditional roles within the family. Women's family roles have centred on activities such as raising children and caring for dependents; cooking, cleaning, and other services essential to enabling family members to hold down jobs; and contributing a secondary income to the family budget roughly in that order. Many employed wives experience a conflict when forced to choose between their job and their family. Their loyalty usually goes to the latter, and employers consequently often view these women as lacking commitment to their work. Barriers to interesting and better-paying jobs consequently persist.[47]

Gender Role Socialization

But how are employers' stereotypes of women, women's expectations and restricted employment opportunities, and women's family roles linked to their employment patterns within the workplace? Are such patterns best explained with reference to women's early socialization, including awareness of family roles and feminine qualities, or as a response to their employment conditions? Clearly, both processes may be involved.

The socialization of girls and boys into traditional gender roles creates cultural norms and expectations that will be carried by them into the workplace as adults. For example, a survey conducted in the early 1980s of children aged 6 to 14 in Ontario, Quebec, and Saskatchewan documented the effects of *gender-role socialization.* While the girls recognized the expanding occupational horizons of women, at a personal level they still held very traditional aspirations. As the researchers conclude: "Many seem to be saying 'Yes, women can become doctors, but I expect to be a nurse'" (Labour Canada 1986: 55). Further discussions with these girls revealed that when they imagined themselves as adults, most saw women who were mothers with small children, supported by a husband.

Have these attitudes changed? Our survey of 1996 Albertan grade 12 students shows that while gender role attitudes are becoming more egalitarian among youth—the vast majority of female and male respondents agree that a woman should have the same job opportunities as a man—more traditional work preferences continue to influence career choices. Nurse, social worker, and teacher were the popular career choices for females, compared with computer programmer/analyst, engineer, and auto mechanic for males.[48] As Jane Gaskell's research illuminates, the choices young working-class women make while they are in school, and upon leaving it, prepare them for domestic labour and employment in female job ghettos. Gaskell (1992: 134–35) explains that the young women whom she studied

> ... end up recreating the world they are not happy with. They see what men are like; they see what jobs pay and how one gets trained for them; they see the lack of child-care options. Within the world as they experience and know it, they do their best. The young men take their gender privilege equally for granted. The result is the reproduction of gender divisions, not because they are desired, but because these young people don't believe the world can be otherwise.

Gender Inequality and the Organization of Work

Also indispensable to an understanding of female work behaviour is how socialization patterns are strengthened and reproduced within the workplace. Rosabeth Moss Kanter's research suggests that the main sources of gender inequality must be located within work organizations. Kanter's (1977: 67) core argument is that "the job makes the person." She elaborates:

> Findings about typical behaviour of women in organizations that have been used to reflect either biologically based psychological attributes or characteristics developed through a long socialization to the female sex role turn out to reflect very reasonable and very universal responses to current organizational situations (Kanter 1977: 67).

In Kanter's view, then, men and women employed in similar jobs in an organization will react in similar ways to their job conditions. We return to this subject in Chapter 8.

A good example of this is Donald Roy's (1959–60) study of male machine operators. These men escaped the drudgery and isolation of their work—"kept from 'going nuts,'" in Roy's words—by engaging in idle chatter, playing games, and fooling around. Female key punch operators, file clerks, or assembly-line workers may seek similar relative satisfactions to cope with the numbing tedium of their work. In either case, management will use the coping behaviour as evidence that these workers are incapable of performing more demanding jobs. This creates a double bind for employees: the most effective ways of personally coping in jobs at the bottom of the organization are also indications to management that workers in these jobs deserve to be kept there.[49]

Kanter does not ignore possible gender differences in socialization or non-work roles. Rather, she underlines the pervasive influence of an individual's job content and organizational position on her or his attitudes and behaviour. This perspective is similar to what Pat and Hugh Armstrong (1994: Chapter 6) call the *materialist* explanation of the gendered division of labour. These researchers document the strong connection between women's self-perceptions and the kinds of work they do. The historical fact that men and women have performed different tasks in the home and in the labour force creates gender differences in work orientations. For example, women may be aware of their subordinate economic role, but they either rationalize it as an outcome of their domestic responsibilities, or else feel powerless to change it.

Gender is a potent controlling device within organizations. Male managers draw on social stereotypes of women as more oriented toward pleasing others, and therefore compliant, to devise paternalistic methods of supervision. Another dominant perception employers have is that women put their domestic responsibilities first, therefore devoting less effort and commitment to their employment. The assumption that women choose to allocate more effort to their domestic than to their employment roles is central to human capital theory's account of why women receive lower wages than men and have limited career opportunities. However, this myth was exploded by Denise Bielby and William Bielby, who document that women do not allocate less physical and mental energy to work than men. In fact, women are more efficient workers, given that the majority put greater effort into their work than men with similar attributes. This finding leads the researchers to suggest that women, therefore, should be preferred by employers.[50]

Kanter advances the analysis of gender divisions in organizations by showing how management is a social process that relies heavily on trust and conformity.[51] To reduce uncertainty in decision making—the essence of managerial activity—a premium is placed on recruiting individuals who are predictable. The best way to achieve this is to recruit only those people who have social characteristics identical to the existing group of managers. This social cloning reproduces male dominance in management and, moreover, creates an enormous barrier to women.

In sharp contrast, the role of the secretary is built on a combination of female stereotypes. Kanter uses the term *office wife* to describe the subordinate, paternalistic, and almost feudal relationship secretaries usually have with their male employers. The job becomes a trap through the dependency of managers on their secretaries and the personal loyalties that result. Many competent secretaries are not promoted because their good performance makes them indispensable to the boss. Unlike other positions in modern bureaucracies, there are no safeguards in place that would curb or restrict the exercise of managerial authority and the expectation that personal services, like fetching coffee, are part of the job. Because secretaries are often stuck in this role, their behavioural responses, such as self-effacement or timidity, may undermine advancement prospects.

Men who have more opportunities take advantage of them, developing behaviours, values, and work attitudes that help them do so. Once young male management trainees are identified as "fast trackers," the resulting halo effect creates the impression that they do not make mistakes and gives them the momentum to move up. Conversely, women in dead-end jobs quite rationally decide to give up, losing both work commitment and motivation. This signals to supervisors that such individuals do not deserve promotions or raises.

Women who succeed in entering management face the problem of *tokenism.* Kanter argues that a goldfish bowl phenomenon, resulting from being an identifiable minority, leads women or members of visible minorities to work harder to prove themselves. In turn, this confirms the dominant group's impression that these individuals are different and, therefore, do not belong. Furthermore, tokens lack the support systems so essential for surviving in the middle and upper ranks of organizations. But the problem is not sex or race, per se; rather, it is one of being part of a group disproportionately underrepresented in a particular environment. Other empirical research into tokenism concludes that it is limited to women in traditionally male occupations and, further, that by focusing on the imbalance in numbers as the causes of the problem, it deflects attention away from the more complex mechanisms of discrimination (Yoder 1991). However, Kanter's more general point still holds: the *structure of opportunities* in an organization—basically, who has access to which positions, resources, and rewards—tends to create self-fulfilling prophecies that only serve to reinforce the subordinate status of women.

Recent feminist analysis moves beyond Kanter's organizational focus by using gender as an explicit analytic category. While acknowledging that women's work experiences are shaped by organizational structure and power,

Rosemary Pringle's study of secretaries adds another crucial dimension: sexuality. Pringle (1989: 162) writes, referring to the boss–secretary relationship:

> Far from being marginal to the workplace, sexuality is everywhere. It is alluded to in dress and self-presentation, in jokes and gossip, looks and flirtations, secret affairs and dalliances, in fantasy, and in the range of coercive behaviours that we now call sexual harassment. Rather than being exceptional in its sexualization, the boss–secretary relation should be seen as an important nodal point for the organization of sexuality and pleasure.

By focusing on sexuality, researchers are able to advance our understanding of how employment relations and work structures contribute to defining "gender," both for men and for women. This new area of *gender studies* challenges us to rethink how masculinity, femininity, and heterosexuality are socially constructed categories reinforced by existing work institutions.[52]

On a larger scale, *sexual harassment* is the most draconian use of male power over women in the workplace. According to the 1993 national Violence Against Women Survey, 23 percent of Canadian women aged 18 and over had experienced some form of workplace sexual harassment, the most common being inappropriate comments about their bodies or sex lives.[53] The secretaries Pringle interviewed also confirmed that sexual harassment is quite pervasive and can drive women to quit jobs. Such harassment, or the fear of it, also deters women from entering nontraditional occupations, all the while reinforcing their subordinate status to men (Pringle 1989: 164).

ACHIEVING WORKPLACE EQUALITY

We have catalogued the inequities women face in terms of work opportunities and rewards. Some of the evidence leads to optimism that the stumbling blocks to equal labour–market opportunities and rewards are slowly being pushed aside. But the agenda of equality in employment can be achieved more effectively and sooner through bold public policy initiatives. This chapter will conclude by assessing two major policy thrusts: employment equity and pay equity. Unions too can play a decisive role in women's quest for greater workplace equality; their role will be examined in Chapter 7.

Employment Equity

The 1984 Royal Commission on Equality of Employment, also called the Abella Commission, defines *employment equity* as a strategy to eliminate the effects of discrimination and to fully open the competition for job opportunities to those who have been excluded historically. Four groups in Canadian society were identified as having been disadvantaged in terms of employment: visible minorities, persons with disabilities, Aboriginal peoples, and women. It is important to recognize that women do not constitute a homogeneous group. Indeed, we can speak of women who are also Aboriginal, or disabled, or members of a visible racial or ethnic minority as facing a double disadvantage. Focusing on women, the Abella Commission asserted that:

> ... equality in employment means first a revised approach to the role women play in the workforce. It means taking them seriously as workers and not assuming that their primary interests lie away from the workplace. At the same time, it means acknowledging the changing role of women in the care of the family by helping them and their male partners to function effectively both as labour force participants and as parents. And it means providing the education and training to permit women the chance to compete for the widest possible range of job options. In practice this means the active recruitment of women into the fullest range of employment opportunities, equal pay for work of equal value, fair consideration for promotions into more responsible positions, participation in corporate policy decision-making through corporate task forces and committees, accessible childcare of adequate quality, paid parental leaves for either parent, and pensions and benefits (Canada 1984: 4).

Far from advocating a workplace revolution, the Abella Commission articulated the growing belief that all individuals, regardless of their personal characteristics, should be treated fairly in recruitment, hiring, promotions, training, dismissals, and any other employment decisions. The commission provided the rationale for the federal 1986 Employment Equity Act by arguing that *systemic discrimination* creates employment barriers that can only be dismantled through strong legislation. Systemic discrimination is the unintentional consequence of employment practices and policies that have a differential effect on specific groups. This form of discrimination is built into the system of employment, rather than being the conscious intent of individuals to discriminate. For example, minimum height and weight requirements (using Caucasian males as the norm) for entry into police or fire departments have the effect of excluding women and members of certain visible minorities, even though this was not the intent.

The 1986 Employment Equity Act covers federal government employees, 370 federally regulated employers and Crown corporations, and employers that have 100 or more employees and bid on government contracts worth more than $200,000. The thrust of the act is twofold. First, it requires these employers to identify and remove employment practices that act as artificial employment barriers to the four *designated groups* (women, visible minorities, Aboriginal peoples, and the disabled). Second, it establishes targets and timetables for achieving a more representative workforce that will reflect the proportion of qualified and eligible individuals from designated groups in the appropriate labour pool (not in the entire population). As the preamble to the act spells out, the ultimate goal is "to achieve equality in the work place so that no person shall be denied employment opportunities or benefits for reasons unrelated to ability" (Canada 1985).

Employment equity policy also recognizes a need for positive measures that will rectify historic imbalances in staff composition (for example, special training programs for Aboriginal peoples) and the reasonable accommodation of differences (such as changing the RCMP's dress code to permit Sikhs to wear turbans and Aboriginal officers to have braids) to make workplaces more accessible and hospitable for a greater diversity of individuals. In this way, organizations are able to become more representative of the increasingly varied composition of Canadian society.

The Employment Equity Act requires employers to file annual reports showing their progress in recruiting and promoting members of the four designated groups. Generally, these reports are a testimony to the slow pace of change. However, recent research does provide a measure of success, suggesting that increased access for designated groups to professional, supervisory, and upper management positions has contributed to reducing the wage gap between these groups and white males.[54] Yet there is wide-ranging criticism of employment equity, to which the Special Committee of the House of

Commons that reviewed the act responded to by recommending stricter monitoring and enforcement; broadening the act to include more workplaces; greater employer commitment to the equity goals, timetables, and plans; and the establishment of a comprehensive national employment equity strategy.[55] Overcoming male resistance to gender equality in organizations and backlash against what some men view as the threat of feminism in action will require these measures and more.[56]

Stronger legislation may indeed speed progress toward equality. But what has brought a growing number of employers to realize that employment equity is good business is the fact that, despite current high levels of unemployment, labour shortages could be expected early in the twenty-first century. Employers are being confronted by the reality that women and members of the other three designated groups will comprise a large majority of new labour force entrants in coming years. Essentially, equity concerns are becoming a human resource management challenge. With respect to women, this is phrased in terms of making better use of their now underutilized talents.

At the forefront of this approach is the Bank of Montreal's 1991 Task Force on the Advancement of Women in the Bank (Bank of Montreal 1991). The task force examined how to correct the following imbalance: three-quarters of the bank's 28,000 employees are women, yet only 9 percent of executives and 13 percent of senior managers are women. The president of the bank committed the institution to the goal of gender equality in the following statement:

> I am convinced ... that establishing equality for our workforce is not just the right thing to do but the smart thing to do. It makes the best of business sense, especially in a world where balance has become a priority. The full participation of women in our enterprise is the giant step that will allow us to take the lead in that world. It will make us more creative and more competitive ... The glass ceiling is now officially smashed (Bank of Montreal 1991).

The task force exposed five dominant myths that had served to justify why women did not make it into senior management ranks: "They're too young or too old"; "they have babies and quit"; "they just need more education"; "they don't have the right stuff" (that is, they show weaker job performance); and "they'll catch up soon." By developing a thorough statistical profile of women and men in the bank, the task force demolished these misconceptions. A survey tapped employees' suggestions regarding how to promote women and help all staff balance multiple commitments to their job, family, community, and education. Employees' main suggestions included training in people development skills, internal posting of management vacancies, crosstraining between departments, flexible work hours, child-care assistance, and time off to care for sick dependents. To bring about the necessary organizational change, the bank has made managers accountable for meeting equity objectives. Starting in 1993, all managers set annual hiring, retention, and advancement goals for women, visible minorities, Aboriginal people, and people with disabilities. To ensure accountability, individual manager's performance appraisals evaluate their success in meeting these goals, as well as their general contributions to workplace equality (Bank of Montreal 1993).

Pay Equity

A related policy initiative is *pay equity*. Pay equity, or *comparable worth* as it is called in the United States, focuses specifically on the most glaring indicator of gender inequality in the labour market: the wage gap. Pay equity is a proactive policy, requiring employers to assess the extent of pay discrimination and then to adjust wages so that women are fairly compensated. Frequently a topic of heated public debate, pay equity recognizes that occupational gender segregation underlies the wage gap. It attempts to provide a gender-neutral methodology for comparing predominantly female jobs with predominantly male jobs that are in different occupational classifications under the same employer. For example, a secretarial job (female) would be compared with the job of maintenance technician (male) in the same organization. A standardized evaluation system assigns points to these jobs on the basis of their skill level, effort, responsibility, and working conditions.

Underpinning the process is the recognition that women's work is valuable but has been under-rewarded in the past. The objective is to pay employees on the basis of their contribution to the employer. This will establish *equal pay for work of equal value*, a more far-reaching concept than *equal pay for the same work*, which only compares women and men in the same (or "substantially similar") jobs. However, developing and applying a truly gender-neutral system for evaluating jobs has proved exceedingly difficult because it challenges long-standing assumptions about the nature of skill (Steinberg 1990).

Pay equity legislation or policies cover most public sector and some private sector employees.[57] Pay equity policies are explicit in their intent. As the British Columbia Public Sector Employers' Council states in the introduction to its pay equity policy: "Pay equity programs address the undervaluation of work traditionally or historically done by women. Employment equity initiatives are required to address other aspects of the wage gap including additudinal barriers and occupational segregation."[58] Opponents claim that the economy cannot afford the resulting wage increases, that some businesses may be driven into bankruptcy, or that it interferes with the operation of the labour market. But for millions of employed women, comparable worth may provide long overdue recognition of their economic contributions to society.

Pay equity legislation has gone some distance toward creating fairer, gender-neutral compensation schemes. One example of the successful implementation of pay equity is found in the Manitoba provincial government. Five thousand women employees received wage adjustments averaging 15 percent at a cost of 3.3 percent of the provincial civil service payroll.[59] Ontario pay equity legislation was heralded as the most comprehensive in North America. Yet loopholes, exclusions, and cumbersome procedures have muted its impact. For instance, casual workers and private-sector firms with fewer than 10 employees are exempted, as are women who are unable to find a suitable male job to use for comparison with their own in their place of employment.[60] Under the scrutiny of feminist analysis, the technical issues and problems of pay equity become the barriers to eliminating the gender wage gap and redefining the value of women's economic worth.[61] So while comparable worth policies cannot eliminate the female–male wage gap, they have contributed to closing it somewhat, and by increasing earnings at the bottom of the female earnings distribution, they also have benefited more than just middle-class women.[62]

Another policy instrument for achieving gender equality in employment is section 15 of the Canadian Charter of Rights and Freedoms. This section of the Charter became law in April 1985. It establishes for the first time in our history a constitutional entitlement to full equality for women in law, as well as in the effects of law. This latter point is a crucial one, for regardless of the wording or intent of a law, if in practice it results in discrimination against women, the courts could rule it to be unconstitutional. This legal process may gradually come to have an influence on gender inequality in the workplace.

CONCLUSION

We are beginning to rectify some of the most glaring problems women confront in the work world. The employment equity and pay equity programs now operating in Canada are reform oriented, aiming to modify existing employment institutions, values, processes, and social relationships. But how effective will workplace reforms be in altering women's traditional nonwork roles—especially within the family—and the supporting socialization processes and ideologies? The limitations of such reforms prompt some feminists, for example, to call for an eradication of the patriarchal relations underpinning the exploitation of women. Clearly any successful strategy must recognize that employment inequities are firmly embedded in the very structure and values of our society. So while we look for ways of reducing the impacts of patriarchy in our families, schools, and other institutions, we also need to continue to focus directly on the organizational barriers that stand in the way of gender equality in the workplace.

NOTES

1. The female labour force participation rate is the number of women in the paid labour force (employed, or unemployed and actively looking for work) divided by the female population 15 (14 prior to 1975) years of age and older. This calculation undervalues women's economic contribution because it overlooks unpaid household work.
2. The role of women in the fur trade is documented by Van Kirk (1980).
3. See Cohen (1988). Useful sources for women's history in Canada are Prentice and Trofimenkoff (1985), Strong-Boag and Fellman (1991), and the labour studies journal *Labour/Le Travail.*
4. Danysk (1995: 150) provides this quotation from a 1923 Prairie farm publication. Danysk's book provides a fascinating historical analysis of the gender construction of work roles in Prairie agriculture.
5. Lowe (1987: 47) presents data from the 1891 Census, the first to break down occupations by sex.
6. For historical background on the transformation of women's work inside and outside the home during the rise of industrial capitalism, see Cohen (1988), Bradley (1989), Armstrong and Armstrong (1994: Chapters 2–3).
7. On the family wage, see Humphries (1977), Land (1980), and Bradbury (1993: 80, and also Chapters 3 and 5). For a related discussion of how the norm of the "male breadwinner" has recently changed in working-class steelworker families in Hamilton, see Livingstone and Luxton (1996).
8. The 25-to-54 age group was chosen because it provides the most accurate crossnational comparison, given national differences in student employment and retirement behaviour.
9. These factors are discussed in Armstrong and Armstrong (1994: Chapter 6) and Jones, Marsden, and Tepperman (1990: Chapters 12). A comprehensive source for trends related to female employment is Statistics Canada (1994c).

10. On lone mothers in the workforce, see Crompton (1994). See Schellenberg and Ross (1997) for a detailed analysis of the working poor in Canada.
11. See Canadian Council on Social Development (1996) and National Council of Welfare (1997).
12. Rashid's (1994: 48) analysis of the top percentile of all families shows that wives in these families had incomes four times greater that the average for all wives, and that without this income 57 percent of these families would not reach the top income percentile. Statistics Canada's National Longitudinal Survey of Children and Youth revealed that, in 1994, 1 in 6 children under the age of 12 lived in lone-mother families, and that these children face far more disadvantages than those in two-parent families (*Canadian Social Trends*, 1997: 7–9).
13. For differing perspectives on patriarchy, compare Johnson (1996), Walby (1990), Hartmann (1976), and Lerner (1986).
14. This post–World War II pattern is described in Ostry (1968). Also see Canada (1958).
15. Logan and Belliveau (1995: 25). This article examines employment among mothers.
16. Statistics Canada, *The Daily* (7 July 1992). Also see Crompton (1994).
17. Hochschild (1989). See Harvey et al. (1991) for a Canadian time-budget study using the General Social Survey.
18. Meissner et al. (1975). For studies of the household division of labour, see Luxton (1980) and Pupo (1997).
19. Marshall (1993: 12). Data are from the 1990 General Social Survey (GSS). As a note of caution, there is some bias in how the GSS measures housework, because one respondent (either male or female) reported their perceptions of who was responsible for which tasks.
20. McKinnon and Odynak (1991: 12); on the need for elder-care policies, see Alvi (1995).
21. Alberta Government, Personnel Administration Office (July 1991).
22. On the changing role of fatherhood and how some men are trying to integrate work and family, see Gerson (1993) and Coltrane (1996). Organizations implementing work-family policies often promote them not just as a women's program, but of benefit to male employees too.
23. For a review of work and family policies in Canada, see Skrypnek and Fast (1996). For a detailed analysis of the U.S. situation, see Spain and Bianchi (1996).
24. See Feuchtwang (1982: 251) for a definition of *job ghetto.* Freedman (1976) discusses the concepts of labour market segments and shelters (see Chapter 3, above, on these concepts).
25. For a fuller discussion of sex labelling, see Lowe (1987).
26. For an overview of the feminization of clerical work, see Lowe (1987).
27. Hughes (1990; 1995). Traditional occupations are those in which women comprise a greater proportion of employment than they do in the labour force as a whole.
28. This paragraph draws on Marshall (1987, 1989). Marshall defines professions as occupations in which 45 percent or more of employees have at least a bachelor's degree. Male-dominated professions are those which were 65 percent male in 1971. Using this methodology, 46 occupations were classified as professional, 34 of which were male-dominated.
29. Statistics Canada (1994c: 20). On the nursing profession, see Sedivy-Glasgow (1992) and Armstrong, Choiniere, and Day (1993).
30. On women in medicine in Canada, see Gorham (1994). Also see Hagan and Kay (1995) for a detailed study of gender issues in Canadian lawyers' careers.

31. International Labour Office (1995: Table 3C). This category includes managers, legislative officials, and government administrators. German data are for 1991. Sweden's classification is not comparable in the 1990s, but 1989 data show that women comprised 64 percent of managers and administrators (ILO, 1991: Table 2B).

32. Data are from annual employment equity reports filed by the employers. Human Resources Development Canada (1996a: Table 5); Employment and Immigration Canada (1990: 33).

33. Based on a survey of *Financial Post 500* corporations. Canadian Labour Market and Productivity Centre (1994: 41). This is a useful report on the impact of economic restructuring on women. *Report on Business Magazine* (July 1997: 67–69) lists the female CEOs of Ford and GM as among the 25 most powerful CEOs in Canada.

34. Statistics Canada (1996b: 33). See National Council of Welfare (1997: 5) on poverty lines in Canada.

35. Calculated by dividing the percentage of employment in this group of occupations made up of women (19.9 percent) by women's share of the total labour force in 1990 (45 percent).

36. *Report on Business Magazine* (July 1996: 83–84); the total 1995 compensation packages of these 50 men ranged from $1.1 million to $13 million.

37. Using the National Graduate Survey, Davies et al. (1996) found a rise in the female–male earnings ratio between 1978 and 1988 from 84 to 91 percent (or stated differently, a closing of the wage gap). Also see Wannell and Caron (1994); Hughes and Lowe (1993).

38. The literature on the wage gap is reviewed by Gunderson (1989a); also see Gunderson (1994). For a more sociological analysis, see Coverman (1988).

39. Labour Canada (1990b: 69–70); refers to bachelor's and first professional degree programs.

40. Refers to undergraduate and first professional degrees. Statistics Canada (1996a: Table 36).

41. Ibid.

42. Canadian Committee on Women in Engineering (1992: 1). On the male culture of engineering see Hacker (1989) and McIlwee and Robinson (1992: Chapter 6).

43. See Feldberg and Glenn (1979). Also see Acker (1988), Beechy (1987), and Calás and Smircich (1996) for critical discussions of the male biases in the sociological study of work and organizations.

44. Various feminist approaches to understanding work are critically assessed by Tancred (1995) and Armstrong and Armstrong (1994). Also see Reskin and Padavic (1994) for a comparative and historical perspective on gender and work.

45. On human capital explanations of sex differences in occupations and earnings, see Blau and Ferber (1986: Chapter 7).

46. For critical discussions of occupational gender segregation, see Siltanen (1994), Phillips and Phillips (1993: Chapter 4), and Armstrong and Armstrong (1990: Chapter 1). Hagan and Kay (1994) critically utilize human capital theory and a more general version of labour market segmentation theory in their study of gender inequalities in the legal profession. Developments in the measurement of occupational gender segregation and the underlying factors are discussed in Rubery and Fagan (1995) and Blackburn, Jarman, and Siltanen (1993).

47. See Garnsey et al. (1985) for this argument.

48. Unpublished data from the 1996 Alberta High School Graduate Survey. Virtually all females (97 percent) and 85 percent of males agreed or strongly agreed with the statement "a woman should have the same job opportunities as a man." Career choices and other study findings are presented in Lowe, Krahn, and Bowlby (1997).

49. For an interesting discussion of the significance of workplace conversations about household work, see Hessing (1991).

50. Bielby and Bielby (1988). Hagan and Kay (1994: 185) make a similar point regarding female lawyers.

51. For a summary of related research, see Powell (1993).

52. The growing area of *mens' studies* examines the social construction of masculinity in work and unemployment (Morgan, 1997); on sexuality and power in organizational life, see Hearn, Sheppard, Tancred-Sheriff, and Burrell (1989).

53. Johnson (1994: 11). Six percent of employed women 18 years of age and over reported sexual harassment in the 12 months prior to the survey, which was conducted by Statistics Canada. Also see Collinson and Collinson (1996) and Giuffre and Williams (1994) for case studies of sexual harassment of women insurance managers and restaurant workers, respectively.

54. Leck, St. Onge, and Lalancette (1995). The study examined 1989–1993 changes in full-time earnings in all organizations covered by the Employment Equity Act.

55. Canada (1992). For a critical analysis of the act, see Canadian Advisory Council on the Status of Women (1992) and Lum (1995). For a summary of the annual equity reports filed under the act, see Human Resource Development Canada (1996).

56. Resistance to equity policies by males and managers (often the same) and the organizational barriers to the elimination of discrimination are analyzed by Cockburn (1991) and Collinson, Knights, and Collinson (1990). Wallace (1995) analyzes resistance to employment equity policy at the University of Alberta.

57. Pay equity laws, policies, or collective agreements negotiated with unions are in place in most provinces and federal jurisdictions, except the Northwest Territories and Alberta. Under the former New Democratic government, Ontario had the most far-reaching pay equity legislation, but the present Conservative government wants to repeal this law, even though employers favour reform rather than outright repeal. *The Globe and Mail* (23 June 1995: B6).

58. British Columbia Public Sector Employers' Council (1995: 1–2).

59. Weiner and Gunderson (1990: Chapter 10). This outlines the methodology of pay equity and its application across Canada. For a comparative perspective see Gunderson (1994).

60. Neale (1992). Under the former New Democratic government, Ontario extended pay equity into the private sector, but the present Conservative government intends to repeal this law, even though employers favour reform rather than outright repeal. *The Globe and Mail* (23 June 1995: B6).

61. See the critique of pay equity in Fudge and McDermott (1991). Quaid (1993) offers a critical analysis of the job evaluation system used in pay equity.

62. Simulations of the U.S. economy show that the wage gap would close 8 to 20 percent if comparable worth was nationally applied (Gunderson, 1994: 111). Figart and Lapidus (1996) provide a more positive evaluation, showing that such policies would generally contribute to reducing earnings inequality between the sexes and among women. However, other researchers suggest that the closing of the wage gap (at least in the United States) is in large part due to the increasing polarization of white male earnings (Bernhardt, Morris, and Handcock, 1995).

5 THE ORGANIZATION AND MANAGEMENT OF WORK

INTRODUCTION

We live in an organizational society (Presthus 1978). Large bureaucratic organizations touch all aspects of our daily lives. Attending school, buying weekly groceries, negotiating a student loan, volunteering at our community foodbank, or watching our favourite TV program are activities that bring us into contact with formal organizations. Even more important, at least from the perspective of an industrial sociologist, are the organizations in which people work. In this chapter, we examine the organization and management of work, sampling selectively from an enormous and diverse literature on organizational analysis and management theory and practice.

Work organizations vary greatly in size, function, and structure. An individual's perceptions of a work organization will differ, depending on his or her vantage point within it. While a manager or executive may assess a particular work organization in terms of efficiency or profitability, other employees may use totally different criteria. Given these variations in the objective features and subjective experiences of work organizations, a number of interrelated questions can be asked.

First, what are the major factors that determine the structure—that is, the patterned regularities of work organizations? Second, looking specifically at process, how are organizations transformed over time? To what degree is organizational change a response to a changing external environment, or to internal forces? Third, how much do the actions and beliefs of managers, employees, and other groups such as clients and customers influence the form, goals, and internal dynamics of an organization? Finally, our discussions of bureaucracy, the division of labour, managerial authority, work groups, and organizational cultures raise a further question: what are the possibilities for reforming work organizations?

Managers have played a key role in constructing modern organizations, mainly because they make critical decisions about goals, structure, personnel, and technology. We will therefore examine various schools of management, including some of the latest management literature, and discuss the current fascination with the Japanese approach to management. This chapter's focus on mainstream organization and management literature is reflected in the prominence given to the themes of *consensus* and *integration*. Then, in Chapter 6, we present a more critical perspective on organizations and management, focusing on the themes of power, control, resistance, and conflict. While some of the basic problems of organizing and managing work in a capitalist economy will be introduced here, a more systematic critique appears in the next chapter.

WHAT'S WRONG WITH BUREAUCRACY?

As we saw in Chapter 1, a major step along the road to industrialization was the division of craftwork into simpler components. Less skilled labourers could then perform each of these narrow tasks more cheaply. But once all the parts of a craftworker's job had been simplified and reassigned, coordinating and integrating these tasks became a problem. This helps to account for the role of managers, who, since the late nineteenth century, have become central actors in most work organizations. Questions about how best to integrate and coordinate the activities of large numbers of workers within a single enterprise gave rise to early theories of management.

Weber, Bureaucracy, and Capitalism

The organizational structure adopted by nineteenth-century businesses was the bureaucratic hierarchy. As we have already seen, Max Weber considered *bureaucracy* to be the organizational form best able to efficiently coordinate and integrate the multitude of specialized tasks conducted in a big factory or office. Without bureaucracy, he predicted, "capitalist production could not continue."[1] Although he described the general features of bureaucracy, Weber did not intend to present a practical guide for managers on how it should be organized. Nevertheless, his description has become the model for a highly mechanistic type of organization. Gareth Morgan defines bureaucratic organizations as those "that emphasize precision, speed, clarity, reliability, and efficiency achieved through the creation of a fixed division of tasks, hierarchical supervision, and detailed rules and regulations."[2]

No doubt bureaucracies were an improvement over the tradition-bound "seat of the pants" methods used in running most nineteenth-century businesses. Their predictability greatly increased the productivity of industrial capitalism. Furthermore, a bureaucracy is a system of authority. Its hierarchical structure, formal lines of authority, and impartial rules and regulations are designed to elicit cooperation and obedience from employees. Given that bureaucracies have a highly specialized division of labour, which can also lead to increased productivity, it would seem that bureaucratic work organizations are ideal.

The Ills of Bureaucracy

All things considered, most sociologists would agree that bureaucracies have serious flaws. Organizational researchers have amassed considerable evidence showing that bureaucracies are often overly complex and, therefore, difficult to manage, resistant to change, and unable to cope with uncertainties. Working conditions in bureaucracies are frequently unsatisfying, as we will show in Chapter 8.[3] Furthermore, a paradox of bureaucracy is that, far from achieving machine-like efficiency, it often unintentionally creates inefficiency, a problem Weber largely failed to see (Albrow 1970: 66).

This point is underlined in many of the classic studies of bureaucracy. For example, Robert Merton described how employees who slavishly obey the rules could undermine the efficiency of a bureaucracy (Merton 1952). The rules become ends in themselves, rather than the means of achieving organizational goals. Officials acquire a *bureaucratic personality*, compulsively following procedural manuals to the last detail. Similarly, Peter Blau's fieldwork in American government agencies revealed how workers behaved according to their own unofficial rules.[4] In doing so, they were directly responding to organizational pressure to attain certain goals, such as handling a quota of clients or cases in a given period. Blau identified the tension between the official rules of the bureaucracy and workers' counter-rules. By striving to make their jobs easier, employees often erode bureaucratic efficiency.

Another example is Alvin Gouldner's (1954) classic study of an American gypsum plant. He argues that organizational life cannot be made as fully predictable as the bureaucratic model would suggest. Events such as promotions, layoffs, or dismissals are unpredictable. Moreover, rules reducing uncertainty for management may be a major source of discontent among employees. In fact, Gouldner argues, often the bureaucratization process is implemented not for reasons of greater efficiency, but as a result of power struggles between workers and managers. In short, there is nothing inevitable about bureaucracy; rather, its many faces reflect the shaky balance of power between workers and managers within an organization.

The notion of bureaucratic efficiency rests, in part, on the assumption that employees will readily submit to *managerial authority*. In Weber's view, bureaucrats accept the legitimacy of the existing authority structure, abide by the rules, and obey their bosses because they believe the basis for such authority is impartial and fair. Underlying capitalist bureaucracies is a *rational–legal value system*. However, the assumption that there is general acceptance of goals is contradicted by the realities of employee–employer relations, which are punctuated by conflict and resistance.

People in positions of power set organizational goals. These goals are, therefore, "rational" from management's perspective, but not necessarily from the perspective of workers. What is rational for them is what reflects their own interests, such as higher pay, a safer and more comfortable work environment, or more scope for making work-related decisions. These goals are often in conflict with those of management. Hence, conflicts over the distribution and use of decision-making power are normal.[5] This line of inquiry will be pursued further in Chapter 6.

Weber's model of bureaucracy neglects employee resistance to such authority. As we will also see below, resistance can frequently be detected in workers' informal group norms and codes of conduct that run counter to the official systems of production. Not surprisingly, a major concern of management has been to find ways of gaining worker cooperation. Managers have gone to great lengths to convince workers to accept organizational goals as their own personal goals, and to justify their decisions to those below them. The development of *management ideology* justifying superior rewards and the right to give orders is part of this process. Reinhard Bendix (1974: 13) explains: "All economic enterprises have in common a basic social relation between the employers who exercise authority and the workers who obey, and all ideologies of management have in common the effort to interpret the exercise of authority in favourable light."

Bureaucracy and Fordism

As an organizing principle, the bureaucratic hierarchy was integrated with technology to create the huge factories that formed the backbone of industrial capitalism. When Henry Ford introduced the moving assembly line in 1914, launching the era of mass-production manufacturing, he was building on the machine-like logic of bureaucratic organization. *Fordism*, based on assembly-line mass production, combined technology with bureaucracy to shape twentieth-century work and economic growth.

Robert Reich (1991), in *The Work of Nations*, provides a trenchant critique of Fordism. Reich's treatise ranges over the sprawling terrain of the emerging global economy, which has shifted the locus of economic activity (as we documented in Chapter 1) from goods production to services. The key to prosperity used to be large volume production in giant factories by corporations that dominated world markets. In the global marketplace of the 1990s, the distinction between goods and services is blurred. Specialized expertise in finance, research and development, and marketing adds value to products and responds to constantly changing market needs. Furthermore, service and production networks tie together working units that are scattered across many countries.

Reich's portrayal of post–World War II corporate America is an indictment of all that is wrong with Fordism and bureaucracy. It is also a recipe for how not to organize work in the new global economy:

> America's corporate bureaucracies were organized like military bureaucracies, for the efficient implementation of preconceived plans. It is perhaps no accident that the war veterans who manned the core American corporations of the 1950s accommodated so naturally to the military-like hierarchies inside them. They were described in much the same terms as military hierarchies—featuring chains of command, spans of control, job classifications, divisions and division heads, and standard operating procedures to guide every decision. When in doubt go by the book. All jobs were defined in advance by pre-established routines and responsibilities. Organization charts graphically mapped out internal hierarchies, starting with a large box at the top containing the chief executive officer, and proceeding downward through levels of ever smaller and more abundant boxes. As in the military, great emphasis was placed upon the maintenance of control—upon a superior's ability to inspire loyalty, discipline, and unquestioning obedience, and upon a subordinate's capacity to be so inspired (Reich 1991).

In short, the triumph of Western industrial capitalism was founded on what is now becoming recognized as an outmoded model of organization and management. This is a leading theme in the new management literature we review below. As Danny Miller (1990) suggests in *The Icarus Paradox*, the life cycle of North American corporations resembles the character Icarus from Greek mythology, who flew so high that the sun melted the wax on his wings and he fell to the sea and drowned. The moral: the strengths of the traditional bureaucratic and Fordist organization have become the source of its downfall.

THEORETICAL PERSPECTIVES ON ORGANIZATIONS

Organizational theory offers a range of perspectives from which to analyze the structure, functions, and dynamics of organizations. This section will touch on the following major theoretical currents in this rich literature: contingency theory, organic models, sociotechnical systems, and strategic choice. Some of these ideas will resurface later in the chapter—for example, the sociotechnical model in our discussion of work redesign, and strategic choice in our discussion of managerial decision making. A newly emerging theoretical interpretation of the changes reshaping organizational life comes from the application of postmodernist theories. As we will see, this critique of conventional organizational theory shares common elements with the much more practically oriented new management literature. The Marxist-inspired radical critique of organizations, itself a distinct perspective, will form part of our exploration of conflict, control, and power in Chapter 6.

Structures, Systems, Strategies

The weaknesses and gaps in the Weberian model of bureaucracy have led to alternative theories of organizations. Weber's thesis that a bureaucratic structure is most appropriate for any type of capitalist economic activity has been largely replaced by *contingency theory.* It proposes that organizational structures and processes are contingent upon the immediate problems posed by their environment. There is no single best way to organize or to manage work. A basic question guiding organizational research today is, what structures and strategies does a particular organization require to survive?[6]

The many possible answers to this question are typically based on an organic model, which views organizations as social systems adapting to internal and external changes. This conventional view of organizations as adapting social systems is grounded in the general sociological theory of *structural functionalism.* Hence, there is an emphasis on goal attainment, functions, structural adaptations, and a value consensus among organizational members. Conventional organization theory has been criticized for being too concerned with structure, per se, and, as a result, losing sight of the larger socioeconomic, political, and historical context of which organizations are a part. Other weaknesses include ignoring the attitudes and behaviours of employees (the informal side of organizations discussed later in this chapter), and glossing over the realities of workplace power and conflict (see Chapter 6).[7] Nonetheless, some useful insights about organizations can be found in this empirical literature.

For example, in the 1950s, Burns and Stalker studied synthetic fibre, electronics, and engineering industries, proposing a continuum of organizational forms from the *mechanistic* (or highly bureaucratic) to the *organic.* More open and flexible organizational structures and management styles were required, they concluded, in industries with rapidly changing technologies and market conditions (Burns and Stalker 1961). Joan Woodward's studies revealed a direct relationship between production technology, on the one hand, and structural forms and management styles on the other. She concluded that bureaucracy and tight management controls are more appropriate in industries with mass production technology. When the workflow is varied, and production processes are nonroutine and complex—as in craft or continuous process technologies—more flexible, organic structures function best (Woodward 1980).[17]

Woodward's research attests to the importance of technology as a key variable in organizational analysis. The concept of a *sociotechnical system*, introduced by researchers at London's Tavistock Institute of Human Relations, takes this idea one step further. In their study of the mechanization of British coal mining, Trist and Bamforth documented how social relations in teams of miners were dependent on the technology used.[8] When the traditional hand method of mining was replaced by mechanical conveyer belts, thus destroying the technical basis for the work teams, the negative social–psychological consequences for workers hampered the operations of the new system. Consequently, the notion of optimizing the fit between social and technical aspects of production has become an important principle in work design.

There is a tendency in this literature to *reify* organizations, that is, to discuss them as if they had a life of their own, independent of the actions and decisions of their members. So, we should remember that organization theory is largely about decision making. Given the constraints of technology, markets, government regulations, labour negotiations, and so on, what are the most appropriate choices for managers to make? This issue is taken up by the *strategic choice perspective* on organizations.[9] In contrast to contingency theory's emphasis on environmental and other constraints imposed on decision making, the concept of strategic choice draws our attention to the ways in which dominant groups (coalitions) actually choose among various strategies for structuring an organization, manipulating its environment, and establishing work standards. To fully comprehend the nature of work organizations, we must examine the guiding theories, actual practices, and supporting ideologies of management.

Despite the persistence of these established approaches, organizational theory is evolving. As Chapter 4 documented, feminist researchers have effectively challenged the one-sided male perspective traditionally found in organizational literature, illuminating how workers' experiences in bureaucracies depend on their gender.[10] The latest attempt to recast it comes from *postmodernism*. This emergent perspective on organizations touches on the major trends reshaping the workplace, thereby contributing to the debate about the nature of post-industrial society. According to this critique, organization theory was the product of *modernity*—the age of the bureaucracy and the assembly line (Clegg 1990; Cooper and Burrell 1988). The driving force was rationality and an increasing division of labour, and everything that flowed from these principles. *Postmodernity* (to risk simplifying an elaborate theory) in organizational life is marked by less differentiation and more unpredictability (Lash 1990). Stewart Clegg argues that a postmodernist view of organizations is more consistent with the assumptions of contemporary North American management writers, reviewed below, or Japanese-style management. Clegg (1990: 181) explains the basic distinction between modernist and postmodernist organizations this way:

> Where modernist organization was rigid, postmodern organization is flexible. Where modernist consumption was premised on mass forms, postmodernist consumption is premised on niches. Where modernist organization was premised on technological determinism, postmodernist organization is premised on technological choices made possible through "de-dedicated" microelectronic equipment. Where modernist organization and jobs were highly differentiated, demarcated and de-skilled, postmodernist organization and jobs are highly de-differentiated, de-demarcated and multi-skilled.

Change Strategies

There is much talk in the management literature about strategic planning in organizations. While reminiscent of strategic choice theory, mentioned above, strategic planning is intended to have a more practical thrust by helping managers to achieve specific goals. Still, it raises sociological questions about how managers (individually or as a group) are able to influence an organization's performance and shape its future. Certainly the new management literature assumes that conscious decisions and strong leadership form the basis of survival strategies. But as Henry Mintzberg (1994) argues, managers have not learned from the failures of strategic planning. The problem with strategic planning, according to Mintzberg, has been its formalization of the planning process, which stifles strategic thinking about creative alternatives and visions for the future of the organization. This is yet another example of how bureaucratic procedures can inhibit innovative behaviour in organizations.

The organization theory literature defines strategy as "a plan for interacting with the competitive environment to achieve organizational goals" (Daft 1995: 45–49). But, as sociologists David Knights and Glenn Morgan (1990) argue, at issue is whether organizations really act according to strategic plans, or whether these plans are post hoc explanations by social scientists trying to make sense of organizational changes and power structures. Strategy, they suggest, is primarily a mechanism of power. To understand it, we must uncover how corporate strategic plans are rooted in power relations and serve to reproduce existing organizational hierarchies and inequities. While it is difficult to know whether a particular strategy actually makes a difference, one can more safely assume that it has the implicit effect of "transforming managers and employees into committed goal-oriented and self-disciplined subjects" (Knights and Morgan 1990).

Understanding Organizational Change

The difficulties of strategic planning reflect the larger challenges of organizational change. How do organizations change? Observing that organizational turmoil became the norm in the 1980s, Bob Hinings and Royston Greenwood (1988) argue that it is essential to recognize and manage change. Their research on local governments in Britain focuses on "strategic organizational design change," which is change that signals a fundamental shift in the orientation of the organization. Their study emphasizes that change and stability are two sides of the same coin. Theoretically, Hinings and Greenwood introduce the concept of a *design archetype* to describe an organization's structure, management system, and supporting beliefs and values. They also suggest that organizations can be classified according to *tracks*. The metaphor of a track captures the extent of change occurring, specifying whether an organization remains within one design archetype over time or moves between archetypes.

Hining's and Greenwood's theory is intended to account for both successful and unsuccessful attempts at organizational redesign. Because recent years have seen a marked increase in organizational decline, this process has become the subject of considerable research. Reviewing this new area of study, William

Weitzel and Ellen Jonsson (1989: 95) distinguish between decline on the one hand and cutbacks and retrenchment on the other. The root cause of decline is the failure of organizations "to anticipate, recognize, avoid, neutralize, or adapt to external or internal pressures that threaten the organization's long-term survival."[11] Thus, the scholarly research on organizational change equips us with analytic concepts for assessing the kinds of reforms now being proposed for work organizations.

Technology has, historically, precipitated huge changes in the organization of work, as we saw in Chapter 1. To more fully understand technological change, it is useful to view it as a process of managerial decision making. This helps to demystify technology by showing how it too reflects organizational and human constraints and choices. John Child (1985) identifies four goals that managers have when they introduce new technology: reducing costs and boosting efficiency; increasing flexibility; quality improvements; and greater control over operations. These goals, which often overlap, are "evolving" and the end results may not be predictable. From this perspective, the same computer hardware or software will, for example, have a varying impact on workers depending on how managers pursue these goals.

However, this view credits managers with too much conscious planning and control. Various case studies underscore major organizational and human constraints on management's ability to plan and implement technological change. The complexity of new technology invariably requires attendant organizational change and job redesign—a tough challenge. Moreover, the full potential of automation cannot be realized without recognition of the human dimension. Only by involving workers in planning and implementing new technology, and giving them the responsibility to operate it, will there be a smooth transition. For instance, often workers' detailed knowledge of old systems is indispensable to making new technology function.[12] Shoshana Zuboff's (1988: 389) conclusion, drawn from her study of several high-tech firms, aptly expresses the contingent and often unpredictable quality of technological change:

> Even where control or deskilling has been the intent of managerial choices with respect to new information technology, managers themselves are also captive to a wide range of impulses and pressures. Only rarely is there a grand design concocted by an elite group ruthlessly grinding its way toward the fulfillment of some

special and secret plan. Instead, there is a concentration of forces and consequences, which in turn develop their own momentum.

THE ROLE OF MANAGERS

We have alluded to the key role managers have in organizing and regulating work, but exactly what do managers do? We know that within any hierarchical organization authority resides at the top. This gives rise to one of the most vexing problems confronting management: how to obtain employee compliance and prevent opposition to authority. In this respect, the workplace is a microcosm of the larger society. Maintaining orderly and harmonious social relations among people who are not equals has always been a problem for those in power.[13] Another pressing concern involves motivating workers to achieve the quantity and quality of output considered necessary by management. Employers do not have complete control over the amount of effort expended by employees (Baldamus 1961). Hence, conflict often erupts over different perceptions of the right amount of effort given a specific wage and work situation. Obviously these concerns—accentuated in periods of rapid economic change—constitute much of the work of managers.

Management Ideology and Practice

Managers became a prominent new social group in the early twentieth century, whose importance lay in their helping to shape the course of economic development. *Cost accounting* techniques for calculating how much each factor of production, including labour, contributes to profits was one way capitalists initially tackled the problems of running increasingly large and complex enterprises. Appointing trained managers, often factory engineers, in the late nineteenth century was an equally important social innovation. As business historian Alfred D. Chandler Jr. suggests, the visible hand of the corporate manager replaced the "invisible hand" of market forces (Chandler 1977; Pollard 1968). Corporate boards of directors, representing the shareholders, delegated to managers the authority to operate the business profitably. Recall from Chapter 1 that this growing power of managers and the separation of corporate ownership from daily control functions has been labelled the *managerial revolution.* In striving to meet their broad mandate, managers undoubtedly have transformed the organization and control of work.

In considering the evolving role of managers, it is important to distinguish among *ideology, theory,* and *practice.*[14] Management ideologies, we noted earlier, are used to justify existing authority relations in organizations. Joseph Smucker's research shows how Canadian managerial ideologies have undergone several shifts since 1900. The self-perception of managers moved away from that of autonomous achieving individuals to one of organizational team workers, while managers' image of workers was transformed from recalcitrants to associates (Smucker 1980: 163). A succession of theories influenced by these views has attempted to specify how to manage. But these theories are merely prescriptions for action.

Henry Mintzberg's distinction between "folklore" and fact is a useful way of deciphering what managers actually do. The words that supposedly guide managers are, he argues, often little more than vague goals: "If you ask managers what they do they will most likely tell you that they plan, organize, coordinate, and control. Then watch what they do. Don't be surprised if you can't relate what you see to those four words" (Mintzberg 1989: 9). This underscores the importance of looking closely at how management theories are actually applied, and at the results.

Another sociological interpretation of managers views their activities as directed at defining and pursuing common problems, goals, and solutions, interpreting their actions as responses to situational constraints.[15] This view helps to demystify management, showing how a group possessing formal authority still faces the limits that institutions place on human agency. Seeing management as a socially constructed practice avoids the trap of reifying organizations. This *social action perspective* on management also raises one of the thorniest problems in studying organizations: how to conceptualize individuals within organizations. As Charles Perrow (1986: 66) puts it, "How can you talk about organizations without talking about individuals?" In response, it should be said that much of organization theory does just that.

Managers as Decision Makers

This leads us into the area of *decision making,* a topic that has received much attention in writings on management. Perrow shows how one of the classic statements about the role of managers, Chester Barnard's 1938 book, *The Functions of the Executive*, falls into the trap of presenting a "nonpersonal" model of organizations (Barnard 1938). For Barnard, even the decisions made by executives are not personal choices (that is, individually determined) because they are embedded in a coordinated system. The logic and rationality often attributed to managers, for him, are actually imposed in a disciplined way by the organizational environment. Barnard's tremendously influential contribution to subsequent thinking about organizations (especially organic theories) is basically flawed, argues Perrow, because it "glorifies the organization and minimizes the person" (Barnard 1938: 76). Organizational policies take on a moral tone, and are assumed to be functional for everyone involved, from executives to workers and customers.

Recent investigations of decision making still grapple with the role of the manager and whether she or he, as an individual, can make a difference in the organization. Reviewing the literature on executive decision making, David Hickson (1987) identifies three major theoretical perspectives. The *incrementalism perspective* emphasizes rational decisions as the ultimate goal, but success in reaching this goal is limited by the information available, biased viewpoints, and the limitations of the decision makers themselves. The second perspective, the *garbage can model*, sees the process as inherently political. All sorts of problems and solutions are thrown into the can, but what comes out in the form of decisions depends on idiosyncratic factors, such as what information is ignored or utilized and disputes among participants. The third model draws on the previous perspectives to view decision making as involving both *politics* and *rational problem solving*.

What these perspectives ignore is the impact of executive decisions on the organization. In fact, the relationship between leadership and corporate performance is subject to ongoing controversy. Media reports of corporate "white knights" and the heroics of turnaround artists, such as Lee Iacocca of Chrysler Corporation, suggest that leaders are like ship captains, some of whose hands are more firmly on the rudder than others. This overly individualistic image of management is challenged by social scientists who document how leadership must be contextualized and, thus, subjected to many situational constraints. Recent empirical studies show that corporate executives do affect the performance of the organization, but that this effect is overshadowed by other performance-related factors (for instance, industrial sector, markets, technology, and size) that differentiate firms (Thomas 1988).

To recap, an overriding management objective to create motivated and cooperative employees. According to virtually all theories of management, this is the basic precondition for meeting organizational goals. But the various management theories have advocated different methods for achieving these goals. During this century, several distinct schools of management have appeared. The two most influential ones have been scientific management and the human relations approach.

SCIENTIFIC MANAGEMENT

Charlie Chaplin's classic movie *Modern Times* humorously depicts the impact of scientific management on working conditions. The little comedian with the distinctive black moustache plays a harried factory worker whose job has been analyzed and redesigned by stopwatch-wielding efficiency experts. Every few seconds, Chaplin tightens a nut as another identical piece of equipment zips past him on the assembly line. Chaplin is little more than an automaton whose actions are programmed by the production system. Once out on the street, he continues repeating the motions on anything that fits his two wrenches.

Taylorism

Scientific management began in the United States as a set of production methods, tools, and organizational systems designed to increase the efficiency of factory production. The term itself was coined in 1911. But this new approach to factory management and organization, popularized by an engineer named Frederick W. Taylor, had been developed by the end of the previous century. Taylor and other "efficiency experts" extolled the virtues of scientific management, and the method soon spread across North America and, to a lesser extent, Britain and Europe. Taylor's theories were at the cutting edge of what Bryan Palmer refers to as the broad "thrust for efficiency" that contributed to the rise of twentieth-century industrial capitalism.[16] These early management consultants advocated workplace reorganization, job redesign, and tighter administrative and employee controls, all in the name of efficiency and profits.

Taylor laid out the following steps for rationalizing the labour process: (1) shift the decision-making responsibility for doing a job from workers to management; (2) use scientific methods to determine the most efficient way of executing a job and redesign it accordingly; (3) provide a detailed description of how to perform each step in a job; (4) select the best worker to perform the job; (5) train workers to execute the job efficiently; and (6) closely monitor workers' performance.[17] Taylor believed his management techniques benefited all parties involved. Yet their overriding effect was to give management tighter control over workers' activities by making all major work decisions. Critics such as Harry Braverman (1974) view Taylorism as the cornerstone of all twentieth-century management. As we will elaborate in Chapter 6, according to the *labour process perspective*, Taylorism degraded labour, minutely fragmenting tasks, reducing skill requirements, and eliminating workers' input about how their jobs should be done.

Taylor was convinced that worker *soldiering*, or deliberate laziness, was the scourge of industry. He believed that workers consciously restricted production by keeping bosses ignorant of how fast a job could be done. In Taylor's rather alarmist language, "there could be no greater crime against humanity than this restriction of output."[18] His solution was to determine "scientifically" the one best way of performing a job through *time-and-motion studies* of each step. A base rate of pay was then tied to a production quota. If workers exceeded the quota, they received a pay bonus. Lazy workers unable to achieve the quota would be forced to quit because their base rate fell below a minimum level. Essentially, scientific management was founded on the assumption that workers were motivated by economic gain alone. Taylor preached that the scientific basis of a "fair day's wage" and the productivity gains through more efficient work methods would bring about a new era of industrial cooperation and harmony.

Taylor's view of human nature was coloured by his preoccupation with technical efficiency. In his mind, the ideal worker was more like a machine than a human being. Taylor was a leading ideologue for early twentieth-century management, articulating its deep concerns about the "labour problem." Industrial cooperation would only replace class conflict, he predicted, once a complete mental revolution had taken hold of both management and labour. As Taylor wrote in a prominent Canadian business magazine just before World War I:

> The new outlook that comes to both sides under scientific management is that both sides very soon realize that if they stop

> pulling apart and both push together as hard as possible in the same direction, they can make that surplus [i.e., profits] so large that there is no occasion for any quarrel over its division. Labour gets an immense increase in wages, and still leaves a large share for capital.[19]

Scientific management failed to provide a successful formula for labour–management cooperation. In fact, the rhetoric of scientific objectivity was little more than an ideological justification for greater management control over labour. In practice, its principles of job design and work organization—like job descriptions, planned work flows, detailed unit accounting, and time-and-motion studies—became standard features of contemporary management.[20] Taylor's package of managerial reforms was seldom adopted completely. Yet various aspects of scientific management were introduced in many shops and factories in Canada around the turn of the century. By the 1920s, these innovations were being used to overhaul large corporate and government offices.[21]

The Legacy of Scientific Management

Basic principles of scientific management can still be found today in many organizations, including some in the expanding service sector. For instance, Burger King attempts to maximize food sales and minimize labour costs by emphasizing SOS—"speed of service" (Reiter 1991: 85). Complying with this motto requires highly standardized work procedures and strict management controls in all Burger King outlets. Time-and-motion studies dictate how long it takes to prepare the fries, burgers, and drinks, exactly how workers should do these tasks, and where they should be positioned depending on the design of the kitchen.

There are few visible signs of resistance to this regimented type of labour process by fast-food workers, which perhaps is not surprising considering that many are teenagers still in high school. However, history has many examples of workers resisting scientific management. Skilled industrial workers besieged by managerial rationalizations in the early twentieth century responded by striking.[22] Autoworkers were one occupational group that experienced a barrage of scientific management, along with extensive technological change.

Chapter 8 will comment further on how Fordism combined scientific management techniques with mass-production, assembly-line technology to create what were among the most alienating and stressful working conditions in modern industrial society.[23]

In many ways, Taylorism represented the practical application of bureaucratic principles to a manufacturing setting. Henry Ford's moving assembly line used technology to develop the logic inherent in scientific management and bureaucracy. The resulting increased monotony and speed of production sparked a huge increase in employee turnover. Only by doubling wages was Ford able to induce workers to accept the new production methods. Worker opposition to Fordism is never far from the surface. When General Motors opened a Vega plant in the early 1970s at Lordstown, Ohio, the relentless pace of the line, coupled with more restrictive management, led to massive labour unrest and sabotage (Aronowitz 1973: Chapter 2). As described in Chapter 6, lean production, the latest Japanese-inspired management system in North American auto factories, has retained elements of Fordism.

In short, major human costs often accompany increased efficiency, productivity, and profits. Other schools of management have attempted to counteract the harshness that resulted from Taylorism and Fordism by developing more humane working conditions. As one organizational researcher aptly concludes, scientific management principles "make superb sense for organizing production when robots rather than human beings are the main productive force, when organizations can truly become machines" (Morgan 1996: 26).

THE HUMAN RELATIONS MOVEMENT

Bureaucracy, scientific management, and mass-production technologies transformed work in the twentieth century. Many jobs became routinized and monotonous, stripped of opportunities for workers to use their minds or develop their skills and abilities. Employee dissatisfaction, often in the form of high turnover and absenteeism rates or industrial unrest, threatened to undermine the machine-like efficiency of the new industrial system. Taylor, Henry Ford, and a host of "efficiency experts" sought to redesign production systems so that control would be firmly in the hands of management. Technical efficiency was paramount.

Toward Normative Control: Workers as Human Beings

However, gaining the cooperation of workers within an increasingly bureaucratized, mechanized, and regimented labour process remained difficult. Some employers responded with programs, broadly known as *corporate welfare* or *industrial betterment*, which emphasized the need to treat workers as human beings. Popular in leading North American firms by the 1920s, corporate welfare programs tried to reduce the alienating effects of bureaucracy and worker dissatisfaction with routinized tasks. The goal was a loyal and productive work force; the means were healthier work settings and improved job benefits. Recreation facilities, cafeterias, cleaner and more pleasant work environments, coherent personnel policies, medical care, and pensions are major examples of corporate welfare efforts.

Taylor and other efficiency experts were quick to dismiss these schemes as a waste of money. Yet many firms committed to scientific management also used corporate welfare measures to gain greater cooperation from staff.[24] More than anything, the corporate welfare movement shows that the principles of bureaucracy and scientific management failed to address the key ingredient in modern industry—human beings. Not until the *human relations school of management* began to systematically examine some of the same concerns in the 1930s did the scientific management model face a serious challenge.

Control within organizations depends upon rank-and-file employees complying with management directives. Such *compliance* can be achieved in three different ways: coercive management techniques that rely on penalties and harsh discipline; utilitarian methods by which employees are motivated by economic self-interest; and normative approaches that assume that workers equate their own interests with organizational goals, thus becoming motivated to work hard (Etzioni 1975). Scientific management combined coercive and utilitarian methods with mixed results at best. The normative approach, which cultivates a community of interests throughout the organization, is typically more effective. Workers are more likely to personally identify with management goals, pursuing them as their own. In short, a normative approach to employee relations sharply contrasts with scientific management in its assumptions regarding human nature and motivation. Theoretically, the big happy corporate family of the human relations school replaced the carrot of incentive wages and the stick of harsh discipline. In practice, however, scientific management and human relations often operate side by side.

The Hawthorne Studies

The human relations school of management originated in the *Hawthorne Studies*, a program of research conducted by Harvard Business School researchers between 1927 and 1932 at Western Electric's Hawthorne Works on the outskirts of Chicago.[25] Western Electric management was initially concerned with the effects of fatigue and monotony on production levels. These were central concerns of industrial psychologists at the time. Various studies examining the impact of rest pauses, hours of work, and lighting levels on productivity led researchers to the unexpected finding that work-group social relations and employee attitudes had a major influence on production. Worker needs and motivation thus became key management concerns. And the workplace came to be viewed as a social system as opposed to a purely technical system.

In the Relay Assembly Test Room study, workers were placed in two separate rooms. Researchers then recorded production while varying light intensity for one group but not the other. To their surprise, productivity in both groups increased regardless of lighting level. Only when light intensity was reduced to that of bright moonlight did productivity decline. Several variations on this study came up with the same puzzling findings. Searching for possible explanations, the researchers speculated that a fundamental change had occurred in the workplace. Involving workers in the study had the unintended effect of raising their morale. They now felt that management cared about them as individuals. Productivity, concluded the researchers, increased as a result. This is the famous *Hawthorne effect*.[26] A basic axiom of human relations management had been discovered: the humane treatment of employees and the creation of an *esprit de corps* improves their motivation to cooperate and be productive.

In a subsequent phase of the research, interviews with employees revealed that work groups were governed by informal behavioural codes. This early attempt at employee counselling also tried to detect grievances and potential trouble spots in the factory (Wilensky and Wilensky 1951). The Bank Wiring Observation Room study further probed work-group behaviour. For 7 months, 14 employees were observed as they wired telephone switching banks. Researchers documented how *informal group norms* replaced formal directives from management. The work team set its own production quotas, making sure that no member worked too hard or too slowly. Infractions of the group's rules, such as reporting violations of company policy to management, were punished. Generally, strong pressures to conform to the group norms prevailed.[27] This exposed the hidden side of the workplace, where workers consciously engage in practices to oppose or subvert established authority.

Re-Evaluating Human Relations Theory

Remarkably, the influential human relations school rests on shaky research foundations. The Hawthorne Studies, according to Alex Carey, were poorly conceived and incompetently executed. Furthermore, the evidence did not really support the conclusions. Economic incentives and coercive supervision, Carey argues, seem to be better explanations of the observed productivity changes than was management's attention to human relations.[28] But leaping to the defence of the studies, Jeffrey A. Sonnenfeld (1985: 111) retorts that the critics "demonstrate how easily the gunsmoke of academic snipers can obscure the conceptual contribution of these pioneering efforts." He asserts that the Hawthorne research advanced organizational theory beyond Taylorism, presenting a more complex social systems approach to organizational life.

Controversy continues to surround the Hawthorne research, perhaps an acknowledgment of the deep imprint it has left on management theory and practice. Two recent contributions to the debate take different sides. Richard Gillespie (1991) examines the history of the Hawthorne experiments and concludes that the official version, strongly influenced by Elton Mayo, obscures the organizational politics and larger context in which the Relay Assembly Test Room studies were carried out and their results interpreted. Gillespie asks: Were these studies really examples of careful, objective scientific discovery as is so often claimed? Did the studies generate adequate evidence of the importance of work-group norms over and above economic incentives in determining worker performance?

Gillespie documents that the Hawthorne researchers initially had conflicting interpretations of inconclusive and contradictory findings. Yet, mainly under Elton Mayo's strong influence, a dominant interpretation was cobbled together. Furthermore, previous literature on Hawthorne has not considered that the outcomes were influenced by how the research process was itself interwoven with the authority structure of the firm. From this perspective, workers took advantage of their participation in the studies to further their own interests. The women in the relay assembly tests did increase their output when working conditions were experimentally improved, but when privileges were withdrawn, they informally set up their own rest breaks and supplied themselves with refreshments. These workers also wanted to take advantage of the special group "piece rate" to earn more by boosting productivity.

However, this interpretation is challenged by Stephen Jones's (1990) statistical reanalysis of the experimental data. Jones shows that worker interdependence, through group interaction, was the basis for joint effort and output decisions. In other words, consistent with the dominant version of the studies, a human relations supervisory style did help to shape worker productivity. In short, there are no signs that the Hawthorne debate has ended.

Cooperation and Conflict in Human Relations Theory

Human relations management theory emphasizes how workers' attitudes, values, emotions, psychological needs, and interpersonal relationships shape their work behaviour. This approach to management seeks the best match between the worker, given her or his personal background and psychological makeup, and the job. Careful recruitment and effective training of employees, as well as good quality of supervision and communications, are therefore essential.

The human relations perspective also assumes that people naturally want to cooperate. This is an explicit rejection of the utilitarian assumption of scientific management. Yet Elton Mayo and other human relations theorists claimed that workers are unaware of their cooperative instincts, acting instead on the basis of irrational sentiments or beliefs. For Mayo, the survival of society depended on cooperation, so he advocated a new industrial order run by an administrative elite. The leadership of this elite would encourage the development of work environments that would bring out the cooperative instincts and productive potential of employees (Mayo 1945).

Mayo and other human relations advocates consider workers unable to act in their own best interests. Less authoritarian leadership, careful selection and training of personnel, an emphasis on human needs and job satisfaction—

these are the central contributions of the human relations approach. Yet lurking behind these management tactics is a contradictory view of the workplace (Burawoy 1979: 7). On the one hand, human relations theory assumes that industrial harmony is normal and healthy and, conversely, that conflict is destructive. The possibility of conflicting interests between management and workers is denied, leaving no place for unions or other collective expressions of workers' interests. On the other hand, human relations theory argues that workers must be closely regulated by management in the greater interests of cooperation and harmony. These inconsistencies have led some critics to label human relations theory as an elaborate justification for management's manipulation of workers (Rinehart 1996: 162–67).

No doubt most human resource (or personnel) managers today sincerely want to treat workers as human beings. But underneath the rhetoric of human relations, problems of power and inequality in organizations remain deeply entrenched. In Charles Perrow's words:

> One may treat slaves humanely, and even ask their opinions on matters with which they are more familiar than the master. But to transform their basic dependence and this presumption of their incompetence with regard to their own interests, there must be an institutional order or public process whereby the opportunity and capacity for legitimate self-assertion is guaranteed. Such a political process does not mean conflict and struggle as such but a setting for ordered controversy and accommodation.[29]

ORGANIZATIONAL CULTURE

This overview of the Hawthorne Studies documents how workers construct their own culture in the workplace, replacing official rules and norms with their own. Consequently, the potential for management–worker conflict is increased, since the official goals of management and the unofficial, more personal goals of workers and work groups are not the same. This issue is taken up further in Chapter 6. Yet informal workplace relations and organizational culture also provide another management tool for increasing employee conformity and integration. This apparent paradox between workplace social relations and culture as means for employee resistance on the one hand, and as the basis for a value consensus on the other, is rooted in the two divergent theoretical traditions we first identified in Chapter 1. The former, which derives from Marx's view of society, emphasizes the dynamics of conflict. The latter draws on the work of French sociologist Émile Durkheim and his concerns about achieving social stability.[30]

The Informal Side of Organizations

By focusing only on the formal structure of organizations and the role of managers, we overlook vital features of life in work organizations. Less visible but equally important in the daily operations of an organization is its *informal* side, where employees reinterpret, resist, or adapt to work structures and management directives. As Blau and Scott (1963: 6) explain:

> In every formal organization there arises informal organization. The constituent groups of the organization, like all groups, develop their own practices, values, norms, and social relations as their members live and work together. The roots of these formal systems are embedded in the formal organization itself and nurtured by the very formality of its arrangements.

Thus, to get a complete picture of a work organization, we must examine it from the vantage point of employees' informal practices and social relations. The glossy organizational charts found in corporate annual reports present management's image of how things ought to operate. Employees further down the hierarchy often see things differently, and act according to these perceptions.

In the seven decades since the Hawthorne studies, the *informal work group* has been under the microscope of social scientists. Some of this research has highlighted the dynamics of conflict and power within work organizations. Despite management's efforts to regiment work procedures, employees often respond in ways that do not fit these plans. Total control of people by bureaucratic structures, management discipline, and technology is difficult to imagine. Furthermore, there is an underlying tension between the cooperation necessary for any organization to function and the internal competition among individuals and groups over the distribution of power, rewards, and other scarce resources.[31]

Research in this tradition also investigates work-group relations, which are frequently a function of how production is organized. For example, assembly-line workers have fewer opportunities to develop strong social ties than do miners or firefighters whose jobs demand close teamwork. Job characteristics, especially technology, shape patterns of communication and interaction among workers.[32] Close interpersonal networks create a more cohesive group, increasing the potential for unified action in modifying or undermining official work directives.

Donald Roy's (1952) participant observer study of a Chicago machine shop graphically portrays work-group dynamics and counter-systems of production. During the 1940s, Roy worked as a machinist in a shop that ran on a *piecework payment system.* Productivity was regulated by management through bonus payments for output that was above established quotas. Machine operators constantly battled over the base wage with time-study personnel trained in scientific management. The machinists invented ingenious shortcuts to maximize their wages while minimizing effort. This required conspiracies with other groups who supplied tools, maintained the machines, or delivered raw materials, all of which violated company rules.

The workers' informal system of production involved what in shop-floor jargon was called "goldbricking" on "stinker jobs." That is, on difficult jobs for which they could not possibly earn a bonus, workers relaxed and enjoyed some free time. On easy jobs, however, they could "make out" by exceeding the quota to receive a bonus. Any production beyond an unofficial quota was stored up in a "kitty" to be used to boost output figures on a slow day. Management rarely challenged the workers' system because production usually fluctuated within an acceptable range. Ironically, the workers had designed a more predictable and efficient production process.[33]

Managers, too, participate in the manipulation of informal work practices, as Roy observed in the machine shop. While able to exercise some authority over rank-and-file workers, many middle- and lower-level managers and supervisors feel constrained in their roles. Consequently, they may not entirely follow the directives of top executives. A revealing study of how managers sometimes operate is Melville Dalton's *Men Who Manage.*[34] Dalton illustrates how managers bend rules and short-circuit bureaucracy in order to achieve their objectives. Especially fascinating is his analysis of how official and unofficial rewards often complement each other, giving management a wider repertoire of means to achieve a particular goal.

On paper, the organizations Dalton studied were formal bureaucracies. In practice, unofficial systems guided actions. Obtaining a promotion depended less on merit than it did on social characteristics such as, for example, being a member of the Masonic Order or the local yacht club. Employees at all organizational levels regularly engaged in what, to the outside observer, was dishonest activity. The company's resources were dispensed as personal rewards in order to keep the bureaucracy running, to acknowledge someone's special services to the firm, or to solidify social relationships in order to get a job done. Workers borrowed tools and equipment; managers had home improvements done at company expense. According to Dalton, this sort of "freewheeling" frequently occurs just beneath the thin veneer of bureaucracy.

Organizational Culture

Based on insights like these about informal group relations, the concept of *organizational culture* has become a prominent theme in literature on management and organizations.[35] Social-anthropological methods are useful in studying organizational culture. Viewed from the perspective of their members, organizations become mini-societies. The shared beliefs, customs, rituals, languages, and myths serve as "social glue," binding together the diverse elements of the organization. *Culture*, then, refers to a system of shared meanings about how organizational life ought to be conducted. It can express how things really get done at an informal level. The culture metaphor, used broadly, shifts our attention from the structure of an organization toward the processes by which employees actually carry out and collectively interpret work activities.[36]

Shaping the *dominant culture* of an organization—that is, encouraging employees to identify strongly with the goals of the corporation—has become a management preoccupation (Pettigrew 1979). Viewed from this perspective, the norms and values of employee work groups become *countercultures* challenging the dominant organizational values. Corporations with strong internal cultures (for instance, Procter and Gamble's obsession with product quality or Hewlett-Packard's culture of constant innovation) send a clear signal to all employees. Bluntly stated, these corporate cultures are meant to be "so strong that you either buy into their norms or get out" (Peters and

Waterman 1982: 76–77). Thus, attempts to develop strong organizational cultures can be seen as the latest effort by management to achieve what Amitai Etzioni calls normative control. Critics argue that this management approach is used to enforce conformity and muzzle troublemakers. To the extent that the "corporate family" values consensus, the open debate often necessary to solve problems may be stifled (Morgan 1996: 138–39; Ray 1986).

Managing Consensus through Culture

Many large public and private sector employers strive to create a strong corporate culture, a dominant system of beliefs and behaviour to which, ideally, all members of the organization are committed. These values are reinforced, for example, by mythology that reveres the founders of the organization and legendary past leaders, or by rituals such as annual awards dinners where employees' achievements are publicly acknowledged. Some organizations have found that transforming their culture can be a powerful tool for renewal and survival. For example, several years ago, the president of the Campbell Soup Company in Canada introduced a "New Age" form of culture into the organization, based on the concept of "breakthrough management," which encourages people to plan from a future perspective, and spread by "power coaches." While the Campbell Soup executive admitted that some people "wonder what we've been smoking," the new thinking fostered by breakthrough management seems to have delivered real results in the form of costs savings and higher profits.[37]

There is also an assumption in some of the organizational culture literature that strong collective values underpin the success of the Japanese approach to management. William Ouchi's research suggests that successful North American corporations that emulate this Japanese approach, have developed clan-like internal cultures. "More than anything," writes Ouchi, "culture implies a company's values, such as aggressiveness, defensiveness, or nimbleness—values that set a pattern for activities, opinions, and actions. Managers instill that pattern in their employees by example and pass it down to succeeding generations of workers" (Ouchi 1981: 195).

Viewing shared values as the cornerstone of organizational culture is a prominent theme in popular literature on management. However, research delving into the nature of organizational culture and analyzing how the culture reflects other characteristics of an organization casts doubt on this view.

Using employee attitude data collected from IBM employees in 64 countries, Geert Hofstede and his colleagues investigated national variations in organizational culture (Hofstede et al. 1990; Hofstede 1984). In particular, the researchers ask whether measurable cultural differences among organizations are a function of the distinctive features of these organizations, or are shaped by the larger environment in which the organization is situated.

Do Organizations Have Different Cultures?

Hofstede's (1984: 252) international study of IBM employees found that organizations are "culture bound" in the sense that national cultures directly influence individuals' behaviour in work organizations, the values they hold, organizational design, and even the theories used to explain organization. Follow-up studies frequently confirm that employee values are not the product of their organization, but are far more likely to vary by nationality, age, or education. Rather than values being at the core of organizational culture, the researchers found shared perceptions of daily practices (what needs to be done and how to do it) to be central (Hofstede et al. 1990: 311). The practical implications of this research are twofold. First, employee values are more likely to enter the organization through the hiring process than through on-the-job socialization that attempts to inculcate the dominant culture. Second, the effectiveness of popular management techniques, organizational design, and work humanization efforts will vary according to national context.

Canadian research by David Zussman and Jak Jabes (1989) comparing senior federal government managers with comparable levels of managers in the private sector also challenges the conception of a dominant culture of shared values. This study documented distinct differences between public and private sector managers in terms of personal and corporate values and leadership styles. Equally pronounced was what they termed "the vertical solitude" between levels of management within the public sector. This suggests morale and leadership problems among federal public service managers, although we hasten to add that all managers did share a commitment to doing a good job serving the Canadian public. What is more, it sensitizes us to how inter-organizational cultural differences may be less pronounced than the differences in values and orientations among groups within a specific organization.

In fact, most organizations have a variety of cultures—dominant and alternative—depending on the degree to which particular groups within them share similar work experiences. The organization of work may create strong occupational or professional alliances, based on values and goals not necessarily congruent with those of management. Under these circumstances, power struggles can erupt. This cultural fragmentation can result in organizations saying one thing in their "philosophy," while their day-to-day operations reflect something quite different. In fact, recent research indicates that an organization's culture can be a barrier to greater employee involvement, the very goal that managers seek to obtain through refashioning culture (Chelte et al. 1989). This suggests that changing the culture of an organization may be a prerequisite to changing its structure.

A Learning Culture

The concept of a *learning organization* has become popular recently. Employers increasingly are turning their attention to gaining a "competitive advantage" through better use of their employees' abilities and potential. This is the stated objective of much human resource management practice. It is assumed, then, that better-trained workers will make an organization more adaptable, innovative, and flexible. So, too, entire organizations must learn by continuously incorporating new knowledge and using it to improve their performance. Simply stated, a learning organization "is an organization skilled at creating, acquiring, and transferring knowledge, and at modifying its behaviour to reflect new knowledge and insights" (Garvin 1993: 80).

A leading advocate of the learning organization is Peter Senge.[38] He advocates that employees and organizations follow five "learning disciplines": expanding your personal abilities and enabling others to do so; breaking out of old ways of thinking; developing a shared vision of the future; team learning; and holistic or systems thinking. These rather abstract principles describe a process, not a set of goals that one day will be reached. Senge claims that there is no "top 10" list of learning organizations, only individuals, work groups, and teams in various organizations engaged in "mastery and self determination" through learning. Such workers are better able to "embrace change." Senge and other champions of organizational learning present a humanistic image of self-development and self-learning in organizations, quite the opposite to the mechanistic model of organizations created by Taylor or described by Weber. Senge and his colleagues level an even more fundamental criticism at traditional organizations in capitalist society:

> Perhaps the most pernicious guiding idea to penetrate to the heart of Western business management over the past thirty to fifty years is that the *purpose* of the enterprise is to maximize return of the shareholders' investment.... Can there be little wonder that people in such organizations are uncommitted, that they view their jobs as mundane and uninspiring, and that they lack any deep sense of loyalty to the organization? (Senge et al. 1994: 23)

Senge stands out among management consultants with this criticism of profits for profits sake. But he is typical of the new breed of management thinkers reviewed later in this chapter. Basically, Senge is saying that in order to escape tradition-bound organizational malaise, work practices and structures must change so that learning can occur. How can this be achieved? Part of the answer is a major transformation in the culture of the workplace. Learning must become a valued and rewarded process that employees have the autonomy to pursue. So, at least in theory, a learning organization has a *learning culture* that empowers employees to take initiatives to solve problems and learn.[39] Some firms have moved toward developing a learning culture. At Harley Davidson Motorcycles, "intellectual curiosity" is now a core value, "Harley University" offers extensive training programs, and the president promotes learning at every opportunity (Gephart et al. 1996: 39). However, as we documented in Chapter 2, relatively few Canadian firms invest in job-related training and, moreover, underemployment is a major problem in many work organizations. Hence, it would appear that in the majority of workplaces a learning culture remains a theoretical ideal.

IN SEARCH OF A NEW MANAGERIAL PARADIGM

Even a cursory glance at recent management literature leaves the strong impression that corporate North America is in a state of crisis. In many respects, the large bureaucracies that have come to dominate the economic landscape are like dinosaurs: cumbersome, slow to respond and adapt, and, according to some critics, a dying breed. The turbulent economic times in which we now live have prompted even the most vocal champions of bureaucracy to search for better ways to manage organizations. Managers, consultants, and some business school academics created a new growth industry in the 1980s and 1990s. They churned out a steady stream of popular management books, all seeking a new *paradigm* that would be capable of inspiring managers to meet the huge challenges of globalization, recession, fierce international competition, and rapid technological advances.[40]

Tom Peters and Bob Waterman Jr. set the tone in their enormously influential 1982 book, *In Search of Excellence*, in which they documented how rigid, inflexible organizations are less able to survive, let alone grow and profit, in today's rapidly changing economy (Peters and Waterman 1982). Despite the fact that many of Peters and Waterman's "excellent" firms later experienced problems,[41] the writers nonetheless fueled debates about the need to rethink old ways of organizing and managing derived from the legacies of Weber, Taylor, and Ford. In this respect, much of the *new management literature* corresponds with the sociological critique of bureaucracy.[42] It also enunciates some additional themes at the core of organizational studies: how change occurs, the role of managers, issues of power, and the possibilities for gaining cooperation and forging a consensus among all organizational participants. A brief review of several of the major contributions to the new management literature will give us its flavour and, at the same time, elaborate these themes.

The Critique from Within

Revolution is a widely used metaphor in this new management literature, as is seen in Joseph H. Boyett and Henry P. Conn's *Workplace 2000: The Revolution Reshaping American Business* (Boyett and Conn 1991). This book begins with a case study of the kind of revolution the authors argue is necessary. Picture a plant employing 130 people, where, in a six-year period, output rises 80 percent, absenteeism drops to 2 percent, and turnover drops to 1 percent. There are no time clocks, no supervisors, no job classifications, and no definite work assignments. Everyone is salaried and productivity levels usually found in plants employing a third more staff are achieved. The ingredients of this apparently remarkable turnaround are captured by Boyett and Conn in their use of terms such as work teams, participative management, employee empowerment, flatter and leaner organization structures, flexibility, creativity, innovation, pay-for-knowledge, continuous learning, quality, service, and doing more with less. This is the language of the new management.

Tom Peters has become one of the best known of the new management gurus. In his book, *Thriving on Chaos: A Handbook for a Management Revolution*, he recants some of the tenets put forward in *In Search of Excellence*, arguing that there is no such thing as an excellent company because a firm can always be run better and rapid change requires constant adaptation (Peters 1987). His model of what he calls a "winner" is based on five sets of characteristics: an obsession with responsiveness to customers; constant innovation in all areas; the full participation and empowerment of all people connected with the organization; leadership that loves change and promotes an inspiring vision; and nonbureaucratic control by simple support systems.

Peters (1987) clearly articulates the necessity of, as he puts it, turning the organization "upside-down and sideways." He has an abundance of anecdotes from the corporate trenches, such as an antibureaucratic inversion of a cherished status symbol, whereby one reformed corporation jokes about still having an "executive dining room"—the Chinese restaurant or the deli across the street from its headquarters (Peters 1987). Finally, Peters obsession with the urgency of embracing change, not running from it, sets a new goal for managers: create internal stability in an organization so that it can be constantly adapting to an ever-changing external environment. Peters drives this message home in an article in the *California Management Review*, with the appropriate title, "Get innovative or get dead" (Peters 1990; 1991).

Echoing similar themes is Henry Mintzberg (1989: 2), who defines organizations simply as "collective action in pursuit of a common mission, a fancy way of saying that a bunch of people have come together under an identifiable label ("General Motors," "Joe's Body Shop") to produce some product or service." Mintzberg's (1989: Chapter 11) work on innovative organizations introduces the concept of *adhocracy*.

Adhocracy is a hallmark of the innovative organization, which has a fluid and decentralized operating structure. This contrasts with the inflexibility of what Mintzberg calls the "machine organization," or traditional bureaucracy, and even with the "entrepreneurial organization," which is too performance-oriented. The work of an adhocracy is performed by multidisciplinary teams. Hierarchical top–down control, rigid lines of authority, and narrow job functions are replaced by a *matrix structure*. This injects elasticity, allowing experts to move between functional units for specialized administrative tasks and multidisciplinary project teams. Mintzberg points to Canada's National Film Board as a good example of an operating adhocracy, with its artists, technical experts, and administrators forming and reforming teams to create the documentaries and animated films for which the agency is famous. Mintzberg's view of fluid, flexible, innovative organizations is shared among management thinkers, and it raises larger questions about how organizations change. Peter F. Drucker (1993: 59), the dean of management gurus, argues that in a knowledge- and technology-based economy, successful organizations must be able to continuously change and renew themselves. Essentially, these writers are elaborating the concept of the "learning organization" introduced earlier in our discussion of organizational culture.

But continuous change is not easy. Rosabeth Moss Kanter evokes the image of elephants learning how to kick up their heels in her book, *When Giants Learn to Dance* (Kanter 1989). In it, she advocates a "post-entrepreneurial revolution." She observes that change has become the new management orthodoxy and wonders if the resulting managerial innovations designed to harness change will infiltrate the old elephantine corporations most in need of reinvigorating. The crux of the problem is that bureaucracy is a hindrance to a cooperative, creative, and flexible workplace. Kanter cautions, however, that the "cowboy management style" typical of many young successful firms—"lean and mean," glamorizing individualism, highly competitive—is not the solution.

Eastman Kodak and Apple Computer exemplify the old elephantine corporation and the new entrepreneurial cowboy, respectively. "Too-bureaucratic Kodak had begun to stagnate," Kanter explains, adding that it "had become burdened with a cumbersome organization that encouraged bureaucratic turf-consciousness and stifled innovation. Too-entrepreneurial Apple, mired in the problems of transition from the founder and the chaotic start-up mode, was caught in internal rivalries that wasted resources, and had not yet harnessed the achievement drives of individuals to shared purposes" (Kanter 1989: 52). These two contrasting firms launched themselves on similar new management strategies. They reorganized according to their strengths, established closer relationships with suppliers and customers, emphasized cooperation and the generation of new ideas, cut out management layers, and developed self-managing employee teams. The result, in Kanter's (1989) words, was "a triumph of process over structure."

In her latest book, *World Class*, Kanter examines successful "cosmopolitan" firms that rely on ever-changing global business networks. Viewing corporate life from this perspective of globalization (see Chapter 1), a more negative picture of management initiatives emerges. The problem, she points out, is that "as cosmopolitan businesses extend their market scope, tap new and better supply sources, and link up with global chains, they inevitably loosen local ties and relationships" (Kanter 1995: 145). This results in increased temporary work, outsourcing, and growing workloads and longer hours for core staff with no guarantee of future security. Kanter advocates human resource policies that create new forms of security within the context of rapid change. She gives examples of global firms that have introduced a "new social contract" based on the concept of employability—ensuring that employees receive the kind of ongoing training, learning opportunities, and career counselling that will keep them employable (Kanter 1995: 156–63).

The Quality Mission

Putting quality and customers first are two axioms of the new management. To this end, some organizations have embraced the *total quality management* or TQM (sometimes called *total quality improvement)* model. Skeptics may view TQM as just a catchy label applied to a particular combination of customer-first innovations prescribed by Peters, Kanter, and others. But TQM champions claim that the model reduces costs, and increases productivity, customer satisfaction, quality of working life, and firm competitiveness.

What is TQM? One consultant defines it as "a cooperative form of doing business that relies on the talents and capabilities of both labour and management to continually improve quality and productivity using teams" (Jablonski 1990: 4). TQM draws its inspiration from Japanese management's obsession with quality, described below. Sociologist Stephen Hill sees TQM as emblematic of management's quest to better utilize human resources. He identifies this management approach as a significant response to more competitive markets and new customer demands. TQM advocates, first and foremost, a customer-based emphasis on quality. But, because the model also incorporates performance measures, improved communications and feedback systems, work teams, participative decision making, and a new organizational culture, it potentially has major implications for employees. TQM's emphasis on continuous improvement is similar to the concept of the learning organization, discussed above.

As with other new management trends, it is difficult to sort out real change from the rhetoric of TQM. But there is evidence that it has encouraged some employers to move in the direction of less bureaucracy, greater customer-responsiveness, organizational flexibility, and employee participation. At Marriott Corporation, a hotel and food service firm, employees are now called "associates" and are "empowered" to make decisions on the spot, rather than get approval from a supervisor, and to take initiatives themselves to satisfy customers (Jablonski 1990: 2). Two of the winners of a national U.S. quality award, Xerox Corporation and Milliken & Company (a textile manufacturer), have made heavy investments in employee training and use teams extensively. But criticisms abound. For example, in the public sector, TQM has been widely applied in health care. Patients are treated as "customers" and quality committees rethink processes and procedures in order to improve the quality of patient care and to cut costs. Yet in an era of health care spending cuts, the end result often is more stressful working conditions for nurses and other health care workers.[43]

Some analysts argue that the "quality movement" has stimulated thinking about how to change workplaces so that employees become the key factor in improved organizational performance (Pfeffer 1994: Chapter 9). While this potential exists, surveys conducted recently by consulting firms suggest that Canada and the United States still lag far behind Japan in the "quality" arena. A mid-1993 survey of Canadian firms determined that just over one-third (half in the manufacturing sector) had adopted some form of TQM.[44] Among those firms using some form of TQM, relatively few have had very positive results. As one major international evaluation of quality management practices concluded, Canadian managers "have learned the jargon, read the books and attended the seminars, but have failed to bring the theory to the shop floor."[45] There frequently is resistance to TQM changes at various levels of the organization. Middle managers balk at the idea of empowering employees, knowing that it is their power that will be redistributed downward. At the same time, employees no doubt have trouble with such TQM concepts as "continuous improvement." With such a vague goal, their best efforts today may not be good enough tomorrow and they will not know why.

The Downside of Downsizing

Despite the people-focus of human resource management in the last decade, the most common management strategy has been *downsizing*. Job cuts, accompanied by organizational restructuring, occurred in close to half of Canadian firms with 100 or more employees between 1991 and 1996, and one-third expected more downsizing to come. Smaller firms, with fewer than 50 employees, were far less likely to downsize, which is not surprising considering that small businesses created the majority of new jobs in the 1990s.[46] A 1993 national survey of over 700 firms in the resource, manufacturing, and business services sectors found that the most common management strategy (reported by over 60 percent) was "cost cutting" through reduced labour and operating costs (Betcherman et al. 1994: 20–21). In the United States, the 100 largest firms in the *Fortune 500* list have downsized an average of 15 times over the past 15 years, eliminating 2.5 million workers from their payrolls (McKay 1996: 56). These figures do not include the public sector, where deep budget cuts aimed at reducing government deficits also have resulted in substantial staff cuts this decade. In the first nine months of 1996, for example, an estimated 50,000 workers in the public sector across Canada lost their jobs (McKay 1996: 55). Profitable corporations and governments with balanced budgets continue to downsize: in March 1995, Bell Canada announced it would eliminate 10,000 jobs over three years, after profits of over $1 billion in the previous year.[47]

Downsizing has been likened to corporate anorexia. Organizations that may have started out reasonably healthy become lean and mean, but sometimes also dysfunctional. Underlying organizational problems are not addressed. There is now considerable evidence that downsizing has inflicted damage not only on individual employees and communities, but also on the downsized organization. There are also signs of public reactions against the downsizing trend, fuelled by widespread feelings of job insecurity (Betcherman and Lowe 1997). *The New York Times* report "The Downsizing of America" observes that the tally of jobs eliminated in the 1990s "...has the eerie feel of battlefield casualty counts. And like waves of strung-out veterans, the psychically frazzled downsized workers are infecting their families, friends, and communities with their grief, fear, and anger."[48] Many of these laid-off workers end up downwardly mobile, unable to find comparable jobs.

A growing body of research by academics and management consultants documents three areas—economic, organizational, and human—in which downsizing can create more problems for organizations than it solves.[49] Economically, the short-term cost savings associated with downsizing often do not translate into improved profits. Expenses actually may increase over time as managers realize they need to rehire workers or contract out work that otherwise would not get done. Organizationally, downsizing too often is a quick fix that is not part of a comprehensive change strategy. When organizations shrink rapidly, structures, processes, values, and goals must also change.

The human costs within the organization are often not anticipated. The term *survivor syndrome* has been coined to describe the negative psychological effects of downsizing on employees who remain behind. A glimmer of this is captured in the black humour of the *Dilbert* comic strip, as Dilbert and his fellow "cubicle dwellers" speculate on where the blunt axe of job cuts will fall next (Adams 1995). Workers experience elevated levels of stress, and generally become demoralized and dissatisfied. Motivation, loyalty, and productivity understandably can suffer as employees avoid taking risks in their jobs and become absorbed in protecting their own interests. This is exacerbated by the inevitable increases in workload (and sometimes wage cuts) as the organization tries to "do more with less." People get reassigned to new duties without adequate training, layers of management may be eliminated without authority being delegated downward, departing employees may take with them vital experience and "organizational memory," long-term planning of any kind becomes very difficult, and customer service and quality can also suffer.

In short, downsizing has had serious unintended consequences, and, in this respect, provides lessons in how not to go about changing organizations. Ironically, downsizing became trendy at the same time as organizational researchers and human resource management experts were preaching the importance of managing employees in ways that empowered them and increased their skills. Recently, the importance of loyalty has been rediscovered, and firms now are being told that a high-loyalty strategy aimed at building committed and long-term staff—the opposite of downsizing, contracting out, or using temporary workers—is directly related to customer loyalty (Reichheld 1996: Chapter 4). Not only is this a longer-term view, but it also treats employees as more than another line in the budget. As organizational theorist Jeffrey Pfeffer (1994: 16) argues:

> Achieving competitive success through people involves fundamentally altering how we think about the work force and the employment relationship. It means achieving success by working *with* people, not by replacing them or limiting the scope of their activities. It entails seeing the work force as a source of strategic advantage, not just as a cost to be minimized or avoided.

Some organizations have reduced staff numbers more humanely. Nova Corporation of Calgary, for example, established the Employment, Transition and Continuity Program to achieve a 10 percent staff reduction. The objective, according to the vice-president of human resources, is "to ensure that those who leave feel good about how they were treated and that those who stay feel energized and ready to move Nova forward."[50] Whether it truly is possible to feel good about being laid off is questionable. But the program does provide employees whose jobs are affected with more options and support, including alternative work arrangements (job sharing, reduced work week, seasonal employment), financial support for education or working in nonprofit community organizations, small business start-up advice and grants, skills upgrading, leaves of absence, and help with relocation costs.

Revolution or Evolution?

Marx theorized that capitalism contained the seeds of its own demise. But, instead of workers revolting to replace capitalism with a worker-run socialist system, the "revolution" has taken an altogether different course. To the extent that the new management commentators such as Peters, Kanter, Mintzberg, and a host of other academics and business consultants are correct, we may be witnessing a management-inspired revolution, driven by an instinct for survival. Or, is it more accurate to call it the latest stage in the evolution of organizational forms and managerial strategies?

Regardless, we can detect a shift away from a mechanistic, bureaucratic model of work organizations and toward a model that strives to better manage its human resources. This greater "people emphasis" indeed may be the most significant feature of the new direction in management, although it is in constant tension with the pressure to downsize and cut labour costs. This people orientation has shown some positive results for both management and employees in the private as well as the public sector. As the Auditor General of Canada (1988: 4.73) found in an analysis of federal government organizations that performed well:

> The most striking attribute of the well-performing organizations is the emphasis they place on their people. People are challenged, encouraged and developed. They are given power to act and to use their judgement. There is a "caring" attitude in these organizations, based on the belief that, in the long run, high performance is a product of people who care rather than of systems that constrain.

Some pressing issues arise from this brief review of the new management literature. The first concerns the nature of change in organizations, as well as the barriers that must be overcome for them to succeed. The changes heralded above as "revolutionary" suggest a shift from traditional approaches to organizing and managing work. Many managers may be talking about these changes, but, in practice, their diffusion is limited. Second, the basic assumptions and prescriptions being advocated fall short of a new paradigm. Many of the ideas are recycled from various streams of earlier thinking, some of which are reviewed below. Third, the likely impact of these changes on employees at all levels of the organization, especially on those in the most subordinate positions, is unclear. Can the management rhetoric of participative management, team work, and employee empowerment now in vogue be taken at face value, or is it a more sophisticated managerial control strategy aiming to get workers to make even greater commitments and sacrifices to the organization and to "do more with less"? This question is taken up in Chapter 6, where we discuss critical perspectives on work. For now, we will demonstrate that the idea that people matter in work organizations is firmly rooted in earlier attempts to reform and humanize work.

WORK HUMANIZATION, JOB REDESIGN, AND THE HIGH-PERFORMANCE WORKPLACE

So far, we have documented the problems of bureaucratic hierarchies, assembly-line technology and a fragmented division of labour, and organizational downsizing. The costs to workers, management, and society take the form of job dissatisfaction, stress and anxiety, poor morale, low productivity, and failure to meet the challenges of today's changing economic environment. Central to the new management approaches just reviewed are team work and greater employee participation in decision making. But, as we document below, these are hardly new ideas. To help locate these ideas historically, we will take a brief journey through the various theories and some of the actual applications of more democratic forms of work organizations and innovative job designs.

Human relations theory has strongly influenced work reform schemes such as job enlargement, job enrichment, participative management, sociotechnical planning, quality circles, and various quality of working life programs. A common ideological thread unites these approaches. Employees should be treated humanely and provided with good working conditions. Even so, beyond a few concessions in the realm of decision making, most of the authority remains with management. However, some reforms in Canada and elsewhere, particularly in Sweden and Norway, have come closer to achieving the dual goals of significantly redistributing power and enhancing the quality of working life. In such instances, more people in the organization stand to benefit, particularly because productivity gains often result.

Swedish Work Reforms

The potential of work humanization has been most fully realized in Sweden, which pioneered work reforms. Decades of social democratic government, a strong labour movement, and legislation giving individuals the right to meaningful jobs provide fertile grounds for the humanistic work reforms that have taken place in Sweden (see Chapter 6). The widely publicized Volvo Kalmar plant, which opened in the early 1970s, is based on a *sociotechnical work design.* The assembly line was replaced by battery-powered robot carriers, which automatically move car bodies to different work teams, each of which is responsible for a phase of assembly. Productivity and quality improved, but a major limitation of the Kalmar plant's sociotechnical design was that a computer (not teams) controlled the movement of the carriers and short task cycles. Despite Kalmar's team approach and elimination of the conventional assembly line, most jobs provide little scope for personal development or for the use of skills and initiative. Workers still complain that their jobs are boring.

A more effective solution to the alienating monotony of assembly-line work can be found in Saab's main auto plant at Trollhattan. The body assembly shop faced problems typical in mass production: high turnover and absenteeism, low quality, widespread dissatisfaction, and a numbingly fast work pace. Reforms initiated in the early 1970s sought to improve the work environment, make jobs intrinsically more satisfying, and boost productivity. As at Volvo, the local union played an active role.

Some remarkable changes resulted. The assembly line was eliminated. Autonomous teams of workers, or *matrix groups*, devote about 45 minutes at a time to completing an integrated cycle of tasks. Robots took over arduous, repetitive welding jobs. Groups of 12 workers control the entire production process in the welding area. This involves programming the computers and maintaining the robots, ensuring quality control, performing related administrative work, and cleaning up their workspace. Buffer zones allow teams to build up an inventory of completed bodies, giving them greater flexibility over how they use their time. (Buffers were an original feature of the Volvo plant but were later removed). Skill development, new learning opportunities, and a broader approach to job design provide the teams with what Saab calls "control and ownership" of their contribution to the production process. Far from being victims of work degradation and deskilling through robotics, these Saab employees have reaped the benefits of upgraded job content and decision-making autonomy.[51]

North American Quality of Working Life Programs

Quality of working life (*QWL*) became a buzzword among managers, public policy makers, academics, and consultants during the 1970s. QWL is an umbrella term covering many different strategies for humanizing work, improving employee–employer cooperation, redesigning jobs, and giving employees greater participation in management. The underlying goal has been to improve employee satisfaction, motivation, and commitment. The expected payoffs are higher productivity, better quality products, and bigger profits. Its proponents have argued that employers and employees alike will benefit: "With QWL there are no losers—everyone wins."[52] These basic concepts of QWL have been appropriated by the new management literature reviewed earlier and are part of TQM and similar schemes.

QWL has diverse intellectual roots. Its core ideas came from Swedish studies on work reform, the Tavistock Institute's sociotechnical systems approach to job design, Norwegian E. Thorsrud's experiments on self-managing groups, and Frederick Herzberg's theory that work is satisfying only if it meets employees' psychological growth needs.[53] In addition, QWL themes are congruent with an emphasis on worker participation in decision making as a means of creating cooperative work relations. *Human resource management*, an influential revision of human relations theory, assumes that employee satisfaction and morale are nurtured in a climate of participative management.[54] Theoretically, QWL claims to combine both humanistic and economic objectives: challenging, involving, and rewarding work experiences for employees and, for the employer, more productive utilization of the firm's human resources. Yet the lofty rhetoric of QWL advocates often fails to translate into successful applications (see Chapter 6).

A quick overview of some of the major QWL techniques would be useful. *Job enlargement* is meant to expand a job horizontally, adding related tasks to put more variety into the work done by an individual worker. *Job enrichment* goes further by combining operations before and after a task to create a more complex and unified job. For example, in the case of a machine operator in a clothing factory, job enrichment might mean that the operator would now be responsible for obtaining necessary materials, doing the administrative paperwork associated with different production runs, and maintaining the machines. This might not be an enormous change, but it would lead to a somewhat more varied, demanding, and responsible job. *Job rotation* has workers moving through a series of work stations, usually at levels of skill and responsibility similar to their original task. This tactic is frequently used to inject variety into highly repetitive, monotonous jobs. When job rotation is combined with more fundamental redesign strategies (especially the use of work teams), an employee can develop a considerable range of new skills.

An *autonomous work team* consists of roughly a dozen employees who are delegated collective authority to decide on work methods, scheduling, inventory, and quality control. They might also perform what previously would have been supervisory tasks, such as administration, discipline, and even hiring. *Quality circles (QCs),* with a narrower mandate of having workers monitor and correct defects in products or services, are perhaps the best-known application of the team concept. But quality circles often fall short of redistributing authority to rank-and-file workers. By the late 1980s, the "team concept" had become quite common in some industries. One-third of Canadian auto industry plants had some kind of QWL or "employee involvement" scheme (Robertson and Wareham 1987: 42). But Richard Long's study of workplace innovation in 946 private sector firms found that only about 10 percent had semiautonomous work groups, while 8 percent had some form of gain (profit) sharing.[55]

Attempts at work reform have generated heated debate between advocates, usually managers and QWL consultants, and critics, who are often trade unionists. As revealed later in the chapter and in Chapter 6, when we discuss "lean production" in the auto industry, team-based production does not necessarily humanize working conditions (Wells 1986a). In fact, the smorgasbord of QWL programs implemented by Canadian employers has resulted in both successes and failures. On the negative side, QWL initiatives have also resulted in declining work performance, heightened union–management tensions, employee dissatisfaction, and a breakdown in communications. Positive effects can include higher employee satisfaction and commitment, better earnings, improved labour relations, and productivity gains.[56] Research also suggests that successful technological change requires QWL-style work reorganization. In one Canadian study, several firms applied a sociotechnical approach to ensure that jobs were redesigned to use technology in ways that increased worker skills, discretion, and responsibility. Workers directly participated in the innovation process and received adequate training to equip them for the new work environment.

Shell's Sarnia Chemical Plant

The flagship of the North American QWL movement is Shell's chemical plant in Sarnia, Ontario.[57] It is unique because union and management actively collaborated in the sociotechnical planning and design of the new plant. In comparison with existing organizations, such "greenfield sites" offer greater scope for innovative work arrangements. Shell's goal was a "post-bureaucratic organization" suitable for the continuous-process technology used in the petrochemical industry that would also facilitate employee control, learning, and participation.

Six teams of twenty workers run the plant around the clock, 365 days a year. Along with two coordinators, a single team operates the entire plant during a shift, and is even responsible for hiring new team members when vacancies occur. Teams are supported by technical, engineering, and managerial personnel, along with a group of maintenance workers, who also teach team members craft skills. The organizational structure is flat, having only three authority levels from top to bottom. Team members have no job titles and rotate tasks. Pay is based on knowledge and skills obtained through job training. It takes about six years of training for an operator to reach the maximum pay level.

This design empowers workers and allows them to utilize and develop their skills. Continuous-process technology may lend itself more readily to this approach because of the huge capital investment per worker and the enormous losses to the firm should the system malfunction. Thus, management has a strong economic incentive to obtain a high level of employee commitment. By tapping the talents of its employees, Shell created a safer and more productive operation. According to the director of the union, the Shell plant eliminated authoritarian bureaucracy and provided members with opportunities to improve the quality of their work life (Reimer 1979: 5).This sociotechnical design seems to have achieved its objectives: a high level of production efficiency, smoothly functioning teams, and mutually beneficial collaboration between union and management (Halpern 1984: 58–59).

On the whole, autonomous work teams appear to have the greatest potential for significantly reallocating decision-making power, as well as for creating more interesting, challenging, socially integrated, and skilled work.[58] Why, then, has the Canadian labour movement often been a vocal critic of QWL? The drawback for unions is that management frequently has used QWL to circumvent collective agreements, rationalize work processes, and co-opt workers into solving problems of quality and productivity.[59] QWL has often been used to undermine union bargaining power and frequently spearheads labour relations schemes intended to keep firms union-free. From labour's perspective, gains in the quality of work life are therefore best achieved through collective bargaining (see Chapter 7).

After considerable internal debate, the Canadian Auto Workers (CAW) adopted a policy on work reorganization such as QWL. Essentially, it supports the involvement and empowerment of workers provided there is a true partnership and union objectives are not undermined. Rarely does this happen, though. But as former CAW president Bob White points out: "Workers should not be misled into believing that with these so-called new programs [QWL], management is offering us a partnership. None of the examples of the new work organization promoted by management includes workers or their union in any meaningful way in the decision-making process" (CAW–Canada 1988). Similarly, the United Autoworkers of America has three preconditions (which are rarely met) for its involvement in QWL: management's main goal must be to improve the quality of working life of employees; productivity gains must be a byproduct of this, not the overriding concern; and changes must in no way weaken the position of the union (UAW 1985: 152).

The Shell experience appears to be atypical. In the Shell chemical plant, the union's involvement came only after guarantees that it would be a full partner in the QWL process, and that its ability to represent the interests of employees would not be undermined. It is noteworthy that members of the same union at an adjacent older refinery wanted nothing at all to do with QWL.

The High-Performance Workplace

Earlier we posed this question: is a new management paradigm emerging? A tentative answer is yes, and perhaps it is most visible in a human resource management approach called the *high-performance workplace (HPW).* Despite the downsizing and rationalizations, a small but growing number of organizations have combined various elements discussed above. A high performance workplace is defined by employee involvement in decision making, team organization and flexible work design, extensive training and learning opportunities, open information sharing and communication, financial incentives for improved performance, support for family responsibilities, and a work environment that improves health and reduces stress. Given these defining characteristics, the working conditions and rewards in such organizations typically are very good, and employers reap the benefits of a productive and loyal workforce.[60]

The Human Resource Management Project at Queen's University conducted an extensive analysis of human resource practices in Canadian private sector workplaces in the early 1990s. It concluded that while an HPW may cost an employer more initially, improved economic performance and worker productivity occurs over time when compared with traditionally run firms.

The study also showed that there is no single model of an HPW, just as we noted in discussions of various approaches to work teams. One typical approach to HPW emphasizes QWL-style employee participation and enhanced job quality; another focuses more on providing employee incentives through improved performance-based compensation. But extensive application of all the HPW elements is found only in a minority of workplaces in Canada; at most, an estimated 30 percent of firms in wood products, metal fabricating, electrical and electronic products, and business services reported varying degrees of an HPW in 1993 (Betcherman 1995: 116). Firms with the most complete applications tend to be large, technologically advanced, and with national and international operations in complex markets.

In some respects, the HPW is a 1990s version of QWL in an internal labour market system (see Chapter 3), but with much greater emphasis on employee participation and human resource development. As such, the HPW approach may contribute to further polarization of the labour market by creating a core of advantaged employees. Yet for this core of employees who have access to good working conditions, high performance appears to mean just that—lots of dedicated hard work and continual upgrading of skills.

JAPANESE INFLUENCES ON MANAGEMENT AND ORGANIZATIONS

Canadians can learn from Swedish experiences of industrial democracy and work humanization, but the Japanese approach to work has captured most of the attention recently. The global success of Japanese corporations has led many people to conclude that their management systems, industrial organization, and technology are superior. Many studies have examined Japanese industry to cast light on what is distinctive about the Japanese approach, why it is so successful, and to what extent it can work in North America. Sociologically, the important issue is whether the Japanese industrial system can be explained by theories of social and economic organization, facilitating its adoption elsewhere, or if Japanese industry's distinctiveness owes more to its culture and history, in which case application outside Japan would be difficult (Lincoln and McBride 1987).

The Japanese Employment System

The four basic elements of the Japanese approach, which typically are found only in the major corporations, include: (1) highly evolved internal labour *markets* (discussed in Chapter 3), with features such as lifetime employment (*Nenko*), seniority-based wages and promotions, and extensive training; (2) a division of labour built around work groups rather than specific positions, a feature that is the basis for the well-known quality circles; (3) a consensual, participative style of decision making involving all organizational levels *(Ringi);* and (4) high levels of employee commitment and loyalty. A closer analysis of these aspects of Japanese firms leads to some interesting conclusions. The differences between North American and Japanese firms and management styles are probably overstated. Moreover, the Japanese system of employment owes more to principles of industrial organization than to any uniqueness in Japan's history or culture (also see Chapter 8).[61] Even so, Japan seems to be at the cutting edge of the new approaches to management and work organization discussed throughout this chapter.

To elaborate briefly, the core of the Japanese work organization is the *internal labour market.* As James R. Lincoln and Kerry McBride observe, Japanese employers strive to maintain a well-functioning internal labour market and to obtain a high level of employee commitment to the firm over the long term.[62] Teams share responsibility and accountability. When this is coupled with the consensus-building networking process used to make decisions, it is easy to see how individual workers are well integrated in their workplace. But how bottom-up is Japanese corporate decision making? Actually, it is a hybrid system, combining both centralized authority in the hands of executives who bear final responsibility for decisions, with consultations that ensure everyone has some input. Ringi refers to lower- or middle-level managers making petitions that circulate and slowly build consensus, thereby gaining a high probability of adoption.

On the shop floor, participation commonly takes the form of *quality circles* (*QCs*). Made famous by Toyota, QCs are now common in Japanese industry. Some, such as those at Toyota, are essential to maintaining and improving high levels of quality. Yet, as Lincoln and McBride observe, others "may be little more than collective suggestion-making exercises, imposed by management, for which workers receive little training."[63] While the contribution of

QCs to Japan's industrial success remains a moot point, sociologist Stephen Wood offers an insightful analysis of how they represent a potentially useful approach to worker participation (Wood 1989a).

Wood notes that the issue of workers' *tacit skills*, or intuitive expertise about how to do their job, figures prominently in debates about the introduction of new technology, deskilling, and management control (also see Chapter 6). For example, without the aid of workers' informal expertise, the bugs in many new automated systems simply would not be overcome. What is especially innovative about Japanese organization, then, is how it harnesses the tacit skills and latent talents of workers. Wood dismisses arguments that this may be just another power grab by management, or Japanese-style Taylorism. Instead, he argues, Japanese industry has shown that production systems can always be improved and that industrial engineers and other technical experts do not have the final word on these matters. QCs and other forms of participation enlarge workers' overall knowledge of the business and sharpen their analytical and diagnostic skills.

The Japanese Approach in North America

How far have these Japanese management and organizational innovations infiltrated North America? Quality, teams, and participative management are the new management buzzwords. Some organizational design concepts, particularly Toyota's *just-in-time (JIT)* system of parts delivery, have been more readily adapted for use outside Japan than have other aspects of Japanese management or work organization.[64] JIT reduces inventory overhead costs, forges a stronger alliance between a firm and its suppliers, and makes it easier to change production specifications, but does not require major changes in job design.

QCs have also become popular among North American firms facing Japanese and other foreign competitors. However, they do not go as far in the delegation of authority to autonomous work teams, as do the systems in place at the Shell chemical plant discussed above. QCs seem to place responsibility for monitoring quality and troubleshooting problems on production workers without a parallel expansion of their authority or increased rewards.[65] As Lincoln and McBride (1987: 301) conclude, QCs are often seen by North American workers as just one more chore imposed on them by management.

The obvious place to look for the successful adaptation of Japanese employment techniques is in *Japanese transplants* (local plants owned and operated by Japanese firms) or in their joint ventures with North American firms. Even here we find very mixed results. At one end of the continuum is the NUMMI plant in California, a unionized joint venture between Toyota and General Motors. Using methods imported by Toyota, employees work in teams and contribute ideas, but the daily management style is distinctly American (Kanter 1989: 274). However, the norm in transplants or joint ventures may be much closer to the other end of the continuum. As Ruth Milkman's investigation of employment conditions in Japanese transplants in California found, these firms closely resembled American firms employing nonunion labour. Few had introduced QCs, and many local managers were unfamiliar with the principles of Japanese work organization or management approaches (Milkman 1991). These firms' employment strategies mainly emphasized cost reduction, leading them to take full advantage of low-wage immigrant labour.

By the early 1990s, Canada had 530 Japanese-owned plants. The most prominent are the Ontario plants of Honda, Toyota, and CAMI (a Suzuki–GM joint venture). The Japanese managers at these three plants have had to develop a hybrid system, modifying aspects of the Japanese approach in a way that is acceptable to Canadian workers (Walmsley 1992). For example, one key to Japanese management's success is "fastidious housekeeping," which emphasizes cleanliness, reduced clutter, and keeping things orderly, as well as consistency in maintaining these goals and mutual respect. Canadian workers at Honda replaced this with their own version of good housekeeping, but dropped the principles of mutual respect and consistency. The major success story among Japanese transplants is Toyota's Cambridge, Ontario, plant, whose Corollas have won the coveted J. D. Power and Associates award for the highest quality car in North America (based on surveys of car owners). From the Toyota workers' point of view, benefits include job flexibility, free uniforms, consensus decision making, team work, good pay, and job security. However, there are drawbacks, including regular overtime, open offices for managers, no replacement workers for absent team members, health problems, close scrutiny of absenteeism and lateness, and only selective implementation of employee suggestions.

Probably the peak performance of the Japanese model described above occurred in the 1970s. Even then it faced criticism, such as the stifling of individual creativity through Nenko and groupism; discrimination against nonpermanent employees, particularly women; labour market rigidities that made the horizontal movement of workers among firms difficult; and long hours of work often at an intense pace.[66] But just like its competitors, Japanese industry faced a barrage of new challenges in the 1980s that altered its employment system.[67] The pressures of new technologies, globalization, the shift to services, a strong yen that drove up the cost of Japanese exports, and a recession have precipitated major changes. Additional stimuli for change included an aging workforce, the different attitudes of young workers, and the growing number of women workers. Firms have struggled to cut jobs without resorting to North American-style downsizing, but this trend also has begun. The pure seniority principle has given way to other means of rewarding and motivating workers. And the mobility of workers during their careers and across firms is increasing. It will be interesting to see if this restructuring signals a growing convergence of Japanese and North American approaches to organizing and managing work.

Flexible Specialization

Standardized mass production techniques have been the hallmark of industrial capitalism for over half a century. The extensive division of labour and elaborate assembly-line technologies in large factories generated huge volumes of goods. But hefty investments in mechanical technology alongside the small amounts spent on training and skill development also meant that the North American manufacturing sector (automobile companies, for example) would be slow to respond to aggressive competition from outside the country. Consequently, according to some observers, assembly-line mass production of standardized goods is becoming much less economically viable, while *flexible specialization* in production is the way of the future. Attention again turns to Japan, where many firms have moved into more flexible, computerized production systems that can be quickly adapted to produce new product lines.

Flexible production systems, which utilize computers at each stage (from designing a product to selling it), link all aspects of production into a coordinated system. Much smaller product runs are possible than with assembly-line systems, and because sales trends and consumer tastes are closely monitored, changes in design or product lines can readily be made. Microelectronic production technology, including advanced programmable robots, is also much more versatile than mass production methods in its ability to produce a wide range of goods, including electronic equipment, automobiles, furniture, clothing and shoes, and engineering products. Computers also reduce stock control costs ("zero inventory") and improve product quality ("zero defects"). In addition to Japan, some firms in Germany, Scandinavia, and northern Italy have implemented this new system. Describing the success of northern Italian consumer goods firms, Piore and Sabel (1984: 17) write:

> Flexible specialization is a strategy of permanent innovation: accommodation to ceaseless change, rather than an effort to control it. This strategy is based on flexible (multi-use) equipment; skilled workers; and the creation, through politics, of an industrial community that restricts the forms of competition to those favouring innovation.

This model of flexible specialization in manufacturing firms is based on the use of advanced microelectronic technology, highly skilled and versatile workers, and a political environment that favours innovative firms but does not protect ailing industries. The emphasis on skilled workers is particularly interesting, given that some labour process critics (reviewed in Chapter 6) take the opposing view, namely that job deskilling results from computerization. Flexible specialization, at least for Piore and Sabel, signals a return to the craft forms of production that were eclipsed with the rise of mass production. These writers also suggest that we may see a greater convergence of interests between workers and management because highly skilled workers are indispensable in such production settings. In addition, because smaller firms will be as or even more competitive in this new manufacturing environment, the global dominance of giant multinational corporations may be reduced.

The evidence of an increase in flexible, computerized manufacturing systems in Japan and other countries is indisputable, but it remains unclear whether the full range of manufacturing industries, in all industrialized countries, can and will move in this direction.[68] There is, to date, only scattered evidence of improvements in working conditions in specialized flexible production settings. As for predictions of a shifting balance of power between workers and management, and between small firms and huge multinationals, these appear to be more in the realm of hope than in reality. As Stephen Wood notes in a detailed assessment of the flexible specialization model, this part of the theory is really "an intellectual manifesto," a description of the type of workplace that Piore and Sabel believe would be preferable (Wood 1989b: 13). In a way, Piore's and Sabel's optimistic predictions are reminiscent of the postindustrial society theorists, such as Daniel Bell, who were convinced that general skill levels would increase while inequality declined.

Piore and Sabel also overlook the potential for job loss that the adoption of new technologies entails. And they do not recognize the possibility of its leading to a two-tiered employment system in which a small group of highly skilled workers, primarily male, would be the main beneficiaries of the new production system, while the majority continue to perform routine, unskilled, or semiskilled work.[69]

The Flexible Firm

While evidence of a significant shift toward flexible specialization production is limited, there are clear indications that many employers, in both the manufacturing and service sectors, have begun to reorganize their workforces to gain greater flexibility and to reduce payroll costs. Frequently, these employer initiatives have involved greater reliance on part-time or part-year workers, as well as on temporary or contract employees. Thus, the economic uncertainties experienced by employers in the past decade have also meant an increase in *nonstandard jobs.* Although some workers prefer part-time or other nonstandard jobs, as Chapter 2 documented, these positions still pay less and typically offer little job security. Consequently, an increase in nonstandard employment also means greater employment insecurity and, potentially, more workplace inequality.[70]

Some observers of these trends suggest that a new type of employment system is needed, with a core of full-time workers and a periphery of low-cost nonstandard workers whose numbers and functions vary with business conditions. John Atkinson labels this the *flexible firm.* The employment practices of such firms are thought to give them a competitive advantage in an environment of quickly changing markets and technologies. This adaptability could be achieved three ways: *functional flexibility* (training workers to perform a variety of different tasks, thus making them more interchangeable);

numerical flexibility (being able to quickly alter the size of the workforce, or the number of hours worked, through hiring of part-time, temporary, subcontracted, and other types of nonstandard workers); and *pay flexibility* (the ability to reduce pay and benefit costs by using alternative wage rates for nonstandard workers and by avoiding traditional collective agreements).[71] Thus, Atkinson's model describes an alternative work organization that is more flexible than a traditional bureaucracy, and that also has lower payroll costs. What more could an employer want?

A number of researchers have examined the employment practices of contemporary private and public sector work organizations to see how well they fit Atkinson's model. The research results show that, despite growing reliance on nonstandard workers, many organizations have not initiated other forms of employment flexibility. Among those that have, however, it is not all that clear that they have done so for the long-term strategic reasons Atkinson identified.[72] Many public sector organizations have begun hiring nonstandard workers, not in order to be more adaptable, but because of pressures to cut public spending and reduce deficits. Furthermore, crossnational differences in the extent to which firms resemble Atkinson's model suggest additional political and cultural factors that must be taken into account.[73]

As with the flexible specialization model of production, we will have to wait and see whether flexible firms become the dominant type of work organization in industrial capitalist societies, or whether traditional bureaucratic organizations remain the norm. Both of these theoretical perspectives describe work organizations that, it is argued, will be more successful in a highly competitive, rapidly changing economic world. However, each has the potential to increase workplace inequalities. As Samuel Rosenberg (1989: 8) cautions: "Behind flexibility—a word with extremely positive connotations—lies the more serious question of the relative balance of power between different groups in society." Competitiveness and productivity are clearly important goals, but so too are employment security and the quality of working life.

Lean Production

Let us return one last time to the question, is a new management paradigm emerging? Earlier, we documented that the high-performance workplace model had the potential to be a new paradigm. The HPW approach drew on various strands of thinking—from work teams and QWL to issues of healthy work environments and family-friendly workplaces. In general terms, the HPW can be interpreted as the latest reincarnation of the human relations tradition: a humanistic view of workers resulting in a strong emphasis on good human resource management practices. But there is yet another alternate management paradigm emerging in Canada—*lean production* (*LP*).[74] Three features of lean production distinguish it from HPW. First, it is modelled directly on the Japanese approach to production described above and is well established in Japanese transplants. Second, it is most fully developed in manufacturing, particularly in the North American auto industry. Third, it revolves around an integration of advanced production technology with team organization, based on a detailed analysis of the work process reminiscent of Taylorism. In this respect, LP exemplifies what is called *re-engineering*, or the radical redesign of a firm's entire business process to achieve maximum output and quality with the least labour by tightly integrating technology and tasks (Hammer and Champy 1993: 65–66).

A number of elements define LP: continuous improvement (*kaizen*), continuous innovation, flexible production, work teams, zero downtime, zero defects, just-in-time inventories and production, and employment security (Drache 1994). Lean production is presented by its advocates as a major improvement over mass production and bureaucratic organization. In other words, it has been held up as the production system for a *post-Fordist* work organization. GM's new Saturn plant in Tennessee and the GM–Toyota NUMMI factory in California are often portrayed as models of lean production. Like the Shell Sarnia plant, both are unionized, but only Saturn was a greenfield site.

At Saturn, workers and the United Auto Workers union played an active role in all phases of designing the plant.[75] A sociotechnical approach was adopted, integrating technology and the social organization of production. Work teams of 6 to 15 members are self-managed, with responsibility for deciding important issues like work flow and quality. Teams also manage human resources, including hiring, absenteeism policies, and replacement of absent workers. Like the high performance workplaces described earlier, but unlike traditional North American auto plants, workers at Saturn are paid 80 percent of the industry wage in an annual salary (as opposed to hourly), but they can receive up to an additional 40 percent if production and customer satisfaction goals are met or exceeded. A unique feature is the partnership approach to strategic planning, operating, and problem-solving decisions, whereby managers are "partnered" with elected union representatives. This approach has generated considerable mutual respect, and productivity and quality also seem to have benefited.

NUMMI differs from Saturn in that it was an old GM factory plagued with labour and production problems. When it reopened as a GM–Toyota joint venture, a new approach to work organization and human resource management was applied (Pfeffer (1994: Chapter 3). The NUMMI system included extensive employee training, job security, teams of multiskilled workers, reduced status distinctions, an elaborate suggestion system, and extensive sharing of what used to be exclusively management's information. Compared with the old GM factory, this new work system resulted in impressive reductions in absenteeism and grievances, and significantly improved quality and productivity. In fact, NUMMI produced high-quality products in less time than other GM plants and was almost as productive as a comparable Toyota plant in Japan. An employee survey showed 90 percent satisfied or very satisfied with work at NUMMI.

Thus, the NUMMI experience shows us that the work environment and industrial relations climate can affect the economic performance of a firm. Both the Saturn and the NUMMI cases demonstrate the potential for lean production to positively alter the worker–management relationship. But, as we will see in Chapter 6, the lean production approach to work organization redesign has also been harshly criticized. As with previous new management models that arrived with great promise, implementation often falls short of the mark.

CONCLUSION

We have covered a vast terrain of research and theory in this chapter. Much has been omitted, however, and we probably have not spent enough time on some major contributions. We have seen that there are many effective ways to structure an organization; the same is true for how to manage one. Yet there is a continuity, a set of unifying themes underlying the various theories and models that attempt to explain what happens inside work organizations. Let us reiterate these dominant themes.

Viewed as structures, most work organizations in capitalist societies (1) have been put together according to the principles of bureaucracy; (2) have a specialized and coordinated division of labour; and (3) have been run by professional managers. Technologies, the nature of markets, the type of product or service being produced or provided, management's strategic preferences, and constraints in the social and political environment are among the factors influencing the specific features of an organization's structure. But we must also look beyond these structural aspects of organizations. The actions and reactions of ordinary employees must all be taken into account if we are to understand the dynamics of work organizations.

Human actors create organizations. Even huge bureaucracies consist essentially of social relationships among individuals and groups. Especially fascinating is how these employees, from the night janitor to the president, compete to varying degrees for control of scarce organizational resources such as rewards, opportunities, power, influence, and status. To draw a fixed battleline between management on one side and subordinate employees on the other would be to caricature the often subtle and complex give-and-take processes at work. This important point will be further explored in Chapter 6. Certainly, worker–management conflict is central to organizational studies. Sometimes conflict erupts, but, typically, truces, negotiations, and tradeoffs create a workable level of stability and cooperation. In sum, the dynamics of conflict and consensus, rooted in unequal power relations, are integral parts of work organizations. But these relationships can assume a myriad of different forms.

In this chapter, we have directly addressed the challenge of workplace reform. How can work be reorganized and tasks redesigned in order to achieve a better balance among the goals of making work satisfying, socially useful, and rewarding on the one hand, and those of achieving economic efficiency and profitability on the other? Is this an impossibility? Are bureaucratic, managerial hierarchies essential for the smooth functioning of capitalism? Can the excesses of Taylorism and Fordism be eradicated? As we have seen, there are some alternative forms of work organization that might be capable of democratizing and humanizing work. The new management literature that calls for a top-down revolution, TQM, QWL, and Japanese-style employment systems all contain potential for meaningful change. How far they go in creating nonbureaucratic, democratic, and fulfilling work environments will likely be the script for the drama of workplace change and conflict in coming decades.

NOTES

1. Weber (1964: 338); also see Weber's essay on bureaucracy (1946: Chapter 6).
2. Morgan (1997: 15–17). This book gives an excellent discussion of the multiple images of organizations portrayed in the literature. Also see Jones (1996: Chapter 2) on theories of bureaucracy.
3. Daft (1995: Chapter 5). A good sociological analysis of bureaucracy and its problems is provided by Perrow (1986); see especially Chapter 1.
4. Blau (1963); also see Crozier (1964), whose case studies of French bureaucracies show workers regularly circumventing formal rules.
5. Johnson (1980) explores the theme of power in the workplace. Also see Hall (1986).
6. Daft (1995: 25); also see Morgan (1996) and Pugh et al. (1985).
7. See Burrell and Morgan (1979: 154–60) for a discussion of the influence of functionalism on organization theory. Donaldson (1989) offers a clear overview and defence of this conventional brand of organization theory. For a critical debate of Donaldson's views, see *Organization Studies* (1988).
8. Trist and Bamforth (1951). The work of Trist and the Tavistock Institute is summarized in Pugh et al. (1985: 84–91). Also see Rankin (1990: Chapter 1).
9. The key source for strategic choice theory is Child (1972). Also see Chandler (1962) for a historical discussion of the importance of managerial strategies in shaping modern business enterprises in the United States.
10. Billing (1994). The new journal *Gender, Work and Organization* is a good resource on this topic.
11. Weitzel and Jonsson (1989: 94); also see Meyer and Zucker (1989) on organizations that become trapped in a pattern of low performance, but somehow avoid total failure.
12. See Hayes and Jaikumar (1988), Forester (1989: Section 11), and Wood (1989a).
13. See Craven (1980: Chapter 1) on the "labour problem."
14. See Kelly (1982: Chapter 2) for an analysis of Taylorism using this typology.
15. Reed (1989). This book reviews the different theoretical perspectives on managers. Also see Godard (1994: Chapter 6).
16. Palmer (1975). For discussions of the spread of scientific management, see Littler (1982), Bendix (1974), and Merkle (1980). See Haber (1964) on the "efficiency craze" that influenced American culture in the 1920s, and Nelson (1980) for a thorough treatment of Taylorism.
17. Based on Morgan (1997: 22–26) and Littler (1982: 51–52).
18. *Industrial Canada* (March 1913: 1106); also see Taylor (1919).
19. *Industrial Canada* (April 1913: 1224–25). On scientific management as an ideology, see Whitaker (1979).
20. Kelly (1982: Chapter 2) distinguishes between the theory, ideology, and practice of Taylorism.

21. The application of scientific management in Canada is discussed in Lowe (1984; 1987: Chapter 2), Palmer (1979: 216–22), and Craven (1980: 90–110).
22. See Heron and Palmer (1977) and Kealey (1986).
23. A classic study of auto assembly-line workers is Walker and Guest (1952). Beynon (1984) describes working conditions and industrial relations at Ford in Britain, while Linhart (1981) focuses on a French Citroen factory. Meyer (1981) offers a good account of Ford's introduction of the assembly line. Hamper (1986) offers a personal account of this type of work.
24. Rinehart (1996: 44–45); Craven (1980: 100–105); Jacoby (1985).
25. The research was originally described in Whitehead (1936) and Roethlisberger and Dickson (1939). For a thorough historical account, see Gillespie (1991).
26. The Hawthorne effect also refers to the problem of reactivity in research methodology. The fact that people are aware of being part of a study may itself confound the results.
27. A good summary is found in Homans (1950: Chapter 3).
28. Carey (1967); Acker and Van Houten (1974); Franke and Kaul (1978); Perrow (1986: 82–85).
29. Perrow (1986: 114). Chapters 2 and 3 of this book summarize the origins of human relations theory and the various strands of organizational research to which it gave rise.
30. On the Durkheimian overtones of the corporate culture literature, see Ray (1986) and Ouchi (1981: Chapter 6).
31. This theme is developed in Hill (1981) and Watson (1987).
32. Meissner (1969: 5) documents how systems of worker relations, based on mutual obligations for recognition, help, and sociability vary according to the extent and type of mechanization.
33. Another study by Roy (1959–1960) showed how work groups also cushion the drudgery of low-skill, monotonous jobs by engaging in games and "goofing off."
34. Dalton (1959). Another insightful investigation of workplace "fiddling," or cheating, is Mars (1982).
35. Trice and Beyer (1993), Frost et al. (1991), Morgan (1997: 129–38).
36. See Morgan (1997: Chapter 5). Ranson et al. (1980) analyze how organizational structures are continually produced and recreated by all members.
37. *The Globe and Mail* (4 August 1992: B18).
38. Senge (1990). For assessments of Senge, see Micklethwait and Wooldridge (1996: Chapter 6); for critical discussions and applications of the concept of "learning organization," see Jones and Hendry (1994) and Maira and Scott-Morgan (1997).
39. See Shien (1992: Chapter 18) on the concept of a "learning culture."
40. In social science, the concept of a paradigm is mostly associated with the work of Kuhn (1970), who described scientific revolutions in terms of the shift from old to new paradigms. More broadly, as used here, a paradigm is a set of assumptions, principles, and guides to action.

41. See *Business Week* (5 November 1984).

42. Wood (1989c) reviews nine books representative of what he calls "new wave management."

43. Little (1992) describes TQM at Edmonton's University of Alberta Hospital. For a critical perspective, see Armstrong et al. (1994).

44. *Report on Business* (August 1993: 21).

45. Enchin (1992: B1); also see *The Globe and Mail* (25 April 1992: B4). A survey by the Arthur D. Little consulting firm of 500 U.S. firms found only one-third reporting that total quality programs significantly improved their competitiveness. A study of 100 firms in the United Kingdom came up with similar findings.

46. *Report on Business* (April 1996: 16). Based on a poll of 880 business owners and senior executives across Canada conducted for *Report on Business* by Dunn & Bradstreet Canada; twenty percent of small businesses had downsized and 10 percent expect to do so.

47. *The Globe and Mail* (28 March 1995: B1–B2; 6 February 1996: A1, A4).

48. *The New York Times* (1997: 21).

49. On the negative impact of downsizing, see Cascio (1993), Hitt et al. (1994), Freeman and Cameron (1993), and Murray Axsmith and Associates (1997).

50. *The Globe and Mail* (21 March 1995: B12); *Nova Now* [monthly employee publication] (July–August 1995).

51. On Volvo Kalmar, see Jonsson (1980) and Aguren et al. (1985). On Saab's work reorganization, see Logue (1981) and Helling (1985). These accounts of the Volvo and Saab factories are also based on Graham Lowe's personal observations and discussions with union officials, management, and shop-floor workers during visits to both plants in late 1985. The two case studies are meant to highlight different applications of sociotechnical principles; the situation in each factory could be quite different now. For a critical view, see Van Houten (1990).

52. See Rinehart (1996: 162–71) for a critical assessment. Newton (1986: 74) defines QWL as encompassing "the total ecology of work, including the linkages uniting individuals and their social relations, their work organizations and the larger society in which they live."

53. Emery and Thorsrud (1969); Thorsrud (1975); Herzberg (1966, 1968); Cherns (1976); Gardell (1977, 1982); Gardell and Gustavsen (1980). On the development of QWL in Canada, see Rankin (1990), Long (1989), and Jain (1990).

54. Miles (1965); also see Perrow (1986: 97–99) and Nightingale (1982: 47–49) for summaries of this perspective.

55. Long (1989); also see Jain (1990) and Mansell (1987).

56. Betcherman et al. (1990); Cunningham and White (1984); Long (1984).

57. This plant is described and evaluated in Rankin (1990), Davis and Sullivan (1980), Halpern (1984), and Reimer (1979).

58. Rinehart (1996: 169–71); Gardell and Gustavsen (1980: 9).

59. For critiques of QWL, see Robertson and Wareham (1987), Swartz (1981), and Rinehart (1984, 1986, 1996).

60. Betcherman et al. (1994); Applebaum and Batt (1994); Osterman (1994); Pfeffer (1994).

61. Lincoln and McBride (1987); Lincoln (1990); Hamilton and Biggart (1988).

62. Lincoln and McBride (1987: 297). This paragraph draws mainly on this source (299–301).

63. Ibid., 300. See Cole (1979) on Toyota's QCs.

64. Wood (1989b); Robertson and Wareham (1987: 12–15).

65. See Knights et al. (1985). On quality circles, see Bradley and Hill (1983) and Rinehart's (1984) Canadian case study.

66. See Kamata's (1983) highly critical personal account of life in a Toyota factory.

67. Whittaker (1990); Mroczkowski and Hanaoka (1989).

68. See Wood (1989b: 11–20), Neis (1991), and Martha Macdonald (1991) for useful discussions and critiques of the flexible specialization perspective.

69. See Jenson (1989) who argues that Piore and Sabel fail to recognize the role of gender in the labour market.

70. Dale and Bamford (1988), Rubery (1988), Polivka and Nardone (1989), and Fevre (1991) are among the many writers who have recently commented on nonstandard employment practices; for information on nonstandard employment in Canada, see the Economic Council of Canada (1990: 11–13), Krahn (1995), Green et al. (1993), and Zeidenberg (1990), who writes about the "just-in-time" workforce.

71. Atkinson (1984, 1985); also see Pinfield and Atkinson (1988) for a Canadian perspective on flexible firms.

72. See Booth (1997) for a critical evaluation of this approach from the employers' perspective.

73. See Rubery (1988), Pollert (1988), and Ryan J. Macdonald (1991) for discussions of the utility of the flexible firm model. Walby (1989) comments on the absence of gender in this theoretical perspective, while Lane (1988, 1989a) provides examples of crossnational variations in employer practices.

74. On lean production in manufacturing, particularly in the auto sector, see Womack et al. (1990), Robertson et al. (1993), Green and Yanarella (1996), Applebaum and Batt (1994: Chapter 8), Pfeffer (1994: Chapter 3), and Drache (1994). Nilsson (1996) examines lean production in a white-collar setting.

75. Applebaum and Batt (1994: Chapter 8).

6 CONFLICT AND CONTROL IN THE WORKPLACE

INTRODUCTION

Throughout the past century, employers have sought new ways of managing workers in order to increase efficiency and productivity and to reduce workers' resistance to authority. Scientific management, with its emphasis on complete managerial control and an extreme division of labour, gave way to the softer human relations approach, which tried to motivate workers by making them feel that they were an integral part of the larger work organization.

By the 1970s, management consultants were advocating changes to organizational structures and job design. Japanese-style management strategies, quality of work life programs, and total quality management models, for example, tried to reduce the negative impacts of bureaucracy, increase job skills, and enhance worker decision making. Downsizing, organizational restructuring, and new technologies have been the favoured approaches to increasing productivity in the past two decades. Even so, the lean production and high-performance workplace models claim to empower workers, enhance their skills, and involve them as partners in the production of goods and services.

If we were to draw a conclusion about consensus, cooperation, skill development, and fairness in today's workplace from the management literature in Chapter 5, it might be that new approaches to management have solved most of the problems of conflict and worker exploitation observed in the past. But this would ignore a great deal of contradictory evidence.

First, we continue to hear about layoffs and factory closures as employers rely on downsizing and restructuring to improve company performance. For example, after purchasing the Bauer hockey equipment company in 1994 and promising to maintain production in Canada, the multinational firm Nike announced the closure of the Cambridge, Ontario, factory in 1997. Four hundred workers were the victims of restructuring. Nike hinted at setting up a new factory in Asia (Heinzl 1997). Along with downsizing, replacement of full-time permanent workers with part-time and temporary employees continues to be the competitive strategy for many Canadian private and public sector work organizations (Betcherman et al. 1994).

Second, despite the rhetoric about the need for better human resource utilization and worker empowerment in order for Canadian firms to be globally competitive, management practices in this regard have been slow to change. A recent study of large Canadian workplaces concluded that a majority of these organizations were "maintaining Taylorist job designs, making low investments in employee training, not integrating human resources into strategic planning, not involving employees, and not responding to their employees' needs for more family-friendly policies" (Betcherman et al. 1994: 58).

Third, in response to such employer practices, we regularly see workers resisting and opposing management policies. In 1992, for example, 99 percent of the employees in the Ingersoll, Ontario, CAMI plant, a state-of-the-art lean production factory, voted to strike. Their union president stated that "if the company's rhetoric of fairness, worker input and commitment to a non-confrontational relationship with our union had been meaningful, this company would have never forced this strike."[1] In 1994, a 17-year-old McDonald's employee tried, unsuccessfully, to organize a union in Orangeville, Ontario. Three years later, in Vancouver, employees of the Starbucks coffee chain approached the Canadian Auto Workers for help in organizing a union. As an employee explained, "The whole idea of being called 'partners' by the company backfired. They used it to brainwash us, and some of us took it seriously. We thought that in order to be a partner, we needed to have a say in what was taking place. And that wasn't happening" (Bourette 1997).

These examples demonstrate the need to counterbalance the discussion in Chapter 5 of management approaches by returning to the themes of power and control, conflict and resistance. These themes are central to an adequate understanding of workplace dynamics. It is also helpful to characterize the management theories and strategies introduced in the previous chapter as sharing a *consensus* perspective. In contrast, this chapter's critical analyses of worker–management relationships have been influenced by the *conflict* perspective in sociological analysis.

It is appropriate, then, to begin by reviewing Karl Marx's critique of work in capitalist society since his arguments shaped the conflict perspective. We then outline the *labour process perspective*, an attempt to update Marx's ideas to explain contemporary worker–management relationships. This alternative approach begins with the assumption that conflict is to be expected in work settings where the interests of owners and managers are in opposition to those of workers. It focuses directly on attempts by management to control workers, and on how workers resist such efforts, trying to gain more control over their own labour. While the labour process approach has itself been criticized on various grounds, it does provide a much more critical assessment of quality of work life, lean production, and other contemporary management strategies, as well as the introduction of new information technologies in the workplace.

This chapter is really a debate with the assumptions and conclusions of the mainstream management and organizational literature reviewed in Chapter 5. But we also go further by asking whether workplace health and safety might be one area in which workers and management have come closer to reaching a consensus. We conclude with a discussion of industrial democracy and worker ownership. Both of these approaches to organizing workplaces help workers to gain more control over the conditions of their work. In Chapter 7, we continue the discussion by examining the origins, functions, and future of trade unions, another vehicle through which workers have attempted to look after their interests.

MARX ON EMPLOYMENT RELATIONSHIPS WITHIN CAPITALISM

As we have observed in Chapters 1 and 3 where some of Karl Marx's theoretical ideas were outlined, class conflict was central to his perspective on social change. Looking back, he argued that feudalism had been transformed into a new mode of production—capitalism, characterized by wage-labour relations of production—because of conflict between different class groupings. Looking forward, he predicted that capitalism would eventually give way to socialism because of the inherently conflictual and exploitative relationships between owners and workers.

Central to Marx's view of social change was a specific economic theory of the capitalist labour market. Beginning with the premise that the value of a product was a direct function of the labour needed to produce it, Marx proposed that, in a capitalist economy, wage labourers produced more than the amount needed to pay their wages. *Surplus value* was being created. Consequently, the relationship between capitalist and worker was exploitative in that the workers who produced the profit were not receiving it.

Unlike feudalism, which greatly restricted the mobility of serfs, workers under capitalism were free. They could always quit and search for another job. However, by purchasing labour, capitalists gained control over the labour process itself. Factory organization and mechanization further increased employer control. Thus, the craftsmen forced into the industrial mills of Marx's time were, according to one commentator, "subjected to inflexible regulations, and driven like gear-wheels by the pitiless movement of a mechanism without a soul. Entering a mill was like entering a barracks or prison."[2]

These relationships of production led, according to Marx, to feelings of *alienation* among workers in a capitalist economy. Lacking control over the process and products of their labour, and deprived of the surplus value (profit) they were creating, workers felt separated (or alienated) from their work. We will discuss alienation in greater depth in Chapter 8, along with other subjective reactions to work. For now, it is sufficient to note that Marx believed that the working class would eventually rise up in revolt against this alienation and exploitation.

But things have changed since Marx's time. The harsh, dangerous, and exploitative working conditions of early industrialization have been largely eliminated. The combination of labour legislation, unions and professional associations, and more sophisticated employers has led to higher incomes and standards of living, safer working conditions, and more responsibility and autonomy for workers, at least in relative terms.

However, earlier chapters have documented the growing number of working poor in Canada, a polarization of work rewards, the rise in involuntary nonstandard employment, and continued high levels of structural unemployment. Unions continue to resist management attempts to reduce wages while most nonunionized workers have little choice but to accept what they are offered. Hundreds of workers are still killed on the job each year, and thousands suffer workplace injuries. Despite the calls from new management approaches to empower workers, some employers continue to act as if control over work belongs to them. As the president of McDonald's Restaurants of Canada explained a few years ago:

> A McDonald's outlet is a machine that produces, with the help of unskilled machine attendants, a highly polished product. Through painstaking attention to total design and facilities planning, everything is built integrally into the technology of the system. The only choice open to the attendant is to operate it exactly as the designers intended.[3]

Marx's descriptions of working conditions in early capitalist society may no longer be applicable, but the core themes in his writings can still help us to gain a better understanding of work in today's economy. These themes—power relationships in the workplace, attempts by owners and managers to control the labour process, resistance to these attempts by workers, and conflict between class groups—are central to the labour process perspective on worker–management relationships.

THE LABOUR PROCESS PERSPECTIVE

Harry Braverman on the "Degradation of Work"

In his influential and provocative book, *Labor and Monopoly Capital,* Harry Braverman argued that twentieth century capitalism was considerably different from the mode of production examined by Karl Marx (1974). A relatively small number of huge, powerful corporations controlled the national and international economies; the role of the state in the production process had expanded; new technologies had evolved; workplace bureaucracies had become larger; and the labour process itself had become increasingly standardized.

Analyzing the transformation of office work in large bureaucracies, Braverman argued that clerical work had once included fairly high-status and responsible jobs. Turn-of-the-century male clerks and bookkeepers had been able to exercise considerable control over their work, and had been responsible for a wide variety of tasks. But this was no longer the case. What the feminization of the occupation masked was how the extensive division of labour in offices had narrowed the scope of the work done by one clerk. Office work had been standardized and mechanized. Clerks essentially processed an endless stream of paper on a white-collar assembly line, their routine tasks devoid of much mental activity. In short, clerical work had been degraded and deskilled.

Braverman attributed these changes to management strategies designed to improve efficiency and gain more control over the office labour process. Thus, office workers experienced the same degradation of work that skilled craft workers had experienced in the nineteenth century when factory-based production was expanding. Many of the management principles introduced to the factory were now also in use in private sector and government white-collar bureaucracies.

For Braverman, Taylorist tendencies lay at the heart of all modern management approaches since they all fragmented and routinized work. As he saw it, these negative trends were also beginning to affect the working conditions of technicians, professionals, and middle-level managers. In other words, both lower- and higher-status white-collar workers were becoming part of the same working class. Management strategies to control workers' every movement, introduce more advanced forms of technology, and refine the division of labour were leading to the deskilling and degradation of work, setting the scene for future class conflict.

Braverman's Contribution to the Sociology of Work

Braverman's analysis of changing employment relationships in twentieth-century capitalism has been widely influential, giving rise to scores of illuminating studies with a labour process perspective. His book encouraged sociologists to look much more closely at the skills used in different jobs, and at the ways in which the labour of employees was controlled by managers. But it has also been severely criticized by researchers sympathetic to its general critical approach.[4]

First, critics point out that Braverman assumed, but did not demonstrate, that all clerical workers in an earlier era were highly skilled and had considerable responsibility in their position. Braverman also overgeneralized from scattered evidence in North America to assert that deskilling was a universal pattern present in all occupations within all industrial capitalist societies. Important cultural differences in the labour process were consequently ignored, as were situations in which automation, work reorganization, and employee relations policies actually provided more autonomy and responsibility to workers. Furthermore, while focusing on declining skills in some occupations, Braverman overlooked the new skills that were required in industrial and postindustrial economies. For example, the management of large numbers of employees involved in different tasks required the development of a wider range of leadership skills, office work in service industries required sophisticated "people skills," and efficient use of new manufacturing and information technologies required the ability to operate computers.[5]

Second, Braverman ignored the gendered nature of workplace skills, as have many other researchers (see Chapter 4). Technical skills, frequently more central to "male" jobs, have been valued more highly than people skills, which figure more prominently in jobs typically held by women.[6] Where Braverman observed the feminization of clerical work, he may have underrated the skill requirements of this rapidly expanding occupational group. Along with his failure to consider the independent effects of gender on workplace relationships, he also overlooked how race and ethnicity have played a major part in determining access to better jobs in North American labour markets (see Chapter 3).

Third, Braverman implied that workers passively accepted management assaults on their job skills and autonomy. Seldom in *Labor and Monopoly Capital* does one find mention of workers resisting management, even though, as we saw in Chapter 5, power struggles have always been part of the informal side of bureaucracy. Furthermore, workers have organized in unions for over a century to collectively oppose their employers (see Chapter 7). The main flaw in Braverman's theory of the degradation of work is its determinism, which suggests that the inner logic of twentieth-century capitalism pushed capitalists to devise Taylorism, Fordism, human relations management approaches, and their many variants.

Why, then, has Braverman's thesis been so influential? The answer is that he challenged work researchers to ask new questions about changes in the labour process in contemporary capitalist societies. The ensuing debate has brought into sharper relief how, to what degree, and under what conditions jobs may have been degraded, deskilled, and subjected to various types of management control. As Vicki Smith notes in her commentary on Braverman's legacy, twenty years after the publication of his book, he brought the sociology of work and organizations back to issues of class and inequality, power and control, resistance and conflict. Even in his failings—overgeneralizing about deskilling, not taking account of gender, and overlooking worker resistance—he motivated other researchers to try to revise the basic labour process perspective (Smith 1994). The following sections on models of managerial control and the deskilling debate review some of this research.

Models of Managerial Control

The diversity of workplace control mechanisms documented by labour process researchers is not easily classified. This is to be expected, if we concede that there is not a single inherent control strategy within capitalism, and that workers have historically resisted efforts to control them, with varying degrees of success. What we find is a patchwork of control strategies that has emerged through the confrontations, compromises, and negotiations that regularly occur between managers and workers. As the editors of a book of Canadian labour process case studies observe, "Workers and their employers are simply too stubborn and too resourceful to conform to an overly tidy theory" (Heron and Storey 1986: 33).

Yet looking back over the past century of maturing capitalism, we do find signs of shifting preferences for control strategies among North American employers. Richard Edwards and his colleagues developed a theory of labour market segmentation around such changes in workplace control systems.[7] As Chapter 3 noted, working conditions and work rewards vary significantly across labour markets in the primary and secondary sectors of the economy. But these radical economists take the idea of segmentation considerably further, asserting that methods of worker control also differ across labour markets.

They distinguish three basic types of managerial control. With *simple control*, most common in secondary labour markets, employers regulate the labour process with coercive or paternalistic methods, or, in larger organizations, through a hierarchy of authority. *Technical control* is achieved by machine-pacing of work (an assembly line is the best example) and can, in part, replace the direct supervision of simple control methods. *Bureaucratic control* has evolved in large corporations in the core sector of the economy. Good salaries, generous benefits, and pleasant work settings are the inducements provided, usually to middle- and upper-level white-collar employees and some groups of skilled manual workers. The internal labour market, and the prospects of an interesting and rewarding career, are part of an employment package designed to win employees' commitment.

Edwards and his colleagues argue that the evolution of segmented labour markets, with their different control systems, has resulted in a socially fragmented and politically weak working class. As they see it, employers in the United States have gained the upper hand over workers in the "contested terrain" of the workplace by developing new and more effective means of control. While impressive in its scope, this historical theory is still quite deterministic, suggesting that changes in the means of production and periodic economic crises forced capitalists to devise new methods for directing, monitoring, evaluating, and disciplining workers. Like Braverman, these economists portray workers as largely passive.

Other observers of the capitalist labour process have emphasized the agency of workers—how they resist, reshape, or participate in management control strategies. Andrew Friedman (1977: 82–85), for instance, describes a shifting *frontier of control*, which is influenced alternately by conflict and accommodation between employers and employees. At issue is who sets the pace of work, hours of work, and order of task execution, and what constitutes fair treatment and just rewards. Sometimes workers gain a say in these matters through union bargaining. Or management may initiate work reforms, giving workers what Friedman calls *responsible autonomy*, which is a way of obtaining cooperation by granting workers some scope for making task-related decisions. Some degree of responsible autonomy is found, for example, in the quality of working life (QWL) programs and other participative management schemes described in the previous chapter.[8] The opposite strategy in Friedman's model is *direct control* (like the simple control described by Richard Edwards) which involves strict supervision with very little job autonomy for workers. These two types of control systems are best viewed as opposite ends of a continuum of employer–employee relationships and work decision-making arrangements, with many combinations in between.

Examples of both types of control are found in the Canadian nickel mining industry. Wallace Clement's study of the International Nickel Company describes the introduction of sophisticated "people technology" at the ultramodern Copper Cliff Nickel refinery (Clement 1981: 204). Inco's emphasis on a "one big happy family feeling," a flatter job hierarchy, and a new on-the-job training system looks rather progressive. However, these changes led to a breakdown of traditional job autonomy and the erosion of the bargaining power of the unionized refinery workers. This increased the level of direct control by management. In contrast, Inco's teams of underground miners possessed considerable responsible autonomy. These small, closely knit groups decided among themselves how and when to do each phase of the mining operation.

A recent study of a nightclub in a Western Canadian city provides an interesting example of the shifting frontier of control. Mike Sosteric (1996) describes the strong informal workplace culture that had emerged in the club, and the considerable degree of job autonomy enjoyed by workers. As a result, they were loyal and committed, and customers received high-quality, personalized service. New management saw some of the norms of the informal workplace culture as problematic, and tried to take charge by implementing what might be seen as a system of responsible autonomy. The workers were put off by the training seminars, disliked the new system of job enlargement, and found that elimination of supervisors made their work more difficult. Consequently, they actively resisted the changes. In turn, management adopted a direct and coercive control strategy that led, ultimately, to workers quitting and the quality of service in the nightclub deteriorating.

While Friedman describes responsible autonomy being offered to selected groups of workers in return for their cooperation, Michael Burawoy (1979; 1984) goes even further, suggesting that in many work settings employees choose to cooperate. Rather than asking why workers resist management initiatives, Burawoy reverses the question and asks why they typically work as hard as they do. His answer is that workers' consent is manufactured, largely through their own actions at the point of production. In his study of machine shop workers, he describes how an unspoken agreement with company goals emerged. Some employees, for example, adapted to management's control system by simply treating wage bonuses as a game they tried to win. Participation in the game of "making out," or earning wage bonuses, was essentially an individualistic response or adaptation to an otherwise boring job. As long as each worker had a fair chance of "winning" bonuses, management's rules went unchallenged. For these workers, coercion (or the *despotic organization of work*, in Burawoy's terms) was unnecessary since, by accepting the rules of the workplace, they basically motivated themselves.

Burawoy also describes the *hegemonic organization of work* in a manner similar to Richard Edwards's bureaucratic control. In large corporations and government departments, employees often see their futures linked with the success of the organization. Hence, management's values are dominant, or hegemonic. The presence of internal labour markets and responsible autonomy helps to maintain management control. Individual workers are encouraged to get ahead, and good job conditions foster long-term commitment to the organization.[9]

The rapid growth of computer-based information technologies appears to be giving rise to yet another type of management control system. *Electronic control* may simply be a replacement for technical control since, like assembly lines, computers can be used to determine the speed of work and reduce job autonomy in some industries. Joel Novek has described, for example, how the individual decision-making opportunities of Thunder Bay grain terminal operators were reduced when computers were installed in the control room (Novek 1988). But electronic control can be much more direct and intrusive when supervisors monitor workers' telephone calls and electronic mail or send warning messages to workers who are not meeting a performance standard.[10] Or it may be somewhat more subtle, although equally controlling, when workplace performance norms (the number of sales made by co-workers, for example) are collected electronically and used to push for higher performance from individuals.[11]

Having reviewed some of the research on managerial control strategies, we can now see the variety of ways in which managers might try to control the labour process. Direct, technical, bureaucratic, hegemonic, and electronic control, along with responsible autonomy, are all possibilities, alone or in some combination. The balance of power and control in any given workplace can range from strictly coercive, with management holding all the cards, to situations where workers have considerable responsibility for regulating their own work, essentially controlling themselves.

Different types of control may be more effective in some industries or with some occupational groups. We have seen examples where control strategies lost their effectiveness as work contexts changed. There may even be cultural differences in control strategies successfully employed by managers. For example, efforts to introduce Japanese forms of management to North American workplaces have frequently been met with considerable resistance by workers. Unaccustomed to paternalistic managers and peer criticism, and perhaps unwilling to give up some of their individuality, North American workers have been reluctant to participate actively in attempts to develop a consensus-based corporate culture.[12]

To conclude, there is not a single control strategy inherent within capitalism. Workers continue to find ways to resist many management control efforts. As Friedman concluded, the labour process is a shifting frontier of control and conflict. At the same time, either through individual adaptation to workplace rules or through participation in internal labour markets and, in a sense, accepting management's values and goals, some workers essentially motivate themselves.

The Skill Debate

Questions about changes in the skill level of workers' jobs are central both to our evaluation of Braverman's thesis (as well as the contrasting theories of postindustrial society) and to current public policy discussions about the link between investments in human resources and Canada's economic competitiveness. Are the forces of globalization, technological change, industrial and labour market restructuring, and new management techniques requiring more or less skill from today's workers?

For Braverman, the application of Taylorist-style management was systematically deskilling both blue-collar and white-collar work in capitalist society. In contrast, Daniel Bell and other postindustrial society theorists argued that a new economy relying heavily on highly skilled "knowledge workers" was taking shape (see Chapter 2). More recently, other writers have put forward a similar *enskilling* argument about the growing number of multiskilled workers required with "flexible specialization," "lean production," and other postindustrial forms of production (see Chapter 5). And public policy debates about competitiveness have been characterized by warnings that more investments in education and training are needed to increase the skill levels of Canadian workers.

Before we can address the skill debate, we need some agreement on definitions. What exactly is skill and how can we measure it accurately?[13] A first basic question is whether skills reside in workers or whether they are characteristics of jobs. In other words, is deskilling something that happens to individual workers or to the jobs they occupy? The answer to both questions is yes, since jobs can be redesigned to increase and decrease skill content, and workers can lose skills if they do not have the opportunity to use them regularly.

Second, are skills such as the ability to use advanced computer software, drive a semi-trailer, or teach children to read completely objective job requirements that can be reliably measured and ranked in terms of their importance and complexity? Or are skills to some extent socially constructed, reflecting the social status, power, and traditions of a particular occupation? Feminist researchers have shown, for example, how the social construction of skill has placed more value on traditionally male skills and devalued those possessed by women.[14] A useful concept in this regard is *tacit skill*, a term describing the informal knowledge workers have gained through experience or from co-workers about how to do their job. Tacit skills obviously are not part of formal job descriptions and, thus, often go unrewarded.

These observations highlight the importance of thinking about skill in a multidimensional way. The research literature contains a variety of detailed skill classifications, and personnel experts who conduct formal job evaluations have their own lists. But there is considerable consensus that, in general terms, work-related skills have two components: *substantive complexity* (the level and scope of intellectually, interpersonally, and manually challenging tasks performed in a job), and *decision-making autonomy* (the opportunity for individual workers to decide how, when, and at what speed to complete a task) (Clement and Myles 1994: 74).

There are also important research design and measurement issues to be addressed in the skill debate. While case studies of specific workplaces or occupations can illuminate deskilling or enskilling processes, they seldom have the breadth to test Braverman's sweeping conclusion about deskilling within capitalism. Hence, larger-scale studies (both in terms of occupational coverage and the time period examined) are needed. Can we assume that jobs typically held by well-educated people are, in fact, highly skilled? Alternatively, do formal job requirements really indicate the skill levels of the work tasks performed? The answer to both questions is "not necessarily." Recall, for example, that rising levels of educational attainment among Canadians, in the absence of enough jobs requiring the skills acquired through education and training, can lead to significant problems of underemployment (Chapter 2). To explore these issues, researchers require multiple measures, including education and training requirements, workers' own perceptions of skill requirements in their job, and independent observations where possible, to provide the most useful approach to studying the skill content of jobs.[15]

Wallace Clement and John Myles (1974: 72) summarize the skill debate by asking if we are faced by "a postindustrial Nirvana of knowledge where everyone will be a brain surgeon, artist, or philosopher (Bell) or, alternatively, a postindustrial Hades where we shall be doomed to labour mindlessly in the service of capital (Braverman)." Some case studies of skill change in specific occupations and work settings have supported the deskilling hypothesis, while others have not. But with larger-scale studies using multiple measures to examine skill shifts over several decades in the complete occupational structure, a more definitive conclusion emerged. On average, the long-term trend in North America has been in the direction of increased skill requirements in the workplace. Although Daniel Bell's overly optimistic predictions of an emerging knowledge society have not been fulfilled, "the net result of the shift to services has been to increase the requirements for people to think on the job."[16]

This conclusion, however, comes with several important caveats. First, Myles and Clement comment on the "net result," acknowledging that deskilling has occurred in some work settings. Second, we also need to recognize that an overall increase in skill requirements need not be accompanied by other improvements in the quality of work life. For example, TQM, lean production, and other recent management innovations may require workers to learn additional skills, but in downsized organizations workers also have to work harder and faster, under more stressful conditions. In fact, some of the critical assessments of these management strategies (summarized below) distinguish between *multitasking* (simply adding more tasks to a worker's job description) and *multiskilling* (adding to the skill repertoire of workers), arguing that the former merely makes employees work harder, not smarter.[17]

Furthermore, none of the large-scale, over-time studies showing increased skill requirements have included data from the 1990s, so we do not know whether the slow positive enskilling trend is continuing. Until the 1980s, growth in higher-skill jobs, most in the upper-tier services and the goods-producing industries, outstripped the expansion of less-skilled positions, many in the lower-tier services. But we have continued to see substantial industrial restructuring and organizational downsizing, and widespread introduction of automated technologies, the sum of which might have slowed or stopped the enskilling trend.[18]

Finally, while providing overall support for the enskilling hypothesis, research also demonstrates an increasing polarization between skilled workers and those with less skill.[19] Some case studies, for example, have shown substantial skill increases for specific groups of workers within an organization, because of automation or new information technologies, while the jobs of other workers have been deskilled.[34] Observing the more general society-wide trend toward skill polarization, Robert Reich (1991) worries about the social implications of growing inequality between "symbolic analysts" and "routine production workers." Clement and Myles (1994: 76) discuss the skill polarization issue in terms of social class (see Chapter 3 for their model of class relations), noting that almost all executives and a majority of the new middle class are in skilled jobs, compared to less than a quarter of the working class. Thus, the polarization of skills may be accenting the already pronounced class differences in income, status, and power in the Canadian labour market.

In their comparative crossnational study, Clement and Myles go further to demonstrate that, in contrast to the United States, a higher proportion of Swedish workers are in high-skill jobs. They explain by noting that a larger proportion of service sector workers in Sweden are employed in the social welfare sector where high-skill, knowledge-based jobs are the norm. In the United States, many more people are employed in lower-tier service jobs that typically have low-skill requirements (Clement and Myles 1994: 77–79). Clement and Myles also show that Canada resembles Sweden more than the United States in this respect, since Canada also developed a relatively broad social safety net in the decades following World War II.

There is some irony in these findings. Clement's and Myles's data were collected in the 1980s, before the provincial and federal governments began to cut back their provision of social services. Cutting services in order to reduce public sector spending may also have the unintended effect of reducing the proportion of higher-skilled jobs in the Canadian labour market (making us more like the United States) at the same time that governments warn that the country's competitiveness is threatened by skill shortages.

TECHNOLOGY AND THE LABOUR PROCESS

Technology is a central concept in the sociology of work. It figures prominently in theories and debates about industrialization and postindustrial society. Most of the management approaches developed over the past century relied on new technologies, at least to some extent, to improve efficiency and increase productivity. In turn, labour process researchers have focused on how employers have used technology to deskill work and increase control over employees. The following sections examine the impacts of new technologies from a critical perspective.

Technology and Social Inequality

Classical theorists like Adam Smith and Karl Marx, and more contemporary observers of postindustrial society such as Daniel Bell, have all emphasized technology's role in social and economic change. Gerhard Lenski, a sociologist analyzing North American industrial society in the 1960s, placed technology at the centre of his theory explaining differences in the level of social inequality. Since critical perspectives on technology focus on inequality in power, skill, income, and job security, it would be useful to begin our discussion with an overview of Lenski's (1966) theory of power and privilege.

Lenski proposed that a society's technological base largely determines the degree of inequality or the structure of the stratification system within it. In simple hunting and gathering societies, he argued, the few resources of the society were distributed primarily on the basis of need. But, as societies became more complex, privilege, or the control of the society's surplus resources, came to be based on power. Ruling elites received a much larger share. In agrarian societies, a governing system had evolved that gave the privileged class control of the political system and access to even more of the society's wealth. However, the arrival of the industrial era reversed this "age old evolutionary trend toward ever-increasing inequality" (Lenski 1966: 308).

Lenski's explanation hinged on the complex nature of industrial technology. Owners of the means of production could no longer have direct control over production. In the interests of efficiency, they had to delegate some authority to subordinates. This led to the growth of a middle level of educated managerial and technical workers who expected greater compensation for their training. Education broadened the horizons of this class of workers, introducing them to ideas of democracy, as well as making them more capable of using the political system to press their demands for a greater share of the profits they produced.

In short, Lenski's theory proposed a causal link between complex industrial technology, rising levels of education, and workers' insistence on sharing in the growing wealth of an industrial society. But why would employers give in to this demand? Lenski believed that the industrial elite needed educated workers; the productive system could not operate without them. Equally important, the much greater productivity of industrial societies meant that the "elite can make economic concessions in relative terms without necessarily suffering any loss in absolute terms" (Lenski 1966: 314). Because so much more wealth was being produced, everyone could have a larger share.

Lenski accurately described the social and economic changes accompanying industrialization. Twentieth-century capitalism had provided a higher standard of living for the working class. Compared to the era observed by Marx, workers were not as exploited and powerless. Social inequality was slowly declining in the decades of economic expansion and full employment immediately following World War II. However, it is virtually impossible to prove that industrial technology was the underlying cause. A better explanation might focus on changing social relations of production. Within capitalism's shifting frontier of control and conflict, workers had gained relatively more collective power, through unions, for example, and the state had legislated rules governing the labour market and provided a social safety net that reduced the level of poverty.

But as we have argued, we are again seeing evidence of growing inequality in North American society. Industrial restructuring, organizational downsizing, the growth of nonstandard jobs, and a reduction in the social safety net are all part of the explanation. But going back to Lenski's starting premise that a society's technological base determines the degree of inequality, is it possible that computer-based technologies have also contributed to the slow increase in social inequality?

The Information Technology Revolution

The new technologies of the industrial age increased productivity largely by reducing the amount of physical labour required in the goods-producing industries. In contrast, today's computer-based information and automated production technologies are reshaping both the physical and mental requirements of work, in both the goods-producing and service sectors. Factory robots, computer networks in offices, electronic databases in the retail sector, automated materials-handling systems in transportation, computer-assisted design in engineering firms, computer-assisted diagnostics in health care, and modems and fax machines in workers' homes are all part of a rapidly changing technological context for work at the end of the twentieth century. And global information links now integrate the production of services and goods in work settings around the world.[21] It would not be an exaggeration to describe the changes occurring as an information technology revolution.

We will not even attempt to catalogue the proliferation of new computer-based information and production technologies and how they are being used.[22] However, several general observations about the trends would be useful. As already noted, the new technologies are reshaping work in all sectors of the economy. Computer-based technologies are now linked throughout entire production and service-delivery processes, within workplaces, across multisite work organizations, and globally.[23] And computer technologies are becoming remarkably sophisticated in their abilities to approximate human thinking. Despite claims about "artificial intelligence," human beings and machines will remain different "species." Yet, it is clear that computer designers are creating machines capable of extremely complex decision-making processes. Two examples make the point. In 1997, for the first time, a world champion chess player was defeated by a computer. And Japanese scientists are working on a robot with human-like features that is intended to "read" people's emotions by comparing their facial expressions to a database and then respond accordingly with changes in its own plastic face (Suplee 1997: 85).

How quickly have computer-based technologies been incorporated into Canadian workplaces? At the beginning of the 1980s, only a small minority of Canadian workers used computers, in any form, in their jobs. By 1985, a survey of Canadian employers indicated that about 16 percent of their workers were using computers (McMullen 1996). By 1989, over one-third (35 percent) did so, and by 1994, almost 1 in 2 (48 percent) Canadian workers were using computers to do their work.[24] However, despite some anecdotal accounts of the rapid growth of *telework* due to the availability of computer modems, in 1995 only 9 percent of all Canadian employees reported doing some or all of their work at home.[25]

How have these new technologies affected employment patterns and the labour process? Technological innovations have contributed to increased productivity. But have these technologies also led to improvements in job quality? Have the skills of workers been enhanced, and have they been able to use the technologies to gain greater control over their work? Have the new technologies eliminated some of the unhealthy and boring jobs of the previous industrial era? Equally important, have the new technologies created more jobs than they have replaced?

Skill Requirements of New Technologies

Having addressed some of these questions in our earlier discussion of the labour process perspective, we will now focus on the role of new technologies in reshaping jobs and workplaces, with particular emphasis on *robotics* (automated production technologies), and *information technologies (IT).*

Automation's potential to eliminate dirty, dangerous, and boring factory jobs has been partly realized through robotics.[26] Robots are ideal for work in cramped spaces, in extreme temperatures, or in otherwise hazardous situations, and they have been used to eliminate dangerous jobs in many factories (welding and painting automobiles is an example). It is possible to organize production around robots in a way that offers workers considerable opportunity for skill improvement and job autonomy. The Saab factory described in Chapter 5 is an example.

Frequently, though, the new jobs involved in operating or maintaining robots have not been organized in this manner. Factory robots are seldom programmed by those running them. In some situations, operators do little more than position the material and the robot does the rest. The retooling of a U.S. automobile plant provides an example (Milkman and Pullman 1991). Until the mid-1980s, the GM factory in Linden, New Jersey, produced luxury-sized cars using traditional assembly-line technology. Around 1985, the factory was retooled in order to start producing smaller cars. Over 200 robots were added to the production system, along with more than 100 automated guided vehicles (AGVs), which moved the cars in production through the system. In addition, management introduced some organizational innovations including just-in-time delivery, quality control circles, and special training programs for workers. However, the basic hierarchy separating production workers on the line from skilled trades workers (electricians, machinists, and carpenters) remained unchanged.

The automated system required 25 percent fewer production workers to do less skilled jobs. This deskilling of production jobs could be traced to the replacement of welders by robots as well as the reorganization of several production processes. Previously, a group of workers with a broad range of skills relieved others, one at a time, from their various positions on the line. With the new technology, everyone took breaks at the same time, so the multiskilled relief workers were no longer needed. Under the old system, production workers frequently repaired defective component parts. With the just-in-time delivery system, defective parts were returned to the suppliers. And even though production workers used computers in the new assembly system, few new skills were needed. As one worker commented, "There is nothing that really takes any skill to operate a computer. You just punch in the numbers, the screen will tell you what to do" (Milkman and Pullman 1991). By contrast, a reduced number of skilled trades workers found themselves doing a larger variety of tasks that required more skills. Compared with the traditional assembly-line technology, the installation and maintenance of the robots and AGVs were challenging jobs with a great deal of variety.

Computer numerical control (CNC) machines, used to make metal parts and tools, have also, in some cases, led to an erosion of workers' knowledge requirements and responsibilities. These machines have been used to replace tool and die makers, who traditionally were among the most skilled manufacturing workers, with cheaper semiskilled CNC operators. As one skilled Canadian machinist described the impact of CNCs on his job:

> You don't even need a man to monitor [the CNC], the machines will monitor themselves. They've got all these electronic scans that tell when the tool edge is wearing, what horsepower the machine is using. They've got all these tool change systems, so they even can change tools whenever they want, so you don't even need a man there.[27]

As for white-collar employees, case studies reveal that the impact of IT has been positive more often than negative.[28] The extent of the improvements in work quality depend on organizational characteristics such as size, industry, and occupation, the specific type of technology, and managerial decisions about how to reorganize work. Thus, some of the dreary filing and typing chores of office work have disappeared, and opportunities to acquire computer skills have provided more challenging, varied, and interesting jobs for some clerical staff.

But the full potential of IT for enhancing the quality of work has not always been realized. On the basis of her case studies, Shoshana Zuboff (1988: 57) concludes that IT "creates pressure for a profound *reskilling*." Yet old-style management control and bureaucracy often prevent workers from learning how to effectively interact with the computers. Fearing loss of power, many middle managers in the firms she studied were reluctant to give workers the training and responsibility they needed to make the leap to *informated* (as opposed to simply *automated)* work.

As these case studies indicate, IT has had mixed effects on the skill levels of workers. But nationwide surveys suggest that skill upgrading has been more common than downgrading, at least from the perspective of workers. In 1989, the General Social Survey showed 29 percent of employed Canadians saying that new computer or automated technologies had "greatly affected" their job in the previous five years. Another 15 percent chose the "somewhat affected" response category. Five years later when the study was repeated, 34 percent of Canadian workers answered "greatly affected" and 17 percent stated that their job had been "somewhat affected" by computer-based technologies. In both studies, about 70 percent of those affected agreed when asked whether their job skills had increased. Almost none said that the skill requirements of their jobs had decreased (Lowe 1997).

However, opportunities to learn a wide range of new skills are usually limited. A 1995 survey of Canadian firms revealed that *know-how skills* (simply knowing how to use a new technology) were more likely to be enhanced than *problem-solving* and individual *decision-making* skills (autonomy). Workers in professional and managerial positions were more likely to have experienced skill upgrading (McMullen 1996: vii). There is also some evidence that the introduction of IT may lead to the loss of informal expertise (tacit skills) that is difficult to build into computer systems (Fearfull 1992: 441).

Furthermore, the spread of new computer-based technologies has led to greater polarization of skills within the labour force. Case studies and the General Social Survey show that workers who already are highly skilled (professionals, managers, and technicians) are more likely to have the opportunity to work with IT and to receive the necessary training.[29] Kathryn McMullen's 1995 survey of Canadian firms reveals that professional positions accounted for 56 percent of new jobs created by IT, while 60 percent of the jobs eliminated were in intermediate-level positions. However, employers appeared to be doing little to upgrade the skills of workers made redundant by IT so that they could move into the new, more skilled jobs (McMullen 1996: viii). As Thomas Idle and Arthur Cordell conclude, "We are beginning to see the creation of a workforce with a bi-modal set of skills. Highly trained people design and implement the technology, and unskilled workers carry out the remaining jobs" (1994: 69).

New Technologies and Control of Workers

Henry Ford's assembly line gave managers a powerful means of controlling the pace of work. As one observer of a Ford plant commented:

> Every employee seemed to be restricted to a well-defined jerk, twist, spasm or quiver resulting in a flivver. I looked constantly for the wire or belt concealed about their bodies which kept them in motion with such clock-like precision.[30]

Such technical control within a rigid bureaucratic setting (Fordism) gave North American industrial workers little autonomy. But as new information technologies became more common, so too did predictions that they would erode organizational power structures. With computers, workers would gain more control over their own labour and there would be less need for direct supervision by managers. John Naisbitt (1982: 282) was one of the enthusiasts:

> The computer will smash the pyramid; we created the hierarchical, pyramidal, managerial system because we needed it to keep track of people and things people did; with the computer to keep track, we can restructure our institutions horizontally.

However, McMullen's 1995 survey of Canadian firms presents a much more cautious assessment. On the basis of employers' responses about the effects of new computer-based technologies, the know-how skills of employees were improved more than their problem-solving and decision-making skills (McMullen 1996: vii). In other words, the new technologies had not provided workers with that much more control over their own work.

Critics of the new technologies have presented case-study evidence to show that computers and other new technologies can also be used by management to expand its control over workers.[31] The most obvious example is electronic control, defined earlier. Specifically, information technology has been used in a range of different settings to monitor workers' productivity and to ensure that they are following rules. One recent study of U.S. companies showed that 30 percent of companies admitted to regularly reading employees' personal electronic mail or computer files.[32]

Nevertheless, it is difficult to draw an overall conclusion about the impact of the new technologies on workplace power structures. The case-study evidence presents a pessimistic picture, but it does not allow us to generalize about the labour market as a whole. In turn, while reaching a somewhat more positive conclusion, the 1995 survey of Canadian firms cannot really tell us what is happening at the point of production, based as it is on employers' responses to general questions about occupational change. Furthermore, new technologies are often introduced along with other managerial initiatives—TQM or lean production, for example—making it difficult to identify the specific causes of improvements or reductions in employee autonomy. The point to remember is that new technologies are almost always chosen and implemented by managers, not by the employees directly affected.

Job Creation or Job Loss?

Early in the 1800s in English milltowns, the Luddites, fearful about the loss of their jobs to new industrial technologies, rioted and smashed weaving machines. In Canada, at the end of that century, skilled workers in Ontario resisted efforts to mechanize their workplaces for the same reason. It is clear, though, that the eventual outcome of the move to factory-based production and, later, the introduction of assembly lines included economic growth, job creation, and a higher standard of living. In the last few decades, the rapid diffusion of new computer-based technologies has also led to economic growth. But will the new technologies create more jobs than they eliminate, and will the eventual outcome be a higher standard of living for more working Canadians?

The industrial revolution eventually produced many more jobs than it destroyed and, later, the service economy expanded to fill the void created by a shrinking manufacturing sector. But the new technologies are replacing "mental" as well as "manual" forms of work. Some futurists like Jeremy Rifkin, therefore, have a pessimistic view of the future. Describing the "end of work" as he sees it, Rifkin writes:

> Within less than a century, "mass" work in the market sector is likely to be phased out in virtually all of the industrialized nations of the world. A new generation of sophisticated information and communication technologies is being hurried into a wide variety of work situations. Intelligent machines are replacing human beings in countless tasks, forcing millions of blue and white collar workers into unemployment lines, or worse still, breadlines.[33]

Canada and other industrialized nations are facing a serious problem of structural unemployment (see Chapter 2). New automated technologies have been introduced to reduce labour costs and have contributed to the unemployment problem.[34] But so have corporate downsizing, the shrinking of the government sector, and global business systems that have moved some jobs overseas. The direct link between the introduction of new information technologies and job loss is not as clear. In some cases, computerization has led to layoffs while, in others, new jobs have been created, although it is evident that workers made redundant by new technologies are seldom first in line for new jobs (McMullen 1996). Thus, there is insufficient evidence to support Rifkin's apocalyptic view of the future, and the targeting of new technologies as the primary cause of job loss. Furthermore, jobs are still being created, even though a larger proportion are less secure and not as well paying as in the past (Chapter 3).

Even so, it is unlikely that we will see sufficient computer-induced job growth in the next decades to counterbalance the effects of a decade of downsizing, automation, and globalization (Menzies 1996: 89–102). As Idle and Cordell conclude in their discussion of the automating of work, "these are not the best of times." High levels of unemployment, increased employment insecurity, and growing income inequality have made life more difficult for millions of Canadians. Reductions in government spending have meant a reduction in support for the unemployed and the working poor. As a society, we are faced with a serious challenge: how do we maintain sustainable economic growth, reduce social inequalities, and ensure social cohesion (Betcherman and Lowe 1997: 40)?

Part of the answer is recognizing, as Charley Richardson puts it, that "computers don't kill jobs, people do" (1996). Technology is a tool that humans have used to their advantage historically, to create jobs and to improve the quality of life. Technology has also been used to eliminate jobs, to destroy the natural environment, and to kill people. There is evidence that the new technologies being developed today can create jobs, increase skill levels, and provide workers with more control over their working environment. New technologies also have the potential to do the opposite, as our quick review of the research literature demonstrates. Hence, as a society, our challenge is to find ways to use technology to provide economic opportunities for as many citizens as possible.

Technological, Economic, or Social Determinism?

We began our critical assessment of technology with Lenski's theory proposing that a society's technological base determines the degree of social inequality. Writing in the 1960s, Lenksi viewed industrial technology positively, arguing that it had led to reduced inequality. At the same time, Marshall McLuhan presented a far more pessimistic analysis of the impact of technology on social life. He concluded that human beings were at risk of becoming the servants of technology. His actual words were stronger; he suggested that if trends continued, we might simply become "the sex organs of the machine world … enabling it to fecundate and to evolve ever new forms."[35]

We do not agree with either of these positions since they attribute too much independent power to technology. *Technological determinism*, the belief that the developmental pattern and effects of a given technology are universal and unalterable, removes the possibility of human agency, the potential for people to shape technology for the greater social good. Furthermore, this position ignores the strong evidence (presented above and in Chapter 5) that technologies have been used in very different ways, with different outcomes, in different work settings and societies.

We also reject *economic determinism*, the belief that the "market knows best" how to choose and implement new technologies. Such a perspective would argue that, despite current problems with job loss, deskilling, and loss of worker autonomy, new technologies will in time lead to more positive than negative outcomes. Behind the free hand of the market are real people, making decisions about how to implement the new technologies. These decisions typically have been made by managers guided by the profit motive, so only a small minority of citizens have participated in making these decisions.

Instead, we prefer a *social determinism* perspective, advocating education, wide-ranging discussion, and open decision making about how technologies will be used, by whom, and for whose benefit. We believe that technology should be used to serve human needs, not merely the needs of a particular company or work organization. Consequently, workers need to be able to participate in decisions about the choice and implementation of new workplace technologies that affect them directly, and citizens need a voice in shaping broader technology strategies.

Because the quest for increased competitiveness through technology has frequently meant job loss or job downgrading for workers, labour movements in North America and Europe generally have opposed the introduction of new technology by management without any input from unions. But this does not mean that unions oppose technological change in principle. Instead, they have insisted that employees be consulted so that the negative effects can be minimized and opportunities for upgrading jobs and improving working conditions maximized. Unions also have argued that any productivity gains should be shared equitably.[36] But while European unions have been successful in obtaining some of these goals, similar gains for organized labour have yet to be achieved in Canada.

Canada presently lacks strong legislation requiring prior consultation with employees on technological change. Legislation at the federal level and in four provinces merely requires up to 120 days' notification of technological changes, but notification does not mean consultation and joint decision making. Fewer than 40 percent of major collective agreements require the employer to notify or consult with the union prior to making technological changes, while fewer than 20 percent establish joint labour–management technological change committees.[37] Clearly, Canadian employers' strong sense of "management rights" extends to decisions regarding automation.

Involving unions and employees in the technological change process in Canada would constitute a major step toward balancing economic and social goals. Crossnational comparisons suggest that in countries with strong labour movements, consultation on technological change is more the norm. Negative effects such as deskilling and income polarization have been less pronounced, and workers have not been as opposed to technological change.[38] Because Sweden and Norway have powerful unions that take an active role in shaping social policy, legislation requires employers to consult with employees prior to automating. Workers have direct input regarding the reorganization of work around new technologies. Widespread layoffs due to technological change have generally been avoided, and, in cases of redundancy, employers have retrained or found other jobs for those affected. In the past few years, however, some of these policies have been weakened and others are being questioned (Smith et al. 1995: 713). It remains to be seen whether Sweden can maintain the system that has provided a model for North American trade unionists.

NEW MANAGEMENT APPROACHES: A CRITICAL PERSPECTIVE

Chapter 5 introduced some of the recent management approaches that have promised to flatten workplace hierarchies, provide workers with additional job autonomy, and enhance their skills. The labour process literature has identified many of the ways in which these promises have not been fulfilled, as documented earlier. Still, it would be useful to itemize some of the specific criticisms of several prominent management approaches. While the management literature itself has addressed problems and contradictions within these models (see Chapter 5), the labour process critique is far more penetrating.

Quality of Working Life (QWL)

The quality of work life (QWL) model of management grew out of several different traditions, including the British sociotechnical systems approach, early Swedish work reforms, and Herzberg's writings on job satisfaction. The emphasis in QWL programs was primarily on workers' immediate job tasks, with job enrichment, job enlargement, job rotation, and autonomous work teams being among the most common innovations. In some settings, management hierarchies were also reduced as work teams took on some of the basic management tasks. The QWL package was typically presented to workers as an effort on the part of management to improve the quality of work life, but obviously managers were hoping to improve productivity as well.

Some QWL initiatives resulted in model "high performance" workplaces, such as the Shell Sarnia refinery and GM's Saturn factory. Unions participated in the design of the program, workers received extensive training, and considerable autonomy and decision-making responsibility was given to self-directed work teams. But more often, critics charge, changes in workers' job tasks were minimal, they did not gain the opportunity to influence decisions on larger workplace changes (the introduction of new technology, for example), and management imposed the programs rather than involving the workers in the decision.[39] In some cases, QWL programs were introduced in a cynical attempt to counter the organizing efforts of unions—if management could provide these benefits, who needs a union?

Total Quality Management (TQM)

Like QWL approaches, total quality management (TQM) programs have been heralded as a "win–win" approach to labour–management relations; workers benefit through improved working conditions and productivity increases. TQM emphasizes customer satisfaction and continuous improvement in addition to job redesign. It also places more emphasis on the need to develop a strong organizational culture. By the 1980s, when TQM was becoming popular, concerns about global competitiveness were becoming more pronounced. Hence, the need for workers to buy into the goals of the program and the values of the corporate culture took on a larger significance. The message for workers was that winning—being part of an ever-improving and more productive company or government workplace—was important not only for the workers and management, but also for the economy. By the same logic, losing meant more than just being part of an unsuccessful work organization. In the new, competitive economy, it might also mean losing one's job.

But TQM efforts have seldom invited workers to participate in decisions about whether to introduce new technologies, or to restructure or downsize organizations. Instead, critics point out, workers have been invited to find ways to work harder, often in an atmosphere of anxiety about possible job loss. Promises of improved working conditions as a result of organizational and job redesign have, consequently, often meant only superficial changes. As in the case of QWL, some TQM initiatives were presented to workers as alternatives to unions. Systems put in place to monitor quality and encourage improvement have also been effective ways to control workers. Ironically, many middle managers also find it stressful to constantly reorganize work processes. Thus, while TQM may have increased productivity in some settings (see Chapter 5), it has done so by requiring employees to work harder. All too often, working conditions have not improved and workers have not been empowered.[40]

Flexible Specialization

Flexible specialization joined the list of new management approaches with considerable fanfare. It promised revolutionary change in Fordist manufacturing systems (computer-coordinated, small-run, flexible production) and the return of craft forms of production (highly skilled, autonomous workers involved in all aspects of the production process). Consequently, bureaucracy should be reduced and workplace conflict should subside. In addition, the power of multinational corporations employing traditional production methods would decline. Essentially, flexible specialization was seen as the production system of a postindustrial economy characterized by less conflict and inequality.

Unlike QWL and TQM, flexible specialization has limited applicability as a management model outside of the manufacturing sector. In fact, it remains unclear just how applicable it is to the full range of manufacturing industries. More important for our discussion here, there is little evidence of working conditions improving and workplace conflict subsiding in firms of this type. Multinational corporations have certainly not become less powerful over the past decade.

Thus, one critique of the flexible specialization model is that it is more a blueprint for a desirable workplace than a description of an emerging trend. However, if it were to become a trend, this model proposes no solution to the social problem of workers made redundant by technological change. Instead, it offers a vision of a severely segmented labour market in which a small elite group of highly skilled workers are the main beneficiaries, while the majority continue to perform routine, unskilled, or semiskilled work.[41]

Lean Production

The *lean production* system of manufacturing also relies heavily on computer-based and automated technology, but without the commitment to the small-scale, highly flexible production processes of flexible specialization. Nevertheless, it goes beyond the rigid and standardized mass production of Fordism by encouraging a flexible approach to product redesign and with its emphasis on quality, continuous improvement in production methods (*kaizen*), and just-in-time delivery. Like QWL and TQM, lean production claims to rely on highly skilled and thinking workers, and promises a reduction in workplace conflicts through its teamwork model of decision making. With all of these features, it is little wonder that lean production has been portrayed by its advocates as the final solution to Taylorism and Fordism (Womack et al. 1990).

Nevertheless, many critics have been harsh in their assessments of lean production's impact on the labour process.[42] They point out that multitasking (one person doing more jobs) is not the same as multiskilling. Instead, it is one of the ways in which management has squeezed more work out of a smaller number of workers. The elimination of replacement workers has also had this effect, as has *kaizen*, the consensus-based approach to continuous improvement. By emphasizing how workers in a particular factory need to outperform their competition elsewhere, management essentially harnesses peer pressure to speed up production.

By way of example, James Rinehart describes a California automobile factory that, before lean production, managed to keep its workers busy for 45 out of every 60 seconds they were on the job. Lean production brought this up to 57 out of 60 seconds. But, as he puts it, "[t]o call kaizen a democratization of Taylorism is to demean the concept of democracy" (1996: 179). Other critics agree, noting that management continues to tightly control the topics discussed in kaizen sessions (Graham 1993: 148). Essentially, lean production has not led to significant skill enhancement or to worker empowerment. It has meant a faster pace of (still repetitive) work, higher stress for employees, and, in some cases, higher injury rates. As a consequence, lean production has also led to resistance by workers—the 1992 strike at the CAMI plant in Ingersoll is an example.[43] Thus, as Rinehart (1996: 181) concludes, "Lean production constitutes an evolution of Fordism, not its transcendence."

High-Performance Workplaces

The *high-performance workplace* is one of the latest additions to the list of new management strategies. This model shares a number of features with other recent management approaches, including an emphasis on reducing bureaucratic hierarchies and rigid job descriptions, increasing workers' decision-making opportunities, and offering them more training to enhance their skills. But it goes further by advocating human resource management programs that are family friendly and emphasizing the importance of a healthy, non-stressful work environment. It also recommends that employers share profits from productivity increases with workers through variable-pay plans that link some compensation to performance.[44]

Like flexible specialization, the high-performance workplace is more a model of a desirable future than a description of current practice, since researchers have demonstrated that only a minority of Canadian organizations are moving in this direction (Betcherman et al. 1994: 58). For workers in a high-performance organization, the potential benefits (skill upgrading, decision-making opportunities, profit sharing, improved working conditions) are considerable. But there are also drawbacks, since one of the assumptions of the model is that employment security can no longer be guaranteed, and that profit sharing also means risk sharing (if the company loses money, so do the workers) (Betcherman et al. 1994: 97). Critics influenced by a labour process perspective would be skeptical of the commitment asked of workers in return for these benefits, pointing to previous examples of companies using QWL, TQM, and other approaches to speed up work and sideline unions.

To the extent that the high-performance workplace becomes a reality, we may see greater labour market segmentation, the result being a society in which a small privileged elite of high-skill, relatively autonomous workers are well rewarded, while the majority of workers face a much greater risk of low-skill, less-rewarding work with greater employment insecurity. This, of course, is not a critique of the high-performance workplace model so much as a recognition that, despite its promise, it does not offer a solution for the larger social problem of growing labour market inequality.

New Management Approaches: A New Labour Process?

The management literature reviewed in Chapter 5, while recognizing some of the flaws and inconsistencies in these approaches, uses labels like *participative management* and *employee empowerment* to describe recent innovations. More critical observers have described them as *neo-Fordist* or *post-Fordist*, suggesting that the changes have not been nearly as significant as their proponents claim. By offering some small concessions to workers, the basic production framework and power structure of industrial capitalist society has been maintained. Some critics go even further, using the term *hyper-Taylorism* to describe how managerial control over the labour process has increased and how "management by stress" requires workers to push themselves and each other to make more profits for their employers (Russell 1997: 28).

But labels are not as important as real outcomes. What do we see when we look back at two decades of new management approaches in North America? Summing up our overview of these initiatives, all of them offer some potential for skill upgrading, increasing worker participation in decision making, and reducing bureaucracy. In some cases (Shell's Sarnia refinery and the Tennessee Saturn plant, for example), the implementation of these approaches has gone a considerable way toward improving the quality of work life for employees. None of these management models, however, really provides avenues for workers to have input on larger organizational decisions, on the introduction of new technologies, for example, or on a decision to restructure the organization.

The two approaches that go the furthest to counter Taylorism and Fordism—flexible specialization and the high-performance workplace—have not been implemented that often. Other approaches typically do not deliver nearly as much as they promise. Furthermore, when we examine them more critically, we frequently find that they have also been used to increase control over workers and to speed up work. In addition, the advent of the new management approaches has been accompanied by widespread organizational restructuring and downsizing. The outcome, for society as a whole, has been a polarization of the labour force in terms of skill, income, and job security, and greater social inequality.

As we concluded about the impacts of new technologies on the labour process, the problem does not lie in the technology but in how it is implemented, by whom, and for what purposes. Overall, new management strategies—we might call them social technologies—have almost always been introduced with productivity and profit as the main goals. Improvements in quality of work life and worker empowerment have been secondary motivations, while reductions in social inequality have seldom figured in the decision. And workers have rarely been involved in the decision to implement new social technologies, either directly or through their unions. With a few exceptions, when invited to participate, workers' input has been restricted to smaller decisions about changes in their immediate work tasks. Consequently, we should not be surprised that much of the promise of the new management approaches has not been realized.

A CRITICAL PERSPECTIVE ON WORKPLACE HEALTH AND SAFETY

Our profile of good jobs and bad jobs in Chapter 3 documented the high costs to workers, employers, and society of workplace health and safety risks. Every year, hundreds of Canadian workers are killed and thousands are injured on the job. Acknowledging that it is impossible to put a price tag on human suffering and death, the magnitude of the problem is nevertheless indicated by the estimate that occupational injuries and deaths cost Canada about $8.6 billion in 1992. Half of this figure was for direct compensation to victims or their families, while the other half was an estimate of indirect costs and lost productivity (Gordon 1994: 547). In addition, the future health of many workers is regularly placed at risk. Every year, a sizable minority of all Canadian workers are exposed to workplace health hazards, including air pollution, excessive noise, physically demanding repetitive work, and stress-inducing work environments (Geran 1992; Grayson 1994).

Workplace health and safety is highly relevant to our discussion of conflict, control, and resistance in the workplace. Historically, dangerous machinery, unsafe work sites, polluted air, and exposure to carcinogenic substances and other risks have taken their toll on the working class in terms of shorter life expectancies and higher illness and disease rates (Reasons et al. 1981: Chapter 11). Most of the progress made over the years in reducing workplace health and safety risks has been the result of workers fighting for improvements, often against the strong opposition of employers. Furthermore, workplace health and safety continues to be a contentious issue in union–management contract disputes and in the larger political arena. At the same time, the area of workplace health and safety provides one example where, at least to some extent, workers and their employers have managed to identify and work together toward common goals (Digby and Riddell 1986).

The Politics of Workplace Health and Safety

In the early years of Canada's industrialization, workers had little protection from what were often extremely unsafe working conditions. Work in the resource industries, in construction of canals and railways, and in factories was hazardous, and the risk of injury and death was high. As in other industrializing countries, an *administrative model of regulation* slowly developed, in which the government set standards for health and safety and tried to enforce them (Lewchuk et al. 1996: 225). Employers frequently opposed these efforts, arguing that their profits were threatened and that the state had no right to interfere in worker–employer relationships. In turn, unions fought for change and the public was mobilized behind some causes, including restrictions on the employment of women and children in factories. Thus, the Factory Acts of the 1880s led to improvements such as fencing around dangerous machines, ventilation standards for factories, and lunchrooms and lavatories in large workplaces. The employment of women and children was also curbed on the grounds of protecting their health.

Over the years, additional safety standards were introduced. In unionized workplaces and industries, *collective bargaining* also made a difference as unions negotiated for better working conditions and the elimination of specific health and safety hazards. By the second decade of the twentieth century, provincial workers' compensation boards had put in place *no-fault compensation systems* that still exist today. Injured workers are provided with some money, the amount depending on the severity of their injury, and with partial compensation for lost wages, no matter whose fault the accident has been. In return, they give up their right to sue for compensation if the employer was at fault. The system is funded by contributions from employers, the amount based, in part, on their safety record. Thus, there is a monetary incentive for employers to reduce workplace health and safety hazards and to encourage safe working practices among employees.

All of these approaches to dealing with health and safety issues—standard setting and enforcement by the state, collective bargaining between unions and employers, and the no-fault compensation system—offer little room for direct involvement on the part of workers who are most directly affected by unsafe and unhealthy working conditions. But the introduction of the *internal responsibility system (IRS)* has changed this. A guiding principle of this approach is that workers' personal experience and knowledge of work practices and hazards are an integral part of any solution to health and safety problems. In addition, they should have the right to participate in the identification and elimination of workplace hazards. Furthermore, health and safety is also management's responsibility. Overall health and safety is a workplace issue—an internal responsibility—too important to be left to government alone. In the IRS system, employees are directly involved with management in monitoring and inspection, and in education and health promotion in their workplaces.

Direct worker involvement in health protection and promotion in the workplace increased dramatically in Europe in the 1970s. This trend grew out of demands for greater industrial democracy (discussed later in this chapter), and government reviews of traditional and unsatisfactory approaches to occupational health and safety (Tucker 1992). In Canada, the first major initiative of this sort was the 1972 Saskatchewan Occupational Health Act. It broke new ground by broadly defining occupational health as "the promotion and maintenance of the highest degree of physical, mental, and social well-being of workers" (Clark 1982: 200), and by making joint health and safety committees (JHSCs) mandatory. Other provinces and the federal government (about 10 percent of Canadian workers are covered by federal labour legislation) followed, and today the internal responsibility system, built around JHSCs, is part of the legislated workplace health and safety system across the country.

JHSCs range in size from two to twelve members, half of whom must be nonmanagerial employees (either elected or appointed by a union if one exists), and are required in any workplace employing twenty or more persons. In most provinces, workplaces with at least five but less than twenty employees must also have at least one nonmanagerial safety representative. The committees keep records of injuries, participate in safety inspections, make recommendations to management about health and safety concerns, inform employees about their rights with respect to such concerns, and develop safety enhancement and educational programs (Gordon 1994: 542–43).

Along with giving JHSCs the *right to be involved* in health and safety issues, legislation also allows workers the *right to refuse unsafe work*, the definition being based on the individual employee's own assessment that a particular task presents a genuine risk. If subsequent inspections determine otherwise, the legislation protects workers from reprisals from employers. Workers also have the *right to be informed* about potentially hazardous materials with which they might be working.

The IRS system appears to be effective. Research has shown that the recommendations of JHSCs to management are usually heeded (Gordon 1994: 548). A recent Ontario study examined data on claims for lost time due to accidents between 1976 to 1989 and concluded that "where management and labour had some sympathy for the co-management of health and safety through joint committees, the new system significantly reduced lost-time accidents" (Lewchuk et al. 1996: 225). If an organization reluctantly introduced JHSCs, the system had little effect. The success of JHSCs in Canada, contrasted with the more traditional and less effective U.S. approach to health and safety issues, has led to recommendations that the Canadian system be copied in the United States (Gordon 1994).

The Labour Process and Workplace Health and Safety

Does the relative effectiveness of JHSCs and the IRS system indicate that workers and management are no longer in conflict over health and safety issues, that this is a win–win situation? We would argue that workers and management have moved further in this direction on health and safety than they have elsewhere. In part, this is due to the economic incentives built into the system for employers; a better safety record means lower costs of production. More important, legislation has reduced some of the power differences between management and workers and directly involved each in addressing health and safety issues.

Even so, workplace health and safety remains a contested terrain. Critics of the IRS system have pointed out that, in many JHSCs, nonmanagement members continue to have much less influence, particularly in nonunionized workplaces. Some employers largely ignore the joint committees, despite legislation (Lewchuk et al. 1996: 228). Research has shown that workers are often unaware of their rights and lack the knowledge needed to address complex health hazards, and that scientific and medical experts give the appearance of impartiality to a system that continues to be dominated by employers for whom profits come first.[45] In some tragic cases like the Westray mine explosion in 1992 in Nova Scotia, the system failed completely. Local miners had warned that the mine site was unstable, and the initial mining plan was rejected for safety reasons. But the mine still opened, and remained open even after repeated problems with methane gas, coal dust, and roof falls. Eventually, twenty-six miners died in an explosion.[46]

Joel Novek's (1992) case study of restructuring within the Canadian meat-packing industry provides another example of how worker health and safety can be jeopardized for profits. Industry-wide consolidation of production in the 1980s led to a rising injury rate among workers. The problem could be traced directly to changes in the labour process, specifically mechanization and speedups. Workers suffered more muscle strains and knife lacerations, and the hazards associated with handling live animals in cold, damp, and noisy environments increased. Productivity also rose, but because of more accidents and worker burnout, the companies faced higher workers' compensation board levies and had difficulty maintaining production. Only at this point did one firm address the problem, approaching a union-run health clinic for assistance.

The definitions and sources of work-related health problems also continue to be contested. For example, there is mounting evidence that job-related stress takes a toll on employees' health. Stress-induced health problems can range from headaches to chronic depression and heart disease.[47] But stress is frequently rejected as a legitimate concern by workers' compensation boards who administer claims.[48] They tend to use a narrow definition of health and illness, focusing mainly on physical injuries and fatalities. Employers and compensation boards sometimes also attempt to place the blame for workers' health problems on their lifestyles or family situations rather than on their jobs. Such a "blaming the victim" ideology assumes that workers are careless, accident-prone, or hypersusceptible to illness.

Rather than accepting a narrow definition of workplace health and safety issues, Bob Sass (1986) argues that we need to

> "stretch" the present legal concept of risk, which covers dust, chemicals, lighting, and other quantifiable and measurable aspects of the workplace to cover all work environment matters: how the work is organized, the design of the job, pace of work, monotony, scheduling, sexual harassment, job cycle, and similar work environment matters of concern to workers.

Sass wrote this more than a decade ago. Since then, he has gone even further to argue that the "weak rights" workers now have within the IRS system need to be extended. "Strong rights," as he sees it, go beyond comanagement and would involve *"worker control* in the area of the work environment."[49] In such a democratized work environment, workers would not have to accept the constant tradeoff between health risks to themselves and the efficiency and profit demanded by employers. Sass sees unions as the only vehicle for such change since they are worker-controlled even though most unions continue to work within the current IRS system and accept its basic premises and goals.

However, with some exceptions, it has not been unions that have been pushing for a broader and more inclusive definition of worker health and well-being. Instead, corporate health promotion, or "wellness programs," emerged in the 1980s as yet another human resource management policy that would help to motivate workers and raise productivity (Conrad 1987; Sloan 1987). The orientation of these wellness programs has typically been to change workers' lifestyles or health-related behaviours (exercising more and quitting smoking, for example). Some have gone further to promote family-friendly and less-stressful employment policies and practices. But they have not addressed job redesign, added to workers' rights, or increased workplace democracy.

Corporate wellness programs no doubt have good intentions, and probably benefit employees who participate in them. But they have no real impact on the unequal distribution of power within work organizations, which contributes to health and safety problems. Furthermore, because they are typically only available in larger work organizations, many workers are unable to participate. While the 1991 Health Promotion Survey showed 61 percent of Canadian workers reporting some kind of health and safety program at work, most were safety or accident-prevention programs. Only one-third of workers had access to counselling programs, fitness classes, smoking cessation programs, or other types of wellness initiatives (Geran 1992: 16). Professionals were much more likely to report that they could participate in such programs. Thus, while offering some assistance to some workers, corporate wellness programs do not address the power structure within the workplace, extend the rights of workers, or improve working conditions for the working class as a whole.

INDUSTRIAL DEMOCRACY: RETHINKING WORKERS' RIGHTS

Our evaluation of new management models concluded that none really offered workers input into decisions beyond their own jobs. New technologies generally have been imposed by management and then, perhaps, workers have been given more freedom to use the technology. Decisions about downsizing and organizational restructuring are rarely negotiated, and unions seldom have been consulted about policies that replace permanent, full-time jobs with nonstandard jobs. The IRS system attempts to go further, acknowledging the need to involve workers in the comanagement of health and safety risks. But even here, critics like Bob Sass call for more control over the work environment by workers.

Within capitalism, ownership carries with it the right to control how work is organized and performed. We have seen some employers relinquishing some of these rights, allowing workers greater autonomy over their immediate work tasks in the belief that efficiency and productivity could be improved and conflict reduced. *Industrial democracy*, in contrast, attempts to involve workers in a much wider range of decisions within the organization.

Industrial democracy applies the principles of *representative democracy* found in the political arena to the workplace. Workers have a voice at the work-group level, as well as indirectly through elected representatives on corporate boards and other key policy-making bodies. A greater degree of open discussion and consensual decision making involving all employees is the goal of democratized work environments. The essence of workplace democracy, according to Donald Nightingale (1982: 49), is "that labour as a legitimate stakeholder in the enterprise has a moral right to play a role in the management of the enterprise."

Even so, industrial democracy in its various forms has not eliminated power differences within work organizations. Typically, owners reserve the right to make the most important decisions themselves, such as closing a factory, for example. Also, the shared decision-making structures of industrial democracy still tend to give owners and managers more influence. Furthermore, industrial democracy does not guarantee less bureaucracy, reduced income inequality, skill upgrading, or even more task-related autonomy for workers. Even if workers are involved extensively in decision making through elected representatives, the debates might not be around these issues.

Job security, for example, or health and safety might be the major concern. Thus, in some settings, industrial democracy has led to job redesign and profit sharing. In others, the results may have been fewer layoffs or more consultation about technological change. Overall, however, industrial democracy has been implemented to a greater degree in European countries than in North America.

Industrial Democracy in North America

Attempts to involve workers in management, at least to an extent, actually have a long history in North America. Following World War I, *works councils* that included elected workers and management representatives, which were set up in large workplaces in a number of industries in both Canada and the United States. The councils met to discuss health and safety, workers' grievances, efficiency, and sometimes even wages. In a number of settings, particularly the coal industry, the impetus for these initiatives was a series of long, bitter, and violent strikes.[50]

Mackenzie King, who later became prime minister, was a labour consultant to some of these companies at the time. He was a strong advocate of the principles of industrial democracy, believing that works councils and related initiatives would reduce industrial conflict and help usher in a new era of social harmony (King 1918). Critics argued that mechanisms to encourage more cooperation between workers and management continued to favour the latter, and that works councils were just a way to deter workers from joining unions. Clearly, in many companies this was the case. With the onset of the Depression at the end of the 1920s, interest in these earlier forms of industrial democracy waned, perhaps because unemployment reduced labour unrest.

Since then, calls have periodically been made for a revival of such worker–management decision-making systems. Not coincidentally, industrial democracy has attracted more interest during periods of labour unrest—immediately after World War II, for example, and again in the 1970s. During those strike-filled eras, employers and politicians looked to Germany and other European countries where industrial democracy has been implemented more widely. North American unions have generally opposed the idea, believing that works councils and other similar forms of industrial democracy undermine collective bargaining, the more traditional means by which workers have negotiated with management for improved working conditions (Guzda 1993: 67).

The spread of industrial democracy in North America has been slow. Most employers have been more interested in avoiding strikes than in really sharing power, and unions have not been supportive. One estimate from the mid-1980s suggested that about one-third of Fortune 500 corporations allowed some form of employee participation in decision making. But the scope of this worker involvement appeared to be limited to joint worker–management consultation committees, special project teams, and problem-solving groups reporting to a top executive. Another estimate from the early 1990s indicates that four out of five Fortune 500 companies have set up "worker involvement programs." This more general term probably includes a wide variety of QWL, TQM, lean production, and other management programs that may provide only limited opportunities for worker involvement in decision making beyond their immediate work tasks (Rothschild and Russell 1986; Guzda 1993: 67).

In the early 1980s, Donald Nightingale conducted an evaluation of *workplace democracy programs* in Canadian companies. He compared 10 firms with varying types of formally instituted participative management with a matched sample of 10 traditionally managed firms.[51] He found that workers received few benefits from participative management. For instance, no significant differences were observed between the two types of organizations in their rates of employee stress symptoms. Workers in democratic organizations experienced slightly higher job satisfaction, but they also expected more from their jobs, especially in the realm of decision making. Recognizing that participative management is only one solution to worker dissatisfaction, he nevertheless concluded that:

> Democratic practices would release human talent and ingenuity which are currently held in check by unchallenging jobs, authoritarian supervision, and a workplace which places little value on employees as creative, responsible, and autonomous human beings. (1982: 194)

Although most North American industrial democracy initiatives have not had a significant impact on the power structure of work organizations, a few examples have gone further toward reaching Nightingale's goal. Shell's Sarnia chemical plant (see Chapter 5), for example, combines QWL principles of job redesign with a commitment to involving workers in decisions about all aspects of the operation. But even this organization has not gone as far as Semco, a fascinating Brazilian case study in worker participation (Semler 1993). The financially successful company with 300 employees (another 200 workers run "satellite" businesses that subcontract to Semco) allows workers to set their own production quotas, redesign products, develop marketing plans, and determine salary ranges. Every six months, workers evaluate their managers. For big decisions, such as buying another company or relocating a factory, every worker gets a vote. Workers also participate in profit sharing and decide how large the shares should be. Thus, Semco appears to have gone beyond basic principles of industrial democracy to give workers rights and obligations normally reserved for owners.

Institutionalized Industrial Democracy in Germany

North American experiments in industrial democracy have usually been introduced by management, occasionally with some pressure from unions. In contrast, in Europe principles of industrial democracy have been institutionalized in a number of countries through government legislation. In Norway, Sweden, Austria, and Germany, for example, legislation gives workers the right to elect representatives to sit on works councils or corporate boards, the right to consultation regarding technological changes, and more grassroots control over health and safety matters.[52]

The German model of *co-determination* has a century-long history. In the 1890s, concerns about widespread labour–management conflict motivated Bismarck to bring in legislation giving works councils the right to advise management on workplace regulations. This legislation was broadened in the 1920s as the Weimar government sought ways to counter the threat of the Russian Revolution spreading into Germany. After World War II, concerned that labour strife would hold back the reconstruction of Germany's devastated economy, the British, American, and French administrators of occupied Germany extended the co-determination legislative framework. A number of additional changes were made in the 1970s and 1980s.

In its current form, German legislation makes works councils mandatory in any workplace with more than five employees.[53] Elected representatives of the workforce (their number proportional to the size of the firm) share decision making with management representatives. The legislation stipulates that in larger work organizations where unions are present, a proportion of the elected members must be from the union. But nonunionized white-collar workers must also be represented. In larger companies, there are several layers of shared decision making. The most powerful management board, a small group of three or four individuals, has only one worker representative, selected from within the larger works council.

The co-determination legislation requires employers to advise and consult with works councils about plans to introduce new technologies, restructure work, reallocate workers to different tasks or locations, or lay off workers. Works councils can demand compensation for workers negatively affected by new technologies or organizational restructuring. Consequently, the North American strategy of downsizing has been much less common. Elected representatives are jointly involved with management in determining hours of work, pay procedures (bonus rates, for example), training systems, health and safety rules, and working conditions. However, collective bargaining between employers and unions about overall pay rates takes place outside the works councils on an industry-wide level. Consequently, the right to strike remains with the larger unions, not with the local works councils. The unions, however, have much less influence in the joint decision-making process at the local level.

The German *dual representation system* of industrial democracy—industry-wide unions and local works councils—is viewed relatively positively by both employers and workers. There are some concerns that unions may be weakened by the dual system of representation (in the long term, this could jeopardize workers' employment security), but union members still constitute a majority of elected representatives on the works councils. Overall, joint decision making has meant better communication between workers and management, greater protection of workers' rights, improved working conditions, and a reduction in labour–management conflict. The latter was, of course, one of the original goals of the co-determination legislation, and this is also what has frequently impressed North American observers concerned about strikes and reduced productivity.

During the 1990s, the German economy began to lose some of its momentum, in part because of the costs of reuniting West and East Germany. Employers have begun to call for changes in the dual system of representation.

In particular, there are pressures to reform the industry-wide collective bargaining system that has meant similar pay rates and conditions of employment in different-size firms and in different parts of the country. Employers argue that they need more flexibility to remain competitive. Whether changes will be made in Germany's labour legislation and whether the rights and working conditions of workers are protected remains to be seen (Beaumont 1995: 107-08).

Sweden: Industrial Democracy as a National Goal

In Germany, concerns about strikes and social unrest led to co-determination legislation. In Sweden, the motivation to implement industrial democracy was somewhat different. An exceptionally strong union movement and the governing Social Democratic Party worked together to improve employment conditions and give workers more rights. In fact, tripartite cooperation and consultation among large and centralized unions (representing over 85 percent of the workforce), the employers' federation, and the state has been a hallmark of Swedish democracy. More than in most other countries, unions and employers have been viewed as social partners (see Chapter 7). Thus, in Sweden in the 1970s and 1980s, industrial democracy was elevated to a national goal within a much broader policy of commitment to reduced inequality and full employment.[54]

The full-employment policy has three key elements. A wage policy, based on the concept of equal pay for equal work, removes pay differentials among regions, industries, and firms by pushing low-wage firms to pay decent wages, and by allowing profitable enterprises to pay less than they would under conventional collective bargaining. The reasoning is that weaker enterprises will either become more efficient or go out of business. The relatively lower wages in expanding industries should stimulate economic growth. Active labour market interventions, including heavy investments in training, assist new labour force entrants, as well as workers displaced from declining industries, in finding work. Selective employment policies also attempt to create jobs in regions or industries affected by structural shifts in the economy.

As in Germany, Swedish law mandates employee representation on corporate boards of directors in all but the smallest firms. Elected members are involved in joint decision making with management in a wide range of areas, but cannot participate in discussions regarding negotiations with unions. But the 1977 Act on Employee Participation in Decision Making extends Swedish employees' rights beyond the rights of German workers. Specifically, in addition to the obligation to inform and consult with workers on major decisions (factory closures, transferring employees, introducing new technologies), Swedish employers must negotiate with unions prior to making such decisions. Unions must also be given complete access to information on the economic status of the firm, its personnel policies, and so forth. In 1984, Sweden went further by setting up Wage Earner Funds that redirected corporate taxes into share purchases on behalf of employees in manufacturing and related industries.

The 1978 Work Environment Act goes beyond the goal of industrial democracy—joint decision making throughout a work organization—to address problems of worker satisfaction and personal fulfillment, a subject we examine in more detail in Chapter 8. The act aims to achieve "working conditions where the individual can regard work as a meaningful and enriching part of existence." It is not enough for work to be free of physical and psychological hazards; it must also provide opportunities for satisfaction and personal growth, and for employees to assume greater responsibility. Thus, unlike QWL and other recent management models that view improved productivity and less conflict as desirable outcomes of worker satisfaction, this legislation makes worker satisfaction and individual growth a high priority.

During the 1970s and 1980s, Sweden's impressive economic performance, low unemployment, and reduction of wage inequalities were seen as strong evidence of the success of its model of society-wide industrial democracy. But the 1990s have brought changes. Some of the active labour market policies encouraging worker mobility and maintaining full employment have been eliminated, and unemployment has been allowed to rise. Employers are seeking more flexibility in the allocation of labour in the production process. Lean production has made its appearance in Swedish factories, some of the most progressive factories (in terms of workers' autonomy and skill enhancement) have closed, and employers have used new technologies to cut jobs.[55] But the framework legislation that supports the Swedish system of industrial democracy is still in place.

Globalization and Industrial Democracy

In 1993, the 12 nations in the European Community at the time formed a single trading and labour market. This required common rules governing labour–management relations. One of the proposed policies would require multinational companies operating in more than one member country to set up works councils. Among the objectives of such a policy would be the desire to reduce worker–management conflict since strikes in one country could seriously affect production in another. All but 1 of the 12 countries agreed to the policy, with Britain being the exception (Guzda 1993: 70). Even though the potential of this form of industrial democracy for reducing conflict and maintaining high production has been demonstrated, the Conservative British government of the day opposed the policy, largely on ideological grounds that it undermined management rights.

Canada has entered into a somewhat similar trading agreement with the United States and Mexico. The North American Free Trade Agreement (NAFTA) has brought calls for the harmonization of labour legislation and labour market policies. Since there is not a tradition of formally legislated industrial democracy in any of the three countries, it is unlikely that a policy promoting works councils or other such initiatives will be developed. Instead, the challenge may be to try to maintain Canada's current labour legislation which, to an extent, protects workers more than American or Mexican legislation.

WORKERS TAKING OVER OWNERSHIP

A basic capitalist principle is that ownership carries with it the right to control how work is performed and how the organization is run. By offering some degree of co-management or co-determination, the various forms of industrial democracy have given workers some of the rights traditionally attached to ownership. But as Stephen Marglin (1976) provocatively asks, are bosses really necessary? Why can workers not run enterprises collectively, thereby dispensing altogether with authority relationships?

In this final section of the chapter, we ask three basic questions about the possibilities of worker ownership: How common is it? Does worker ownership provide more opportunity for control over the labour process? And, how economically viable is worker ownership within a capitalist economy?

Employee Share Ownership Plans

In North America, *employee share ownership plans (ESOPs)* have been widely promoted as a way for workers to share in the profits of production and as a means of generating more consensus in the workplace. If workers are part-owners, the reasoning goes, they should be more likely to identify with the company, work harder, and cooperate with management. An additional factor in the popularity of ESOPs is that they may provide companies with tax advantages (Nightingale 1982: 166).

In companies with ESOPs, shares in the company are purchased for employees and provided as part of a benefit package. Depending on the details of the plan, some categories of employees might receive more shares than others. In some ESOPs, employees can also make additional share purchases for themselves. Thus, employees receive some of the company profits, in the same way as would other shareholders. However, when shares available through the ESOP are provided as benefits in lieu of wages, employees will also lose when the company is losing money, since their shares would then lose value.

A recent estimate indicates that there are over 10,000 ESOPs in existence in the United States. Since such benefit programs are more common in larger firms, a considerable number of employees would be participants. In Canada, about two-thirds of the firms listed on the Toronto Stock Exchange have ESOPs. About half of these are available to all employees with the company paying at least some of the cost. Similar plans are in existence in a number of European countries, frequently as part of a legislated industrial democracy strategy. In Sweden, for example, the Wage Earner Funds have been used to make share purchases for employees in some industries since 1984. Because the principles of industrial democracy have not been widely promoted in Britain in recent years, ESOPs are less common. Currently, less than 100 are in operation in Britain.[56]

In North America, ESOPs have been set up primarily to provide additional benefits to workers or to allow them to purchase shares, but not to promote joint decision making. In workplaces where employees participate in an ESOP as well as some form of joint decision making, it is usually because some other managerial model (QWL, for example) has also been implemented. A British study of the recently privatized bus industry shows that firms with ESOPs are somewhat more likely to have workers on the board of directors, although there is no evidence that share ownership by employees led to this weak form of industrial democracy. The study also reveals that workers participating in ESOPs were no more likely to have control over their own work tasks, although management was concerned that workers might begin to demand more control. Unions representing the workers were more interested in using their seats on the board of directors to preserve jobs than to gain control over the labour process (Pendleton et al. 1996).

Employee Buyouts

Economic restructuring and factory closures over the past several decades have made worker ownership of a different kind a frequent news item in Canada. Workers have bought out their employers (or attempted to do so) in an effort to save their jobs when the company was about to close. In some cases, huge firms were bought out, while in others, much smaller enterprises were involved. *Employee buyouts* or attempted buyouts have occurred in both the service industries (the attempted buyout of Canadian Airlines, for example) and the manufacturing sector. One of the most prominent recent examples of the latter was the purchase of Algoma Steel in Sault Ste. Marie in 1992. The company had been operating in the community since 1901 and employed about 5,000 workers at the beginning of the 1990s. If the company had folded, the community would have been devastated.[57]

Through their union (the United Steel Workers of America) and with the assistance of loan guarantees from the New Democratic provincial government, workers negotiated the purchase of a majority of shares in the company. Cost savings were obtained by a voluntary pay reduction and through a plan to eliminate 1,600 jobs through attrition. The company has been running successfully since the employee buyout, under the direction of a 13-person board of directors, four of whom are nominated by the union. When the workers bought the company, they also took the opportunity to reorganize the front-line management system, replacing a hierarchical system with a teamwork approach. Thus, in this case, aspects of both an industrial democracy model and a participative management system were introduced. The employee buyout was economically successful and also led to greater control over the labour process by workers.

When failing companies are rescued by their employees, the new management systems can take many different forms. However, more often than not, traditional management schemes are maintained. The Algoma Steel example is an exception in this respect. Typically, new worker-owners do not attempt to introduce industrial democracy or innovative participative management schemes. Instead, as shareholders they delegate authority back to a management team, although job security in return for wage concessions is usually negotiated at the same time. Thus, after the buyout has occurred and production resumes, the worker–management relationship would resemble that in a company with an employee share ownership plan (ESOP). But, there is still one critical difference. With majority ownership, workers retain the option to change the governance structure of the organization.

Research has shown that worker-owners typically report more job satisfaction and exhibit more commitment to the organization than workers in conventional companies. But it is unclear whether it is ownership per se that makes the difference. However, the research is clear on the viability of firms bought by their employees. Most companies bought by workers become successful once again. The chances of success are increased when all the participants, including the union if one is present, support the buyout plan. In addition, workers typically need expert advice to assist them in deciding how to restructure the organization since major changes (often in wage rates and staffing) are usually needed. Government support is also critical, particularly with respect to financing, since many lenders are reluctant to gamble on worker buyouts, despite their better-than-average track record.

Producer Cooperatives

Producer cooperatives have a long history in North America and Europe. The first examples appeared in Britain over a century ago as workers looked for alternatives to the exploitative excesses of early capitalism. However, the producer cooperative movement was overshadowed by another form of collective response by workers, the formation of trades unions (see Chapter 7). Nevertheless, the cooperative alternative continues. In Atlantic Canada, for example, records show that 221 worker cooperatives were founded between 1900 and 1987. Three-quarters came into existence after 1975. Recent estimates indicate that about 300 producer cooperatives are functioning in Canada, with a total of about 6,000 members.[58] While producer cooperatives are not a widespread phenomenon, and those that exist are quite small, they nonetheless offer another alternative to conventional employer–employee relationships.

Producer cooperatives must be distinguished from other collective enterprises, including consumer cooperatives (such as co-op food stores) or housing co-ops in which a number of individuals or families jointly own and maintain a dwelling or housing complex. They are also different than marketing co-ops (the wheat pools set up by Western farmers are the best example), and financial services co-ops, such as credit unions. While sharing with these other organizations a general commitment to collective ownership and shared risk-taking, *producer cooperatives* are distinguished by their function as collective producers of goods or services.[59]

Distinguishing producer cooperatives from other types of worker-owned enterprises is not quite as easy. However, there are several characteristics that do stand out. First, to a much greater extent, producer cooperatives have typically been established because of a desire to collectively solve problems faced by their members. Difficulties in obtaining high-quality reliable child care, for example, have led to the formation of child-care co-ops. On a much larger scale, some employee buyouts of a company have been instigated by immanent job loss and the possibility of a community's economic base disappearing. Thus, unlike most enterprises in a capitalist economy where profit-making is the first priority, producer cooperatives have a social purpose interwoven with the need to be successful in the marketplace. Second, central to the philosophy of producer cooperatives is a commitment to the democratic principle of "one person—one vote." This defining characteristic would eliminate companies with employee share ownership plans (ESOPs) and many examples of employee buyouts. Third, and related to the second point, producer cooperatives typically do not allow nonmembers to own shares. As a result, members cannot benefit financially from the success of the cooperative by selling shares. Instead, some arrangements are usually made to reimburse members for their own contributions when they leave the organization.

It has often been assumed that producer cooperatives, like employee buyouts, are typically a response to difficult economic times. In other words, workers decide to set up a cooperative, or take over a company and reshape it into a cooperative, because their jobs are at risk. However, analysis of the cooperative experience in Atlantic Canada over the course of this century indicates no relationship between economic cycles and the formation of producer cooperatives (Staber 1993). This suggests that the social goals of producer cooperatives' members may be as important as their economic goals.

Small producer cooperatives can survive in a capitalist economy. The study of Atlantic Canada cooperatives showed an estimated median life span of 17 years for rural producer cooperatives and 25 years for those in urban settings (Staber 1993: 140). But producer cooperatives face many challenges. It is difficult to finance such enterprises, since banks are often skeptical of their ability to survive. This problem is also faced by other small businesses and by employees attempting to buy out their company. In situations where producer cooperatives are set up as a solution to high unemployment caused by economic downturns, the new worker-owned enterprises are at a disadvantage from the outset. And, as with any attempts to democratize workplaces, participants in producer cooperatives have to learn how to work collectively toward common goals, something that is not taught or encouraged in a competitive capitalist society.

Do producer cooperatives offer workers greater control over their work tasks and the organization as a whole? Some accounts suggest that many are organized much like other profit-oriented work organizations (Nightingale 1982: 227), but this conclusion may be the result of including as examples companies with ESOPs and employee buyouts that maintain traditional management approaches. Leslie Brown draws the opposite conclusion, arguing that producer cooperatives actually incorporate many of the democratizing and work-humanizing features of workplace reform promised, but not always delivered, by the many new management approaches of the past decades. She also concludes that producer cooperatives are a viable solution to problems of community economic development that have not been solved by attempts to encourage traditional forms of capitalist enterprise in underdeveloped regions of the country.[60]

The most successful producer cooperative is found in Mondragon, a city in the Basque region of Spain, where some 20,000 worker-owners run a wide range of firms, including heavy equipment manufacturers and consumer goods and services companies. Each worker has an economic stake in the enterprise where she or he works and, as a member of the firm's general assembly, establishes policies, approves financial plans, and elects members to a supervisory board, which, in turn, appoints managers. Mondragon co-ops have replaced the private ownership of industry in this region with a system of collective ownership and control. By all accounts, these co-ops have achieved high levels of growth, productivity, and employment creation, strong links with the community, harmonious labour relations, a satisfying and non-alienating work environment, and a close integration between workplace and community (Whyte and Whyte 1988).

Mondragon's success is linked, among other things, to the Basque region's decades-long struggle for greater autonomy from Spain, the destruction of the area's industrial base during the Spanish Civil War in the 1930s, and support from the local Catholic church and unions. This unique historical mix of political, cultural, and economic circumstances has sometimes been used as an argument that producer cooperatives could not be successful in other settings such as North America. Granted, it is never possible to easily transplant production systems from one cultural and political context to another. But, if we are willing to accept that Japanese lean production or German co-determination, for example, offer alternatives to the North American approach to organizing workplaces, we should not ignore the Mondragon-style producer cooperative alternative.

CONCLUSION

In this chapter, we have debated the assumptions and conclusions of the mainstream management literature outlined in Chapter 5. From a critical perspective influenced by the labour process research tradition, we focused on power relationships within the workplace, management attempts to control workers, and their efforts to regain control over their labour. We questioned whether new management models and new computer-based technologies really empower workers and allow them to enhance their skills. And we critically scrutinized the systems that have been put into place to improve workers' health and safety. We then shifted our focus to an examination of alternative ways of organizing work that might reduce conflict and provide workers with more control over the labour process and their work organizations.

Several general conclusions sum up this discussion. First, concentration of power in the hands of owners and managers continues to characterize workplaces within our society, and the desire to increase profits continues to overshadow any commitment to empowering workers. Managers continue to systematically control workers, although their methods have changed. Second, employees' expectations of reasonable wages and working conditions, and their desire for more control over the labour process, are frequently at odds with the goals of management. Consequently, conflict and resistance are often frequently present in the workplace, manifested in many different ways.

Third, it is apparent that the new management models intended to empower workers and enhance their skills, while reducing conflict and improving productivity, have frequently not lived up to their potential. In fact, in some cases, the rhetoric of new management models has been used to gain additional control over workers. New technologies have the potential to raise workers' skill levels, humanize the workplace, and improve the quality of life for society as a whole. We have seen evidence of this but have also observed how information technology has been used to control workers and to eliminate jobs. Fourth, computers and management models are created and implemented by human beings. The social problems generated by these "hard" and "soft" technologies are a result of human choices. By the same reasoning, it is our responsibility to try to use these technologies to improve working conditions, empower workers, create jobs, and reduce social inequality.

Workplace health and safety continues to be a contested issue in the workplace. Even so, our assessment of the systems put in place to address health and safety concerns reveals some evidence of workers and management finding common ground. When we examine different approaches to creating industrial democracy and examples of worker ownership, we observe that these alternative methods of organizing work offer some potential for worker empowerment and conflict reduction. Hence, our last and most general conclusion is that there are alternatives to traditional employment relationships within capitalism that deserve serious consideration.

Despite our emphasis on the need to examine worker resistance when analyzing the labour process, resistance has been only one of many themes in this chapter. In fact, we have talked more about management control systems, the deskilling debate, the impact of new technologies, and alternative approaches to organizing the workplace. In the next chapter, we examine the primary collective vehicle for worker resistance in Canada over the past century, namely, the organized labour movement.

NOTES

1. CAW–Canada Research Group on CAMI (1993: 55).
2. Paul Mantoux, quoted by Beaud (1983: 66).
3. George Cohon, president of McDonald's Restaurants of Canada, Ltd., quoted in *Report on Business* (October 1990: B8).
4. See Zimbalist (1979), Littler (1982), Thompson (1989), Tanner et al. (1992), and Smith (1994) for useful critical assessments. Also see Zimbalist (1979), Wood (1989), Heron and Storey (1986), and Sturdy et al. (1992) for case studies based on this perspective.
5. See Littler and Salaman (1982), Spenner (1983), Penn and Scattergood (1985), Attewell (1987), Form (1987), Diprete (1988), Gallie (1991), Stewart and Graham (1995), and Lewis (1995) for contributions to the deskilling debate. Canadian studies addressing this issue include Heron and Storey (1986), Lowe (1987, 1991a, 1997), Myles (1988), Hunter (1988), Boyd (1990), Clement and Myles (1994: Chapter 4), and Russell (1995).
6. See Jenson (1989), Horrell et al. (1990), Gaskell (1991), Wacjman (1991), and Hughes (1996) on the gendered nature of occupational skills.
7. Edwards (1979); also see Gordon et al. (1982). For critiques of their theory, see Penn (1982) and Nolan and Edwards (1984).
8. In his elaboration of the Edwards (1979) typology of control, Hodson (1996) uses the term "participative management" in much the same way as Friedman (1977) describes "responsible autonomy."
9. Wallace (1995) uses the term "corporatist control" in a somewhat similar manner to describe the high level of organizational commitment among professionals.
10. See Howard (1985: 31), Booth (1987), DeTienne (1993), and Menzies (1996: 117–22) on electronic surveillance.
11. Frenkel et al. (1995) label such practices as "info-normative control."
12. Walmsley (1992); Graham (1993, 1995); CAW–Canada Research Group on CAMI (1993: 30).
13. See Spenner (1983, 1990), Form (1987), Jenson (1989), Myles and Fawcett (1990), Vallas (1990), Steinberg (1990), Gallie (1991), and Clement and Myles (1994: 74–75) on the definition and measurement of skill.
14. Jenson (1989); Steinberg (1990); Gaskell (1991).
15. See Myles and Fawcett (1990) and Gallie (1991) for Canadian and British examples, respectively.
16. Clement and Myles (1994: 72); also see Spenner (1983), Myles (1988), and Hunter (1988). However, on the basis of his review of the evidence, Lewis (1995) concludes that Braverman has not yet been refuted.
17. See Russell (1995, 1997), Menzies (1996), and Rinehart (1996: 180) for examples.
18. McMullen (1996) and Lowe (1997) both present recent Canadian data showing workers who use computers reporting increases in the skill content of their jobs as a result. However, such studies cannot tell us about the impacts of other labour market changes, or about longer-term, economy-wide changes in skill requirements.
19. Myles and Fawcett (1990), Myles (1988), Gallie (1991).

20. Attewell (1987); Milkman and Pullman (1991); Stewart and Garrahan (1995).

21. See Kaplinsky (1984), Shallis (1984), Howard (1985), Gill (1985), Ebel (1986), Hughes (1989, 1996), Zuboff (1988), Block (1990), Idle and Cordell (1994), Rifkin (1995), Noble (1995), and Menzies (1996) to trace the debate about the impact of new technologies on work.

22. See Rifkin (1995: Chapter 4) for some interesting examples.

23. See Hughes (1996: 231) for a useful description of first- and second-wave computer-based technologies.

24. Lowe (1997) presents data from the 1989 and 1994 General Social Surveys; McMullen (1996) presents similar over-time results from her survey of Canadian firms.

25. Akyeampong (1997b: 48); Dickinson and Sciadas (1996: 3–2) report that 16 percent of Canadian households had a computer with a modem, up from 8 percent two years earlier.

26. On robotics, see Robertson and Wareham (1987, 1989), Howard (1985: 36–43), Ebel (1986), Block (1990: 100–03), and Suplee (1997).

27. Robertson and Wareham (1987: 28); also see Noble (1985, 1995) and Block (1990: 100–03).

28. See, for example, Feldberg and Glenn (1983), Barker and Downing (1985), Osterman (1986), Hughes (1989, 1996), Zuboff (1988), Fearfull (1992), Menzies (1996), and McMullen (1996).

29. Lowe (1997); also see Dickinson and Sciadas (1996: 3–4) who show that more affluent Canadian households are more likely to own computers and to be linked to the "information highway."

30. Ewan (1976: 11), quoted by Swift (1995: 30).

31. See Howard (1985), Fearfull (1992), Noble (1995), and Menzies (1996) for examples.

32. *Edmonton Journal* (10 June 1993). Also see Howard (1985: 31), Booth (1987), DeTienne (1993), and Menzies (1996: 117–22) on electronic surveillance of employees.

33. Rifkin (1995: 3); for equally concerned but somewhat less pessimistic views, see Idle and Cordell (1994), Sherman and Judkins (1995), Nobel (1995), Swift (1995), Menzies (1996), and Richardson (1996).

34. A 1986 survey of Canadian employers indicated that increased productivity was the most common reason for adoption of new technologies, followed by reduced labour costs and increased quality control (Newton, 1989: 42); also see Idle and Cordell (1994) and Rinehart (1996: 156–62).

35. McLuhan (1964: 56), quoted by Menzies (1996: 44).

36. On technology and industrial relations, see Grayson (1985: 216–54), Gill (1985), Howard (1985: 197–210), Mahon (1987), Robertson and Wareham (1987, 1989).

37. Giles and Jain (1989: 339); also see Kumar et al. (1991: 62–65).

38. Mahon (1987); see Smucker and van den Berg (1991) and Smith et al. (1995, 1997) for comparisons of the industrial relations environment in Canada and Sweden. Yun (1995) comments on the Singapore situation where, even though management has seldom consulted with workers, opposition on their part to technological change has been limited because unemployment rates are low.

39. See Swartz (1981), Wells (1986), Robertson and Wareham (1987), Rinehart (1996: 162–76) on QWL.

40. See Webb (1996), Sosteric (1996), Rinehart (1996: 181–83), Menzies (1996: 102–108), and Redman et al. (1997) on TQM.

41. See Wood (1989), Thompson (1989: 218–29), Jenson (1989), Neis (1991), and MacDonald (1991) on flexible specialization.

42. Robertson et al. (1992), Graham (1993, 1995), Rinehart et al. (1994), Drache (1994), Stewart and Garahan (1995), Rinehart (1996: 176–81); see Nilsson (1996) for a somewhat more positive assessment.

43. See CAW–Canada Research Group on CAMI (1993).

44. Betcherman et al. (1994: 96); the Auditor General of Canada (1988) presents a similar model of desirable organizational characteristics.

45. Walters and Haines (1988), Walters (1985); also see Sass (1995).

46. *The Globe and Mail* (29 March 1993: A1).

47. See Karasek and Theorell (1990) and Lowe and Northcott (1986: Chapter 1) on job stress research; also see Geran (1992) on the incidence of job stress in Canada.

48. Kompier et al. (1994) note that Sweden, the United Kingdom, and the Netherlands recognize work-related stress in their health and safety legislation, while Germany and France do not.

49. Sass (1995: 123); in another essay, Sass (1996) criticizes the organized labour movement for accepting the status quo in terms of legislation and policies regarding health and safety.

50. See Russell (1990: Chapter 3) and Rinehart (1996: 49–51) on early work councils in Canada. Also see Guzda (1993) on the U.S. situation.

51. Included in the ten democratic firms studied by Nightingale (1982) were several producer cooperatives and other firms with a mix of worker–management decision-making structures.

52. Spinrad (1984); Adams (1989); Guzda (1993); Beaumont (1995: 101–08).

53. This discussion of the German co-determination system draws mainly on Guzda (1993) and Beaumont (1995: 101–08).

54. This discussion of Sweden draws on Erikson et al. (1986–1987), Alestalo and Kuhnle (1986–1987), Milner (1989), and Olsen (1991). Also see Smith et al. (1995, 1997) who compare the effects of different labour market policies in Canada and Sweden on workers' reactions to technological change.

55. Sandberg (1994); Smith et al. (1995, 1997); Nilsson (1996).

56. See Pendleton et al. (1996: 212) for the U.S. and British estimates, and Gunderson et al. (1995: 418) for the Canadian estimate. For additional discussion of employee ownership in Canada, see Nightingale (1982) and Quarter and Melnyk (1989).

57. Most of this discussion of worker buyouts, including the Algoma Steel example, is based on Gunderson et al. (1995).

58. Staber (1993) provides the Atlantic Canada figures while Rinehart (1996: 190–92) provides the recent estimate.

59. This discussion of producer cooperatives is based on Nightingale (1982: 224–33), Quarter and Melynk (1989), Staber (1993), Rinehart (1996: 190–92), and Brown (1997).

60. Brown (1997); also see Staber (1993), who makes a similar argument.

UNIONS, INDUSTRIAL RELATIONS, AND STRIKES

INTRODUCTION

At midnight on March 25, 1997, over 10,000 unionized workers at 73 Canada Safeway supermarkets in Alberta went on strike, rejecting the company's "final offer." The battle lines were drawn in what became a long and bitter dispute. The workers, represented by the United Food and Commercial Workers Union, had been attempting to negotiate a new contract with the California-based corporation for over a year. The issues at stake—a living wage, concessions, flexibility—resonate throughout workplaces in the 1990s, making this strike emblematic of the current and future shape of industrial relations in Canada.

The striking workers wanted more hours for part-time workers and a new contract that would restore the $2.85 per hour they gave up in rollbacks in 1993. Since then, the company had become very profitable, partly by vigorously adopting a "flexible employment" strategy.

Over 80 percent of its employees were part-timers, with 35 percent working fewer than 12 hours weekly, and only 5 percent receiving any benefits. Employees hired since 1993 could only work up to 20 hours weekly and will likely never qualify for benefits or reach the top of the wage scale. Having won wage and benefit concessions totalling $40 million in the 1993 contract, Safeway had its sights set on cutting wages an average of $2,000 to $10,000 per employee over five years. Safeway was determined to continue operating during the strike, running prominent ads in local newspapers for $6-per-hour "replacement workers." Surprisingly, the Alberta public, not known for its pro-union views, widely supported the striking workers on the principle of fairness. The firm lost an estimated 70 percent of its customers for the duration of the strike. Still, the dispute dragged on for 11 weeks. Despite pressure from clergy and other community leaders, the government would not intervene. In the end, workers made very modest gains—part-timers are now guaranteed 12 hours weekly—but the company got a two-tier wage structure with three-quarters of its workers in the lower tier.[1]

Viewed from a distance, the Safeway strike raises questions that go to the very heart of contemporary employee–employer relations, a topic we raised in Chapter 6 and continue here. The confrontation pitted the free-market principles of capitalism against the rights of workers to collective bargaining, a decent wage, and job security. Do corporations have any responsibility to the communities in which they operate? Is there an inherent conflict between workers' desires for good jobs and employers' goals of profits and competitiveness? Conversely, to what degree are interests between workers and employers shared? Are there circumstances under which labour and management can cooperate to their mutual benefit? What is the role of government in regulating the relations between labour and capital? Why do workers join a union in the first place? Finally, what improvements in wages and working conditions have unions achieved through collective bargaining?

These are the sorts of industrial relations issues that will be examined in this chapter. From a sociological perspective, we will focus on power, conflicts, and compromises over the distribution of resources in the workplace, and on employee collective action. These themes are highlighted in the study of unions, the major organizations representing the interests and aspirations of employees in capitalist societies. As we concluded in Chapter 6, much of the resistance to employers by North American workers has been channelled through their unions. We will, therefore, explore the nature and development of the labour movement in Canada, as well as how union–management relations are regulated through a complex legal framework. The causes and implications of industrial conflict are the subject of later sections in this chapter.

THEORETICAL PERSPECTIVES ON THE LABOUR MOVEMENT

We can begin to understand why unions developed in the first place by reviewing some of the early theories of the labour movement. No single issue stands out as the driving force of unionization. Rather, workers historically have rallied collectively to oppose the imposition of arbitrary management power to protect their jobs and retain some semblance of control over the labour process, and to obtain improvements in rights, wages, and working conditions.

Why Do Workers Unionize?

In a classic work on British trade unionism, Sidney and Beatrice Webb (1894; 1911) suggested that workers' pursuit of higher wages expressed a more basic desire to reduce employer domination. Collective action could improve working conditions and reduce the competition for jobs that drives wages down. Furthermore, the Webbs argued that it could curb an employer's authority by instituting common rules governing the employment relationship. Selig Perlman (1928) later stressed the role of unions in controlling jobs. After studying the International Typographical Union, the oldest union in America, Perlman concluded that workers develop an awareness that jobs are scarce and must, therefore, be protected through unionization. Michael Poole sheds additional light on the emergence of the labour movement in his discussion of the various goals it pursued.[2] Unions thus can be viewed five different ways: as moral institutions, fighting against the injustices and inequities of capitalist industrialization; as revolutionary organizations intent on overthrowing capitalism; as psychological or defensive reactions against the threat early capitalism posed to workers' jobs; as responses to economic realities, aimed at achieving better wages and working conditions; and as political organizations extending workers' rights further into the industrial arena.

Generally speaking, the harsh working conditions endured by industrial workers in the late nineteenth century sparked the first major surge of unionization. Yet the basic idea that workers are motivated to unionize by the desire to gain greater control over their jobs, as well as fair treatment and just rewards, remains a dominant theme in industrial relations. Mainstream industrial relations theory views the *system of job regulation* as the core of worker–management relations.[3] In other words, the rules and regulations that form the basis of collective agreements are assumed to inject stability into employment relations by tilting the balance of power slightly away from management and toward workers.

However, this perspective overplays the importance of predictable and harmonious industrial relations, and downplays the frequency of conflict. That is, by focusing on the system of rules, regulations, and institutions governing industrial relations, the mainstream perspective does not question the existing distribution of power between workers and management. It also presents an incomplete picture of industrial relations, due to a narrow focus on the formal aspects of the system, such as legislation and collective bargaining. An equally important informal side involves the daily interaction between workers and employers, as "the rules of the game" are constantly being negotiated. It is, therefore, helpful to acknowledge that work is a power relationship in which conflict is always a possibility.[4] As Richard Hyman (1975: 26) explains, "in every workplace there exists an invisible frontier of control, reducing some of the formal powers of the employer: a frontier which is defined and redefined in a continuous process of pressure and counter-pressure, conflict and accommodation, overt and tacit struggle." Echoing themes from Chapter 6, Hyman proposes a more critical perspective on industrial relations, defining it as the process of control over work relations—a process that especially involves unions.

Conflict and Cooperation in Union–Management Relations

It is important to understand the role of conflict in union management relations. Collective agreements, negotiated and administered under provincial and federal labour laws, seek to avoid open conflict. Indeed, the main thrust of modern industrial relations practice is the avoidance of conflict. Thus, for the system to operate with some degree of fairness and equity for workers, who on the whole are in the weaker bargaining position, there must be the threat of conflict that could disrupt the employer's business. A stock criticism of the Canadian industrial relations scene concerns its adversarial nature. A federal government task force on labour relations, responding to these concerns, explained the underlying conflict in these words:

> Paradoxical as it may appear, collective bargaining is designed to resolve conflict through conflict, or at least through the threat of conflict. It is an adversary system in which two basic issues must be resolved: how available revenue is to be divided, and how the clash between management's drive for productive efficiency and the workers' quest for job, income and psychic security are to be reconciled.[5]

We must also view industrial relations as a continuous process. New problems regularly confront the parties in collective bargaining. Solutions for one side may create difficulties for the other, as in cases of wage rollbacks. Or an agreement may be based on compromises that both sides have trouble living with (for example, when a third-party arbitrator imposes a solution). Part of the difficulty is that workers and management have different definitions of social justice and economic reality.[6] Safeway considered competition from Superstore adequate justification for pursuing further economic concessions from its Alberta workers. Safeway employees considered it grossly unfair that the corporation would not share some of its healthy profits with them and replace the wage reductions they had already taken to improve its competitive position. We are thus wise to remember Tom Keenoy's (1985: 12) comment that "at best, most solutions in industrial relations should be seen as no more than temporary arrangements between employer and employee. Indeed, this relationship is best thought of as one in which there is a *permanent* potential for differences of opinion and conflict...."

There is another paradox here. As pointed out in Chapter 5, work organizations typically have a division of labour that requires collective interdependence. Management, therefore, must balance the need to control employees with the necessity of achieving a workable level of cooperation and commitment from them. Stephen Hill has explored this basic tension and concludes that workers and managers must cooperate to provide goods or services.[7] Yet in doing so, Hill notes, each side also strives to maximize its own interests. Workers aim for more wages, better working conditions, and more autonomy in their jobs. Employers pursue higher profits, lower costs, and increased productivity. The chronic tension between these opposing interests forces tradeoffs on both sides, and may also generate open conflict. Of course, we must recognize that not all union–management negotiations are *a zero-sum game*. That is, the only way one side can gain something is for the other to give up something. Indeed, on some issues, such as improved health and safety conditions (see Chapter 6), negotiations can produce a win–win situation in which both workers and management benefit.

Unions as "Managers of Discontent"

There is a general consensus among scholars that the industrial relations systems in modern capitalist societies "keep the lid on conflict." Having observed the oppressive conditions under which mid-nineteenth-century factory workers toiled, Marx concluded that eventually their misery and poverty would ignite a revolution. But, as Stephen Hill (1981: Chapter 7) points out, even Marxists, committed to the belief that capitalism pits the workers and bosses against each other in constant struggle, acknowledge that collective bargaining integrates workers into the existing economic system. For many Marxists, unionism itself embodies a basic contradiction by striving to solve workers' problems within the confines of capitalism. This is why Lenin, father of the Russian Revolution, dismissed trade unions as capable only of reform, not revolution. But to lay all the blame on capitalism is to ignore the basic dilemma of the distribution of scarce resources, which all societies must face.[8]

In some respects, then, unions function as *managers of discontent*.[9] Unions in Canada and other advanced capitalist societies channel the frustrations and complaints of workers into a carefully regulated dispute-resolution system. Unions help their members to articulate specific work problems, needs, or dissatisfactions. Solutions are then sought through collective bargaining, or through grievance procedures. In Canada, for example, labour legislation prohibiting strikes during the term of a collective agreement puts pressure on union leaders to contain any actions by rank-and-file members that could disrupt the truce with management. This may seem ironic, since unions developed in response to the deprivations suffered by workers in the early stages of industrial capitalism. But unions today operate in ways that contribute to the maintenance of capitalism, seeking reforms that smooth its rough edges. In James Rinehart's (1996: 185) critical assessment, "... unions nibble away at the margins of power, modifying but not altering in any fundamental sense relations of dominance and subordination."

In order to channel the discontent of their members, unions must legitimately represent the views of the majority of members. This raises the issue of internal *union democracy*. Generally speaking, unions are democratic organizations whose constitutions allow members to elect leaders regularly. Theoretically, this should make leaders responsive and accountable to rank-and-file members, translating their wishes into tangible collective bargaining goals. But, despite this, there has long been a sociological debate about the pitfalls on the road to union democracy.

Robert Michels was the first to investigate the problems of union bureaucracy and democracy. His study of German trade unions and the Social Democratic Party prior to World War I concluded that leaders in working-class organizations always dominate members. Michels's famous *iron law of oligarchy* draws on technical, organizational, and psychological explanations. According to this theory, leaders develop expert knowledge, which gives them power; once in office, leaders can control the organization to maintain their power; and, finally, the masses tend to identify with leaders, and expect them to exercise power on their behalf. But in Canada and elsewhere, we have recently witnessed the emergence of strong rank-and-file movements challenging entrenched union leadership cliques and, in effect, opposing oligarchic rule. Most unions today espouse democratic principles, but some have been more successful in putting these into practice than others. In fact, union officials seem to be constantly trying to increase the participation of rank-and-file members in union activities. Images of corrupt and autocratic leaders, while headlined by the media and reinforced by the history of a few unions (such as the infamous Seafarers' International Union led by Hal Banks) are far from typical. Thus, what Michels discovered was not a universal trait of unions, but a potential problem faced by all large bureaucratic organizations.[10]

WHAT DO UNIONS DO?

How do unions set goals and devise strategies to attain them? Of great interest to sociologists is why unions, rather than espousing revolutionary or even reformist aims, have engaged in largely conservative and defensive actions.

Typically, the daily activities of unions focus on two types of goals: control over work and the rewards of work (Crouch 1982: Chapter 4). It is not inconceivable that demands for control over the work process could, if they escalated, spark radical challenges to the capitalist system of business ownership. Yet, historically, such demands often involved skilled craft workers fighting to defend their relatively privileged position in the labour market against the onslaught of modern production methods. Their goal, in short, was to preserve the status quo.

There are frequently compromises between control over the labour process and economic rewards. Workers may be forced by their immediate economic needs to pursue the latter to the exclusion of the former. In addition, employers are sometimes willing to give up more of their profits rather than concede to workers' greater decision-making authority. The emphasis on material gain rather than job control, known as *business unionism*, has become a hallmark of the North American labour movement. In the last decade, we can detect a shift away from business unionism toward what can be called *social unionism*. Public sector unions, along with some leading private sector unions such as the Canadian Auto Workers, have taken on a much broader agenda of reform, entering national debates about issues such as free trade, the Goods and Services Tax, and the preservation of medicare.[11]

Public Opinion about Unions

How does the public view the activities of unions? Since the 1950s, Canadian public opinion has become somewhat less favourable toward the role of unions in our society. Gallup polls routinely ask respondents if they think unions are good or bad for the country. In polls taken between 1950 and 1958, 12 to 20 percent of respondents said unions were bad, while 60 to 69 percent said they were good. However, responses to the same question during the 1980s show a shift in public opinion, with "bad" as a response increasing to between 30 and 42 percent. Even so, the majority of Canadians still views them in a positive light.[12]

Public attitudes toward unions are, however, usually more ambiguous than suggested by Gallup polls. For example, in a study of Winnipeg and Edmonton residents made in 1984, we found that individuals hold both positive and negative images of unions, depending on the specific issues at stake.

Many respondents believed that unions contributed to inflation, while also recognizing that they had achieved material gains for members. At a general level, this study identified two different images of unionism: a *big labour image* that sees unions as too powerful believes that they inflict harm on society, and thinks, therefore, that they require greater government regulation; and a business unionism image that focuses on the positive gains in wages and working conditions unions have made through collective bargaining.[13] Both images are reinforced by the media, which frequently portrays unions in a negative light (Hackett 1982).

Moreover, views about labour unions are part of the public's overall assessment of the major institutions affecting their lives. Opinion polls taken between 1969 and 1989 reveal a growing disenchantment with government and corporations, compared with unions. Responses to the question, "Which do you think will be the biggest threat to Canada in the years to come: big business, big labour or big government?" document that Canadians' concerns over government and business have come to overshadow their concern about unions (Coates et al. 1989: 118).

The Economic Impact of Unions

There is no question that unions benefit their members financially. Recent research by Canadian economists suggests that, on average, unionized workers earn between 13 and 16 percent more than nonunion workers do. Furthermore, union members are 22 to 25 percent more likely to have pension plans provided by their employer (Swidinsky and Kupferschmidt 1991). A study of women employed in full-year jobs in the service sector found that unionized workers had a 27-percent wage advantage (Clemenson 1989: 39). Unions also have the effect of somewhat reducing overall wage inequality in the labour market.[14]

The better wages, benefits, and job security of union members is partly a function of employer size: unionization is significantly higher in large firms. Only 6 percent of employees in firms with fewer than 20 workers, and 19 percent of those in firms with between 20 and 99 workers, belong to unions, compared with close to half of workers in firms with 1000 or more employees.[15] Recall from earlier chapters that large firms make up much of the "core" sector of the economy, providing better wages and benefits, and are more likely to introduce new technologies and innovative forms of work organization. They are in a better competitive position than are smaller firms to provide decent wages and working conditions (Morissette 1991).

Does the conventional wisdom that unions further their members' interests at public expense have a basis in fact? The most thorough analysis of what trade unions actually do is a study by two Harvard economists, Richard Freeman and James Medoff (1984: 5–11), who make a useful distinction between the two "faces" of unionism. The *monopoly* face represents unions' power to raise members' wages at the expense of employers and other workers. The *collective voice* face shifts attention to how unions democratize authoritarian workplaces, giving workers a collective voice in dealing with management. Freeman and Medoff admit that unions do impose some social and economic costs, but think that these are far outweighed by their positive contributions. Unions significantly advance workers' economic and political rights and freedoms. And, to the chagrin of their opponents, unions also boost productivity. As these researchers explain, unions improve productivity through lower employee turnover, better management performance, reduced hiring and training costs, and greater labour–management communication and cooperation.[16] But because of higher wage costs, productivity gains do not necessarily make unionized firms more profitable.

Even though they are examining American unions, Freeman's and Medoff's conclusions deserve careful attention. They show that, in addition to raising members' wages relative to those of nonmembers', unions

> alter nearly every other measurable aspect of the operation of workplaces, from turnover to productivity to profitability to the composition of pay packages. The behaviour of workers and firms and the outcomes of their interactions differ substantially between the organized and unorganized sectors. On balance, unionization appears to improve rather than to harm the social and economic system.[17]

THE DEVELOPMENT OF THE CANADIAN LABOUR MOVEMENT

The Canadian labour movement has long been a major force in the economic life of the nation. Its history is tied to the development of capitalism. But, as workers in the late nineteenth and early twentieth centuries reacted to the inequities and deprivations of their employment by organizing unions, they also had to fight to gain the right to do so. The story of unions is a human drama in which groups of workers often struggled against strong-willed employers and a reluctant state to gain higher wages, better working conditions, and some control over their daily working lives.

Craft Unionism

Skilled craft workers were the first to unionize. The earliest union in Canada was organized by printers in York (now Toronto). Carpenters, bricklayers, masons, cabinetmakers, blacksmiths, shoemakers, tailors—these were the pioneers of the union movement before the days of modern industry. A strike by Toronto printers in 1872 resulted in the Trade Unions Act, which for the first time legalized union activity. Prior to that, unions had been considered a conspiracy against the normal operations of business. Other significant events that laid the foundations for trade unionism in Canada were the Nine-Hour Movement in the 1870s, involving working-class agitation for shorter working hours, and the creation of the Trades and Labour Congress (TLC) in 1883 as the first central labour body.[18]

Craft pride based on the special skills acquired through a long apprenticeship, solidarity with fellow artisans, and a close integration of work and communities were the hallmarks of these early *craft unions.* Craftsmen (there were no women among them) were the aristocrats of the working class. Printers, for example, reinforced their status by referring to their work as a "profession." Like other crafts, shoemakers drew on a long heritage to bolster craft pride. "From medieval craft lore, the shoemakers brought forth St. Crispin as a symbol of their historic rights and their importance to the community," reports historian Greg Kealey (1980: 292).[32]

Craft unions were organized according to specialized craft skills, and served their members in several important ways. They were benevolent societies, providing members with a form of social insurance years before the rise of the welfare state. They also protected their members' position in the labour market by regulating access to the craft, thus monopolizing its unique skills. Today, this would be referred to as a "labour market shelter" (see Chapter 3). And, as small local enterprises of the nineteenth century gave way to the factories and large corporations of the twentieth, unions provided craftsmen with a defence against the erosion of their way of life. Artisans opposed scientific management, the mechanization and reorganization of craft production in factories, and other attempts by employers to undermine the skills and responsibilities on which their craft traditions were based. Moreover, the tightly knit social relations of working-class artisan communities—reinforced by educational institutes, parades, picnics, and other neighbourhood events—bolstered these reactions to the march of modern industry.[19]

Craft unions dominated the young Canadian labour movement well into the twentieth century. These *international unions* were American-based and affiliated with the conservative American Federation of Labour (AFL). The iron moulders' union was the first international Union to set down permanent Canadian roots, in 1859. This was a time when the labour market for many skilled trades spanned both sides of the Canada–U.S. border. The internationals quickly came to control the Canadian labour scene. At the 1902 convention of the TLC, the AFL unions purged their Canadian-based rivals by banning any organization duplicating one already in the AFL, and stole power from more radical Canadian labour leaders (Babcock 1974).

Industrial Unionism

The craft principle underlying the early AFL unions contrasts with *industrial unionism*, where all workers in an industry are represented by the same union, regardless of their occupational skills. The Knights of Labour, the earliest industrial union in Canada, organized its first local assembly in Hamilton in 1875. For a brief period in the 1880s, they challenged the dominance of the AFL craft unions. Driven by an idealistic radicalism, the Knights' immediate goal was to organize all workers into a single union, regardless of sex, skill level, craft, or industry of employment. They saw their efforts ultimately leading to the abolition of the capitalist wage system and the creation of a new society. Their membership peaked in 1887, with more than 200 local assemblies representing workers in 75 occupations. A combination of factors led to the Knights' demise: rapid membership growth that made it difficult to maintain an idealistic philosophy; regular defeats at the hands of employers; internal political rivalries; the union's growing hostility with the AFL unions; and a recognition among craft workers that uniting with unskilled workers in industrial unions would jeopardize their privileged position. The Knights survived longer in Canada than south of the border, although by the early years of the twentieth century they had all but disappeared (Kealey 1981b).

Only a handful of industrial unions surfaced in the early twentieth century. Several were part of the rising tide of labour radicalism that reached a crest with the 1919 Winnipeg General Strike. There was a distinctive regional flavour to these working-class protests, as most were rooted in Western Canada. The Western Federation of Miners, an international union but archrival of the AFL, gained a foothold in British Columbia mines. The radical ideology of the Chicago-based Industrial Workers of the World (the "Wobblies") attracted unskilled immigrants employed in lumbering, mining, agriculture, and railways in the West prior to World War I. The Wobblies advocated a form of *syndicalism*, which held that international industrial unions and general strikes are the main vehicles for working-class emancipation.

Our discussion would be incomplete without mention of the One Big Union (OBU). This revolutionary industrial union received widespread support in the Western provinces, particularly among miners, loggers, and transportation workers, around the time of the Winnipeg General Strike. The OBU called for secession from the conservative AFL and its Canadian arm, the TLC. Its support for the Russian Revolution brought counterattacks from employers, governments, and craft unions, and caused the union's eventual defeat in the 1920s.[20]

Not until the 1940s did industrial unionism become firmly established in Canada. The opening round was the United Auto Workers' (UAW) milestone victory in 1937 against General Motors in Oshawa, Ontario. The UAW sprang up under the banner of the left-leaning Congress of Industrial Organizations (CIO) in the 1930s to organize unskilled and semiskilled workers in mass-production industries. Many of the initial forays into the auto, electrical, rubber, and chemical factories of corporate North America were led by communist organizers. Craft union leaders opposed the CIO largely on political grounds, despite the fact that Canadian workers embraced the CIO form of industrial unionism.[21]

In 1956 Canadian craft and industrial unions buried their differences, uniting skilled and unskilled workers within a single central labour organization. This marked the merger of the craft-based TLC and the industrial unions of the Canadian Congress of Labour, resulting in the creation of the Canadian Labour Congress (CLC). A similar merger of the AFL and the CIO had occurred one year earlier in the United States. The CLC remains Canada's "house of labour." Its affiliated unions represent 63 percent of union members in the country.[22]

The CLC promotes the economic, political, and organizational interests of affiliated unions by providing research, education, and organizational and collective bargaining services, as well as by eliminating jurisdictional conflicts and organizational duplication. It sometimes becomes embroiled in interunion disputes over jurisdictions and complaints about unions *raiding* each other's members. Prominent examples of such rivalries include the Canadian Auto Workers (CAW) recruitment of Newfoundland fishery workers who were represented by the United Food and Commercial Workers International Union, and the raid on the Canadian Union of Postal Workers by the International Brotherhood of Electrical Workers. The CLC also has strong ties to the New Democratic Party, having taken a leading role in founding the party in 1961. The CLC has become active on the national political stage, for example, by forming coalitions with other community-based groups to oppose free trade. This more broadly based political action increased with the election of Bob White, the high-profile former head of the CAW, as CLC president in 1992.

Quebec Labour

The history and present character of the labour movement in Quebec contributes to the distinctiveness of social and economic life in that province.[23] Quebec labour's history is a fascinating topic in its own right, and deserves more than the brief treatment we can afford to give it here. Many of the issues central to Canada's ongoing constitutional debates are amplified in the arena of labour relations. For example, industrial relations have been shaped by a different legal framework in Quebec (its laws are derived from the Civil Code of France, rather than British-based common law). A more interventionist state role has created a higher degree of centralized bargaining than in other provinces, as well as resulting in some innovative legislation such as the 1977 antistrikebreaking law. And nationalist politics have left an indelible mark on union policies and priorities. Indeed, the question of special representation for Quebec on the executive of the Canadian Labour Congress at the 1992 CLC convention raised the spectre of a split between the CLC and the Quebec Federation of Labour, which represents CLC affiliates in that province.

The development of unions in Quebec followed a different path from that of the rest of Canada. For example, in the early twentieth century the Catholic church organized unions that, unlike their counterparts elsewhere, emphasized the common interests of employers and employees. During the years that Premier Maurice Duplessis and the ultraconservative Union Nationale party held power (from 1936 to 1960), repressive state actions attempted to stifle union development. Worker militancy flared up in response, the most violent manifestations being the 1949 strike of miners at Asbestos and the 1957 Murdochville copper miners' strike. Some analysts view these strikes as major catalysts in Quebec's Quiet Revolution, which ushered in major social, economic, and political reforms in the 1960s.

During this period, the old Catholic unions cut their ties with the church, becoming one of the main central labour organizations in the province (the CNTU, or Confederation of National Trade Unions) and adopting an increasingly radical stance. Hence, as is not the case in other provinces, the Quebec Federation of Labour, made up of CLC-affiliated unions, represents a minority of union members in the province and operates in a more independent manner. Another influential union organization is the Quebec Teachers' Federation. Thus, there is not a unified Quebec labour movement, although these central organizations have banded together on occasion, the most notable example being the 1972 Common Front strike by some 200,000 public sector workers against government policies.

THE ROLE OF THE CANADIAN STATE IN INDUSTRIAL RELATIONS

Canada's contribution to the quest for industrial peace has been the development of a legislative and administrative framework that casts the state into the role of *impartial umpire*, mediating between labour and capital. The architect of this system was William Lyon Mackenzie King, the first federal minister of labour and later a Liberal prime minister. King's 1907 Industrial Disputes Investigation Act (IDIA) became the cornerstone of Canada's modern industrial relations policy. The act provided for compulsory *conciliation* (fact finding) in disputes during a "cooling off" period, a tripartite board of *arbitration*, and special treatment of public interest disputes involving public services. At first the act was applied to disputes in coal mines and railways. Its scope was extended during World War I, and, in the 1950s its principles were incorporated into provincial legislation. In some instances, the state used the powers of the act to legislate an end to strikes. There is little question that this sort of intervention has shaped the pattern of industrial conflict in Canada (some would argue in the interests of employers).[24]

State intervention in industrial conflict is not a twentieth-century invention, however. Claire Pentland, for example, documents the role of the British army in suppressing unrest among colonial labourers building the Rideau Canal in 1827. He concludes: "Intervention by the Canadian state on behalf of employers in more recent years should not be regarded as novelties, but as fruits of what employers and officials learned about labour problems in the middle of the nineteenth century" (Pentland 1981: 196). Yet, it was the 1907 IDIA that marked the first major step toward the institutionalization of industrial conflict through the control of law.[25]

We can identify four major phases in the development of the legal framework for industrial relations in Canada.[26] In the first, or pre-Confederation phase, common law prohibited collective bargaining. The second phase was entered with the 1872 Trade Unions Act, passed by the Conservative government of Sir John A. Macdonald. This neutralized the legal restrictions on unionism, but did not grant workers positive legal rights or protections that facilitated collective bargaining. The National War Labour Order, regulation P.C. 1003, launched the third, or modern, phase in 1944. Modelled on the 1935 U.S. National Labour Relations Act (Wagner Act), P.C. 1003 granted employees in the private sector collective bargaining rights, set down union certification procedures, spelled out a code of unfair labour practices, and established a labour relations board to administer the law. These measures paved the way for a postwar labour–management pact designed to maintain industrial peace. This truce was enshrined in federal legislation in 1948 and in subsequent provincial legislation.

Another milestone in the legal entrenchment of *collective bargaining rights* came out of a 1945 strike by the United Auto Workers at the Ford Motor Company in Windsor. The *Rand Formula*, named after Justice Ivan Rand of the Supreme Court, whose ruling was instrumental in settling the strike, provided for union security through a *union shop* and *union dues checkoff*. According to the Rand Formula, while no one should be required to join a union because a union must act for the benefit of all employees in a workplace, it is justifiable to automatically deduct union dues from the paycheques of all employees in a workplace regardless of whether or not they actually belong to the union.

The fourth phase involved the rise of public sector unions. The movement toward full-fledged public sector unionism began in Saskatchewan in 1944. The real push, however, started when Quebec public employees were granted collective bargaining rights in 1964. Another major breakthrough was the 1967 Public Service Staff Relations Act, which opened the door to unions in the federal civil service.

The intent of all these legislative changes was to establish industrial peace. It is obvious that one of their unintended effects was to spur the growth of unions. But the goal of conflict reduction should not be underestimated. The centrepiece of the 1907 IDIA was the regulation of work stoppages through compulsory postponement of strikes and lockouts, provisions for mediation or conciliation, the banning of strikes or lockouts during the term of a collective agreement, and alternative means of dispute resolution. The act also made strikes or lockouts illegal in key industries (transportation, communications, mines, and public utilities) until a board of inquiry had studied the problem and its conciliation report had been made public. These methods of *institutionalizing conflict* have been fine-tuned over the years. But work stoppages are still illegal during the term of a collective agreement (although they do occur) and the state has taken away the right to strike altogether from certain public employees who perform essential services.

Some analysts would argue that industrial relations entered a coercive phase during the 1980s. Leo Panitch and Donald Swartz view government imposition of wage controls, more restrictive trade union legislation, and the use of courts to end strikes as signals of the end of "free collective bargaining" as established by the industrial relations system set out in the 1948 federal legislation. Panitch and Swartz characterize this new era as *permanent exceptionalism*, reflecting how the suspension of labour's rights and more heavy-handed state intervention that were once the exception have become the rule.[27] As we shall see below, there is now considerable debate over whether Canadian industrial relations have entered troubled times.

UNION MEMBERSHIP TRENDS

Canadian Union Membership Growth and Stabilization

Figure 7.1 traces union membership growth in Canada since 1911. In 1996, there were over 4 million union members, representing 33.9 percent of the nonagricultural paid workforce.[28] Considering that only 4.9 percent of all nonagricultural paid employees belonged to unions in 1911, this is an impressive record of expansion. This percentage measures *union density* and reflects the proportion of actual union members to potential members. The exclusion of agriculture, where most workers are self-employed and are, therefore, ineligible for union membership, allows more accurate comparisons with earlier historical periods (when agriculture was a much larger sector) and with other countries at different levels of industrialization. But the measure is still problematic. For

FIGURE 7.1 *Union Membership in Canada, 1911–1996*

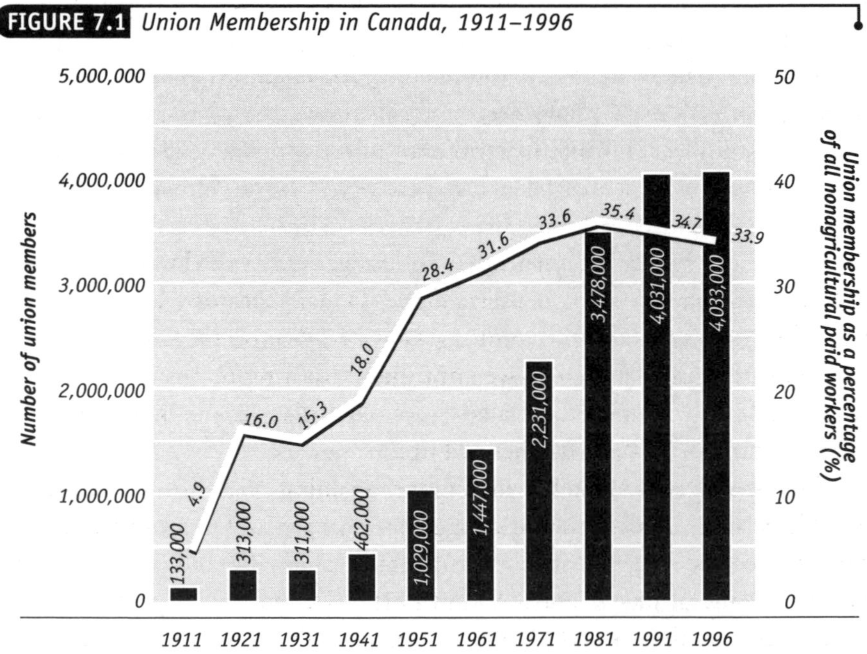

Source: Reproduced with the permission of the Minister of Public Works and Government Services Canada, 1997.

example, some employees in agriculture belong to unions, and legislation in Canada usually prohibits managers and supervisors from joining.[29] A slightly higher percentage of workers are covered by collective agreements since, in some cases, nonmembers in a unionized organization are entitled to the wages and benefits negotiated by unions.[30]

Scanning the chart, we can identify three major spurts in membership growth. The first two coincided with the two World Wars. This is not surprising because national mobilization for these wars resulted in economic growth, labour shortages, and the need for a high level of cooperation between employers and employees, all of which are key ingredients for successful union recruitment.

In the years during and immediately following World War II, Canada's contemporary industrial relations system took shape. Massive changes in the size, composition, legal rights, and goals of unions have occurred since the 1940s. The third growth spurt took place in the 1970s. The rise of *public sector unions* in that decade, largely facilitated by supportive legislation, brought many civil servants, teachers, nurses, and other public employees into organized labour's fold.

In the 25 years since 1971, union density has remained at about one-third of nonagricultural paid employment, hitting a peak of 37.2 percent in 1984.[31] In part, this is because labour force expansion outpaced the growth of union membership. Two recessions and industrial restructuring also cut deeply into the traditional membership strength of unions in manufacturing and other blue-collar occupations. Similarly, recent budget cuts and downsizing in the public sector have eroded membership ranks. Furthermore, employer pressures for concessions and the whittling away of collective bargaining rights by governments and the courts have contributed to a more hostile climate for labour relations. Despite these adversities, Canadian unions have held their own by adapting to these harsher realities.

The labour movement has undergone organizational changes as well. A notable trend is consolidation, resulting from mergers and membership growth since the 1960s. In 1968, there were 14 large unions (30,000 or more members), accounting for just under half of total union membership. By 1996, 34 unions had memberships of 30,000 or more, and these made up 75 percent of total union membership in the country.[32] There has also been an upswing in the number of small unions (under 1000 members), but this has had a minor impact on the process of consolidation. One of the defining features of the Canadian labour movement is the large number of locals. In 1996, the 275 national and international unions chartered 17,149 *locals*, the basic self-governing unit of the labour movement and the legal entity for collective bargaining. Membership in locals ranges from as few as 10 to over 45,000, with an average size of around 235. In short, despite consolidations, Canadian labour remains fragmented and, consequently, collective bargaining is very decentralized. Unlike some European nations, where industry-wide national bargaining is the norm, the Canadian pattern of single-establishment, single-union bargaining results in over 22,000 collective agreements in effect at any one time (Kumar 1986: 121–22).

A Comparative Perspective on Canadian Unions

A comparative perspective on Canada's unions provides insights about the nature of union–employer relations, and how these are "institutionalized" into national systems of industrial relations. Figure 7.2 provides two key measures for 12 countries: union density and collective bargaining coverage.[33] Keep in mind, though, that these comparisons are approximate because countries collect these data in somewhat different ways. As we noted above, density measures the extent of union membership. *Collective bargaining* is the decision-making process in which union and management negotiate wages, benefits, hours, and other employment conditions for a group of workers, resulting in a *collective agreement* (or contract).

In terms of union density, Canada is higher than the United States and Japan, but lower than most European countries, Australia, and New Zealand. In Europe, it is more common than in Canada, the United States, or Japan for workers who are not union members to have terms and conditions of employment set by collective agreements. For example, in France and Germany, 10 and 33 percent, respectively, of wage and salary earners are union members, yet 90 percent or more are covered by the provisions of collective agreements.

What accounts for these crossnational differences? In North America, key factors are management's traditional opposition to unions, labour laws that make the "certification" process for new bargaining units difficult, and a decentralized industrial relations system based in local workplaces. In Japan, where density and coverage are similar, collective bargaining also is decentralized and

FIGURE 7.2 *Union Density and Collective Bargaining Coverage in Selected Industrialized Countries, 1990**

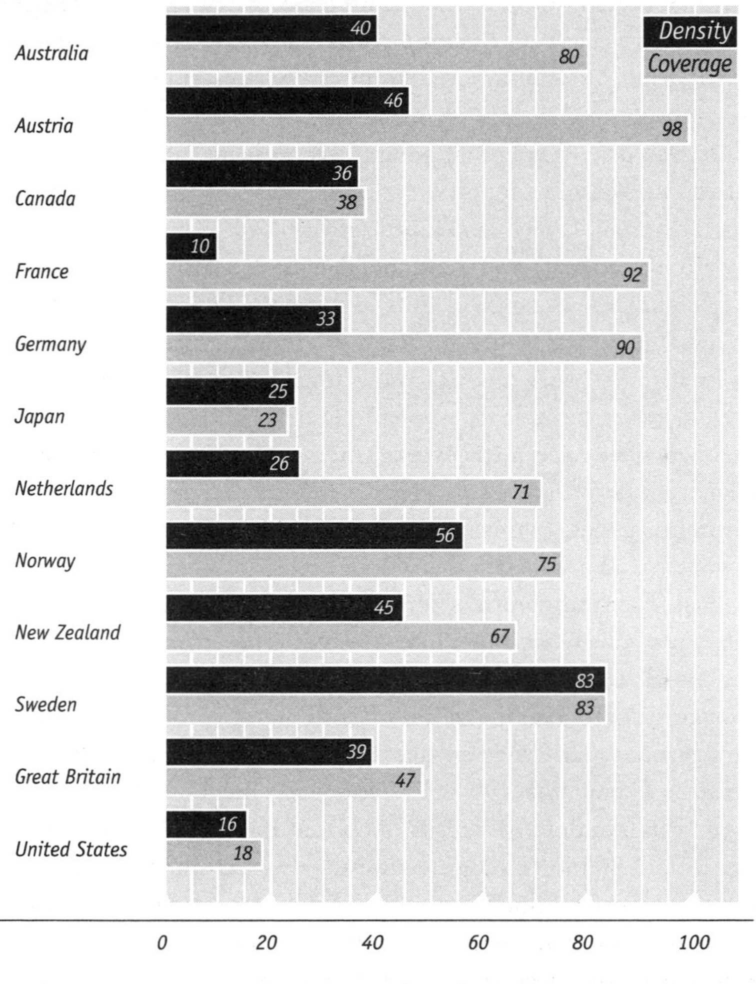

* Union density refers to the number of trade union members as a percentage of wage and salary earners. Collective bargaining coverage rate refers to the number of workers covered by collective agreements negotiated by unions as a percentage of wage and salary earners. Methodological differences in how countries collect these data make direct comparability difficult.

Source: ©OECD, 1994, *Employment Outlook July 1994*. Reproduced by permission of the OECD.

firm-based. But, unlike North America, there is much greater coordination within each industrial sector, and annual rounds of bargaining occur within a national framework. In Europe, with the exception of Sweden, where the vast majority of workers eligible for union membership actually belong, countries with even moderate levels of union density can have extensive collective bargaining coverage.

The European pattern is a result of highly coordinated and centralized collective bargaining systems, supported by law, in which national unions negotiate with large employers' federations. Pay and other basic working conditions are set nationally or by industrial sector, greatly reducing competition among individual workplaces on these issues (unlike Canada, where a firm may resist union pay demands because it would increase its wage costs relative to local competitors). So, in France, for example, despite a union density of only 10 percent, employer associations are legally required to regularly negotiate broad agreements with unions, the benefits of which are extended to virtually all employers and employees. In addition, Chapter 6 documented that industrial democracy systems at the firm level in some European countries give workers and unions a voice in a wide range of local issues, from technological change to work arrangements. European systems of collective bargaining recently have become more decentralized, in some cases bringing greater industrial democracy to workplaces, and providing more scope for worker participation in management decisions.

We noted earlier that Canadian union density has been stable for the last several decades. Comparing 23 OECD countries, including those in Figure 7.2, between 1970 and 1990 density increased in 10 and decreased in 12 countries (OECD 1994: 184–85). However, this did not result in parallel declines in collective bargaining coverage. Declines in both density and coverage were more likely to occur in nations with employer-centred, decentralized industrial relations systems—notably the United States and Japan. Drops in coverage were less likely in countries with strong sectoral or national bargaining, regulated by the state to balance employers' and employees' interests. Britain and New Zealand, two countries with previously centralized systems, stand out with declining density and coverage in the 1980s. In each case, market-oriented governments deregulated and decentralized industrial relations systems in attempts to weaken the power of unions. There are also various signs in other European countries and Australia of a shift in collective bargaining from national or sectoral levels down to firms, largely due to the introduction of more flexible forms of work organization, although the extent and implications of this decentralization process varies considerably (Katz 1993).

The Decline of U.S. Unions

Canada's union density and coverage have surpassed those of Japan and the United States, the two other countries with employer-centred industrial relations. This stability of Canadian unions relative to the rate of growth or decline in other countries, especially the United States, is a significant development. Canadian unions appear to have weathered the economic storms of the 1970s and 1980s rather well. U.S. unions, in contrast, are engaged in a struggle for survival. Membership has plunged from one-third of the workforce in the mid-1950s to less than 16 percent today. Observers attribute this decline to a number of factors, but in particular to fierce anti-union campaigns launched by private sector employers, labour laws that permit these coercive tactics, and ineffective responses from unions to these changes. Also significant is the shift of employment away from the union strongholds of the northeastern industrial regions to the Sun Belt states, where *right-to-work laws* undermine union security by prohibiting as a condition of employment either union membership or payment of union dues.[34]

Some industrial relations scholars have concluded that the American industrial relations system, which grew out of the New Deal in the 1930s and institutionalized collective bargaining, was replaced in the 1970s and 1980s by a nonunion approach to industrial relations. The breakdown of the old union-based industrial relations system can be traced to three trends: (1) *concession bargaining* (that is, unions agreeing to rollbacks in wages, benefits, and collective rights); (2) management innovations such as teamwork and greater employee participation; and (3) explicitly nonunion human resource management strategies.[35] Taking a more historical view, Goldfield links the decline of American unions to changing class relations. He argues that the failure to form a solid working-class base for the labour movement during its period of greatest membership strength, from the 1930s to the 1950s, seriously weakened it as a political force. Hence, U.S. labour lacked the strategies, leadership, and membership solidarity necessary to survive in a more hostile environment (Goldfield 1987). Another perspective is offered by S.M. Lipset, probably the best-known student of Canadian–American differences. According to Lipset, a core difference between the two societies is the traditionally stronger commitment among Americans to individualistic values, and the greater conviction held by Canadians that state intervention, social democratic politics, and unions will improve individuals' living conditions. For Lipset, these value differences underpin the greater propensity of Canadians to belong to unions. His thesis is, however, disputed by a number of Canadian scholars.[36]

To recap, several distinctive features of Canadian unions, as well as their social and political environment, help to explain why they have not suffered the same fate as their American counterparts. Most important are the somewhat more militant character of Canadian unions, widespread public sector collective bargaining that has been facilitated through legislation, and demands for greater local control of union affairs in Canada. The U.S. experience, on the other hand, clearly shows the decisive role legislation can play in encouraging or inhibiting free collective bargaining.

THE CURRENT STATE OF UNIONS IN CANADA

Membership Patterns

The likelihood of a Canadian worker being a union member, or joining one in the future, varies according to gender, province of residence, industry, and occupation. Figure 7.3 shows that in 1994, 33 percent of wage and salary earners (excluding the unemployed and self-employed) belonged to a union.[37] Provincial differences in labour legislation, industrial mix, and economic performance influence union membership. The provinces with the highest rates of unionization are Newfoundland and Quebec, each at over 40 percent, followed by Manitoba at about 39 percent. Newfoundland's high rate is due to the disproportionately large size of the unionized public sector in an otherwise depressed economy and the strength of unions in the fishing industry. At the opposite end of the scale, Alberta's union density is only 25 percent. A critical perspective would suggest that Alberta industrial relations have moved closer to the American model, given this province's more restrictive labour legislation, the decimation of its construction industry unions in the early 1980s, and American-style nonunion human resource policies found in key industries such as oil and gas.[38]

FIGURE 7.3 *Unionization Rates by Province, Canada, 1994*

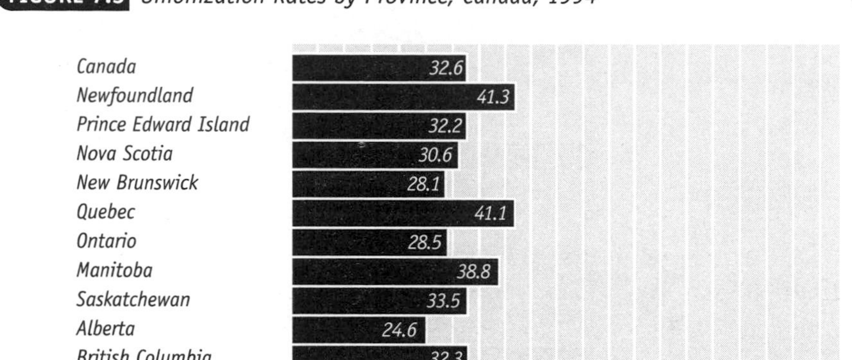

* Currently employed only; unemployed and self-employed excluded.

Source: Statistics Canada, "Unionization Rates by Province, Canada, 1994," from "General Social Survey, 1994," Catalogue No. 11-612. Reprinted with permission.

Figure 7.4 provides a detailed industrial breakdown of union membership for men and women. In the paid labour force, men have a slightly higher rate of union membership than women (34 and 31 percent, respectively). However, the rate for women and men is identical among full-time workers, while a higher proportion of women working part-time are union members (Statistics Canada 1994c: 58). This gender gap has closed recently, considering that the comparable figures in 1989 were 38 percent and 29 percent, respectively (Statistics Canada 1992c: 48). Public administration is the only industry in which women are more unionized, probably because of the overall high level of unionization and the fact that more males are managers, and, therefore, excluded from unions. It is clear that industry of employment is more crucial than gender in explaining membership trends. We note, for example, that the two industrial sectors with the greatest union density—education, health, and social services (59 percent unionized), and public administration (64 percent unionized)—have small or reversed gaps between male and female membership. The low rates of union membership in service industries, such as business services or consumer services and retail trade, support this argument from the other side: the lack of opportunities to join a union,

FIGURE 7.4 *Unionization Rates by Industrial Sector and Gender, Canada, 1994*

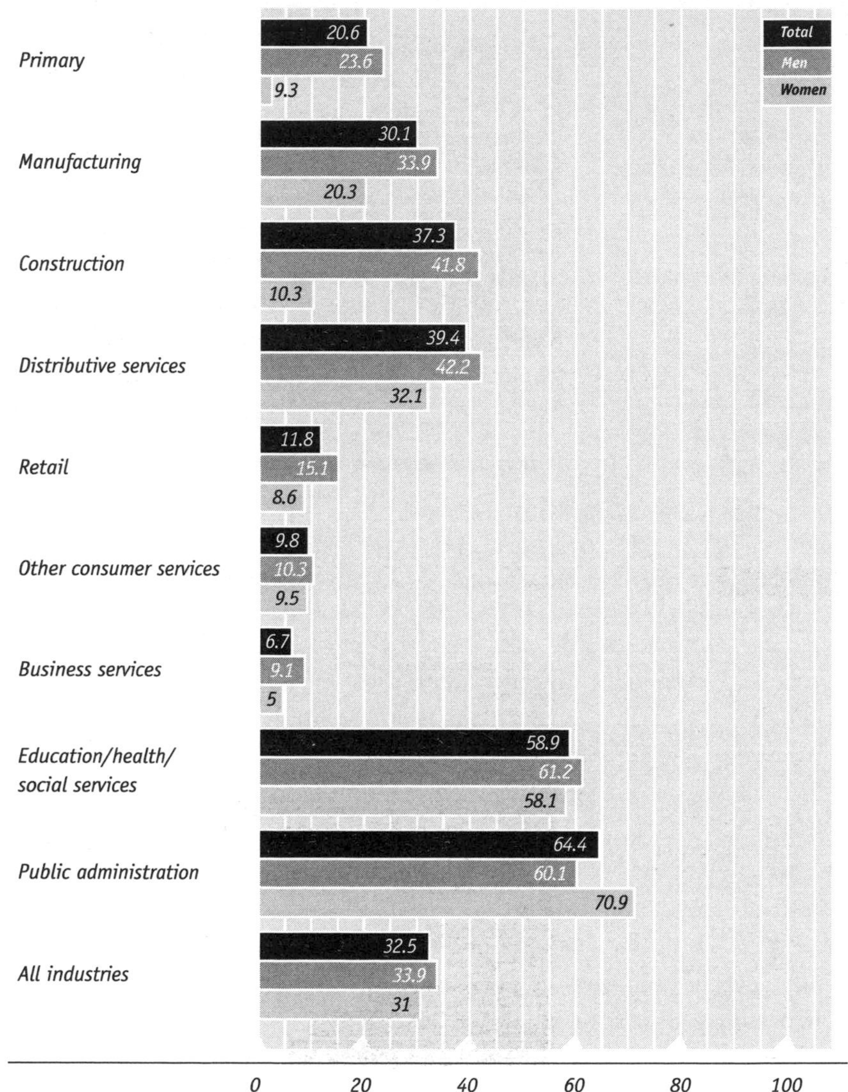

* Currently employed only; unemployed and self-employed excluded.

Source: Statistics Canada, "Unionization Rates by Industrial Sector and Gender, Canada, 1994," from "General Social Survey, 1994," Catalogue No. 11-612. Reprinted with permission.

or difficulties in organizing one, affects men and women equally. Unions' lack of success in these industries does not bode well for the future of unions, given our discussion in Chapter 3 about the importance of these sectors in job growth.

Unionization density is well above the national average in construction and distributive services (37 and 39 percent, respectively). However, here we find a large gender gap in membership levels, mainly due to the gender division of labour in these predominantly male, blue-collar areas of employment. Few women work in these industries. Those who do are located in clerical, secretarial, and administrative jobs, which unions have either ignored or have encountered major hurdles in their attempts to organize.

Another way of examining union membership is by occupation. Figure 7.5 shows that individuals in sales, managerial and administrative, primary, and artistic and recreation occupations are least likely to be union members.

FIGURE 7.5 *Unionization Rates by Occupation, Canada, 1994*

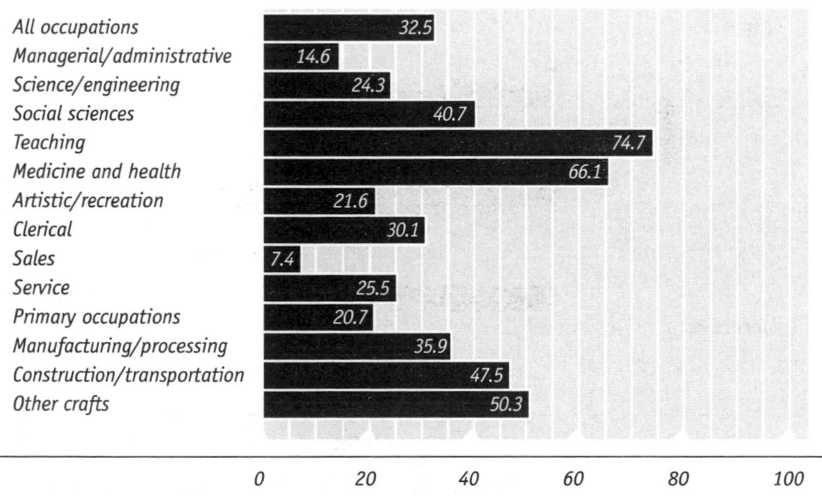

* Currently employed only; unemployed and self-employed excluded.

Source: Statistics Canada, "Unionization Rates by Occupation, Canada, 1994," from "General Social Survey, 1994," Catalogue No. 11-612. Reprinted with permission.

Conversely, the most highly unionized jobs are in teaching, and medicine and health (75 and 66 percent respectively). The recent unionization of such white-collar workers, many of whom are women, has given a whole new complexion to the labour movement. The traditional, blue-collar union strongholds in craft jobs, manufacturing and processing, transportation, and construction now have union densities ranging from 36 to 50 percent.

Other factors are also associated with union membership. In terms of sociodemographic characteristics, age and education are strongly related.[39] In 1994, only 13 percent of young workers (aged 15 to 24 years) belonged to unions, compared with 35 percent of 25- to 44-year-olds, and 41 percent of those over age 45. This pattern poses a major challenge for unions to bolster their recruitment efforts, given their aging membership. Better-educated workers also have higher rates of union membership. For example, the unionization rate among workers with university degrees is 38 percent, compared with 28 percent among those with a high school diploma or less. However, while these worker characteristics help to predict who is a member of a union, far more determinant are one's employment characteristics. As noted earlier, workplace size is one of the strongest predictors of union membership. So too is one's employment status. Specifically, being a full-time, permanent worker improves your chances of being a union member, or, in other words, of having the opportunity to join. Unions represent 25 percent of part-time workers, compared with 35 percent of full-time workers, 27 percent of temporary workers, and 36 percent of permanent workers (Schellenberg and Clark 1996: 19).

In short, the composition of the labour movement has been transformed since the 1960s. The typical unionist today is a white-collar worker employed in one of the service industries, most likely in the public sector. Women are joining the ranks of organized labour faster than men, so chances are that new union recruits will be women. Labour's traditional bastion, the male-dominated manufacturing, construction, and resource sectors of the economy, has been shaken by the forces of industrial restructuring, downsizing, recessions, international competition and the globalization of production, and weak prices for natural resources. Between 1977 and 1986, for example, union density and the actual number of members dropped considerably in forestry, mining, manufacturing, transportation, and construction industries (Kumar and Coates 1989: 27). The two major unions in manufacturing, the United Steel Workers (USW) and the Canadian Auto Workers (CAW), suffered the greatest membership losses of any labour organization in Canada during the 1981–82 recession (Kumar 1986: 140). However, both unions were able to increase membership during the most recent recession through organizing efforts, diversification, and mergers.

The Rise of Public Sector Unions

In marked contrast, membership grew in both relative and absolute terms during this time throughout the service sector. An example of this expansion is that of the Canadian Union of Public Employees (CUPE), the largest union in Canada since the early 1980s. The key to CUPE's success is membership diversification: the union has moved into new areas such as universities, airlines, and nursing homes in this period. This strategy also seems to be paying dividends for some industrial unions. Witness, for instance, the CAW's recruitment of workers in airlines and fisheries, and the USW's organizing campaigns among security guards and taxi drivers.[40]

The present character of the labour movement is reflected in its largest organizations. Table 7.1 lists the ten largest unions in 1996, which, as a group, account for close to half of all union members in Canada. The top two, CUPE and NUPGE, represent government and other public sector employees. CUPE members work in a wide spectrum of jobs in municipalities, electrical utilities, social services, child-care centres, schools, libraries, colleges and universities, hospitals, nursing homes, and many other public institutions. Typical of many government employee unions, CUPE evolved from a traditional and rather docile staff association. Established in the 1960s, it grew to 97,000 members by 1967. CUPE's fourfold growth in three decades made it the first union in the country to break the 400,000 membership mark. In 1996, it represented 11 percent of all union members in Canada. NUPGE is the umbrella organization for the various provincial government employee unions. Two other public sector unions are among the top ten—one is based in Quebec, and the other, PSAC, represents federal government workers. The largest private-sector union is the U.S.-based United Food and Commercial Workers. It has been actively organizing new members in service industries, growing by 20 percent between 1983 and 1989.[41] This is the union involved in the 1997 Alberta Safeway strike.

A watershed in the Canadian labour movement was reached in 1967 when the federal government passed the Public Service Staff Relations Act. This

TABLE 7.1 *Ten Largest Unions, Canada, 1996*

Union	*Membership (000s) in 1996*
Canadian Union of Public Employees	*455.8*
National Union of Public and General Employees	*310.6*
National Automobile, Aerospace, Transportation and General Workers Union of Canada (Canadian Auto Workers, or CAW)	*205.0*
United Food and Commercial Workers International Union	*185.0*
United Steelworkers of America	*170.0*
Public Service Alliance of Canada	*167.8*
Communications, Energy and Paperworkers Union of Canada	*165.2*
Fédération des affaires sociales inc. (Quebec)	*97.0*
International Brotherhood of Teamsters	*95.0*
Service Employees International Union	*80.0*
Total union membership	*4,033.0*
Membership of ten largest unions	*1,931.4*
Percentage of total membership in the ten largest unions	*47.9%*

Source: Human Resources Development Canada, Workplace Information Directorate, *Directory of Labour Organizations in Canada 1996* (Ottawa: Canada Communications Groups—Publishing, 1996): xiv, xvii. Reproduced with the permission of the Minister of Public Works and Government Services Canada, 1997.

opened the door to collective bargaining for federal civil servants. Provincial government employees were already moving in this direction, with the granting of collective bargaining rights to Quebec public employees in 1965. Unionism soon spread into municipal governments, hospitals, schools, prisons, social services, and other expanding public institutions. Consequently, the international unions representing mainly male craft and industrial workers have lost their once-dominant position in the Canadian labour movement. Thus, the large unions in Table 7.1 represent the wave of public sector unionism that began in the late 1960s. They also signal a new brand of worker militancy. Nurses, teachers, librarians, social workers, clerks, university professors, and other white-collar employees have taken to the picket lines to pressure their employers (ultimately, the government) into improving wages and working conditions and maintaining the quality of public services.

"Canadianizing" Unions

The rise of public sector unions has also helped to *Canadianize* the labour movement. At the turn of the century, U.S.-based international unions represented about 95 percent of all unionized workers in Canada. By 1969, this had dropped to 65 percent and, with the groundswell of nationalism since the 1970s, has continued to decline to 31.9 percent in 1990.[42] Not surprisingly, the recent upsurge in union growth is largely because of the efforts of national public sector unions (such as CUPE, mentioned above). Equally important in explaining the Canadianization trend is the push for greater autonomy, or outright independence, within Canadian sections of international unions.

The vulnerability of Canada's branch-plant economy taught growing numbers of workers the need for greater local control of union activities. A strong argument in support of international unions is that they are labour's best defence against the global strategies of multinational corporations. Yet the internationals have not always been effective in dealing with the sorts of problems multinational corporations created for Canadian employees. For example, officials at the U.S. headquarters of these unions sometimes equated layoffs or plant closures in Canada—associated with multinational firms shifting production to their U.S. facilities—with more jobs for their much larger American memberships. The North American Free Trade Agreement and the rising tide of protectionism south of the border have compounded these problems.

Different bargaining agendas also tended to arise in the two countries, reflecting their distinctive industrial relations environments. Canadian auto workers, for instance, roundly rejected the concessions made to employers by the U.S. wing of their union. The issue of national autonomy came to a head in the 1984 strike against General Motors by the Canadian division of the United Auto Workers. These Canadian autoworkers found themselves pitted against not only GM, but also the UAW leadership in Detroit, who wanted Canadian workers to accept the concessions agreed to by their American counterparts. While autonomy was not the goal of the Canadian workers going into the strike, it became an inevitable result. Reflecting on the formation of the Canadian Auto Workers union in December 1984, Sam Gindin, research director with the CAW, offers this analysis:

> While the anti-concession objectives of the Canadian UAW was, of itself, a modest goal, it was another strong reminder that collective bargaining remains at the heart of unionism ... The story of this fight against concessions obviously includes struggles beyond the Canadian autoworkers ... But if the autoworkers, with their

> reputation for militancy, for being at the leading edge of collective bargaining developments, had fallen into line with their American parent, concessions would not only have been legitimated in Canada but an aura of fatalism would have enveloped them. The Canadian autoworkers were faced with either becoming the vehicle for spreading concessions into Canada or risking the uncertainty of establishing their own Canadian union. Their choice was critical to maintaining the vitality of the Canadian labour movement.[43]

Beyond having different bargaining priorities and strategies, some Canadian branches of international unions felt that their dues were flowing into the American headquarters with few services flowing back. These and other factors have prompted a growing number of separations. In addition to the Canadian Auto Workers Union, the Communications and Electrical Workers, the Energy and Chemical Workers, and the Canadian Paperworkers Union were all created in this way.[44] Usually, good working relations are maintained, however, with their former U.S. parents.

WOMEN AND UNIONS

Why has the level of unionization historically been lower among female workers compared with male workers? At one time, it was assumed that women would be less interested in unions because of their family responsibilities and presumed lower commitment to paid employment. Because of their domestic roles, the argument went, women's ties to the labour force were weak. Hence, work problems that might prompt unionization were of secondary concern. Old myths die hard, but close scrutiny of recent membership trends totally shatters this one. Women made up only 16.4 percent of all union members in 1962, yet by 1991, this figure had jumped to 41 percent. In fact, women have been joining unions at a much faster rate than men. Between 1983 and 1991 alone, female membership increased by 34 percent, compared with only a 4 percent increase among men. These membership patterns strongly parallel the remarkable jump in female labour force participation outlined in Chapter 2, especially in the service sector, and the rapid growth of public sector unions. It seems obvious that women are not apathetic, passive, or indifferent to unions—if, in fact, they ever were.[45]

Indeed, women are often more pro-union than men because of their inferior positions in firms.[46] Kate Purcell rejects the "passive woman worker" argument on the grounds that industrial patterns of unionism are most decisive in who joins. Men and women alike join unions and engage in militant action according to the established patterns of their industries or occupations (Purcell 1979: 122–23). Miners and forestry workers are highly unionized, as we noted above, and have a history of militancy. But because these are non-traditional areas of women's employment, we would not expect to find many female unionists in these industries.

Thus, gender segregation in the labour market (discussed in Chapter 4) is the key factor in women's unionization patterns.[47] We have seen how, historically, women's employment has been restricted to a few predominantly female jobs. The oppressive and unrewarding character of this type of work, not the fact of being a woman, underlies the lower rate of female unionization. Such conditions in themselves can undermine collective action as a way of solving problems: workers, be they male or female, may be more likely to quit than to stay and fight for change.

What has been the role of male-dominated unions in keeping women out of certain jobs and, therefore, out of unions? There are numerous examples of craft and industrial unionists adopting policies that restricted female access to their jobs, mainly due to fears about having their wages undercut. Early this century, craft unions lobbied with middle-class reformers to keep women out of the industrial labour force (allegedly to protect them). Such efforts discouraged union initiatives by women, thereby defining the union movement as a male institution. In Canada, for example, the failure of the 1907 strike by female Bell Telephone operators in Toronto was partly due to the lack of support their unionization campaign received from the International Brotherhood of Electrical Workers, an exclusively male craft union (Sangster 1978).

Consequently, for many women the option of joining a union has not existed. Only in the last 20 years, for example, were major organizing efforts launched in the largely female retail and financial industries. Massive counterattacks were mounted by management in banks and in retail stores. Despite a huge investment of organizing resources since the late 1970s, the CLC has achieved only limited success in unionizing banks. Breakthroughs during the 1980s in achieving union certification in big department stores, such as Eaton's, initially augured well for union expansion in the retail sector. Yet the

1987 *decertification* of unions by employees in five Ontario Eaton's stores was a major setback.[48] While some areas of the retail industry, such as grocery stores, have moderate levels of unionization, vast areas of the service sector still pose large hurdles, as witnessed in recent unionization attempts at McDonald's, Wal-Mart, and Starbucks coffee shops.

Recent feminist scholarship has cast new light on the collective struggles of women to achieve fairness and equality through unions. In predominantly female occupations, women have a long tradition of collective action. As professionals, female teachers have been organized for decades. While not based on trade union principles, the 1918 founding of the Ontario Federation of Women Teachers' Associations showed the growing commitment of women to organize for improved working conditions (Strong-Boag 1988: 69). Also, a history of union activism exists among women in the garment and textile industries, particularly in unions such as the International Ladies' Garment Workers.[49] Moreover, women have exerted pressure on the male-dominated unions to which they belong to have their concerns addressed. As Pamela Sugiman shows in her study of women's struggle for gender equality within the Canadian wing of the United Auto Workers during the 1960s, feminists active in the union used "gendered strategies of coping and resistance," drawing on women's combined experiences as auto workers, unionists, wives, and mothers. Sugiman documents the often contradictory stance of unions on the issue of women's equality. While formally espousing this goal, male UAW members had difficulty getting beyond their patriarchal ideology:

> As their struggle unfolded, female activists recognized that industrial unionism, *as practiced by UAW men*, was not sufficient to achieve equality in the workplace. Male union leaders had long juggled the democratic principles of industrial unionism on the one hand and exclusive notions of a male breadwinner and family wage on the other. These were inherently contradictory philosophies, however, and male unionists therefore displayed ambivalence and sometimes resistance toward their feminist sisters. Thus, marginal to the UAW power structure, women auto workers were forced to draw on the support of feminists across class lines, and mobilize on their own within the union. The gendered politics in the union and company forced these women to

> turn to a social movement that extended beyond the workplace and union.[50]

Sugiman underscores a prominent theme in women's growing influence in unions, namely the importance of coalitions with the organized women's movement outside the workplace. *Pay equity* has become a major new workplace objective, largely due to a broad alliance of feminists and some major unions. Indeed, the central thrust of pay equity is to challenge the gendered division of labour as enshrined in many union-negotiated job classifications. It also places equality squarely on the collective bargaining agenda, especially given that legislation in Ontario and elsewhere requires unions to negotiate pay equity with employers. Perhaps the most prominent example of how pay equity for women workers has become a rallying point for unions is the national Public Service Alliance (PSAC) strike of federal civil servants in 1991. The union gained considerable public support for taking a stand on behalf of women in low-paid clerical and administrative jobs, who made up the majority of its members. Thus, if unions can demonstrate tangible improvements in women's wages and working conditions, their appeal to unorganized women workers may be enhanced (Cuneo 1990; Fudge and McDermott 1991).

In sum, women's demands for equality of opportunities and rewards in the workplace already have had a major impact on Canadian unions. The CLC elected its first female president, Shirley Carr, in 1986, and women are making up a growing share of elected union officers and paid staff, especially in public sector unions. The largest union in Canada, CUPE, elected Judy Darcy as its president in 1991. And a few unions, such as the Canadian Union of Postal Workers, have given top priority to concerns most often expressed by women (for example, paid maternity leave, sexual harassment, child care, and fair treatment of part-time workers) (Julie White 1990). Gradually, "women's issues"—which really are issues for all workers—have come to have higher stature in labour's collective bargaining and social action. Important bargaining items, at least for large unions, now include gender-neutral contract language and clauses dealing with discrimination, sexual harassment, family-related leaves, child care, technological change, and rights for part-time workers.[51] Labour's success in achieving this bargaining agenda is obviously crucial to its future. The combination of women's increasing labour-force participation and their still lower level of unionization make them prime targets for organizing drives in the future.

MANAGEMENT OPPOSITION TO UNIONS

Despite laws giving each employee the right to join a union and to participate in free collective bargaining, employer opposition to unionism frequently has been a major obstacle to putting these rights into practice. Workers who encounter strong management opposition to their union organizing activities may legitimately fear for their jobs, and this will have a chilling effect on the union campaign. Moreover, if an employer chooses not to recognize a union after it has been legally certified in the workplace, it is very difficult for members of that union to exercise their legal rights. Prior to the introduction of a legal framework for *union certification* and *collective bargaining* procedures during World War II, many industrial disputes occurred over the employer's refusal to recognize the workers' union. Surveying the historical record, Pentland observes: "It is sad but true that Canadian employers as a group and Canadian governments have never taken a forward step in industrial relations by intelligent choice, but have had to be battered into it."[52]

Positive Labour Relations

White-collar workers in the private sector remain the largest unorganized group in the labour force. Strenuous efforts by employers to remain union-free, with the help of the new human resource management practices already mentioned, and government inaction with regard to promoting private sector union recognition, have created an inhospitable climate for unionism. There are several additional reasons for this climate (Bain 1978: 23). White-collar employees often have direct contact with management and, therefore, may identify more closely with the company ideology than do blue-collar workers. The fact that management openly disapproves of unions can make white-collar workers reluctant to join one. Workers join unions for the benefits, such as better working conditions, higher wages, job security, or access to a grievance procedure. Concrete proof that unions can "deliver the goods" is obviously lacking in industries that have never had high levels of unionization. The difficulty of overcoming these obstacles discourages unions from launching recruitment drives. Consequently, the option of joining a union has not been available to many private sector white-collar workers.

The form of employee relations usually preferred by management is to deal with each worker individually. This creates a "David and Goliath" situation, pitting individual employees against the power of a corporation. However, the once virulent anti-unionism of Canadian business has softened somewhat into a grudging acceptance. Joseph Smucker's (1980: Chapter 7). analysis of changing *managerial ideologies* from 1901 to 1970 indicates that collective bargaining has come to be accepted as a "necessary evil." Instead of fighting unions head on, managers now often criticize them as being unrepresentative organizations under misguided leadership. An underlying concern is over the issue of what constitutes *management's rights.* There are still some employers today who zealously believe that the owners of a business should unilaterally define the employment relationship. In such cases, the right to manage takes absolute priority.

Some leading corporations have adopted a velvet-gloved strategy. This *positive labour relations* approach is based on maintaining high-quality human resource policies and good working conditions, and encouraging employee participation and commitment. Both lean production and high-performance workplace models, discussed in Chapter 5, have been adapted by some employers to maintain a union-free workplace. In some cases, a *company union* is even set up to create the façade of democratic employee representation. The basic assumption, derived from the human relations management tradition, is that if management treats employees well and listens to their concerns, a union will be unnecessary. IBM is a prime example of positive industrial relations in action. In Britain, the corporation's 13,000 employees were balloted at the request of the government's industrial relations board to find out if they desired union recognition. Only about 4 percent of the staff favoured unionization. This vote was not the result of corporate coercion or intimidation, as is becoming increasingly common in the United States (although not at IBM). Rather, it reflects the great deal of attention and resources that the company devotes to employee relations.

IBM can afford to do this, given its size and profitability. Here are some of its key company policies: the same fringe benefits package for all staff (an attempt to eliminate major status differences); merit pay and a sophisticated job evaluation system (the firm is the industry leader in salaries); open communication channels between management and employees; a form of internal grievance system, which acts as a safety valve for discontent; the development of people skills among managers so that dissatisfaction can be pre-empted; and, until recently, no layoffs. These human resource management policies produce a corporate culture based on strong employee loyalty and identification with management's goals.[53] Wherever corporations such as IBM, Xerox, or Hewlett-Packard operate, this approach is implemented. Some Canadian firms, most notably the Hamilton steel producer Dofasco, have developed their own unique brand of positive labour relations to obtain the cooperation of employees.[54]

Workplace reforms, particularly lean production and high-performance work systems, pose major dilemmas for unions. However, some of the most successful innovations of this kind suggest that union involvement is a prerequisite (Kumar 1995: 148). The examples of Saturn, Shell, and NUMMI (see Chapter 5) make this point. But in most cases, unions have tended to respond with either passive acceptance of these initiatives or active rejection.[55] The CAW, after extensive experience with lean production, adopted a policy of very carefully assessing the benefits and costs of participation (CAW 1993: 12). Only if workers' interests can be advanced and the union as an organization strengthened will the CAW enter into such change programs with management. Crucial ingredients are worker education and openness on management's part to share information (Martin 1995: 118–21). Kumar (1995: 148–49) explains why "workplace innovation" poses difficulties for unions as well as management:

> ... unions and management have different views of the goals of workplace innovations. Management goals are primarily efficiency-oriented. The general mission of HRM [human resource management] is to improve organizational effectiveness and achieve competitive advantage through a more efficient utilization and development of human resources ... Unions, on the other hand, are voluntary organizations of workers that serve as their collective voice in order to improve their physical, economic, social, and political well-being. The underlying values of the unions are inherently pluralistic and collective. Union activities extend beyond the workplace to legislative and political action to effect economic and social change. Consequently, if the unions are to have an independent role in workplace change, the objective of HR innovations must be more than simply enhancing organizational effectiveness: it must include improving the lot of the individual worker and promoting societal well-being.

Unions in an Era of Continuous Restructuring

Crystal-ball gazing is not a very scholarly activity, but we should at least contemplate likely future scenarios in Canadian industrial relations. The collective bargaining agenda is being transformed. Declining productivity growth since the mid-1960s, recessions in the early 1980s and early 1990s, privatization and cuts in government spending, high taxes and shrinking real incomes, and the increasing use of legislation and courts to restrict labour's rights have forced unions to rethink their negotiating priorities. For organized labour, the challenge of the 1990s has been to protect members' jobs and incomes (Kumar and Coates 1991: 41–43). Unions also face employer demands for wage and benefit concessions and greater flexibility in hiring practices. Concession bargaining began seriously in 1983, and, partly as a result of it, wage settlements have dropped sharply.

The 1985 strike by 3,000 Air Canada ticket agents brought together for the first time issues that have since become prominent. These included the use of part-time employees, technological change, the rights of women workers, and the effects of industry deregulation. Deregulation in 1984 forced airlines to reduce labour costs because of mounting competition. The union was concerned that management wanted to make ticket agents into part-time workers, because it intended to use machines to issue tickets and check in passengers. At stake were full-time incomes for female employees. The big issue raised by this dispute was the necessity of involving workers directly in the process of workplace change. In the 1990s, examples of concession bargaining include the 1996 restructuring of Canadian Airlines that depended, in part, on substantial employee wage rollbacks, and the Alberta government's 1993 5-percent pay cut for all public sector employees in the name of deficit reduction.

In an era of industrial restructuring, downsizing, and public sector cutbacks, employers increasingly are using work reorganization, flexible employment systems, and contracting out ("privatization" in the public sector) to their advantage. There is little doubt that these are major collective bargaining challenges in the future. When 26,000 members of the Canadian Auto Workers union went on strike in October 1996 against General Motors Canada, the key issue was "outsourcing" of work (using other companies to make parts previously made by GM workers). The union gained some ground in its fight to restrict GM's ability to sell plants or to contract out "non-core" jobs.[56] In the public sector, similar issues arose in November 1995 when 120 laundry workers at two Calgary hospitals staged an illegal "wildcat" strike, protesting the contracting out of their work to a private Edmonton company. They had previously taken a 28-percent wage cut that they thought would preserve their jobs. Other unionized hospital workers joined the picket line and there was considerable support from citizens fearful about the general deterioration of health services. Within a few days, the regional health authority and the provincial government had backed down on this particular privatization initiative, but the larger trend was unchecked.[57]

This realignment in collective bargaining in favour of management reflects underlying economic trends. Many factors are motivating employers to slash labour costs, boost employee productivity, intensify the work process, or even relocate jobs out of Canada. Included among these are globalization; pressures from NAFTA to bring Canadian employment standards into line with lower standards in the U.S., Mexico, or elsewhere; the acceleration of technological innovations; government deregulation of industry; the desire to obtain greater flexibility in staffing and production systems; and pressures to cut government deficits. Some analysts argue that, in response, organized labour must develop truly international strategies, given that large multinational corporations are leading the way in these respects. Not surprisingly, the impact of these trends on national and workplace industrial relations is a growing area of research.[58]

THE NATURE OF COLLECTIVE ACTION

So far, we have assumed that union members' common interests and objectives make it likely that they will bargain collectively with their employer. But how do workers come to act collectively? We recognize the importance of work-group dynamics, informal norms, and social relations, topics already discussed in Chapter 5. But this is only a partial answer. A more complete understanding of collective action requires us to examine the underlying basis for unionization, which is the predominant form of collective worker action in industrial society. What makes this particularly interesting is that the very idea of collective action seems contrary to the individualistic norms of capitalist employment relations.

The Dilemmas of Collective Action

Drawing on the insights of informal group dynamics, sociologists portray unions as *social movements* that unite members so they can actively seek shared goals. But, as with bureaucracies, unions also require rules and sanctions to regulate the behaviour of members. As Alan Flanders (1970: 44) writes, "trade unions need organization for their power and movement for their vitality." Both qualities are essential for unions to achieve their social and economic objectives. At the individual level, this perspective focuses on why employees would organize themselves into unions to collectively pursue common goals. In addition, it incorporates an analysis of the economic and social conditions that encourage or inhibit unionism and, moreover, raises questions about the internal dynamics of unions.

It is helpful to consider two dilemmas that a worker must resolve if she or he is to seriously consider joining a union or, if already a member, becoming an activist. The first is the *free-rider problem.* Mancur Olson asserts that individuals will not naturally organize to further their collective interest. "The rational worker," explains Olson, "will not voluntarily contribute to a union providing a collective benefit since [s]he alone would not perceptibly strengthen the union, and since [s]he would get the benefits of any union achievements whether or not [s]he supported the union."[59] Just like social movements concerned with environmental, peace, or feminist issues, unions provide *collective goods.* In other words, all potential members have access to the organization's achievements—a sustainable environment, a world with fewer weapons, employment equity programs, or a grievance procedure and negotiated regular wage increases—whether they have assisted in achieving these objectives or not. Returning to our discussion of crossnational unionization trends, this is one reason that unionization levels remain low in European countries such as France, the Netherlands, and Germany. Given that the centralized, state-regulated industrial relations systems in these countries guarantee many nonmembers the full benefits of union-negotiated wage agreements, the incentive to join is considerably reduced. In contrast, in the United States where such legislation is absent, "right to work" laws weaken unions by taking advantage of the "free rider" dilemma.

The second dilemma involves Albert Hirschman's (1970) *exit* and *voice* methods of expressing discontent. According to Hirschman, a dissatisfied employee can either leave her or his employer or stay and push for changes. The presence of a union increases the chances that the employee will pursue the latter strategy. But in nonunion workplaces, the poor employment conditions that could spark an organizing drive also increase the chances of an individual opting to quit. This is a major obstacle to unionization in low-wage job ghettos in the service industries today.

However, as we have already noted, many people do not have employment options. Unemployment may be high in their community, or their particular skills may not be in demand. Consequently, as we document in Chapter 8, such individuals adapt to their limited opportunities to find a better job, perhaps becoming increasingly apathetic and alienated from their work. But, while it is true that apathy and alienation stifle collective action, it would be wrong to assume that these conditions cannot be overcome. Instead, we should ask why some groups of employees mobilize while others do not.

The Mobilization Process

The process of mobilizing initial support for a union requires the obtaining of signed union cards from the majority of employees in the workplace. It also requires the financial assistance and organizational expertise of an established union. Once organized, a union faces the problem of rallying members in support of collective bargaining goals. Ultimately, this could involve strike action. According to Charles Tilly's (1979) research on the causes of social protest, what is essential here is a sense of shared identity with the group. Collective action in the workplace will be easier when the work group is an important part of each employee's life. Strong social ties inside and outside the workplace integrate employees into the group. Individual interests become synonymous with group interests, acting as a springboard to collective action. Good examples of groups possessing this *solidarity* are printers, miners, fishers, and members of other occupations in which the occupational culture encompasses all of a worker's life.[60] Levels of unionization and industrial militancy tend to be high under these conditions.

Assuming the existence of a cohesive group, what pushes its members into common action? The role of the group leader is obviously central. Especially important are *organic leaders* who, by virtue of being part of the group, are best able to tap its potential for collective action. This is because they understand the experiences of group members and can gain their trust better than an outsider could. In short, an effective leader will build up group solidarity, create an awareness of common interests, map out a realistic program of action, and seize opportunities to launch the plan.

But we are not suggesting that all union activity can be reduced to the characteristics of a particular group, its members, and its leaders. Also important is the environmental context, which might involve a supportive community, a hostile employer, or fair labour legislation—all factors that can either nurture or dampen union activity. Even if such conditions are favourable, employees ripe for unionization may still not act. Similarly, unionized workers facing a deadlock in negotiations with management over a new collective agreement may not strike. Often missing is one or more precipitating factors: an arbitrary change in work practices; the denial of a long-awaited salary increase; the dismissal of co-workers; or a pent-up sense of being treated unfairly by management. Such perceived injustices could serve as the catalysts for mobilization.

Research on the inner workings of two Canadian unions gives us glimpses of how some of these factors actually contribute to *militancy*. Julie White's study of the Canadian Union of Postal Workers (CUPW) quotes a woman worker in a Saint John post office: "We're a militant union, and I really believe that Canada Post has made us that way."[61] This view is typical of CUPW members, White argues. The union has developed a "culture of struggle," based on the belief that management does not have the interests of workers at heart and, further, that any past improvements have been extracted from management by militant action. Against a background of unsuccessful attempts to resolve disputes through negotiation, mediation, and conciliation, this culture of struggle has been cultivated by an openly democratic structure based on rank-and-file involvement.

The importance of internal union dynamics was also a crucial factor in the militancy of Canadian autoworkers in the 1980s. Charlotte Yates attributes CAW's success at holding back on concessions demanded by North American auto firms to its greater membership solidarity, compared with the United Auto Workers union in the United States, which agreed to concessions. Some of the key features of union organization that contributed to CAW's militancy were members' influence over union decision making, including the rank and file's ability to mobilize opposition to the leadership if unpopular positions were being imposed, and effective communication channels linking all levels in the union (Yates 1990: 77).

In summary, a solid organizational base, strong leadership, union democracy that encourages rank-and-file participation, a shared understanding of who is responsible for employees' grievances, and support from other groups in the community are key ingredients for collective action. Equipped with this understanding, we can now turn our attention to the most common manifestation of collective action—strikes.

STRIKES

According to conventional wisdom, unions in this country are strike-happy, and our entire industrial relations system is far too adversarial. In this section, we will evaluate the popular complaint that Canadian workers are strike-prone. We will also probe beneath the surface of these conflicts, locating strikes within the context of the larger political arena. Are strikes a sign of worker militancy? Does industrial conflict have any connection with working-class politics? After all, many of the grievances fuelling strikes could be blamed generally on the capitalist system itself. But do union members and nonunion workers themselves make such connections?

What Are Strikes?

Strikes are high drama on the stage of industrial relations. The public views strikes as an inconvenience or even as a major social problem. Many politicians and business leaders argue that strikes harm the economy. The participants seldom want strikes, least of all the union members who will never recoup the wages lost should the dispute drag on. But if conflict has been largely *institutionalized*, as described earlier, why do strikes occur at all? What motivates workers to strike, and what are the larger social and economic implications of their actions?

Let us begin with a widely accepted definition of a *strike* or *lockout:* "A temporary stoppage of work willfully effected by a group of workers, or by one or more employers, with a view to enforcing a demand."[62] Workers initiate strikes typically after a legally required strike vote, while lockouts (which account for relatively few work stoppages) are initiated by employers. Between

1980 and 1993 in Canada, 13 percent of private sector and 4 percent of public sector collective agreements were signed after a strike. This strike rate has declined since the late 1960s.[63] Thus, strikes may accurately be described as infrequent events. Contrary to public opinion, settlement of union–management disputes without recourse to work stoppages is clearly the norm in Canada. There is evidently some truth to the argument that conflict has been institutionalized through the elaborate legal framework that regulates union–management relations.

Strikes are, nonetheless, central to the wage-labour relationship. If workers are selling their labour power to an employer in return for wages, their ultimate bargaining lever is to withdraw that labour. Even before the emergence of industrial capitalism in Canada, strikes erupted as workers protested against harsh treatment. For example, carpenters imported to build ships in colonial New France staged a slowdown to win living expenses above basic wages (Pentland 1981: 27). We have already mentioned that the struggling nineteenth-century labour movement mounted several landmark strikes, most notably the 1872 Toronto printers' strike and the Nine-Hour Movement agitations that happened around the same time.

But strikes are only one possible form of workplace conflict. Richard Hyman distinguishes between *unorganized* and *organized conflict* (1978: Chapter 3). The former is not a calculated group action, and typically involves workers responding to oppressive situations by individual absenteeism, quitting, or sabotage. The latter is a planned collective strategy, the aim of which is to change the source of the discontent. Recall that strikes in Canada are only legal after the collective agreement has expired and specific conditions, such as a strike vote, have been met. Unauthorized strikes during the term of an agreement, often spontaneous responses by rank-and-file workers to an immediate problem in the workplace, are known as *wildcat strikes*.[64] The Calgary laundry workers that we discussed earlier provide a recent example.

Not all strikes are over economic issues, nor do they exclusively involve working-class unionists. They can be political, as in the case of the Canadian Labour Congress's 1976 "national day of protest," when over one million employees marched on the streets to register their opposition to the federal government's imposition of wage and price controls. The British Columbia Federation of Labour's concerted opposition in 1983 to new legislation that would seriously weaken unions is another example. So too are the 1996 "days of action" initiated by the Ontario Federation of Labour to protest the newly elected Conservative government's massive public-sector funding cuts. Strikes can involve work stoppages by high-status professionals. Examples include the 1986 Ontario doctors' strike over the right to extra-bill patients and the 1997 faculty strike at York University over collective bargaining rights and deteriorating working conditions. Finally, strikes do not necessarily entail all members of the union leaving the worksite as a group. Under certain situations, *rotating strikes*, across a number of worksites, working-to-rule (doing the minimum required), or staging work stoppages by "sitting down" on the job are variants of strike activity that can also communicate workers' demands to management.

Our emphasis on strike activity may leave the impression that workers are the disruptive factor in what otherwise would be harmonious labour relations. The key word here is *relations*, for there are two parties (three if the government intervenes, and possibly four if the public is directly affected) in every strike. Seldom is the employment relationship a balanced one, however, since employers inevitably wield greater power. After all, management holds the final bargaining chip—the keys to the factory gate or office door, and, therefore, to the workers' jobs. Nonetheless, in the public mind, unions are usually the "cause" of strikes and labour unrest.

The United Auto Workers (now the CAW) attempted to set the record straight in their 1985 brief to the Royal Commission on the Economic Union and Development Prospects for Canada, saying, in part, "No matter how legitimate our demands are, it is the unions who have to initiate strike action. This reinforces the public bias of blaming workers for management–labour conflict."[65] The brief debunks the myth that unions are too powerful and strike-happy by outlining the underlying causes of what, at the time, were three UAW disputes. These included the unwillingness of an employer to recognize a legitimately organized union local, employer attempts to force wage and benefit rollbacks, and concerns about plant closures. These are not isolated instances. Rather, they are typical of how employers are able to muscle unions into a tight economic corner from which strike action is often the only rational escape.

Canadian Strike Trends

On an annual basis, work stoppages rarely account for more than 0.5 percent of all working time in Canada (Table 7.2). This indicates that the seriousness of the strike "problem" often gets blown out of proportion. But, historically, we can identify eras when strikes were more common and widespread. There have been four particularly stormy periods of industrial conflict in Canada during the twentieth century, gauged by the percentage of total working time lost due to strikes and lockouts.

TABLE 7.2 *Work Stoppages Involving One or More Workers, Canada, 1976–1996**

Period	*Number in existence during year*	*Total number of workers involved*	*Average number of workers per stoppage*	*Total person-days not worked*	*Average days lost per worker involved*	*Days lost as a percentage of estimated total working time*
1976	1,040	1,586,221	1525	11,544,170	7.3	0.53
1977	806	217,647	270	3,320,050	15.3	0.15
1978	1,057	400,622	379	7,357,180	18.4	0.32
1979	1,049	462,386	441	7,819,350	16.9	0.33
1980	1,028	439,003	427	9,129,960	20.8	0.37
1981	1,050	341,852	326	8,850,560	25.9	0.35
1982	680	464,181	683	5,712,500	12.3	0.23
1983	645	329,472	511	4,440,900	13.5	0.18
1984	716	186,916	261	3,883,400	20.8	0.15
1985	829	162,333	196	3,125,560	19.3	0.12
1986	748	484,255	647	7,151,470	14.8	0.27
1987	668	581,882	871	3,810,170	6.5	0.14
1988	548	206,796	377	4,901,260	23.7	0.17
1989	627	444,747	709	3,701,360	8.3	0.13
1990	579	270,471	467	5,079,190	18.8	0.17
1991	463	253,334	547	2,516,090	9.9	0.09
1992	404	149,940	371	2,110,180	14.1	0.07
1993	381	101,784	267	1,516,640	14.9	0.05
1994	374	80,856	216	1,606,580	19.9	0.06
1995	328	149,159	455	1,582,321	10.6	0.05
1996	328	283,744	865	3,339,560	11.8	0.11

* Work stoppages refers to strikes and lockouts.

Source: Human Resources Development Canada, Labour Program, Workplace Information Directorate. (Obtained from Human Resources Development Canadaís Internet site.) Reproduced with the permission of the Minister of Public Works and Government Services Canada, 1997.

A number of issues were at stake in early twentieth-century strikes. Skilled artisans in the nineteenth century had been able to retain much of their craft status, pride, and economic security through their control of the production process. This privileged position was eroded by industrialization after 1900, as advancing technology and scientific management techniques undermined craft workers' autonomy. Thus, craft workers angrily resisted rationalization of their work, sparking many of the 421 strikes and lockouts that occurred between 1901 and 1914 in southwestern Ontario manufacturing cities (Heron and Palmer 1977).

Prior to union recognition and compulsory collective bargaining becoming encoded in law during World War II, many strikes were precipitated by an employer's refusal to recognize the existence of a union, much less bargain with it. The historic peak in labour militancy occurred at the end of World War I. Workers across the country were agitating against oppressive working conditions, low wages, and declining living standards due to soaring wartime inflation. Most of all, they wanted recognition of their unions. Western Canadian unions were far more militant and inclined toward radical politics than those in the rest of the country. Thus, in 1919 when Winnipeg building and metal trades employers refused to recognize and negotiate with unions over wage increases, the Winnipeg Trades and Labour Council called a *general strike.*

A massive display of working-class solidarity erupted, bringing the local economy to a halt. Sympathy strikes spread to other cities across Canada, and even into the United States. The battlelines of open class warfare (one of the few instances of this in Canadian history) were drawn when, fearing a revolution, Winnipeg's upper class fought back with the help of the state. For several days, strikers squared off against police and employer-sponsored armed vigilantes. The confrontation ended in violence after the Royal Northwest Mounted Police, sent in by the federal government, charged a crowd of demonstrators. Strike leaders were arrested and jailed, while the workers' demands were still unmet.[66]

Strike activity declined with rising unemployment during the Depression of the 1930s. As a rule, unions are less likely to strike in tough economic times. Conversely, when industry is booming and there is a relative shortage of labour, reflected in low unemployment rates, a strike becomes a more potent bargaining lever. The World War II era marked the rise of industrial unionism in manufacturing industries. Organizing drives accelerated as military production demands helped to restore the ailing economy. Again, union recognition was a dominant issue, driving workers in automobile factories, steel plants, and mines onto the picket line. As mentioned earlier in the chapter, the 1945 Ford strike led to the introduction of the Rand Formula to protect union security. Subsequently, this became a standard feature of collective agreements, setting the tenor of post–World War II labour relations by legitimizing unions while simultaneously ensuring orderly collective bargaining.[67]

Canada experienced a series of strikes in the mid-1960s. The fact that about one-third of these work stoppages involved wildcat strikes (mainly over wages) led the government to perceive a serious crisis in industrial relations. A task force, chaired by Professor H. D. Woods of McGill University, was set up to investigate the causes of industrial unrest and to recommend ways of achieving labour peace. Yet rampant inflation during the 1970s, and an increasingly militant mood among public sector workers, escalated labour–management confrontations.

The most recent strike wave reached its apex in 1976. The Trudeau government's imposition of wage and price controls in 1975 as part of its anti-inflation program, made strikes over higher wages a futile exercise.[68] But in the 20 years since 1976, lost time due to work stoppages dropped to post–World War II lows. The recession-plagued 1980s and 1990s have dampened strike activity. Ironically, the fact that Canada's lost working time due to strikes and lockouts had dropped by the late 1980s was used by the federal government to attract foreign investors looking for a stable industrial relations environment.[69]

Table 7.2 profiles the labour relations patterns of the past two decades by reporting the four ingredients of strike activity: *frequency* (number of strikes), *size* (number of workers involved), *duration* (days lost), and overall *volume* (days lost as percentage of total working time). Thus, in 1996 for example, the 328 work stoppages that occurred involved an average of 865 workers, with each striking worker on the picket line an average of 11.8 days. In comparison, there were more than three times the number of strikes in 1980, each involving fewer workers (an average of 427) but lasting considerably longer (20.8 days on average). A comparison of the average size and duration of strikes in the 1980s and 1990s reveals two important changes: fewer workers on average were involved in the recent period (456 in the 1990s, compared with 567 in the 1980s); and there has been a decline in average days lost per worker (from 18 days in the 1980s to 14 in the 1990s). Changing economic and industrial relations conditions since 1980 have resulted in somewhat smaller and shorter strikes.

A Comparative Perspective on Strikes

How does Canada's strike record compare with that of other industrial nations? Recognizing the difficulties involved in making international comparisons of strike activity (due to differences in how strikes are defined and measured), we can, nonetheless, get a rough idea of where Canada stands in this regard from Figure 7.6 below.[70] Based on the annual averages of working days lost in nine industrialized countries between 1970 and 1992, Canada's rate was the second highest after Italy.

Are Canadian workers really more strike-prone than their counterparts in other countries, or do other factors underlie the ranking in Figure 7.6? This is a very complex question, but it is fairly clear that a major reason for Canada's record is the length of strikes in this country. For example, the average duration

FIGURE 7.6 *Strike Volume in Selected Industrialized Countries, Annual Averages, 1970–1992*

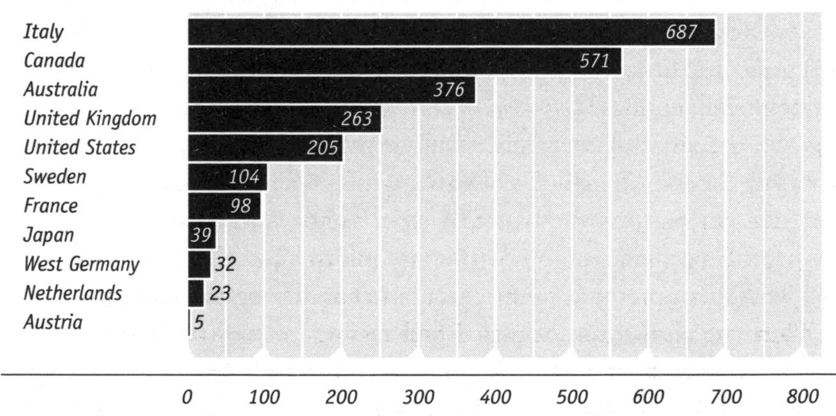

Note: Comparisons across countries should be made cautiously due to national differences in data collection methods.

Source: Roy J. Adams, "Canadian industrial relations in comparative perspective." In Morley Gunderson and Allen Ponak (eds.), Union–Management Relations in Canada, 3rd edition (Don Mills: Addison-Wesley, 1995): 512. Copyright ©1995 Addison-Wesley Publishers Limited. All Rights Reserved. Reproduced by permission.

of work stoppages between 1977 and 1981 was 20 days in Canada, 7 in the United Kingdom, 5 in Germany and Sweden, and less than 4 in France, Italy, and Japan.[71] Italy has such a high strike rate because disputes, while short, are frequent and involve many workers. By contrast, the Swedish system of centralized bargaining, along with the country's powerful unions and their huge strike funds, mean that a work stoppage could quickly cripple the economy. This imposes considerable pressure to peacefully resolve potential disputes. In Japan, unions are closely integrated into corporations in what really amounts to a type of company unionism. Strikes are infrequent; workers voice their grievances by wearing black armbands or by making other symbolic gestures calculated to embarrass management. German union–management collective bargaining is centrally coordinated, but, at the individual workplace, employee-elected works councils frequently negotiate employment conditions (see Chapter 6). German laws require these participatory councils; they also make it very difficult to strike.

Thus, legislation governing the structure of collective bargaining is vitally important. The North American system of bargaining is highly decentralized and fragmented, involving thousands of separate negotiations between a local union and a single employer, each of which could result in a strike. Low-strike nations such as Austria, Germany, and Sweden avoid these problems by having national or industry-wide agreements, and by legislating many of the quality of working life issues that Canadian unions must negotiate with employers on a piecemeal basis. As Roy Adams (1995: 515) concludes, "As long as uncoordinated decentralized bargaining continues in North America, it is unlikely that the overall level of conflict will be reduced to the levels common in Northern Europe." In addition, as discussed in Chapter 6, laws in these countries give employees greater participation rights in enterprise-level decision making. This provides unions with more information about the firm's operations and opens up more communication channels with management.

There are also major industrial and regional variations in strikes, which may be the result of how industries are organized. The least strike-prone Canadian industries are finance, trade, and services, which makes sense given their low unionization levels. Of the highly unionized industries, mining has historically been the most strife ridden. Similarly, Newfoundland and British Columbia have significantly higher-than-average strike rates because of their high concentration of primary and other strike-prone industries.[72]

Explaining Strikes

One prominent but widely challenged interpretation of inter-industry differences in strike behaviour is Kerr and Siegel's *isolation hypothesis*. These writers propose that isolated industries have higher strike rates than those where workers are integrated into the larger society. Isolated workers "... live in their own separate communities: the coal patch, the ship, the waterfront district, the logging camp, the textile town. These communities have their own codes, myths, heroes, and social standards."[73] Canada has always had large numbers of remote, resource-based, single-employer towns (see Chapter 2), where a combination of social isolation and a limited occupational hierarchy moulds workers into a cohesive group in opposition to management.

Research by Eric Batstone and his colleagues in a British auto plant adds to our understanding of strikes by highlighting the day-to-day processes that may culminate in a strike (Batstone et al. 1978). Strikes, argue these researchers, do not just happen. Rather, as a form of collective action, strikes require a high degree of *mobilization*. How production is organized, the type of technology used, and the formal institutions regulating union–management relations shape the context for this mobilization. But a crucial (yet largely ignored) ingredient of mobilization is how the social relations within the union allow certain individuals and groups to shape the course of events leading up to a strike. This mainly occurs through the identification of potential strike issues and through the use of rhetoric, by which the escalation of collective action is justified.

At the time of Batstone's study, most British strikes were unofficial stoppages initiated on the shop floor, not by top union leaders or by a democratic vote by all members. Laws more strictly regulate Canadian strikes, although recent British legislation has also moved in this direction. But the Batstone study offers some important insights about strikes in general. Workers usually do not want to strike, so they must develop a vocabulary to justify such action. This requires the translation of specific grievances into the language of broad principles and rights. Furthermore, disputes over wages also typically involve *effort bargaining*.[74] That is, even if management refuses to grant wage increases, workers can informally shift their bargaining tactics to the other side of the "wage-effort equation" through slowdowns, refusal of overtime, and unauthorized work breaks. Finally, the study refutes the common view that the most powerful unions throw their weight around by striking. A basic contradiction of trade unionism, especially when examined in the workplace, is that "... the groups of workers most able to strike (in terms of bargaining awareness and collective strength) may rarely have to resort to strike action" (Gannagé 1995).

Case studies of strikes involving women workers add new insights to the dynamics of industrial disputes. Industrial conflicts in the past two decades more often were in the public sector and involved women, immigrants, and other workers new to collective bargaining. Jerry White's analysis of the 1981 illegal strike in Ontario hospitals highlights how the pressures of cutbacks and the resulting work reorganization in health care have the potential to push workers onto the picket line. White dismisses the "agitator" explanation of strikes, pointing out that, in this case, the union leadership generally did not support the strike. Rather, the strike was a grassroots protest by nonprofessional service workers such as orderlies, housekeepers, food handlers, registered nursing assistants, lab technicians, and maintenance workers. In the end, the strike won the workers slight wage improvements, but at a price: thousands of strikers were suspended, 34 were fired, and 3 union leaders were jailed.

Interestingly, the motivations to strike were different for men and women in this dispute. At issue was the transformation of the labour process associated with patient care due to massive cost-cutting. Male workers wanted compensation in the form of higher pay, reduced workload, and guaranteed benefits. Women, in contrast, were far more concerned with how cutbacks had deteriorated their relationships with patients. As White explains, for women:

> There was a complex of rewards, including formal *recognition* of the usefulness of the work, an *interaction* with other workers, and an intrinsic sense of a *job well done*. The hospital work provided this complex of rewards. Care-giving was a key aspect of this. Labour process changes broke this care-giving bond for many women workers. The desire to reestablish this bond was one consideration in the decision to strike.[75]

WORKER MILITANCY AND CLASS POLITICS

Social scientists often use strikes as a measure of worker *militancy*. Are strikes actually deeply rooted in class antagonisms, reflecting basic working-class discontent? Or do unionized workers act simply out of economic self-interest?

General strikes have temporarily disrupted the economies of several advanced capitalist societies in recent years, and there is debate over how to interpret these events. Are they signs of heightened *class consciousness*, or are they merely pressure tactics to force changes in specific government or employer policies? Economists have calculated that strikes have only a modest impact on the economy.[76] As sociologists, we are equally interested in the broader implications of strikes for class consciousness, and for working-class political action.

Comparative Perspectives on Working-Class Radicalism

Michael Mann's (1970) comparative study of industrial conflict addresses this question. Workers in France and Italy, he found, were more politically radical than those in Britain or the United States, who identified more closely with management. But the political potential of the French and Italian working classes was frequently limited by their failure to articulate an alternative social system and to chart a course toward it. Mann argues that strikes can be *explosions of consciousness*. But the working-class solidarity they generate rarely gathers momentum beyond the immediate event. For example, a test of the "explosion of consciousness" hypothesis among Hamilton, Ontario, postal workers who had participated in a strike found increased positive identification with fellow workers and the union, but little impact on class consciousness (Langford 1996). Ultimately, then, strikes by even politically radical workers are transformed into tactical manoeuvres to obtain concessions from employers.

Most workers, according to Mann, possess a *dual consciousness*. Instead of having a unified understanding of how their work dissatisfactions are organically linked to the operations of capitalism—real class consciousness in the Marxist sense—workers tend to compartmentalize their work experiences from the rest of their lives. They develop a "pragmatic acceptance" of the alienation and subordinate status they endure at work. Satisfactions in life are found in the basic pleasures of family, friends, and community, not in the quest for a new society.

Several other comparative studies have carried this discussion further, trying to identify which factors may transform varying degrees of working-class consciousness into collective action. This question gets at what perhaps is the weakest link in Marxist theories of class (Form 1983: 175). Duncan Gallie (1983) investigated the nature and determinants of worker attitudes to class inequality in France and Britain. At the time, these two countries had similar levels of socioeconomic development, but the French working class was radical, while its British counterpart was moderate. Indeed, Gallie (1983) points out that the May 1968 general strike in France was "arguably the most powerful strike movement unleashed in the history of capitalist society, shaking its very foundations." Why is it, asks Gallie, that British workers accept major social inequities as inevitable, while for the French they are a source of resentment and a catalyst for industrial militancy and political radicalism?

Gallie's evidence shows that workers in both France and Britain recognize class-based inequities in opportunity, wealth, and privilege. They differ, however, in their attitudes toward these inequities. For French workers, class position is an important part of personal identity. They identify with the larger working class, resent the system that puts them at the bottom, and believe that political action can improve their situation. British workers, in contrast, are more concerned about changing things in the workplace rather than in society as a whole.

Gallie's explanation of these differences hinges on the role of left-wing political parties in translating workplace experiences into a radical critique of society. French employers exercise greater unilateral power than do their British counterparts, and workplace industrial relations in France are not governed by mutually agreed-upon rules. Thus, social inequality is more pronounced than in Britain. Furthermore, France has a revolutionary political tradition going back to the late eighteenth century. Hence, French workers' grievances with their employers are more intense and more readily carried outside the workplace, where they are moulded into a broad counterideology by exposure to trade unions and radical politics (especially the Communist Party).

Scott Lash (1990) provides another perspective on the determinants of worker militancy, with conclusions echoing those of Duncan Gallie. He compares the radical French with the conservative American working classes. Data collected at industrial sites in both countries show that differences in objective employment conditions cannot account for variations in militancy. Lash's alternative explanation focuses on how ideological and cultural factors shape militancy. Trade unions and political parties in a society or region are vehicles for socialization, transmitting to workers ideologies of natural rights in the workplace and in the political arena. Exposure to left-wing political parties determines societal radicalism. Socialization by trade unions, "industry's alternative rule-makers," is the most important cause of industrial radicalism (Lash 1984). Both kinds of *radicalism* aim to achieve the kinds of broader legal rights that would give power to individual workers. Militant workers do not, therefore, necessarily try to overthrow existing institutions; rather, they use them to their collective advantage.

Class and Politics in Canada

What about the Canadian situation? Gallie and Lash conclude that unions and political parties are the main vehicles for channelling general working-class discontent into collective action. Have Canadian unions, which are basically reformist in orientation, had the same role?[77] The Canadian Labour Congress helped to found the New Democratic Party in 1961, and remains closely affiliated with it. However, if all union members voted for the NDP, it should have formed the government by now. And, despite the tough economic times that many workers have endured since the early 1980s, there are few signs that widespread discontent is on the rise. When New Democratic Party governments were elected in Ontario, British Columbia, and Saskatchewan in the last decade, it was achieved with little change from previous elections in the NDP's share of the popular vote. Nor have two major recessions made the unorganized members of the working class more inclined to seek union representation. If anything, they have tended to blame their economic woes partly on unions.[78]

Despite theories suggesting that involvement in strikes may have a radicalizing effect on workers' political consciousness, our earlier discussion showed that this is seldom the case. Because strikes involve the organized and better-off members of the working class, resulting improvements in wages and working conditions may further divide the working class. Michael Smith claims that if strikes bring gains for the unionized workers involved, the more disadvantaged, unorganized workers may see this as proof of the unfairness of the system.[79] Cynicism, political alienation, and antiunion feelings may result. So, even though strikes may briefly kindle the flames of class consciousness among strikers, their overall political impact within the Canadian working class appears small.

One of the few Canadian studies to probe these theoretical issues examined the ideologies of male manual workers in an aircraft repair plant where skill levels were high, and in a home insulation factory employing low-skilled labourers. No significant differences in political attitudes or class ideologies were found between the two groups (Tanner 1984; Keddie 1980). Furthermore, among those who were committed to left- or right-wing political beliefs, these were not related to other attitudes about work and society (Tanner and Cockerill 1986). The researchers concluded that a coherent and integrated set of political views was absent among the male blue-collar workers they studied. Worker consciousness regarding class and politics tended to be fragmented and often contradictory. For example, some of the same individuals who believed that corporate profits should be more equally distributed (a left-wing position) also agreed that trade unions are too powerful (a right-wing stance). But this does not demonstrate an acceptance of the capitalist status quo or, alternatively, a rejection of socialism. Rather, it suggests that workers' limited encounters with alternative ideologies lead them to question the system only on certain issues.

Other attitude surveys reinforce this assessment of class consciousness among Canadian workers. For instance, William Johnston and Michael Ornstein (1985) examined the political ideologies of employed men and women. They found class differences in support for social welfare programs and the redistribution of income, with the working class being the more egalitarian. But, despite being slightly to the left in political ideology, members of the working class were not more active in politics. "Left-wing political organizations and trade unions," conclude Johnston and Ornstein (1985), "have evidently failed to transform class differences in attitudes to social policy into coherent and durable perceptions of class structure and the political system." Even the economic crisis of the late 1970s and early 1980s, marked by high inflation and rising unemployment, did not further polarize class ideologies (Baer, Grabb, and Johnston 1991). However, a more recent Alberta study did reveal that individuals personally affected by the recession were somewhat more likely to be critical of the distribution of wealth in society (Krahn and Harrison 1992).

The Future of Worker Militancy

Despite the absence of a strong working-class radical ideology and, moreover, a decline in strike activity in Canada, there have been several examples of worker militancy that deserve careful scrutiny. Can we expect to see an upswing in industrial conflict in the future, coupled perhaps with a leftward shift in working-class politics? Some observers believe that future working-class mobilization could be provoked by employer and government demands for greater productivity, economic concessions, and more management rights.

A graphic illustration of this is the British Columbia Solidarity Movement, which sprang up in opposition to the Social Credit government's 1983 public sector restraint program. Proposed legislation would have limited the scope of public sector bargaining, allowed the firing of employees at will, cut back on social services, ended rent controls, and abolished the B.C. Human Rights Commission. The launching of Operation Solidarity by the B.C. Federation of Labour was a delayed reaction, which followed the more militant responses by the grassroots Lower Mainland Budget Coalition.

Bryan Palmer's (1986) analysis of the B.C. Solidarity Movement raises some provocative questions. Class relations in Canada have begun to realign themselves, argues Palmer, and the 1983 events in British Columbia signal that class conflict may be on the rise. Palmer goes as far as calling the protest marches, public rallies, picket lines, and community-based resistance during the summer of 1983 "class warfare." These actions reflected mass opposition to the proposed legislation, rather than being merely the response of union leaders. In fact, the moderate leadership of Operation Solidarity rejected calls for a general strike that would have deepened the conflict. Negotiations between the government and mainstream union leaders eventually resulted in minor revisions to the legislation.

Not everyone would agree with Palmer's Marxist interpretation of the events in British Columbia. In hindsight, it may have been premature to draw conclusions about realignments in class relations on the basis of this case alone. It is interesting to speculate about other possible outcomes of this confrontation if organized labour had not become involved. What seems clear, though, is that government offensives against employee rights and social programs have the potential for provoking the labour movement into more broadly-based political action. Even though these reactions often are defensive, with unions scrambling to preserve past gains or members' jobs, public opinion can sometimes be rallied against unpopular government decisions, as in the case of the Calgary hospital laundry workers. Ontario recently has experienced a series of mass protests in five cities against the Harris government's cuts in health care, education, and a wide range of community and social services. This is an example of social movement unionism, as Ontario unions have forged a broad coalition with community-based organizations to oppose sweeping government policies that undercut the "welfare state." On a separate front, unions themselves have united to oppose Bill 136, which, if passed, would remove government workers' right to strike, scrap job security, and cut wages.[80] The political goals of both initiatives are practical and immediate: pressure the Harris government to rethink its agenda and defeat it in the next election.

In general terms, however, the environment of labour relations became more restrictive after the recession of the early 1980s. Canadian employers increasingly resorted to lockouts. Several provincial governments introduced public sector restraint legislation during this period, and the use of court injunctions and legislation to end strikes has escalated. Major private sector strikes, such as the 1997 Alberta Safeway dispute, have been accompanied by the increased use of strikebreakers. On the other hand, there have been positive breakthroughs for labour, such as Quebec's antistrikebreaking legislation. But these are exceptions, and some analysts believe that the new developments may undercut the post–World War II labour–management accord by placing severe restrictions on free collective bargaining, especially by public employees.[81]

These backward steps violate international labour conventions. In fact, the International Labour Organization (ILO) investigated two Alberta laws, one restricting the right of public servants to strike, and the other making unions liable to having up to six months' worth of union dues forfeited in the event of illegal walkouts. It also investigated Ontario's Inflation Restraint Act of 1982, which suspended public sector collective bargaining rights for two years, and a 1983 Newfoundland law banning rotating public sector strikes and preventing certain public employees from joining unions.[82] Organized labour took these cases to the Supreme Court of Canada, hoping that the new Charter of Rights and Freedoms would disallow these laws restricting workers' rights. But, in the spring of 1987, the Supreme Court ruled that the Charter neither guarantees the right to strike nor the right to bargain collectively. Clearly, this particular interpretation of the Charter's guarantee of *freedom of association* could, in time, reshape industrial relations in Canada.[83]

CONCLUSION

To return to the themes of conflict and cooperation introduced at the start of this chapter, do the stark economic realities of the 1990s require that unions and management strive for greater cooperation? This nonadversarial approach is now being actively promoted. While laudable in principle, there are (as with everything in industrial relations) two competing perspectives on what cooperation may entail. Many people, especially in business and government circles, believe that labour–management relations in Canada are too confrontational. Craig Riddell (1986b: 2) articulates the case in favour of less conflict and more cooperation:

> Labour–management cooperation is advocated not for its own sake but because it may yield tangible returns, both to those involved in labour relations and to society more generally. Increased cooperation, employee involvement in planning and decision making, and consultation, although not without some costs, can yield higher levels of job satisfaction and a more enjoyable work environment for employees. Greater employee involvement in planning and decision making may also result in improved productivity, better product quality and more competitiveness. Each of these improvements can benefit both employers and employees by producing both higher profits *and* job satisfaction and wages, as well as more employment opportunities. In addition, the need for flexibility and adaptability in our economy is more likely to be met in an open labour relations environment. Finally, reductions in labour–management conflict, expressed through strikes, lockouts, grievances, absenteeism and so on, could also occur.

Unions have a very different perspective on labour–management cooperation. In organized labour's experience, management wants workers to cooperate on its terms, and often substitutes this for tangible improvements in working conditions. Only in bad times do employers want cooperation, just as they want concessions. Cooperation is, therefore, defined by management as a way of improving competitiveness and efficiency and lowering costs, rather than as a means of balancing legitimate worker concerns with economic objectives (UAW 1985: 151–52). As one labour leader explained at a roundtable discussion of this issue:

> ... authoritarian managerial practices and unwillingness to share power are at the root of many of Canada's problems of competitiveness. When all the bunting is stripped off, a worker in Canada is still just a unit of production in the eyes of most employers, not a valued individual. Therefore, when labour is called upon these days to cooperate with employers and governments in the name of competitiveness, labour is skeptical ... We are usually the only ones in the process being asked to altruistically deny our interests and sacrifice our goals ... this route to competitiveness is inherently confrontational and thus incompatible with genuine cooperation. Yet it is the route chosen by most employers and governments who have tried to mask intent by calling it cooperation.[84]

It is not that unions dismiss the importance of productivity, competitiveness, or organizational flexibility. They simply want cooperation and consultation on these issues to be fully open and democratic. As documented elsewhere in the book (Chapters 5 and 6), there are models of a more equal partnership between labour and management, such as attempts at industrial democracy or at Shell's Sarnia chemical plant, where the union was actively involved in designing the plant and its innovative team-based work organization.[85] But this approach requires a fundamental shift away from adversarialism and toward full recognition of the rights of workers. This will require greater trust between workers and management. The end result could be significant benefits for labour, management, and society as a whole.

NOTES

1. *Edmonton Journal* (19 March 1997: A1, A16; 20 March 1997: B1; 26 March 1997: A1, A20; 10 April 1997: B1; 19 April 1997: H1, H2; 26 April 1997: H1; 12 June 1997: B7; *The Globe and Mail* (9 June 1997: B1, B4).
2. Poole (1981: Chapter 1). This classification is based on Perlman (1958). Godard (1994: Chapter 7) provides a useful discussion of the role and function of unions as institutions.
3. Bain and Clegg (1974). The systems model of industrial relations was pioneered by John

Dunlop (1971). For critical assessments, see Poole (1981: Chapter 2); Crouch (1982: Chapter 1); and Hyman (1975: Chapter 1). A modified systems approach is applied to Canada by Gunderson and Ponak (1995).

4. For a discussion of work as a power relationship between employees and employers, see T. Johnson (1980).
5. Canada (1969: 1, 19). On the same theme, also see Barbash (1979).
6. See Poole (1981: Chapter 8) for a discussion of the importance of workers' values and perceptions (which are the basis of their actions) in the study of industrial relations. Also see Hyman and Brough (1975) on value systems in industrial relations. Keenoy (1985: 15–20) elaborates the point that workers and managers have different definitions of reality.
7. See Hill (1981), especially Chapter 7 on unions.
8. Crouch (1982: 37–38). This paragraph draws on Crouch's distinction between radical and Marxist approaches to trade unionism.
9. The phrase "managers of discontent" was coined by C.W. Mills (1948). An especially interesting discussion of the mobilization and management of discontent is provided by Batstone et al. (1978: Chapter 16).
10. Michels (1959); also see Crouch (1982: 163–74); Lipset, Trow, and Coleman (1956); and Freeman (1982). On the CSU and Hal Banks, see Kaplan (1987).
11. On the social unionism of the CAW, see Gindin (1995).
12. The data in this paragraph are derived from Riddell (1986a: 5) and Coates, Arrowsmith, and Courchene (1989: 119); also see Lowe and Krahn (1989); Bowden (1989); Lipset and Meltz (1996); and Galenson (1994: Chapter 7).
13. Krahn and Lowe (1984); Lowe and Krahn (1989).
14. Swidinsky and Kupferschmidt (1991); also see Gunderson and Hyatt (1995).
15. 1994 General Social Survey, microdata file (Statistics Canada, 1995b).
16. See Freeman and Medoff (1984: Chapter 11) on the impact unions have on productivity.
17. Freeman and Medoff (1984: 19); also see Gunderson and Hyatt (1995) on how unions affect compensation, productivity, and management practices in Canada.
18. Basic sources for historical accounts of the rise of the Canadian labour movement include Heron (1989), Morton (1989), Smucker (1980: Chapters 7 and 8), and Godard (1994: Chapter 4). The Canadian labour history journal, *Labour/Le Travail*, is an excellent source, as occasionally are *Relations Industrielles/Industrial Relations* and *Studies in Political Economy*.
19. Palmer (1979); Kealey (1980); Heron (1989).
20. On labour radicalism during the early twentieth century, see Robin (1968), McCormack (1978), Bercuson (1974), and Frager (1992).
21. Two key CIO organizing drives are described in Abella (1974) and Moulton (1974).
22. Human Resources Development Canada, Workplace Information Directorate (1996: xv).
23. On Quebec labour, see Boivin and Déom (1995) and Lipsig-Mummé (1987).

24. See Craven (1980); Pentland (1979); Huxley (1979).

25. The institutionalization of conflict thesis was put forward by sociologists to explain the relative peacefulness of union–management relations in the immediate postwar period. Some U.S. academics went so far as to suggest that the decline in industrial disputes signalled a lessening of class distinctions and class conflict. See Crouch (1982: 106–9), Hill (1981: 124–27), and Ingham (1974).

26. This account is from Riddell (1986a).

27. Panitch and Swartz (1988). Also see Haiven, McBride, and Shields (1991); Reshef (1990); Russell (1990); Kettler, Struthers, and Huxley (1990); Drache (1994). Similar concerns about collective bargaining in the United States and the United Kingdom are discussed in Freeman (1995).

28. Note that the data in Figure 7.1 for 1981 and later are based on revised labour force estimates, to reflect changes to the Labour Force Survey in 1995 (see Chapter 2). This results in higher estimates of nonagricultural paid employment, and, therefore, lower levels of union density than obtained using earlier labour force data series (as in the second edition of this text). See Human Resources Development Canada, Workplace Information Directorate (1996: vii).

29. See Murray (1995: 161–62), OECD (1994: Chapter 5), and Chang and Sorrentino (1991) on measurement issues regarding union membership.

30. In 1990, collective bargaining coverage was about 4.5 percentage points higher than union density (Murray 1995: 162).

31. Human Resources Development Canada, Workplace Information Directorate (1996: xiv).

32. 1996 data in this paragraph are from Human Resources Development Canada, Workplace Information Directorate (1996).

33. This discussion is based on OECD (1994: Chapter 5), and Adams (1995).

34. For an assessment of right-to-work leglislation from a Canadian perspective, see Ponak and Taras (1995); for a critical U.S. analysis, see AFL–CIO (1995).

35. Kochan, Katz, and McKersie (1986). Also see Milton (1986), who argues that this new system of industrial relations holds few prospects for greater democracy in the workplace.

36. See Lipset (1990: Chapter 9). Also see the criticism of Lipset's thesis by Bowden (1989) and Lipset's reply (1990). For general discussions of the decline in U.S. union membership, with comparisons to the Canadian scene, see Freeman and Medoff (1984: 228–43), Chaison and Rose (1990), Kettler, Struthers, and Huxley (1990), and Reshef (1990).

37. It is important to note that the union membership data in Figures 7.3, 7.4, and 7.5 come from Statistics Canada's (1995b) 1994 General Social Survey, a national probability sample of individuals. Surveys such as these, which ask individuals whether they belong to a union, are more precise than the membership information provided by unions (and reported in Figure 7.1), whose records may not be completely accurate or up-to-date. For 1994, the GSS density rate was 32.6, compared with 35.6 based on union-provided data (from the Corporations and Labour Unions Return Act). As of January 1997, the Monthly Labour Force survey will also record union membership.

38. See, for example, Panitch and Swartz (1993); Noël and Gardiner (1990); Reshef (1990); Aikenhead (1991).

39. Data in this paragraph were obtained from Statistics Canada's (1995b) 1994 General Social Survey microdata file.

40. This paragraph draws on Kumar and Coates (1989: 25, 29–30).

41. Kumar and Coates (1989: 25); also see Kumar and Coates (1991).

42. Labour Canada's annual publication, *Directory of Labour Organizations*, contains complete data on membership according to type of union. See Gindin (1989), Roberts (1990), and Chaison and Rose (1990) on the Canadianization trend.

43. Gindin (1989: 81–82); also see Gindin (1995).

44. A history of the Energy and Chemical Workers Union and its drive for a Canadian approach is found in Roberts (1990). The Communications Workers, the Energy and Chemical Workers, and the Canadian Paperworkers Union have since merged to form the Communications, Energy, and Paperworkers Union of Canada.

45. Data on female union membership are from *Corporations and Labour Unions Return Act* (CALURA), Statistics Canada (1973: 13; 1994: 58–59). On women in unions in Canada, see Canadian Labour Congress (1997); Briskin and McDermott (1993); Creese (1995); Gannagé (1995); Clemenson (1989); Julie White (1990); and J.P. White (1990).

46. Based on a major U.S. study of employee voting in union representation elections. See Farber and Saks (1980) and Antos et al. (1980). Once members, women are no less committed to their union than are men; see Wetzel et al. (1991).

47. Kumar and Cowan (1989). The authors' statistical analysis reveals that industry and occupation of employment account for more than 80 percent of the gender differential in unionization rates, after controlling for other demographic and labour market variables.

48. Decertification refers to unionized workers voting to terminate their relationship with the union representing them. On the bank organizing drive, see Lowe (1981); Ponak and Moore (1981); and Beckett (1984). For an account of the unsuccessful 1948–1952 Eaton's organizing drive, see Sufrin (1982). The labour magazine *Our Times* covers recent organizing drives and generally is a good source of information on union issues.

49. See Gannagé (1986, 1995); Lipsig-Mummé (1987); Frager (1992).

50. Sugiman (1992: 24); also see Creese (1995).

51. Kumar and Acri (1991); Briskin and McDermott (1993).

52. Pentland (1979: 19); also see Jamieson (1971: 51–52). See Bendix (1974) on U.S. employers' anti-union tactics.

53. This account of IBM is from Keenoy (1985: 98–102).

54. See Storey (1983) on the "Dofasco Way" of employee relations.

55. Downie and Coates (1995: 177). For differing perspectives on this issue, see Rinehart, Huxley, and Robertson (1994); Pfeffer (1994); Wells (1986); Applebaum and Batt (1994); and Green and Yanarella (1995).

56. *The Globe and Mail* (23 October 1996: A1, A6).

57. *The Globe and Mail* (23 November 1995: A13; 25 November 1995: A3). See Taylor (1995) for a discussion of organized labour's response to the Klein government's deficit reduction strategy.

58. See Robinson (1994); Bélanger, Edwards, and Haiven (1994); Kumar (1995).

59. Olson (1965: 88); also see Crouch (1982: 51–67).

60. Tilly's (1979: 64) example is Lipset, Trow, and Coleman's (1956) study of union democracy, which found that printers' union locals "have both distinct, compelling identities and extensive, absorbing interpersonal networks," and incorporate much of the members' lives. Clement's studies of miners (1981) and fishery workers (1986) provide Canadian examples. See Conley (1988) for a useful theoretical treatment of working-class action. Crouch's (1982) rational-choice model of trade unionism focuses even more directly on the attitudes and beliefs of individual employees, as well as on the larger contextual constraints on their actions.

61. Julie White (1990: 147); also see Langford (1996).

62. Lacroix (1986: 172). This definition is used by the International Labour Organization.

63. Gunderson, Hyatt, and Ponak (1995: 381); Riddell (1986a: 32). In this discussion, we use the term *strike* to refer to both strikes and lockouts.

64. Gouldner (1955) is the classic study of a wildcat strike. Jamieson (1971: Chapter 7) discusses the wildcat strikes that characterized the turbulent industrial relations climate in Canada during the 1960s. Also see Fisher (1982) and Zetka (1992) on wildcat strikes.

65. United Auto Workers (1985: 153). Also see Finn (1984) and Hackett (1982) on the role of the media in shaping public perceptions of unions.

66. On the Winnipeg General Strike and its context, see Bercuson (1974), Jamieson (1971: Chapter 3), and Kealey (1984).

67. Russell (1990); for an account of the Ford strike, see Colling (1995).

68. On the impact of wage and price controls, see Reid (1982).

69. *The Globe and Mail* (4 April 1987: A3).

70. See Lacroix (1986: 172–74) for a discussion of these methodological problems.

71. Riddell (1986a: 40). Adams (1995) examines these international differences, including how industrial dispute patterns have varied within nations over time.

72. See Gunderson, Hyatt, and Ponak (1995) for a discussion of these trends. For historical perspectives on militancy and industrial conflict in mining, see Craven (1980: Chapter 8), Frank (1986), and Seager (1985).

73. Kerr and Siegel (1954: 191). For critiques, see Shorter and Tilly (1974: 287–305) and Stern (1976). Fisher (1982) finds empirical support in Canada for the Kerr and Siegel thesis.

74. See Gannagé (1995) for a discussion of effort bargaining.

75. Jerry P. White (1990: 124–25). Also see Luxton and Corman (1991) and Ferland (1989) on strike action and other forms of militancy among women.

76. For an analysis of the economic costs of strikes, see Gunderson, Hyatt, and Ponak (1995: 400–02) and Freeman and Medoff (1984: 218–20).

77. Smucker (1980: Chapter 11) examines historically the ideologies of the Canadian labour movement in the context of his broader discussion of working class consciousness.

78. Palmer (1992: Chapter 7); Baer, Grabb, and Johnston (1991).

79. Smith (1978). Also see Form's (1985) discussion of the political consequences of divisions within the American working class.

80. *The Globe and Mail* (28 October 1996: A6; 8 July 1997: A1, A7).

81. Compare Panitch and Swartz (1993) with Russell (1990).

82. *The Globe and Mail* (3 April 1985: A4).

83. On the implications of the Charter for unions, see Kumar and Coates (1991: 17–19).

84. Quoted in Kumar and Coates (1991: 42).

85. See Rankin (1990). Compare this with the position of the Canadian Auto Workers Union (CAW Canada, 1988).

THE MEANING AND EXPERIENCE OF WORK

INTRODUCTION

In previous chapters, we have presented a largely structural analysis of work in Canada. Among other topics, we discussed labour markets, the occupational structure, work organizations, labour unions, and gender and other forms of stratification. Some of this material addressed individual reactions to work—workers' problems in balancing work and family responsibilities, and resistance and conflict in the workplace, for example. But in this final chapter, we get to the very core of the individual–job relationship by examining the meaning of work in our society and workers' subjective response to their employment situation.

The chapter begins with an overview of general work values. We ask: What does "work" mean in our society today, and how do our work values differ from those in pre-industrial and early industrial societies? What can the experiences of the unemployed tell us about the meaning of work in contemporary society? Are there cultural differences in work values? Do we need a new set of values in a society where many citizens are having difficulty obtaining satisfactory employment?

We then become somewhat more specific in our analysis, asking about the types of work orientations (or preferences) held by individual Canadians. How are these work orientations shaped? Are we observing the emergence of alternative work orientations in response to industrial restructuring, high levels of unemployment, the growth in nonstandard employment relationships, and demographic shifts in Canadian society?

The last section of the chapter focuses on job satisfaction. In general, how satisfied are Canadian workers with their employment situation? Is this changing? What factors influence job satisfaction and dissatisfaction? We then continue our discussion of individual responses to work by examining the related issues of alienation and job-related stress.

This micro-level analysis of individuals' responses to their work situation complements our more macro analysis in the previous chapters. It encourages us to ask two basic types of questions. First, how does the structure of work influence individuals' experiences of work? Second, and related to the first question, what can individuals do to improve their work situation? More broadly, the manner in which societal work values influence workplace structure, employer–employee relationships, and individual responses to work is of interest. Equally important, though, is the question about how unequal power relationships in society might influence work values and workers' behaviours. Thus, this chapter brings together many of the book's themes by focusing on the core distinction in sociology between *individual agency* and *social structure.*

DEFINING WORK VALUES, WORK ORIENTATIONS, AND JOB SATISFACTION

Values, as sociologists use the term, are "standards used by members of a society to judge behaviour and to choose among various possible goals" (Spencer 1985: 16). We could talk about how personal attributes such as honesty and industriousness are valued in our society, about how we value the freedom of speech, or about the value placed on getting a good education. And we might ask how work is valued, or, in other words, what the meaning of work is in a particular society.

Having identified work values as societal standards, we can define *work orientations* more narrowly as the meaning attached to work by particular individuals within a society. Blackburn and Mann (1979: 141) define an orientation as "a central organizing principle which underlies people's attempts to make sense of their lives." Thus, studying work orientations involves determining what people consider important in their lives. Does someone continue to work primarily for material reasons (a desire to become wealthy or because of economic necessity), because income from the job allows him or her to enjoy life away from work, or to get enjoyment and personal fulfillment from work? Even more specifically, what types of work and work arrangements do individuals prefer?

The distinction between work values and work orientations is not always that clear, since it hinges on the extent to which the latter are broadly shared within a society. As we will argue below, several different sets of work values can co-exist within a society, influencing the work orientations of individuals within that society. In fact, as our earlier discussion of managerial ideologies and practices showed, particular work values have often been promoted by employers to gain the cooperation of their workers. On this point, R.M. Blackburn writes:

> Ideologies of work ... provide forms of understanding and evaluation which help to sustain and reproduce the existing socio-economic structure, a structure in which there are great inequalities in the rewards derived from work.[1]

An individual's work orientations are also shaped by specific experiences on the job. Indeed, a worker whose job is dissatisfying may begin to challenge dominant work values. Thus, over the long term, shifting work orientations on the part of many workers might also influence societal work values. *Job satisfaction* (or dissatisfaction), then, is the most individualized and subjective response of an individual to the extrinsic and intrinsic rewards offered by her or his job.

WORK VALUES ACROSS TIME AND SPACE

Historical Changes in the Meaning of Work

The meaning attached to work has changed dramatically over the centuries.[2] The ancient Greeks and Romans viewed most forms of work negatively, considering it brutalizing and uncivilized. In fact, the Greek word for "work," *ponos*, comes from the Latin root word for "sorrow." According to Greek mythology, the gods had cursed the human race by giving them the need to work. Given these dominant work values, the ruling classes turned their attention to politics, warfare, the arts, and philosophy, leaving the physical work to slaves.

Early Hebrew religious values placed a different but no more positive emphasis on work. Hard work was seen as divine punishment for the "original sin" of the first humans who ate from the "tree of the knowledge of good and evil." According to the Old Testament, God banished Eve and Adam from the Garden of Eden, where all of creation was at their easy disposal, to a life of hard labour, telling them that "In the sweat of thy face shalt thou eat bread till thou return unto the ground."[3] This perspective on work remained part of the early Christian world view for many centuries.

A more positive view of work was promoted by Saint Thomas Aquinas in the thirteenth century. In ranking occupations according to their value to society, Aquinas rejected the notion that all work is a curse or a necessary evil. Instead, he argued that some forms of work were better than others. Priests were assigned the highest ranks, followed by those working in agriculture, and then craft workers. Because they produced food or products useful to society, these groups were ranked higher than merchants and shopkeepers. A comparison of this scheme to contemporary occupational status scales (see Chapter 3) reveals some interesting reversals. The status of those involved in commercial activity—bankers, corporate owners, and managers, for example—has increased, while farmers and craft workers have experienced substantial declines in occupational status.

During the sixteenth-century Protestant Reformation in Europe, Martin Luther's ideas marked a significant change in dominant work values. He argued that work was a central component of human life. Although he still viewed work for profit negatively, Luther went beyond the belief that hard work was an atonement for original sin. When he wrote, "There is just one best way to serve God—to do most perfectly the work of one's profession" (Burstein et al. 1975: 10), he was articulating the idea of a "calling," that is, industriousness and hard work within one's station in life, however lowly that might be, was how one must fulfil God's will. Whether or not rural peasants or the urban working class actually shared these values is difficult to determine. However, to the extent that the ruling classes could convince their subordinates that hard work was a moral obligation, power and privilege could be more easily maintained.

The Protestant Work Ethic

The Industrial Revolution transformed the social and economic landscape of Europe and also generated a new set of work values. In his famous book, *The Protestant Ethic and the Spirit of Capitalism*, Max Weber emphasized how the Calvinists, a Protestant group that had broken away from the mainstream churches, embraced hard work, rejected worldly pleasures, and extolled the virtues of frugality.[4] Weber was not attempting to prove that Calvinist beliefs were the cause of capitalism. Instead, he argued that religious doctrines that encouraged individuals to make and reinvest profits gave rise to work values conducive to the growth of capitalism.

Since then, other scholars have questioned whether these early Protestant entrepreneurs really acted solely on religious beliefs, and whether other groups not sharing these beliefs might have been equally successful.[5] Nonetheless, Weber did draw our attention to the role of work values in capitalist societies. He also recognized that such an *ideology of work*, while justifying the profit-seeking behaviour of capitalists, might also help control their employees. As one contemporary observer wryly notes:

> The engagement of God as the supreme supervisor was a most convenient device; a great part of the efforts of modern management has been aimed at finding a secular but equally omnipotent equivalent in the worker's own psyche. (Anthony 1977: 43)

Freedom and equality are additional secular values that fit into the belief system of capitalist democracies. A central assumption is that workers are participants in a labour market where they can freely choose their job. It must follow that some people are wealthier and more powerful than others because of hard work and prior investments in education. Hence, within this ideology of work, equality does not refer to the distribution of wealth and power, but to access to the same opportunities for upward mobility in a competitive labour market. But, as demonstrated in our discussion of labour market processes (Chapter 3), some workers are advantaged by birth, and some occupational groups are more protected in the labour market. Consequently, for many workers, the daily realities of the labour market often contradict the dominant set of work values.

Work as Self-Fulfillment: The Humanist Tradition

The importance of hard work and wealth accumulation are only one perspective on work in a capitalist society. The belief that work is virtuous in itself gave rise to another set of values in the seventeenth and eighteenth centuries.[6] The *humanist tradition* grew out of Renaissance philosophies that distinguished humans from other species on the basis of our ability to consciously direct our labour. A view of human beings as creators easily led to the belief that work was a fulfilling and liberating activity, and that it constituted the very essence of humanity. From this perspective, work was the means through which humans could fulfil their potential.

Karl Marx fashioned these ideas into a radical critique of capitalism and a formula for social revolution. He agreed that the essence of humanity was expressed through work, but argued that this potential was stifled by capitalist relations of production. Because they had little control over their labour and its products, workers were engaged in alienating work. For Marx, capitalist economic relations limited human independence and creativity. Only when capitalism was replaced by socialism, he argued, would work be truly liberating.

Marx's theory of alienation has had a major impact on the sociology of work, as we discuss below. Interestingly, a similar set of beliefs about the centrality of work to an individual's sense of personal well-being underlies a number of contemporary management approaches, which are decidedly non-Marxist in their assumptions (see Chapter 5). It is often argued, for example, that workers would be more satisfied if they were allowed to use more of their skills and abilities in their job. But these management perspectives do not see capitalism as the problem. Rather, they advocate better organizational systems and job designs within capitalism.

Humanistic beliefs about the essential importance of work have also been espoused by some contemporary theologians who address economic issues from a "social justice" perspective. For example, in response to rising levels of unemployment in Canada, a group of Catholic bishops recently prepared a discussion paper on "the crisis of work." In their call for greater government involvement in the economy and more corporate responsibility for job creation, they argued that:

> It is through the human activity of work, that people are able to develop their sense of self-identity and self-worth, acquire an adequate income for their personal and family needs, and to participate in the building-up of one's community and society.[7]

Experiencing Unemployment: Identifying the Meaning of Work in Its Absence

Many studies tell us that unemployment is extremely traumatic for jobless individuals and their families.[8] But the Catholic Bishops suggest that the unemployed are disadvantaged in ways that go beyond lost income, a lower standard of living, personal and family stress, and health problems. They take the humanist position that work gives meaning in our lives. Thus, by examining the experience of unemployment, the gaps left by the loss of a paid job, we can gain further insights about the personal and social functions of work.

Based on her research among the unemployed during the Depression of the 1930s, Marie Jahoda identified some of the *latent functions* of work, which, if absent because of unemployment, can be very distressing.[9] While the *manifest function* of work is, primarily, maintaining or improving one's standard of living, the latent (less obvious) functions contribute to an individual's personal well-being. Thus, work can provide experiences of creativity and mastery, and foster a sense of purpose. It can be self-fulfilling, although, clearly, some jobs offer much less fulfillment than others. When hit by unemployment, an individual loses these personal rewards, as illustrated by the following comments by a female nutritionist about her 14 months of unemployment:

> I feel like I'm wasting time. I feel like I'm not accomplishing anything. I don't really feel like I'm contributing to the marriage, to society, or anything like that.[10]

Work also provides regularly shared experiences and often enjoyable interactions with co-workers. When the job is gone, so are such personally satisfying routines. The unemployed individual quickly comes to miss these social rewards, and may also find that relationships away from work are no longer the same. Such feelings are expressed in the following way by an unemployed teacher:

> The whole feeling that I had … [was] that nobody really understood where I was, what I was going through, what I cared about, what was important to me. Because I was no longer talking about my job as a teacher, in fact I wasn't talking about my job as anything. I had a strong sense of not fitting in.

In addition, work structures time. Individuals who have lost their job frequently find that their days seem not only empty, but disorienting. A divorced mother of a four-year-old, living with her own mother to make ends meet, explains:

> If you went to work, at least you're coming home in the evening. When I'm home all day … I get confused. My whole metabolism's gone crazy, because it's, like, I'm coming back from … where I have been. Or I've gone and I'm still waiting to come home.

Being unemployed often requires that one seek financial assistance, sometimes from family members, but more often through government agencies. Dealing with the bureaucracy can be frustrating. Even more problematic, receiving social assistance carries a great deal of *stigma*. As a former factory worker, the mother of two small children explains:

> When I went down there, I felt that I just stuck right out. I thought, "Oh, my God, people think I'm on welfare … You used to think "It's those people who are on welfare," and now you discover you're one of those people.

The same value system that rewards individuals for their personal success also leads them to blame themselves for their own problems. A common research finding is that the unemployed internalize their problems and blame themselves for their lack of success. As a male computer operator, who had been jobless for two months, said: "Right now I would consider being unemployed as my problem. If I am unemployed a year from now, that is my fault."

These glimpses into the lives of unemployed Canadians reflect the value placed on work in our society as a potential source of self-fulfillment and social integration. At the same time, a set of more materialistic work values are highlighted through the stigma and self-blame that can result from joblessness, seen by some unemployed as a mark of their own labour market failure. Thus, while career success and wealth accumulation are at the core of one of the value-systems in capitalist society, the humanist perspective on work as a source of self-identity and personal satisfaction reflects an equally important alternative set of work values.

Cultural Variations in Work Values

Max Weber argued that the Protestant work ethic provided a set of work values that were conducive to the emergence of a new capitalist mode of production. Today, when we compare the economic performance of different countries in the global economy, we might be tempted to make a similar "cultural differences" argument. Do Japan and the Southeast Asian tiger economies owe some of their success to a different set of work values in these societies?

As Japan's economy outperformed the rest of the world in the 1980s, a common explanation was that Japanese workers simply had a much stronger work ethic. They willingly worked long hours, often went without holidays, and were more strongly committed to their employers than were "Western" workers.[11] Typically, explanations of this behaviour focused on cultural differences, suggesting that the Japanese have always exhibited strong patterns of conformity and social integration. In modern times, the corporation has assumed the once-central roles of the family and the community in the lives of Japanese workers. Hence, Japanese workers exhibit great loyalty to their employers and work extremely hard. From the vantage point of North America, the presumably stronger work ethic of Japanese employees appeared to be a key ingredient in the Japanese "economic miracle."

As the economies of Singapore, South Korea, Taiwan, and Hong Kong expanded rapidly, similar cultural explanations about different underlying work values have been proposed for their success. Like descriptions of the presumably more-motivated Japanese workers, this "Confucian work ethic" argument attributed the economic success of these economies to traditional habits of hard work, greater willingness to work toward a common social goal, and employees' ready compliance with authority.[12] Without such willing and motivated workers, it was reasoned, these economies could not have grown as quickly as they did.

Undoubtedly, there are crossnational differences in the way people respond to work in general, to new technologies, and to their employers' demands for compliance and/or new employment relationships. North American workers, for example, may be somewhat less accepting of Japanese-style management approaches that expect workers to show unwavering loyalty to company goals. Workers in Asian countries may think of their work organization in less individualistic and more family-like terms.[13] That said, it is overstating such differences to argue that a Confucian work ethic explains the rapid growth of the East Asian economies. If it does, why did the rapid growth not begin earlier? Why are there significant differences among the four "tigers" in the way firms are organized (see Chapter 1), in the extent to which democratic rights of workers are respected, and in the role of the state in economic development?[14]

Conceding that there are cultural differences in work values, we would argue that they are not central to explanations of national differences in economic development in today's global economy. Far more crucial are the production decisions of firms regarding technology, employment practices, and research and development, and the extent to which governments actively participate in economic development strategies.[15] In fact, research suggests that the cause-and-effect relationship may frequently operate in the opposite direction—work values and, in turn, employee behaviour can be influenced by employment practices and labour market institutions.[16]

The Japanese labour market is highly segmented, even more so than in Canada. Only a minority of Japanese workers are employed in the huge, profitable, high-technology corporations so admired by Western observers. Most people work in the smaller businesses that subcontract to make parts or provide services for the giant firms (Rose 1985: 37). The major advantages of this arrangement for the large corporations include the flexibility of being able to expand and contract their labour force without hiring permanent employees, and the reduction in inventory costs through the just-in-time delivery of components from the subcontracting businesses.

Along with higher wages, major Japanese firms have frequently offered their employees lifetime employment guarantees, a variety of fringe benefits, and opportunities for skill development and upward advancement within the corporation. Thus, while loyalty and commitment to the firm may be part of Japanese corporate culture, internal labour markets (see Chapter 3) play a major role in maintaining the stability of the system (Hill 1988: 246–47). In fact, some critics have argued that company loyalty is built on fears of job loss, and that the economic benefits provided to workers in major firms simply make it easier for their employers to demand compliance and hard work.[17] By contrast, in small firms and family businesses, low pay, few benefits, and little job security mean workers have to work long hours to make a living. Thus, for both core- and periphery-sector Japanese employees, the willingness to work long and hard may have much more to do with organizational and economic factors than is often recognized.

Evidence supportive of this "internal labour market" explanation comes from a large comparative study that found Japanese workers more likely than U.S. workers to be employed in firms where benefits were extensive, where some employee participation in decision making was encouraged, and where mobility opportunities and job security were provided. However, given a similar organizational context, there were few differences in commitment to one's firm between the two countries. So for workers employed in core-sector Japanese firms, economic and organizational factors have a significant influence on workplace behaviours and work values, just as they do in North America (Lincoln and Kalleberg 1985; 1990).

Yet global economic pressures are forcing even the largest Japanese corporations to alter their employment practices. High wages for all company employees are no longer the norm, and subcontracting of production tasks to periphery firms has increased. New technologies have made more workers redundant and, perhaps most importantly, traditional patterns of lifelong employment have begun to disappear. As the Japanese labour force rapidly ages, it is frequently the older employees, with the most years of service, who are now finding themselves without employment security (Kumazawa and Yamada 1989: 10; Whittaker 1990). This suggests a convergence in Japanese and North American management approaches and, perhaps, work ethics.

A Need for New (Nonpaid) Work Values?

Unemployment levels have risen in most of the Western industrialized economies since 1980. This shortage of jobs is a structural problem that is not about to quickly disappear. Nonstandard employment has increased significantly, placing more workers in jobs with limited hours and low pay. At the same time, other workers face a longer and more stressful work week. Thus, social inequality has increased as a result of labour market polarization, and work-related anxieties have become widespread.

Given this industrial restructuring, new employment relationships, and growing work-related anxiety, perhaps what is needed is a change in dominant work values. If more citizens came to recognize that there is a world outside the workplace, and began to value the benefits of nonpaid work and the pleasures of leisure activities, perhaps we would get back on track to a better society. This is not a new idea. Two decades ago in his provocative book, *Farewell to the Working Class*, Andre Gorz (1982) argued that we need to recognize that higher levels of unemployment also mean more free time for individuals to participate in nonpaid work and leisure activities. Recognizing that people still need to work to make a living, he suggested that new technologies have reduced the time it takes to produce what is needed for a decent standard of living. Consequently, Gorz called for a new set of values that replaced hard work, labour market competition, and consumption of material goods with more emphasis on the personal fulfillment that comes from nonpaid work activities and leisure pursuits.

Similar ideas have been promoted in a number of recent books about the future of work in Western societies. Jamie Swift concludes his description of growing labour market inequality in Canada by noting that, along with many more poorer workers, we have another more advantaged group of workers, overworked and stressed from the long hours they put into their jobs. He reflects on "the lunacy of lives driven by the compulsions of work, speed, and consumption," and calls for more attention to "the good life" rather then "the goods life."[18] Like Gorz, Swift recommends a new set of work values that emphasize working less, consuming less, and seeking self-fulfillment not only in paid work but also in healthy leisure pursuits and in (nonpaid) caring for others around us. We need, he writes, a "radical rethinking of how we spend our time and what we find rewarding" (Swift 1995: 240).

Jeremy Rifkin develops similar ideas, arguing that the industrial transformations occurring today will be more traumatic for workers than were previous industrial revolutions. While manufacturing jobs replaced agricultural jobs and, in turn, service jobs replaced manufacturing jobs, new technologies and global production patterns essentially mean the "end of work" as we know it for many people (Rifkin 1995). Like Gorz and Swift, Rifkin advocates redefining work values, proposing that we need to involve more people in the voluntary sector of the economy. By doing so, individuals without paid employment would find personal fulfillment in caring for others, improving the environment and making a contribution to society in other ways.

Clearly, labour market polarization and growing social inequality are social problems that need to be addressed. Emphasizing the value of nonpaid work and reducing inequities in access to paid work are all part of a solution. So too are stressing the importance of caring for others and the environment, and emphasizing that there is more to a good life than earning high incomes and acquiring and consuming material goods. But writers like Gorz, Swift, and Rifkin fail to tell us how such a transformation of social values can be achieved. Nor do they explain how high levels of inequality between those with paid jobs and those without will be avoided.[19] In a society where women have traditionally been expected to do most of the "caring work" (see Chapter 4), would nonpaid voluntary work continue to be seen as "women's work"? There is also an intergenerational equity concern: since older workers are often more economically secure, is it fair to encourage young Canadians to change their values and reduce their career aspirations, arguing that they are the ones who will face the "end of work"?

While it is important to rethink dominant work values, an overemphasis on changing work values as *the* solution to labour market polarization can also divert our attention from the sources of growing inequality. The "new ruthless economy" (Head 1996) is not simply the product of natural market forces. Real people in positions of power make decisions to change technologies, to move factories, and to push workers to accept less income and fewer hours of work. Consequently, there is room for individuals, unions, and the government to either resist some of these trends or to reshape them (Noble 1995). In fact, we would argue that the work values of employers need to be reshaped as well, with commitments to profits at all costs being balanced with greater responsibility to employees and the larger community.

Since many well-paid workers put in long hours while others have trouble making a living on part-time jobs, work redistribution must be part of the solution.[20] Alternative forms of work organizations such as worker-owned cooperatives can help reduce labour market inequalities and, in some settings, can also contribute to improvements in community life.[21] A greater emphasis on industrial democracy in its various forms (see Chapter 6) might reduce labour market polarization. And, as we have argued, there is still an important role to be played by government through labour legislation, income support, and retraining programs and industrial strategies that encourage job creation.

Critics might dismiss such efforts to reduce labour market inequalities as out of step with today's political and economic reality. In fact, evidence suggests that they are in line with the dominant social values of Canadians. A recent study concluded that concerns about people being self-reliant rather than relying on government, and about the government being fiscally responsible, were prominent among Canadians. But equally central to the core *social values* of Canadians were compassion and a feeling of collective responsibility for others, a concern about opportunities for future generations, and a belief that government had a role to play in reducing inequalities.[22] For example, in 1987, about 50 percent of Canadians agreed that government has a responsibility to see that everyone has a job and a decent standard of living. By 1993, the proportion agreeing had risen to 60 percent.

WORK ORIENTATIONS

Having discussed how societal work values have changed over time, might vary across cultures, and need to be re-examined in light of today's economic realities, we now shift our analysis to individuals' job expectations—the type of work orientations they bring to their jobs. Are most Canadians motivated by a desire to be successful and become wealthy? Do they merely work to earn money in order to purchase satisfaction elsewhere, or is their work a source of personal fulfillment? Do women and men have similar orientations to work? Are specific groups of labour force participants beginning to exhibit different types of work orientations, and if so, why?

Instrumental Work Orientations

Several decades ago, David Lockwood commented on some of the differences he observed in male British working-class "images of society." Lockwood was interested in the issue of *working-class consciousness*, how British workers perceived social inequality. He identified three distinct world views originating in different community and workplace experiences. *Proletarian workers*, argued Lockwood, saw the world in much the way Marx had predicted: they perceived themselves to be in an "us against them" conflict with their employers. Lockwood (1966) concluded that this image of society was more pronounced in industries such as shipbuilding and mining where large differences between management and workers in terms of income, power, and opportunities for upward mobility had produced heightened class consciousness.

Deferential workers also recognized class differences, but accepted the status quo, believing that wealth and power inequities were justified. Provided they were treated decently, deferential workers were unlikely to engage in militant actions against employers. Lockwood located this world view in the traditional service industries and in family firms where paternalistic employment relationships foster acceptance of the existing stratification.

Both of these traditional orientations to work, Lockwood argued, were found primarily in declining industries. The third type, *instrumental work orientations*, were more typical of the attitudes of the contemporary (1960s) working class, whose members Lockwood labeled *privatized workers*. This group tended to see society separated into many levels on the basis of income and possessions. Rather than expressing antagonism or attachment to their employers, the dominant feeling of these workers was one of indifference. Similarly, they were unlikely to develop strong ties with other workers and to participate in union activities. According to Lockwood, the "cash nexus" (the pay received), and not feelings of antagonism or deference, constituted the employment relationship for such workers. Work was simply a means of obtaining a better standard of living, an "instrument" used to achieve other nonwork goals.

Lockwood and his colleagues went on to conduct a major study of the work orientations, political attitudes, and work and community behaviours of a group of male auto workers in Luton, a manufacturing town north of London, England (Goldthorpe et al. 1969). These "affluent workers" had chosen to move to this new industrial town because the jobs available would provide them with the money and security needed to enjoy a middle-class standard of living. The fact that work in the Vauxhall automobile factory was not intrinsically rewarding did not seem to matter. Indeed, the researchers argued that the workers' choice of community reflected their preferences for extrinsic work rewards and the value they placed on making money and achieving a middle-class lifestyle (MacKinnon 1981).

Critics argue that contemporary workers appear to be instrumental only in comparison with an idealized proletarian worker of the past, and that the conclusions drawn from this study were overgeneralizations (Bulmer 1975; MacKinnon 1981: 259). Based on their study of the male labour market in another British city, Robert M. Blackburn and Michael Mann found that most workers reported a variety of work orientations. In addition, there was often little congruence between an individual's expressed work preferences and the characteristics of his job. Blackburn and Mann (1979: 155) explained this finding by arguing that the major flaw with an *orientations model* of labour market processes is that many people have few job choices, taking whatever work they can get, even if it is not what they would prefer. A further criticism of these studies, of course, is that they studied only men but assumed that the findings applied to all workers.

Even so, we should not be surprised if some workers do have instrumental work orientations, given the strong emphasis on material success in our society, and current fears about job security. By way of example, in 1996, 35 percent of a national sample of employed Canadians agreed that "[m]y current job is a way to make money—it's not a career." In another study conducted several years earlier, almost 2,500 private sector and crown corporation employees across the country were asked to rank the relative personal importance of a number of job rewards. This 1991 survey showed that about one in four workers (23 percent) ranked pay higher than any other work reward.[23]

Individuals' work preferences can also be modified in the workplace. If a job offers few intrinsic rewards or little opportunity to develop a career, workers may adjust their values and priorities accordingly. This would explain why studies have shown instrumental work orientations to be more common among workers in monotonous, assembly-line jobs (MacKinnon 1981; Rinehart 1978). Richard Sennett and Jonathan Cobb examined this theme in their book, *The Hidden Injuries of Class*. Their discussions with American blue-collar workers revealed a tendency to downplay intrinsic work rewards while emphasizing pay and job security. Workers interviewed by Sennett and Cobb also redefined the meaning of personal success, frequently talking about how hard they were working in order to provide their children with the chance to go to college.[24]

But most employed Canadians do not appear to be motivated primarily by instrumental work orientations. Instead, research shows that a majority state preferences for work that is interesting, that allows them to be creative, and to use and develop their skills (Burstein et al. 1975: 31). In fact, few people are motivated by a single reason for working. Instead, they are likely to express commitment to a number of interrelated work orientations, even though one type of preference might be stronger.[25]

Indeed, there is a diversity of work preferences. We probably all know people who work extremely hard, driven by the goal of success. In fact, some individuals become almost pathological in their work habits, devoting so much time and energy to their job that the label *workaholic* becomes appropriate.[26] Other individuals may have a strong preference for physical or outside work, for computer work, or work involving machines. Some people are strongly motivated by a desire to help others.

GENDER AND WORK ORIENTATIONS

A quick glance at the studies we have reviewed indicates that most focused only on men. When the work orientations of women were mentioned, it was often assumed that their interests were directed primarily toward the home, and less toward paid employment (Grint 1991: 29–30). The argument that *gender role socialization* might encourage women to place less value on intrinsic and extrinsic job rewards, and more on social relationships in the family, the community, and on the job seemed plausible in the 1960s and early 1970s when many of these studies were completed. In fact, a national survey in 1973 revealed that Canadian women were somewhat more likely than men to value social relationships in their workplace, a finding replicated in several other studies in that era.[27]

There is another more compelling structural explanation of gender differences in work orientations. Women and men work in very different labour market locations, and women typically receive fewer job rewards. Hence, the somewhat different work orientations and preferences of women and men might also be adaptations to the type of work they typically perform. Using the same logic we employed to explain why unskilled blue-collar workers might have more instrumental work orientations—their low-level jobs discourage other types of work preferences—we could also argue that female work orientations, to the extent that they differ from those of men, are a function of workplace differences.[28]

In addition, the domestic and child-care responsibilities that many women continue to carry force some of them to readjust their work and career goals. As a part-time nurse explains:

> My career is important to me. I don't want to give that up. But my main concern is the children ... So I give about 100 percent to the children and maintain a career at the same time. (Duffy and Pupo 1992: 116)

But once again, this example points to structural determinants—the gendered household division of labour—rather than to female personality characteristics.

An American study from the mid-1980s compared the work values of women and men in managerial and professional jobs, as well as in lower-status clerical, service, and blue-collar positions. In the upper-level positions, men and women reported very similar work orientations. In the less rewarding jobs, women were more likely than men to state that good social relationships in the workplace were important to them (men at this occupational level placed more emphasis on extrinsic work rewards). If gender role socialization was the major determinant of differing work orientations, we would expect women in both the primary and secondary labour markets to exhibit similar work orientations. These results suggest that at least some of the gender differences in work preferences found in lower-level occupations may represent an accommodation on the part of women to less rewarding work situations (Mottaz 1986: 372).

CHANGING ORIENTATIONS TO WORK

In the 1960s, during a period of economic expansion and rising standards of living in the industrialized capitalist economies, the Affluent Worker research team concluded that a new set of work orientations—the instrumental sentiments of privatized workers—were emerging. Today, we are observing substantial industrial restructuring, along with a shift in the nature of employment relationships. The characteristics of the labour force are changing as well (see Chapter 2). It is not surprising, then, to find observers of these changes concluding that work orientations may also be in flux (Braus 1992). While the comparable over-time data needed to fully substantiate claims of changing work orientations are seldom available, it would still be useful to examine some of these arguments.

Work or Leisure as a Central Life Interest?

Do most Canadians continue to see their jobs as central to their lives, or are we beginning to see a greater emphasis on leisure and satisfactions deriving from nonwork activities? The analysts of an *Environics* survey conducted in the late 1980s concluded that the latter was the case, quoting a young male Winnipeg technologist: "I like toys, and to pay for those toys I have to work. But if I could have four days of work and three days of leisure, I'd take it." The pollsters concluded that there is "a growing insistence on personal pleasure" (Maynard 1987: 114). At about the same time, in a book about "motivating and leading the new generation," Michael Maccoby (1988: 20) wrote that:

> Motivated to succeed in family life as well as in a career, and to balance work with play, they [the new generation] continually question how much of themselves to invest in the workplace. They want to know why they are working, as opposed to expressing themselves outside of the job.

This argument suggests that the types of (nonpaid) work values desired by Andre Gorz, Jamie Swift, and Jeremy Rifkin have already taken root in our society. It is interesting, however, to see such value systems being promoted as "new," given that industrial sociologists have been debating questions about work as a central life interest for many decades.[29] Thus, broad generalizations about the more diverse personal goals of today's workers may be based on an oversimplified one-dimensional view of the life interests of previous generations.

Nevertheless, American public opinion surveys indicate that, during the 1980s, the proportion of U.S. workers who said that their leisure time was more important than their work time increased until, by 1989, the leisure advocates were in the majority (Waldrop 1992). However, a more recent

Ontario study introduced an important qualification. Three-quarters of the over 1,500 employed subjects in the study stated that they would be interested in reduced time spent at work if they could maintain their income levels. The authors interpret this finding as indicating an increase in instrumental work orientations (Reid and Mannell 1994: 262). However, it might simply indicate a realistic assessment of the precarious employment climate in Canada today, and a sense of anxiety over possible permanent income loss if one decided to cut back on time spent at work.

In fact, the better-paid workers in the Ontario study were more likely to predict that their work time would decrease in the future. Similarly, a 1994 national survey revealed that more affluent Canadians were much more likely to be planning to retire before age 65. Specifically, 59 percent of those with annual household incomes greater than $60,000 were planning an early retirement, compared to only 34 percent of those with incomes below $20,000.[30] Thus, individuals employed in the secondary labour market, where pay is lower and pensions are less common, may not have the luxury of thinking about leisure pursuits as alternatives to paid work.

The baby boom generation may also have helped to create the appearance of growing leisure interests among North American workers. As this very large cohort moves through middle age, many of its members are reaching their career peak in terms of both promotions and earning potential.[31] These employees may be finding that other personal and community interests are now as compelling as their jobs. The same aging process no doubt affected the life interests of previous generations of workers. But because the baby boom is such a large cohort, their mid-life responses would dominate public opinion surveys conducted today. Rather than societal values shifting, perhaps a larger proportion of today's workers are at that point in their life course when nonwork interests begin to compete with work interests.[32]

The Work Orientations of Youth

Socrates is reputed to have said that "[c]hildren today are tyrants. They contradict their parents, gobble their food and terrorize their teachers." If he had lived today, he might also have added that "they don't want to work hard" since such concerns about deficient work orientations have frequently been part of the public stereotype of youth. In the 1960s and 1970s, for example, the counterculture activities of some North American youth led to fears that the work ethic of this new generation was declining. Most members of that cohort are now settled into their careers, thus demonstrating that these fears were largely unfounded. It seems that each generation, when observing the generation following, sees lifestyle experimentation, forgets its own similar experiences, and concludes that values are slipping.

What are the concerns about the work orientations of today's youth? At first glance, debates about the possibly inadequate *employability skills* of young Canadians seem to have little to do with the subject of work orientations. The Conference Board of Canada, an organization representing large public and private sector employers, published an *Employability Skills Profile (ESP)* in 1993. In this pamphlet, the Conference Board (1993) listed a set of "critical skills required for the Canadian workplace" as identified by employers. Included in the list are *academic skills* (communication, thinking, ability to learn), *personal management skills* (positive attitudes and behaviours, responsibility, adaptability), and *teamwork skills* (the ability to work with others). The ESP has been influential, focusing debate on the types of skills that schools should be developing in students in order to prepare them for employment in the rapidly changing labour market. It has also shaped public criticisms of the educational system. A 1995 Angus Reid poll, for example, revealed that two-thirds of Canadian adults believed that high school graduates were inadequately prepared for employment.[33]

Clearly, all of the skills identified in the ESP are important, not only for young workers, but for all labour force participants, even though not all of these skills would be equally necessary in all jobs. However, more careful scrutiny of the public education system suggests that, with respect to teaching academic skills, Canadian schools are performing quite well.[34] Furthermore, research indicates that when hiring young people for entry-level positions, many employers focus mainly on motivation, perceived work ethic, and the personality of the applicant—in other words, on work orientations rather than on skills.[35] Young job seekers are told that "proper attitude earns a job."[36]

Are today's youth less willing to "work hard" and to make a commitment to an employer? Unfortunately, there is little reliable data documenting shifts in the "soft" employability skills of youth. But a majority of high school students work part-time at some point while completing school, suggesting that there is a strong desire to work, even if only for the money. Continued high rates of participation in post-secondary education indicate that youth are willing to work hard to obtain the credentials needed for better jobs. Surveys of youth continue to show high levels of general work commitment. For example, our 1996 survey of almost 2,700 Alberta twelfth-grade students showed only 6 percent agreeing that "I'd rather collect welfare than work at a job I don't like." Seven out of ten stated that they would be willing to move out of the province to take a job (Lowe et al. 1997: 50, 53). Such facts leave us skeptical about the supposed "work attitude" problem of today's youth.

The employment difficulties faced by Canadian youth are real, as we have demonstrated in Chapters 2 and 3. Continuing high levels of structural unemployment, corporate and public sector downsizing, and an increase in nonstandard jobs have made it much more difficult for young people to cash in their educational investments for good jobs. It may also have led to a prolonged entry into adult roles, such as marriage and parenthood (Côté and Allahar 1994: 52). Recognizing these trends, in 1993, Douglas Coupland wrote a fictional account of the experiences of today's youth moving between jobs and relationships. *Generation X: Tales for an Accelerated Culture* was a best-seller. Its portrayal of the post–baby boom generation as cynical and alienated, with largely instrumental work orientations, became part of popular culture. Journalists picked up the theme, and headlines such as "job vacuum sucks graduates' hopes" were used to introduce anecdotal accounts of the sagging career aspirations and work orientations of today's youth.[37]

The Generation X view of changing work orientations differs from public concerns about employability skills. It focuses on somewhat older, more educated youth rather than on recent high school graduates, and diagnoses "the problem" more specifically, pointing to a devaluing of careers and intrinsic work rewards, rather than simply a reluctance to work hard. It points to structural changes in the labour market—a lack of satisfactory employment opportunities—as the source of the problem, rather than at schools and their presumed failure to socialize appropriate work attitudes in youth.

Is there evidence of the emergence of Generation X work orientations? The answer appears to be no. A majority of young Canadians continue to invest in higher education, despite rising tuition fees, hoping to get good jobs. Many continue to pursue additional work-related training after obtaining formal qualifications (Lowe and Krahn 1995). Surveys of youth fail to reveal a decline in commitment to work or a reduced interest in intrinsic work rewards. For example, in 1985 we surveyed graduates of the five largest faculties at the University of Alberta, asking them about their work goals and career ambitions. In 1996, we repeated the study, asking identical questions of graduates from the same faculties. In response to a question about "how important would the following be to you when looking for a full-time job after leaving school?" 92 percent of the class of 1985 agreed that "work that is interesting" would be important to them, compared to 96 percent of the class of 1996. Similarly, over 90 percent of both cohorts agreed that "work that gives a feeling of accomplishment" would be important to them. For both questions, the proportion who answered "very important" increased over time. Other findings from these studies lead to the same conclusion: young Canadians continue to aspire to good jobs and satisfying careers.[38]

The 1996 survey also showed 74 percent of the university graduates agreeing that "it will be harder for people in my generation to live as comfortably as previous generations," a sentiment echoed by 65 percent of Alberta Grade 12 students (Lowe et al. 1997: 53). Thus, while the basic work orientations of youth may not have changed, and while their work ethic has not declined, there is considerably more anxiety about future employment prospects. A generation ago, an expanding economy allowed a larger proportion of youth to launch satisfying careers. Today, labour market restructuring has made career entry more difficult for Canadian youth and heightened their employment anxiety.

At the same time, reduced loyalty and commitment by many employers to their workers, as reflected in greater reliance on part-time and temporary workers, may also translate into less commitment and loyalty to the work organization by employees, both young and old. However, rather than indicating a decline in the work ethic, this points to a change in the relationship between workers and their employers. It also indicates a problem that employers, not schools, need to address. How do you motivate workers without offering them some degree of employment security and satisfaction in return? As nonstandard work becomes more common, employers will be forced to face this issue more directly.[39]

Welfare Dependency and an Emerging Underclass?

The poor also have been the frequent target of public concern about a "declining work ethic," since it is often easier to blame them for their plight than to try to understand the structural conditions that create poverty (Kluegel 1987; Wright 1993). During the 1970s, growing awareness of extensive poverty, particularly among Black Americans, prompted fears that fewer people were willing to work. In 1972, U.S. President Richard Nixon stated that American society was threatened by the "new welfare ethic that could cause the American character to weaken." One study of the issue revealed that 79 percent of managers believed that a declining work ethic was responsible for a national drop in productivity, compared with only 35 percent of union leaders. The difference in response demonstrates how the declining work ethic argument sometimes gets used to shift the blame for economic problems to other groups.[40]

As in the United States, results from national surveys conducted in Canada in the early 1970s did not find a declining work ethic. For example, few Canadian respondents agreed that they would rather collect unemployment insurance than hold a job. Most stated that, given the choice, they would prefer working to not having a job, and that work was a central aspect of their lives. Paradoxically, these same respondents doubted the work commitment of other Canadians. Four out of five agreed that "[t]here is an atmosphere of welfare for anybody who wants it in this country."[41] People seemed to be saying that they personally wanted to work, but that our social institutions made it easy for others to avoid working.

Public opinion about social assistance programs and the work orientations of recipients seems to have changed little over the past 20 years. National surveys conducted in 1994 showed 68 percent of Canadians agreeing that "the existence of our social programs makes it too easy for people to give up looking for work." A smaller majority (55 percent) agreed that "if people just took more responsibility for themselves and their families we wouldn't need all of these social programs." Sixty-three percent supported lower unemployment insurance benefits for frequent users of the UI system, presumably because they felt they were less deserving (Peters 1995: 115–16).

What has changed, however, are the social assistance programs themselves. During the 1990s, the Unemployment Insurance program (now called Employment Insurance) has been altered, making it more difficult for seasonal workers to obtain benefits. In several provinces, social assistance benefits have been cut back for "able-bodied" recipients, and *workfare* programs that require recipients to work in public projects have been introduced.[42] Thus, in the past decade, long-standing beliefs that many of the poor are reluctant to work, perhaps because the *social safety net* is too comfortable, have had a significant influence on public policy.

In fact, with the number of long-term unemployed increasing in many Western industrialized countries, and with income inequality rising, some observers have begun to label the most marginalized members of society as an *underclass*, even though the term has been used very imprecisely (see Chapter 3). Some discussions of this new underclass are sympathetic, arguing that this level of social inequality is unacceptable. Other commentators treat the trend toward greater inequality as largely inevitable, worrying instead about welfare dependency. The argument, simply put, is that prolonged receipt of social assistance and unemployment insurance benefits lead to changed attitudes: both the stigma of receiving assistance and the desire to seek paid employment decline. Even more troubling, such accounts suggest, these welfare dependency orientations can be passed on to the children of the poor.

Is there any basis to such fears about a declining work ethic within the poorest members of society, or are we simply seeing ideological justifications for reducing social assistance benefits to the poor and unemployed? The best test would be to determine whether the presumed weak work ethic of the poor translates into little effort to seek paid work or other sources of income. Research that has taken this approach invariably leads to the same conclusion —a weak work ethic and a lack of effort are seldom the problem. Much more often, the problem is one of not enough good jobs.

The majority of Canada's poor are not welfare-dependent but "working poor," seeking to maintain their standard of living on jobs with low pay and short hours. While long-term unemployment has increased in Canada, there is still, in fact, a considerable amount of movement in and out of poverty as individuals lose jobs, move from social assistance to a low-paying job, become divorced, or enter retirement without an adequate pension.[43] In regions where unemployment is high, a great deal of productive work continues to take place in the nonpaid economy (Felt and Sinclair 1992). Even among street people and the homeless, we find many engaged in casual work and the informal economy in an effort to maintain their existence (Wagner 1994; Edin 1991). When offered jobs that pay only a few dollars more than the minimum wage, welfare recipients have demonstrated a great willingness to work.[44] As for the argument that welfare dependency attitudes are passed from one generation to the next, research shows little of this happening (Duncan et al. 1988). Thus, while we are concerned about rising social inequality, we are not convinced by accounts of welfare dependency among the poor.

Anxious Workers: Growing Anxiety over Job and Income Security

Despite weak evidence for popular beliefs about changing work orientations in our society, there is growing anxiety about job and income security in response to continued high unemployment, an increase in nonstandard work, and cutbacks in government social assistance programs. This is reflected in the hesitant interest in early retirement among workers concerned about maintaining their incomes, in the concerns of youth about their chances to begin a satisfying career, and in the daily worries of the employed and unemployed poor struggling to support themselves.

Recent public opinion surveys reinforce this impression of rising job and income-related anxiety in our society. A 1996 Angus Reid national survey sponsored by the Royal Bank showed 22 percent of employed Canadians worried that they might lose their job in the coming year. The youngest and oldest workers surveyed felt the least secure. An Ekos Research poll in the same year asked about fears of job loss in the next several years. Forty-four percent of the employed thought this was a possibility. When asked whether they thought that, by the year 2000, the Canada Pension Plan would have worse funding or be bankrupt, 70 percent of the respondents in the *Maclean's* 1995 year-end poll agreed. A year later, in a similar poll, 80 percent of the sample stated that, by the year 2005, "[m]any people will never find full-time work throughout their lives." Half of the Canadians surveyed (48 percent) thought this scenario was "very likely."[45]

Such concerns about job security and income maintenance do not necessarily mean that other work orientations are declining in importance. Some workers continue to exhibit instrumental work orientations, being motivated primarily by a hope for higher income and the nonwork satisfactions it can purchase. A larger number want jobs that provide a range of intrinsic work rewards. Both work and family are central life interests for a majority of Canadian labour force participants. Thus, as one observer of recent American workforce trends concludes:

> American workers ... want time for work, family, friends, and themselves. They also want interesting jobs, financial security, and a chance to get ahead. Sometimes they want all these things at once; more often, they want different things at different points in

> their lives. And what they want most of all from employers is a confusing mix of flexibility and security. (Braus 1992: 30)

Economic growth and rising standards of living during the mid-twentieth century led to observations that "affluent workers" with instrumental work orientations were the new majority. At the end of the twentieth century, we see a broader mix of work orientations in Canadian society. But it is also clear that anxious workers, along with the even more anxious jobless, have grown in number.

JOB SATISFACTION AND DISSATISFACTION

We began this chapter with an overview of societal work values, and then examined the work orientations or preferences of individuals. Now we will focus on job satisfaction and dissatisfaction, the subjective reactions of individual workers to the particular set of rewards, intrinsic or extrinsic, provided by their job (Blackburn and Mann 1979: 167).

What do Canadians find most and least satisfying about their jobs? Are most of them satisfied? Do people's work orientations influence what they find satisfying in a job? Can job satisfaction or dissatisfaction affect workers off the job? Some researchers assume that productivity is a function of job satisfaction. Their goal has been to discover how to organize work and manage employees in a way that leads to increased satisfaction, productivity, and profits. Others, adopting the humanistic view that work is an essential part of being human, view satisfying and self-fulfilling work for as many people as possible as a desirable societal goal in itself.

The Prevalence of Job Satisfaction

The standard measure of job satisfaction in survey research is some variation of "All in all, how satisfied are you with your job?" In response, a large majority of workers typically report some degree of satisfaction. For example, a 1996 Angus Reid survey of 850 employed Canadians revealed that 45 percent were "very satisfied" while a similar proportion were "satisfied" with their job. These results, and many similar findings over the past few decades, imply that job dissatisfaction is not a serious problem.[46]

However, there are several reasons why we could question such a conclusion. James Rinehart points out that workers' behaviours—strikes, absenteeism, and quitting—all indicate more dissatisfaction with working conditions than do attitude surveys. Rinehart (1978: 7) proposes that answers to general questions about job satisfaction are "pragmatic judgements of one's position vis-à-vis the narrow range of available jobs." Most workers look at their limited alternatives and conclude, from this frame of reference, that they are relatively satisfied with their work.

Essentially, responses to general job satisfaction questions may be similar to replies to the question, "How are you today?" Most of us would say "fine," whether or not this was the case. Hence, more probing questions may be needed to uncover specific feelings of job dissatisfaction. We should also recognize that in a society with highly individualistic work values, people may be unwilling to express dissatisfaction with their jobs because it could reflect negatively on their own ability and efforts. General satisfaction measures may "strike too closely and too directly at the worker's self-esteem."[47]

This is why more refined measures of job satisfaction are useful. For example, a 1987 Environics survey asked Canadian workers whether they would choose the same occupation if they had another chance to choose. Almost half (46 percent) said that they would stay in their occupation, 42 percent said they would change occupations, and the rest were uncertain. The 1996 Angus Reid poll revealed 32 percent of employed Canadians agree that "I would take a comparable job at another company if it were offered to me."[48] Thus, *behavioural intention* measures typically reveal somewhat more widespread job dissatisfaction. As Sandy Stewart and Bob Blackburn put it, "satisfaction is expressed within a framework of what is possible, liking is expressed within a framework of what is desirable."[49]

Age and Job Satisfaction

A consistent finding in job satisfaction research is that older workers generally report more satisfaction. For example, the 1989 General Social Survey showed that 48 percent of 15-to-24-year-old Canadian workers were "very satisfied" with their job, compared with 51 percent of those aged 25 to 34, 58 percent of 35-to-44-year-old workers, 64 percent of 45-to-54-year-olds, and 69 percent of those who were 55 to 64 years old.[50] Typical of the research on differences in job satisfaction, explanations for this age-related pattern take two basic forms. Some are individualistic, focusing on motivations and work orientations, while others are more structural, pointing to characteristics of the job and the workplace (Hall 1986: 94; Ospina 1996: 181).

Perhaps older workers have reduced their expectations, becoming more accepting of relatively unrewarding work. This is an *aging* effect. Alternatively, a *cohort* explanation emphasizes lower expectations (and consequently higher satisfaction) on the part of a generation of older workers, assuming that older workers grew up in an era when simply having a secure job was all one desired and when little self-fulfillment at work was expected. Third, a *life-cycle* effect argues that older workers are more likely to have family and community interests that might compensate for nonsatisfying work. A fourth explanation emphasizes the nature of the work performed (a *job effect*), suggesting that older people have been promoted into more rewarding and satisfying jobs, or have changed jobs until they found one they liked. A final explanation points to *self-selection*, arguing that less satisfied workers will drop out of the labour force as they get older, leaving behind the more satisfied workers.

Which is the best explanation? No clear answer emerges from the many studies on this topic although, with today's high unemployment rates, fewer workers will have the luxury of changing jobs until they find one they like or of quitting work because of job dissatisfaction. Regardless, we know that older workers are more likely to report satisfaction with their work, and that this is due mainly to the better jobs they have obtained over time and to their cumulative social experiences and adaptations in the workplace and society.[51]

Several recent studies have suggested that the relationship between age and job satisfaction is U-shaped: satisfaction is moderately high among the youngest workers, lower in the next cohort, and then higher again in each successive cohort. The explanation is that young workers are usually reasonably satisfied with their entry-level jobs, but only for a while. Then the mismatch between low-level jobs and high aspirations begins to have an effect, and job satisfaction is lower among workers in their late twenties and early thirties. With time, however, the combination of better jobs and declining expectations again leads to higher levels of job satisfaction.[52] This argument points to both individualistic and structural determinants of job satisfaction. It also raises an interesting question for future research. Because today's youth seem to be facing many more barriers to entry into good jobs, will we continue to observe the overall strong, positive relationship between age and job satisfaction in the future?

Gender and Job Satisfaction

Given that women are more likely to work part-time in the secondary labour market, are they less satisfied with their jobs? The research evidence offers a clear answer: despite large differences in work rewards, there is typically little difference between men and women in self-reported job satisfaction.[53] Again, as with age differences in job satisfaction, an explanation of this nondifference brings us back to the subject of work orientations. Some researchers suggest that women have been socialized to expect fewer intrinsic and extrinsic work rewards. Hence, the argument goes, women are more likely to be satisfied with lower-quality jobs, focusing instead perhaps on satisfying social relationships within the workplace.[54]

However, we should not explain the job satisfaction of women with a *gender model* (differences due to prior socialization) while employing a *job model* (differences due to the nature of the job) to account for the satisfaction of men.[55] In fact, it makes more theoretical sense to explain the satisfaction of both women and men with reference to the type of jobs they hold and their roles outside the workplace. While, on average, men might report high satisfaction with their relatively good jobs, women might be equally satisfied with less rewarding jobs, having modified their expectations because of the time spent in these same jobs. And as Chapter 4 discussed, men's and women's involvement in family roles differs greatly. This also needs to be taken into account when explaining the nondifferences in job satisfaction between women and men.

The critical test would compare women and men doing similar work, as in a study of post office employees in Edmonton where men and women performed identical tasks. The researchers found very few gender differences in job satisfaction or in work orientations after accounting for both job content and family roles.[56] Thus, while gender differences in work orientations may exist, characteristics of the jobs women typically hold and family responsibilities, rather than prior socialization, are probably responsible.

Educational Attainment and Job Satisfaction

Educational attainment and job satisfaction might be linked in several different ways. Following human capital theory (see Chapter 3), we might hypothesize that higher education should lead to a better job and, in turn, more job satisfaction. A second more complex hypothesis begins with the assumption that better-educated workers have higher expectations regarding their careers but recognizes that not all well-educated workers will have good jobs. Hence, well-educated workers in less-rewarding jobs would be expected to report low job satisfaction. As one commentator wrote several decades ago, "the placing of intelligent and highly qualified workers in dull and unchallenging jobs is a prescription for pathology—for the worker, the employer, the society" (O'Toole 1977: 60).

Job satisfaction studies covering a complete range of occupations typically find that education has little effect on job satisfaction, perhaps because the two hypothesized effects cancel each other. Even when comparing well-educated and less-educated workers in the same blue-collar jobs, few differences in job satisfaction are observed. Perhaps the more educated workers anticipate future upward mobility, and so are willing to tolerate less rewarding work for a time.[57] Thus, research evidence suggests that intrinsically unrewarding jobs have the same negative effect on all workers, regardless of their education.

However, these studies of education and job satisfaction were conducted almost two decades ago. They focused on the match between education and job content and, noting that education levels were rising, questioned whether the mismatch might be increasing. We have considered the other half of the equation in previous chapters, arguing that the labour market has also been changing, particularly in the 1990s. Unemployment has risen, nonstandard employment has increased, large employers have cut back on hiring, and the labour market appears to have become more polarized. We may be seeing a greater degree of education–work mismatch than in the past, not because of rising expectations but because of declining opportunities.

If today's well-educated young workers are unable to find jobs that even come close to their expectations, will we perhaps begin to see more job dissatisfaction? Research has yet to compare the relationships among age, education, and job satisfaction today with the situation several decades ago. However, one recent study did show that workers who considered themselves to be underemployed in terms of their education and skill were much more likely to be dissatisfied with their jobs (Johnson and Johnson 1995). Given the extent to which youth, including the well educated, have been negatively affected by recent labour market changes, this is a trend that needs to be monitored.

Job Conditions, Work Orientations, and Job Satisfaction

Our review of the effects of age, gender, and education on job satisfaction indicates that work orientations are frequently part of the explanation. Nevertheless, research clearly demonstrates that "[j]ob conditions are more strongly related to job satisfaction than are the social characteristics of the workers or the predispositions they bring to the job" (Miller 1980). In fact, hundreds of studies have attempted to identify the specific job conditions that workers are most likely to find satisfying. Such studies have focused on pay, benefits, promotion opportunities, and other *extrinsic rewards;* autonomy, challenge, social relationships in the workplace and a range of *intrinsic rewards; work organization features* (for example, bureaucracy, health and safety concerns, and the presence of a union); and *job task design* characteristics, including the use of new technologies.

A popular theory developed several decades ago by Frederick Herzberg drew on all of these traditions, emphasizing both the extrinsic and intrinsic rewards of work. *Hygiene factors* like pay, supervisory style, and physical surroundings in the workplace could reduce job dissatisfaction, Herzberg argued. But only *motivators*, such as opportunities to develop one's skills and to make decisions about one's own work, could increase job satisfaction.[58] Herzberg also insisted that the presence of such motivators would lead, by way of increased job satisfaction, to greater productivity on the part of workers. We will return to that issue below.

Influenced by Herzberg's *two-factor theory*, most job satisfaction researchers now utilize multidimensional explanatory frameworks incorporating both intrinsic and extrinsic work rewards, as well as organizational and task characteristics. Although researchers categorize the specific features of work in somewhat different ways, there is considerable consensus at a broader level. Arne Kalleberg, for example, identifies six major dimensions of work. The first, an intrinsic reward dimension, emphasizes interesting, challenging, and self-directed work that allows personal growth and development. Career opportunities form a second dimension, and financial rewards (pay, job security, and fringe benefits) a third. Relationships with co-workers, convenience (the comfort and ease of work), and resource adequacy (availability of information, tools, and materials necessary to do a job) complete the list.[59]

It is also clear from the research we have reviewed that work orientations or preferences must remain part of the job satisfaction equation. Indeed, Kalleberg argues that it is the specific match between work rewards (characteristics of the job) and work orientations that determines one's degree of job satisfaction. This would apply, he suggests, to both extrinsic and intrinsic dimensions of work. Kalleberg found that job rewards had positive effects on expressions of job satisfaction in the U.S. labour force, as predicted. But he also observed that, other things being equal, work preferences had negative effects on satisfaction. In other words, the more one values some particular feature of work (the chance to make decisions, for example), the less likely it is that one's desires can be satisfied. However, job rewards had substantially greater effects on satisfaction than did work preferences. In addition, Kalleberg's analysis led him to conclude that intrinsic job rewards were more important determinants of job satisfaction than were extrinsic rewards.[60]

Canadian Research on Intrinsic Job Rewards

What does Canadian research tell us about intrinsic work rewards and their fit or mismatch with the work orientations of workers? Respondents in the 1973 national Job Satisfaction Survey were given a list of more than 30 specific job characteristics and asked to assess, first, how important each was to them and, second, how their own job rated on these characteristics. The analysts then compared the average "importance" and "evaluation" scores, and examined the gap between them. The largest discrepancies appeared in the areas of "opportunities for promotion" and "potential for challenge and growth" (Burstein et al. 1975: 31–34). These are not unusual findings since most workers seek intrinsic rewards from their work and wish to "get ahead" in their careers. But has labour market restructuring, particularly downsizing and greater reliance on nonstandard workers, changed this pattern?

A study comparing U.S. and Canadian data over a ten-year period (1977–87) showed that employees' perceptions of opportunities for advancement had declined. In 1989, only 57 percent of employed Canadians agreed (somewhat or strongly) that, in their job, "the chances for promotion or career development are good." A 1991 survey revealed that "career development and training" were evaluated considerably less positively than were other job characteristics such as pay, benefits, and supervision. Thus, it appears that concerns about career development continue to be widespread and may even have increased. A 1996 poll showing 44 percent of the employed being fearful about losing their job indicates that these concerns now extend to basic job security.[61]

What does it mean to have "opportunities for challenge and growth"? Researchers agree that, for most workers, jobs that provide considerable autonomy, complexity, and variety are fulfilling. The opportunity to make decisions about how a job should be done, to develop and use a wide range of skills, and to complete projects can also increase a worker's satisfaction. Repetitive jobs with little variety often have the opposite effect.[62] In the following quotations, compare the variety and challenge that are so satisfying for the male oil-field service company manager and the sense of accomplishment reported by the professional engineer (also male) with descriptions of repetitive, low-skill work by a female food-processing factory worker and a male assembly-line worker.[63]

> Every morning even now, I'm happy to come to work; I look forward to it. I think it's because this business is, well, you never know when you come in here in the morning what's going to be asked of you. It could be different every day; generally it is.
>
> I love it. I think I have one of the best jobs I know of ... I enjoy working on projects from start to finish as opposed to just having a small piece of them ... I have found over the years that I am very easily bored and in this field and this environment you don't get bored very often.
>
> Basically, I stand there all day and slash the necks of the chickens ... The chickens go in front of you on the line and you do every other chicken or whatever. And you stand there for eight hours on one spot and do it.
>
> Your brain gets slow. It doesn't function the way it should. You do the same thing day in and day out and your brain goes. I'm like a robot. I walk straight to my job and do what I have to do.

Fortunately, the jobs held by the majority of Canadians appear to be more challenging than those described in these last two quotations. Data comparing the complexity, autonomy, and skill requirements in jobs today compared to a decade or two ago are not available. But an overview of contemporary data would be useful. A 1996 Angus Reid survey reveals, for example, that 71 percent of employed Canadians agree (somewhat or strongly) that "[m]y work is challenging and interesting." The 1989 General Social Survey asked employed respondents whether, in their job, "there is a lot of freedom to decide how to do your work." Over half (54 percent) strongly agreed with this statement while 27 percent agreed somewhat. In response to the statement "your job requires a high level of skill," 46 percent agreed strongly; 29 percent agreed somewhat; and 1 in 4 workers (24 percent) disagreed (strongly or somewhat). Thus, about one-half of employed Canadians evaluate their jobs very positively with respect to challenge, decision making (autonomy), and skill requirements (complexity), and about one-quarter are somewhat positive in their assessments of these intrinsic work rewards. At the same time, a sizable minority evaluate these aspects of their work negatively. [64]

When asked to agree or disagree with "you do the same things over and over," one-third (32 percent) of the 1989 survey respondents agreed strongly; about the same portion (30 percent) agreed somewhat; while 37 percent disagreed. These results suggest that repetitious work (a lack of variety) is more common than nonchallenging, low-skill work, or work with little autonomy. The same study also asked workers to respond with a yes or no to the question: "considering your experience, education, and training, do you feel that you are overqualified for your job?" One in four workers (23 percent) said "yes." More recently, a 1994 national survey of literacy skills indicated that about 1 in 5 employed Canadian workers are underemployed with respect to their reading and writing skills.[65]

The 1989 General Social Survey found women more likely to agree that they were overqualified and required to do repetitious work, but somewhat less likely to agree that their job provided considerable autonomy and required a high level of skill. Younger workers also evaluated these aspects of their jobs more negatively. It is noteworthy that feelings of overqualification among university-educated respondents (22 percent) were not that different from the total sample average (23 percent).[66] This suggests that *underemployment* may be fairly widespread among well-educated Canadian workers, a conclusion we have already drawn in our earlier discussions of changing employment trends over the past decade. As we also have noted, there is strong evidence that underemployment may lead to job dissatisfaction (Johnson and Johnson 1995).

Aggregate statistics conceal a great deal of variation in job quality across occupations and industries and across different types of employment relationships. The jobs assessed most favourably tend to be in the upper-tier services and in some of the goods-producing industries. Compared with those in full-time and permanent positions, workers in nonstandard employment, particularly in the lower-tier services, evaluate their jobs much less positively. For example, while two-thirds of Canadians in full-time, permanent jobs in the education, health and welfare industries report that their job requires a high level of skill, only 10 percent of nonstandard workers in the retail trade sector say this about their jobs (Krahn 1992: Chapter 5). These survey results indicate that a labour market segmentation perspective (see Chapter 3) can help us explain variations in job satisfaction. Along with better pay, more benefits, and greater job security, jobs in the primary labour market also offer greater intrinsic rewards.

Consequences of Job Satisfaction and Dissatisfaction

"If the job's so bad, why don't you quit?" Many of us may have thought this about an unsatisfying job, but fewer have actually done so. There may be some features of the job—pay, hours, location, friendly workmates—that make it palatable, despite the absence of other work rewards. In addition, unless other jobs are available, most employees simply cannot afford to quit. This would be particularly true today, given high levels of unemployment and widespread downsizing in both the private and the public sectors. Thus, job dissatisfaction, even if it is extreme, will not necessarily translate into quitting behaviour. It might, on the other hand, encourage individuals to call in sick or come in late more frequently.[67]

Studies have also shown a relationship between job dissatisfaction and overt acts of employee deviance, such as theft of company property, or the use of drugs and alcohol on the job and away from work.[68] Dissatisfaction with work is also correlated with the number of complaints and grievances filed in unionized work settings. As for nonunionized workers, surveys have shown that those dissatisfied with their work are more likely to view unions positively and are more likely to join a union, if given the chance.[69]

From an employer's perspective, however, the critical issue is whether increases in job satisfaction will boost productivity. If dissatisfaction leads to tardiness, absenteeism, deviance, or quitting, will improvements in the quality of working life lead to a happier and more productive workforce? Although one can find examples of research showing such a relationship, the safest answer to the question would be "don't count on it." Research consistently has shown that the relationship between satisfaction and productivity is very weak, or is only present in some work settings.[70]

There are several possible explanations for this. First, productivity is more often a function of technology and workers' skills than of their attitudes. Thus, even if high levels of satisfaction are evident, low skill levels, inadequate on-the-job training, or obsolete machinery will limit opportunities for productivity increases.[71] Second, work-group norms and expectations must be taken into consideration. Managers and consultants who have introduced job enrichment programs, and have perhaps even found higher levels of satisfaction as a consequence, have frequently been disappointed when productivity increases did not follow. They failed to realize that workers might view an improved quality of working life as their just reward, or that informal work norms and long-standing patterns of behaviour are difficult to alter.[72]

Finally, it may be that productivity can be influenced by job satisfaction, but only under certain conditions. Our earlier discussion suggested that workers in low-level jobs might report job satisfaction because they were assessing their work with a limited set of alternatives in mind. Workers in higher-status jobs might, on the other hand, report satisfaction because of tangible work rewards. If so, perhaps productivity increases due to job satisfaction might only be expected in the latter group. In fact, a review of over 40 studies on this topic supports this hypothesis, demonstrating that the productivity–satisfaction link is strongest among professional, managerial, and supervisory workers (Petty et al. 1984).

WORK AND ALIENATION

William Faulkner once wrote that "You can't eat for eight hours a day nor drink for eight hours a day nor make love for eight hours a day—all you can do for eight hours is work. Which is the reason why man makes himself and everybody else so miserable and unhappy."[73] Faulkner didn't use the term *alienation*, but he might have since his cryptic observations about the misery of work capture some of the many meanings of the term as used by social philosophers and researchers.

Typically, the concept refers in some way to negative subjective reactions to work, but beyond that there is little consensus on its meaning. We might, for example, come across references to the causes and consequences of "job dissatisfaction and alienation," but seldom are the two concepts distinguished from each other. However, alienation is really a much broader philosophical concept. In fact, with reference to our earlier discussion of the meaning of work, we might conceive of alienation as the human condition resulting from an absence of fulfilling work.

Karl Marx and Alienating Work within Capitalism

The verb "alienate" refers to an act of separation, or to the transfer of something to a new owner. Marx used the term in the latter sense when he discussed the "alienating" effects of capitalist production relations on the working class. The noun "alienation" refers to the overall experience of work under these conditions.

Marx identified a number of sources of alienation under capitalism. Products did not belong to those who produced them. Instead, ownership of the product remained with those who owned the enterprise and who purchased the labour of workers. Decisions about what to produce and about the sale of the finished products were not made by the workers, and profits generated in the exchange remained with the owners of the enterprise. In fact, given an extensive division of labour, many of the workers involved in the productive process might never see the finished product. Thus, workers were alienated from the product of their own work.

Marx also emphasized alienation from the activity of work. Transfer of control over the labour process from individual workers to capitalists or managers meant that individual workers lost the chance to make decisions about how the work should be done. In addition, extensive fragmentation of the work process had taken away most intrinsic work rewards. Alienation also involved the separation of individual workers from others around them. Obviously, bureaucratic hierarchies could have this effect. But more importantly, because capitalist employment relationships involve the exchange of labour for a wage, work was transformed from a creative and collective activity to an individualistic, monetary activity. Work itself had become a commodity. As a consequence, Marx argued, workers were alienated from themselves. Capitalist relations of production had reduced work from its role as a means of human self-fulfillment to being a market transaction.[74]

This structural perspective on alienation from work rests on several key assumptions. First, alienation occurs because workers have little or no control over the conditions of their work, and few chances to develop to their fullest potential as creative human beings. Second, the source of alienation can be traced to the organization of work under capitalism. Third, given that alienation is characteristic of capitalism, it exists even if workers themselves do not consciously recognize it.

Alienation, then, is a "condition of objective powerlessness" (Rinehart 1996: 11–21). Whether individual workers become aware of the cause of their discontent with work depends on a variety of factors. In the absence of a well-defined alternative to the current economic system, we would not expect most workers to be able to clearly articulate their alienation, or to act on it.[75] Apathy, or an attempt to forget about work as soon as one leaves it behind, are the common responses of many workers to a situation to which they see no viable alternative. But as we have seen in Chapter 7, discontent does exist, as demonstrated by the frequency of strikes, walkouts, and other behaviours showing frustration and unhappiness with the conditions of work.

The Social–Psychological Perspective on Alienation

The social–psychological perspective on alienation shares with the structural perspective an emphasis on the powerlessness of workers, and the conclusion that many jobs offer limited opportunities for personal growth and self-fulfillment. While the structural perspective emphasizes separation from the product and the activity of work, from co-workers and from oneself, the social–psychological approach attempts to measure feelings of powerlessness, meaninglessness, social isolation, self-estrangement, and normlessness.[76] Thus, the main focus of the social–psychological perspective is on the absence of intrinsic job rewards.[77]

Social–psychological studies of alienation, moreover, are unlikely to lay all or much of the blame on capitalism itself. Instead, technologies that allow workers few opportunities for self-direction, bureaucratic work organizations, and modern mass society in general are identified as the sources of alienation. This perspective also differs from the structural approach in its emphasis on feelings of alienation—the subjective experience of alienating work conditions. Researchers within this approach have relied primarily on the self-reports of workers, in contrast with the Marxist focus on the organization and content of work (Hall 1986: 105–09).

Consequently, social–psychological accounts of alienation resemble job dissatisfaction, although their explanations of the sources of alienation have pointed more explicitly to the negative consequences of work fragmentation and powerlessness. The general job satisfaction literature examines a broader array of causal variables (work orientations, for example). But since some social–psychological studies of alienation actually define the phenomenon as an "extrinsic orientation to work" (Seemen 1975: 273), there is really more congruence between the two research traditions than first impressions would suggest. Hence, it is not surprising to find studies that examine alienation and job dissatisfaction simultaneously, or writers who use the terms interchangeably.

Robert Blauner on "Alienation and Freedom"

Four decades ago, Robert Blauner published *Alienation and Freedom*, a classic study of industrial differences in workers' responses to their jobs.[78] Following the social–psychological tradition, he defined alienation in terms of powerlessness, meaninglessness, isolation (or social alienation), and self-estrangement. The centrality of powerlessness in Blauner's theory of alienation is clear from his use of the word *freedom* to refer to the ability to choose how one does one's work.

Blauner compared work in four different industries to test his theory that technology (and the attendant division of labour) is a major determinant of the degree of alienation experienced at work. He argued that the traditional printing industry, which at the time still operated largely in a craft-work mode, produced low levels of alienation because of the considerable autonomy of workers and the high levels of skill required. The textile manufacturing industry represented an intermediate step in the process of technological development, while the culmination occurred with the assembly lines of the automobile industry. Here, alienation was most acute because of low-skilled, repetitive tasks that deprived workers of control over their actions.

Blauner argued that new automated technologies reversed this trend. In work settings such as oil refineries, skill levels were higher, tasks were varied, and individuals could make a number of decisions about how they would do their work. Since this industry was providing us with a glimpse of the future of industrialized societies, he reasoned, the prospects for individual freedom were good. By predicting that alienation would decline as fewer workers were employed in mass production settings, Blauner was rejecting Marx's argument that work in a capitalist society was alienating.

Alienation and Freedom has been both influential and controversial. Blauner was undoubtedly correct about the negative consequences of continued exposure to low-skill, routinized work. But critics have argued that a social–psychological definition does not address alienation in the broader way that Marx had defined it.[79] Furthermore, Duncan Gallie's (1978) comparative study of refinery workers in France and England has highlighted crosscultural differences in workers' responses to technology, an important point Blauner overlooked. And as we have argued earlier, effects of technology are not predetermined. A position of *technological determinism* conveniently overlooks why different technologies are designed or chosen by those who control an enterprise, and how these technologies are built into the organizational structure of the workplace.

WORK AND STRESS

If we take a broader *work and well-being* approach to the subject of how workers' experience and react to their jobs, both physical and psychological reactions to work become part of our subject matter. This approach also encourages us to consider how paid work might affect an individual's life in the family and the community. Workplace health and safety issues, discussed earlier, are also central to the work and well-being subject area, as are concerns about balancing work and family responsibilities (see Chapter 4). Here, we look more specifically at work and stress.

Defining Work-Related Stress

Defining *work-related stress* independent of job dissatisfaction is not easy. In fact, many researchers studying stress and its consequences rely on measures that might, in a different context, be considered indicators of job dissatisfaction. However, it is possible to feel dissatisfied with work without experiencing a great deal of stress. It is useful, then, to conceive of stress as a many-sided problem—with job dissatisfaction as one of its components—that can lead to serious mental and physical health disorders.

It is also helpful to distinguish *stressors* (or *strains*) from an individual worker's reactions to them. Stressors are objective situations (for example, noisy work environments or competing job demands) or events (a dispute with a supervisor or news that some workers are about to be laid off) that have the potential to produce a negative subjective or physical response. Thus, work-related stress is an individually experienced negative reaction to a job or work environment.[80] Obviously, the absence of stress does not imply the presence of job satisfaction. What distinguishes stress reactions are the wide range of ill health (physical and psychological) symptoms.

Causes and Consequences of Work-Related Stress

Research in many different settings has shown that physical reactions to stress can include fatigue, insomnia, muscular aches and pains, ulcers, high blood pressure, and even heart disease. Depression, anxiety, irritation, low self-esteem, and other mental health problems are among the documented psychological reactions to stressful work. The research literature has also shown that the effects of work-based stressors can be conditioned by individuals' psychological coping mechanisms and by the amount of social support they receive from family, friends, and co-workers.[81]

Constant worry over paying bills or losing one's job, concerns that have been increasing over the past decades, can be considered a form of work-related stress. For example, a recent U.S. study of automobile workers revealed that the strongest predictor of symptoms of ill health was a chronic concern over job loss (Heaney et al. 1994). And, as Chapter 4 documented, equally stressful for some workers, especially women, are the pressures of looking after family responsibilities while trying to devote oneself to a job or career.

But most research in this area has concentrated on stressors in the work environment.[82] Continual exposure to health and safety hazards, sexual harassment, working in a physically uncomfortable setting, shift work, or long hours can all be stressors. Similarly, fast-paced work (especially when the pace is set by a machine) and inadequate resources to complete a task can generate stress. In addition, working at tasks that underutilize one's skills and abilities, or that allow little latitude for decision making, are stressful for many workers. Finally, there is the stress that an unreasonable and overly demanding supervisor can create.

Statistics Canada's 1990 Health Promotion Survey asked employed Canadian adults whether, in the previous six months, they had experienced any of a long list of possible workplace stressors. About 1 in 4 responded that they had encountered unreasonable deadlines, conflicts with other people at work, lack of feedback about their work performance, unclear duties, and not having sufficient influence over doing their own job. In fact, half of the sample (49 percent) reported experiencing at least one of these sources of stress (Geran 1992: 16).

The "Demand–Control" Model of Work-Related Stress

A useful perspective for understanding workplace stress is the *demand–control model*, which redefines stressors as *job demands* but also introduces the concept of worker control.[83] It distinguishes between active jobs where individual decision-making potential is high, and passive jobs where it is largely absent. If psychological demands on a worker are high, but she or he can do something about it, stress is less likely to result. If demands are high and control is low, stress and the health problems that can follow are far more often the outcome.

From this perspective, we can see why researchers have repeatedly found highly routinized, machine-paced work to be extremely stressful. Assembly-line or data-entry jobs are often considered to be among the most stressful.[84] Demand is constant, the physical work can be extremely taxing, and worker control is virtually absent. Earlier we suggested that instrumental work attitudes may be a coping mechanism—the paycheque becomes the only relevant work reward. Some people adapt to assembly-line work by "tuning out" the boredom and waiting for the chance to get away from the job. Ben Hamper (1986: 88), better known as "Rivethead," describes how he was introduced to his new job on a truck-assembly line in Flint, Michigan:

> "Until you get it down, your hands will ache, your feet will throb and your back will feel like it's been steamrolled … "

> "Are there any advantages to working down here?" I asked pitifully.
>
> The guy scratched at his beard. "Well, the exit to the time clocks and the parking lot is just down these stairs. Come lunchtime or quittin' time, you can usually get a good jump on the rest of the pack."

But psychological problems can also arise. Robert Linhart (1981: 57) describes an extreme reaction to the assembly line in a French automobile factory:

> He was fixing parts of a dashboard into place with a screwdriver. Five screws to fix on each car. That Friday afternoon he must have been on his five hundredth screw of the day. All at once he began to yell and rushed at the fenders of the cars brandishing his screwdriver like a dagger. He lacerated a good ten or so car bodies before a troop of white and blue coats rushed up and overcame him, dragging him, panting and gesticulating, to the sick bay.

Highly routine, monotonous, mechanized, and closely supervised jobs are also found in the service industries. A study of Canada Post mail sorters and letter carriers in Edmonton revealed that the most stressful job in the organization involved "keying" postal codes using automated machinery. The relentless pace of the machinery, conflicting demands imposed by management, constant repetition, and lack of challenges and job autonomy were associated with diminished mental and physical health among coders. The use of pain relievers and tranquilizers was significantly higher among the coders using automated technology compared with those sorting mail by hand (Lowe and Northcott 1986).

With the rapid spread of computerized technologies, electronic surveillance has added a new source of stress. This practice might involve monitoring the telephone calls of workers who deal with the public by phone, recording output in settings where workers use computers to conduct their work, or even delivering warnings to those performing below certain levels. As e-mail and voice-mail systems have become more common, some employers have recognized their potential for maintaining control of workers. In 1993, for example, a study of large U.S. companies indicated that, in more than 30 percent of these firms, managers routinely read employees' e-mail or examined their personal computer files.[85]

Frederick Taylor would have applauded, but employees do not. A data entry clerk whose workgroup had been told that they had not met management productivity goals the previous week comments:

> I feel so pressured, my stomach is in knots. I take tons of aspirin, my jaws are sore from clenching my teeth, I'm so tired I can't get up in the morning, and my arm hurts from entering, entering, entering. (Nussbaum and duRivage 1986: 18)

It is not difficult to see how such working conditions—high demands and virtually no worker control—can be stressful, and lead to physical and psychological ill health.

The "Person–Environment Fit" Model

A different theoretical model of work-related stress emphasizes the *person–environment fit.*[86] According to this model, stress results when there is a significant gap between an individual's needs and abilities and what the job offers, allows, or demands. To take a specific example, reports of "burnout" among social workers, teachers, and nurses are common. Individuals in these helping professions have work orientations (the desire to solve problems and help people) and useful skills (training in their profession) that are frequently thwarted by the need to deal with an excessive number of clients, limited resources, and administrative policies that make it difficult to be effective.[87]

We might also use this perspective to help us understand the stress many workers feel when they attempt to juggle their work and family roles. A paid job requires you to be present and involved; at the same time, family responsibilities demand time and attention. Because women continue to carry a large share of domestic and child-care responsibilities, they are much more likely to experience role conflict and stress.

> When I worked full-time, I felt very guilty about the children. If they were sick and I went to work, I felt guilty. If I stayed home

> with them, I felt guilty about work. Part-time work could offer the flexibility that full-time work cannot.
>
> I started working nights about seven years ago, so we wouldn't have to pay for day care. There was no way around it—we couldn't afford a babysitter. I find it hard to sleep regularly. I get home at 1:00 A.M., then I must prepare my husband's meal for the next day. I need to wake up early to get the children ready for school.[88]

These two women chose part-time work and shift work to deal with their problems. The first gave up additional income and career options (which are limited in most part-time jobs), while the second traded one source of stress (not enough money) for another (irregular hours and a limited family life). From a person–environment fit perspective, they were attempting to improve the fit between demands of their family and their job (or the financial need to work). But that fit could also have been improved if structural, rather than just individual, changes were implemented.

Thus, while the person–environment fit model of stress broadens our explanatory framework by bringing in work orientations, its individualistic focus advocates personal solutions. From the demand–control perspective, we are more inclined to seek solutions to the lack of worker control. In this case, if more men accepted an equal share of the responsibilities in their homes, if more employers offered flexible work schedules to their workers, and if affordable, quality child care was more accessible, would the women quoted above have been forced to make these choices? With respect to professional burnout, how could organizational structures and administrative policies be changed to allow social workers and nurses to be more effective? How can we use new technologies to reduce stress and increase job satisfaction, rather than merely to control workers?

CONCLUSION: THE "LONG ARM OF THE JOB"

Early in this chapter, we described how individuals are exposed to at least two competing work-value systems: the first suggests that monetary rewards are paramount; the second emphasizes how work can be personally self-fulfilling. This raises the possibility that, because of different socialization experiences, some workers would be primarily instrumentally oriented while others would be more motivated by the intrinsic rewards of a job. In short, it could be argued that work orientations or preferences are brought to the job, and will influence feelings of satisfaction or alienation.

But most research tends to support an alternative explanation, namely, that participation in low-skill or routinized work can produce instrumental work attitudes. For many workers, such attitudes may be a means of adapting to employment that has little but a paycheque to offer. Even so, studies of job satisfaction, alienation, and stress highlight the negative consequences of work that is repetitive and routine, offers few chances for individual decision making, and does not develop a person's skills and abilities. While it is important to recognize that work orientations affect how an individual feels about his or her job, the nature of the work itself is likely to have a stronger impact, both on an individual's feelings of satisfaction, alienation, and stress, as well as on her or his work orientations.

We have suggested that work-related stress does not get left behind at the end of the workday. Chronic work pressures, as well as anxiety about potential job or income loss, can undermine an individual's overall quality of life. At the same time, it is apparent that satisfaction with work translates into a broader sense of well-being. But are there any other more long-term, perhaps even permanent, psychological effects a job can have on an individual? The answer appears to be yes—continued exposure to some kinds of work can have long-lasting effects on nonwork behaviours and on one's personality.

Martin Meissner has argued that the "long arm of the job" has an impact on one's life away from work. In a study of male British Columbia sawmill workers, he tested two rival hypotheses about how the nature of work might affect after-work behaviours. The *compensatory leisure* hypothesis proposes that people will look for activities away from work that will compensate for what is absent in their jobs. Thus, workers who have little opportunity to develop their skills and abilities on the job might seek these opportunities away from work. The *spillover* hypothesis suggests that the effects of work will influence one's choice of after-work activities. Meissner concluded that there is a spillover effect. Workers who had little chance to make decisions about how their work should be done were considerably less likely to engage in free-time activities that required or allowed this kind of individual discretion.

Similarly, those who had few opportunities for social interactions at work were more inclined toward solitary leisure-time activities (Meissner 1971: 260).

One could argue that the subjects in Meissner's study had chosen their jobs in order to satisfy their personal preferences. Such an emphasis on work orientations would explain, for example, that individuals with a preference for solitary activities would choose both their jobs and their leisure activities with this in mind. While plausible, this explanation is not convincing for several reasons. First, it suggests that individuals have a much greater range of job choices than is typically the case. Second, subsequent studies comparing these two hypotheses have agreed with Meissner.[89] Third, there is research demonstrating even more conclusively that work with limited scope has a negative effect on personality.

Melvin Kohn and his associates have examined this relationship for many years using the concept of *occupational self-direction*. Kohn argues that work that is free from close supervision, that involves considerable complexity and independent judgment, and that is nonroutine will have a lasting positive effect on one's personality and psychological functioning. Specifically, individuals whose work allows self-direction are more likely to develop a personality that values such opportunities and a more self-confident, less fatalistic and less conformist approach to life. They also exhibit greater flexibility in dealing with ideas. Alternatively, jobs allowing little self-direction are more likely to lead to psychological distress, a finding we have already documented from stress research.

Kohn presents a convincing case, since he used longitudinal data in his studies. By comparing the jobs and personalities of workers at two points in time (up to ten years apart), he clearly demonstrated the personality changes in those who had and those who did not have the opportunity to work in jobs allowing self-direction. Hence, he has also been able to demonstrate that "both ideational flexibility and a self-directed orientation lead, in time, to more responsible jobs that allow greater latitude for occupational self-direction."[90] The overall conclusion of Kohn's studies and related research[91] is that because of the "long arm of the job," intrinsically rewarding work, particularly work that allows self-direction, can have important long-term consequences for the personalities and careers of those fortunate enough to participate in it.

NOTES

1. Blackburn (1988: 226). Also see Anthony (1977) for a provocative analysis of the "ideology of work."
2. Burstein et al. (1975: 10–11); Anthony (1977; Chapter 1); Smucker (1980: 280–81); Peitchinis (1983: 160–62); Rose (1985: 27–30); Byrne (1990: Chapter 3).
3. Genesis (2: 17; 3: 19), *The Bible*, King James Version.
4. Weber (1958) emphasized the Calvinist belief in "predestination," a doctrine proposing that entry into heaven could not be influenced by good works on earth because it was already determined by God. According to Weber, hard work and economic success served to reduce anxiety about being among the "chosen." After all, the "chosen" must have been placed on earth to glorify God through their work and success.
5. See Marshall (1982) and Dickson and McLachlan (1989) on these debates and Furnham (1990), who reviews social–psychological research on the Protestant work ethic and related topics.
6. See Anthony (1977: 45–51) for an interesting discussion of the common roots of these two different ideologies of work.
7. Canadian Conference of Catholic Bishops (1991: 2).
8. See Kelvin and Jarrett (1985), Burman (1988, 1996), Newman (1989), Feather (1990), Kirsh (1992), Swift (1995), and Tanner et al., (1995: Chapter 6) for an introduction to the large research literature on the social and psychological consequences of unemployment and the poverty that often accompanies it.
9. Jahoda (1982); also see Warr (1987).
10. The quotations in this section are from Burman (1988: 161, 113, 144, 86, 200).
11. See Horvat (1983); Freeman (1993) comments on a greater pursuit of leisure activities in Japan in the 1990s.
12. Harrison (1992) suggests that the absence of such work values in Latin America has resulted in limited economic growth. See *The Economist* (1996) for a critique of such "cultural explanations" of economic growth, and the World Bank (1993) for a structural explanation of East Asian economic growth.
13. Jiang et al. (1995) suggest that family involvement in the work organization may be more important to Chinese than to American workers; Walmsley (1992) and Graham (1993, 1995) comment on problems experienced by Japanese firms setting up factories in North America. Also see Sivesind (1995) on cultural differences in work values in Norway and Germany.
14. Siu-Kai and Hsin-Chi (1988) describe how the political and social values of the Hong Kong Chinese reflect both Confucian and Western influences; they also comment on differences between the "tiger economies" in commitment to democratic rights of individuals.
15. *The Economist* (1996: 26).
16. Kalleberg and Stark (1993: 182); Schooler (1996).

17. See Kamata (1983), Gill (1985: 32), and Thompson (1990). The National Defense Counsel for Victims of Karoshi (1990:11) argue that corporate demands for total commitment to one's job in return for advancement within the company are responsible for an increasing rate of "karoshi," defined as "death from overwork."

18. Swift (1995: 221, 224); also see Schor (1991) on *The Overworked American,* a source for some of Swift's ideas.

19. Among other strategies, Rifkin (1995: 255–57) proposes tax deductions for voluntary work and a "social wage" for the unemployed who participate in voluntary work. But he does not really address the clear possibility that such policies, even if they were introduced, would still produce a very unequal income distribution.

20. See Reid (1985), Best (1990), and Report of the Advisory Group on Working Time and the Distribution of Work (1994).

21. See Brown (1997) on worker cooperatives as a solution to problems of community development and worker empowerment.

22. Peters (1995: 5, 69–71) presents data from public opinion polls spanning two decades, and from focus groups (group interviews) conducted in the mid-1990s.

23. The 1996 survey was conducted for the Royal Bank by Angus Reid (*Edmonton Journal,* 8 October 1996: F1). Wyatt Canada (1991: 11) completed the 1991 survey.

24. Sennett and Cobb (1972); also see Chinoy (1955) on the same theme.

25. Blackburn and Mann (1979: 145, 162); Loscocco (1989).

26. See Furnham (1990: 158–62) on workaholics and National Defence Counsel for Victims of Karoshi (1990) on overwork in Japan.

27. Burstein et al. (1975: 57); also see Mottaz (1986) and Neil and Snizek (1987).

28. Dex (1988); Lorence (1987a); Loscocco (1990); Grint (1991: 30); Rowe and Snizek (1995: 226).

29. See, for example, Dubin (1956) and Dubin et al. (1975).

30. Statistics Canada, "Age at retirement: a different perspective for men and women." 1994 General Social Survey fact sheet (n.d.: 2).

31. See Foot and Venne (1990) and Foot and Stoffman (1996).

32. See Lorence (1987b) and Lorence and Mortimer (1985) for discussions of work involvement through the life course.

33. *Edmonton Journal* (7 January 1996: E1); also see the Economic Council of Canada (1992b) for criticisms of the Canadian education system.

34. Barlow and Robertson (1994: 25–38); Osberg et al. (1995: 161–71).

35. Environics (1986); National Centre on Education and the Economy (1990: 24); Borman (1991: 33-34). Holzer (1996) examines the skills required in jobs for less-educated workers, rather than the factors employers consider when making a decision to hire.

36. "Proper attitude earns a job: employers impressed by eagerness to work, counsellors advise" (*Edmonton Journal,* 18 May 1997: B7); also see Cappelli (1992: 6) on employers' attitudes toward young workers. Ainley (1993: 24) argues that, for many employers,

"skill" refers less to technical competency than to whether an individual is a "good employee" in terms of commitment, flexibility, responsibility, and hard work.

37. Coupland (1993); *The Globe and Mail* (3 October 1995: A8).

38. Unpublished results from research conducted by the authors; also see Krahn and Lowe (1997b).

39. Angus Reid Interactive (1996) reports a U.S. opinion poll showing 29 percent of employed respondents stating that they felt less loyal to their employer, compared to several years earlier (22 percent reported feeling more loyal). A 1996 Canadian survey conducted for the Royal Bank by Angus Reid shows only 7 percent of young workers agreeing that "my company cares about me" (*Edmonton Journal*, 8 October 1996: F1). See Johnson and Grey (1988), Leinberger and Tucker (1991), Feldman et al. (1994), Nollen and Axel (1996), and Booth (1997) on reduced loyalty among today's workers, and Wallace (1995b) for a study showing organizational commitment by professionals to be a function of their perceptions of available career opportunities.

40. Nixon's comment was quoted in *Time* (7 September 1987: 42), Also see Furnham (1990: 195) on the shifting of blame for economic problems.

41. Burstein et al. (1975: 12, 22, 60); also see Economic Council of Canada (1976; Chapter 9). Hamilton and Wright (1986: 288) and Furnham (1990: 196–208) review a range of similar U.S. studies and draw the same conclusion.

42. See Burman (1996: 42–45) on welfare state restructuring, and Richards et al. (1995) for debates about "workfare" programs.

43. See Economic Council of Canada (1992c), Schellenberg and Ross (1997), and Statistics Canada (1997b) on the working poor in Canada; also see Newman (1989); Morris and Irwin (1992); and Payne and Payne (1994).

44. For a recent Canadian example, see Social Research and Demonstration Corporation (1996). MacDonald (1994) describes how British social assistance recipients work in the informal economy in order to supplement low incomes.

45. For the Angus Reid–Royal Bank poll, see *Edmonton Journal* (8 October 1996: F1). The Ekos poll is discussed by Betcherman and Lowe (1997: 5); also see *Maclean's* (25 December 1995: 28); (30 December, 1996: 46–47).

46. The Angus Reid–Royal Bank survey results were reported in the *Edmonton Journal* (8 October 1996: F1). Also see Krahn (1992: 113) and Maynard (1987: 115) for similar findings from the 1989 General Social Survey conducted by Statistics Canada and a 1987 Environics survey, respectively. Firebaugh and Harley (1995) document similar levels of satisfaction in U.S. studies over the past 20 years.

47. Burstein et al. (1975: 28); Hall (1986: 92).

48. Maynard (1987: 115); *Edmonton Journal* (8 October 1996: F1); also see Burstein et al. (1975: 29) and Levitan and Johnson (1982: 76–79).

49. Stewart and Blackburn (1975: 503); also see Kalleberg and Griffin (1978: 390).

50. Krahn (1992: 130) presents results from Statistics Canada's 1989 General Social Survey. Firebaugh and Harley (1995) document the same pattern in the United States, while Jiang et al. (1995) observe it in China.

51. Kalleberg and Loscocco (1983) conclude that all of the explanations have some relevance; Hamilton and Wright (1986: 288) favour the "job effect," while Firebaugh and Harley (1995: 97) believe that "aging" and "life cycle" explanations best fit the observed data.

52. Clark et al. (1996: 75). Also see Birdi et al. (1995), who report a U-shaped pattern in data from nine different countries.

53. The 1989 General Social Survey conducted by Statistics Canada revealed virtually no gender differences in job satisfaction (Krahn, 1992: 130); also see Mottaz (1986); Northcott and Lowe (1987); de Vaus and McAllister (1991).

54. Murray and Atkinson (1981); Glenn and Weaver (1982); Phelan (1994).

55. Feldberg and Glenn (1979); de Vaus and McAllister (1991).

56. Northcott and Lowe (1987). Also see Mottaz (1986) for similar findings.

57. Ross (1992) suggest that the two effects cancel each other; also see Martin and Shehan (1989); Glenn and Weaver (1982); and Wright and Hamilton (1979).

58. Herzberg (1966, 1968). For a recent study of Canadian teachers based on Herzberg's model, see Knoop (1994).

59. Kalleberg (1977: 128). Also see Burstein et al. (1975: 80) and Nightingale (1982: 129–33) for somewhat more detailed typologies of job and workplace characteristics that can influence job satisfaction. Ospina (1996) focuses on workers' perceptions about the justness of the opportunity structure in addition to work rewards and work orientations as determinants of job satisfaction.

60. Kalleberg (1977) uses the term "work values" to describe what we have been calling "work orientations" or "work preferences." Hall (1986: 95–99) reviews job satisfaction literature from several decades and also concludes that work preferences are less important than job characteristics and that intrinsic rewards have a larger impact than do extrinsic rewards.

61. Johnson and Grey (1988: 21); Krahn (1992: 80–81); Wyatt Canada (1991: 3); Betcherman and Lowe (1997: 5). A large Canadian study of management in the public sector shows similar concerns about promotions and career opportunities (Jabes and Zussman, 1988; Zussman and Jabes, 1989).

62. Kalleberg (1977); Nightingale (1982); Hall (1986); Hodson and Sullivan (1990: 101).

63. In order, the quotations are from House (1980: 335), Bailyn and Lynch (1983: 281), Armstrong and Armstrong (1983: 129), and Robertson and Wareham (1987: 29). For additional "tales from the assembly line," see Hamper (1986).

64. The Angus Reid survey was completed for the Royal Bank (see *The Edmonton Journal,* 9 February 1997: B4). Also see Krahn (1992: Chapter 5) for results from the 1989 General Social Survey conducted by Statistics Canada.

65. Krahn (1997: 18). Also see Krahn and Lowe (1997a) for additional results from the Canadian component of the International Adult Literacy Survey (IALS).

66. The 1994 literacy survey (Krahn and Lowe, 1997a) also showed women and youth more likely to be underemployed with respect to use of their reading and writing skills.

67. Hall (1986: 93); Argyle (1989: 250–59).

68. Mars (1982); Hollinger and Clark (1982); Hall (1986: 110); Martin and Roman (1996).

69. See Locke (1976: 1332) on job dissatisfaction and filing grievances. Kochan (1979: 25) links dissatisfaction to willingness to join a union. Berger et al. (1983), Pfeffer and Davis-Blake (1990), Northcott and Lowe (1995), and Gordon and Denisi (1995) reverse the question by asking about the effects of union membership on job satisfaction.

70. Locke (1976: 1333); Macarov (1982); Petty et al. (1984); Iaffaldano and Muchinsky (1985); Hall (1986: 92); Fincham and Rhodes (1988: 96).

71. High levels of productivity in Japanese industry, despite relatively low levels of worker satisfaction (Lincoln and Kalleberg, 1985: 738), suggest that productivity is determined primarily by other factors.

72. Macarov (1982: 71). Tausky (1978: 106–7) suggests that higher training and other costs associated with job redesign might counter any productivity increases due to increased worker satisfaction.

73. Faulkner is quoted by Studs Terkel (1971: xi).

74. See Archibald (1978: 35–43), Grabb (1990: 24–26), Erikson (1990), and Rinehart (1996: 11–21) for additional discussion of Marx's writings on alienation.

75. See Mann (1970) on the "social cohesion of liberal democracy," and Abercrombie et al. (1980) on the "dominant ideology."

76. Seeman (1959, 1967, 1975) has been most influential in developing this conceptual framework.

77. Seeman (1967: 273), for example, defines alienation as "work which is not intrinsically satisfying." Hill (1981: 91) suggests that the social–psychological tradition draws more on Durkheim's analysis of "anomie" than on Marx's writings on alienation.

78. Blauner (1964). Also see Hall (1986: 105–8), who reviews more recent research in response to Blauner's study, and Hodson (1996) who elabortes Blauner's thesis and links it to labour process debates about control.

79. See Archibald (1978: 124–30); Hill (1981: 90–102).

80. Kessler (1983); also see Geran (1992).

81. McDonald and Doyle (1981); Baker (1985); House (1981, 1987); Quick et al. (1987); Geran (1992).

82. See Selye (1976); Kasl (1978); Lowe and Northcott (1986); Lowe (1989); Karasek and Theorell (1990); and Roberts and Baugher (1995).

83. Karasek (1979); Karasek and Theorell (1990); Sauter et al. (1989).

84. Hamilton and Wright (1986: 266); also see Lowe and Northcott (1986).

85. The study, conducted by *Macworld* magazine, also revealed that 65 percent of the managers surveyed felt this practice was ethically acceptable (*Edmonton Journal*, 10 June 1993). Also see Howard (1985: 31), Booth (1987), DeTienne (1993), and Menzies (1996: 117–22) on electronic surveillance.

86. Kahn (1981). Also see Johnson (1989) for a comparison with the "demand–control" model.

87. Leiter (1991). Also see Wallace and Brinkerhoff (1991) on the measurement of "burnout."

88. Quotations from Duffy and Pupo (1992: 134) and Johnson and Abramovitch (1987: 2); also see Lowe (1989) on "women, paid/unpaid work, and stress."

89. Staines (1980); also see Martin and Roman (1996), who link excessive use of alcohol away from work to job dissatisfaction.

90. Kohn and Schooler (1983: 152); also see Kohn (1990); Miller et al. (1979); and Miller et al. (1985).

91. Menaghan (1991) makes similar arguments about "work experiences and family interactions." Krahn and Lowe (1997a) propose that underutilization of literacy skills at work can lead to the loss of such skills. Schooler (1984) develops a more general theory of "psychological effects of complex environments" that has applicability beyond the workplace.

CONCLUSION

This discussion of work, industry, and Canadian society has ranged widely over many different topics. We have tried to review and synthesize key theoretical debates in the sociology of work and industry and, at the same time, document emerging industrial, technological, labour market, and workplace trends. Instead of attempting a detailed summary of all the issues we have covered, we conclude by highlighting some of the major themes in current debates about changing labour markets and workplaces. If there is one metatheme linking the many subjects addressed in this book, it is this: a clear understanding of the factors affecting work and of the alternatives to existing workplace arrangements are essential preconditions for initiating and directing changes that could benefit more Canadians.

Debates about the emerging postindustrial society have been part of sociological discourse for several decades and will no doubt continue. But it is already clear that, like all major industrialized nations, Canada has become a service-based society. Natural resource, construction, and manufacturing industries will continue to play an important, if diminished, role in the economy. But it is the service sector, and the kinds of jobs it provides, that now dominates. Today, 3 out of 4 employed Canadians depend on the service sector for their livelihood. Some service industry jobs are highly skilled and well paying, yet a substantial number are relatively unskilled and less rewarding. Clearly one of the characteristics of the new postindustrial economy is the sharp distinction between "good jobs" and "bad jobs." In particular, while a majority of working Canadians are still employed in permanent, full-time jobs, nonstandard work continues to increase.

Equally important demographic changes have been quietly transforming the Canadian workforce. In particular, the population is slowly aging and the implications of this trend are only beginning to be understood. As the baby boom generation moves into middle age during an era of economic retrenchment, many members of this large and privileged cohort are finding their careers have plateaued. At the same time, younger labour force participants, many of them well educated, are having considerable difficulty finding good jobs. Will this situation change as older workers retire, allowing a smaller cohort of younger labour force participants to fill their positions? Will there be a generation that was bypassed in the process? And will most of the larger cohort of older workers be able to retire with income security, or will the large group of working poor Canadians become a large group of retired poor?

These questions highlight the issue of growing social inequality in Canadian society, clearly the most disturbing trend we have observed. After three decades of growth, family incomes are no longer increasing in real terms. Nonstandard jobs have become more common. The ranks of the working poor are growing and structural unemployment continues to be problematic. The causes are complex and intertwined, but involve transformation of the global economy, the use of new technologies as labour replacements, shrinking employment in the goods-producing sector, polarization within the growing service sector, changing skill requirements in both sectors, and the popularity of downsizing and the growing reliance on nonstandard workers by employers. Together, these trends are creating a more segmented labour market in terms of income and benefits, job security, and skill requirements.

However, we are not convinced by the overly pessimistic futurists like Jeremy Rifkin (1995) who predict "the end of work" and a society in which the majority do not have employment. Current labour market and economic trends simply do not support such predictions. Nor do we accept that the future labour market will be "dejobbed," that traditional paid jobs will be largely replaced by a fluid arrangement of postmodern contractual employment relationships (Bridges 1994). From our perspective, such predictions are more ideological justifications for the current heavy reliance on nonstandard workers than generalizations based on real trends. Nevertheless, there is evidence of growing polarization in the labour market, greater inequality in society as a whole, and increased anxiety among Canadians about their employment future and standard of living (Betcherman and Lowe 1997). The important question is whether we can do something about it.

Overlaid on the trend toward a more polarized labour market are inequities based on gender, age, race and ethnicity, disability, and region. With respect to the latter, some regions of the country remain underdeveloped, largely bypassed by the economic growth experienced by others. The lack of opportunities, outright discrimination, and other employment barriers faced by women, people with disabilities, racial and ethnic minorities, and Aboriginal Canadians are still very evident in Canadian society. When we look back at the long and difficult battles fought by organized labour to obtain the employment rights and standard of living we take for granted today, we are reminded that social inequities such as these are not easily eliminated. And as we look into the future, we recognize once again that some of the disturbing employment trends are age-differentiated. Because of the downsizing and work organization restructuring that has occurred in the past decade, the youngest labour force participants are having difficulty starting careers while the oldest are worried about income security in retirement.

Even so, there are a few signs of positive change. Over the past few decades, women have made some progress in their quest for labour market equality. Acknowledging the present flaws of employment equity and pay equity policies, their very existence has nevertheless begun a slow process of institutional change. Although members of visible minorities continue to encounter labour market barriers, there is some evidence that discrimination against them is becoming less acceptable. Unfortunately, beyond the fact that their disadvantaged situation has been officially recognized in federal government employment equity initiatives, we can identify fewer positive employment trends for Aboriginal groups and people with disabilities. Recently, government and employers have begun to concern themselves (again, since we have seen this before) with the "youth employment problem," but as yet, the initiatives intended to address the problem have not been very effective.

Shifting topics, we draw attention to how the computer revolution has placed information technology at the centre of everyday life, at work and in the home. Most Canadians believe that these new technologies have had a positive impact on their work situation, and it is clear that new and challenging jobs have been created. There is also evidence of the new technologies being used to eliminate jobs, deskill others, and increase management control over the labour process. But we need to remember that the effects of technology are not predetermined. Instead, the outcomes are a result of social choices made within particular organizational contexts by real people. Unfortunately, too often workers have not been involved as equal partners in the process of technological change, and the goals of such change have not included job creation and an improved quality of working life. Few would seriously advocate blocking the diffusion of new computer-based technology, given the potential it offers for economic prosperity and an improved quality of life. Rather, the public policy issue is how we can collectively manage technological change in a way that will benefit as many people as possible.

Our examination of new management approaches within Canadian work organizations also identifies conflicting trends. On the one hand, we have documented how downsizing and an overreliance on nonstandard workers have frequently been the substitute for innovative approaches to increasing productivity. Similarly, despite their promise for humanizing work and empowering workers, the new management schemes have frequently been used to push workers harder with no compensation in terms of autonomy, skill enhancement, or improved incomes. Yet, on the other hand, some of the management literature advocates major workplace reforms that put people first, and there are positive examples of the implementation of such reforms. Furthermore, there are important alternatives, including legislated industrial democracy and incentives to encourage worker ownership, that could lead to more worker autonomy, increased job security, and reduced social inequality. The challenge will be to convince employers of the benefits of real workplace reform and to assist workers in their struggle to obtain it.

The organized labour movement in Canada has reacted to the new technologies and new management schemes with some uncertainty. Some unions have strongly resisted change while others have been willing to accept it, so long as job and income security have been maintained. Others have insisted on being active partners in the change process, in return for their cooperation. Where equal-partner status has been obtained, and where real consultation took place, the outcomes have often been positive. Recognizing that unions have been responsible for many of the gains made by working Canadians over the past century, it is extremely important, in our opinion, to maintain and strengthen the labour legislation that has allowed this to happen. At the same time, we need to find ways to support and protect workers not currently covered by union contracts. The alternative may be a more segmented and polarized labour market, and greater social inequality.

Over the past decade, there has been some public policy debate about the social issues of unemployment, poverty, and growing inequality. But more often, the debate has had an economic tone, focusing on concerns about flexibility and competitiveness. Clearly, we have no quarrel with the desire to be competitive in the global economy, and recognize that greater labour market flexibility may be useful. But, as our comments throughout this book suggest, we are critical of single-factor solutions to the competitiveness problem that do not take job creation, the need for good jobs, and social equality into account.

Becoming more competitive could mean more than just leaner and meaner ways to increase corporate profits. From the perspective of individual workers, it could reflect the removal of barriers that prevent them from competing for good jobs and improving their standard of living. From the perspective of communities and regions in the country, it might indicate increased opportunities to benefit equally from economic growth. We are also unwilling to accept that flexibility has only one meaning, namely, that Canadian workers should be willing to accept whatever work opportunities they are offered by employers. Flexibility can also describe labour market and workplace policies that provide workers with a wider array of options to improve their standard of living and quality of life (Kamerman and Kahn 1987). It might also refer to the willingness of corporations to consider job creation, local economic development, and other social goals as being on par with profit-making.

Training and education have been heavily promoted in the past decade as a solution to the disadvantaged labour market position of some workers and, in the aggregate, as a way of improving Canada's economic position. Clearly, human resource development of this sort is important. By obtaining additional education and training, some individuals can better compete for good jobs. Similarly, with a better stock of human capital, Canada can be more competitive. Investments in human capital may, perhaps, even lead to more job creation. But this is a long-term solution that, by itself, will not solve current problems of unemployment (Osberg et al. 1995; Swift 1995). Nor will it alter the position of the thousands of well-educated but underemployed working Canadians. In fact, in the absence of employment opportunities that allow workers to use their education and skills, we may be at risk of losing some of our current stock of human capital (Krahn 1997; Krahn and Lowe 1997a). Thus, the larger and more immediate problem is simply one of not enough good jobs. And this is a problem that is not being addressed by employers, who are cutting more jobs than they create, or by the provincial and federal governments, which have been backing away from active labour market intervention.

The critical question is really about our societal goals. Is economic competitiveness at any social cost our objective? Or would Canadians prefer that the primary goal be a better quality of life, achieved through a reasonable standard of living, employment security, and good opportunities for personally rewarding work? If it is the latter, and we believe it should be, then a political response is also needed. As we have argued at various places in this book, a "let the market decide" approach (basically the position of the federal and most provincial governments over the past decade) is unlikely to assist us in reaching these social goals. This crucial point is echoed by Daniel Drache and Meric Gertler (1991: 19):

> When trade sets the economic agenda for a society, a society is also letting market forces set the social and political agenda … a society that puts competitiveness ahead of any other single concern is prevented from dealing with challenges posed by a labour surplus policy and by its need to harmonize its public policies with those of its trading partners. To prevent the growth of short- and long-term unemployment and the worsening of wage and household inequality, innovative measures are needed to create a fundamentally different policy mix.

What form might these innovative measures take? The solutions proposed by Drache and Gertler acknowledge the need for a comprehensive industrial strategy involving government, employers, and organized labour. Such a strategy would improve the chances of a successful transition to a high-technology, information-based economy by promoting coordinated planning and encouraging innovation through increased research and development. Equally important are income security (perhaps through a guaranteed annual income for all adult Canadians), improved training, job creation, flexible production processes but with the maintenance of employment and pay standards, pay equity and antidiscrimination legislation, legislation to assist workers dislocated through industrial restructuring, and a broad-based environmental agenda based on sustainable development. This is a long "wish list," to be sure. Yet, as Drache and Gertler argue, the basic question really is about the direction in which Canadians wish to go at this critical time in our history:

> [T]he most important decision facing Canada is whether to let itself be shaped by the global market or whether … Canadians will determine their own future. The choice is essentially a political one. If governments do not invest in people and protect their citizens from the uncertainty of global competition, positive economic change will not happen on the ground where it counts most. No amount of persuasion will convince people to accept

> change as a normal part of modern economic life, let alone accept the need for greater flexibility in the workplace and outside of it.[1]

Recognizing a similar trend toward greater social inequality in their country, a number of American writers have also begun to call for an industrial policy with social as well as economic goals. Seymour Bellin and S.M. Miller, for example, argue that governments must reject the idea that high unemployment is natural, or necessary, for global competitiveness. They recommend that employment growth should be driven less by defence spending and more by investments in people. They call for a higher minimum wage to lift the bottom tier of workers out of poverty; stronger plant shutdown legislation to protect workers at risk of losing their jobs; national health insurance; affirmative action programs; and more training programs (Bellin and Miller 1990; Lonnroth 1994).

Robert Reich, commenting on American society but with observations relevant to Canada as well, also alerts us to the connection between economic globalization and polarization within national economies. In his view, left as things are, we will see further inequality between nations and within industrialized capitalist nations. In his words:

> The choice is ours to make. We are no more slaves to present trends than to vestiges of the past. We can, if we choose, assert that our mutual obligations as citizens extend beyond our economic usefulness to one another, and act accordingly (Reich 1991: 313).

We agree.

NOTES

1. Drache and Gertler (1991: 22). Also see Myles (1991), Osberg et al. (1995), Osberg and Fortin (1996), and a special issue of *Policy Options* (July–August 1996) for additional discussion of policy responses to unemployment and inequality. John Raulston Saul (1995) addresses similar questions in his discussions of the tension between marketplace economics and democratic principles.

REFERENCES

Abella, Irving **1974** "Oshawa 1937." In Irving Abella, ed., *On Strike: Six Key Labour Struggles in Canada 1919–1949.* Toronto: James Lewis and Samuel.

Abercrombie, Nicholas, S. Hill, and B. S. Turner **1980** *The Dominant Ideology Thesis.* London: George Allen and Unwin.

Acker, Joan **1988** "Women and work in the social sciences." In Ann Helton Stromberg and Shirley Harkess, eds., *Women Working: Theories and Facts in Perspective.* 2nd ed. Mountain View, CA: Mayfield Publishing.

Acker, Joan, and Donald R. Van Houten **1974** "Differential recruitment and control: the sex structuring of organizations." *Administrative Science Quarterly* 19: 152–63.

Adams, Roy J. **1989** "Industrial relations systems: Canada in comparative perspective." In John C. Anderson, Morley Gunderson, and Allen Ponak, eds., *Union–Management Relations in Canada.* 2d ed. Don Mills, ON: Addison-Wesley.

———**1995** "Canadian industrial relations in comparative perspective." In Morley Gunderson and Allen Ponak, eds., *Union–Management Relations in Canada,* 3d ed. Don Mills, ON: Addison-Wesley Publishers.

Aguren, Stefan, Christer Bredbacka, Reine Hansson, Kurt Ihregren, and K. G. Karlson **1985** *Volvo Kalmar Revisited: Ten Years of Experience.* Stockholm: Efficiency and Participation Development Council.

Aikenhead, Sherri **1991** "Has amended labour code crippled the unions?" *The Edmonton Journal* (3 February): E1, E3.

Ainley, Pat **1993** *Class and Skill: Changing Divisions of Knowledge and Labour.* London: Cassell Educational Limited.

Akyeampong, Ernest B. **1989** "Discouraged workers." *Perspectives on Labour and Income* (Autumn): 64–69.

———**1992a** "Absences from work revisited." *Perspectives on Labour and Income* (Spring): 44–53.

———**1992b** "Discouraged workers—where have they gone?" *Perspectives on Labour and Income* 4: 38–44.

———**1995** "Missing work." *Perspectives on Labour and Income* (Spring) 12–16.

———**1997a** "The labour market: year-end review." *Perspectives on Labour and Income* (Spring): 9–17.

———**1997b** "Work arrangements: 1995 overview." *Perspectives on Labour and Income* (Spring): 48–52.

Alberta Government, Personnel Administration Office **1991** *Balancing Work and Family: Survey Results.* Edmonton: Personnel Administration Office, Alberta Government, July.

Albrow, Martin **1970** *Bureaucracy.* London: Macmillan.

Alestalo, Matti, and Stein Kuhnle **1986–1987** "The Scandinavian route: economic, social, and political developments in Denmark, Finland, Norway, and Sweden." *International Journal of Sociology* 16: 3–38.

Althauser, Robert P. **1989** "Internal labor markets." *Annual Review of Sociology* 15: 143–61.

Althauser, Robert P., and Arne L. Kalleberg **1981** "Firms, occupations and the structure of labor markets: a conceptual analysis." In Ivar Berg, ed., *Sociological Perspectives on Labor Markets.* London: Academic Press.

Alvi, Shahid. **1995** *Eldercare and the Workplace..* Ottawa: Conference Board of Canada, 150–95.

References

American Federation of Labour (AFL–CIO) 1995 *What's Wrong With Right-to-Work: A Tale of Two Nations.* Revised ed. Washington, DC: AFL–CIO.

Amin, Samir 1976 *Unequal Development.* New York: Monthly Review.

Anderson, Kay J. 1991 *Vancouver's Chinatown: Racial Discourse in Canada, 1875–1980.* Montreal & Kingston: McGill–Queen's University Press.

Angus, Charlie, and Brit Griffin 1996 *We Lived a Life and Then Some: The Life, Death, and Life of a Mining Town.* Toronto: Between the Lines.

Angus Reid Interactive 1996 "Loyalty at work." (17 October): 1–3.

Anisef, Paul, and Paul Axelrod, eds. 1993 *Transitions: Schooling and Employment in Canada.* Toronto: Thompson Educational Publishing.

Anisef, Paul J., Gottfried Paasche, and Anton H. Turrittin 1980 *Is the Die Cast? Educational Achievements and Work Destinations of Ontario Youth.* Toronto: Ontario Ministry of Colleges and Universities.

Anthony, P. D. 1977 *The Ideology of Work.* London: Tavistock.

Antoniou, Andreas, and Robin Rowley 1986 "The ownership structure of the largest Canadian corporations, 1979." *Canadian Journal of Sociology* 11: 253–68.

Antos, Joseph R., Mark Chandler, and Wesley Mellow 1980 "Sex differences in union membership." *Industrial and Labor Relations Review* 33: 162–69.

Apostle, Richard, and Gene Barrett 1992 *Emptying Their Nets: Small Capital and Rural Industrialization in the Nova Scotia Fishing Industry.* Toronto: University of Toronto Press.

Apostle, Richard, D. Clairmont, and L. Osberg 1985 "Segmentation and wage determination." *Canadian Review of Sociology and Anthropology* 22: 30–56.

Applebaum, Eileen, and Rosemary Batt 1994 The New American Workplace: Transforming Work Systems in the Unites States. Ithaca, NY: ILR Press.

Archibald, W. Peter 1978 *Social Psychology as Political Economy.* Toronto: McGraw-Hill Ryerson.

Argyle, Michael 1989 *The Social Psychology of Work.* 2d ed. London: Penguin.

Armstrong, Pat, and Hugh Armstrong 1983 *A Working Majority: What Women Must Do for Pay.* Ottawa: Canadian Advisory Council on the Status of Women.

———**1990** *Theorizing Women's Work.* Toronto: Garamond Press.

———**1994** *The Double Ghetto: Canadian Women and Their Segregated Work.* 3rd ed. Toronto: McClelland and Stewart.

Armstrong, Pat, Jacqueline Choiniere, and Elaine Day 1993 *Vital Signs: Nursing in Transition.* Toronto: Garamond Press.

Armstrong, Pat, Jacqueline Choiniere, Gina Feldberg, and Jerry White 1994 "Voices from the ward: a study of the impact of cutbacks." In Hugh Armstrong, Jacqueline Choiniere, Gina Feldberg, Jerry White, Pat Armstrong, eds., *Take Care: Warning Signals for Canada's Health System.* Toronto: Garamond Press.

Aronowitz, S. 1973 *False Promises: The Shaping of American Working Class Consciousness.* New York: McGraw-Hill.

Arsen, David D. 1996 "The NAFTA debate in retrospect: U.S. perspectives." *Policy Choices: Free Trade Among NAFTA Nations.* Karen Roberts and Mark I. Wilson, eds. East Lansing: Michigan State University Press.

Arsen, David D., Mark I. Wilson, and Jonas Zoninsein 1996 "Trends in manufacturing employment in the NAFTA region: evidence of a giant sucking sound?" *Policy Choices: Free Trade Among NAFTA Nations,* Karen Roberts and Mark I. Wilson, eds. East Lansing: Michigan State University Press.

Ashton, David 1986 *Unemployment Under Capitalism: The Sociology of British and American Labour Markets.* Brighton: Wheatsheaf Books.

Ashton, David, and Graham Lowe, eds. 1991 *Making Their Way: Education, Training and the Labour Market in Canada and Britain.* Toronto: University of Toronto Press.

Aston, T. H., and C. H. E. Philpin, eds. 1985 *The Brenner Debate: Agrarian Class Structure and Economic Development in Pre-Industrial Europe.* Cambridge: Cambridge University Press.

Atkinson, J. 1984 *Flexibility, Uncertainty and Manpower Management.* Brighton: Institute of Manpower Studies Report No. 89.

———1985 "Flexibility: planning for an uncertain future." *Manpower Policy and Practice* 1 (Summer): 26–29.

Attewell, Paul 1987 "The deskilling controversy." *Work and Occupations* 14: 323–46.

Auditor General of Canada 1988 *Attributes of Well-Performing Organizations.* Extract from the 1988 Annual Report of the Auditor General of Canada. Ottawa: Supply and Services Canada.

Avery, Donald H. 1995 *Reluctant Host: Canada's Response to Immigrant Workers, 1896–1994.* Toronto: McClelland and Stewart.

Babcock, Robert H. 1974 *Gompers in Canada: A Study in American Continentalism Before the First World War.* Toronto: University of Toronto Press.

Baer, Douglas E., Edward Grabb, and William A. Johnston 1991 "Class, crisis and political ideology in Canada: recent trends." *Canadian Review of Sociology and Anthropology* 24: 1–22.

Bailyn, Lotte, and John T. Lynch 1983 "Engineering as a life-long career: its meaning, its satisfactions, its difficulties." *Journal of Occupational Behaviour* 4: 263–83.

Bain, George S. 1978 *Union Growth and Public Policy in Canada.* Ottawa: Labour Canada.

Bain, George S., and H. A. Clegg 1974 "A strategy for industrial relations research in Britain." *British Journal of Industrial Relations* 12: 91–113.

Baker, D.B. 1985 "The study of stress at work." *Annual Review of Public Health* 6: 367–81.

Baldamus, W. 1961 *Efficiency and Effort: An Analysis of Industrial Administration.* London: Tavistock Publications.

Bank of Montreal 1991 *Task Force on the Advancement of Women in the Bank.* Report to Employees.

———1993 *Advancing Workplace Equality.* Second Milestone Report.

Barbash, Jack 1979 "Collective bargaining and the theory of conflict." *Relations industrielles/Industrial Relations* 34: 646–49.

Barker, Jane, and Hazel Downing 1985 "Word processing and the transformation of patriarchal relations of control in the office." In Donald Mackenzie and Judy Wajcman, eds., *The Social Shaping of Technology.* Milton Keynes: Open University Press.

Barlow, Maude, and Heather-Jane Robertson 1994 *Class Warfare: The Assault on Canada's Schools.* Toronto: Key Porter Books.

Barnard, Chester 1938 *The Functions of the Executive.* Cambridge, MA: Harvard University Press.

Barnet, Richard J., and John Cavanagh 1994 *Global Dreams: Imperial Corporations and the New World Order.* New York: Touchstone.

Basset, Penny 1994 "Declining female labour force participation." *Perspectives on Labour and Income* (Summer): 36–39.

Batstone, Eric, Ian Boraston, and Stephen Frenkel 1978 *The Social Organization of Strikes.* Oxford: Basil Blackwell.

Baureiss, Gunter 1987 "Chinese immigration, Chinese stereotypes, and Chinese labour." *Canadian Ethnic Studies* 19: 15–34.

Beach, Charles M., and George A. Slotsve 1996 "The distribution of earnings and income in Canada." *Policy Options* (July–August): 42–45.

Beaud, Michel 1983 *A History of Capitalism 1500–1980.* New York: Monthly Review.

Beaumont, P. B. 1995 *The Future of Employment Relations.* London: Sage.

Becker, Gary S. 1975 *Human Capital: A Theoretical and Empirical Analysis with Special Reference to Education.* 2d. ed. Chicago: University of Chicago Press.

Beckett, Elizabeth 1984 *Unions and Bank Workers: Will the Twain Ever Meet?* Ottawa: Labour Canada, Women's Bureau.

Beechy, Veronica 1987 *Unequal Work.* London: Verso.

Bélanger, Jacques, P. K. Edwards, and Larry Haiven, eds. 1994 *Workplace Industrial Relations and the Global Challenge.* Ithaca, New York: ILR Press.

Bell, Daniel 1973 *The Coming of Post-Industrial Society.* New York: Basic Books.

Bellamy, Lesley Andres 1993 "Life trajectories, action, and negotiating the transition from high school." In Paul Anisef and Paul Axelrod, eds., *Transitions: Schooling and Employment in Canada.* Toronto: Thompson Educational Publishing.

Bellin, Seymour S., and S. M. Miller 1990 "The split society." In Kai Erikson and Steven Peter Vallas, eds., *The Nature of Work: Sociological Perspectives.* New Haven: American Sociological Association and Yale University Press.

Bendix, Reinhard 1974 *Work and Authority in Industry.* Berkeley: University of California Press.

Bercuson, David J. 1974 *Confrontation at Winnipeg: Labour, Industrial Relations, and the General Strike.* Montreal: McGill–Queen's University Press.

Berg, Maxine 1988 "Women's work, mechanization and the early phases of industrialization in England." In R. E. Pahl, ed., *On Work: Historical, Comparative and Theoretical Approaches.* Oxford: Basil Blackwell.

Berger, Chris. J., C. A. Olson, and J. W. Boudreau 1983 "Effects of unions on job satisfaction: the role of work-related values and perceived rewards." *Organizational Behavior and Human Performance* 32: 289–324.

Berle, Adolf A., and Gardiner C. Means 1968 *The Modern Corporation and Private Property.* rev. ed. New York: Harcourt, Brace and World. [Originally published in 1932.]

Bernard, Richard B., and Michael R. Smith 1991 "Hiring, promotion, and pay in a corporate head office: an internal labour market in action?" *Canadian Journal of Sociology* 16: 353–74.

Bernhardt, Annette, Martina Morris, and Mark S. Handcock 1995 "Women's gains or men's losses? A closer look at the shrinking gender gap in earnings." *American Journal of Sociology* 101: 302–28.

Bernier, Suzanne 1995 "Youth combining school and work." *Education Quarterly Review* 2: 10–23.

Best, Fred J. 1990 "Work sharing: an underused policy for combating unemployment?" In Kai Erikson and Steven Peter Vallas, eds. *The Nature of Work: Sociological Perspectives.* New Haven: American Sociological Association and Yale University Press.

Betcherman, Gordon 1993 "Research gaps facing training policy-makers." *Canadian Public Policy* 19: 18–28.

———**1995** "Workplace transformation in Canada: policies and practices." *Managing Human Resources in the 1990s and Beyond.* Bryan Downie and Mary L. Coates eds. Kingston, ON: IRC Press, Queen's University.

Betcherman, Gordon, and Graham Lowe 1997 *The Future of Work in Canada: A Synthesis Report.* Ottawa: Canadian Policy Research Networks Inc.

Betcherman, Gordon, and Norm Leckie 1995 "Age structure of employment in industries and occupations." Ottawa: Human Resources Development Canada, Applied Research Branch, Research Paper (no. R-96–7E).

———1997 *Youth Employment and Education Trends in the 1980s and 1990s.* Ottawa: Canadian Policy Research Networks (CPRN) Working Paper no. W03.

Betcherman, Gordon, and Rene Morissette 1994 *Recent Youth Labour Market Experiences in Canada.* Ottawa: Analytic Studies Branch, Statistics Canada.

Betcherman, Gordon, Kathryn McMullen, Norm Leckie, and Christina Caron, eds. 1994 *The Canadian Workplace in Transition.* Kingston: IRC Press.

Betcherman, Gordon, Keith Newton, and Joanne Godin, eds. 1990 *Two Steps Forward: Human Resource Management in a High-Technology World.* Ottawa: Economic Council of Canada.

Beynon, H. 1984 *Working for Ford.* 2d ed. Harmondsworth, England: Penguin Books.

Bielby, Denise B., and William T. Bielby 1988 "She works hard for her money: household responsibilities and the allocation of work effort." *American Journal of Sociology* 93: 1031–59.

Billing, Yvonne D. 1994 "Gender and bureaucracies—a feminist critique of Ferguson's 'The feminist case against bureaucracy.'" *Gender, Work and Organization* 1: 179–93.

Birdi, Kamal, Peter Warr, and Andrew Oswald 1995 "Age differences in three components of employee well-being." *Applied Psychology: An International Review* 44: 345–373.

Black, Don, and John Myles 1986 "Dependent industrialization and the Canadian class structure: a comparative analysis of Canada, the United States and Sweden." *Canadian Review of Sociology and Anthropology* 23: 157–81.

Blackburn, R. M. 1988 "Ideologies of work." In David Rose, ed., *Social Stratification and Economic Change.* London: Hutchinson.

Blackburn, R.M., and Michael Mann 1979 *The Working Class in the Labour Market.* London: Macmillan.

Blackburn, Robert M., Jennifer Jarman, and Janet Siltanen 1993 "The analysis of occupational gender segregation over time and place: considerations of measurement and some new evidence." *Work, Employment & Society* 7: 335–62.

Blau, Francine D., and Marianne A. Ferber 1986 *The Economics of Women, Men and Work.* Englewood Cliffs, NJ: Prentice-Hall.

Blau, Peter M. 1963 *The Dynamics of Bureaucracy.* 2d ed. Chicago: University of Chicago Press.

Blau, Peter M., and Otis Dudley Duncan 1967 *The American Occupational Structure.* New York: John Wiley and Sons.

Blau, Peter M., and W. Richard Scott 1963 *Formal Organizations: A Comparative Approach.* London: Routledge and Kegan Paul.

Blaug, Mark 1985 "Where are we now in the economics of education?" *Economics of Education Review* 4: 17–28.

Blauner, Robert 1964 *Alienation and Freedom: The Factory Worker and His Industry.* Chicago: University of Chicago Press.

Bleasdale, Ruth 1981 "Class conflict on the canals of Upper Canada in the 1840s." *Labour/Le Travailleur* 7: 9–39.

Blishen, Bernard R., W. K. Carroll, and C. Moore 1987 "The 1981 socioeconomic index for occupations in Canada." *Canadian Review of Sociology and Anthropology* 24: 465–88.

Block, Fred 1990 *Postindustrial Possibilities: A Critique of Economic Discourse.* Berkeley, CA: University of California Press.

Bloom, Michael 1990 *Reaching for Success: Business and Education Working Together.* Ottawa: Conference Board of Canada.

———1995 *Ethical Guidelines for Business–Education Partnerships.* Report 153-95. Ottawa: Conference Board of Canada.

Bluestone, Barry, and Bennett Harrison 1982 *The Deindustrialization of America.* New York: Basic Books.

Bognanno, Mario F., and Kathryn J. Ready, eds. 1993 *The North American Free Trade Agreement: Labor, Industry, and Government Perspectives.* Westport, CT: Praeger.

Boivin, Jean, and Esther Déom 1995 "Labour–management relations in Quebec." *Union–Management Relations in Canada,* 3d ed. Morely Gunderson and Allen Ponak, eds. Don Mills, ON: Addison-Wesley Publishers.

Bonacich, Edna 1972 "A theory of labour market antagonism: the split labour market." *American Sociological Review* 37: 547–59.

Boone, Louis E., David L. Kurtz, and C. Patrick Fleenor 1988 "The road to the top." *American Demographics* (March): 34–37.

Booth, Patricia 1997 *Contingent Work: Trends, Issues and Challenges for Employers.* Report 192–97. Ottawa: Conference Board of Canada.

Booth, William 1987 "Big Brother is counting your keystrokes." *Science* (2 October): 17.

Boothby, Daniel 1993 "Schooling, literacy and the labour market: towards a 'literacy shortage'?" *Canadian Public Policy* 19: 29–35.

Borman, Kathryn M. 1991 *The First "Real" Job: A Study of Young Workers.* Albany, NY: State University of New York Press.

Boulet, Jac-Andre, and Laval Lavallée 1984 *The Changing Economic Status of Women.* Ottawa: Supply and Services Canada (Economic Council of Canada).

Bourdieu, Pierre 1986 "The forms of capital." In J.C. Richardson, ed., *Handbook of Theory and Research for the Sociology of Education.* New York: Greenwood Press.

Bourette, Susan 1997 "Organized labour lures growing number of youth." *The Globe and Mail* (4 July 1997): B1.

Bowden, Gary 1989 "Labour unions in the public mind: the Canadian case." *Canadian Review of Sociology and Anthropology* 26: 723–42.

Bowier, Rita 1991 "Education and change for Aboriginal people in Canada." In R. Ghosh and D. Day, eds., *Social Change and Education in Canada.* Toronto: Harcourt Brace Jovanovich.

Bowles, Roy T. 1982 *Little Communities and Big Industries: Studies in the Social Impact of Canadian Resource Extraction.* Toronto: Butterworths.

Boyd, Monica 1985 "Revising the stereotype: variations in female labour force interruptions." Paper presented at the annual meetings of the Canadian Sociology and Anthropology Association and the Canadian Population Society, Montreal.

———1990 "Sex differences in occupational skill: Canada, 1961–1986." *Canadian Review of Sociology and Anthropology* 27: 285–315.

Boyd, Monica, J. Goyder, F. E. Jones, H. A. McRoberts, P. C. Pineo, and J. Porter 1985 *Ascription and Achievement: Studies in Mobility and Status Attainment in Canada.* Ottawa: Carleton University Press.

Boyer, Robert, and Daniel Drache, eds. **1996** *States Against Markets: The Limits of Globalization.* London: Routledge.

———**1996** "Introduction." In *States Against Markets: The Limits of Globalization.* London: Routledge.

Boyett, Joseph H., and Henry P. Conn **1991** *Workplace 2000: The Revolution Reshaping American Business.* New York: Dutton.

Bradbury, Bettina **1993** *Working Families: Age, Gender, and Daily Survival in Industrializing Montreal.* 3d ed. Toronto: McClelland and Stewart.

Bradley, Harriet **1989** *Men's Work, Women's Work: A Sociological History of the Sexual Division of Labour in Employment.* Cambridge: Polity Press.

Bradley, Keith, and Stephen Hill **1983** "After Japan: the quality circle transplant and productive efficiency." *British Journal of Industrial Relations* 21: 291–311.

Bradwin, Edmund **1972** *The Bunkhouse Man: A Study of Work and Pay in the Camps of Canada.* Toronto: University of Toronto Press. [Originally published in 1928.]

Braus, Patricia **1992** "What workers want." *American Demographics* (August): 30–37.

Braverman, Harry **1974** *Labor and Monopoly Capital: The Degradation of Work in the Twentieth Century.* New York: Monthly Review Press.

Breen, Richard, and David B. Rottman **1995** *Class Stratification: A Comparative Perspective.* London: Harvester Wheatsheaf.

Bridges, William **1994** *JobShift: How to Prosper in a Workplace without Jobs.* Don Mills, ON: Addison-Wesley.

Briskin, Linda, and Patricia McDermott **1993** *Women Challenging Unions: Feminism, Democracy, and Militancy.* Toronto: University of Toronto Press.

British Columbia Public Sector Employers' Council **1995** *Pay Equity Policy Framework.* (website: www.bcpsca.bc.ca)

Brown, Leslie H. **1997** "Organizations for the 21st century? Co-operatives and 'new' forms of organization." *Canadian Journal of Sociology* 22: 65–93.

Brown, Lorne **1987** *When Freedom Was Lost: The Unemployed, The Agitator, and the State.* Montreal: Black Rose Books.

Brym, Robert **1996** "The third Rome and the end of history: notes on Russia's second communist revolution." *Canadian Review of Sociology and Anthropology* 33: 391–406.

Bulmer, Martin **1975** *Working Class Images of Society.* London: Routledge and Kegan Paul.

Burawoy, Michael **1979** *Manufacturing Consent: Changes in the Labor Process under Monopoly Capitalism.* Chicago: University of Chicago Press.

———**1984** "Karl Marx and the satanic mills: factory politics under early capitalism in England, the United States, and Russia." *American Journal of Sociology* 90: 247–82.

Burchell, Brendan, and Jill Rubery **1990** "An empirical investigation into the segmentation of the labour supply." *Work, Employment & Society* 4: 551–75.

Burman, Patrick **1988** *Killing Time, Losing Ground: Experiences of Unemployment.* Toronto: Wall & Thompson.

———**1996** *Poverty's Bonds: Power and Agency in the Social Relations of Welfare.* Toronto: Thompson Educational Publishing.

Burnham, J. **1941** *The Managerial Revolution.* Harmondsworth, England: Penguin.

Burns, T., and G. M. Stalker **1961** *The Management of Innovation.* London: Tavistock Publications.

Burrell, Gibson, and Gareth Morgan **1979** *Sociological Paradigms and Organizational Analysis: Elements of the Sociology of Corporate Life.* London: Heinemann.

Burstein, M., N. Tienharra, P. Hewson, and B. Warrander **1975** *Canadian Work Values: Findings of a Work Ethic Survey and a Job Satisfaction Survey.* Ottawa: Information Canada.

Butler, Peter M. **1980** Establishments and the work–welfare mix. *Canadian Review of Sociology and Anthropology* 17: 138–53.

Butlin, George **1995** "Adult women's participation rate at a standstill." *Perspectives on Labour and Income* (Autumn): 30–33.

Byrne, Edmund F. **1990** *Work, Inc.: A Philosophical Inquiry.* Philadelphia: Temple University Press.

Calás, Marta B., and Linda Smircich **1996** "From 'the woman's point of view': feminist approaches to organization studies." In *Handbook of Organization Studies,* Eds. Stewart R. Clegg, Cynthia Hardy, and Walter R. Nord. London: Sage, 218–57.

Calliste, Agnes **1987** "Sleeping car porters in Canada: an ethnically submerged split labour market." *Canadian Ethnic Studies* 19: 1–20.

Campbell, Robert M. **1991** "The full-employment objective in Canada in the postwar period." In Surendra Gera, ed., *Canadian Unemployment: Lessons from the 80s and Challenges for the 90s.* Ottawa: Economic Council of Canada.

Canada **1969** *Canadian Industrial Relations: The Report of the Task Force on Labour Relations.* Ottawa: Queen's Printer.

———**1984** *Report of the Commission on Equality in Employment* [The Abella Report]. Ottawa: Supply and Services.

———**1985** *Employment Equity Act.* Chapter 23, 2nd Supplement, Revised Statutes of Canada.

———**1992** *A Matter of Fairness. Report of the Social Committee on the Review of the Employment Equity Act.* Ottawa: House of Commons.

Canada, Department of Labour **1958** *Survey of Married Women Working for Pay in Eight Canadian Cities.* Ottawa: Queen's Printer.

Canadian Advisory Council on the Status of Women **1992** *Re-Evaluating Employment Equity: A Brief to the Special House of Commons Committee on the Review of the Employment Equity Act.* Ottawa: CACSW.

Canadian Committee on Women in Engineering **1992** *More than Just Numbers: Report of the Canadian Committee on Women in Engineering.* Fredericton: Faculty of Engineering, University of New Brunswick.

Canadian Conference of Catholic Bishops **1991** "The crisis of work." Canadian Conference of Catholic Bishops, Work and Solidarity Project.

Canadian Council on Social Development **1996** *The Progress of Canada's Children 1996.* Ottawa: Canadian Council on Social Development.

Canadian Labour Congress (CLC) **1991** *Two Years Under Free Trade: An Assessment.* Ottawa: CLC Free Trade Briefing Document no. 7.

———**1997** *Women's Work: A Report.* Ottawa: Canadian Labour Congress.

Canadian Labour Market and Productivity Centre **1994** *Women and Economic Restructuring: A Report by the Committee on Women and Economic Restructuring.* Ottawa: Canadian Labour Market and Productivity Centre.

Canadian Social Trends **1996** "Projections of visible minority groups, 1991 to 2016." *Canadian Social Trends* (Summer): 3.

———**1997** "Canadian children in the 1990s: selected findings of the National Longitudinal Survey of Children and Youth." *Canadian Social Trends* 44 (Spring): 2–9.

Cant, Sarah, and Ursala Sharma 1995 "The reluctant profession–homeopathy and the search for legitimacy." *Work, Employment & Society* 9: 743–62.

Cappelli, Peter 1992 "Is the 'skills gap' really about attitudes?" Philadelphia: National Center on the Educational Quality of the Workforce, University of Pennsylvania.

Caragata, Warren 1979 *Alberta Labour: A Heritage Untold.* Toronto: James Lorimer.

Carey, Alex 1967 "The Hawthorne studies: a radical criticism." *American Sociological Review* 32: 403–16.

Carroll, William K., John Fox, and Michael D. Ornstein 1982 "The network of directorate links among the largest Canadian firms." *Canadian Review of Sociology and Anthropology* 19: 44–69.

Cascio, Wayne F. 1993 "Downsizing: what do we know? what have we learned?" *Academy of Management Executive* 7: 95–104.

———1996 *Issues of an Aging Workforce in a Changing Society: Cases and Comparisons.* Toronto: University of Toronto, Centre for Studies of Aging.

CAW–Canada (National Automobile, Aerospace and Agricultural Implements Workers Union of Canada) 1988 *CAW Statement on the Reorganization of Work.* North York, ON: CAW.

CAW–Canada Research Group on CAMI 1993 *The CAMI Report: Lean Production in a Unionized Auto Plant.* Willowdale, ON: Canadian Auto Workers Research Department.

Centre for Studies of Aging. 1996. *Issues of an Aging Workforce in a Changing Society: Cases and Comparisons.* Toronto: University of Toronto, Centre for Studies of Aging.

Chaison, Gary N., and Joseph B. Rose 1990 "New directions and divergent paths: the North American labor movements in troubled times." *Proceedings of the Spring Meeting of the Industrial Relations Research Association.* Madison, WI: IRRA.

Chandler, Jr., Alfred D. 1962 *Strategy and Structure: Chapters in the History of the American Industrial Enterprise.* Cambridge, MA: MIT Press.

———1977 *The Visible Hand: The Managerial Revolution in American Business.* Cambridge, MA: Harvard University Press.

Chang, Clara, and Constance Sorrentino 1991 "Union membership statistics in 12 countries." *Monthly Labor Review* (December): 46–53.

Chawla, Raj K. 1992 "The changing profile of dual-earner families." *Perspectives on Labour and Income* (Summer): 22–29.

Chelte, Anthony F., Peter Hess, Russell Fanelli, and William P. Ferris 1989 "Corporate culture as an impediment to employee involvement: when you can't get there from here." *Work and Occupations* 16: 153–64.

Chen, Mervin Y. T., and Thomas G. Regan 1985 *Work in the Changing Canadian Society.* Toronto: Butterworths.

Cherns, A. 1976 "The principles of socio-technical design." *Human Relations* 29: 783–92.

Child, John 1972 "Organizational structure, environment and performance: the role of strategic choice." *Sociology* 6: 2–22.

———1985 "Managerial strategies, new technology and the labour process." In David Knights, Hugh Willmott, and David Collison, eds., *Job Redesign: Critical Perspectives on the Labour Process.* Aldershot, England: Gower.

Chinoy, Ely 1955 *Automobile Workers and the American Dream.* Boston: Beacon Press.

Chirot, Daniel 1986 *Social Change in the Modern Era.* San Diego: Harcourt Brace Jovanovich.

Chui, Tina, and Mary S. Devereaux 1995 "Canada's newest workers." *Perspectives on Labour and Income* (Spring): 17–23.

Church, Elizabeth 1996 "CEO pay packages not always 'justified.'" *The Globe and Mail* (25 September: B12).

Clairmont, Donald, R. Apostle, and R. Kreckel 1983 "The segmentation perspective as a middle-range conceptualization in sociology." *Canadian Journal of Sociology* 8: 245–71.

Clark, Andrew, Andrew Oswald, and Peter Warr 1996 "Is job satisfaction U-shaped in age?" *Journal of Occupational and Organizational Psychology* 69: 57–81.

Clark, R. D. 1982 "Worker participation in health and safety in Canada." *International Labour Review* 121: 199–206.

Clark, S. D. 1978 *The New Urban Poor.* Toronto: McGraw-Hill Ryerson.

Clegg, Stewart R. 1990 *Modern Organizations: Organization Studies in the Postmodern World.* London: Sage.

Clemenson, Heather A. 1989 "Unionization and women in the service sector." *Perspectives on Labour and Income* (Autumn): 30–44.

———**1992** "Are single industry towns diversifying? a look at fishing, mining and wood-based communities." *Perspectives on Labour and Income* (Spring): 31–43.

Clement, Wallace 1981 *Hardrock Mining: Industrial Relations and Technological Changes at INCO.* Toronto: McClelland and Stewart.

———**1986** *The Struggle to Organize: Resistance in Canada's Fishery.* Toronto: McClelland and Stewart.

———**1990** "Comparative class analysis: locating Canada in a North American and Nordic context." *Canadian Review of Sociology and Anthropology* 27: 462–86.

Clement, Wallace, and John Myles 1994 *Relations of Ruling: Class and Gender in Postindustrial Societies.* Montreal and Kingston: McGill–Queen's University Press.

Coates, Mary Lou, David Arrowsmith, and Melanie Courchene 1989 *The Canadian Industrial Relations Scene in Canada 1989: The Labour Movement and Trade Unionism Reference Tables.* Kingston: Industrial Relations Centre, Queen's University.

Cobb, Clifford, Ted Halstead, and Jonathan Rowe 1995 "If the GDP is up, why is America down?" *Atlantic Monthly* (October): 60–74.

Cockburn, Cynthia 1991 *In the Way of Women: Men's Resistance to Sex Equality in Organizations.* Ithaca, New York: ILR Press.

Cohen, Gary L. 1991 "Then and now: the changing face of unemployment." *Perspectives on Labour and Income* (Spring): 37–45.

———**1992** "Hard at work." *Perspectives on Labour and Income* (Spring): 8–14.

Cohen, Marjorie Griffen 1988 *Women's Work, Markets and Economic Development in Nineteenth Century Ontario.* Toronto: University of Toronto Press.

Cole, Robert E. 1979 *Work, Mobility, and Participation.* Berkeley CA: University of California Press.

Colling, Herb 1995 *Ninety-Nine Days: The Ford Strike in Windsor, 1945.* Toronto: NC Press.

Collins, James C., and Jerry I. Porras 1994 *Built to Last: Successful Habits of Visionary Companies.* New York: HarperCollins.

Collins, Randall 1990 "Market closure and the conflict theory of professions." In Michael Burrage and Rolf Torsten-dahl, eds., *Professions in Theory and History: Rethinking the Study of the Professions.* London: Sage.

Collinson, David L., David Knights, and Margaret Collinson 1990 *Managing to Discriminate.* London: Routledge.

Collinson, Margaret, and David Collinson 1996 "'It's only Dick': the sexual harassment of women managers in insurance sales." *Work, Employment & Society* 10: 29–56.

Coltrane, Scott 1996 *Family Man: Fatherhood, Housework, and Gender Equity.* New York: Oxford University Press.

Conference Board of Canada 1993 *Employability Skills Profile.* Ottawa: Conference Board of Canada.

Conley, James R. 1988 "More theory, less fact? social reproduction and class conflict in a sociological approach to working-class history." *Canadian Journal of Sociology* 13: 73–102.

Conrad, Peter 1987 "Wellness in the workplace: potentials and pitfalls of work-site health promotion." *Milbank Quarterly* 65: 255–75.

Cooper, Robert, and Gibson Burrell 1988 "Modernism, postmodernism and organizational analysis: an introduction." *Organization Studies* 9: 91–112.

Copp, Terry 1974 *The Anatomy of Poverty: The Condition of the Working Class in Montreal, 1897–1929.* Toronto: McClelland and Stewart.

Corak, Miles 1993 "Unemployment insurance once again: the incidence of repeat participation in the Canadian UI program." *Canadian Public Policy* 19:162–76.

Coser, Lewis A. 1971 *Masters of Sociological Thought: Ideas in Historical and Social Context.* New York: Harcourt Brace Jovanovich.

Côté, James E., and Anton L. Allahar 1994 *Generation on Hold: Coming of Age in the Late Twentieth Century.* Toronto: Stoddart.

Côté, Michel G. 1991 "Visible minorities in the Canadian labour force." *Perspectives on Labour and Income* (Summer): 17–26.

Coupland, Douglas 1993 *Generation X: Tales for an Accelerated Culture.* New York: St. Martin's Press.

Coverman, Shelley 1988 "Sociological explanations of the male–female wage gap: individual and structuralist theories." In Ann Helton Stromberg and Shirley Harkess, eds., *Women Working: Theories and Facts in Perspective.* 2d ed. Mountain View, CA: Mayfield.

Craven, Paul 1980 *An Impartial Umpire: Industrial Relations and the Canadian State, 1900–1911.* Toronto: University of Toronto Press.

Creese, Gillian 1988–1989 "Exclusion or solidarity? Vancouver workers confront the oriental problem." *B.C. Studies* 80: 24–51.

———**1995** "Gender equity or masculine privilege? union strategies and economic restructuring in a white collar union." *Canadian Journal of Sociology* 20 (2): 143–66.

Creese, Gillian, Neil Guppy, and Martin Meissner 1991 *Ups and Downs on the Ladder of Success: Social Mobility in Canada.* Ottawa: Statistics Canada, General Social Survey Analysis Series 5 (Cat. No. 11-612E, No. 5).

Crompton, Susan 1991 "Who's looking after the kids?: child care arrangements for working mothers." *Perspectives on Labour and Income* (Summer): 68–75.

———**1992** "Studying on the job." *Perspectives on Labour and Income* (Summer): 30–38.

———**1994** "Left behind: lone mothers in the labour market." *Perspectives on Labour and Income* (Summer): 23–28.

———**1995a** "Work and low income." *Perspectives on Labour and Income* (Summer): 12–14.

———**1995b** "Full-year employment across the country." *Perspectives on Labour and Income* (Autumn): 25–29.

Crompton, Susan and Leslie Geran. 1995 "Women as main wage-earners." *Perspectives on Labour and Income* (Winter): 26–29.

Cross, Phillip 1992 "The labour market: year-end review." *Perspectives on Labour and Income* (Spring): 3–14.

Crouch, Colin 1982 *Trade Unions: The Logic of Collective Action.* Glasgow: Fontana.

Crozier, Michel 1964 *The Bureaucratic Phenomenon.* Chicago: University of Chicago Press.

Cuneo, Carl J. 1990 *Pay Equity: The Labour–Feminist Challenge.* Toronto: Oxford University Press.

Cunningham, J. B., and T. H. White, eds. 1984 *Quality of Working Life: Contem-porary Cases.* Ottawa: Labour Canada.

Daft, Richard L. 1992 *Organization Theory and Design.* 4th ed. St. Paul, MN: West Publishing.

———**1995** *Organization Theory & Design.* Minneapolis/St. Paul, MN: West Publishing Company.

Dai, S. Y., and M. V. George 1996 *Projections of Visible Minority Population Groups, Canada, Provinces and Regions, 1991–2016.* Cat. No. 91-541-XPE. Ottawa: Statistics Canada.

Dale, Angela, and Claire Bamford 1988 "Temporary workers: cause for concern or complacency?" *Work, Employment & Society* 2: 191–209.

Dalton, Melville 1959 *Men Who Manage: Fusions of Feeling and Theory in Administration.* New York: John Wiley and Sons.

Dana, Leo-Paul 1992 "Why we must join NAFTA." *Policy Options* 13 (27): 6–8.

Das Gupta, Tania 1996 *Racism and Paid Work.* Toronto: Garamond Press.

Davies, Scott, Clayton Mosher, and Bill O'Grady 1994 "Trends in labour market outcomes of Canadian post-secondary graduates, 1978–1988." In Lorna Erwin and David MacLennan, eds., *Sociology of Education in Canada: Critical Perspectives on Theory, Research, and Practice.* Toronto: Copp Clark Longman.

———**1996** "Educating women: gender inequalities among Canadian university graduates." *Canadian Review of Sociology and Anthropology* 33: 125–42.

Davis, Kingsley, and Wilbert E. Moore 1945 "Some principles of stratification." *American Sociological Review* 10: 242–49.

Davis, Louis E., and Charles Sullivan 1980 "A labour–management contract and quality of working life." *Journal of Occupational Behaviour* 1: 29–41.

Dei, George J. Sefa 1996 "Critical perspectives in antiracism: an introduction." *Canadian Review of Sociology and Anthropology* 33: 247–67.

DeTienne, Kristen Bell 1993 "Big brother or friendly coach? Computer monitoring in the 21st century." *Futurist* 27 (September–October): 33–37.

de Vaus, David, and Ian McAllister 1991 "Gender and work orientation: values and satisfaction in Western Europe." *Work and Occupations* 18: 72–93.

Dex, Shirley 1988 *Women's Attitudes Towards Work.* London: Macmillan.

Dhingra, Harbans L. 1983 "Patterns of ownership and control in Canadian industry: a study of large non-financial private corporations." *Canadian Journal of Sociology* 8: 21–44.

Dickinson, P., and G. Sciadas 1996 "Access to the information highway." *Canadian Economic Observer* (December): 3–1—3–15.

Dickson, Tony, and Hugh V. McLachlan 1989 "In search of the spirit of capitalism: Weber's misinterpretation of Franklin." *Sociology* 23: 81–89.

Digby, Caroline, and W. Craig Riddell 1986 "Occupational health and safety in Canada." In W. Craig Riddell, ed., *Canadian Labour Relations.* Toronto: University of Toronto Press.

Diprete, Thomas A. 1987 "Horizontal and vertical mobility in organizations." *Administrative Science Quarterly* 32: 422–44.

———**1988** "The upgrading and downgrading of occupations: status redefinition vs. deskilling as alternative theories of change." *Social Forces* 66: 725–46.

Diprete, Thomas A., and Whitman T. Soule 1988 "Gender and promotion in segmented job ladder systems." *American Sociological Review* 53: 26–40.

Donaldson, Lex 1995 *In Defence of Organization Theory: A Reply to Critics.* Cambridge: Cambridge University Press.

Donner, Arthur W. 1991 "Recession, recovery, and redistribution: the three R's of Canadian state macro-policy in the 1980s." In Daniel Drache and Meric S. Gertler, eds., *The New Era of Global Competition: State Policy and Market Power.* Montreal and Kingston: McGill–Queen's University Press.

Downie, Bryan, and Mary L. Coates 1995 "Barriers, challenges, and future directions." *Managing Human Resources in the 1990s and Beyond: Is the Workplace Being Transformed?* Bryan Downie and Mary L. Coates, eds. Kingston, Ontario: IRC Press.

Drache, Daniel 1994 "Lean production in Japanese auto transplants in Canada." *Canadian Business Economics* (Spring): 45–59.

———**1995** "The decline of collective bargaining: is it irreversible?" *Proceedings of the XXXIst Conference.* Anthony Giles, Anthony E. Smith, and Kurt Wetzel, eds. Quebec: Canadian Industrial Relations Association.

Drache, Daniel, and Meric S. Gertler 1991 "The world economy and the nation-state: the new international order." In D. Drache and M.S. Gertler, eds., *The New Era of Global Competition: State Policy and Market Power.* Montreal and Kingston: McGill–Queen's University Press.

Drost, Helmar 1996 "Joblessness among Canada's Aboriginal peoples." In Brian MacLean and Lars Osberg, eds., *The Unemployment Crisis: All for Nought?* Montreal and Kingston: McGill–Queen's University Press.

Drucker, Peter F. 1993 *Post-Capitalist Society.* New York: HarperBusiness.

Dubin, Robert 1956 "Industrial workers' worlds: a study of the central life interests of industrial workers." *Social Problems* 3: 131–42.

Dubin, Robert, J. E. Champoux, and L. W. Porter 1975 "Central life interests and organizational commitments of blue-collar workers." *Administrative Science Quarterly* 20: 411–21.

Duffy, Ann, and Norene Pupo 1992 *Part-Time Paradox: Connecting Gender, Work and Family.* Toronto: McClelland and Stewart.

Duncan, Greg J., Martha S. Hill, and Saul D. Hoffman 1988 "Welfare dependence within and across generations." *Science* (January): 467–71.

Dunlop, John T. 1971 *Industrial Relations Systems.* Carbondale, IL: Southern Illinois University Press. [Originally published in 1958.]

Durkheim, Émile 1960 *The Division of Labour in Society.* New York: Free Press. [Originally published in 1897.]

Easterlin, Richard 1980 *Birth and Fortune: The Impact of Numbers on Personal Welfare.* New York: Basic Books.

Ebel, Karl H. 1986 "The impact of industrial robots on the world of work." *International Labour Review* 125: 39–51.

Economic Council of Canada 1976 *People and Jobs: A Study of the Canadian Labour Market.* Ottawa: Supply and Services Canada.

———**1982** *In Short Supply: Jobs and Skills in the 1980s.* Ottawa: Supply and Services Canada.

———**1990** *Good Jobs, Bad Jobs: Employment in the Service Economy.* Ottawa: Supply and Services Canada.

———**1991a** *Employment in the Service Economy.* Ottawa: Supply and Services Canada.

———**1991b** *New Faces in the Crowd: Economic and Social Impacts of Immigration.* Ottawa: Supply and Services Canada.

———**1992a** *Pulling Together: Productivity, Innovation and Trade.* Ottawa: Supply and Services Canada.

———**1992b** *A Lot to Learn: Education and Training in Canada.* Ottawa: Supply and Services Canada.

———**1992c** *The New Face of Poverty: Income Security Needs of Canadian Families (Summary).* Ottawa: Supply and Services Canada.

Economist, The **1996** "Cultural explanations: the man in the Baghdad café." (9 November): 23–26.

Edin, Kathryn 1991 "Surveying the welfare system: how AFDC recipients make ends meet in Chicago." *Social Problems* 38: 462–74.

Edwards, Richard C. 1979 *Contested Terrain: The Transformation of the Workplace in the Twentieth Century.* New York: Basic Books.

Emery, F. E., and Einar Thorsrud 1969 *Form and Content in Industrial Democracy.* London: Tavistock Publications.

Employment and Immigration Canada 1990 *1990 Annual Report, Employment Equity Act.* Ottawa: Supply and Services Canada.

Enchin, Harvey 1992 "Canada loves quality, in theory." *The Globe and Mail* (15 May): B1–B2.

Engels, Friedrich 1971 *The Condition of the Working Class in England.* Oxford: Basil Blackwell. [Originally published in 1845.]

Environics 1986 *Youth Unemployment and Entry-Level Jobs: A Survey of Ontario Employers.* Toronto: Environics Research Group.

Erikson, Kai 1990 "On work and alienation." In Kai Erikson and Steven Peter Vallas, eds., *The Nature of Work: Sociological Perspectives.* New Haven: American Sociological Association and Yale University Press.

Erikson, Robert, et al., eds. 1986–1987 *International Journal of Sociology* 16. [Special issue on the Scandinavian model.]

Etzioni, Amitai 1975 *A Comparative Analysis of Complex Organizations.* 2d ed. New York: Free Press.

Evans, John M., and Raj K. Chawla 1990 "Work and relative poverty." *Perspectives on Labour and Income* (Summer): 32–40.

Ewan, Stuart 1976 *Captains of Consciousness: Advertising and the Social Roots of the Consumer Culture.* New York: McGraw-Hill.

Farber, Henry S., and Daniel H. Saks 1980 "Why workers want unions: the role of relative wages and job characteristics." *Journal of Political Economy* 88: 349–69.

Fast, Janet E., and Judith A. Frederick 1996 "Working arrangements and time stress." *Canadian Social Trends* 43 (Winter): 14–19.

Fearfull, Anne 1992 "The introduction of information and office technologies: the great divide?" *Work, Employment & Society* 6 (3): 423–42.

Feather, Norman T. 1990 *The Psychological Impact of Unemployment.* New York: Springer-Verlag.

Feldberg, Roslyn, and Evelyn Nakano Glenn 1979 "Male and female: job versus gender models in the sociology of work." *Social Problems* 26: 524–38.

———**1983** "Technology and work degradation: effects of office automation on women clerical workers." In Joyce Rothschild, ed., *Machina Ex Dea: Feminist Perspectives on Technology.* New York: Pergamon Press.

Feldman, Daniel C., Helen I. Doerpinghaus, and William H. Turnley 1994 "Managing temporary workers: a permanent HR challenge." *Organizational Dynamics* 23: 49–63.

Felstead, Alan, Harvey Krahn, and Marcus Powell 1997 "Contrasting fortunes across the life course: non-standard work among women and men in Canada and the United Kingdom." Leicester: Centre for Labour Market Studies, University of Leicester, Working Paper no. 17.

Felt, Lawrence, and Peter Sinclair 1992 "Everybody does it: unpaid work in a rural peripheral region." *Work, Employment & Society* 6: 43–64.

Ferland, Jacques 1989 "In search of the unbound Prometheia: a comparative view of women's activism in two Quebec industries, 1869–1908." *Labour/Le Travail* 24: 11–44.

Feuchtwang, Stephen 1982 "Occupational ghettos." *Economy and Society* 11: 251–91.

Fevre, Ralph 1991 "Emerging alternatives to full-time and permanent employment." In Phillip Brown and Richard Scase, eds., *Poor Work: Disadvantage and the Division of Labour.* Milton Keynes: Open University Press.

Figart, Deborah M., and June Lapidus 1996 "The impact of comparable worth on earnings inequality." *Work and Occupations* 23: 297–318.

Fincham, Robin, and Peter S. Rhodes 1988 *The Individual, Work and Organization: Behavioural Studies for Business and Management Students.* London: Weidenfeld and Nicolson.

Finn, Ed 1984 "Ten labour myths." In G. S. Lowe and H. J. Krahn, eds., *Working Canadians: Readings in the Sociology of Work and Industry.* Toronto: Methuen.

Firebaugh, Glenn, and Brian Harley 1995 "Trends in job satisfaction in the United States by race, gender, and type of occupation." *Research in Sociology of Work* 5: 87–104.

Fisher, E. G. 1982 "Strike activity and wildcat strikes in British Columbia: 1945–1975." *Relations industrielles/Industrial Relations* 37: 284–312.

Flanders, Allen 1970 *Management and Unions: The Theory and Reform of Industrial Relations.* London: Faber and Faber.

Foot, David K., and Daniel Stoffman 1996 *Boom, Bust & Echo: How to Profit From the Coming Demographic Shift.* Toronto: Macfarlane Walter & Ross.

Foot, David K., and Jeanne C. Li 1986 "Youth employment in Canada: a misplaced priority?" *Canadian Public Policy* 12(3):499–506.

Foot, David K., and Rosemary A. Venne 1990 "Population pyramids and promotional prospects." *Canadian Public Policy* 16: 387–98.

Forester, Tom 1989 *Computers in the Human Context: Information Technology, Productivity, and People.* Cambridge, MA: MIT Press.

Form, William 1983 "Sociological research on the American working class." *Sociological Quarterly* 24: 163–84.

———**1985** *Divided We Stand: Working Class Stratification in America.* Urbana, IL: University of Illinois Press.

———**1987** "On the degradation of skills." *Annual Review of Sociology* 13: 29–47.

Fortin, Pierre 1996 "The unbearable lightness of zero-inflation optimism." In *The Unemployment Crisis: All for Nought?* Brian K. MacLean and Lars Osberg, eds. Montreal and Kingston: McGill–Queen's University Press, 14–38.

Fox, John, and Carole Suschnigg 1989 "A note on gender and the prestige of occupations." *Canadian Journal of Sociology* 14: 353–60.

Frager, Ruth A. 1992 *Sweatshop Strife: Class, Ethnicity, and Gender in the Jewish Labour Movement of Toronto 1900–1939.* Toronto: University of Toronto Press.

Frank, David 1986 "Contested terrain: workers' control in the Cape Breton coal mines in the 1920s." In Craig Heron and Robert Storey, eds., *On the Job: Confronting the Labour Process in Canada.* Montreal and Kingston: McGill–Queen's University Press.

Franke, Richard Herbert, and James D. Kaul 1978 "The Hawthorne experiments: first statistical interpretation." *American Sociological Review* 43: 623–43.

Frederick, Judith A. 1995 *As Time Goes By: Time Use of Canadians.* Ottawa: Statistics Canada. (Cat. No. 89–544E).

Freedman, Marcia 1976 *Labor Markets: Segments and Shelters.* Montclaire, NJ: Allanheld, Osmun and Co.

Freeman, Alan 1993 "Japan gets a life." *The Globe and Mail* (13 March): D1.

Freeman, Bill 1982 *1005: Political Life in a Union Local.* Toronto: James Lorimer.

Freeman, Chris, and Luc Soete 1994 *Work for All or Mass Unemployment? Computerised Technical Change into the 21st Century.* London: Pinter.

Freeman, R. B., and J. L. Medoff 1984 *What Do Unions Do?* New York: Basic Books.

Freeman, Richard B. 1995 "The future for unions in decentralized collective bargaining systems: US and UK unionism in an era of crisis." *British Journal of Industrial Relations* 33: 519–36.

Freeman, Sarah J., and Kim S. Cameron 1993 "Organizational downsizing: a convergence and reorientation framework." *Organization Science* 4: 10–29.

Frenkel, Steve, Marek Korczynski, Leigh Donoghue, and Karen Shire 1995 "Reconstituting work: trends towards knowledge work and info-normative control." *Work, Employment & Society* 9: 773–96.

Friedman, Andrew L. 1977 *Industry and Labour: Class Struggle at Work and Monopoly Capitalism.* London: Macmillan.

Frost, Peter J., Larry F. Moore, Meryl Reis Louis, Craig C. Lundberg, and Joanne Martin, eds. 1991 *Reframing Organizational Culture.* Newbury Park, CA: Sage.

Fudge, Judy, and Patricia McDermott, eds. 1991 *Just Wages: A Feminist Assessment of Pay Equity.* Toronto: University of Toronto Press.

Furlong, Andy, Andy Biggart, and Fred Cartmel 1996 "Neighbourhoods, opportunity structures and occupational aspirations." *Sociology* 30: 551–65.

Furnham, Adrian 1990 *The Protestant Work Ethic: The Psychology of Work-Related Beliefs and Behaviours.* London: Routledge.

Galenson, Walter 1994 *Trade Union Growth and Decline.* Westport, CT: Praeger.

Gallie, Duncan 1978 *In Search of the New Working Class: Automation and Social Integration within the Capitalist Enterprise.* Cambridge: Cambridge University Press.

———1983 *Social Inequality and Class Radicalism in France and Britain.* Cambridge: Cambridge University Press.

———1991 "Patterns of skill change: upskilling, deskilling or the polarization of skills?" *Work, Employment & Society* 5: 319–51.

Gannagé, Charlene 1986 *Double Day, Double Bind: Women Garment Workers.* Toronto: Women's Press.

———1995 "Union women in the garment industry respond to new managerial strategies." *Canadian Journal of Sociology* 20 (4): 469–95.

Ganzeboom, Harry B. B., Paul M. de Graaf, and Donald J. Treiman 1992 "A standard international socio-economic index of occupational status." *Social Science Research* 21: 1–56.

Gardell, B. 1977 "Autonomy and participation at work." *Human Relations* 30: 515–33.

———1982 "Scandinavian research on stress in working life." *International Journal of Health Services* 12: 31–41

Gardell, B., and B. Gustavsen 1980 "Work environment research and social change: current developments in Scandinavia." *Journal of Occupational Behavior* 1: 3–17.

Gardiner, Arthur 1995 "Their own boss: the self-employed in Canada." *Canadian Social Trends* 37 (Summer): 26–29.

Garnsey, E., J. Rubery, and F. Wilkinson 1985 "Labour market structure and work-force divisions." In R. Deem and G. Salaman, eds., *Work, Culture and Society.* Milton Keynes and Philadelphia: Open University Press.

Garvin, David A. 1993 "Building a learning organization." *Harvard Business Review* (July/August) 78–91.

Gaskell, Jane 1991 "What counts as skill? Reflections on pay equity." In Judy Fudge and Patricia McDermott, eds., *Just Wages: A Feminist Assessment of Pay Equity.* Toronto: University of Toronto Press.

———1992 *Gender Matters from School to Work.* Milton Keynes, UK: Open University Press.

Gaskell, Jane, and Deirdre M. Kelly, eds. 1996 *Debating Dropouts: New Policy Perspectives.* New York: Teachers College Press.

Gephart, Martha A., Victoria J. Marsick, Mark E. Van Buren, and Michelle S. Spiro 1996 "Learning organizations come alive." *Traning & Development* (December): 35–45.

Gera, Surendra, ed. 1991 *Canadian Unemployment: Lessons from the 80s and Challenges for the 90s.* Ottawa: Economic Council of Canada.

Geran, Leslie 1992 "Occupational stress." *Canadian Social Trends* (Autumn): 14–17.

Gerson, Kathleen 1993 *No Man's Land: Men's Changing Commitments to Family and Work.* New York: Basic Books.

Gilbert, Sid, L. Barr, W. Clark, M. Blue, and D. Sunter 1993 *Leaving School: Results from a National Survey Comparing School Leavers and High School Graduates 18 to 20 Years of Age.* Ottawa: Minister of Supply and Services.

Giles, Anthony, and Hem C. Jain 1989 "The collective agreement." In John C. Anderson, Morley Gunderson, and Allen Ponak, eds., *Union–Management Relations in Canada.* 2d ed. Don Mills: Addison-Wesley.

Gill, Colin 1985 *Work, Unemployment and the New Technology.* Cambridge: Polity Press.

Gillespie, Richard 1991 *Manufacturing Knowledge: A History of the Hawthorne Experiments.* New York: Cambridge University Press.

Gindin, Sam 1989 "Breaking away: the formation of the Canadian Auto Workers." *Studies in Political Economy* 29: 63–89.

———1995 *The Canadian Auto Workers: The Birth and Transformation of a Union.* Toronto: James Lormier.

Giuffre, Patti A., and Christine L. Williams 1994 "Boundary lines: labeling sexual harassment in restaurants." *Gender & Society* 8: 378–401.

Glenn, Norval D., and Charles N. Weaver 1982 "Further evidence on education and job satisfaction." *Social Forces* 61: 46–55.

Godard, John 1994 *Industrial Relations: The Economy and Society.* Toronto: McGraw-Hill Ryerson.

Gold, Mark, and David Leyton-Brown, eds. 1988 *Trade-Offs on Free Trade: The Canada–U.S. Free Trade Agreement.* Toronto: Carswell.

Goldfield, Michael 1987 *The Decline of Organized Labor in the United States.* Chicago: University of Chicago Press.

Goldthorpe, John H., D. Lockwood, F. Bechhofer, and J. Platt 1969 *The Affluent Worker in the Class Structure.* Cambridge: Cambridge University Press.

Gordon, Brett R. 1994 "Employee involvement in the enforcement of the occupational safety and health laws of Canada and the United States." *Comparative Labor Law Journal* 15: 527–60.

Gordon, David. M., R. Edwards, and M. Reich 1982 *Segmented Work, Divided Workers: The Historical Transformation of Labor in the United States.* New York: Cambridge University Press.

Gordon, Michael E., and Angelo S. Denisi 1995 "A re-examination of the relationship between union membership and job satisfaction." *Industrial and Labor Relations Review* 48: 222–36.

Gorham, Deborah 1994 "'No longer an invisible minority?': Women Physicians and medical practice in late twentieth-century North America." In *Caring and Curing: Historical Perspectives on Women and Healing in Canada.* Dianne Dodd and Deborah Garham, eds. Ottawa: University of Ottawa Press, 183–211.

Gorz, Andre 1982 *Farewell to the Working Class: An Essay on Post-Industrial Socialism.* London: Pluto Press.

Gouldner, Alvin W. 1954 *Patterns of Industrial Bureaucracy.* New York: Free Press.

———1955 *Wildcat Strike.* New York: Free Press.

Gower, David 1989 "Canada's unemployment mosaic." *Perspectives on Labour and Income* (Summer): 16–26.

———1995 "Men retiring early: how are they doing?" *Perspectives on Labour and Income* 7: 30–34.

Grabb, Edward G. 1990 *Theories of Social Inequality: Classical and Contemporary Perspectives.* 2d ed. Toronto: Holt, Rinehart and Winston.

Graham, Laurie 1993 "Inside a Japanese transplant: a critical perspective." *Work and Occupations* 20 (2): 147–73.

———1995 *On the Line at Subaru–Isuzu: The Japanese Model and the American Worker.* Ithaca, NY: ILR Press.

Grayson, Paul 1985 *Corporate Strategies and Plant Closures: The SKF Experience.* Toronto: Our Times.

Grayson, Paul J. 1994 "Perceptions of workplace hazards." *Perspectives on Labour and Income* (Spring): 41–47.

Green, Francis, and David Ashton 1992 "Skill shortages and skill deficiency: a critique." *Work, Employment & Society* 6: 287–301.

Green, Francis, H. Krahn, and J. Sung 1992 "Non-standard work in Canada and the United Kingdom." *International Journal of Manpower* 14(5): 70–85.

Green, William C., and Ernest J. Yanarella, eds. 1995 *North American Auto Unions in Crisis: Lean Production as Contested Terrain.* Albany, NY: State University of New York Press.

Grenon, Lee 1996 "Are service jobs low-paying?" *Perspectives on Labour and Income* (Spring): 29–34.

Grint, Keith 1991 *The Sociology of Work: An Introduction.* Cambridge: Polity Press.

Grubb, W. Norton, and Robert H. Wilson 1989 "Sources of increasing inequality in wages and salaries, 1960–80." *Monthly Labor Review* (April): 3–13.

Gunderson, Morley 1994 *Comparable Worth and Gender Discrimination: An International Perspective.* Geneva: Organization for Economic Cooperation and Development.

Gunderson, Morley, L. Muszynski, and J. Keck 1990 *Women and Labour Market Poverty.* Ottawa: Canadian Advisory Council on the Status of Women.

Gunderson, Morley, and Douglas Hyatt 1995 "Union impact on compensation, productivity, and management of the organization." *Union–Management Relations in Canada,* 3d ed. Morely Gunderson and Allen Ponak, eds. Don Mills, ON: Addison-Wesley Publishers.

Gunderson, Morely, and Allen Ponak 1995 "Industrial relations." *Union– Management Relations in Canada,* 3d ed. Morely Gunderson and Allen Ponak, eds. Don Mills, ON: Addison-Wesley Publishers.

Gunderson, Morely, Douglas Hyatt, and Allen Ponak 1995 "Strikes and dispute resolution." *Union–Management Relations in Canada,* 3d ed. Morely Gunderson and Allen Ponak, eds. Don Mills, ON: Addison-Wesley Publishers.

Gunderson, Morley, Jeffrey Sack, James McCartney, David Wakely, and Jonathan Eaton 1995 "Employee buyouts in Canada." *British Journal of Industrial Relations* 33: 417–42.

Guppy, Neil, and Krishna Pendakur 1989 "The effects of gender and parental education on participation within post-secondary education in the 1970s and 1980s." *Canadian Journal of Higher Education* 19: 49–62.

Guzda, Henry P. 1993 "Workplace partnerships in the United States and Europe." *Monthly Labor Review* (October): 67–72.

Haber, Samuel 1964 *Efficiency and Uplift: Scientific Management in the Progressive Era, 1890–1920.* Chicago: University of Chicago Press.

Hachen Jr., David S., 1988 "Gender differences in job mobility rates in the United States." *Social Science Research* 17: 93–116.

Hacker, Sally 1989 *Pleasure, Power and Technology: Some Tales of Gender, Engineering, and the Cooperative Workplace.* Boston: Unwin Hyman.

Hackett, Robert 1982 "Is TV news biased against labour?" *Canadian Labour* 28: 12–15.

Hagan, John, and Fiona Kay 1995 *Gender in Practice: A Study of Lawyers' Lives.* New York: Oxford University Press.

Hagey, N. Janet, G. Larocque, and C. McBride 1989 *Highlights of Aboriginal Conditions, 1981–2001: Part III.* Ottawa: Indian and Northern Affairs, Quantitative Analysis & Socio-Demographic Research Working Paper Series 89–3.

Haiven, Larry, Stephen McBride, and John Shields, eds. 1991 *Regulating Labour: The State, Neo-Conservativism and Industrial Relations.* Toronto: Garamond.

Hall, Richard H. 1986 *Dimensions of Work.* Beverly Hills, CA: Sage.

Halpern, Norman 1984 "Sociotechnical systems design: the Shell Sarnia experience." In J. B. Cunningham and T. H. White, eds., *Quality of Working Life: Contemporary Cases.* Ottawa: Labour Canada.

Hamilton, Gary G., and Nicole Woolsey Biggart 1988 "Market, culture, and authority: a comparative analysis of management and organization in the Far East." *American Journal of Sociology* 94: S52–S94.

Hamilton, Richard F., and James D. Wright 1986 *The State of the Masses.* New York: Aldine.

Hammer, Michael, and James Champy 1993 *Reengineering the Corporation: A Manifesto for Business Revolution.* New York: HarperBusiness.

Hamper, Ben 1986 *Rivethead: Tales From the Assembly Line.* New York: Warner Books.

Harding, Philip, and Richard Jenkins 1989 *The Myth of the Hidden Economy: Towards a New Understanding of Informal Economic Activity.* Milton Keynes: Open University Press.

Harrison, Lawrence E. 1992 *Who Prospers? How Cultural Values Shape Economic and Political Success.* New York: Basic Books.

Hartmann, Heidi 1976 "Capitalism, patriarchy, and job segregation by sex." *Signs* 1: 137–69.

Harvey, Andrew S., Katherine Marshall, and Judith A. Frederick 1991 *Where Does Time Go?* Ottawa: Statistics Canada, General Social Survey Analysis Series 4 (Cat. no. 11-612E, no. 4).

Hayes, Robert H., and Ramchandran Jaikuma 1988 "Manufacturing's crisis: new technologies, obsolete organizations." *Harvard Business Review* (September/October): 77–85.

Head, Simon 1996 "The new, ruthless economy." *The New York Review of Books* (29 February): 47–52.

Heaney, Catherine, Barbara A. Israel, and James S. House 1994 "Chronic job insecurity among automobile workers: effects on job satisfaction and health." *Social Science and Medicine* 38: 1431–37.

Hearn, Jeff, Deborah L. Sheppard, Peta Tancred-Sheriff, and Gibson Burrell, eds. 1989 *The Sexuality of Organization.* London: Sage.

Heinzl, John 1997 "Nike's hockey plans put Bauer on thin ice." *The Globe and Mail* (2 July 1997): B2.

Helling, Jan 1985 *Innovations in Work Practices at Saab–Scania* (Saab–Scania Personnel Division). Paper delivered at the U.S.–Japan Automotive Industry Conference, Ann Arbor, MI., March 5–6.

Henry, Frances, and Effie Ginzberg 1985 *Who Gets the Work? A Test of Racial Discrimination in Employment.* Toronto: The Urban Alliance on Race Relations and the Social Planning Council of Metropolitan Toronto.

Henson, Kevin D. 1996 *Just a Temp.* Philadelphia: Temple University Press.

Heron, Craig 1980 "The crisis of the craftsmen: Hamilton's metal workers in the early twentieth century." *Labour/Le Travailleur* 6: 7–48.

———**1989** *The Canadian Labour Movement: A Short History.* Toronto: James Lorimer.

Heron, Craig, and Bryan Palmer 1977 "Through the prism of the strike: industrial conflict in southern Ontario, 1910–14." *Canadian Historical Review* 58: 423–58.

Heron, Craig, and Robert Storey, eds. 1986 *On the Job: Confronting the Labour Process in Canada.* Montreal and Kingston: McGill–Queen's University Press.

Herzberg, Frederick 1966 *Work and the Nature of Man.* New York: World.

———**1968** "One more time: how do you motivate employees?" *Harvard Business Review* 46: 53–62.

Hessing, Melody 1991 "Talking shop(ping): office conversations and women's dual labour." *Canadian Journal of Sociology* 16: 23–50.

Hickson, David J. 1987 "Decision making at the top of organizations." *Annual Review of Sociology* 13: 165–92.

Hill, Stephen 1981 *Competition and Control at Work.* London: Heinemann.

———**1988** "Technology and organizational culture: the human imperative in integrating new technology into organization design." *Technology in Society* 10: 233–53.

Hilton, Rodney, ed. 1976 *The Transition from Feudalism to Capitalism.* London: New Left Books.

Hinings, C. R., and Royston Greenwood 1988 *The Dynamics of Strategic Change.* Oxford: Basil Blackwell.

Hirsch, Eric 1980 "Dual labor market theory: a sociological critique." *Sociological Inquiry* 50: 133–45.

Hirschman, A.O. 1970 *Exit, Voice and Loyalty.* Cambridge, MA: Harvard University Press.

Hirst, Paul, and Grahame Thompson 1995 "Globalization and the future of the nation state." *Economy and Society* 24: 408–42.

Hitt, Michael A., Barbara W. Keats, Herbert F. Harback, and Robert D. Nixon 1994 "Rightsizing: building and maintaining strategic leadership and long-term competitiveness." *Organizational Dynamics* (Autumn): 18–32.

Hochschild, Arlie 1989 *The Second Shift: Working Parents and the Revolution at Home.* New York: Viking Penguin.

Hodson, Randy 1996 "Dignity in the workplace under participative management: alienation and freedom revisited." *American Sociological Review* 61: 719–38.

Hodson, Randy, and Robert L. Kaufman 1982 "Economic dualism: a critical review." *American Sociological Review* 47: 727–39.

Hodson, Randy, and Teresa A. Sullivan 1990 *The Social Organization of Work.* Belmont, CA: Wadsworth.

Hofstede, Geert 1984 *Culture's Consequences: International Differences in Work-Related Values.* Beverly Hills, CA: Sage.

Hofstede, Geert, Bram Neuijen, Denise Daval Ohayv, and Geert Sanders 1990 "Measuring organizational cultures: a qualitative and quantitative study across twenty cases." *Administrative Science Quarterly* 35: 286–316.

Hollinger, Richard, and John Clark 1982 "Employee deviance: a response to the perceived quality of the work experience." *Work and Occupations* 9: 97–114.

Holzer, Harry J. 1996 *What Employers Want: Job Prospects for Less-Educated Workers.* New York: Russell Sage Foundation.

Homans, George C. 1950 *The Human Group.* New York: Harcourt, Brace and World.

Horrell, Sara, J. Rubery, and B. Burchell 1990 "Gender and skills." *Work, Employment & Society* 4: 189–216.

Horvat, Andrew 1983 "Work comes before pleasure for Japanese." *The Edmonton Journal* (15 June): F6.

House, J. D. 1980 *The Last of the Free Enterprisers: The Oilmen of Calgary.* Toronto: Macmillan.

House, J. S. 1981 *Work, Stress and Social Support.* Reading, MA: Addison-Wesley.

———**1987** "Chronic stress and chronic disease in life and work: conceptual and methodological issues." *Work and Stress* 1: 129–34.

Howard, Robert 1985 *Brave New Workplace: America's Corporate Utopias: How They Create Inequalities and Social Conflicts in our Working Lives.* New York: Penguin.

Hsiung, Ping-Chun 1996 *Living Rooms as Factories: Class, Gender, and the Satellite Factory System in Taiwan.* Philadelphia: Temple University Press.

Hughes, Everett C. 1943 *French Canada in Transition.* Chicago: University of Chicago Press.

Hughes, Karen D. 1989 "Office automation: a review of the literature." *Relations Industrielles/Industrial Relations* 44: 654–79.

———**1990** "Trading places: men and women in non-traditional occupations, 1971–86." *Perspectives on Labour and Income* (Summer): 58–68.

———**1995** "Women in non-traditional occupations." *Perspectives on Labour and Income* (Autumn): 14–19.

———**1996** "Transformed by technology? The changing nature of women's 'traditional' and 'non-traditional' white-collar work." *Work, Employment & Society* 10: 227–50.

Hughes, Karen, and Graham S. Lowe 1993 "Unequal returns: gender differences in intitial employment among university graduates." *Canadian Journal of Higher Education* 23: 37–55.

Hughes, Karen D., Graham S. Lowe, and Allison L. McKinnon 1996 "Public attitudes towards budget cuts in Alberta: biting the bullet or feeling the pain?" *Canadian Public Policy* 22: 268–84.

Hum, Derek, and Wayne Simpson 1996 "Canadians with disabilities and the labour market." *Canadian Public Policy* 22: 285–97.

Human Resource Development Canada 1994 *Report of the Advisory Committee on Working Time and the Distribution of Work.* Ottawa: Supply and Services Canada.

———**1996a** *Annual Report, Employment Equity Act, 1996.* Hull, QC: Human Resources Development Canada.

———**1996b** *Job Futures 1996: Occupational Outlooks.* Ottawa: Human Resources Development Canada.

Human Resources Development Canada (and Statistics Canada) 1997 *Adult Education and Training in Canada: Report of the 1994 Adult Education and Training Survey.* (Cat. No. 81-583).

Human Resources Development Canada, Workplace Information Directorate 1996 *Directory of Labour Organizations in Canada 1996.* Ottawa: Canada Communication Group-Publishing.

Humphries, Jane 1977 "Class struggle and the persistence of the working class family." *Cambridge Journal of Economics* 1: 241–58.

Hunter, Alfred A. 1986 *Class Tells: On Social Inequality in Canada.* 2d ed. Toronto: Butterworths.

———**1988** "Formal education and initial employment: unravelling the relationships between schooling and skills over time." *American Sociological Review* 53: 753–65.

Hunter, Alfred A., and Michael C. Manley 1986 "On the task content of work." *Canadian Review of Sociology and Anthropology* 23: 47–71.

Huxley, Christopher 1979 "The state, collective bargaining and the shape of strikes in Canada." *Canadian Journal of Sociology* 4: 223–39.

Hyman, Richard 1975 *Industrial Relations: A Marxist Introduction.* London: Macmillan.

———**1978** *Strikes.* 2d ed. Glasgow: Fontana.

———**1987** "Strategy or structure? capital, labour and control." *Work, Employment & Society* 1: 25–55.

Hyman, Richard, and Ian Brough 1975 *Social Values and Industrial Relations.* Oxford: Basil Blackwell.

Iaffaldano, Michelle T., and Paul M. Muchinsky 1985 "Job satisfaction and job performance: a meta-analysis." *Psychological Bulletin* 97: 251–73.

Idle, Thomas R., and Arthur J. Cordell 1994 "Automating work." *Society* 36 (September–October): 65–71.

Ilg, Randy E. 1995 "The changing face of farm employment." *Monthly Labor Review* (April): 3–12.

Ingham, G. K. 1974 *Strikes and Industrial Conflict: Britain and Scandinavia.* London: Macmillan.

International Labour Office (ILO) 1991 *Year Book of Labour Statistics, 1991.* Geneva: ILO.

———**1995** *Yearbook of Labour Statistics.* Geneva: ILO.

Jabes, Jak, and David Zussman 1988 "Motivation, rewards, and satisfaction in the Canadian federal public service." *Canadian Public Administration* 31: 204–25.

Jablonski, Joseph 1990 *Implementing Total Quality Management: Competing in the 1990s.* Albuquerque, NM: Technical Management Consortium, Inc.

Jackson, Chris 1996 "Measuring and valuing household's unpaid work." *Canadian Social Trends* 42 (Autumn): 25–29.

Jacobs, Jerry 1983 "Industrial sector and career mobility reconsidered." *American Sociological Review* 48: 415–21.

Jacoby, Sanford M. 1985 *Employing Bureaucracy: Managers, Unions, and the Transformation of Work in American Industry, 1900–1945.* New York: Columbia University Press.

Jahoda, M. 1982 *Employment and Unemployment: A Social-Psychological Approach.* Cambridge: Cambridge University Press.

Jain, Hem C. 1990 "Worker participation in Canada: current developments and challenges." *Economic and Industrial Democracy* 11: 279–90.

James, Carl E. 1990 *Making It: Black Youth, Racism and Career Aspirations in a Big City.* Oakville ON: Mosaic Press.

Jamieson, Stuart Marshall 1971 *Times of Trouble: Labour Unrest and Industrial Conflict in Canada, 1900–66.* Ottawa: Queen's Printer.

Jenness, Diamond 1977 *Indians of Canada.* 7th ed. Toronto: University of Toronto Press.

Jenson, Jane 1989 "The talents of women, the skills of men: flexible specialization and women." In Stephen Wood, ed., *The Transformation of Work: Skill, Flexibility and the Labour Process.* London: Unwin Hyman.

Jiang, Shanhe, Richard H. Hall, Karyn L. Loscocco, and John Allen 1995 "Job satisfaction theories and job satisfaction: a China and U.S. comparison." *Research in the Sociology of Work* 5: 161–78.

Johnson, Carol 1996 "Does capitalism really need patriarchy? some old issues reconsidered." *Women's Studies International Forum* 19: 193–202.

Johnson, Gail Cook, and Ronald L. Grey 1988 "Trends in employee attitudes: signs of diminishing employee commitment." *Canadian Business Review* (Spring): 20–23.

Johnson, Gloria Jones, and Roy W. Johnson 1995 "Subjective underemployment and job satisfaction." *International Review of Modern Sociology* 25: 73–84.

Johnson, Holly 1994 "Work-related sexual harassment." *Perspectives on Labour and Income* (Winter): 9–12.

Johnson, Jeffrey V. 1989 "Control, collectivity and the psychosocial work environment." In S. L. Sauter, J. J. Hurrell Jr., and C. L. Cooper, eds., *Job Control and Worker Health.* New York: Wiley.

Johnson, Laura, and Rona Abramovitch 1987 "Rush hours: a new look at parental employment patterns." *Social Planning Council of Metropolitan Toronto, Social Infopac* 6: 1–4.

Johnson, Terry 1980 "Work and power." In Geoff Esland and Graeme Salaman, eds., *The Politics of Work and Occupations.* Toronto: University of Toronto Press.

Johnston, William A., and Michael D. Ornstein 1985 "Social class and political ideology in Canada." *Canadian Review of Sociology and Anthropology* 22: 369–93.

Jones, Alan M., and Chris Hendry 1994 "The learning organization: adult learning and organizational transformation." *British Journal of Management* 5: 153–62.

Jones, Charles, Lorna Marsden, and Lorne Tepperman 1990 *Lives of Their Own: The Individualization of Women's Lives.* Don Mills, ON: Oxford University Press.

Jones, Frank E. 1996 *Understanding Organizations: A Sociological Perspective.* Toronto: Copp Clark Ltd.

Jones, Stephen R. G. 1990 "Worker interdependence and output: the Hawthorne Studies reevaluated." *American Sociological Review* 55: 176–90.

Jonsson, Berth 1980 "The Volvo experiences of new job design and new production technology." *Working Life in Sweden* 18 (September).

Kahn, R.L. 1981 *Work and Health.* New York: Wiley.

Kalleberg, Arne L. 1977 "Work values and job rewards: a theory of job satisfaction." *American Sociological Review* 42: 124–43.

———**1988** "Comparative perspectives on work structures and inequality." *Annual Review of Sociology* 14: 203–25.

Kalleberg, Arne, and Ivar Berg 1987 *Work and Industry: Structures, Markets and Processes.* New York: Plenum.

Kalleberg, Arne, and Karyn A. Loscocco 1983 "Aging, values and rewards: explaining age differences in job satisfaction." *American Sociological Review* 48: 78–90.

Kalleberg, Arne, and Larry J. Griffin 1978 "Positional sources of inequality in job satisfaction." *Sociology of Work and Occupations* 5: 371–401.

Kalleberg, Arne L., and David Stark 1993 "Career strategies in capitalism and socialism: work values and job rewards in United States and Hungary." *Social Forces* 72: 181–98.

Kalleberg, Arne L., and Mark E. Van Buren 1996 "Is bigger better? explaining the relationship between organization size and job rewards." *American Sociological Review* 61: 47–66.

Kamata, Satoshi 1983 *Japan in the Passing Lane: An Insider's Account of Life in a Japanese Factory.* New York: Pantheon.

Kamerman, Sheila B., and Alfred J. Kahn 1987 *The Responsive Workplace: Employers and a Changing Labor Force.* New York: Columbia University Press.

Kanter, Rosabeth M. 1977 *Men and Women of the Corporation.* New York: Basic Books.

———**1989** *When Giants Learn to Dance: Mastering the Challenges of Strategy, Management, and Careers in the 1990s.* New York: Simon and Shuster.

———**1995** *World Class: Thriving Locally in the Global Economy.* New York: Simon & Shuster.

Kaplan, William 1987 *Everything That Floats: Pat Sullivan, Hal Banks and the Seamen's Union of Canada.* Toronto: University of Toronto Press.

Kaplinsky, Raphael 1984 *Automation: The Technology and Society.* Harlow, England: Longman.

Kapstein, Ethan B. 1996 "Workers and the world economy." *Foreign Affairs* 75: 16–37.

Karasek, Robert 1979 "Job demands, job decision latitude and mental health implications for job redesign." *Administrative Science Quarterly* 24: 285–308.

Karasek, Robert, and Töres Theorell 1990 *Healthy Work: Stress, Productivity, and the Reconstruction of Working Life.* New York: Basic Books.

Kasl, S. V. 1978 "Epidemiological contributions to the study of work stress." In C. L. Cooper and R. Payne, eds., *Stress at Work.* New York: Wiley.

Katz, Harry C. 1993 "The decentralization of collective bargaining: a literature review and comparative analysis." *Industrial and Labor Relations Review* 43 (1): 3–22.

Kaufman, Robert L. 1986 "The impact of industrial and occupational structure on Black–white employment allocation." *American Sociological Review* 51: 310–23.

Kealey, Gregory S. 1980 *Toronto Workers Respond to Industrial Capitalism, 1867–1892.* Toronto: University of Toronto Press.

———**1981a** "Labour and working-class history in Canada: prospects in the 1980s." *Labour/Le Travailleur* 7: 67–94.

———**1981b** "The bonds of unity: The Knights of Labour in Ontario, 1880–1900." *Histoire sociale/Social History* 14: 369–411.

———**1984** "1919: the Canadian labour revolt." *Labour/Le Travail* 13: 11–44.

———**1986** "Work control, the labour process, and nineteenth-century Canadian printers." In Craig Heron and Robert Storey, eds., *On the Job: Confronting the Labour Process in Canada.* Montreal and Kingston: McGill–Queen's University Press.

———**1995** *Workers and Canadian History.* Montreal and Kingston: McGill–Queen's University Press.

Keddie, V. 1980 "Class identification and party preference among manual workers." *Canadian Review of Sociology and Anthropology* 17: 24–36.

Keenoy, Tom 1985 *Invitation to Industrial Relations.* Oxford: Basil Blackwell.

Kelly, John E. 1982 *Scientific Management, Job Redesign and Work Performance.* London: Academic Press.

Kelly, Karen 1995 "Visible minorities: a diverse group." *Canadian Social Trends* (Summer): 2–8.

Kelvin, Peter, and Joanna E. Jarrett 1985 *Unemployment: Its Social–Psychological Effects.* Cambridge: Cambridge University Press.

Kerckhoff, Alan C., Richard D. Campbell, and Idee Winfield-Laird 1985 "Social mobility in Great Britain and the United States." *American Journal of Sociology* 91: 281–308.

Kerr, Clark, and Abraham Siegel 1954 "The interindustry propensity to strike: an international comparison." In Arthur Kornhauser et al., eds., *Industrial Conflict.* New York: McGraw-Hill.

Kerr, Clark, J. T. Dunlop, F. H. Harbison, and C .A. Myers 1973 *Industrialization and Industrial Man.* London: Penguin.

Kessler, Ronald C. 1983 "Methodological issues in the study of psychosocial stress." In Howard B. Kaplan, ed., *Psychosocial Stress: Trends in Theory and Research.* New York: Academic Press.

Kettler, David, James Struthers, and Christopher Huxley 1990 "Unionization and labour regimes in Canada and the United States." *Labour/Le Travail* 25: 161–87.

King, W. L. Mackenzie 1918 *Industry and Humanity: A Study in the Principles Underlying Industrial Reconstruction.* Toronto: Thomas Allen.

Kirsh, Sharon 1992 *Unemployment: Its Impact on Body and Soul.* Toronto: Canadian Mental Health Association.

Kluegel, James R. 1987 "Macro-economic problems, beliefs about the poor and attitudes toward welfare spending." *Social Problems* 34: 82–99.

Knight, Rolf 1978 *Indians at Work: An Informal History of Native Indian Labour in British Columbia 1858–1930.* Vancouver: New Star Books.

Knights, David, and Glenn Morgan 1990 "The concept of strategy in sociology: a note of dissent." *Sociology* 24: 475–83.

Knights, David, Hugh Willmott, and David Collison, eds. 1985 *Job Redesign: Critical Perspectives on the Labour Process.* Aldershot, England: Gower.

Knoop, Robert 1994 "Work values and job satisfaction." *Journal of Psychology* 128: 683–90.

Knottnerus, J. David 1987 "Status attainment research and its image of society." *American Sociological Review* 52: 113–21.

Kochan, Thomas A. 1979 "How American workers view labor unions." *Monthly Labor Review* 102 (April): 23–31.

Kochan, Thomas A., Harry C. Katz, and Robert B. McKersie 1986 *The Transformation of American Industrial Relations.* New York: Basic Books.

Kohn, Melvin L. 1990 "Unresolved issues in the relationship between work and personality." In Kai Erikson and Steven Peter Vallas, eds., *The Nature of Work: Sociological Perspectives.* New Haven: American Sociological Association and Yale University Press.

Kohn, Melvin L., and Carmi Schooler 1983 *Work and Personality: An Inquiry into the Impact of Social Stratification.* Norwood, NJ: Ablex.

Kompier, M., E. Degier, P. Smulders, and D. Draasisma 1994 "Regulations, policies and practices concerning work stress in five European countries." *Work and Stress* 8: 296–318.

Kopinak, Kathryn 1996 *Desert Capitalism: Maquiladoras in North America's Western Industrial Corridor.* Tucson: University of Arizona Press.

Krahn, Harvey 1991 "Non-standard work arrangements." *Perspectives on Labour and Income* (Winter): 35–45.

———**1992** *Quality of Work in the Service Sector.* Ottawa: Statistics Canada, General Social Survey Analysis Series 6 (Cat. no. 11 612E, No. 6).

———**1995** "Non-standard work on the rise." *Perspectives on Labour and Income* (Winter): 35–42.

———**1997** "On the permanence of human capital: use it or lose it." *Policy Options* (July/August): 16–19.

Krahn, Harvey, and Graham S. Lowe 1984 "Public attitudes towards unions: some Canadian evidence." *Journal of Labor Research* 5: 149–64.

———**1990** *Young Workers in the Service Economy.* Ottawa: Economic Council of Canada, Working Paper No. 14.

———**1991** "Transitions to work: findings from a longitudinal study of high school and university graduates in three Canadian cities." In David Ashton and G. S. Lowe, eds., *Making Their Way: Education, Training and the Labour Market in Canada and Britain.* Toronto: University of Toronto Press.

———**1993** *The School-to-Work Transition in Edmonton, 1985–1992.* Edmonton: Population Research Laboratory, University of Alberta.

———**1997a** *Literacy Utilization in Canadian Workplaces.* Ottawa: Human Resources Development Canada.

———**1997b** "School–work transitions and post-modern values: what's changing in Canada?" In Walter Heinz, ed., *From Education to Work: Cross-National Perspectives.* Cambridge: New York: Cambridge University Press.

Krahn, Harvey, and Trevor Harrison 1992 "Self-referenced relative deprivation and economic beliefs: the effects of the recession in Alberta." *Canadian Review of Sociology and Anthropology* 29: 191–209.

Krymkowski, Daniel H., and Tadeusz K. Krauze 1992 "Occupational mobility in the year 2000: projections for American men and women." *Social Forces* 71: 145–57.

Kuhn, Thomas S. 1970 *The Structure of Scientific Revolutions,* 2d ed. Chicago: University of Chicago Press.

Kumar, Krishnan 1995 *From Post-Industrial to Post-Modern Society: New Theories of the Contemporary World.* Oxford: Blackwell.

Kumar, Pradeep **1986** "Union growth in Canada: retrospect and prospect." In W. Craig Riddell, ed., *Canadian Labour Relations.* Toronto: University of Toronto Press.

———**1995** *Unions and Workplace Change in Canada.* Kingston, ON: IRC Press.

Kumar, Pradeep, and Lynn Acri **1991** "Women's issues and collective bargaining." In Donald Carter, ed., *Women and Industrial Relations, Proceedings of the 28th Conference of the Canadian Industrial Relations Association* (June 2–4): 581–95.

Kumar, Pradeep, and Mary Lou Coates **1989** *Industrial Relations in 1989: Trends and Emerging Issues.* Kingston, ON: Industrial Relations Centre, Queen's University.

———**1991** *Industrial Relations in 1991: Trends and Emerging Issues.* Kingston: Industrial Relations Centre, Queen's University.

Kumar, Pradeep, David Arrowsmith, and Mary Lou Coates **1991** *Canadian Labour Relations: An Information Manual.* Kingston, ON: Industrial Relations Centre, Queen's University.

Kumar, Pradeep, and David Cowan **1989** *Gender Differences in Union Membership Status: The Role of Labour Market Segmentation.* Kingston: Industrial Relations Centre, Queen's University.

Kumazawa, Makoto, and Jun Yamada **1989** "Job skills under the lifelong nenko employment practice." In Stephen Wood, ed., *The Transformation of Work: Skill, Flexibility and the Labour Process.* London: Unwin Hyman.

Kutscher, Ronald E. **1995** "Summary of BLS projections to 2005." *Monthly Labor Review:* 3–9.

Kuttner, Bob **1983** "The declining middle." *Atlantic Monthly* (July): 60–72.

Labour Canada **1986** *Women in the Labour Force, 1985–86 Edition.* Ottawa: Labour Canada, Women's Bureau.

———**1990** *Women in the Labour Force 1990–91 Edition.* Ottawa: Women's Bureau, Labour Canada.

Lacroix, R. **1986** "Strike activity in Canada." In W. Craig Riddell, ed., *Canadian Labour Relations.* Toronto: University of Toronto Press.

Land, Hillary **1980** "The family wage." *Feminist Review* 6: 55–77.

Landes, David S. **1986** "What do bosses really do?" *Journal of Economic History* 46: 585–623.

Lane, Christel **1988** "Industrial change in Europe: the pursuit of flexible specialisation in Britain and West Germany." *Work, Employment & Society* 2: 141–68.

———**1989** "From welfare capitalism to market capitalism: a comparative review of trends toward employment flexibility in the labour markets of three major European societies." *Sociology* 23: 583–610.

Langford, Tom **1996** "Effects of strike participation on the political consciousness of Canadian postal workers." *Relations Industrielles/Industrial Relations* 51 (3): 651–82.

Lash, Scott **1990** *Sociology of Postmodernism.* London: Routledge.

Laxer, Gordon **1989** *Open for Business: The Roots of Foreign Ownership in Canada.* Don Mills, ON: Oxford University Press.

———**1995** "Social solidarity, democracy and global capitalism." *Canadian Review of Sociology and Anthropology* 32: 287–313.

Leadbeater, David, and Peter Suschnigg **1997** "Training as the principal focus of adjustment policy: a critical view from northern Ontario." *Canadian Public Policy* 23: 2–19.

Leck, Joanne D., Sylvie Onge, and Isabelle Lalancette **1995** "Wage gap changes among organizations subject to the Employment Equity Act." *Canadian Public Policy* 21: 387–400.

Leinberger, Paul, and Bruce Tucker 1991 *The New Individualists: The Generation after the Organization Man.* New York: HarperCollins.

Leiter, Michael P. 1991 "The dream denied: professional burnout and the constraints of human service organizations." *Canadian Psychology* 32: 547–55.

Lenski, Gerhard 1966 *Power and Privilege: A Theory of Social Stratification.* New York: McGraw-Hill.

Lerner, Gerda 1986 *The Creation of Patriarchy.* New York: Oxford University Press.

Levitan, Sar A., and Clifford M. Johnson 1982 *Second Thoughts on Work.* Kalamazoo, MI: W. E. Upjohn Institute for Employment Research.

Lewchuk, Wayne, A. Leslie Robb, and Vivienne Walters 1996 "The effectiveness of Bill 70 and joint health and safety committees in reducing injuries in the workplace: the case of Ontario." *Canadian Public Policy* 22: 225–43.

Lewis, Alan 1995 "The deskilling thesis revisited: Peter Armstrong's defence of Braverman." *Sociological Review* 43: 478–500.

Li, Peter 1982 "Chinese immigrants on the Canadian prairie, 1919–47." *Canadian Review of Sociology and Anthropology* 19: 527–40.

Lincoln, James R. 1990 "Japanese organization and organization theory." *Research in Organizational Behavior* 12: 255–94.

Lincoln, James R., and Arne L. Kalleberg 1985 "Work organization and workforce commitment: a study of plants and employees in the U.S. and Japan." *American Sociological Review* 50: 738–60.

———1990 *Culture, Control, and Commitment: A Study of Work Organization and Work Attitudes in the United States and Japan.* Cambridge: Cambridge University Press.

Lincoln, James R., and Kerry McBride 1987 "Japanese industrial organization in comparative perspective." *Annual Review of Sociology* 13: 289–312.

Lindsay, Colin 1989 "The service sector in the 1980s." *Canadian Social Trends* (Spring): 20–23.

Lindsay, Colin, and Mary Sue Devereaux 1991 *Canadians in the Pre-Retirement Years: A Profile of People Aged 55–64.* Ottawa: Statistics Canada (Cat. no. 89–521E).

Lindsay, Colin, Mary S. Devereaux, and Michael Bergob 1994 *Youth in Canada.* 2d ed. Ottawa: Statistics Canada. Catalogue no. 89-511E.

Linhart, Robert 1981 *The Assembly Line.* London: John Calder.

Lipset, Seymour Martin 1990a *Continental Divide: The Values and Institutions of the United States and Canada.* New York: Routledge.

———1990b "Trade unionism in Canada and the United States: a reply to Bowden." *Canadian Review of Sociology and Anthropology* 27: 531–35.

Lipset, Seymour Martin, Martin Trow, and James Coleman 1956 *Union Democracy: The Internal Politics of the International Typographical Union.* Garden City, NJ: Anchor Books.

Lipset, Seymour M., and Noah Meltz 1996 "Canadian and American unions: attitudes and participation." Paper prepared for AFL-CIO/Cornell University Conference on Union Organizing (Washington, DC, 31 March–2 April).

Lipset, Seymour Martin, and Reinhard Bendix 1959 *Social Mobility in Industrial Society.* Berkeley, CA: University of California Press.

Lipsig-Mummé, Carla 1987 "Organizing women in the clothing trades: homework and the 1983 garment strike in Canada." *Studies in Political Economy* 22: 41–71.

Little, Bruce 1992 "Curing what ails the system." *The Globe and Mail* (18 January): A1, A6.

Littler, Craig R. 1982 *The Development of the Labour Process in Capitalist Societies.* London: Heinemann.

Littler, Craig R. and Graeme Salaman 1982 "Bravermania and beyond: recent theories of the labour process." *Sociology* 16: 251–69.

Livingstone, David W. 1993 "Lifelong Education and Chronic Underemployment." In Paul Anisef and Paul Axelrod, eds., *Transitions: Schooling and Employment in Canada.* Toronto: Thomson Educational Publishing.

Livingstone, D. W., and Meg Luxton 1996 "Gender consciousness at work: modification of the male breadwinner norm." In *Recast Dreams: Class and Gender Consciousness in Steeltown.* David W. Livingstone and J. M. Mangan, eds. Toronto: Garamond Press, 100–29.

Locke, Edwin A. 1976 "The nature and causes of job satisfaction." In Marvin B. Dunnette, ed., *Handbook of Industrial and Organizational Psychology.* Chicago: Rand-McNally.

Lockwood, David 1966 "Sources of variation in working class images of society." *Sociological Review* 14: 249–67.

Logan, Ron, and Jo-Anne Belliveau 1995 "Working mothers." *Canadian Social Trends* 36 (Spring): 24–28.

Logan, Ronald 1991 "Immigration during the 1980s." *Canadian Social Trends*, (Spring): 11–13.

Logue, John 1981 "Saab/Trollhattan: reforming work life on the shop floor." *Working Life in Sweden* 23 (June).

Loh, S. 1995 *Projections of Population With Aboriginal Ancestry, Canada, Provinces/Regions and Territories, 1991–2016.* Ottawa: Statistics Canada. (Cat. No. 91–539OXPE)

Long, Richard J. 1984 "Introducing employee participation in ownership and decision making." In J. B. Cunningham and T. H. White, eds., *Quality of Working Life: Contemporary Cases.* Ottawa: Labour Canada.

———**1989** "Patterns of workplace innovation in Canada." *Relations industrielles/Industrial Relations* 44: 805–26.

Lonnroth, Juhani 1994 "Global employment: issues in the year 2000." *Monthly Labor Review* (September): 5–15.

Looker, Dianne 1993 "Interconnected transitions and their costs: gender and urban– rural differences in the transition from school to work." In Paul Anisef and Paul Axelrod, eds., *Transitions: Schooling and Employment in Canadian Society.* Toronto: Thompson Educational Publishers.

———**1994** "Active capital: the impact of parents on youthes' educational performance and plans." In Lorna Erwin and David MacLennan, eds. *Sociology of Education in Canada: Critical Perspectives on Theory, Research and Practice.* Toronto: Copp Clark Longman.

Looker, E. Dianne, and Karen L. McNutt 1989 "The effect of occupational expectations on the educational attainments of males and females." *Canadian Journal of Education* 14: 352–67.

Lorence, Jon 1987a "A test of gender and job models of sex differences in job involvement." *Social Forces* 66: 121–42.

———**1987b** "Age differences in work involvement." *Work and Occupations* 14: 533–57.

———**1987c** "Gender differences in occupational labor market structure." *Work and Occupations* 14: 23–61.

Lorence, Jon, and Jeylan T. Mortimer 1985 "Job involvement through the life course: a panel study of three age groups." *American Sociological Review* 50: 618–38.

Loscocco, Karyn A. 1989 "The instrumentally oriented factory worker: myth or reality?" *Work and Occupations* 16: 3–25.

———**1990** "Reactions to blue-collar work: a comparison of women and men." *Work and Occupations* 17: 152–77.

Love, Roger, and Susan Poulin 1991 "Family income inequality in the 1980s." *Perspectives on Labour and Income* (Autumn): 51–57.

Lowe, Graham S. 1981 "Causes of unionization in Canadian banks." *Relations Industrielles/Industrial Relations* 36: 865–92.

———**1984** "The rise of modern management in Canada." In G. S. Lowe and H. J. Krahn, eds., *Working Canadians.*Toronto: Methuen.

———**1987** *Women in the Administrative Revolution: The Feminization of Clerical Work.* Toronto: University of Toronto Press.

———**1989** *Women, Paid/Unpaid Work, and Stress.* Ottawa: Canadian Advisory Council on the Status of Women.

———**1991a** "Computers in the workplace." *Perspectives on Labour and Income* (Summer): 38–49.

———**1991b** "Retirement attitudes, plans and behaviour." *Perspectives on Labour and Income* (Autumn): 8–16.

———**1997** "Computers in the workplace." *Perspectives on Labour and Income* (Summer): 29–36.

Lowe, Graham S., and Harvey Krahn 1985 "Where wives work: the relative effects of situational and attitudinal factors." *Canadian Journal of Sociology* 10: 1–22.

———**1989** "Recent trends in public support for unions in Canada." *Journal of Labor Research* 10: 391–410.

———**1992** "Do part-time jobs improve the labor market chances of high school graduates?" In B. D. Warme, K .L. P. Lundy, and L. A. Lundy, eds., *Working Part-time: Risks and Opportunities.* New York: Praeger.

———**1995** "Job-related education and training among young workers." *Canadian Public Policy* 21: 362–78.

Lowe, Graham S., and Harvey Krahn, eds. 1993 *Work in Canada: Readings in the Sociology of Work and Industry.* Scarborough, ON: Nelson Canada.

Lowe, Graham S., and Herbert C. Northcott 1986 *Under Pressure: A Study of Job Stress.* Toronto: Garamond Press.

———**1995** "Stressful working conditions and union dissatisfaction." *Relations Industrielles/Industrial Relations* 50: 420–42.

Lowe, Graham S., Harvey Krahn, and Jeff Bowlby 1997 *1996 Alberta High School Graduate Survey: Report of Research Findings.* Edmonton, AB: Population Research Laboratory, University of Alberta.

Lucas, Rex A. 1971 *Minetown, Milltown, Railtown.* Toronto: University of Toronto Press.

Lum, Janet M. 1995 "The Federal Employment Equity Act: goals vs. implementation." *Canadian Public Administration* 38: 45–76.

Lush, Patricia 1987 "Going, going, gone." *Report on Business* (January): 36–40.

Luxton, Meg 1980 *More Than a Labour of Love.* Toronto: Women's Press.

Luxton, Meg, and June Corman 1991 "Getting to work: the challenge of the Women Back Into Stelco Campaign." *Labour/Le Travail* 28: 149–85.

Macarov, David 1982 *Worker Productivity: Myths and Reality.* Beverly Hills: Sage.

Maccoby, Michael 1988 *Why Work: Motivating and Leading the New Generation.* New York: Simon and Schuster.

Macdonald, Keith, and George Ritzer 1988 "The sociology of the professions: dead or alive?" *Work and Occupations* 15: 251–72.

Macdonald, Martha 1991 "Post-Fordism and the flexibility debate." *Studies in Political Economy* 36: 177–201.

MacDonald, Robert 1994 "Fiddly jobs, undeclared working and the something for nothing society." *Work, Employment & Society* 8: 507–30.

MacKinnon, Malcolm H. 1981 "The industrial worker and the job: alienated or instrumentalized?" In K. L. P. Lundy and B. Warme, eds., *Work in the Canadian Context.* Toronto: Butterworths.

MacLean, Brian K., and Lars Osberg, eds. 1996 *The Unemployment Crisis: All for Nought?* Montreal and Kingston: McGill–Queen's University Press.

Mahon, Rianne 1984 *The Politics of Industrial Restructuring: Canadian Textiles.* Toronto: University of Toronto Press.

———**1987** "From Fordism to?: new technology, labour markets and unions." *Economic and Industrial Democracy* 8: 5–60.

Maira, Arun, and Peter Scott-Morgan 1997 *The Accelerating Organization: Embracing the Human Face of Change.* New York: McGraw-Hill.

Mandell, Nancy, and Stewart Crsydale 1993 "Gender tracks: male–female perceptions of home–school–work transitions." In Paul Anisef and Paul Axelrod, eds. *Transitions: Schooling and Employment in Canada.* Toronto: Thompson Educational Publishing.

Mann, Michael 1970 "The social cohesion of liberal democracy." *American Sociological Review* 35: 423–39.

Mansell, Jacquie 1987 *Workplace Innovation in Canada.* Ottawa: Economic Council of Canada.

Marchak, M. Patricia 1981 *Ideological Perspectives on Canada.* 2d ed. Toronto: McGraw-Hill Ryerson.

Marchak, Patricia, Neil Guppy, and John McMullan 1987 *Uncommon Property: The Fishing and Fish-Processing Industries in British Columbia.* Toronto: Methuen.

Marglin, Stephen A. 1976 "What do bosses do? the origins and functions of hierarchy in capitalist production." In Andre Gorz, ed., *The Division of Labour.* New York: Humanities Press.

Marquardt, Richard 1996 *Youth and Work in Troubled Times: A Report on Canada in the 1990s.* Ottawa: Canadian Policy Research Networks, Inc. Working Paper no. W01.

Mars, Gerald 1982 *Cheats at Work: An Anthropology of Workplace Crime.* London: Unwin Paperbacks.

Marsh, Catherine, R. McAuley, and S. Penlington 1990 "The road to recovery? some evidence from vacancies in one labour market." *Work, Employment & Society* 4: 31–58.

Marshall, G. 1982 *In Search of the Spirit of Capitalism: An Essay on Max Weber's Protestant Ethic Thesis.* London: Hutchinson.

Marshall, Katherine 1987 *Who Are the Professional Women?* Ottawa: Statistics Canada (Cat. No. 99–951).

———**1989** "Women in the professional occupations: progress in the 1980s." *Canadian Social Trends* (Spring): 13–16.

———**1993** "Dual Earners: who's responsible for housework?" *Canadian Social Trends* (Winter): 11–14.

———1996 "A job to die for." *Perspectives on Labour and Income* (Summer): 26–31.

———1997 "Job sharing." *Perspectives on Labour and Income* (Summer): 6–10.

Martin, Jack K., and Constance L. Shehan 1989 "Education and job satisfaction: the influences of gender, wage-earning status, and job values." *Work and Occupations* 16: 184–99.

Martin, Jack K. and Paul M. Roman 1996 "Job satisfaction, job reward characteristics, and employees' problem drinking behaviors." *Work and Occupations* 23: 4–25.

Matthews, Roy A. 1985 *Structural Change and Industrial Policy: The Redeployment of Canadian Manufacturing, 1960–80.* Ottawa: Supply and Services Canada.

Maynard, Rona 1987 "How do you like your job?" *Report on Business Magazine* (November): 112–22.

Mayo, Elton 1945 *The Social Problems of an Industrial Civilization.* Cambridge, MA: Harvard University Press.

McBride-King, Judith L. 1990 *Work and Family: Employment Challenge of the '90s.* Ottawa: Conference Board of Canada, Report.

McCormack, A. Ross 1978 *Reformers, Rebels and Revolutionaries: The Western Canadian Radical Movement, 1899–1919.* Toronto: University of Toronto Press.

McDonald, N., and M. Doyle 1981 *The Stresses of Work.* Don Mills, ON: Nelson Canada.

McDonald, P.L., and R.A. Wanner 1990 *Retirement in Canada.* Toronto: Butterworths.

McDonald, Ryan J. 1991 "Canada's off-reserve Aboriginal population." *Canadian Social Trends* (Winter): 2–7.

McIlwee, Judith S., and J. Gregg Robinson 1992 *Women in Engineering: Gender, Power, and Workplace Culture.* Albany, NY: State University of New York Press.

McKay, Shona 1991 "Willing and able." *Report on Business Magazine* (October): 58–63.

———1996 "You're (still) hired." *Report on Business Magazine* (December): 54–60.

McKinnon, Allison L., and Odynak, D. 1991 *Elder Care, Employees, and Employers: Some Canadian Evidence.* Discussion paper prepared for the Demographic Review Secretariat, Health and Welfare Canada. Edmonton: Population Research Laboratory, University of Alberta.

McLuhan, Marshall 1964 *Understanding Media: The Extensions of Man.* New York: McGraw-Hill.

McMullen, Kathryn 1996 *Skill and Employment Effects of Computer-Based Technology: The Results of the Working with Technology Survey III.* Ottawa: Canadian Policy Research Networks Inc. Study no. W01.

McSkimmings, Judie 1990 "The farm community." *Canadian Social Trends* (Spring): 20–23.

Meissner, Martin 1969 *Technology and the Worker: Technical Demands and Social Processes in Industry.* San Francisco: Chandler.

———1971 "The long arm of the job: a study of work and leisure." *Industrial Relations* 10: 239–60.

Meissner, Martin, E. W. Humphreys, S. M. Meis, and W. J. Scheu 1975 "No exit for wives: sexual division of labour and the cumulation of household demands." *Canadian Review of Sociology and Anthropology* 12: 424–39.

Menaghan, Elizabeth G. 1991 "Work experiences and family interaction processes: the long reach of the job?" *Annual Review of Sociology* 17: 419–44.

Menzies, Heather 1996 *Whose Brave New World? The Information Highway and the New Economy.* Toronto: Between the Lines.

Mergenhagen, Paula 1994 "Job benefits get personal." *American Demographics* (September): 31–38.

Merkle, Judith A. 1980 *Management and Ideology: The Legacy of the International Scientific Management Movement.* Berkeley, CA: University of California Press.

Merton, Robert K. 1952 "Bureaucratic structure and personality." In Robert K. Merton, A .P. Gray, B. Hockey, and H. C. Selvin, eds., *Reader in Bureaucracy.* New York: Free Press.

Meyer, Marshall W., and Lynne G. Zucker 1989 *Permanently Failing Organizations.* Newbury Park, CA: Sage.

Meyer, Stephen 1981 *The Five Dollar Day: Labor Management and Social Control in the Ford Motor Company, 1908–1921.* Albany, NY: State University of New York Press.

Michaud, Jean-Francois, M. V. George, and S. Loh 1996 *Projections of Persons With Disabilities (Limited at Work/Perception), Canada, Provinces and Territories, 1993–2016.* Ottawa: Statistics Canada. (Cat. No. 91–538E).

Michels, Robert 1959 *Political Parties: A Sociological Study of the Oligarchical Tendencies of Modern Democracy.* New York: Dover Publications. [Originally published in 1915.]

Micklethwait, John, and Adrian Wooldridge 1996 *The Witch Doctors: Making Sense of the Management Gurus.* New York: Times Books.

Middleton, Chris 1988 "The familiar fate of the *famulae:* gender divisions in the history of wage labour." In R. E. Pahl, ed., *On Work: Historical, Comparative and Theoretical Approaches.* Oxford: Basil Blackwell.

Miles, Raymond E. 1965 "Human relations or human resources." *Harvard Business Review* 43 (July-August): 148–63.

Milkman, Ruth 1991 *Japan's California Factories: Labor Relations and Economic Globalization.* Los Angeles: Institute of Industrial Relations, University of California, at Los Angeles.

Milkman, Ruth, and Cydney Pullman 1991 "Technological change in an auto assembly plant: the impact on workers' tasks and skills." *Work and Occupations* 18: 123–47.

Miller, Danny 1990 *The Icarus Paradox: How Exceptional Companies Bring About Their Own Downfall.* New York: Harper/Business.

Miller, Joanne 1980 "Individual and occupational determinants of job satisfaction: a focus on gender differences." *Sociology of Work and Occupations* 7: 337–66.

Miller, Joanne, C. Schooler, M. L. Kohn, and K. A. Miller 1979 "Women and work: the psychological effects of occupational conditions." *American Journal of Sociology* 85: 66–94.

Mills, C. Wright 1948 *The New Men of Power.* New York: Harcourt-Brace.

———**1956** *White Collar: The American Middle Classes.* New York: Oxford University Press.

Milner, Henry 1989 *Sweden: Social Democracy in Practice.* Oxford: Oxford University Press.

Milton, David 1986 "Late capitalism and the decline of trade union power in the United States." *Economic and Industrial Democracy* 7: 319–49.

Mintzberg, Henry 1989 *Mintzberg on Management: Inside Our Strange World of Organizations.* New York: Free Press.

———**1994** "The fall and rise of strategic planning." *Harvard Business Review* 72: 107–14.

Minus, Rolf, Roger J. Smith, and Vladimir Karoleff 1994 "Canadian underground economy revisited: update and critique." *Canadian Public Policy* 20: 235–52.

Mitchell, Alanna 1997 "The poor fare worst in schools." *The Globe and Mail* (18 April: A1).

Monette, Manon 1996a "Retirement in the 90s: retired men in Canada." *Canadian Social Trends* 42 (Autumn): 8–11.

———**1996b** "Retirement in the 90s: going back to work." *Canadian Social Trends* 42 (Autumn): 12–14.

Moreau, Joanne 1991 "Employment equity." *Canadian Social Trends* (Autumn): 26–28.

Morgan, Gareth 1997 *Images of Organization.* Thousand Oaks, CA: Sage Publications.

Morissette, René 1991 "Are jobs in large firms better jobs?" *Perspectives on Labour and Income* (Autumn): 40–50.

Morissette, René, J. Myles, and G. Picot 1994 "Earnings inequality and the distribution of working time in Canada." *Canadian Business Economics* 2: 3–16.

Morris, Lydia, and Sarah Irwin 1992 "Employment histories and the concept of the underclass." *Sociology* 26: 401–20.

Morton, Desmond 1989 "The history of the Canadian labour movement." In John C. Anderson, Morley Gunderson, and Allen Ponak, eds., *Union–Management Relations in Canada.* 2d ed. Don Mills: Addison-Wesley.

Mottaz, Clifford 1986 "Gender differences in work satisfaction, work-related rewards and values, and the determinants of work satisfaction." *Human Relations* 39: 359–78.

Moulton, David 1974 "Ford Windsor 1945." In Irving Abella, ed., *On Strike: Six Key Labour Struggles in Canada 1919–1949.* Toronto: James Lewis and Samuel.

Mroczkowski, Tomasz, and Masao Hanaoka 1989 "Continuity and change in Japanese management." *California Management Review* 31: 39–53.

Murray Axmith and Associates 1997 *1997 Canadian Hiring and Dismissal Practices Survey.* Toronto: Murray Axmith and Associates.

Murray, Gregor 1995 "Unions: membership, structures, and actions." In *Union–Management Relations in Canada,* 3d ed. Morley Gunderson and Allen Ponak, eds. Don Mills, ON: Addison-Wesley Publishers.

Murray, Michael A., and Tom Atkinson 1981 "Gender differences in correlates of job satisfaction." *Canadian Journal of Behavioural Science* 13: 44–52.

Muszynski, Leon, and David A. Wolfe 1989 "New technology and training: lessons from abroad." *Canadian Public Policy* 15: 245–64.

Myles, John 1988 "The expanding middle: some Canadian evidence on the deskilling debate." *Canadian Review of Sociology and Anthropology* 25: 335–64.

———**1991** "Post-industrialism and the service economy." In Daniel Drache and Meric S. Gertler, eds., *The New Era of Global Competition: State Policy and Market Power.* Montreal and Kingston: McGill–Queen's University Press.

———**1992** "Is there a post-Fordist life-course?" In Walter R. Heinz, ed., *Institutions and Gatekeeping in the Life Course.* Weinheim: Deutscher Studien Verlag.

———**1996** "Public policy in a world of market failure." *Policy Options* (July–August): 14–19.

Myles, John and Debra Street 1995 "Should the economic life course be redesigned? old age security in a time of transition." *Canadian Journal on Aging* 14: 335–59.

Myles, John, and Gail Fawcett 1990 *Job Skills and the Service Economy.* Working paper no. 4. Ottawa: Economic Council of Canada, Working Paper no. 7.

Myles, John, G. Picot, and T. Wannell 1988 "The changing wage distribution of jobs, 1981–86." Statistics Canada, *The Labour Force* (October): 85–138.

Naisbitt, John 1982 *Megatrends: Ten New Directions Transforming Our Lives.* New York: Warner.

National Center on Education and the Economy (NCEE) 1990 *America's Choice: High Skills or Low Wages! Report of the Commission on the Skills of the American Workforce.* Rochester, NY: NCEE.

National Council of Welfare 1997 *Poverty Profile 1995.* Ottawa: National Council of Welfare.

National Defense Counsel for Victims of Karoshi 1990 *Karoshi: When the "Corporate Warrior" Dies.* Tokyo: Mado-Sha.

Neale, Deborah 1992 "Will Bob Rae deliver on his promise?" *Policy Options* (January–February): 25–28.

Nee, Victor, and Rebecca Matthews 1996 "Market transformation and societal transformation in reforming state socialism." *Annual Review of Sociology* 22: 401–35.

Neil, Cecily C., and William E. Snizek 1987 "Work values, job characteristics, and gender." *Sociological Perspectives* 30: 245–65.

Neis, Barbara 1991 "Flexible specialization: what's that got to do with the price of fish?" *Studies in Political Economy* 36: 145–76.

Nelson, Daniel 1980 *Frederick W. Taylor and the Rise of Scientific Management.* Madison, WI: University of Wisconsin Press.

Nelson, Joel I. 1995 *Post-Industrial Capitalism: Exploring Economic Inequality in America.* Thousand Oaks, CA: Sage.

Newman, Katherine S. 1989 *Falling from Grace: The Experience of Downward Mobility in the American Middle Class.* New York: Vintage Books.

Newton, Keith 1986 "Quality of working life in Canada: a survey." In W. Craig Riddell, ed., *Labour–Management Cooperation in Canada.* Toronto: University of Toronto Press.

———1989 "Technological and organizational change in Canada." *New Technology, Work and Employment* 4: 40–45.

New York Times, The 1996 *The Downsizing of America: Millions of Americans are Losing Good Jobs. This Is Their Story.* New York: Times Books.

Niezen, Ronald 1993 "Power and dignity: the social consequences of hydro-electric development for the James Bay Cree." *Canadian Review of Sociology and Anthropology* 30: 510–529.

Nightingale, Donald 1982 *Workplace Democracy: An Enquiry into Employee Participation in Canadian Work Organizations.* Toronto: University of Toronto Press.

Nilsson, Tommy 1996 "Lean production and white collar work: the case of Sweden." *Economic and Industrial Democracy* 17: 447–72.

Noble, David 1985 "Social choice in machine design: the case of automatically controlled machine tools." In Donald Mackenzie and Judy Wajcman, eds., *The Social Shaping of Technology.* Milton Keynes: Open University Press.

———1995 *Progress without People: New Technology, Unemployment, and the Message of Resistance.* Toronto: Between the Lines.

Noël, Alain, and Keith Gardner 1990 "The Gainers strike: capitalist offensive, militancy, and the politics of industrial relations in Canada." *Studies in Political Economy* 31: 31–72.

Nolan, Peter, and P. K. Edwards 1984 "Homogenise, divide and rule: an essay on *Segmented Work, Divided Workers.*" *Cambridge Journal of Economics* 8: 197–215.

Nollen, Stanley, and Helen Axel 1996 *Managing Contingent Workers: How to Reap the Benefits and Reduce the Risks.* New York: American Management Association.

Noreau, Nathalie 1996 "The many faces of unemployment." *Perspectives on Labour and Income* (Spring): 35–42.

Northcott, Herbert C., and Graham S. Lowe 1987 "Job and gender influences in the subjective experience of work." *Canadian Review of Sociology and Anthropology* 24: 117–31.

Novek, Joel 1988 "Grain terminal automation: a case study in the control of control." *Labour/Le Travail* 22: 163–80.

———1989 "Peripheralizing core labour markets: the case of the Canadian meat packing industry." *Work, Employment and Society* 3: 157–77.

———**1992** "The labour process and workplace injuries in the Canadian meat packing industry." *Canadian Review of Sociology and Anthropology* 29: 17–37.

Nussbaum, Karen, and Virginia duRivage 1986 "Computer monitoring: mismanagement by remote control." *Business and Society Review* 56 (Winter): 16–20.

Oderkirk, Jillian 1993 "Educational achievement: an international perspective." *Canadian Social Trends* (Autumn): 8–12.

———**1996** "Computer literacy—a growing requirement." *Education Quarterly Review* (Autumn): 9–29.

Oderkirk, Jillian, Cynthia Silver, and Marc Prud'homme 1994 "Traditional-earner families." *Canadian Social Trends* 32 (Spring): 19–25.

O'Hara, Bruce 1993 *Working Harder Isn't Working.* Vancouver: New Star Books.

Olsen, Gregg 1991 "Labour mobilization and the strength of capital: the rise and stall of economic democracy in Sweden." *Studies in Political Economy* 34: 109–45.

Olson, Mancur 1965 *The Logic of Collective Action.* Cambridge, MA: Harvard University Press.

O'Neill, Jeff 1991 "Changing occupational structure." *Canadian Social Trends* (Winter): 8–12.

Organization for Economic Co-operation and Development (OECD) 1986 *OECD Employment Outlook.* Paris: OECD.

———**1989** Paris: OECD.

———**1991** Labour Force Statistics 1969

———**1994** *Employment Outlook, July 1994.* Paris: OECD.

***Organization Studies* 1988** "Offence and defence: a symposium with Hinings, Clegg, Child, Aldrich, Karpik, and Donaldson." *Organization Studies* 9: 1–32.

Orme, Jr. W. A. 1996 *Understanding NAFTA: Mexico, Free Trade, and the New North America.* Austin: University of Texas Press.

Osberg, Lars, and Pierre Fortin, eds. 1996 *Unnecessary Debt.* Toronto: Lorimer.

Osberg, Lars, Fred Wein, and Jan Grude 1995 *Vanishing Jobs: Canada's Changing Workplace.* Toronto: Lorimer.

Ospina, Sonia 1996 *Illusions of Opportunity: Employee Expectations and Workplace Inequality.* Ithaca and London: Cornell University Press.

Osterman, Paul 1986 "The impact of computers on employment of managers and clerks." *Industrial and Labor Relations Review* 39: 175–86.

———**1994** "How common is workplace transformation and who adopts it?" *Industrial and Labor Relations Review* 47: 173–88.

Osterman, Paul, ed. 1984 *Internal Labor Markets.* Cambridge, MA: MIT Press.

Ostry, Sylvia 1968 *The Female Worker in Canada.* Ottawa: Queen's Printer.

O'Toole, James, ed. 1977 *Work, Learning and the American Future.* San Francisco: Jossey–Bass.

Ouchi, William 1981 *Theory Z: How American Business Can Meet the Japanese Challenge.* Reading, MA: Addison-Wesley.

Owram, Doug 1996 *Born at the Right Time: A History of the Baby Boom Generation.* Toronto: University of Toronto Press.

Pahl, R.E. 1984 *Divisions of Labour.* Oxford: Basil Blackwell.

Palmer, Bryan 1975 "Class, conception and conflict: the thrust for efficiency, managerial views of labor and the working class rebellion, 1902–22." *Radical Review of Political Economics* 7: 31–49.

———**1979** *A Culture in Conflict: Skilled Workers and Industrial Capitalism in Hamilton, Ontario, 1860–1914.* Montreal and Kingston: McGill–Queen's University Press.

———**1986** *The Character of Class Struggle: Essays in Canadian Working Class History, 1850–1985.* Toronto: McClelland and Stewart.

———**1992** *Working Class Experience: Rethinking the History of Canadian Labour, 1800–1991.* 2d ed. Toronto: McClelland and Stewart.

Panitch, Leo, and Donald Swartz 1993 *The Assault on Trade Union Freedoms: From Wage Controls to Social Contract.* Toronto: Garamond.

Paris, Hélène 1989 *The Corporate Response to Workers with Family Responsibilities.* Ottawa: Conference Board of Canada, Report 43–89.

Parr, Joy 1990 *The Gender of Breadwinners: Women, Men and Change in Two Industrial Towns 1880–1950.* Toronto: University of Toronto Press.

Patterson, E. Palmer II 1972 *The Canadian Indian: A History Since 1500.* Don Mills, ON: Collier–Macmillan.

Pauls, Syd 1996 "Racism and Native schooling: a historical perspective." In Ibrahim Alladin, ed., *Racism in Canadian Schools.* Toronto: Harcourt Brace Canada.

Pauly, Edward, H. Kopp, and J. Haimson 1995 *Homegrown Lessons: Innovative Programs Linking School and Work.* San Francisco, CA: Jossey–Bass.

Payne, Joan, and Clive Payne 1994 "Recession, restructuring and the fate of the unemployed: evidence in the underclass debate." *Sociology* 28: 1–19.

Peitchinis, Stephen G. 1983 *Computer Technology and Employment: Retrospect and Prospect.* London: Macmillan.

Pendleton, Andrew, John McDonald, Andrew Robinson, and Nicholas Wilson 1996 "Employee participation and corporate governance in employee-owned firms." *Work, Employment & Society* 10: 205–26.

Penn, Roger 1982 "The contested terrain : a critique of R.C. Edwards' theory of working class fractions and politics." In Graham Day, ed., *Diversity and Decomposition in the Labour Market.* Aldershot, England: Gower.

Penn, Roger, and Hilda Scattergood 1985 "Deskilling or enskilling? an empirical investigation of recent theories of the labour process." *British Journal of Sociology* 36: 611–30.

Pentland, H. Claire 1979 "The Canadian industrial relations system: some formative factors." *Labour/Le Travail* 4: 9–23.

———**1981** *Labour and Capital in Canada, 1650–1860.* Toronto: James Lorimer.

Perlman, Mark, ed. 1958 *Labor Union Theories in America: Background and Development.* Evanston, IL: Row, Peterson.

Perlman, Selig 1928 *A Theory of the Labor Movement.* New York: Macmillan.

Perrow, Charles 1986 *Complex Organizations: A Critical Essay.* 3d ed. New York: Random House.

Peters, Thomas J., and Robert H. Waterman Jr. 1982 *In Search of Excellence.* New York: Warner.

Peters, Tom 1987 *Thriving on Chaos: Handbook for a Management Revolution.* New York: Alfred A. Knopf.

———**1990** "Get innovative or get dead, Part I." *California Management Review* 33, 1: 9–26.

———**1991** "Get innovative or get dead, Part II." *California Management Review* 33, 2: 9–23.

Peters, Suzanne 1995 *Exploring Canadian Values: Foundations for Well-Being.* Ottawa: Canadian Policy Research Networks Study Inc.

Pettigrew, Andrew M. 1979 "On studying organizational culture." *Administrative Science Quarterly* 24: 570–81.

Petty, M. M., G. McGee, and J. Cavender 1984 "A meta-analysis of the relationship between individual job satisfaction and individual performance." *Academy of Management Review* 9: 712–21.

Pfeffer, Jeffrey 1994 *Competitive Advantage through People: Unleashing the Power of the Workforce.* Boston: Harvard University Press.

Pfeffer, Jeffrey, and Alison Davis-Blake 1990 "Unions and job satisfaction: an alternative view." *Work and Occupations* 17: 259–83.

Phelan, Jo 1994 "The paradox of the contented female worker: an assessment of alternative explanations." *Social Psychology Quarterly* 57: 95–107.

Phillips, Paul, and Erin Phillips 1993 *Women & Work: Inequality in the Canadian Labour Market.* Toronto: James Lorimer & Company.

Philp, Margaret 1997 "Child-care plan makes Quebec distinct." *The Globe and Mail* (June 17): A1, A6.

Picard, Andre 1994 "Who Gets UI?" *Perspectives on Labour and Income* (Summer): 29–35.

Picot, W. Garrett 1987 "The changing industrial mix of employment, 1951–1985." *Canadian Social Trends* (Spring): 8–11.

Pineo, Peter C. 1984 "Revisions of the Pineo-Porter-McRoberts socioeconomic classification of occupations for the 1981 census." Hamilton: McMaster University, Program for Quantitative Studies in Economics and Population, Research Paper No. 125.

Pineo, Peter C., and John Porter 1967 "Occupational prestige in Canada." *Canadian Review of Sociology and Anthropology* 4: 24–40.

Pinfield, Lawrence T., and John S. Atkinson 1988 "The flexible firm." *Canadian Business Review* (Winter): 17–19.

Piore, Michael J. 1975 "Notes for a theory of labor market segmentation." In Richard Edwards, M. Reich, and D. Gordon, eds., *Labor Market Segmentation.* Lexington: D.C. Heath and Company.

Piore, Michael J., and Charles F. Sabel 1984 *The Second Industrial Divide: Possibilities for Prosperity.* New York: Basic Books.

Piva, Michael J. 1979 *The Condition of the Working Class in Toronto, 1900–1921.* Ottawa: University of Ottawa Press.

Polanyi, Karl 1957 *The Great Transformation.* Boston: Beacon Press.

Pold, Henry, and Fred Wong 1990 "The price of labour." *Perspectives on Labour and Income* (Autumn): 42–49.

***Policy Options* 1996** *Special Issue on Unemployment.* (July–August).

Polivka, A. E., and T. Nardone 1989 "On the definition of contingent work." *Monthly Labor Review* (December): 9–16.

Pollard, Sidney 1968 *The Genesis of Modern Management.* Harmondsworth, England: Penguin.

Pollert, Anna 1988 "The flexible firm: fixation or fact?" *Work, Employment & Society* 2: 281–316.

Pomfret, Richard 1981 *The Economic Development of Canada.* Toronto: Methuen.

Ponak, Allen and Daphne Taras 1995 *Right-to-Work.* Submission to Alberta Economic Development Authority Joint Review Committe

Ponak, Allen, and Larry F. Moore 1981 "Canadian bank unionism: perspectives and issues." *Relations Industrielles/Industrial Relations* 36: 3–30.

Poole, Michael 1981 *Theories of Trade Unionism.* London: Routledge and Kegan Paul.

Porter, John, Marion Porter, and Bernard R. Blishen 1982 *Stations and Callings: Making It through the School System.* Toronto: Methuen.

Powell, Gary N. 1993 *Women & Men in Management.* 2nd ed. Newbury Park, CA: Sage.

Praeger, Carol A. 1988 "Poverty in North America: losing ground?" *Canadian Public Policy* 14: 52–65.

Presthus, Robert 1978 *The Organizational Society.* 2d ed. New York: St. Martin's Press.

Price, D. G., and A. M. Blair 1989 *The Changing Geography of the Service Sector.* London: Belhaven.

Pringle, Rosemary 1989 "Bureaucracy, rationality and sexuality: the case of secretaries." In Jeff Hearn, Deborah L. Sheppard, Peta Tancred-Sheriff, and Gibson Burrell, eds., *The Sexuality of Organization.* London: Sage.

Pugh, D. S., D. J. Hickson, and C. R. Hinings 1985 *Writers on Organizations.* Beverly Hills, CA: Sage.

Pupo, Norene 1997 "Always working, never done: the expansion of the double day." pp. 144–65 in *Good Jobs, Bad Jobs, No Jobs: The Transformation of Work in the 21st Century.* Ann Duffy, Daniel Glenday, and Norene Pupo, eds. Toronto: Harcourt-Brace Canada.

Purcell, Kate 1979 "Militancy and acquiescence amongst women workers." In Sandra Burman, ed., *Fit Work for Women.* London: Croom Helm.

———**1988** "Gender and the experience of employment." In Duncan Gallie, ed., *Employment in Britain.* Oxford: Basil Blackwell.

Quaid, Maeve 1993 *Job Evaluation: The Myth of Equitable Assessment.* Toronto: University of Toronto Press.

Quarter, Jack, and George Melnyk, eds. 1989 *Partners in Enterprise: The Worker Ownership Phenomenon.* Montreal: Black Rose Books.

Quick, J. D., R. S. Horn, and J. C. Quick 1987 "Health consequences of stress." *Journal of Organizational Behavior Management* 8: 19–36.

Randle, Keith 1996 "The white-coated worker: professional autonomy in a period of change." *Work, Employment & Society* 10: 737–53.

Rankin, Tom 1990 *New Forms of Work Organization: The Challenge for North American Unions.* Toronto: University of Toronto Press.

Ranson, Stewart, Bob Hinings, and Royston Greenwood 1980 "The structure of organizational structures." *Administrative Science Quarterly* 25: 1–17.

Rashid, Abdul 1993 "Seven decades of wage changes." *Perspectives on Labour and Income* (Summer): 9–21.

———**1994** "High income families." *Perspectives on Labour and Income* (Winter): 46–57.

Ray, Carol Axtell 1986 "Corporate culture: the last frontier of control?" *Journal of Management Studies* 23: 287–97.

Reagan, Barbara B., and Martha Blaxall 1976 "Occupational segregation in international women's year." In M. Blaxall and B. B. Reagan, eds., *Women and the Workplace.* Chicago: University of Chicago Press.

Reasons, Charles E., Lois L. Ross, and Craig Paterson 1981 *Assault on the Worker: Occupational Health and Safety in Canada.* Toronto: Butterworths.

Redman, Tom, Adrian Wilkinson, and Ed Snape 1997 "Stuck in the middle? managers in building societies." *Work, Employment & Society* 11: 101–14.

Redpath, Lindsay 1994 "Education–job mismatch among Canadian university graduates: implications for employers and educators." *Canadian Journal of Higher Education* 24: 89–114.

Reed, Mike 1989 *The Sociology of Management.* London: Harvester Wheatsheaf.

Reich, Robert B. 1991 *The Work of Nations: Preparing Ourselves for 21st-Century Capitalism.* New York: Alfred A. Knopf.

Reichheld, Frederick F. 1996 *The Loyalty Effect: The Hidden Force Behind Growth, Profits, and Lasting Value.* Boston: Harvard Business School Press.

Reid, Angus 1996 *Shakedown: How the New Economy is Changing Our Lives.* Toronto: Doubleday.

Reid, Donald G., and Roger C. Mannell 1994 "The globalization of the economy and potential new roles for work and leisure." *Society and Leisure* 17: 251–66.

Reid, Frank 1982 "Wage-and-price controls in Canada." In John Anderson and Morley Gunderson, eds., *Union–Management Relations in Canada.* Don Mills ON: Addison-Wesley.

———**1985** "Reductions in work time: an assessment of employment sharing to reduce unemployment." In W. Craig Riddell, ed., *Work and Pay: The Canadian Labour Market.* Toronto: University of Toronto Press.

Reimer, Neil 1979 "Oil, chemical and atomic workers international union and the quality of working life: a union perspective." *Quality of Working Life: The Canadian Scene* (Winter): 5–7.

Reiter, Ester 1991 *Making Fast Food: From the Frying Pan into the Fryer.* Montreal and Kingston: McGill–Queen's University Press.

Reitz, Jeffrey G. 1988 "Less racial discrimination in Canada, or simply less racial conflict?: implications of comparisons with Britain." *Canadian Public Policy* 14: 424–41.

Renaud, Viviane, and Jane Badets 1993 "Ethnic diversity in the 1990s." *Canadian Social Trends* 30 (Autumn): 17–22.

Reshef, Yonatan 1990 "Union decline: a view from Canada." *Journal of Labor Research* 9: 25–39.

Reskin, Barbara, and Irene Padavic 1994 *Women and Men at Work.* Thousand Oaks, CA: Pine Forge Press.

Richards, John, Aidan Vining, David M. Brown, Michael Krashinsky, William J. Milne, Ernie S. Lightman, and Shirley Hoy 1995 *Helping the Poor: A Qualified Case for "Workfare."* Ottawa: C. D. Howe Institute.

Richardson, Charley 1996 "Computers don't kill jobs, people do: technology and power in the workplace." *Annals of the American Academy of Political and Social Science* (March): 167–79.

Riddell, W. Craig 1985 "Work and pay: the Canadian labour market: an overview." In W. Craig Riddell, ed., *Work and Pay: The Canadian Labour Market.* Toronto: University of Toronto Press.

———**1986a** "Canadian labour relations: an overview." In W. Craig Riddell, ed., *Canadian Labour Relations.* Toronto: University of Toronto Press.

———**1986b** "Labour–management cooperation in Canada: an overview." In W. Craig Riddell, ed., *Labour–Management Cooperation in Canada.* Toronto: University of Toronto Press.

———**1996** "Assessing recent experience." *Policy Options* (July–August): 9–14.

Rifkin, Jeremy 1995 *The End of Work: The Decline of the Global Labor Force and the Dawn of the Post-Market Era.* New York: Putnum.

Riley, Matilda W., ed. 1988 *Social Structure and Human Lives.* Newbury Park, CA: Sage.

Rinehart, James 1978 "Contradictions of work-related attitudes and behaviour: an interpretation." *Canadian Review of Sociology and Anthropology* 15: 1–15.

———**1984** "Appropriating workers knowledge: quality control circles at a General Motors plant." *Studies in Political Economy* 14: 75–97.

———**1986** "Improving the quality of working life through job redesign: work humanization or work rationalization?" *Canadian Review of Sociology and Anthropology* 23: 507–30.

———**1996** *The Tyranny of Work: Alienation and the Labour Process.* 3d ed. Toronto: Harcourt Brace Canada.

Rinehart, James, Christopher Huxley, and David Robertson 1994 "Worker commitment and labour–management relations under lean production at CAMI." *Relations Industrielles/Industrial Relations* 49: 750–75.

Rioux, Marcia H. 1985 "Labelled disabled and wanting to work." In *Research Studies of the Commission on Equality in Employment* (Abella Commission) Ottawa: Supply and Services Canada.

Roberts, Karen, Doug Hyatt, and Peter Dorman 1996 "The effect of free trade on contingent work in Michigan." *Policy Choices: Free Trade Among NAFTA Nations,* Karen Roberts and Mark I. Wilson, eds. East Lansing, MI: Michigan State University Press.

Roberts, J. Timmons, and John E. Baugher 1995 "Hazardous workplaces and job strain: evidence from an eleven nation study." *International Jounal of Contemporary Sociology* 32: 235–249.

Roberts, Wayne 1990 *Cracking the Canadian Formula: The Making of the Energy and Chemical Workers Union.* Toronto: Between the Lines.

Robertson, David, and Jeff Wareham 1987 *Technological Change in the Auto Industry.* Willowdale, ON: Canadian Auto Workers (CAW).

———**1989** *Changing Technology & Work: Northern Telecom.* Willowdale, ON: Canadian Auto Workers (CAW).

Robertson, David, James Rinehart, and Christopher Huxley 1992 "Team concept and kaizen: Japanese production management in a unionized Canadian plant." *Studies in Political Economy* (Autumn): 77–107.

Robin, Martin 1968 *Radical Politics and Canadian Labour: 1880–1930.* Kingston: Queen's University Industrial Relations Centre.

Robinson, Ian 1994 "NAFTA, social unionism, and labour movement power in Canada and the United States." *Relations Industrielles/Industrial Relations* 49 (4): 657–93.

Roethlisberger, F. J., and W. J. Dickson 1939 *Management and the Worker.* Cambridge, MA: Harvard University Press.

Rónas-Tas, Ákos. 1994 "The first shall be last? entrepreneurship and Communist Cadres in the transition from socialism." *American Journal of Sociology* 100: 40–69.

Rose, Michael 1985 *Re-Working the Work Ethic: Economic Values and Socio-Cultural Politics.* London: Batsford.

Rosenberg, Samuel, ed. 1989 *The State and the Labor Market.* New York: Plenum.

Ross, David P. 1992 "Action needed on education for Indians." *Perception* 15–4/16–1: 27–30.

Ross, David P., and Richard Shillington 1991 *Flux: Two Years in the Life of the Canadian Labour Market.* Findings of the Statistics Canada Labour Market Activity Survey 1986–87. Ottawa: Statistics Canada (Cat. No. 71–538E Occasional).

Rothschild, Joyce, and Raymond Russell 1986 "Alternatives to bureaucracy: democratic participation in the economy." *Annual Review of Sociology* 12: 307–28.

Rowe, Reba, and William E. Snizek 1995 "Gender differences in work values: perpetuating the myth." *Work and Occupations* 22: 215–29.

Roy, Donald 1952 "Quota restriction and goldbricking in a machine shop." *American Journal of Sociology* 57: 427–42.

———**1959–60** "'Bananatime': job satisfaction and informal interaction." *Human Organization* 18: 158–68.

Rubery, Jill 1988 "Employers and the labour market." In Duncan Gallie, ed., *Employment in Britain.* Oxford: Basil Blackwell.

Rubery, Jill, and Colette Fagan 1995 "Gender segregation in societal context." *Work, Employment & Society* 9: 213–40.

Rubery, Jill, F. Wilkinson, and R. Tarling 1989 "Government policy and the labour market: the case of the United Kingdom." In S. Rosenberg, ed., *The State and the Labor Market.* New York: Plenum.

Russell, Bob 1990 *Back to Work? Labour, State, and Industrial Relations in Canada.* Scarborough, ON: Nelson.

———**1995** "The subtle labour process and the great skill debate: evidence from a potash mine-mill operation." *Canadian Journal of Sociology* 20: 359–385.

———**1997** "Rival paradigms at work: work reorganization and labour force impacts in a staple industry." *Canadian Review of Sociology and Anthropology* 34: 25–52.

Ryerson, Stanley B. 1968 *Unequal Union: Confederation and the Roots of Conflict in the Canadas, 1815–1873.* Toronto: Progress Books.

Ryscavage, Paul 1995 "A surge in growing income inequality?" *Monthly Labor Review* (August): 5l–61.

Sandberg, Ake 1994 "'Volvoism's at the end of the road?" *Studies in Political Economy* 45: 170–82.

Sangster, Joan 1978 "The 1907 Bell telephone strike: organizing women workers." *Labour/Le Travailleur* 3: 109–30.

Sass, Robert 1986 "Workplace health and safety: report from Canada." *International Journal of Health Services* 16: 565–82.

———**1995** "A conversation about the work environment." *International Journal of Health Services* 25: 117–128.

———**1996** "A message to the labor movement: stop and think!" *International Journal of Health Services* 26: 595–609.

Satzewich, Victor, and Peter S. Li 1987 "Immigrant labour in Canada: the cost and benefit of ethnic origin in the job market." *Canadian Journal of Sociology* 12: 229–41.

Saul, John R. 1995 *The Unconscious Civilization.* Toronto: Anansi.

Saunders, John 1997 "Dollars and sense." *The Globe and Mail* (12 April: B1).

Sauter, Steven L., J. J. Hurrell Jr., and C. L. Cooper 1989 *Job Control and Worker Health.* New York: Wiley.

Schein, Edgar H. 1992 *Organizational Culture and Leadership.* 2d ed. San Francisco: Jossey–Bass.

Schellenberg, Grant, and Christopher Clark 1996 *Temporary Employment in Canada: Profiles, Patterns and Policy Considerations.* Ottawa: Canadian Council on Social Development.

Schellenberg, Grant, and David P. Ross 1997 *Left Poor by the Market: A Look at Family Poverty and Earnings.* Ottawa: Canadian Council on Social Development.

Schooler, Carmi 1984 "Psychological effects of complex environments during the life span: a review and theory." *Intelligence* 8: 259–81.

———**1996** "Cultural and social-structural explanations of cross-national psychological differences." *Annual Review of Sociology* 22: 323–49.

Schor, Juliet 1991 *The Overworked American: The Unexpected Decline of Leisure.* New York: Basic Books.

Schwartz, Joe 1992 "Low-wage workers growing rapidly." *American Demographics* (July): 12, 17.

Scott, John 1988 "Ownership and employer control." In Duncan Gallie, ed., *Employment in Britain.* Oxford: Basil Blackwell.

Seager, Allen 1985 "Socialists and workers: the Western Canadian coal miners, 1900–21." *Labour/Le Travail* 16: 25–39.

Secretariat of the Commission for Labor Cooperation. 1996 *North American Labor Markets: A Comparative Profile 1984–1995. Preliminary Findings.* Dallas: Commission for Labor Cooperation.

Sedivy-Glasgow, Marie 1992 "Nursing in Canada." *Canadian Social Trends* (Spring): 27–29.

Seeman, Melvin 1959 "On the meaning of alienation." *American Sociological Review* 24: 783–91.

———1967 "On the personal consequences of alienation in work." *American Sociological Review* 32: 273–85.

———1975 "Alienation studies." *Annual Review of Sociology* 1: 91–125.

Selye, Hans 1976 *Stress in Health and Disease.* Boston: Butterworths.

Semler, Ricardo 1993 "Workers' paradise?" *Report on Business Magazine* (December): 39–48.

Senge, Peter M. 1990 *The Fifth Discipline: The Art and Practice of the Learning Organization.* New York: Doubleday.

Senge, Peter, Art Kleiner, Charlotte Roberts, Richard B. Ross, and Bryan J. Smith 1994 *The Fifth Discipline Fieldbook: Strategies and Tools for Building a Learning Organization.* New York: Currency Doubleday.

Sennett, Richard, and Jonathon Cobb 1972 *The Hidden Injuries of Class.* New York: Knopf.

Shadd, Adrienne L. 1987 "Dual labour markets in core and periphery regions of Canada: the position of Black males in Ontario and Nova Scotia." *Canadian Ethnic Studies* 19: 91–109.

Shain, Alan 1995 "Employment of people with disabilities." *Canadian Social Trends* (Autumn): 8–13.

Shallis, Michael 1984 *The Silicon Idol: The Micro Revolution and Its Social Implications.* Oxford: Oxford University Press.

Sharpe, Andrew 1990 "Training the workforce: a challenge facing Canada in the 90s." *Perspectives on Labour and Income* (Winter): 21–31.

Sharpe, Dennis B., and Gerald White 1993 *Educational Pathways and Experiences of Newfoundland Youth.* St. John's: Centre for Educational Research and Development, Memorial University.

Sherman, Barrie, and Phil Judkins 1995 *Licensed to Work.* London: Cassel.

Shieh, G. S. 1992 *"Boss" Island: The Subcontracting Network and Micro-Entrepreneurship in Taiwan's Development.* New York: Peter Lang.

Shorter, Edward, and Charles Tilly 1974 *Strikes in France, 1830–1968.* Cambridge, MA: Cambridge University Press.

Siltanen, Janet 1994 *Locating Gender: Occupational Segregation, Wages and Domestic Responsibilities.* London: UCL Press.

Sinclair, Peter R., and Lawrence F. Felt 1992 "Separate worlds: gender and domestic labour in an isolated fishing region." *Canadian Review of Sociology and Anthropology* 29: 55–71.

Singelmann, J. 1978 *From Agriculture to Services.* Beverly Hills, CA: Sage.

Siu-Kai, Lau, and Kuan Hsin-Chi 1988 *The Ethos of the Hong Kong Chinese.* Hong Kong: Chinese University Press.

Sivesind, Karl Henrik 1995 "The indispensable role of culture: explaining different understandings of work through a comparison of German and Norwegian factories." *Comparative Social Research* 15: 35–101.

Skrypnek, Berna J., and Janet E. Fast 1996 "Work and family policy in Canada." *Journal of Family Issues* 17: 793–812.

Sloan, Richard P. 1987 "Workplace health promotion: a commentary on the evolution of a paradigm." *Health Education Quarterly* 14: 181–94.

Smith, Adam 1976 *The Wealth of Nations.* Chicago: University of Chicago Press. [Originally published in 1776.]

Smith, Michael R. 1978 "The effects of strikes on workers: a critical analysis." *Canadian Journal of Sociology* 3: 457–72.

Smith, Michael R., Anthony C. Masi, Axel van den Berg, and Joseph Smucker 1995 "External flexibility in Sweden and Canada: a three industry comparison." *Work, Employment & Society* 9: 689–718.

———**1997** "Insecurity, labour relations, and flexibility in two process industries: a Canada/Sweden comparison." *Canadian Journal of Sociology* 22: 31–63.

Smith, Vicki 1994 "Braverman's legacy: the labour process tradition at 20." *Work and Occupations 21*: 403–21.

Smucker, Joseph 1980 *Industrialization in Canada.* Scarborough, ON: Prentice-Hall.

Smucker, Joseph, and Axel van den Berg 1991 "Some evidence of the effects of labour market policies on workers' attitudes toward change in Canada and Sweden." *Canadian Journal of Sociology* 16: 51–74.

Social Research and Demonstration Corporation 1996 *When Work Pays Better Than Welfare: A Summary of the Self-Sufficiency Project's Implementation, Focus Group, and Initial 18-Month Impact Reports.* Vancouver: Social Research and Demonstration Corporation.

Sonnenfeld, Jeffrey A. 1985 "Shedding light on the Hawthorne Studies." *Journal of Occupational Behaviour* 6: 111–30.

Sorrentino, Constance 1995 "International unemployment indicators, 1983–93." *Monthly Labor Review* (August): 31–50.

Sosteric, Mike 1996 "Subjectivity and the labour process: a case study in the restaurant industry." *Work, Employment & Society* 10: 297–318.

Spain, Daphne, and Suzanne M. Bianchi 1996 *Balancing Act: Motherhood, Marriage, and Employment among American Women.* New York: Russell Sage Foundation.

Spencer, Metta 1985 *Foundations of Modern Sociology.* 4th ed. Scarborough: Prentice-Hall.

Spenner, Kenneth I. 1983 "Deciphering Prometheus: temporal change in the skill level of work." *American Sociological Review* 48: 824–37.

———**1990** "Skill: meanings, methods, and measures." *Work and Occupations* 14: 399–421.

Spinrad, William 1984 "Work democracy: an overview." *International Social Science Journal* 36: 195–215.

Staber, Udo 1993 "Worker cooperatives and the business cycle: are cooperatives the answer to unemployment?" *The American Journal of Economics and Sociology* 52: 129–43.

Stabler, Jack C., and Eric C. Howe 1990 "Native participation in northern development: the impending crisis in the NWT." *Canadian Public Policy* 16: 262–83.

Staines, Graham L. 1980 "Spillover versus compensation: a review of the literature on the relationship between work and non-work." *Human Relations* 33: 111–29.

Stark, David 1988 "Rethinking internal labour markets: new insights from a comparative perspective." In R.E. Pahl, ed., *On Work: Historical, Comparative and Theoretical Perspectives.* Oxford: Basil Blackwell.

Statistics Canada 1973 *Corporations and Labour Unions Returns Act (CALURA). Report for 1970.* Part II— Labour Unions (Cat. No. 71–202).

———**1991** *Income Distributions by Size in Canada, 1990.* (Cat. No. 13–207).

———**1992a** *Labour Market Activity Survey, Canada's Women: A Profile of Their 1988 Labour Market Experience.* (Cat. No. 71–205).

———**1992b** *Labour Market Activity Survey, Canada's Men: A Profile of Their 1988 Labour Market Experience.* (Cat. No. 71–206).

———**1992c** *CALURA Part II Labour Unions 1989.* (Cat. No. 71–202).

———**1993** *1991 Census, Industry and Occupation: Occupation, The Nation.* (Cat. No. 93–327). Ottawa: Statistics Canada.

———**1994a** *Schooling, Work and Related Activities, Income, Expenses and Mobility: 1991 Aboriginal Peoples Survey.* Ottawa: Statistics Canada. (Cat. No. 89–534–XPB)

———**1994b** *Work Injuries 1991–1993.* (Cat. No. 72–208).

———**1994c** *Women in the Labour Force, 1994 Edition.* Ottawa: Statistics Canada. (Cat. No. 75–507E).

———**1994d** *Population Projections for Canada and the Provinces 1976–2001.* (Cat. No. 91–520C) Ottawa: Statistics Canada

———**1995a** "Moving with the times: introducing change to the LFS" *The Labour Force* (December): C–2–C–19.

———**1995b** *1994 General Social Survey (Cycle 9) Microdata File.* Ottawa: Statistics Canada.

———**1996a** *Education in Canada, 1995.* (Cat. No. 81–229).

———**1996b** *Income Distribution by Size in Canada 1995.* (Cat. No. 13–207).

———**1996c** *Canada's Retirement Income Programs: A Statistical Overview.* Ottawa: Statistics Canada. Cat. No. 74–507–XPB).

———**1996d** *Historical Labour Force Statistics.* (Cat. No. 71–201).

———**1997a** *Earnings of Men and Women 1995.* (Cat. No.13–217).

———**1997b** "Crossing the low-income line, 1993–1994." *The Daily* (7 July 1997): 5–7.

———**1997c** *Labour Force Annual Averages 1996.* (Cat. No. 71–220–XPB).

———**1997d** *Income After Tax, Distributions by Size in Canada, 1995.* (Cat. No. 13–210–XPB). Ottawa: Statistics Canada.

Statistics Canada and Human Resources Development Canada 1996 *Reading the Future: A Portrait of Literacy in Canada.* (Cat. No. 89–551).

Steinberg, Ronnie J. 1990 "Social construction of skill: gender, power, and comparable worth." *Work and Occupations* 17: 449–82.

Stern, David, N. Finkelstein, J. R. Rose III, J. Latting, and C. Dornsife 1995 *School to Work: Research on Programs in the United States.* Washington: Falmer.

Stern, Robert N. **1976** "Intermetropolitan pattern of strike frequency." *Industrial and Labor Relations Review* 29: 218–35.

Stewart, A., and R. M. Blackburn **1975** "The stability of structured inequality." *Sociological Review* 23: 481–508.

Stewart, Paul, and Phillip Garahan **1995** "Employee responses to new management techniques in the auto industry." *Work, Employment & Society* 9: 517–36.

Stone, Leroy **1994** *Dimensions of Job–Family Tension.* Ottawa: Statistics Canada.

Storey, Robert **1983** "Unionization versus corporate welfare: the Dofasco way." *Labour/Le Travailleur* 12: 7–42.

———**1991** "Studying work in Canada." *Canadian Journal of Sociology* 16: 241–64.

Strong-Boag, Veronica **1988** *The New Day Recalled: Lives of Girls and Women in English Canada, 1919–1939.* Markham, ON: Penguin Books.

Sturdy, Andrew, David Knights, and Hugh Willmott, eds. **1992** *Contemporary Studies in the Labour Process.* London: Routledge.

Sufrin, Eileen **1982** *The Eaton Drive: The Campaign to Organize Canada's Largest Department Store, 1948 to 1952.* Toronto: Fitzhenry and Whiteside.

Sugiman, Pamela **1992** "That wall's comin' down: gendered strategies of worker resistance in the UAW Canadian region (1963–1970)." *Canadian Journal of Sociology* 17: 24–27.

Sunahara, Ann Gomer **1981** *The Politics of Racism: The Uprooting of Japanese Canadians during the Second World War.* Toronto: James Lorimer.

Sunter, Deborah **1997** "Youths and the labour market." *Canadian Economic Observer* (May): 3.1–3.7.

Sunter, Deborah, and Rene Morissette **1994** "The hours people work." *Perspectives on Labour and Income* (Autumn): 8–13.

Suplee, Curt **1997** "Robot revolution." *National Geographic* (July): 76–93.

Swartz, Donald **1981** "New forms of worker participation: a critique of quality of working life." *Studies in Political Economy* 5: 55–78.

Swidinsky, R., and M. Kupferschmidt **1991** "Longitudinal estimates of the union effects on wages, wage dispersion and pension fringe benefits." *Relations Industrielles/Industrial Relations* 46: 819–38.

Swift, Jamie **1995** *Wheel of Fortune: Work and Life in the Age of Falling Expectations.* Toronto: Between the Lines.

Szelényi, Iván, and Eric Kostello **1996** "The market transition debated: toward asynthesis?" *American Journal of Sociology* 10: 1082–96.

Tancred, Peta **1995** "Women's work: a challenge to the sociology of work." *Gender, Work and Organization* 2: 11–20.

Tanner, Julian **1984** "Skill levels of manual workers and beliefs about work, management, and industry: a comparison of craft and non-craft workers in Edmonton." *Canadian Journal of Sociology* 9: 303–18.

Tanner, Julian, and Rhonda Cockerill **1986** "In search of working-class ideology: a test of two perspectives." *Sociological Quarterly* 27: 389–402.

Tanner, Julian, and Harvey Krahn **1991** "Part-time work and deviance among high school seniors." *Canadian Journal of Sociology* 16: 281–302.

Tanner, Julian, Scott Davies, and Bill O'Grady **1992** "Immanence changes everything: a critical comment on the labour process and class consciousness." *Sociology* 26: 439–53.

Tanner, Julian, Harvey Krahn, and Timothy F. Hartnagel **1995** *Fractured Transitions from School to Work: Revisiting the Dropout Problem.* Don Mills, ON: Oxford University Press.

Tausky, Curt **1978** *Work Organizations: Major Theoretical Perspectives.* 2d ed. Ithasca, IL: F. E. Peacock Publishers.

Taylor, Frederick W. **1919** *Shop Management.* New York: Harper.

Taylor, Jeff **1995** "Labour in the Klein Revolution." *In the Trojan Horse: Alberta and the Future of Canada.* Trevor Harrison and Gordon Laxer, eds. Montreal: Black Rose Books.

Teachman, Jay D. **1987** "Family background, educational resources, and educational attainment." *American Sociological Review* 52: 548–57.

Teeple, Gary **1972** "Land, labour and capital in pre-Confederation Canada." In Gary Teeple, ed., *Capitalism and the National Question in Canada.* Toronto: University of Toronto Press.

Terkel, Studs **1971** *Working.* New York: Pantheon.

Thomas, Alan Berkeley **1988** "Does leadership make a difference to organizational performance?" *Administrative Science Quarterly* 33: 388–400.

Thompson, Elizabeth **1990** "Worked to the bone." *Perception* 14: 45–47.

Thompson, Paul **1989** *The Nature of Work: Introduction to Debates on the Labour Process.* 2d ed. London: Macmillan.

Thompson, Tim **1991** "The labour market: mid-year review." *Perspectives on Labour and Income* (Autumn): 2–10.

Thorsrud, Einar **1975** "Collaborative action research to enhance the quality of working life." In L. E. Davis and A. B. Cherns, eds., *The Quality of Working Life.* Vol. 1. New York: Free Press.

Thurow, Lester C. **1975** *Generating Inequality: Mechanisms of Distribution in the U.S. Economy.* New York: Basic Books.

Tilly, Charles **1979** *From Mobilization to Revolution.* Reading, MA: Addison-Wesley.

Tindale, Joseph A. **1991** *Older Workers in an Aging Workforce.* Ottawa: National Advisory Council on Aging.

Tobin, James **1996** "Business cycles and economic growth: current controversies about theory and policy." *Unnecessary Debts.* Lars Osberg and Pierre Fortin, eds. Toronto: Lorimer.

Toffler, Alvin **1980** *The Third Wave.* New York: Bantam.

Toscano, Guy, and Janice Windau **1993** "Fatal work injuries: results from the 1992 national census." *Monthly Labor Review* (October): 39–48

Trice, Harrison M., and Janice M. Beyer **1993** *The Cultures of Work Organizations.* Englewood Cliffs, NJ: Prentice-Hall.

Trist, E. L., and K. W. Bamforth **1951** "Some social and psychological consequences of the longwall method of coal-getting." *Human Relations* 4: 3–38.

Tucker, Eric **1992** "Worker participation in health and safety regulation: lessons from Sweden." *Studies in Political Economy* 37: 95–127.

United Auto Workers **1985** "Can capital and labour cooperate?" In Daniel Drache and Duncan Cameron, eds., *The Other Macdonald Report.* Toronto: James Lorimer.

Useem, Michael, and Jerome Karabel **1986** "Pathways to top corporate management." *American Sociological Review* 51: 184–200.

Vallas, Steven Peter **1990** "The concept of skill." *Work and Occupations* 14: 379–98.

Van den Berg, Axel, and Joseph Smucker, eds. **1997** *The Sociology of Labour Markets: Efficiency, Equity, Security.* Scarborough, ON: Prentice-Hall.

Van Houten, Donald R. 1990 "The political economy and technical control of work humanization in Sweden during the 1970s and 1980s." *Work and Occupations* 14: 483–513.

Van Kirk, Sylvia 1980 *Many Tender Ties: Women in Fur-Trade Society, 1670–1870.* Winnipeg: Watson and Dwyer.

Veltmeyer, Henry 1983 "The development of capitalism and the capitalist world system." In J. Paul Grayson, ed., *Introduction to Sociology: An Alternative Approach.* Toronto: Gage.

Wagner, David 1994 "Beyond the pathologizing of nonwork: alternative activities in a street community." *Social Work* 39: 718–27.

Wajcman, Judy 1991 "Patriarchy, technology, and conceptions of skill." *Work and Occupations* 18: 29–45.

Walby, Sylvia 1989 "Flexibility and the changing sexual division of labour." In Stephen Wood, ed., *The Transformation of Work?* London: Unwin Hyman.

———**1990** *Theorizing Patriarchy.* Oxford: Basil Blackwell.

Waldram, James B. 1987 "Native employment and hydroelectric development in northern Manitoba." *Journal of Canadian Studies* 22: 62–76.

Waldrop, Judith 1992 "Less work, more play, same pay." *American Demographics* (August): 13.

Walker, C. R., and R. H. Guest 1952 *Man on the Assembly Line.* Cambridge, MA: Harvard University Press.

Wallace, Jean E. 1995a "Corporatist control and organizational commitment among professionals: the case of lawyers working in law firms." *Social Forces* 73: 811–39.

———**1995b** "Organizational and professional commitment in professional and nonprofessional organizations." *Administrative Science Quarterly* 40: 228–55.

Wallace, Jean E., and Merlin B. Brinkerhoff 1991 "The measurement of burnout revisited." *Journal of Social Service Research* 14: 85–111.

Wallace, Jo-Ann 1995 "'Fit and qualified': the equity debate at the University of Alberta." In *Beyond Political Correctness: Toward the Inclusive University,* Stephen Richer and Lorna Weir, eds. Toronto: University of Toronto Press.

Walmsley, Ann 1992 "Trading places." *Report on Business Magazine* (March): 17–27.

Walsh, Janet 1997 "Employment systems in transition? a comparative analysis of Britain and Australia." *Work, Employment & Society* 11: 1–25.

Walters, Vivienne 1985 "The politics of occupational health and safety: interviews with workers health and safety representatives and company doctors." *Canadian Review of Sociology and Anthropology* 22: 57–79.

Walters, Vivienne, and Ted Haines 1988 "Workers use and knowledge of the internal responsibility system: limits to participation in occupational health and safety." *Canadian Public Policy* 14: 411–23.

Wannell, Ted, and Nathalie Caron 1994 *The Gender Earnings Gap among Recent Postsecondary Graduates, 1984–92.* Ottawa: Statistics Canada. Analytic Studies Branch, Research Paper Series, No. 64.

Wanner, Richard A. 1993 "Patterns and trends in occupational mobility." In James Curtis, Edward Grabb, and Neil Guppy, eds., *Social Inequality in Canada: Patterns, Problems, Policies.* 2d ed. Scarborough: Prentice-Hall.

Wanner, Richard A., and Bernadette C. Hayes 1996 "Intergenerational occupational mobility among men in Canada and Australia." *Canadian Journal of Sociology* 21: 43–76.

Warme, B.D., K.L.P. Lundy, and L.A. Lundy, eds. 1992 *Working Part-Time: Risks and Opportunities.* New York: Praeger.

Warr, Peter 1987 *Work, Unemployment, and Mental Health.* Oxford: Clarendon Press.

Watkins, Mel 1977 "From underdevelopment to development." In Mel Watkins, ed., *Dene Nation: The Colony Within.* Toronto: University of Toronto Press.

———**1991** "A staples theory of economic growth." In Gordon Laxer, ed., *Perspectives on Canadian Economic Development.* Toronto: Oxford University Press.

———**1997** "Canadian capitalism in transition." pp. 19–42 in *Understanding Canada: Building on the New Canadian Political Economy,* Wallace Clement, ed. Montreal and Kingston: McGill–Queen's University Press.

Watson, Tony J. 1987 *Sociology, Work and Industry.* 2d ed. London: Routledge and Kegan Paul.

Webb, Janette 1996 "Vocabularies of motive and the 'new' management." *Work, Employment & Society* 10: 251–71.

Webb, Sidney, and Beatrice Webb 1894 *The History of Trade Unionism.* London: Longmans, Green.

Weber, Max 1946 "Bureaucracy." In H. H. Gerth and C. Wright Mills, eds., *From Max Weber.* New York: Oxford University Press.

———**1958** *The Protestant Ethic and the Spirit of Capitalism.* New York: Scribner.

———**1964** *The Theory of Social and Economic Organization.* New York: Free Press.

Weiner, Nan, and Morley Gunderson 1990 *Pay Equity: Issues, Options and Experiences.* Toronto: Butterworths.

Weiss, Donald D. 1976 "Marx versus Smith on the division of labour." *Monthly Review* 28: 104–118.

Weitzel, William, and Ellen Jonsson 1989 "Decline in organizations: a literature integration and extension." *Administrative Science Quarterly* 34: 91–109.

Wells, Don 1986 *Soft Sell: Quality of Working Life Programs and the Productivity Race.* Ottawa: Canadian Centre for Policy Alternatives.

Westergaard, John 1995 *Who Gets What? The Hardening of Class Inequality in the Late Twentieth Century.* Cambridge: Polity Press.

Wetzel, Kurt, Daniel G. Gallagher, and Donna E. Soloshy 1991 "Union commitment: is there a gender gap?" *Relations Industrielles/Industrial Relations* 46: 564–83.

Whitaker, R. 1979 "Scientific management theory as political ideology." *Studies in Political Economy* 2: 75–108.

White, Jerry P. 1990 *Hospital Strike: Women, Unions, and Public Sector Conflict.* Toronto: Thompson Educational Publishing.

White, Julie 1990 *Male and Female: Women and the Canadian Union of Postal Workers.* Toronto: Thompson Educational Publishing.

White, Lynn, Jr. 1962 *Medieval Technology and Social Change.* Oxford: Oxford University Press.

Whitehead, T. N. 1936 *Leadership in a Free Society.* Cambridge, MA: Harvard University Press.

Whitley, Richard 1992 *Business Systems in East Asia: Firms, Markets and Societies.* London: Sage.

Whittaker, D. H. 1990 "The end of Japanese-style employment?" *Work, Employment & Society* 4: 321–47.

Whyte, William Foote, and Kathleen King Whyte 1988 *Making Mondragon: The Growth and Dynamics of the Worker Cooperative Complex.* Ithaca, NY: ILR Press.

Wiatrowski, William J. 1994 "Employee benefits for union and nonunion workers." *Monthly Labor Review* (February): 34–37.

Wilensky, Jeanne L., and Harold L. Wilensky 1951 "Personnel counseling: the Hawthorne case." *American Journal of Sociology* 57: 265–80.

Wilgosh, Lorraine R., and Deborah Skaret 1987 "Employer attitudes toward hiring individuals with disabilities: a review of the recent literature." *Canadian Journal of Rehabilitation* 1: 89–98.

Wilson, William J. 1997 *When Work Disappears: The World of the New Urban Poor.* New York: Alfred A. Knopf.

Winson, Anthony. 1996 "In search of the part-time capitalist farmer: labour use and farm structure in central Canada." *Canadian Review of Sociology and Anthropology* 33: 89–110.

Womack, James P., Daniel T. Jones, and Daniel Roos 1990 *The Machine That Changed the World.* New York: Harper Perennial.

Wood, Stephen 1987 "The deskilling debate, new technology and work organization." *Acta Sociologica* 30: 3–24.

———**1989a** "The Japanese management model." *Work and Occupations* 16: 446–60.

———**1989b** *The Transformation of Work? Skill, Flexibility and the Labour Process.* London: Unwin Hyman.

———**1989c** "New wave management?" *Work, Employment & Society* 3: 379–402.

Woodward, Joan 1980 *Industrial Organization: Theory and Practice.* 2d ed. Oxford: Oxford University Press.

World Bank 1993 *The East Asian Miracle: Economic Growth and Public Policy.* New York: Oxford University Press.

World Commission on Environment and Development 1987 *Our Common Future.* Oxford: Oxford University Press.

Worsley, Peter 1984 *The Three Worlds: Culture and World Development.* London: Weidenfeld and Nicolson.

Wotherspoon, Terry 1995 "Transforming Canada's education system: the impact on educational inequalities, opportunities, and benefits." In B. Singh Bolaria, ed., *Social Issues and Contradictions in Canadian Society.* 2d ed. Toronto: Harcourt Brace Jovanovich.

Wright, Eric Olin, C. Costello, D. Hachen, and J. Sprague 1982 "The American class structure." *American Sociological Review* 47: 709–26.

Wright, James D., and Richard F. Hamilton 1979 "Education and job attitudes among blue-collar workers." *Sociology of Work and Occupations* 6: 59–83.

Wright, Susan 1993 "Blaming the victim, blaming society, or blaming the discipline: fixing responsibility for homelessness." *Sociological Quarterly* 34: 1–16.

Wyatt Canada 1991 *The New National Benchmark on Worker Attitudes.* Vancouver: The Wyatt Company.

Wylie, William N. T. 1983 "Poverty, distress, and disease: labour and the construction of the Rideau Canal, 1826–1832." *Labour/Le Travailleur* 11: 7–30

Yalnizyan, Armine, T. Ran Ide, and Arthur J. Cordell 1994 *Shifting Time: Social Policy and the Future of Work.* Toronto: Between the Lines Press.

Yates, Charlotte 1990 "The internal dynamics of union power: explaining Canadian autoworkers militancy in the 1980s." *Studies in Political Economy* 31: 73–105.

Yoder, Janice D. 1991 "Rethinking tokenism: looking beyond numbers." *Gender & Society* 5: 178–92.

Yun, Hing Ai 1995 "Automation and new work patterns: cases from Singapore's electronics industry." *Work, Employment & Society* 9: 309–27.

Zeidenberg, Jerry 1990 "The just-in-time workforce." *Small Business* (May): 31–34.

Zeitlin, Irving M. 1968 *Ideology and the Development of Sociological Theory*. Englewood Cliffs, NJ: Prentice-Hall.

Zeitlin, M. 1974 "Corporate ownership and control." *American Journal of Sociology* 79: 1073–1119.

Zetka, James R. Jr., 1992 "Work organization and wildcat strikes in the U.S. automobile industry, 1946–1963." *American Sociological Review* 57: 214–26.

Zimbalist, Andrew, ed. 1979 *Case Studies on the Labor Process*. New York: Monthly Review Press.

Zuboff, Shoshana 1988 *In the Age of the Smart Machine: The Future of Work and Power*. New York: Basic Books.

Zussman, David, and Jak Jabes 1989 *The Vertical Solitude: Managing in the Public Sector*. Halifax: Institute for Research on Public Policy.

INDEX

Abella Commission, 190
Aboriginals. *See* Native Canadians
Absenteeism, 163
Academic skills, 401
Adams, Roy, 365
Additional employment benefits, 99–101
Adhocracy, 230, 231
Administrative model of regulation, 292
Age discrimination, 135
AGVs, 278
Air Canada strike, 353
Algoma Steel, 306
Alienation, 262, 417–421
Alienation and Freedom (Blauner), 420, 421
Alternative work schedules, 78. *See also*
    Nonstandard work arrangements
Anxious workers, 406, 407
Apple Computer, 231
Aquinas, Saint Thomas, 384
Armstrong, Pat and Hugh, 187
Assembly-line factories, 20
Assembly-line work, 423, 424
Atkinson, John, 250, 251
Authors' conclusions, 435
Automated guided vehicles (AGVs), 278
Autonomous work team, 240

Babbage, Charles, 20
Baby boom generation, 39, 400
Bad job syndrome, 128
Bad jobs vs. good jobs, 95–104
Bank Wiring Observation Room study, 218
Banks, Hal, 321
Barnard, Chester, 211, 212
Barriers to mobility, 127–129
Batstone, Eric, 366
Beaudoin, Laurent, 98
Bell, Daniel, 24, 250, 270
Bellin, Seymour, 441
Bendix, Reinhard, 118, 203
Betcherman, Gordon, 89
Bielby, Denise, 187
Bielby, William, 187
Big labour image, 323
Bill 136, 373
Blackburn, Robert M., 383, 396, 408
Blacks, and racial discrimination, 131, 132
Blaming the victim ideology, 295
Blau, Peter, 202
Blauner, Robert, 420, 421
Blishen, Bernard, 407
Blishen scores, 407
Blue-collar occupations, 59
Bluestone, Barry, 136
Boom, Bust and Echo (Foot), 39
Boss–secretary relationship, 189
Bourdieu, Pierre, 116
Bourgeoisie, 17
Boyett, Joseph H., 229
Bradbury, Bettina, 248
Bradwin, Edmund, 9
Braverman, Harry, 214, 263–266, 270
British Columbia Solidarity Movement, 372
Brown, Leslie, 309
Brym, Robert, 15
Buffer zones, 239
Bunkhouse Man, The (Bradwin), 9
Burawoy, Michael, 268, 269
Bureaucracy, 21, 22, 201–203
Bureaucratic control, 267
Bureaucratic personality, 202
Burger King, 124
Burnout, 425
Business services, 56
Business unionism, 322
Business unionism image, 323

Calvinists, 385
Campbell Soup, 225
Canada
    class structure, 108–111
    demographic shifts, 39–46
    educational attainment, 43–46
    free trade, 29–31
    future trends, 87–89
    history of industrialization, 6–9
    hours of work, 78–80
    industrial relations, role of, in, 329–331

industrial restructuring, 26, 27
intrinsic job rewards, 413–416
labour force participation, 46–53
labour movement, development of, 324–329
mobility studies, 119
nonstandard work arrangements, 80–87
occupational changes, 58–63
regional variations, 65–68
self-employment, 64, 65
service sector, 54–57
statistical sources, 38, 39
strike trends, 361–364
unemployment, 68–77
unions, 332–349
workforce aging, 39–42
workforce diversity, 42, 43
Canadian Auto Workers (CAW), 242, 342, 352, 353, 357
Canadian Census, 38
Canadian Labour Congress (CLC), 327, 328, 349, 359, 370
Canadian Union of Postal Workers (CUPW), 357
Capitalism, 2
Capitalist-executive class, 110
Capitalists, 108
Capitalist system of production, 2
Career ladders, 125
Carey, Alex, 219
Carr, Shirley, 349
CEOs, 98, 112, 180
Chaebol, 13
Chandler, Alfred D., Jr., 220
Chaplin, Charlie, 213
Chief executive officers (CEOs), 98, 112, 180
Child, John, 209
China, 14, 15
Chinese Canadian workers, 130, 131
Circulatory mobility, 118
Class conflict, 17
Clegg, Stewart, 207
Clement, Wallace, 110, 175, 268, 272, 273
Clerical work, 167, 169
CNC machines, 278
Co-determination, 300, 301
Cobb, Jonathan, 396
Coefficient of representation, 170
Cohen, Marjorie, 151
Collective bargaining, 134
Collective voice face of unionism, 324
Collins, Randall, 127
Commercial capitalism, 3
Company union, 351
Comparable worth, 193
Compensatory leisure hypothesis, 427
Compressed work weeks, 165
Computer-based technologies, 276–280
Computer numerical control (CNC) machines, 278
Computer use in workplace, 104–106
Concession bargaining, 337, 353
Conclusion, 435
Conditions of the Working Class in England, The (Engels), 16
Confederation of National Trade Unions (CNTU), 329
Conflict and control in workplace, 259–311
flexible specialization, 287
high-performance workplace, 289
industrial democracy, 297–304
labour process perspective, 263–274
lean production, 288
managerial control, 266–270
Marxian capitalism, 262, 263
new management approaches, 285–291
quality of working life, 285, 286
skill debate, 270–274
technology, 274–285
total quality management, 286, 287
worker ownership, 304–310
workplace health and safety, 291–296
Conflict perspective, 18
Confucian work ethic, 390
Conn, Henry P., 229
Consensus approach, 21
Contingency theory, 205
Convergence thesis, 10
Cordell, Arthur, 280, 282
Core sector firms, 123, 124
Corporate welfare, 217

Corporate wellness programs, 296
Cost accounting, 210
Countercultures, 224
Coupland, Douglas, 402
Craft unions, 325, 326
Craft work, 20
Cultural capital, 116
CUPE, 343, 349
Cyclical unemployment, 75

Dalton, Melville, 223, 224
Darcy, Judy, 349
Days of action, 359, 360
Decision-making autonomy, 271
Declining middle class, 139
Deferential workers, 395
Deindustrialization, 8, 26, 27
Deindustrialization of America, 136
Demand-control model of work-related stress, 423
Demographic shifts, 39–46
Design archetype, 208
Deskilled, 104
Despotic organization of work, 269
Dilbert, 235
Direct control, 267
Disabled workers, 134
Disabling injury/illness, 101, 103
Discouraged workers, 69
Discrimination
  age, 135
  blacks, 131, 132
  ethnic stratification, 130, 131
  Native Canadians, 129, 130
  sexual orientation, 135
  systemic, 190
  wage, 181
Distributive services, 56
Division of labour, 19–21
Doctors, 127
Domestic division of labour, 159–162
Dominant culture, 224
Double day, 159, 160
Downsizing, 136, 234–236
Drache, Daniel, 27, 440
Drucker, Peter F., 231
Dual consciousness, 368
Dual-earner families, 48, 159, 160, 162
Dual economies, 122–125
Dual labour market theory. *See* Labour market segmentation
Dual representation system, 301
Duplessis, Maurice, 329
Durkheim, Emile, 21, 222

East Asian Tigers, 11–14, 390
Eastman Kodak, 231
Economic determinism, 284
Educational aspirations, 114
Educational attainment, 43–46, 411
Edwards, Richard, 267, 268
Effort bargaining, 366
1872 Toronto printers' strike, 325, 359
Elder care, 160
Electronic control, 269
Electronic surveillance, 424
Employability Skills Profile (ESP), 401
Employee buyouts, 306, 307
Employee share ownership plans (ESOPs), 305, 306
Employment benefits, 99–101
Employment equity, 190–193
End of Work, The (Rifkin), 76
Engels, Friedrich, 16
Enskilling, 270, 273
Equal pay for the same work, 193
Equal pay for work of equal value, 193
Equality of educational opportunity, 114, 115
Equity programs, 141
Esprit de corps, 218
Ethnic business enclaves, 131
Ethnic discrimination, 129–135
Ethnic stratification, 130
Etzioni, Amitai, 225
Exchange mobility, 118
Exit and voice methods of expressing discontent, 355, 356
Explosion of consciousness, 368

Family enterprise, 14
Family forms, 159
Family ownership, 23

Family wage ideology, 152–154
Farewell to the Working Class (Gorz), 392
Fast, Janet, 164
Fastidious housekeeping, 247
Faulkner, William, 417
Female job ghettos, 165, 166
Female labour force participation rates, 154
Female-to-male earnings ratio, 97, 176
Feminization, 169
Flanders, Alan, 355
Flexible firm, 250, 251
Flexible production systems, 248
Flexible specialization, 248–250, 287
Flextime, 78, 165
Foot, David, 39
Forced division of labour, 37–43
Ford, Henry, 20, 203, 216
Fordism, 203, 280
Former Soviet Union, 15
Four Tigers, 11–14, 390
Frederick, Judith, 164
Free-rider problem, 355
Free Trade Agreement (FTA), 29, 30
Freeman, Richard, 324
Freewheeling, 224
Frictional unemployment, 75
Friedman, Andrew, 267, 270
Fringe benefits, 99–101
Frontier of control, 267
FTA, 29, 30
Functional flexibility, 250
Functions of the Executive, The (Barnard), 212

Gallie, Duncan, 268, 369, 421
Garbage can model, 212
Gaskell, Jane, 185
Gender
  defined, 150
  human capital theory, 117
  income differences, 97
  job satisfaction, 410
  labour force participation, 47–49
  nonstandard work arrangements, 83
  occupations, 59–63
  part-time work, 85
  service sector employment, 56, 57
  unemployment, 72, 73
  work orientations, 397, 398
  See also Women
Gender labelling, 166
Gender role socialization, 185, 397
Gender studies, 189
Gender wage gap, 97, 178
General Motors strikes, 345, 353
General strike, 362
Generation X: Tales for an Accelerated Culture (Coupland), 402
Germany, industrial democracy, 300–302
Gertler, Meric, 27, 440
Gillespie, Richard, 219
Glass ceiling, 165
Globalization, 27–29
Goldbricking, 223
Good jobs vs. bad jobs, 95–104
Gordon, David, 135
Gorz, Andre, 392
Gouldner, Alvin, 202
Great leap backward, 32
Great transformation, 5, 6
Greenfield sites, 241
Greenwood, Royston, 208
Gunderson, Morley, 181

Hagan, John, 174
Hamper, Ben, 423
Harley Davidson Motorcycles, 228
Harrison, Bennett, 136
Hawthorne effect, 218
Hawthorne Studies, 218, 219
Health and safety, 101–104, 291–296
Hegemonic organization of work, 269
Herzberg, Frederick, 240, 412
Hewlett-Packard, 224
Hickson, David, 212
Hidden economy, 52, 53
Hidden Injuries of Class, The (Sennett/Cobb), 396
High-performance workplace (HPW), 243, 244, 289
Hill, Stephen, 232, 319, 320
Hinings, Bob, 208
Hirschman, Albert, 355

Hochschild, Arlie, 160, 162
Hofstede, Geert, 226
Homogenization of labour, 135
Hong Kong, 14
Hours of work, 78–80
Household managers, 152
Hughes, Karen, 170
Human capital model, 95, 111–122, 142
  economic advantage/cultural capital, 115, 116
  equality of educational opportunity, 114, 115
  gender inequities, 184
  gender/region, 117
  occupational mobility research, 117–119
  social structure/occupational choice, 113, 114
  status attainment research, 119–122
Human relations movement, 216–221
Human resource management, 240
Humanist tradition, 386
Hygiene factors, 412
Hyman, Richard, 318, 359

Iacocca, Lee, 212
IBM, 351
Icarus Paradox, The (Miller), 204
Ideal-type bureaucracy, 22
Idle, Thomas, 280, 282
In-person services, 25
In Search of Excellence (Peters/Waterman), 229
Inco, 268
Income differences, 96–99, 137–139
Incrementalism perspective, 212
Individualization process, 157
Individuals' responses to work, 381–452
  alienation, 417–421
  job satisfaction/dissatisfaction, 407–417
  long arm of the job, 426–428
  stress, 421–426
  unemployment, 387–389
  work values, 382–394
Industrial betterment, 217
Industrial capitalism, 3–6
Industrial classification system, 54
Industrial democracy, 297–304
Industrial Disputes Investigation Act (IDIA), 329–331
Industrial fatality rates, 101, 102
Industrial mill, 5
Industrial relations, 315–395
  Canada, role of, 329–331
  Charter guarantee of freedom of association, 373
  collective action, nature of, 354–358
  conflict, role of, 318–320
  development of Canadian labour movement, 324–329
  restrictive environment of labour relations, 373
  worker militancy, 357, 367–373
    See also Unions
Industrial restructuring, 26, 27
Industrial Revolution, 385
Industrial society, 2
Industrial unionism, 326–328
Industrialization, 2
Informal group norms, 219
Informal work, 51–53
Informal work group, 222
Information technologies (IT), 104
Information technology revolution, 276–280
Information workers, 25
Initial proletarianization, 135
Innis, Harold, 66
Instrumental work orientations, 395–397
Intergenerational mobility, 118
Intergenerational transfer of advantage, 114
Internal labour markets, 125, 126
Internal responsibility system (IRS), 293, 294
International Ladies' Garment Workers, 348
Intragenerational mobility, 117, 118
Intrinsic job rewards, 413–416
Involuntary part-time workers, 85
Iron law of oligarchy, 321
Isolation hypothesis, 366

Jabes, Jak, 226
Jahoda, Marie, 387
Japan
  influences on management, 244–253
  work values, 389–391

Japanese transplants, 247
Job enlargement, 240
Job enrichment, 240
Job-family conflict, 162
Job ghettos, 124, 165
Job rotation, 240
Job satisfaction/dissatisfaction, 407–417
  age, and, 408–410
  consequences of, 416, 417
  educational attainment, and, 411, 412
  gender, and, 410
  intrinsic job rewards, and, 413–416
  job conditions/work orientations, and, 412, 413
  prevalence of, 407, 408
Job sharing, 165
Jobs. *See* Labour markets
Johnston, William, 371
Joint health and safety committees (JHSCs), 293, 294
Jones, Charles, 156
Jones, Stephen, 220
Jonsson, Ellen, 209
Just-in-time (JIT), 246

Kaizen, 252, 258
Kalleberg, Arne, 412, 413
Kanter, Rosabeth Moss, 162, 186–188, 231, 232
Kay, Fiona, 174
Kealey, Greg, 325
Keenoy, Tom, 319
Keynesian economic principles, 32
King, William Lyon Mackenzie, 298, 329
Knights, David, 208
Knights of Labour, 326
Knowledge economy, 136
Knowledge workers, 24
Kohn, Melvin, 428

Labor and Monopoly Capital (Braverman), 263, 265
Labour force participation, 46–53
  gender, 47–49
  older Canadians, 50, 51
  unpaid work, 51–53
  youth, 49, 50
Labour Force Survey, 38, 39
Labour market polarization, 136, 137
Labour market processes, 111
Labour market segmentation, 122–139, 142
  barriers to primary market entry, 127–129
  disadvantaged groups, 131–135
  dual economies, 122–125
  gender inequities, 184
  income inequality, 137–139
  internal labour markets, 125, 126
  labour market polarization, 136, 137
  labour market shelters, 126, 127
  racial/ethnic discrimination, 129–135
Labour markets, 93–142
  Canada's class structure, 111–114
  computer use, 104–106
  defined, 94
  employment benefits, 99–101
  human capital model, 111–122
  income differences, 96–99, 137–139
  labour market segmentation, 122–139
  occupational status, 106, 107
  policy responses to inequalities, 139–141
  risks to health and safety, 101–104
Labour market shelters, 126, 127
Labour process perspective, 214
Lash, Scott, 369
Latent functions of work, 387
Laxer, Gordon, 27
Lean production (LP), 251–253, 288
Learning culture, 227, 228
Learning organizations, 45, 229
Leisure, 399
Lenin, Vladimir Ilyich, 320
Lenski, Gerhard, 274, 275, 283
Let the market decide approach, 439
Li, Peter, 131
Life chances, 165
Life-course perspective, 50
Lifelong learning, 45
Lincoln, James R., 245, 246
Linhart, Robert, 424
Lipset, Seymour Martin, 118, 337
Lockout, 358
Lockwood, David, 395
Logic of industrialism, 10
Lone-parent families, 159

Long, Richard, 241
Long arm of the job, 426–428
Looker, Dianne, 128
Low income line, 99
Lowe, Graham, 89
Lower-tier services, 56, 57
Luddites, 5
Luther, Martin, 384

Maccoby, Michael, 399
Management ideologies, 203, 211
Management theory and practice, 199–254
  bureaucracy, 200–203
  downsizing, 234–236
  flexible firm, 250, 251
  flexible specialization, 248–250
  high-performance workplace, 243, 244
  human relations movement, 216–221
  Japanese influences, 244–253
  lean production, 251–253
  managers, 210–213
  new management literature, 228–237, 285–291
  organization theory, 204–210
  organizational culture, 221–228
  quality movement, 232, 233
  quality of working life, 239–241
  scientific management, 213–216
  Swedish work reforms, 238, 239
  work humanization/job redesign, 237–243
Management's rights, 351
Managerial authority, 202
Managerial control, 266–270
Managerial decision making, 211–213
Managerial revolution, 210
Managerial revolution theory, 24
Managers, 210–213
Manifest function of work, 387
Mann, Michael, 368, 396
Maquiladora, 30, 31
Marginal work world, 129
Marglin, Stephen, 304
Market closure, 127
Marriott Corporation, 233
Marsden, Lorna, 156
Marshall, Katherine, 173
Marx, Karl, 16–18, 108, 236, 262, 263, 320, 386, 418, 419
Materialist explanation of gendered division of labour, 187
Matrix groups, 239
Matrix structure, 230
Mayo, Elton, 219, 220
McBride, Kerry, 245, 246
McClung, Nellie, 1
McLuhan, Marshall, 283
McMullen, Kathryn, 280, 281
McNab, Donald, 9
Means of production, 16
Medoff, James, 324
Megatrends (Naisbitt), 25
Meissner, Martin, 160, 427
Men Who Manage (Dalton), 228
Mercantile period, 3
Meritocracy, 118
Merton, Robert, 201
Michels, Robert, 321
Microelectronic production technology, 249
Milliken & Company, 233
Milkman, Ruth, 247
Miller, Danny, 204
Miller, S.M., 441
Mills, C. Wright, 19
Minimum wages, 98
Minorities, 43
Mintzberg, Henry, 207, 211, 230, 231
Mobility chains, 125
Mode of production, 16
Modern Times, 213
Mondragon co-ops, 309, 310
Monopoly face of unionism, 324
Morgan, Gareth, 201
Morgan, Glenn, 208
Motivators, 412
Mulroney, Brian, 32
Multilateral Agreement on Investment (MAI), 28
Multiskilling, 272
Multitasking, 272
Myles, John, 110, 141, 175, 272, 273

NAFTA, 29–31, 304
Naisbitt, John, 25, 280
National Action Committee on the Status of Women, 158
National day of protest, 359
National Occupational Classification (NOC), 58, 60, 61
National War Labour Order (P.C. 1003), 330
Native Canadians
  disadvantaged labour market position, 133
  discrimination, 129, 130
  hunting/gathering societies, 52
  unemployment, 72
Natural rate of unemployment, 75
Nenko, 245
New Democratic Party, 370
New management literature, 228–237
New middle class, 110
New social contract, 232
Newly industrializing countries (NICs), 13
Nightingale, Donald, 297, 299
Nike, 27
Nine-Hour Movement, 325
Nixon, Richard, 404
No-fault compensation systems, 292
NOC, 58, 60, 61
Nonpaid work, 51–53
Nonstandard work arrangements
  part-time work, 84–86
  part-year work, 87
  temporary employment, 86, 87
  varieties of, 80–83
Normative control, 225
Nortel, 27
North American Free Trade Agreement (NAFTA), 29–30, 304
North American Institute, 37
Nova Corporation, 236
Novek, Joel, 269, 295
Numerical flexibility, 251
NUMMI, 247, 252, 253
NUPGE, 343

O'Hara, Bruce, 79
Occupational changes, 58–63
Occupational choice, 114
Occupational gender segregation, 165, 173
Occupational mobility research, 117–119
Occupational self-direction, 428
Occupational status, 106, 107
Office wife, 187
Old middle class, 110
Older workers
  age discrimination, 135
  job satisfaction, 408–410
  labour force participation, 50, 51
  nonstandard work arrangements, 82
  part-year work, 87
  service sector employment, 57
  See also Youth
Olson, Mancur, 355
One Big Union (OBU), 327
Ontario Federation of Women Teachers' Associations, 348
Operation Solidarity, 372
Organic leaders, 356
Organization theory, 204, 205
Organizational analysis. *See* Management theory and practice
Organizational change, 208–210
Organizational culture, 221–228
Organized conflict, 359
Orientation, 383
Orientations model, 396
Ornstein, Michael, 371
Ouchi, William, 225
Owram, Doug, 39

P.C. 1003, 330
Palmer, Bryan, 213, 372
Panitch, Leo, 331
Parr, Joy, 156
Part-time work, 84–86, 164
Part-year work, 87
Patriarchy, 158
Pay equity, 193–195, 349
Pay flexibility, 251
Pentland, Claire, 330, 350
Periphery sector, 123, 124
Perlman, Selig, 317
Permanent exceptionalism, 331
Perrow, Charles, 211, 212, 221

Person-environment fit, 425
Personal management skills, 401
Peters, Tom, 229, 230
Petite bourgeoisie, 17, 108, 109
Piecework payment system, 223
Pineo, Peter, 107
Pineo scale, 107
Pink collar, 62
Polanyi, Karl, 6
Poole, Michael, 317
Population aging, 39
Ports of entry, 125
Positive labour relations, 350, 351
Postindustrial society, 24, 25
Postmodernity, 207
Poverty line, 99
Pre-capitalist economy, 4
Pre-market economy, 4
Primary labour market, 137
Primary sector, 54
Pringle, Rosemary, 189
Privatized workers, 395
Procter and Gamble, 224
Producer cooperatives, 307–310
Professions, 126, 127
Proletarian workers, 395
Proletariat, 17, 108
Protestant Ethic and the Spirit of Capitalism (Weber), 385
Protestant Reformation, 384
Protestant work ethic, 385–389
Public sector unions, 343, 344
Public Service Alliance (PSAC), 343, 349
Public Service Staff Relations Act, 331, 343
Purcell, Kate, 347
Putting out system, 4, 5

Quality circles (QCs), 240
Quality movement, 233, 234
Quality of working life (QWL), 239–241, 285, 286
Quebec Federation of Labour, 329
Quebec labour, 328, 329

Racial discrimination, 129–135
Racially split labour market, 131
Rand Formula, 330, 363
Rational-legal value system, 202
Re-engineering, 252
Reagan, Ronald, 32
Real earnings, 178
Regional variations, 65–68, 71
Reich, Robert, 25, 26, 203, 273, 441
Reiter, Ester, 124
Relations of ruling, 108
Relay Assembly Test Room study, 218
Representative democracy, 297
Reskilling, 279
Responsible autonomy, 267
Richardson, Charley, 283
Riddell, Craig, 374
Rifkin, Jeremy, 78, 282, 393, 436
Right to refuse unsafe work, 294
Right-to-work laws, 337
Rinehart, James, 288, 320, 408
Ringi, 245
Robotics, 277
Rosenberg, Samuel, 251
Rotating strikes, 360
Routine production work, 25
Roy, Donald, 186, 223
Royal Commission on Equality of Employment (Abella Commission), 190

Saab, 239
Safeway strike, 315, 316, 319
Sass, Bob, 295, 296
Saturn, 252
Saul, John Ralston, 32
School-work transition programs, 141
Schumpeter, Joseph, 26
Scientific management, 213–216
Seafarers' International Union, 321
Second shift, 160
Secondary labour market, 124, 137, 184
Secondary sector, 56
Segmentation of labour, 136
Segmentation theories. *See* Labour market segmentation
Self-employment, 64, 65
Semco, 300
Semi-autonomous workers, 109

Senge, Peter, 227, 228
Sennett, Richard, 396
Service, 54
Service categories, 56
Service sector, 54–57
SES measures, 107
Sex, 150
Sexual harassment, 189
Sexual orientation, 135
Shell's Sarnia chemical plant, 241–243, 300
Shorter work weeks, 78, 79
Simple control, 267
Singapore, 14
Skill debate, 270–274
Skilled craft workers, 8
Smith, Adam, 18–20
Smith, Vicki, 266
Smucker, Joseph, 211, 351
SOC, 58, 62
Social assistance, 405, 406
Social class, 108
Social determinism, 284
Social glue, 225
Social mobility, 117
Social relations of production, 16
Social safety net, 404
Social unionism, 322
Socialist society, 17
Socioeconomic status (SES) scales, 107
Sociotechnical system, 206
Sociotechnical work design, 238
Socrates, 400
Soldiering, 214
Sonnenfeld, Jeffrey A., 219
Sosteric, Mike, 268
South Korea, 13
Spillover hypothesis, 427
Standard Occupational Classification (SOC), 58, 62
Staple theory of economic growth, 66
Status attainment, 119–122
Stewart, Sandy, 408
Stinker jobs, 223
Strategic choice, 206
Strategic planning, 207
Strategy, 208
Stress, 295, 421–426
Stressors, 422
Strikes, 358–367
Structural employment, 282
Structural functionalism, 205
Structural mobility, 118
Structural unemployment, 75
Structure of opportunities, 188
Student labour market, 137
Subcontracting systems, 13
Subsistence work, 52
Substantive complexity, 271
Sugiman, Pamela, 348, 349
Sunset industries, 26
Surplus value, 262
Survey of Work Arrangements, 78, 79
Survivor syndrome, 235
Swartz, Donald, 331
Sweden
  industrial democracy, 302, 303
  wage earner funds, 305
  work reforms, 238, 239
Swift, Jamie, 392
Symbolic analysts, 25
Syndicalism, 327
System of job regulation, 318
Systemic discrimination, 190

Tacit skills, 246, 271
Taiwan, 13
Taylor, Frederick W., 213–215, 217
Taylorism, 213–216
Teamwork skills, 401
Technical control, 267
Technological determinism, 283, 421
Teleworking, 78
Temporary/contract labour market, 137
Temporary employment, 86, 87
Tepperman, Lorne, 156
Tertiary sector, 54
Thatcher, Margaret, 32
Thorsrud, E., 240
Thriving on Chaos: A Handbook for a Management Revolution (Peters), 230
Tilly, Charles, 356
Time-and-motion studies, 214, 215

Time budget studies, 159, 160
Time-crunch stress, 162–165
Tokenism, 188
Total quality management (TQM), 232, 233, 286, 287
Toyota, 247
TQM, 232, 233, 286, 287
Tracks, 208
Trade Unions Act, 325, 330
Trades and Labour Congress (TLC), 325
Two-factor theory, 412

Under-the-table payments, 53
Underclass, 139, 405
Underemployment, 141, 415
Underground economy, 52, 53
Unemployment
  causes of, 74–76
  counting the unemployed, 68, 69
  gender, 72, 73
  history of, 69–71
  international comparisons, 76, 77
  meaning of work, and, 387–389
  regional variations, 71, 73
  youth, 73, 74
Unemployment rate, 68
Union democracy, 321
Union density, 332, 341
Unions
  activities, 321, 322
  American, 337, 338
  class consciousness, 368, 370, 371
  economic impact, 323, 324
  industrial restructuring, and, 353, 354
  labour market shelter, as, 126
  management opposition to, 350–354
  managers of discontent, 320, 321
  membership trends, 332–343
  mobilization process, 356–360
  politics, and, 370, 371
  public opinion, 322, 323
  public sector, 343, 344
  raiding, 328
  reduction of inequalities, and, 141
  strikes, 358–367
  why unionize, 317, 318
  women, and, 346–349
  workplace health and safety, and, 292
  workplace innovation, and, 352
  See also Industrial relations
United Auto Workers, 357, 360
United Autoworkers of America, 243
United Food and Commercial Workers, 343
United Steel Workers (USW), 342
Unorganized conflict, 359
Unpaid domestic labour, 152
Unpaid household and child care work, 52
Upper-tier services, 56, 57

Values, 382
Vertical solitude, 226
Visible minorities, 43, 133
Volunteer work, 52
Volvo Kalmar plant, 238

Wage discrimination, 181
Waterman, Bob, Jr., 229
Wealth of Nations (Smith), 18, 19
Webb, Sidney and Beatrice, 317
Weber, Max, 21, 22, 165, 201–203, 385, 389
Weitzel, William, 209
Welfare dependency, 403–405
Wellness programs, 296
Western Federation of Miners, 227
Westray mine disaster, 295
When Giants Learn to Dance (Kanter), 231
White, Bob, 242
White, Jerry, 367
White, Julie, 357
White-collar occupations, 59
Whitley, Richard, 14
Wildcat strikes, 359
Winnipeg general strike, 359
Wobblies, 327
Women, 149–195
  boss-secretary relationship, 189
  earnings/wages, 178–183
  education, 172, 182, 183
  employment equity, 190–193
  family wage ideology, 152–154
  female job ghettos, 165, 166
  gender role socialization, 185, 186

gender segregation, 165–178
gender stratification, 134, 173–178
glass ceiling, 175, 177
historical sketch, 150–154
horizontal occupational segregation, 167–173
human capital theory, 184
labour force participation, 154–158
labour market segmentation, 184
leading female occupations, 169
nontraditional jobs, 170, 171
organization of work, 186–189
pay equity, 193–195
professional occupations, 173
sexual harassment, 189
strikes, 367
theoretical perspectives, 183–189
time-crunch stress, 162–165
unions, 346–349
vertical segregation, 134, 173–178
wage gap, 178–183
work and family, 158–165
See also Gender
Wood, Stephen, 246, 250
Woods, H.D., 363
Woodward, Joan, 205, 206
Work of Nations, The (Reich), 25, 203
Work orientations
anxiety over job/income security, 406, 407
defined, 382, 383
gender, and, 397, 398
instrumental, 395–397
job satisfaction, 412
welfare dependency, 403–405
work vs. leisure, 399, 400
youth, and, 400–403
Work-related death, 101
Work-related stress, 421–426
Work values, 382–394
Work Well Network, 79
Workaholic, 397
Worker involvement programs, 299
Worker militancy, 357, 367–373
Worker ownership, 304–310
Workfare, 404
Workforce aging, 39–42
Workforce diversity, 42, 43
Working class, 110
Working-class consciousness, 395
Working-class radicalism, 368–370
Working poor, 139, 405
Workplace democracy programs, 299
Workplace hazards, 103
Workplace health and safety, 101–104, 291–296
Workplace 2000: The Revolution Reshaping American Business (Boyett/Conn), 229
Works councils, 298
World Class (Kanter), 232
Wright, Eric Olin, 109

Xerox Corporation, 233

Yates, Charlotte, 357
Youth
age discrimination, 135
job satisfaction, 408–410
labour force participation, 49, 50
nonstandard work arrangements, 82
part-year work, 87
service sector employment, 57
student labour market, 137
temporary employment, 87
unemployment, 73, 74
work orientations, 400–403
See also Older workers

Zero-sum game, 320
Zuboff, Shoshana, 209, 279
Zussman, David, 226